Global Marketing

Global Marketing

THIRD EDITION

KATE GILLESPIE
University of Texas at Austin

H. DAVID HENNESSEY
Babson College, Wellesley, Massachusetts
Ashridge Management College, Berkhamsted, United Kingdom

SOUTH-WESTERN
CENGAGE Learning

Australia • Brazil • Japan • Korea • Mexico • Singapore • Spain • United Kingdom • United States

SOUTH-WESTERN
CENGAGE Learning

Global Marketing, Third Edition
Kate Gillespie, H. David Hennessey

Vice President of Editorial, Business: Jack W. Calhoun

Editor-in-Chief: Melissa Acuna

Executive Editor: Mike Roche

Managing Development Editor: Joanne Dauksewicz

Editorial Assistant: Kayti Purkiss

Vice President Marketing: Bill Hendee

Senior Marketing Communications Manager: Sarah Greber

Senior Content Project Manager: Kim Kusnerak

Production Technology Analyst: Emily Gross

Media Editor: John Rich

Frontlist Buyer, Manufacturing: Miranda Klapper

Production Service: KnowledgeWorks Global Limited (KGL)

Compositor: KnowledgeWorks Global Limited (KGL)

Senior Art Director: Stacy Jenkins Shirley

B/W Image: Getty Images / Hisham Ibrahim

Color Image: Shutterstock Images / Scott Rothstein

Senior Rights Acquisition Account Manager: Katie Huha

Permissions Acquisition Manager—Images: Deanna Ettinger

Photo Researcher: Don Schlotman

For product information and technology assistance, contact us at
Cengage Learning Customer & Sales Support, 1-800-354-9706

For permission to use material from this text or product, submit all requests online at **www.cengage.com/permissions**

Further permissions questions can be emailed to **permissionrequest@cengage.com**

Library of Congress Control Number: 2009937990
International Student Edition ISBN-13: 978-0-538-47339-2
International Student Edition ISBN-10: 0-538-47339-8

Cengage Learning International Offices

Asia
cengageasia.com
tel: (65) 6410 1200

Australia/New Zealand
cengage.com.au
tel: (61) 3 9685 4111

Brazil
cengage.com.br
tel: (011) 3665 9900

India
cengage.co.in
tel: (91) 11 30484837/38

Latin America
cengage.com.mx
tel: +52 (55) 1500 6000

UK/Europe/Middle East/Africa
cengage.co.uk
tel: (44) 207 067 2500

Represented in Canada by Nelson Education, Ltd.
nelson.com
tel: (416) 752 9100/(800) 668 0671

For product information: **www.cengage.com/international**
Visit your local office: **www.cengage.com/global**
Visit our corporate website: **www.cengage.com**

Printed in Canada
1 2 3 4 5 6 7 13 12 11 10

Brief Contents

© Photodisc/Getty Images

v

Contents

CHAPTER **3**

Cultural and Social Forces 47

CASES

APPENDIX **CASES**

Preface

Today, virtually every major firm must compete in a global marketplace. Buyers can comprise ordinary consumers or local businesses in international markets, multinational corporations, or foreign governments. Competitors can be local firms or global firms. Although some consumer needs and wants may be converging across national markets, and multilateral agreements seek to bring order to the international economic and legal environment, global marketers must still navigate among varied cultures where unexpected rules apply. Addressing this varied and increasingly competitive marketplace and developing strategies that are both efficient and effective are the tasks that face the global marketer.

Whether they oversee foreign markets or face international competitors at home, students who plan to enter marketing as a profession will need to understand and apply the essentials of global marketing. This text prepares them for that challenge.

Why This Book?

There are a number of global marketing texts on the market. Our approach differs from that of other books in several ways.

A Dual Focus: International Buyers and Global Competition

Whereas most texts envisage global marketing as an understanding of international buyers, we envisage it as *competing* for those buyers. Immediately following our chapter on global markets and buyers, we present the student with a chapter on global and local competitors. From then on, we keep students focused on both buyers and competitors throughout the book.

A Global View Combined with a Strong Appreciation for Cultural Differences

Some global marketing texts downplay culture. Others make cultural differences their focus. Our approach is to recognize that cultural differences do exist and influence global marketing in a plethora of ways. To this end, we introduce students early to cultural issues and ways of analyzing culture that are reinforced throughout the book. But we also present students with a global view of managing cultural differences. For example, if you know you are going to sell a new product in 70 countries, why not consider this when you first design the product? What is the best design that will allow for necessary adaptations with the least effort and cost?

Regional Balance

For a text to be a true guide to global marketing, it must present students with a regional balance. Most texts concentrate on the markets of the United States, Europe, and China. Our book delivers a balance of developed and developing markets, including insights into the often-overlooked markets of Africa, Latin America, and the Middle East. We also encourage students to think of competitors as coming from all countries, including emerging markets such as China, India, Korea, and Mexico.

Current Coverage across a Wide Variety of Topics

Our combined research and consulting experience allows us to speak with enthusiasm and conviction across the many areas covered by a global marketing text, including global strategy, cross-cultural consumer behavior, and marketing organization, as well as the effects government policy can have on international markets and global marketing. Our text combines recent academic research along with in-the-news corporate stories.

Gender Representation

We have taken care to present examples of women as well as men in roles of global marketers. This is apparent in our end-of-chapter cases as well as the many real-life examples in the text.

An Interactive Approach

Because the field of global marketing changes so quickly, perhaps no subject is better suited to take advantage of Internet technology. The Internet offers a variety of respected sites that allow students to do research and formulate preliminary marketing plans. Our goal is to familiarize each student with these tools that are available to the global marketer.

Application Opportunities

To help students better internalize their knowledge of global marketing, this text offers various opportunities to apply knowledge of global marketing concepts and skills to business situations. These opportunities include full-length cases, shorter end-of-chapter cases, and an online Country Market Report guide. This guide assists students in assessing whether a firm should enter a foreign market. For example, should Marriott Hotels and Resorts enter Uzbekistan? Should Yoshinoya, a Japanese casual dining chain, enter Brazil? The guide walks students through subsequent marketing mix questions such as what adaptations a U.S.-based dating service would have to make if it were to enter the French market. What pricing, promotion, and distribution strategies should it employ?

Why This New Edition?

Updated Coverage of Evolving Issues in Global Marketing

Global marketing doesn't stand still! The new edition of this text includes insights and frameworks from recent academic and consulting research. Just some of the new questions addressed include:

- The Japanese score lower than Americans on uncertainty avoidance yet intentionally use ambiguous clauses in business contracts. How should global marketers deal with such cultural paradoxes?
- How are global marketers using the new social media to reach young consumers worldwide?
- In tough times, governments seek ways to help their national firms export goods and services. Where can marketers go to tap into this government support?
- Why do global marketers use both emic research and etic research to understand international markets? What are the pros and cons of each?
- Rethinking country of origin: How does consumer animosity pose new threats to global brands?

- Halal certification has become increasingly important in Muslim markets in the past few years. How does this affect multinational firms such as McDonald's, KFC, and Nestlé?
- What is BRIC? What is BRICK? Does it make sense to focus on only four or five major emerging markets?
- How should global marketers respond to a major currency devaluation in a foreign market? Do they have to lower prices or are there other strategies available to preserve margins and market share?
- So-called parallel firms are on the rise. Why do global marketers have to watch out for joint venture partners that compete with them on the side?

New and Updated Cases

New and updated cases are provided to capture recent developments in global marketing. These cases are located at the end of the text. For example:

- ***Diaspora Marketing*** World migration has doubled in the past 35 years. How can marketers from both host and home countries help meet the needs of the new diaspora markets?
- ***Procter & Gamble Targets Emerging Markets*** The world's largest packaged goods company decides to target developing countries and transitional economies. What are the advantages and dangers of such a strategy?
- ***Work versus Leisure*** In some countries people are working more hours and in others they are working less. Koreans now have more leisure time, but many find it stressful and expensive. Is this an opportunity or a challenge for global marketers?
- ***ShanghaiCosmopolitan.com*** Young Chinese cosmopolitans love their social networking site, but can the site's owners attract advertising from multinational firms without offending the site's users?
- ***Cars for Emerging Markets*** Ford heads to India and GM to Russia, but can GM's joint venture survive when an arms exporter takes over its Russian partner?
- ***Fighting AIDS in Asia*** A former global product manager in packaged foods has turned social marketer and must prioritize markets and programs to help alleviate the spread of AIDS in Asia. Can her skills in global marketing be put to use in this new context? And what can she learn from a major donor that entered the market and then quickly exited the market?

Expanded Test Bank with Both Factual and Problem-Oriented Questions

We now provide more than 1,500 questions in the test bank. More than 450 are application-oriented questions. To enrich the number and types of application questions, we have added to this edition mini-cases with questions.

Content and Organization of the Book

Chapter 1 presents an introduction to global marketing. In this chapter, we describe the development of global marketing and the importance of global marketing to both firms and the managers of the future. We explore the need for a global mindset and set forth the structure of the book.

Part 1 is entitled "Understanding the Global Marketing Environment." In this early section, we investigate the key ways that the macro environment can affect global marketers. Although the concepts may be macro, we constantly show how they apply to a variety of firms trying to succeed in a vibrant international marketplace. In Chapter 2, "The Global Economy," we present the student with basic theories of trade, explain how exchange rates work and affect marketing decisions, and explore issues of protectionism and trade restrictions as well as economic integration and the challenges of outsourcing. In Chapter 3, "Cultural and Social Forces," we explore the impact on marketing of factors such as religion, family structure, education, and attitudes toward time. We describe the Hofstede measures of culture and present ratings for nearly 70 countries—ratings that can be used time and again when analyzing cultural underpinnings of marketing dilemmas later in the book. The chapter continues with a discussion of issues relating to language and communication, such as the difference between high- and low-context cultures and the social acceptability (or not) of showing emotion. We conclude with insights into overcoming language barriers and dealing with culture shock. In Chapter 4, "Political and Regulatory Climate," we begin by asking the question, "What do governments want?" We then explore the varied ways that both host and home countries can impact global marketers. We describe how legal systems and attitudes toward rules vary around the world. We continue by explaining to the global marketer the difference between the task of forecasting and managing regulatory change and the task of managing political risk, and we offer concrete ideas on how to do both. The chapter concludes with a discussion of how terrorism impacts global marketing.

Part 2 concentrates on "Analyzing Global Opportunities." Beginning with Chapter 5, "Global Markets," we introduce students to segmentation in international markets and discuss cross-cultural aspects of consumer, business, and government markets, including a discussion of bribery and international contracts. Chapter 6, "Global Competitors," introduces students to issues of global firm versus global firm, as well as global firm versus local firm. In particular, we present ways in which one global firm can successfully engage another, as well as ways in which a local firm can respond to an encroaching global firm—including going global itself. We then explore cultural attitudes toward competition that can help explain why government regulation of corporate behavior varies around the world and why firms from different countries can be expected to behave differently. We describe how home countries' actions can affect the global competitiveness of their firms. In addition to discussing firms from the developed world—the United States, Europe, and Japan—we devote a separate section to better understanding firms from the emerging markets of the developing world. We conclude by examining the country-of-origin advantage (or sometimes disadvantage) that affects global competition, and we discuss the increasingly visible phenomenon of consumer animosity toward firms from particular countries. In Chapter 7, "Global Marketing Research," we present issues of research design and organization in a global setting and discuss the collection of secondary and primary data across cultures.

Part 3, "Developing Global Participation Strategies," examines the key decisions of determining where and how to compete and how to enter foreign markets. In Chapter 8, "Global Market Participation," we look at traditional patterns of how firms internationalize as well as the more recent phenomenon of born-global firms that enter foreign markets from their inception. We identify the pros and cons of geographic market choices, such as targeting developed versus developing economies, and explore the concepts of stand-alone attractive markets and strategically important markets. We then provide a format for country selection. In Chapter 9, "Global Market Entry Strategies," we cover the varied options of how to enter (and sometimes leave) a foreign market, including production and ownership decisions, portal or e-business entry options, and when to consider exiting markets.

Part 4, "Designing Global Marketing Programs," covers the global management of the marketing mix and the cross-cultural challenges involved in decisions concerning products, pricing, distribution, and promotion. Chapter 10, "Global Product Strategies," explores necessary and desirable product (including packaging and warranty) adaptations for international markets, and it explains the importance of managing a global product line. We examine a new paradigm—designing a product with multiple national markets in mind. We also explore the decision to design (rather than adapt) a product for an important foreign market. We identify different sources for new products, whether developed in-house or outsourced, and conclude with an examination of global rollouts for new products. In Chapter 11, "Global Strategies for Services, Brands, and Social Marketing," we present the particular cross-cultural challenges of services marketing and discuss branding decisions, including issues of brand protection. The chapter concludes with a discussion of the possibilities and challenges of applying global marketing concepts to social marketing internationally. In Chapter 12, "Pricing for International and Global Markets," we examine how cost and market factors as well as environmental factors, such as exchange rate movements and inflation, can affect pricing in international markets. We then explore managerial issues such as determining transfer prices, quoting prices in foreign currencies, dealing with parallel imports, and deciding when and how to participate in countertrade arrangements.

Part 4 continues with Chapter 13, "Managing Global Distribution Channels." This chapter reviews global channels and logistics and introduces the potential differences that exist among local channels, with special emphasis on accessing and managing these channels. Recent trends are examined, including the globalization of retail chains and the growth of direct marketing worldwide, as well as the peculiar challenges of smuggling and the increasing presence of organized crime in the global movement of consumer goods. Chapter 14, "Global Promotion Strategies," begins by exploring global selling and cross-cultural differences in local selling and sales force management. It continues with a discussion of international sports sponsorship and public relations, as well as cross-cultural differences in sales promotions, product placement, and managing word of mouth. Part 4 concludes with Chapter 15, "Managing Global Advertising," which explores issues of global versus local advertising, as well as global media strategies and agency selection.

Chapter 16, "Organizing for Global Marketing," in Part 5, identifies the elements that will determine the most appropriate organization for a firm's global marketing and outlines the characteristics of various organizational options. The chapter also examines issues of control and discusses the particular problem of conflict between headquarters and national subsidiaries. We conclude with a discussion of global marketing as a career.

Pedagogical Advantages

Our book incorporates several features to help students learn about global marketing.

Chapter-Opening Stories

Each chapter begins with a short recap of a recent marketing experience that illustrates key issues in the chapter that follows. This helps students grasp immediately the real-life relevance and importance of issues presented in the chapter.

Chapter Outlines and Learning Objectives

At the beginning of each chapter, we present both a chapter outline and a list of clear learning objectives to help focus students on the understanding they can expect to take away from the chapter.

"World Beat" Boxed Inserts

Numerous and timely examples of market challenges from around the world help students further explore international issues.

Internet Icons

Throughout the text we draw the student's attention to readings, exercises, or hyperlinks provided on our website that have particular relevance to the subject under discussion.

Pictures and Full-Color Text and Graphics

We believe that engaging the student visually enhances the learning experience.

Discussion Questions

We provide discussion questions at the end of each chapter that challenge a student's creativity to stretch beyond the chapter.

Short but Evocative End-of-Chapter Cases

We believe cases can be short but conceptually dense. We have included two or three such cases at the end of each chapter. These cases were written or chosen to work with the chapter content. The end-of-case questions often refer specifically to chapter content in order to test a student's ability to apply the chapter to the case.

Longer Cases for More In-Depth Analysis

We are aware that some instructors like to augment shorter cases with several longer ones, either throughout the course or at the end of a course. For these instructors, we have provided several longer cases that challenge students to apply and synthesize their knowledge.

An Internet-Based Country Market Report

This exercise presents students with an opportunity to apply concepts from the chapters in the book, as well as introduces them to Internet sites that are useful to global marketers.

A Complete Supplements Package

The comprehensive *Instructor's Manual* includes chapter outlines, suggested review questions and answers, answers to the discussion questions at the end of each chapter, and comments on cases and case questions. Teaching notes are also provided for the end-of-text cases, and a *Video Guide* is included at the end of the manual.

The *Test Bank* provides true/false, multiple-choice, and fill-in questions for each chapter, and includes a mix of objective and application questions. New to this edition are mini-cases with questions. These mini-cases can be used to test a student's ability to apply knowledge to new situations and to think across chapters. *Exam-View*, a computerized version of the Test Bank, provides instructors with all the tools they need to create, author/edit, customize, and deliver multiple types of tests. Instructors can import questions directly from the Test Bank, create their own questions, or edit existing questions.

Videos

A DVD is also available to support the third edition. The segments can be used across several chapters, and the *Video Guide* includes summaries of each video as well as teaching guidelines and issues for discussion.

Instructor Companion Site

The Instructor Companion Site can be found at www.cengage.com/international. It includes the complete Instructor's Manual in PDF form, Word files for both the Instructor's Manual and Test Bank, and PowerPoint slides for easy downloading.

Student Companion Site

The Student Companion Site can also be found at www.cengage.com/international. It includes the Country Market Report, which is referred to throughout the text, giving students an opportunity to apply the concepts from the chapters in the book. The Student Companion Site also includes important Web links that are useful to global marketers and online study aids, such as interactive quizzes, glossary flashcards, crossword puzzles, and student PowerPoint® slides.

Availability of resources may differ by region. Check with your local Cengage Learning representative for details.

ACKNOWLEDGMENTS

We very much appreciate the contributions of case studies from Anna Andriasova, William Carner, Dae Ryun Chang, Nigel Goodwin, Charles W. L. Hill, Jaeseok Jeong, Michael Magers, Laurie Milton, Monica Park, Sam Perkins, Liesl Riddle, K. B. Saji, Bernd Schmitt, Chi Kin Yim, and Jie Zhang. We are especially thankful to Jean-Pierre Jeannet, our coauthor on the first two editions of this book, for his dedication to making global marketing accessible and enjoyable to students around the world.

In addition, we are grateful to the following instructors for their insights and guidance:

Thomas L. Ainscough, *University of South Florida, St. Petersburg*

Steven J. Anderson, *Austin Peay State University*

Sally Andrews, *Linn-Benton Community College*

David Andrus, *Kansas State University*

Subir Bandyopadhyay, *Indiana University Northwest*

Walter H. Beck Sr., *Reinhardt College*

Tom Bilyeu, *Southwestern Illinois College*

Gloria Christian, *Butler County Community College*

Joyce A. Claterbos, *University of Kansas*

Andrew Czaplewski, *University of Colorado at Colorado Springs*

Tevfic Dalgic, *University of Texas, Dallas*

Les Dlabay, *Lake Forest College*

Bob Eddy, *Diablo Valley College*

Darrell Goudge, *University of Central Oklahoma*

John M. Guarino, *Averett University*

Paul Herbig, *Tri-State University*

Glen Johns, *Cedar Crest College*

Keith C. Jones, *North Carolina A&T State University*

Theodore Jula, *Stonehill College*

William J. Kehoe, *University of Virginia*

William Lesch, *University of North Dakota*

Marilyn Liebrenz-Himes, *George Washington University*

Ann B. Little, *High Point University*

Steven Lysonski, *Marquette University*

Michel Marette, *Northern Virginia Community College*

Maria McConnell, *Lorain County Community College*

Sanjay Mehta, *Sam Houston State University*

Mark Mitchell, *University of Southern California*

Jennifer Nevins Henson, *Appalachian State University*

Karen G. Palumbo, *University of St. Francis*

Barnett R. Parker, *Pfeiffer University*

Fred Pragasam, *University of North Florida*

Alfred Quinton, *The College of New Jersey*

Liesl Riddle, *George Washington University*

H. Rika Houston, *California State University—Los Angeles*

Martin Shapiro, *Berkeley College, New York*

Fred Tennant, *Webster University*

Frank Tian Xie, *Drexel University*

Hope Torkornoo, *Kennesaw State University*

Thuhang Tran, *Middle Tennessee State University*

Michael Weinstein, *Brooklyn College*

Global Marketing

© Antony V. Giblin/Lonely Planet Images

© Inmagine/18439GNG

1

Introduction to Global Marketing

LEARNING OBJECTIVES

After studying this chapter, you should be able to:

- Describe the development of global marketing.
- Explain the importance of global marketing and the need for a global mindset.

WHEN MTV first went international, it aired the same videos it used in the United States, essentially blaring Michael Jackson at the world. In Europe, this strategy worked well in attracting the top 200 largest pan-European advertisers. But to reach other advertisers, MTV had to adopt a more national approach, tailoring music and programming to local tastes and languages. However, over time the rising costs of production ($200,000–$350,000 per half-hour episode) caused MTV to reevaluate its multidomestic strategy. Now local subsidiaries are encouraged to create products that will play across regions or even globally.[1] Thus global firms must constantly balance the unique needs of national markets with global imperatives.

One important job of global marketers is to address the many different cultures and regulatory environments of various international markets. For example, Metro, a free newspaper that targets urban commuters, originated in Sweden then spread to 70 cities across Europe, Asia, and the United States. It prospered in spite of copycat competitors. However, when a credit crisis hit and advertisers cut back on spending, Metro saw its profits plummet. In response, the company realized that it needed to better adapt its newspapers to the different markets in which they were sold. So, Hong Kong readers were provided more business news and Italian readers received more coverage of politics.[2]

Yet, the demands of local consumers are multifaceted and often changing. The Japanese are now eating more sweets than ever. When Krispy Kreme Doughnuts opened its first store in Japan, 10,000 customers arrived in the first three days alone. The Japanese are craving larger portions as well. McDonald's Mega Macs were a great hit, selling 1.7 million in four days.[3] Therefore, global marketers must not only understand the current status of international markets, they must also be cognizant of key trends in these markets and prepare for the future. This is true despite the fact that no one ever agrees about the future or what to do about it. When Starbucks entered China, it decided to emphasize its premium coffee with the goal of changing China's tea-drinking culture. When Dunkin' Donuts entered the market, however, it announced that it would emphasize new tea drinks at first and only later ease into coffee.[4]

Though national markets remain unique, they are increasingly interdependent. Aided by technology, local consumers are more and more aware of products and prices from around the world, and large retailers and multinational firms have become powerful global buyers that demand special attention. Competition increasingly occurs across markets, and competitive moves cross national borders at an alarmingly fast rate. In addition, global marketers must also exploit economies of scale in order to deliver quality and value in a competitive global marketplace. Thus, a final job of global marketing is to manage these interdependencies across international markets.

This first chapter introduces you to the field of global marketing. Initially, we explore why companies seek global markets and examine the differences among domestic, international, multidomestic, and global types of marketing. We then explain why mastering global marketing skills can be valuable to your future career. A conceptual outline of the book concludes the chapter.

THE IMPORTANCE OF GLOBAL MARKETS

Global markets are expanding rapidly. The combined value of merchandise exports has exceeded $15 trillion annually. In addition, exports of commercial services account for more than $3 trillion. For many years, international trade has grown faster than domestic economies, further contributing to the ever-increasing pace of globalization.

Furthermore, international trade statistics do not reflect a substantial portion of international marketing operations. In particular, overseas sales of locally manufactured and locally sold products produced by foreign investors are not included in world trade figures. Consequently, the total volume of international marketing far exceeds the volume of total world trade. Sales of overseas subsidiaries for U.S. companies are estimated at three times the value of these companies' exports. Although no detailed statistics are available, this pattern suggests that the overall volume of international marketing amounts to a multiple of the world trade volume.

The scope of global marketing includes many industries and many business activities. Boeing, the world's largest commercial airline manufacturer, engages in global marketing when it sells its aircraft to airlines across the world. Likewise, Ford Motor Company, which operates automobile manufacturing plants in many countries, engages in global marketing, even though a major part of Ford's output is sold in the country where it is manufactured. Large retail chains, such as Wal-Mart, search for new products abroad to sell in the United States. As major global buyers, they too participate in global marketing.

A whole range of service industries are involved in global marketing. Major advertising agencies, banks, investment bankers, accounting firms, consulting companies, hotel chains, airlines, and even law firms now market their services worldwide. Many of these multinational services companies enjoy more sales abroad than they do at home. India-based Tata Consultancy Services derives over 50 percent of its sales from North America.[5] Leading orchestras from Vienna, Berlin, New York, and Philadelphia command as much as $150,000 per concert. Booking performances all over the world, they compete with new global entrants from St. Petersburg and Moscow.

Headquartered on the shores of Lake Geneva, Swiss-based Nestlé is the world's largest foods company. Its products are sold in virtually every country.

Why Companies Seek Global Markets

Companies become involved in international markets for a variety of reasons. Some firms simply respond to orders from abroad without making any organized efforts of their own. Most companies take a more active role. Many firms enter foreign markets to increase sales and profits. Some companies pursue opportunities abroad when their domestic market has reached maturity. For example, Coca-Cola, the market leader worldwide in the soft-drinks business, finds that on a per-capita basis, most foreign consumers drink only a fraction of the cola that Americans drink. Consequently, Coca-Cola sees enormous growth potential in international markets.

Sometimes a domestic competitive shock provides the impetus to globalize. After Mexico joined the North American Free Trade Association (NAFTA), Mexican companies realized that they would face increased competition from U.S. firms. Bimbo, Mexico's market leader in packaged foods, entered the U.S. market to better understand the competition it would inevitably face back home in Mexico.[6]

Other firms launch their international marketing operations by following customers who move abroad. Major U.S. banks have opened branches in key financial centers around the world to serve their U.S. clients better. Similarly, advertising agencies in the United States have created networks to serve the interests of their multinational clients. When Japanese automobile manufacturers opened plants in the United States, many of their component suppliers followed and built operations nearby. Failing to accommodate these important clients could result in the loss not only of foreign sales but of domestic sales as well.

For some firms, however, the reason to become involved in global marketing has its roots in pure economics. Producers of television shows in Hollywood can spend more than $1.5 million to produce a single show for a typical series. Networks in the United States pay only about $1 million to air a single show, and the series producers rely on international markets to cover the difference. Without the opportunity to market globally, they would not even be able to produce the shows for the U.S. market.

Online shopping giant eBay is serious about international market opportunities. Nonetheless, expanding into the important Asian market has not been easy. Tough competition from Yahoo! forced eBay to exit the Japanese market. In China, eBay shut down its own website and retreated to owning a minority share in a locally owned site. Despite these setbacks, eBay commands a 13 percent *global* market share of online shopping, and its PayPal unit accounts for a 9 percent share of online payments worldwide. Like any successful global marketer, eBay must continually rethink its global strategy.[7] Global expansion is not just a decision to venture abroad. It is a commitment to learn from experience.

THE DEVELOPMENT OF GLOBAL MARKETING

The term *global marketing* has been in use only since the 1980s. Before that decade, *international marketing* was the term used most often to describe marketing activities outside one's domestic market. Global marketing is not just a new label for an old phenomenon, however. Global marketing provides a new vision for international marketing. Before we explain global marketing in detail, let us first look at the historical development of international marketing as a field in order to gain a better understanding of the phases through which it has passed (see Figure 1.1).

FIGURE 1.1
International and Global Marketing

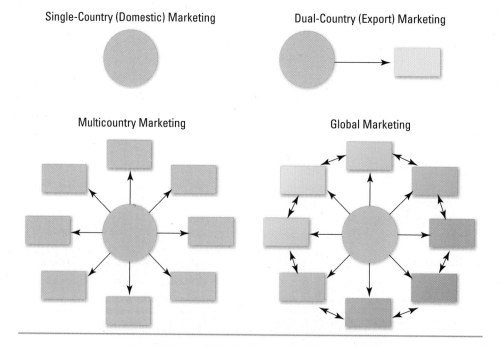

Single-Country (Domestic) Marketing

Dual-Country (Export) Marketing

Multicountry Marketing

Global Marketing

Domestic Marketing

Domestic marketing marketing activities aimed at a firm's domestic market

Marketing that is aimed at a single market, the firm's domestic market, is known as **domestic marketing**. In domestic marketing, the firm faces only one set of competitive, economic, and market issues. It essentially deals with only one set of national customers, although the company may serve several segments in this one market.

Export Marketing

Export marketing marketing activities undertaken when a firm sells its products abroad and when those products are shipped from one country to another

Export marketing covers marketing activities that are involved when a firm sells its products outside its domestic base of operation and when products are physically shipped from one country to another. The major challenges of export marketing are the selection of appropriate markets or countries through marketing research, the determination of appropriate product modifications to meet the demand requirements of export markets, and the development of export channels through which the company can market its products abroad. In export marketing, the firm may concentrate mostly on product modifications, running its export operations as a welcome and profitable byproduct of its domestic strategy. Other aspects of marketing strategy, such as pricing, channel management, and promotion, may be outsourced either to foreign agents or distributors or to specialist export management companies located in the firm's home country. Although export marketing probably represents the most traditional and least complicated form of nondomestic marketing, it remains an important feature for many firms.

International Marketing

International marketing marketing activities undertaken when a company becomes significantly involved in local marketing environments in foreign countries

A company that practices **international marketing** goes beyond exporting and becomes much more directly involved in the local marketing environment within a given country. The firm is likely to have its own sales subsidiaries and will participate in and develop entire marketing strategies for foreign markets. At this point, the necessary adaptations to the firm's domestic marketing strategies become of greater concern. Table 1.1 illustrates typical adaptations in international marketing. Companies need to decide how to adjust an entire marketing strategy, including how they sell, advertise, and distribute products, in order to fit new market demands. Understanding different cultural, economic, and political environments becomes increasingly necessary for success.

Typically, much of the field of international marketing has been devoted to making the environment understandable and helping managers navigate the differences.

Multidomestic Marketing

Multinational corporation (MNC) a company that possesses extensive investments in assets abroad and operates in a number of foreign countries as though it were a local company

Multidomestic strategy a strategy pursued by a multinational firm in which various marketing strategies are developed, each tailored to a particular local market

The focus on multidomestic marketing came as a result of the development of the **multinational corporation (MNC)**. These companies, characterized by extensive investments in assets abroad, operate in a number of foreign countries as though they were local companies. For many years multinationals pursued a **multidomestic strategy**, wherein the multinational firm competes by applying many different strategies, each one tailored to a particular local market. Often, MNCs would attempt to appear "local" wherever they competed. The major challenge confronting the multidomestic marketer is to find the best possible adaptation of a complete marketing strategy to each individual country. This more extreme approach to international marketing led to a maximum amount of localization and to a large variety

<table>
<tr><td>**TABLE 1.1**</td><td>**ADAPTING TO NATIONAL DIFFERENCES**</td></tr>
</table>

Brazil:
In Latin America, 25 percent of the population lives on less than $2 a day. Consumers often require smaller packages at lower prices. Sales of Nestlé's Bono cookies increased 40 percent in a single year when the company decreased the package size in Brazil from 200 grams to 149 grams.

China:
Cadillacs sold in China provide more legroom for rear-seat passengers because many wealthy Chinese ride in chauffeur-driven cars.

Finland:
Finland wants more vitamin D added to foods because Finns are exposed to less sunlight. This is one reason why cereal manufacturer Kellogg has to produce variations of its corn flakes and other cereals for the European market.

France:
Apples and pears require different labels across the EU. For example, in France labels on fruit must specify chemical treatments, preservation methods, and wax treatments—all in French of course!

India:
Disney sells school bags in India that are larger than those sold in the United States because Indian schools don't have student lockers.

Japan:
The Japanese are said to be in love with the ephemeral. They like products that are here today but gone tomorrow. To tap into this cultural trait, Nestlé offers limited edition candy for each season of the year.

Mexico:
To foster loyalty within its distribution system, Coca-Cola has offered life insurance to small retailers in Mexico.

Middle East:
When Coty Inc. ran an ad aimed at the Middle East market for its Jennifer Lopez perfume, it placed the ad in the newly launched Middle East edition of *Elle*. But the ad only showed the singer's face instead of her signature curvy silhouette that ran in the original ad.

Sources: Merissa Marr, "Small World," *Wall Street Journal*, June 11, 2007, p. A1; Antonio Regalado, "Marketers Pursue the Shallow-Pocketed," *Wall Street Journal*, January 26, 2007, p. B3; Mei Fong, "IKEA Hits Home in China," *Wall Street Journal*, March 2, 2006, p. B1; Christina Passariello, "Chic under Wraps," *Wall Street Journal*, June 20, 2006, p. B1; Gordon Fairclough, "Chinese Cadillac Offers Glimpse of GM's Future," *Wall Street Journal*, November 17, 2006, p. B1; and Kenji Hall, "Fad Marketing's Balancing Act," *BusinessWeek*, August 6, 2007, p. 42.

of marketing strategies. Ironically, the traditional multidomestic strategies of MNCs failed to take advantage of the global reach of these firms. Lessons learned in one domestic market were often not applied elsewhere. Good ideas in product development or promotions were not always shared among national subsidiaries. Similarly, multinationals often failed to take advantage of their global size in negotiating with suppliers and distributors.

Pan-Regional Marketing

Given the diseconomies of scale that plague individualized marketing strategies, each tailored to a specific local environment, many companies have begun to emphasize strategies for larger regions. These regional strategies encompass a number of

Global reach: AT&T is a multinational firm that operates in over 200 countries.

markets, such as pan-European strategies for Europe, and have come about as a result of regional economic and political integration. Such integration is also apparent in North America, where the United States, Canada, and Mexico have committed themselves to the far-reaching NAFTA trade pact. Companies considering regional strategies seek synergies in marketing operations in one region with the aim of achieving increased efficiency. Many firms are presently working on such solutions, moving from many multidomestic strategies toward selected pan-regional strategies.

Global Marketing

Global marketing strategy a single transnational strategy for a product, service, or business that nonetheless incorporates flexibility for local adaptation

Over the years, academics and international companies alike have become aware that opportunities for economies of scale and enhanced competitiveness are greater if firms can manage to integrate and create marketing strategies on a global scale. A multinational or **global marketing strategy** involves the creation of a single strategy for a product, service, or company for the entire global market. It encompasses many countries simultaneously and is aimed at leveraging the commonalities across many markets. Rather than tailoring a strategy perfectly to any individual market, a firm that pursues global marketing settles on a basic strategy that can be applied throughout the world market, all the while maintaining flexibility to adapt to local market requirements where necessary. Such strategies are inspired by the fact that many markets appear increasingly similar in environmental and customer requirements. The management challenges are to design marketing strategies that work well across multiple markets, while remaining alert to the possible adaptations that may be advisable on a market-to-market basis.

Thinking globally has its advantage. As we will see later in this book, global marketers enjoy several benefits beyond those of international marketers. Global marketing can allow firms to offer better products and services at a lower cost, even when adapting for local market conditions. These lower costs can be passed on to customers in the form of lower prices. Alternatively, global marketers can use their increased profits to invest in product development or increase promotion. Global marketers can often move quicker than international marketers, introducing new products rapidly into many foreign markets. They are also better armed to engage competition worldwide.

Even though global marketers face the unique challenge of finding marketing strategies that involve many countries at once, the skills and concepts that have been critical since the earliest stages in the history of marketing remain important and continue to be needed. Firms that pursue global strategies must be adept at international marketing as well because designing a global strategy does not mean ignoring national differences. Instead, a global strategy must reflect a sound understanding of the cultural, economic, and political environment of many countries. Few global marketing strategies can exist without local tailoring, which is the hallmark of international and multidomestic marketing. Managing global marketing is the last in a series of skills that managers must acquire to be successful in the global marketplace.

WHY STUDY GLOBAL MARKETING?

You have probably asked yourself why you should study global marketing. Each year multinational companies hire large numbers of marketing professionals. As these firms become increasingly globalized, competence in global marketing will become even more important in the future—and many marketing executives will be pursuing global marketing as a career. Other career opportunities exist with a large number of exporters, where job candidates will require international marketing skills. Even newly formed companies are now entering foreign markets at a young age.

With the service sector becoming increasingly globalized, many graduates joining service industries find themselves confronted with international opportunities at early stages of their careers. Today, consulting engineers, bankers, brokers, public accountants, medical services executives, and e-commerce specialists all need global marketing skills to compete in a rapidly changing environment. Consequently, a solid understanding and appreciation of global marketing will benefit the careers of most business students, regardless of the field or industry they choose to enter.

A Need for Global Mindsets

The Swedish firm IKEA is today one of the world's largest furniture retailing chains. IKEA entered the important U.S. market and quickly become a dominant player. IKEA's success was largely attributable to a new concept that it introduced to the United States: setting up large stores where consumers could browse, buy, and take furniture home in disassembled form at the end of their visit. IKEA is but one example of an international competitor entering a previously "safe" market with new ideas, bringing global competition to the doorstep of strictly domestic companies.

Few firms can avoid the impact of global competition today. Foreign competition has made enormous inroads into the manufacture of apparel, textiles, shoes, electronic equipment, and steel. Although foreign competition for many consumer goods has been evident for years, inroads by foreign firms into the industrial and capital goods markets have been equally spectacular.

The need to become more competitive in a global economy will force many changes on the typical company. Firms will have to compete in global markets to defend their own domestic markets and to keep up with global competitors based in other countries. These firms will need an increasing cadre of managers who can adopt a global perspective. This requires not only a knowledge of other countries, economies, and cultures but also a clear understanding of how the global economy works. Managers with a global perspective will also have to integrate actions taken in one national market with actions in another national market. This means that global marketers will be required to use ideas and experiences from a number of other countries so that the best products can be marketed the most efficiently and effectively. Managers with a global mindset will need to deal with new strategies that were not part of the domestic or older international business scenes.

To compete successfully in today's global marketplace, companies and their management must master certain areas. *Environmental competence* is needed to navigate the global economy. This area of expertise includes knowledge of the dynamics of the world economy, of major national markets, and of political, social, and cultural environments. *Analytic competence* is necessary to pull together a vast array of information concerning global markets and competitors. *Strategic competence* helps executives focus on the where, why, and how of global market participation. A global marketer must also possess *functional competence,* or a thorough background in all areas of marketing, such as product development, channel management, pricing, and promotion. *Managerial competence* is the ability to implement programs and to organize effectively on a global scale. In addition to these basic competencies, global marketers must attain an overarching **global competence** or the ability to balance local market needs with the demands of global efficiency and the opportunities of global synergies.

Global competence the ability to balance local market needs with the demands of global efficiency and the opportunities of global synergies

Organization of This Book

This text is structured around the basic requirements for making sound global marketing decisions, as depicted in Figure 1.2.

Part 1, Chapters 2 through 4, is concerned with the global marketing environment. Special emphasis is placed on the economic, cultural, political, and legal environments that companies must address in order to be successful.

Part 2, Chapters 5 through 7, concentrates on global market opportunity analysis. Chapters in this section discuss global buyers, competitors, and the research methods that are necessary to apply in order to understand marketing opportunities globally.

Chapters 8 and 9, which make up Part 3, deal with global market participation. Chapter 8 introduces key issues relating to market choices. Chapter 9 describes the various modes of entry that companies can employ once they decide to enter a foreign market.

Part 4, which comprises Chapters 10 through 15, aims at developing competence in designing global marketing programs consistent with a global strategy. The chapters in this section cover product and service strategies, global branding, social marketing, pricing, channel management, promotion, and advertising.

The text concludes with Part 5, which consists of Chapter 16. Here the emphasis is on building managerial competence in a global environment. Chapter 16

FIGURE **1.2**
Global Marketing Management

COMPETENCE LEVEL	DECISION AREA	
Environmental Competence	**Understanding the Global Marketing Environment**	
	Ch 2	The Global Economy
	Ch 3	Cultural and Social Forces
	Ch 4	Political and Regulatory Climate
Analytic Competence	**Analyzing Global Opportunities**	
	Ch 5	Global Markets
	Ch 6	Global Competitors
	Ch 7	Global Marketing Research
Strategic Competence	**Developing Global Participation Strategies**	
	Ch 8	Global Market Participation
	Ch 9	Global Market Entry Strategies
Functional Competence	**Designing Global Marketing Programs**	
	Ch 10	Global Product Strategies
	Ch 11	Global Strategies for Services, Brands, and Social Marketing
	Ch 12	Pricing for International and Global Markets
	Ch 13	Managing Global Distribution Channels
	Ch 14	Global Promotion Strategies
	Ch 15	Managing Global Advertising
Managerial Competence	**Managing the Global Marketing Effort**	
	Ch 16	Organizing for Global Marketing

discusses how firms organize for effective global marketing and also explores career issues of concern to the global marketer.

At the end of each of Chapters 2 through 16, two or three short cases are included to help you think concretely about global marketing and apply concepts from the chapter. At the end of the book, we have placed several longer, capstone cases that will give you a chance to synthesize what you have learned across chapters. For those of you wishing to put your knowledge to immediate use, the book website provides you with a guide to developing a Country Market Report (complete with research advice and numerous Internet links) to help you evaluate a national market for a product or service and determine the best form of market entry. Subsequently, the guide leads you through the steps to determine how your product or service should be adapted for the local market, what location or distribution channel is most appropriate, what price you should charge, and what promotional strategy you should pursue.

CONCLUSION

As a separate activity of business, global marketing is of great importance to nations, to individual companies, and to prospective managers. With markets and industries becoming increasingly globalized, most companies must become active participants in global marketing. The competitive positions of most companies, both abroad and in their domestic markets, rest on their ability to succeed in global markets. At the same time, the economies of entire countries depend on the global marketing skills of managers. The standard of living of many people will be governed by how well local industry performs in the global marketplace. These forces will place a premium on executive talent that is able to direct marketing operations from a global perspective. Clearly, many business professionals will need to understand the global dimension of the marketing function if they are to progress in their careers.

Although the need to develop a global competence may be clear, the circumstances that determine successful marketing practices for foreign markets are far less clear. The foreign marketing environment is characterized by a wide range of variables not typically encountered by domestic firms. This makes the job of global marketing extremely difficult. Despite the complexities involved, there are concepts and analytic tools that can help global marketers. By learning to use these concepts and tools, you can enhance your own global marketing competence. As a result, you will be able to contribute to the marketing operations of a wide range of firms, both domestic and foreign.

QUESTIONS FOR DISCUSSION

1. How is global marketing as a field related to your future career? How would you expect to come into contact with global marketing activities?

2. What do you think are the essential skills of a successful "global marketer"?

3. Which important skills make up an effective "global mindset"?

4. List ten things that are important to you that you hope to be able to understand or accomplish after studying this book.

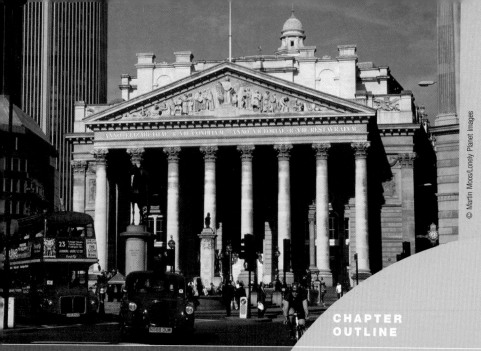

© Martin Moos/Lonely Planet Images

© Inmagine/18439GNG

2
The Global Economy

LEARNING OBJECTIVES

After studying this chapter, you should be able to:

- Distinguish among the basic theories of world trade: absolute advantage, comparative advantage, and competitive advantage.

- Discuss the pros and cons of global outsourcing.

- List and explain the principal parts of the balance-of-payments statement.

- Describe how and why exchange rates fluctuate.

- List and describe the major agencies that promote world trade, as well as those that promote economic and monetary stability.

- Describe common trade restrictions and explain their impact on international marketers.

- Compare the four different forms of economic integration.

WHEN EURODISNEY OPENED outside Paris, French attendance at the theme park was disappointing. Some attributed low ticket sales to a cultural snub of this American icon. Others noted a particularly wet and cold season. Still others blamed the strength of the local currency against the U.S. dollar. French consumers could buy—and spend—dollars at bargain prices. If the French wanted Disney, they could catch a plane to Florida's Disney World for not much more than they would pay for a weekend at EuroDisney.

The global economy constantly affects international marketing. Billions of dollars of goods and services are traded among nations each day. Currency exchange rates fluctuate, affecting sales and profits. Businesses establish operations and borrow funds in locations throughout the world. Banks lend and arbitrage currencies worldwide. When these transactions are interrupted or threatened, we can truly appreciate the scope and significance of the international economy.

This chapter introduces the important aspects of world trade and finance. We begin by explaining the concept of comparative advantage, the basis for international trade. Then we explain the international system to monitor world trade, particularly the balance-of-payments measurement system. From this base, we describe the workings of the foreign exchange market and the causes of exchange rate movements. We discuss the international agencies that promote economic and monetary stability, as well as the strategies that countries use to protect their own economies. We conclude with a look at economic integration as a means of promoting trade.

INTERNATIONAL TRADE: AN OVERVIEW

Few individuals in the world are totally self-sufficient. Why should they be? Restricting consumption to self-made goods lowers living standards by narrowing the range and reducing the quality of the goods we consume. For this reason, few nations have economies independent from the rest of the world, and it would be difficult to find a national leader willing or able to impose such an economic hardship on a country. This interdependency of global markets is apparent in even the most isolated regions of the world. When a recession in the United States causes consumers to cut back on purchasing cashmere sweaters and coats, nomadic herders in Mongolia who supply cashmere to manufacturers around the world see their earnings plummet.[1]

International Dependence of Nations

Foreign goods are central to the living standards of all nations. But as Table 2.1 shows, countries vary widely in their reliance on foreign trade. Imports are 14 percent of the gross domestic product (GDP) of Japan and 15 percent of the GDP of the United States, whereas Switzerland and Mexico have import-to-GDP ratios of 39 and 31 percent, respectively.

TABLE 2.1

IMPORTS AND EXPORTS AS A PERCENTAGE OF GDP (IN BILLIONS OF DOLLARS)

	GDP	IMPORTS	IMPORTS/GDP	EXPORTS	EXPORTS/GDP
Industrial Countries					
France	2,562	611	23%	539	21%
Germany	3,297	1,059	32	1,328	40
Canada	1,326	380	28	420	32
Japan	4,376	622	14	714	16
Italy	2,107	511	24	500	24
Switzerland	415	161	39	172	41
United Kingdom	2,727	624	23	439	16
United States	13,811	2,017	15	1,162	8
Developing Countries					
Argentina	262	44	17%	55	21%
Brazil	1,314	120	9	160	12
China	3,280	955	29	1,217	37
India	1,171	218	19	145	12
Mexico	893	281	31	271	30
Russian Federation	1,291	199	15	352	27
South Africa	277	79	29	64	23

Source: Adapted from United Nations Comtrade Database 2007 and World Bank Group, Data Profiles, 2007 (http://www.worldbank.org).

The figures given in Table 2.1 are useful for identifying the international dependence of nations, but they should be viewed as rough indicators only. In any widespread disruption of international trade, there is little doubt that the United States would be harmed much less than the Netherlands. Yet this is not to say a disruption of trade would not be harmful to countries with large domestic markets such as the United States and Japan, which both depend heavily on world trade for growth. In the United States, $1 billion of exports supports the creation, on average, of about 11,500 jobs.[2]

The Growth in World Trade

After its stock market crash of 1929, the United States turned its back on free trade. Fearing losses of jobs at home, this country tried to assist local industries by sharply increasing taxes on imports from other countries. Unfortunately, other countries retaliated with similar measures. In less than a year, world trade collapsed, sending the world into a global depression. Two hard-hit countries were Germany and Japan. Many believe that this severe economic downturn encouraged the militaristic regimes that precipitated World War II. After the war, the United States and other industrialized nations were eager for world trade to be promoted and to expand.

Their vision has certainly come to pass. World trade has increased over 22-fold since 1950, far outstripping the growth in world GDP. This growth has been fueled by the continued opening of markets around the world. The Bretton Woods conference of world leaders in 1944 led to the establishment of the General Agreement on Tariffs and Trade (GATT), which we will discuss in detail later. GATT, and subsequently the World Trade Organization (WTO), helped to reduce import tariffs from 40 percent in 1947 to an estimated 4 percent today. The principle of free trade has led to the building of market interdependencies. International trade has grown much more rapidly than world GDP output, demonstrating that national economies are becoming much more closely linked and interdependent via their exports and imports. This interdependence has created many opportunities for international marketers but has made world trade more vulnerable to global recessions. The WTO predicted a 9 percent drop in world trade as a result of collapsing global demand in 2009.[3]

Foreign direct investment, another indication of global integration, increased over 100 percent in a single decade, and services are an important and growing part of the world's economy. Industries such as banking, telecommunications, insurance, construction, transportation, tourism, and consulting make up over half the national income of many rich economies. A country's **invisible exports** include services, transfers from workers abroad, and income earned on overseas investments.

Invisible exports a country's earnings abroad from intangibles such as services, remittances, and income earned on overseas investments

THE BASIC THEORIES OF WORLD TRADE: ABSOLUTE, COMPARATIVE, AND COMPETITIVE ADVANTAGE

Internationally traded goods and services are important to most countries, as shown in Table 2.1. Because jobs and standard of living seem to be so closely tied to these inflows and outflows, there is much debate about why a particular country finds its comparative advantages in certain goods and services and not in others.

The past 25 years have witnessed not only a dramatic rise in the volume of trade but also numerous changes in its patterns. Countries that once exported vast amounts of steel, such as the United States, are now net importers of the metal. Other nations, such as India, once known for producing inexpensive handicrafts now compete globally in high-tech products. What caused these changes in trade patterns? Why do countries that are able to produce virtually any product choose to specialize in certain goods? Where do international cost advantages originate? As the 21st century continues, will we still think of Indonesia and China as having the greatest advantage in handmade goods, or will they come to be like Japan and Taiwan are today?

The early work of Adam Smith provides the foundation for understanding trade today. Smith saw trade as a way to promote efficiency because it fostered competition, led to specialization, and resulted in economies of scale. Specialization supports the concept of absolute advantage—that is, sell to other countries the goods that utilize your special skills and resources, and buy the rest from those who have some other advantage. This theory of selling what you are best at producing is known as *absolute advantage.* But what if you have no advantages? Will all your manufacturers be driven out of business? David Ricardo, in his 1817 work *Principles of Political Economy,* offered his theory of *comparative advantage.* This theory maintains that it is still possible to produce profitably what one is best at producing, even if someone else is better. The following sections further develop the concepts of absolute and comparative advantage, the economic basis of free trade and hence of all global trade.

Absolute Advantage

Although many variables may be listed as the primary determinants of international trade, productivity differences rank high on the list. Take, for example, two countries—Vietnam and Germany. Suppose the average Vietnamese worker can produce either 400 machines or 1,600 tons of tomatoes in one year. Over the same time period, the average German worker can produce either 500 machines or 500 tons of tomatoes. (See Example 1 in Table 2.2.) In this case, German workers can produce more machinery, absolutely, than Vietnamese workers can, whereas Vietnamese workers can produce more tomatoes, absolutely, than can their German counterparts. Given these figures, Vietnam is the obvious low-cost producer of tomatoes and should export them to Germany. Similarly, Germany is the low-cost producer of machines and should export them to Vietnam.

Currently China has an absolute advantage in garlic production. Chinese farm labor receives $1 per day versus $5 in Mexico and $8.50 an hour in California. Garlic has a shelf life of up to nine months and can be easily shipped. Not unexpectedly, the California producers have been devastated.[4]

Comparative Advantage

We should not conclude from the previous examples that absolute differences in production capabilities are necessary for trade to occur. Consider the same two countries in the first example—Vietnam and Germany. Now assume that the average Vietnamese worker can produce either 200 machines or 800 tons of tomatoes each year, whereas the average German worker can produce either 500 machines or 1,000 tons of tomatoes (see Example 2 in Table 2.2). Germany has an absolute advantage in both goods, and it appears that Vietnam will benefit from trade

TABLE 2.2	ABSOLUTE VERSUS COMPARATIVE ADVANTAGE: WORKER PRODUCTIVITY EXAMPLES	
	VIETNAM	**GERMANY**
Example 1		
Yearly output per worker		
Machinery	400	500
Tomatoes	1,600 tons	500 tons
Absolute advantage	Tomatoes	Machinery
Example 2		
Yearly output per worker		
Machinery	200	500
Tomatoes	800 tons	1,000 tons
Opportunity costs of production	1 machine costs	1 machine costs
	4 tons tomatoes *or*	2 tons tomatoes *or*
	1 ton tomatoes costs	1 ton tomatoes costs
	0.25 machine	0.50 machine
Absolute advantage	None	Tomatoes
		Machinery
Comparative advantage	Tomatoes	Machinery

because it can buy from Germany cheaper goods than Vietnam can make for itself. Even here, however, the basis for mutually advantageous trade is present. The reason lies in the concept of comparative advantage.

Comparative advantage measures a product's cost of production not in monetary terms but in terms of the forgone opportunity to produce something else. It focuses on tradeoffs. To illustrate, the production of machines means that resources cannot be devoted to the production of tomatoes. In Germany, the worker who produces 500 machines will not be able to grow 1,000 tons of tomatoes. The cost can be stated as follows: Each ton of tomatoes costs 0.5 machine, or 1 machine costs 2 tons of tomatoes. In Vietnam, producing 200 machines forces the sacrifice of 800 tons of tomatoes. Alternatively, this means that 1 ton of tomatoes costs 0.25 machine, or 1 machine costs 4 tons of tomatoes.

From this example, we see that even though Vietnam has an absolute disadvantage in both commodities, it still has a comparative advantage in tomatoes. For Vietnam the cost of producing 1 ton of tomatoes is 0.25 machine, whereas for Germany the cost is 0.5 machine. Similarly, even though Germany has an absolute advantage in both products, it has a comparative cost advantage only in machines. It costs Germany only 2 tons of tomatoes to produce a single machine, whereas in Vietnam the cost is 4 tons of tomatoes.

The last step in examining the concept of comparative advantage is to choose a mutually advantageous trading ratio and show how it can benefit both countries. Any trading ratio between 1 machine = 2 tons of tomatoes (Germany's domestic trading ratio) and 1 machine = 4 tons of tomatoes (Vietnam's domestic trading ratio) will benefit both nations (see Table 2.3). Suppose we choose 1 machine = 3 tons of tomatoes. Because Germany will be exporting machinery, it gains by

TABLE 2.3	MUTUALLY ADVANTAGEOUS TRADING RATIOS	
TOMATOES		**MACHINES**
Germany, 1 ton tomatoes = 0.50 machine		Vietnam, 1 machine = 4 tons tomatoes
Germany, 1 machine = 2 tons tomatoes		Vietnam, 1 ton tomatoes = 0.20 machine

getting 3 tons of tomatoes rather than the 2 tons it would have produced domestically. Likewise, because Vietnam will be exporting tomatoes, it gains because 1 machine can be imported for the sacrifice of only 3 tons of tomatoes, rather than the 4 tons it would have to sacrifice if it made the machine in Vietnam.

Our discussion of comparative advantage illustrates that relative rather than absolute differences in productivity can form a determining basis for international trade. Although the concept of comparative advantage provides a powerful tool for explaining the rationale for mutually advantageous trade, it gives little insight into the source of the differences in relative productivity. Specifically, why does a country find its comparative advantage in one good or service rather than in another? Is it by chance that the United States is a net exporter of aircraft, machinery, and chemicals but a net importer of steel, textiles, and consumer electronic products? Or can we find some systematic explanations for this pattern?

The notion of comparative advantage requires that nations make intensive use of those factors they possess in abundance—in particular, land, labor, natural resources, and capital. Thus Hungary, with its low labor cost of US$1 per hour, will export labor-intensive goods, such as unsophisticated chest freezers and table linen, whereas Sweden, with its high-quality iron ore deposits, will export high-grade steel.

Competitive Advantage

Michael Porter argues that even though the theory of comparative advantage has appeal, it is limited by its traditional focus on land, labor, natural resources, and capital. His study of ten trading nations that account for 50 percent of world exports and one hundred industries resulted in a new and expanded theory.[5] This theory postulates that whether a country will have a significant impact on the competitive advantage of an industry depends on the following factors:

- The elements of production
- The nature of domestic demand
- The presence of appropriate suppliers or related industries
- The conditions in the country that govern how companies are created, organized, and managed, as well as the nature of domestic rivalry

Porter argues that strong local competition often benefits a national industry in the global marketplace. Firms in a competitive environment are forced to produce quality products efficiently. Demanding consumers in the home market and pressing local needs can also stimulate firms to solve problems and develop proprietary knowledge before foreign competitors do.

A good example of a country that enjoys a competitive advantage in digital products is South Korea. South Koreans are among the most "wired" people on earth. More than half of Korea's households have broadband service, and more than 60 percent of Koreans own cell phones. Seventy percent of share trades in the Korean securities market are done online. Korean companies can use entire urban populations in their home market as test markets for their latest digital ideas. This in turn gives these Korean companies an advantage when they want to export new products or know-how abroad.[6] Similarly, Japan has a competitive advantage in energy conservation. With few domestic sources of energy, Japan has been at the forefront of designing manufacturing processes that consume the least amount of energy. When the price of oil rises, this gives Japan an advantage—especially compared with other Asian countries.[7]

A nation's competitive advantage can change over time. China was once known for ultra-cheap labor and a business environment relatively free of government regulaton. Many believe those days are now over. Manufacturing costs are increasing in China, threatening the country's previously successful export model that was based on low export prices.[8]

GLOBAL OUTSOURCING

For 200 years, most economists have agreed with the theory of comparative advantage: Nations gain if they trade with each other and specialize in what they do best. However, advances in telecommunications, such as broadband and the Internet, have created for the first time a global market for skilled workers that threatens traditional ideas of national specialization. According to comparative advantage, India, with its vast numbers of low-paid, low-skilled workers, should specialize in low-wage standardized products. Yet the country competes successfully in a global market for white-collar workers, undercutting the wages of highly skilled Americans and Europeans.[9] Tata Consultancy Services, the largest outsourcing company in India, derives 50 percent of its income from North America and another 10 percent from continental Europe.[10] Increasingly, information technology (IT) jobs and back-office services (such as credit collection, benefits and pension administration, insurance claims processing, and tax accounting) are outsourced to cheaper labor in developing countries.[11]

A study published by the McKinsey Global Institute on the national impact of outsourcing back-office services and IT jobs to India reveals that outsourcing need not be a zero-sum game. This is not to say there are not national winners and losers.[12] To date, as depicted in Table 2.4, the United States and India would appear to be net winners, whereas Germany would be a loser.

Direct benefits of outsourcing are captured by India, such as wages, profits to local firms, and taxes collected by the Indian government. Indian workers in the

TABLE 2.4 NATIONAL NET GAINS FOR EACH U.S. DOLLAR SPENT IN INDIA ON OUTSOURCING BACK-OFFICE SERVICES AND IT FUNCTIONS

	INDIA	USA	GERMANY
Outsourced wages, profits, taxes	$ .33	—	—
Cost savings	—	$ .58	$ .52
New revenues from India	—	.05	.03
Repatriated earnings	—	.04	—
Redeployment of workers	—	.46	.25
Total	$ .33	$1.13	$ .80

Many multinational firms now outsource customer service to call centers overseas such as this one in India.

Masterfile (Royalty-Free Div.)

back-office services and IT fields, who are usually college educated and proficient in English, have seen their wages soar in recent years—though not enough to stop the outsourcing to India. However, new revenues and repatriated earnings from multinationals selling to firms in India are captured in Germany and the United States. Because U.S. multinationals have a larger presence in the Indian market than do German multinationals, the United States captures more of these particular benefits than does Germany. Cost savings from outsourcing is an important benefit as well. Again, this benefit is lower for Germany than the United States because Indian businesses in these areas operate in English. This raises the relative coordination costs for German companies working with Indian firms. The biggest advantage in realized benefits for the United States over Germany lies in the redeployment of workers (particularly to higher-value-added jobs). Workers in the United States who are displaced by outsourcing are more likely to find new jobs, and find them more quickly, than are similar workers in Germany.

However, even if the United States currently gains as a whole from global outsourcing, the losses and benefits of outsourcing accrue differently to different groups. For this reason global outsourcing remains very controversial and politically explosive. New revenues from India and repatriated earnings accrue primarily to investors, not workers. How the cost savings from outsourcing are distributed depends on the relative power of the different groups—investors, labor, and buyers. As labor in the United States loses its bargaining power in the new global labor market, most of the savings are likely again to accrue to investors, not labor.

If white-collar job losses rise to 6 percent in the United States, the wages for remaining workers could be depressed by 2 to 3 percent. This is similar to the wage-level losses due to earlier outsourcing in manufacturing. Another concern is whether the United States can continue to realize gains from redeployment of labor as the type of job outsourced becomes increasingly sophisticated. Despite the greater worker mobility in the United States, only about 30 percent of laid-off workers earn the same or more after three years. When only manufacturing jobs moved to developing countries, about 25 percent of the U.S. labor force was affected. With the addition of professional jobs at risk to outsourcing, a majority of American workers could lose more from job losses and the depression of wages than they gain from lower prices of goods.[13]

BALANCE OF PAYMENTS

Newspapers, magazines, and nightly TV news programs are filled with stories related to aspects of international business. Often, media coverage centers on the implications of a nation's trade deficit or surplus or on the economic consequences of an undervalued or overvalued currency. What are trade deficits? What factors will cause a currency's international value to change? The first step in answering these questions is to gain a clear understanding of the contents and meaning of a nation's balance of payments.

The **balance of payments (BOP)** is an accounting record of the transactions between the residents of one country and the residents of the rest of the world over a given period of time. Transactions in which domestic residents either purchase assets (goods and services) from abroad or reduce foreign liabilities are considered *outflows of funds*, because payments abroad must be made. Similarly, transactions in which domestic residents either sell assets to foreign residents or increase their liabilities to foreigners are *inflows of funds*, because payments from abroad are received.

Listed in Table 2.5 are the principal parts of the balance-of-payments statement: the current account, the capital account, and the official transactions account. There are three items under the **current account**. The **goods category** states the monetary values of a nation's international transactions in physical goods. The **services category** shows the values of a wide variety of transactions, such as transportation services, consulting, travel, passenger fares, fees, royalties, rent, and investment income. Finally, **unilateral transfers** include all transactions for which there is no quid pro quo. Private remittances, personal gifts, philanthropic donations, relief, and aid are included within this account. Unilateral transfers have less impact on the U.S. market but are important to markets elsewhere. For example, remittances from workers abroad have fueled demand for consumer products in many developing countries, such as Egypt, Mexico, and the Philippines.

The **capital account** is divided into two parts on the basis of time. *Short-term transactions* refer to maturities less than or equal to one year, and *long-term*

Balance of payments (BOP) an accounting record of the transactions between the residents of one country and the residents of the rest of the world over a given period of time

Current account a principal part of the balance of payments statement that includes the key sub-accounts of goods, services, and unilateral transfers

Goods or merchandise account BOP account stating the monetary value of a country's international transactions in physical goods

Services account BOP account stating a country's international transactions in intangibles such as transportation services, consulting, royalties on intellectual property, and dividends on foreign investment

Unilateral transfers all the transactions for which there is no quid pro quo, such as private remittances, personal gifts, philanthropic donations, and aid

Capital account principal BOP account that records a country's international financial assets and liabilities over the BOP period

TABLE 2.5	BALANCE OF PAYMENTS		
		USES OF FUNDS	**SOURCES OF FUNDS**
Current Account			
1. Goods		Imports	Exports
2. Services		Imports	Exports
3. Unilateral transfers		Paid abroad	From abroad
Capital Account			
1. Short-term investments		Made abroad	From abroad
2. Long-term investments		Made abroad	From abroad
a. Portfolio investment			
b. Direct investment			
Official Transactions Account			
Official reserve changes		Gained	Lost

transactions refer to maturities longer than one year. Purchases of Treasury bills, certificates of deposit, foreign exchange, and commercial paper are typical short-term investments. Long-term investments are separated further into portfolio investments and direct investments.

In general, the purchaser of a **portfolio investment** holds no management control over the foreign investment. Debt securities, such as notes and bonds, are included under this heading. **Foreign direct investments** are long-term ownership interests, such as business capital outlays in foreign subsidiaries and branches. Stock purchases are included as well, but only if such ownership entails substantial control over the foreign company. Countries differ in the percentage of total outstanding stock an individual must hold in order for an investment to be considered a direct investment in the balance-of-payment statements. These values range from 10 percent to 25 percent.

Because it is recorded in double-entry bookkeeping form, the balance of payments as a whole must always have its inflows (sources of funds) equal its outflows (uses of funds). Therefore, the concept of a deficit or surplus refers only to selected parts of the entire statement. A deficit occurs when the particular outflows (uses of funds) exceed the particular inflows (sources of funds). A surplus occurs when the inflows considered exceed the corresponding outflows. In this sense, a nation's surplus or deficit is similar to that of individuals or businesses. If we spend more than we earn, we are in a deficit position. If we earn more than we spend, we are running a surplus.

The most widely used measure of a nation's international payments position is the statement of balance on current account. It shows whether a nation is living within or beyond its means. Because this statement includes unilateral transfers, deficits (in the absence of government intervention) must be financed by international borrowing or by selling foreign investments. Therefore, the measure is considered to be a reflection of a nation's financial claims on other countries.

EXCHANGE RATES

The purchase of a foreign good or service can be thought of as involving two sequential transactions: the purchase of the foreign currency, followed by the purchase of the foreign item itself. If the cost of buying either the foreign currency or the foreign item rises, the price to the importer increases. A ratio that measures the value of one currency in terms of another currency is called an **exchange rate**. An exchange rate makes it possible to compare domestic and foreign prices.

When a currency rises in value against another currency, it is said to **appreciate**. When it falls in value, it is said to **depreciate**. Therefore, a change in the value of the U.S. dollar exchange rate from 0.50 British pound to 0.65 British pound is an appreciation of the dollar and a depreciation of the pound. The dollar now buys more pounds, whereas a greater number of pounds must be spent to purchase 1 dollar.

The Foreign Exchange Market

Foreign exchange transactions are handled on an over-the-counter market, largely by phone or e-mail. Private and commercial customers as well as banks, brokers, and central banks conduct millions of transactions on this worldwide market daily.

As Figure 2.1 shows, the foreign exchange market has a hierarchical structure. Private customers deal mainly with banks in the retail market, and banks stand ready either to buy or to sell foreign exchange as long as a free and active market for the currency exists. Banks that have foreign exchange departments trade with private commercial customers on the retail market, but they also deal with other

Portfolio investments investments, such as the purchase of stocks and bonds, over which investors assume no direct management control

Foreign direct investments foreign investments over which investors assume some if not all direct management control

Exchange rate the ratio that measures the value of one currency in terms of another currency

Appreciation an increase in value or price of a currency

Depreciation a decrease in value or price of a currency

banks (domestic or foreign) and brokers on the wholesale market. Generally, these wholesale transactions are for amounts of US41 million or more. Not all banks participate directly in the foreign exchange market. Smaller banks may handle customers' business through correspondent banks.

Central banks play a key role in the foreign exchange markets because they are the ultimate controllers of domestic money supplies. When they enter the market to influence the exchange rate directly, they deal mainly with brokers and large money market banks. Their trading is done not to make a profit but to attain some macroeconomic goal, such as altering the exchange rate value, reducing inflation, or changing domestic interest rates. In general, even if central banks do not intervene in the foreign exchange markets, their actions influence exchange rate values because large increases in a nation's money supply increase its inflation rate and lower the international value of its currency.

FIGURE 2.1
Structure of the Foreign Exchange Market

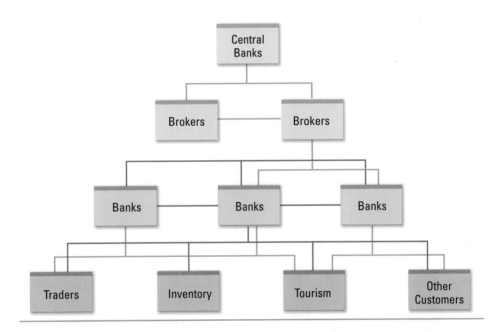

A sign for currency exchange at the airport in Osaka, Japan. When the Japanese yen increases in value against the U.S. dollar, American products can become less expensive and more appealing to Japanese buyers. But Japanese products become more costly in the U.S. marketplace.

Causes of Exchange Rate Movements

Exchange rates are among the most closely watched and politically sensitive economic variables. Regardless of which way the rates move, some groups are hurt and other groups are helped. When a currency's value rises, domestic businesses find it more difficult to compete internationally, and the domestic unemployment rate may rise. When the value of a currency falls, foreign goods become more expensive, the cost of living increases, and domestically produced goods become cheaper to foreign buyers. What are the causes of these exchange rate movements, and to what extent can governments influence them?

Freely floating currency a currency whose exchange rate is determined by the market forces of supply and demand

Most major currencies are **freely floating**. Their exchange rates are determined by the forces of supply and demand. Consumers in different countries can affect the supply and demand for these national currencies. An increase in a nation's GDP gives consumers in that country the wherewithal to purchase more goods and services. Because many of the newly purchased goods are likely to be foreign, increases in GDP will raise the demand for foreign products and therefore raise the demand for foreign currencies.

Similarly, a relatively high inflation rate can shift consumer demand and weaken a currency. If the U.S. inflation rate exceeds that of Japan, then U.S. goods will become progressively more expensive than Japanese goods. Consequently, U.S. consumers will begin to demand more Japanese goods, thereby increasing the supply of dollars to the foreign exchange market while increasing the demand for Japanese yen. For the same reason, Japanese consumers will reduce their demand for dollars (that is, reduce their supply of yen) as they purchase fewer U.S. goods. Therefore, inflation in the United States will cause the international value of the dollar to fall and the value of other currencies to rise.

Supply and demand for currencies are also affected by investors and speculators. If, for example, Japanese interest rates were greater than U.S. interest rates (adjusted for such things as risk, taxes, and maturity), then investors would have an incentive to sell dollars and purchase yen in order to place their funds where they earned the highest return—in Japan. Speculators buy and sell currencies in anticipation of changing future values. If there were a widespread expectation that the Japanese yen would rise in value relative to the dollar, speculators would try to purchase yen now (that is, sell dollars) in anticipation of that change.

Finally, governments affect foreign exchange markets in a variety of ways. Because governments exercise strong and direct controls over domestic money supplies, their activities affect inflation rates and interest rates, which, in turn, affect the exchange rates of their currencies. Perhaps the most pronounced impact governments have is as buyers and sellers in foreign exchange markets. Suppose the United States and Japan agreed to lower the dollar's value relative to the yen. For this to occur, dollars would have to be supplied—and yen demanded—in the foreign exchange markets. For the United States, this would mean putting upward pressure on the domestic money supply as newly created dollars were exchanged for circulating Japanese yen. For Japan, this type of intervention would mean putting downward pressure on its money supply as dollar reserves were used to take yen off the market.

Managed Currencies

The foreign exchange market just described is not applicable to all currencies. Small, less developed countries often have currencies that attract little global demand. No effective international markets develop for these **soft currencies**. Also, until recently, most foreign exchange rates in developing countries were set by the

Soft currency a currency that attracts little global demand

WORLD BEAT 2.1

ADOPTING THE DOLLAR

MANY DEVELOPING COUNTRIES currently link their national currency to the U.S. dollar. However, a peg to the dollar is not always an easy ride. Ask Dubai and Vietnam.

Dubai is one of seven emirates that comprise the United Arab Emirates (UAE), whose national currency, the dirham, is linked to the dollar. Dubai has successfully diversified its economy beyond oil and become a regional hub for tourism and financial services. To support this expansion and its consequent construction boom, the emirate imports a vast number of foreign laborers. Many of these laborers come from India and are responsible for billions of dollars of remittances sent home to their families. However, as the Indian rupee revalued against the U.S. dollar, it consequently revalued against the dirham. Salaries denominated in dirham translated to far less rupees. Furthermore, as demand for housing and imports soared in boomtown Dubai, so did inflation. However, because of the dollar peg, the UAE's Central Bank was unable to raise interest rates to discourage inflation as long as the United States kept rates low to encourage its own sluggish economy. The result: widespread labor protests and dozens of arrests in Dubai. Despite this strife, the UAE decided to maintain its peg to the dollar.

Vietnam pegged its currency, the dong, to the U.S. dollar in the 1990s when this communist country first began to court foreign investors. Vietnamese Americans regularly send dollars to relatives in their homeland. Similar to Dubai, Vietnam experienced a period of rapid growth accompanied by high inflation. Vietnam has since increased the band around the dollar price in which the dong can be traded. In response, the dollar has declined against the dong. This is not good news for Vietnamese processors of seafood who saw exports tumble as the dong revalued.

Sources: Chip Cummins, "Dollar's Slide Fuels Strife in Dubai," *Wall Street Journal*, November 1, 2007, p. 8; Joanna Slater and Chip Cummins, "Wealthy Nations in Gulf Rethink Peg to Dollar," *Wall Street Journal*, November 20, 2007, p. A1; Polya Lesova, "U.A.E. Task Force to Study Dirham's Peg to Dollar," *MarketWatch*, March 10, 2008; and James Hookway, "Vietnam Tries to Cut Loose from Falling Dollar," *Wall Street Journal*, March 19, 2008, p. A8.

Pegged currency a currency whose price is fixed by its government to another currency or basket of currencies

government. This is still true in many countries today. Managed currencies are usually **pegged** to the currency of a developed country that is a major trading partner. Many are pegged to the U.S. dollar. Some are pegged to a combination, or basket, of major currencies. The value of the local currency relative to the major currency is sometimes kept stable and other times allowed to fluctuate a few percentage points based on market demand.

Pegged currencies are not immune to the forces of supply and demand. Defending a peg from devaluation requires keeping a relatively strong demand for the local currency in line with the price set by the government. If domestic inflation is higher than that of trading partners, local goods can quickly become too overpriced to sell on export markets. However, governments cannot indefinitely prop up currencies if there is little demand for them because of such factors as low levels of export earnings or low levels of inward-bound foreign investment. Trying to defend a peg too long can result in sudden large devaluations in developing countries instead of more gradual ones.

For example, Venezuela experienced several years of depressed export earnings because of continued low prices on oil, its major export. The Venezuelan bolivar plunged against the U.S. dollar after the Venezuelan government relinquished a six-year-old system to keep the bolivar steady with the dollar. Even with the collapse of the bolivar, Venezuela experienced capital flight as people hurried to exchange bolivars for dollars. Although few currencies today are nonconvertible, Venezuela was forced to establish currency controls to restrict access to foreign exchange. This caused problems for foreign firms in the country such as General

Motors, Ford, and Procter & Gamble. These firms waited months for the government to approve requests to change local currency into U.S. dollars for purposes of paying foreign suppliers.[14]

Although it has evolved into a major currency in world trade, the Chinese yuan doesn't trade freely but has been kept pegged primarily to the U.S. dollar by the Chinese government. Neighboring Asian countries have sometimes seen their currencies appreciate against a weakening U.S. dollar. When this occurs, manufacturers in Korea, Thailand, and Taiwan have to decide whether to raise prices in the United States or cut into their already thin margins at home. This puts manufacturers in these countries at a disadvantage compared with manufacturers in China, where the yuan remains more aligned to the dollar. For example, 30 to 40 percent of Korean exports compete directly with Chinese exports.[15] Consequently, a major debate has emerged regarding managed and floating currencies. Is an exchange rate system in which currencies such as the Chinese yuan are pegged but the euro and the yen float freely the best way to balance the world's trade and capital flows?[16]

Implications for Global Marketers

Intuitively, citizens may be proud of a strong national currency. A strong currency can, however, present challenges to international marketers and particularly to firms that export products manufactured in their home country. The strengthening of a domestic or home currency against the currency of that country's trading partners can have a negative effect on exporters. Currency fluctuations can also affect global marketers in other ways, such as the valuation of overseas sales, profits, and licensing fees. Currency fluctuations also impact the costs of marketing investments in foreign markets and may serve as the catalyst for a firm to expand operations in a foreign market or even leave a market.

Impact on Export Markets. When the currency of a foreign market devalues against an exporter's home currency, there are immediate implications for export pricing. The costs of producing the product increase immediately when translated into the foreign currency in which the product is priced and sold. Marketers must decide between two options. They can raise prices in the export market to preserve profit margins or they can keep prices steady in hopes of sustaining or even increasing market share.

Maintaining the Export Price. An exporter may decide against raising prices in an export market in which currency devaluation has occurred. Choosing this option means that the firm decides to accept lower margins and consequently lower profits on its export sales. Such a decision is not an easy one to make. However there are good reasons to consider this option.

Significant currency devaluation often denotes a period of economic stress. Some necessary goods that are imported, such as energy and food, will increase in price. This leaves local buyers with less discretionary income. Many consumers look for bargains and cut back on nonessential products. Following a major devaluation of the ruble, Russian consumers saw their purchasing power plummet. Consequently, sales of Coca-Cola fell 60 percent in Russia.[17] Similarly, business buyers put off capital purchases such as buying new machinery. Raising prices in this environment may result in a significant loss of sales volume. This loss of sales volume may not be offset by the product's increased price.

Another reason to maintain prices is a competitive concern. Some competitors may enjoy a currency advantage as the result of the devaluation in the export mar-

Currency devaluations in overseas markets elicit various corporate responses. After a 50 percent devaluation in the peso, major automakers reported multimillion dollar losses in the Argentine market. Incomes in real local currency were significantly depressed, making financing options for car purchases all the more important to the marketing mix. Ford Argentina also launched a program in which farmers could exchange crops for vehicles.

ket. Local producers in the export market will not immediately experience a rise in costs. Consequently, locally produced products become more competitive compared to imported products. In addition, certain global competitors may also experience a currency advantage if their home currencies do not revalue as much against the currency of the export market. For example, were the Australian dollar to revalue more against the euro than the Brazilian real revalued against the euro, then Brazilian beef exporters would experience a currency advantage over Australian beef exporters when selling to the euro zone. Brazilian suppliers might feel little need to raise prices in the European market, thus forcing Australian producers to keep prices down as well. Therefore, exporters must not only consider the impact of currency fluctuations on customers; exporters must also monitor their major competitors whose home currencies could provide them an advantage as a result of currency fluctuation.

For example, such a competitive currency advantage has helped many nontraditional destinations increase their share of the American study abroad market. Nearly a quarter million U.S. students study abroad every year, and a favorite destination is Europe. However, when the U.S. dollar depreciates too much against the euro, universities seek cheaper overseas opportunities for their students. As a result, African countries such as Ghana, Mali, and South Africa have increased their market share of American students studying abroad.[18]

In the case of exporters that compete fully or partially on cost, raising prices can be especially problematic. When India's rupee strengthened against the U.S. dollar, it particularly hurt India's IT services industry, whose export sales total $35 billion annually. Although industry costs rose in dollar terms, Indian IT firms did not increase their prices to U.S. customers to fully cover these increased costs. Profitability in the industry fell an estimated 8 percent.[19]

If management decides that prices cannot be increased, they may seek ways to contain costs instead. When the U.S. dollar reached a 16-year high against most foreign currencies, the cost of American-made products (translated into those foreign currencies) soared. This forced U.S. manufacturers to find creative ways to compete overseas as well as to protect their own home market from foreign competitors that enjoyed a cost advantage. Automatic Feed Company of Ohio embarked on its most extensive product redesign in its 52-year history trying to offset the cost advantage of its foreign competitors.[20]

Another way to contain costs is to source the export market from a cheaper location. For many years, O.R.T. Technologies resisted moving any operations outside its home base of Israel. However, when the Israeli shekel soared 31 percent against the U.S. dollar, the company was forced to transfer some of its development work to Eastern Europe.[21] Many Canadian exporters are hurt when the Canadian dollar increases in value against the U.S. dollar, especially since 85 percent of merchandise exports go to the United States. However, some Canadian exporters can better weather the revaluation of the Canadian currency because they have U.S. manufacturing operations as well.[22]

Of course the ability to enact cost containment varies by situation as well as by firm. If devaluation of a currency in an overseas market is large and swift, this makes adapting to it more difficult than if it is more predictable and gradual. In any case, larger firms usually have more resources to respond with cost-cutting measures than do smaller firms.

Raising the Export Price. Exporters may also decide to raise prices in an export market in response to devaluation of a foreign currency. This is an attempt to pass on to buyers some or all of the exporter's increased costs. In order to successfully employ this strategy, a global marketer must answer the following questions:

Can the brand command a higher price? As we will discuss in Chapter 11, the value of a brand is the difference between a price the branded product commands and the price a buyer would pay for the product without a brand. A strong global brand may be able to sustain increased prices without losing as many buyers as would a lesser known brand or a generic product.

Are you selling a prestige product? Some consumer goods and services are bought largely for prestige. In such cases, consumers may be more likely to accept higher prices, since price is not their major purchase criteria. High prices may in fact bestow increased prestige on the product. Hermes, a European firm that sells luxury scarves and ties, marked up its entire U.S. line by 5 percent when the U.S. dollar devalued against the euro.[23]

Can you deliver more value to the buyer in return for charging a higher price? Marketers should be wary, however, about relying on a product's brand or prestige. During the most recent global downturn, even luxury products with prestigious global brands experienced declines in sales. If companies raise prices in export markets, they may need to invest in more salespeople and market research in order to deliver better value to customers. One creative way to offer value to buyers is to mitigate some of their foreign exchange risk. One year when the U.S. dollar was tumbling against the euro, many European hotels offered guaranteed prices in dollars to American tourists seeking to book rooms.[24]

Impact on Subsidiary Earnings.   Many global marketers own subsidiaries abroad where products sold in that market are produced in that market. In such cases, devaluation of the local currency does not cause an immediate increase in production costs for the local subsidiary of the foreign firm. (If the subsidiary imports a significant portion of their products' inputs, however, production costs will eventually rise as import costs rise.)

Nonetheless, currency fluctuations overseas affect the reporting of earnings in the market where a devaluation or revaluation has occurred. In the year following a major devaluation of the Argentine peso, consumer expenditures on leisure and recreation remained steady when measured in pesos. However, these expenditures fell 68 percent when measured in U.S. dollars.[25] A U.S.-based entertainment firm operating in the Argentine market would inevitably report a significant drop in dollar earnings. Alternatively, if the peso revalues against the U.S. dollar, reported earnings in Argentina rise in dollar terms even when sales in pesos remain the same.

Multinational firms tend to think primarily in terms of their own home currencies and sometimes evaluate the attractiveness of a market solely on those terms. However, global marketers should differentiate between market realities and currency fluctuations. The Turkish sales force of a U.S. multinational pharmaceutical firm was congratulated for attaining the highest sales per salesperson of any of the firm's national sales forces. Two weeks later after a major devaluation of the Turkish lira, headquarters told the Turkish sales force that their contribution (measured in U.S. dollars) no longer looked good. Of course the Turkish sales force had no control over the fluctuations of their national currency. Needless to say, headquarters' attitude resulted in a morale crisis at their Turkish subsidiary.

Impact on Licensing and Franchising Fees.   Some firms do not directly sell their products or services abroad. Instead they license or franchise them to local companies overseas. (These modes of market entry are discussed in Chapter 9.) Multinationals that license or franchise collect fees from their foreign partners. These fees are usually determined as a percentage of local sales and are therefore subject to the same translation issues that face subsidiary earnings.

Reevaluating Market Participation.   Sometimes a relative change in currencies causes marketers to reevaluate their participation in certain international markets. Some currency fluctuations create new market opportunities. Once when the U.S. dollar was dropping against most major currencies, New York City saw this as an opportunity to attract more foreign tourists. The city advertised to potential tourists residing in London to visit New York and "shop while the dollar drops."[26]

Currency fluctuations can also cause marketers to leave a foreign market. This can occur if exporters decide that they cannot reasonably raise prices in response to currency devaluation in an export market. However many multinational firms take a longer-term view of the situation. They remain in the market, temporarily accept lower margins, and attempt to defend their market share. A local currency devaluation can even make buying assets or purchasing companies cheaper for those holding foreign currency. At the same time the Indian IT firms faced export difficulties because of a strong rupee, they also took advantage of a strong rupee to purchase U.S. companies. The dollar prices of these companies, translated into rupees, appeared to be real bargains.

INTERNATIONAL AGENCIES FOR PROMOTING ECONOMIC AND MONETARY STABILITY

Stability in the international economy is a prerequisite for worldwide peace and prosperity. It was for this reason that at the end of World War II, representatives from several countries met at Bretton Woods, New Hampshire, and formed both the International Monetary Fund and the World Bank (the International Bank for Reconstruction and Development). With headquarters in Washington, DC, these two agencies continue to play major roles on the international scene.

International Monetary Fund (IMF)

The core mission of the International Monetary Fund (IMF) is to help stabilize an increasingly global economy. The IMF's original goals were to promote orderly and stable foreign exchange markets, restore free convertibility among the currencies of member nations, reduce international impediments to trade, and provide assistance to countries that experienced temporary balance-of-payments deficits.

Over the years, the IMF has shifted its focus from exchange rate relations among industrialized countries to the prevention of economic instability in developing countries and countries from the former Eastern European bloc. The Mexican economic crisis in 1994 prompted an unprecedented bailout of $47 billion and launched the recent trend of providing rescue packages to major economies in the developing world. In the past several years, the IMF approved a $19 billion rescue package for Turkey and led a $17.2 billion rescue for Thailand, a $42 billion package for Indonesia, and a $41.5 billion deal for Brazil. South Korea got a whopping $58.4 billion when it was on the verge of bankruptcy. These rescue packages helped stabilize the respective economies and avoid total economic collapse of the countries involved.

For more information about the IMF, check out the link on the student companion website at http://www. cengage.com/ international.

To qualify for assistance, the IMF may require that countries take drastic economic steps, such as reducing tariff barriers, privatizing state-owned enterprises, curbing domestic inflation, and cutting government expenditures. Although many nations have resented such intervention, banks worldwide have used the IMF as a screening device for their private loans to many developing countries. If countries qualify for IMF loans, they are considered for private credit. A growing world economy in the early 21st century resulted in fewer crises for the IMF to manage. Its loan portfolio fell to the lowest level since the 1980s, and its influence over countries and their economies diminished.

World Bank

The World Bank (International Bank for Reconstruction and Development) acts as an intermediary between the private capital markets and the developing nations. It makes long-term loans (usually 15 or 25 years) carrying rates that reflect prevailing market conditions. By virtue of its AAA credit rating, the bank is able to borrow private funds at relatively low market rates and pass the savings along to the developing nations. However, because it must borrow to obtain capital and is not funded by members' contributions, the World Bank must raise lending rates when its costs (that is, market interest rates) rise. Table 2.6 lists typical projects that the World Bank finances.

When private funds were pouring into developing economies, some critics questioned the future role of the World Bank. However, a pan-Asian economic crisis caused the flow of private funds to developing countries to drop by more than $100 billion in 1998. The World Bank has expanded its role from mostly loans to partial guarantees of government bonds for investment projects. In Thailand, the World Bank partially guaranteed the Electricity Generating Authority of Thailand. The guarantee attracted investors and spawned interest in similar programs in South Korea and the Philippines. In addition, the bank is encouraging governments to improve financial supervision and reduce red tape.

TABLE 2.6	SELECTED WORLD BANK PROJECTS
COUNTRY	**PROJECT**
Albania	Social Service Delivery Project
Azerbaijan	Second National Water Supply and Sanitation Project
Bangladesh	Higher Education Quality Improvement
Bulgaria	Second Trade and Transport Facilitation Project
Cambodia	Land Administration Management and Distribution
China	Hubei Yiba Highway Project
Colombia	Columbia Rural Education Project
Croatia	Coastal Cities Pollution Control Project 2
Ethiopia	General Education Quality Improvement Project
India	Power System Development
Indonesia	Public Expenditure Support Facility
Kenya	Energy Sector Recovery—Additional Financing
Mexico	Mexico Sustainable Rural Development
Morocco	Waste Sector Development
Nigeria	Commercial Agriculture Development Project
Pakistan	Pakistan Poverty Reduction and Economic Support Operation
Peru	Health Reform Program
Poland	Road Maintenance and Rehab
Russia	Housing and Communal Services Project
Senegal	Sustainable Management of Fish Resources
Ukraine	Roads and Safety Improvement Project
West Bank/Gaza	Food Price Crisis Response Program
Yemen, Republic of	Civil Service Modernization Project

Source: World Bank Projects 2008 from http://www.worldbank.org. Copyright © 2008 by World Bank. Reproduced by permission of World Bank via Copyright Clearance Center.

Group of Seven

The world's leading industrial nations have established a Group of Seven, which meets regularly to discuss the world economy. Finance ministers and central bank governors from the United States, Japan, Germany, France, Britain, Italy, and Canada make up this group, which is often referred to as the *G7*. (When Russia joins the talks, the group calls itself the *G8*.) The members work together informally to help stabilize the world economy and reduce extreme disruptions. For example, the G7 developed proposals to reduce the debt of 33 impoverished nations, mostly in Africa, by 70 percent. The G8 agreed to help rebuild the Balkans, including Serbia if it continued to demonstrate a full commitment to economic and democratic reforms.

European Monetary System

The European Union (EU) single currency, the euro, has replaced 16 national currencies in Europe. The countries comprising the euro zone are Austria, Belgium, Cyprus, Finland, France, Germany, Greece, Ireland, Italy, Luxembourg, Malta, the

The EU's single currency, the euro, has replaced numerous national currencies across Europe.

©iStockphoto.com/MistikaS

Netherlands, Portugal, Slovakia, Slovenia, and Spain. The European Central Bank (ECB) has control over the euro and is obliged to maintain price stability and avoid inflation or deflation.

The changeover to the euro was not easy, however. One study showed that a vending machine in France that dispensed coffee for two French francs could not charge the equivalent in euros. The conversion rate turned out to be .3049. The coffee could be repriced at .30 euro, causing the vendor to lose 1.5 percent of gross revenue. Alternatively, the vending machine could be expensively reconfigured to dribble out slightly less coffee.[27]

Nonetheless, supporters of the euro believed it would reduce transaction costs and foreign exchange risk within Europe and provide a strong viable currency alternative to the dollar. To date, their faith appears to be justified. A report by 11 economists estimates that trade among the euro-zone members increased by 30 percent in the first four years alone. Britain didn't adopt the euro, and U.K. trade with the euro zone rose by only 13 percent.[28]

PROTECTIONISM AND TRADE RESTRICTIONS

It is a fact of life that like virtually all changes, free trade creates both beneficiaries and victims. By increasing competition, free trade lowers the price of imported goods and raises the overseas demand for efficiently produced domestic goods. In these newly stimulated export industries, sales will increase, profits will rise, and stock prices will climb. Clearly, consumers of the imported good and producers of the exported good benefit from these new conditions. However, it is equally clear that other groups are harmed. Domestic producers of the import-competing goods are one of the most visible of such groups. They experience noticeable declines in market share, falling profits, and deteriorating stock prices.

Herein lies the major reason for protectionist legislation. The victims of free trade are highly visible and their losses quantifiable. Governments use protectionism as a means of lessening the harm done to these easily identified groups. Conversely, the individuals who are helped by free trade tend to be dispersed throughout the nation rather than concentrated in a specific region. However, when too many citizens face economic hardship, governments reconsider protectionist measures. Despite an overall trend toward trade liberalization, protectionism rose in 2009 in response to a worldwide economic crisis. Large and small countries alike raised taxes on imports, and national economic stimulus packages unabashedly favored national suppliers.[29]

Protectionist legislation tends to take the form of tariffs, quotas, or qualitative trade restrictions. This section describes these barriers and their economic effects.

Tariffs

Tariff a tax on goods or services moving across an economic or political boundary

Tariffs are taxes on goods moving across an economic or political boundary. They can be imposed on imports, exports, or goods in transit through a country on their way to some other destination. In the United States, export tariffs are constitutionally prohibited, but in other parts of the world they are quite common. Export tariffs can provide a source of government funding. Brazil taxes agricultural exports such as soybeans, and revenues from these export tariffs fund various social programs.[30] Export tariffs may also be employed to assure that the local population has adequate supply at reasonable prices. Argentina temporarily banned beef exports to keep foreign demand from pushing up prices within the country.[31]

The most common type of tariff is the import tariff. Import tariffs have a dual economic effect. First, they tend to raise the price of imported goods and thereby protect domestic industries from foreign competition. Second, they generate tax revenues for the governments imposing them. Regardless of what the goals are, tariffs may not be the most direct or effective means of attaining them. For example, foreign sellers may lower their prices to offset any tariff increase. The net effect is for the consumer-paid price to differ only slightly, if at all, from the price before the tariff was imposed. Consequently, the nation has greater tariff revenues but little additional protection for the domestic producers.

When tariffs do raise the price of an imported good, consumers are put at a disadvantage, whereas the import-competing industries are helped. However, tariffs can have wider implications. For example, when the U.S. Department of Commerce imposed a high duty on advanced flat screens used on laptop computers, the duty helped some small U.S. screen manufacturers. But it hurt computer companies such as Apple, Compaq, and IBM, who argued that the high duty inflated the cost of their products, undermined their ability to compete abroad, and would force them to shift production to other countries.

Quotas

Quota a physical limit on the amount of goods that can be imported into or, less commonly, exported from a country

Quotas are physical limits on the amount of goods that can be imported into a country. Unlike tariffs, which restrict trade by directly increasing prices, quotas increase prices by directly restricting trade. Naturally, to have such an effect, imports must be restricted to levels below the free-trade level.

For domestic producers, quotas are a much surer means of protection. Once the limit has been reached, imports cease to enter the domestic market, regardless of whether foreign exporters lower their prices. Consumers have the most to lose with the imposition of quotas. Not only are their product choices limited and the prices increased, but the goods that foreign exporters choose to ship often carry the highest profit margins. Restrictions on imported automobiles, for instance, result in the import of more luxury models with high-cost accessories. Because foreign producers are restricted in the number of cars they can sell, they seek the highest margin per car.

Orderly Marketing Arrangements and Voluntary Export Restrictions

Orderly marketing arrangement (or voluntary export restriction) an agreement between countries in which one country agrees to limit its exports to the other

An **orderly marketing arrangement** or **voluntary export restriction (VER)** is an agreement between countries to share markets by limiting foreign export sales. Usually, these arrangements have a set duration and provide for some annual increase in foreign sales to the domestic market. The euphemistic terms are intended to give the impression of fairness. After all, who can be against anything that is orderly or voluntary?

Scratch the surface of these so-called negotiated settlements, however, and a different image appears. First, the negotiations are initiated by the importing country with the implicit threat that unless concessions are made, stronger unilateral sanctions will be imposed. They are really neither orderly nor voluntary. They are quotas in the guise of negotiated agreements. For example, the U.S. Commerce Department reached an agreement whereby Russia would voluntarily limit its steel imports into the United States to 750,000 tons per year, compared with 3.5 million tons in the prior year. If Russia had not agreed to the limits, the Commerce Department was prepared to announce duties of 71 to 218 percent on Russian steel.[32]

At one time there were approximately 300 VERs worldwide, most protecting the United States and Europe. Today signatories to the WTO agree not to enact such agreements. However, exceptions can be granted to protect a single sector of a national economy.

Nontariff Trade Barriers

Nontariff barriers nonmonetary restrictions on trade

The final category of trade restrictions is perhaps the most problematic and certainly the least quantifiable. **Nontariff barriers** include a wide range of charges, requirements, and restrictions, such as surcharges at border crossings, licensing regulations, performance requirements, government subsidies, health and safety regulations, packaging and labeling regulations, and size and weight requirements. Not all of these barriers are discriminatory and protectionist. Restrictions dealing with public health and safety are certainly legitimate, but the line between social well-being and protection is a fine one.

At what point do consular fees, import restrictions, packaging regulations, performance requirements, licensing rules, and government procurement procedures discriminate against foreign producers? Is a French tax on automobile horsepower targeted against powerful U.S. cars, or is it simply a tax on inefficiency and pollution? Are U.S. automobile safety standards unfair to German, Japanese, and other foreign car manufacturers? Does a French ban on advertising bourbon and Scotch (but not cognac) serve the public's best interest?

Sometimes, nontariff barriers can have considerable impact on foreign competition. For decades, West German authorities forbade the sale of beer in Germany unless it was brewed from barley malt, hops, yeast, and water. If any other additives were used—a common practice elsewhere—German authorities denied foreign brewers the right to label their products as beer. The law was eventually struck down by the European Court of Justice.

Courtesy of Roger Simmermaker, www.howtobuyamerican.com

Although trade restrictions have decreased worldwide, there remains a market for home-grown products such as those promoted on this Made in the USA search engine.

Nevertheless, many nontariff barriers continue in many creative ways. For example, under China's WTO commitments, quotas for imported cars were to be abolished. However, a Chinese policy paper that outlined China's plan to become a major car manufacturer suggested a number of nontariff ideas to support the local automobile industry, such as restricting the number of ports where foreign imports can be offloaded and requiring Chinese-made and foreign-made automobiles to use different sales outlets. The latter would increase the cost of introducing new brands and effectively slow imports.[33]

General Agreement on Tariffs and Trade (GATT)

Because of the harmful effects of protectionism, which were most painfully felt during the Great Depression of the 1930s, 23 nations banded together in 1947 to form the General Agreement on Tariffs and Trade (GATT). Over its life, GATT has been a major forum for the liberalization and promotion of nondiscriminatory international trade between participating nations.

The principles of a world economy embodied in the articles of GATT are reciprocity, nondiscrimination, and transparency. The idea of *reciprocity* is simple. If one country lowers its tariffs against another's exports, then it should expect the other country to do the same. *Nondiscrimination* means that one country should not give one member or group of members preferential treatment over other members of the group. This principle is embodied in the **most favored nation (MFN) status**. MFN does not mean that one country is most favored, but rather that it receives no less favorable treatment than any other. *Transparency* refers to the GATT policy that nations make any trade restrictions overt, such as replacing nontariff barriers with tariffs. Through these principles, trade restrictions have been effectively reduced.

Most favored nation (MFN) status a guarantee in a trade agreement between countries binding signatories to extend trade benefits to each other equal to those accorded any third state

Although its most notable gains have been in considerably reducing tariff and quota barriers on many goods, GATT has also helped to simplify and homogenize trade documentation procedures, discourage government subsidies, and curtail dumping (that is, selling abroad at a cost lower than the cost of production).

The Uruguay Round of GATT talks, which lasted seven years, was finally completed in late 1993. This agreement covered several controversial areas, such as patents and national protection of agriculture and the textile and clothing industry.

World Trade Organization (WTO)

The final act of GATT was to replace itself with the World Trade Organization in 1996. The WTO continues to pursue reductions in tariffs on manufactured goods as well as liberalization of trade in agriculture and services. With 148 member countries in 2005, the WTO is the global watchdog for free trade. Even China became part of the WTO in 2001 after 14 years of negotiations concerning its vast semiplanned economy, with its formidable array of import quotas, trade licenses, and import inspections. Since its inception the WTO has established an agreement on tariff-free trade in information technology among 40 countries, as well as a financial services agreement that covers 95 percent of trade in banking and insurance. An agreement on intellectual property covering patents, trademarks, and copyrights has also been negotiated.

A major advantage that the WTO offers over GATT involves the resolution of disputes. Under GATT, any member could veto the outcome of a panel ruling on a dispute. WTO panels are stricter. They must report their decisions in nine months and can be overturned only by consensus. Countries that break the rules must pay compensation, mend their ways, or face trade sanctions.

The use of quotas and voluntary export restrictions is declining with the strengthening of the WTO and with increased compliance by its member countries. Whereas GATT presided over 300 disputes over its lifetime (1947–1994), the WTO dealt with over 300 complaints in its first eight years. The WTO has not been used by the big countries solely to control the smaller ones, as some feared. Costa Rica, for example, asked the WTO to rule against American barriers to its export of men's underwear. It won the case, and the United States was forced to change its import rules.

The WTO's current concerns focus on several challenges. First, the WTO continues to push for liberalization of foreign investment. Other challenges comprise the "new issues" of trade policy, such as competition policy, labor standards, and even censorship. Taiwan, for example, has a strong modern dance culture that is accepting of nudity onstage. Mainland Chinese authorities consider this pornographic. Did joining the WTO mean that China could no longer ban performing arts from Taiwan that it considered offensive?[34]

Find the WTO link on the student companion website at http://www.cengage.com/international.

ECONOMIC INTEGRATION AS A MEANS OF PROMOTING TRADE

Another important issue facing the WTO is the spread of regional trading agreements. The WTO exempts members of regional trade agreements from the MFN principle. In other words, the United States could extend Israel a lower tariff rate under a free-trade agreement that it would not have to extend to other countries under the MFN principle expected by WTO membership. Recently there has been

TABLE 2.7	SELECTED INTEGRATION AGREEMENTS		
AGREEMENT	**COUNTRIES**	**FOUNDING DATE**	**AGREEMENT TYPE**
NAFTA (North American Free Trade Agreement)	Canada, Mexico, United States	1994	Free-trade area
EU (European Union)	Austria, Belgium, Bulgaria, Cyprus, Czech Republic, Denmark, Estonia, Finland, France, Germany, Greece, Hungary, Ireland, Italy, Latvia, Lithuania, Luxembourg, Malta, Netherlands, Poland, Portugal, Romania, Slovak Republic, Slovenia, Spain, Sweden, United Kingdom	1951	Common market
AFTA (ASEAN Free Trade Area)	Brunei Darussalam, Cambodia, Indonesia, Laos, Malaysia, Myanmar, Philippines, Singapore, Thailand, Vietnam	1992	Free-trade area
MERCOSUR (Southern Common Market)	Argentina, Brazil, Paraguay, Uruguay	1991	Customs union
CAN (Andean Community)	Bolivia, Colombia, Ecuador, Peru, Venezuela	1969	Customs union
CIS (Commonwealth of Independent States)	Azerbaijan, Armenia, Belarus, Georgia, Moldova, Kazakhstan, Russian Federation, Ukraine, Uzbekistan, Tajikistan, Kyrgyz Republic	1999	Free-trade area
GCC (Gulf Cooperation Council)	Bahrain, Kuwait, Oman, Qatar, Saudi Arabia, United Arab Emirates	1981	Customs union (as of 2003)
EFTA (European Free Trade Association)	Iceland, Liechtenstein, Norway, Switzerland	1960	Free-trade area
CACM (Central American Common Market)	Costa Rica, El Salvador, Guatemala, Honduras, Nicaragua	1960	Customs union

a significant increase in the number of such agreements. There are nearly 250 regional agreements between countries granting preferential access to each other's markets. Nearly all members of the WTO belong to at least one regional pact. Table 2.7 lists examples of such agreements.

Some believe that the increase in these bilateral agreements (very much in favor with the United States) will undermine the multilateral vision of the WTO. By dangling access to its large market, the United States has special negotiating power over smaller, developing countries. Furthermore, bilateral deals fragment negotiating power of coalitions of smaller markets.[35]

Although the degree of economic integration can vary considerably from one organization to another, four major types of integration can be identified: free-trade areas, customs unions, common markets, and monetary unions.

Free-Trade Areas

The simplest form of integration is a free-trade area. The most famous is the North American Free Trade Association (NAFTA), which includes the United States, Canada, and Mexico. Within a **free-trade area**, nations agree to drop trade barriers among themselves, but each nation is permitted to maintain independent trade relations with countries outside the group. There is little attempt at this level to

Free-trade area two or more countries that formally sign an agreement to drop trade barriers among themselves but to allow each member country to maintain independent trade relations with nonmember countries

coordinate such things as domestic tax rates, environmental regulations, and commercial codes. Generally such areas do not permit resources (that is, labor and capital) to flow freely across national borders. Moreover, because each country has autonomy over its money supply, exchange rates can fluctuate relative to both member and nonmember countries.

Despite the apparent simplicity of this form of economic integration, unexpected complications can arise. When NAFTA was being negotiated, U.S. business groups demanded that foreign investors be protected, noting that the Mexican government had a history of nationalizing U.S. assets. Consequently, arbitration procedures established by the World Bank ensure that governments in the United States, Mexico, and Canada will pay compensation to any foreign investor whose property is seized. Arbitration panels cannot make new law. However, they can interpret law, and their rulings cannot be appealed. One NAFTA panel issued its own interpretation of the Mexican constitution and awarded $16.7 million to a California waste disposal company after the governor of the state of San Luis Potosi and a town council refused to honor the company's permit to open a toxic-waste site. The idea that NAFTA law may give foreign investors privileges over those enjoyed by local companies has many concerned in all NAFTA countries.[36]

Free-trade areas have been less successful among many developing countries. A case in point is the Asian Free Trade Area (AFTA). AFTA was envisaged to create a regional free-trade zone by slashing tariffs. However, the actual free trade that ensued has fallen far short of the rhetoric. For example, Malaysia refused to remove protective tariffs for its auto industry. Furthermore, the association's member countries represent widely disparate development levels, political institutions, and economic philosophies. Some countries are democracies, others military dictatorships.[37]While trade within NAFTA grew by 17 percent in its first seven years, interregional trade in AFTA dropped 19 percent in the same amount of time. Some of the key problems that persist are different product standards across countries and unpredictable policy implementation.[38]

Check out the NAFTA links on the student companion website at http://www. cengage.com/ international.

Customs Unions

Customs union two or more countries that formally sign an agreement to drop trade barriers among themselves and to establish common external barriers between member and nonmember countries

Customs unions, a more advanced form of economic integration, possess the characteristics of a free-trade area but with the added feature of a common external tariff/trade barrier for the member nations. Individual countries relinquish the right to set trade agreements outside the group independently. Instead, a supranational policy-making committee makes these decisions.

Common Markets

Common market a form of economic integration with all the characteristics of a customs union and in which the free flow of resources, such as labor and capital, is encouraged among member nations

The third level of economic integration is a **common market**. This arrangement has all the characteristics of a customs union, but the organization also encourages the free flow of resources (labor and capital) among the member nations. For example, if jobs are plentiful in Germany but scarce in Italy, workers can move from Italy to Germany without having to worry about severe immigration restrictions. In a common market, there is usually an attempt to coordinate tax codes, social welfare systems, and other legislation that influences resource allocation. Finally, although each nation still has the right to print and coin its own money, exchange rates among nations often are fixed or are permitted to fluctuate only within a narrow range. The most notable example of a common market is the European Union. The EU has been an active organization for trade liberalization and continues to increase its membership size.

See the EU link on the student companion website at http://www.cengage.com/international.

When Vincente Fox was elected president of Mexico, he called for expanding NAFTA into a common market. He admitted, however, that this would be a long-term project that would gradually evolve over 20 to 40 years. As an initial step, however, he wanted the United States to accept more Mexican labor, expanding its temporary-worker program so that 300,000 or more Mexicans a year could be legally employed in the United States.[39]

Monetary Unions

The highest form of economic integration is a monetary union. A monetary union is a common market in which member countries no longer regulate their own currencies. Rather, member-country currencies are replaced by a common currency regulated by a supranational central bank. With the passage of the Maastricht Treaty by EU members, the European Monetary System became the first monetary union in January 1999.

THE GLOBALIZATION CONTROVERSY

On the eve of the new millennium, groups representing organized labor, human rights, and environmental interests confronted the WTO in what has come to be known as the Battle of Seattle. The WTO had convened in the American city for a new round of negotiations to reduce trade barriers. Thirty thousand protesters from around the world, angered by what they believed was a failure of the WTO to properly address their concerns relating to poverty, labor conditions, and the environment, blocked traffic and in a few cases engaged in vandalism and violence. The police responded with tear gas and rubber bullets. The next meeting of the WTO was subsequently scheduled in the Arab Gulf state of Qatar, described by a U.S. State Department report as a country that "severely limits freedom of assembly and prohibits workers from organizing unions."[40]

Clearly a final challenge facing the WTO is how to handle an increasingly global and organized opposition to its agenda. Some parties believe that the globalization fostered by the WTO favors developed countries seeking to sell to developing countries and not vice versa. For example, the United States, Japan, and Europe maintain some of their highest tariffs on agricultural products, which account for a large portion of exports from the developing world. Agricultural subsidies in the developed world further undermine the ability of developing countries to compete in the global marketplace. Developing countries also claim that food safety standards imposed by developed countries are often discriminatory. Thailand sued Australia for requiring chicken parts to be precooked at such a high temperature that it renders the product inedible.[41]

Other opposition to globalization comes from traditional labor unions in industrialized countries as well as new groups opposed to the outsourcing of professional jobs. Both conservatives and liberals in developed and developing countries are concerned that the WTO usurps sovereignty from governments. For example, the state of Utah outlawed gambling for 110 years, and this prohibition was later extended to Internet gambling. However, the WTO ruled that the Utah law discriminated against foreign providers of "recreational services." Such rulings fuel the fears of those who believe that the WTO is an attempt to impose a one-world government.[42]

Is globalization bad or good? As we saw with the case of global outsourcing, this depends on who you are. The distribution of income in the United States reflects increased inequality over the past 25 years. Geoffrey Garret argues that this pattern can also be observed at a national level. Twenty years of increased globalization

WORLD BEAT 2.2

THE WTO GAMBLE

FIRST THE TINY ISLAND OF ANTIGUA COMPLAINED: The United States would not allow American citizens to place bets on Antiguan online gambling sites. The United States government forbade American banks and credit card companies from processing payments made to online and offshore gambling operations. The prohibition was included with little political debate in a port security bill. In doing so it invoked a rarely used WTO rule that allows a country to deny open access to its market. The clause does require a nation that pursues this option to compensate others affected by the change. Consequently, Antigua asked the United States to pay it $3.4 billion in compensation for lost gambling revenues. Soon others countries including Australia, Canada, India, Japan, and the EU submitted similar demands.

Still U.S. lawmakers were unusually united in their opposition to online gambling, noting the ease by which minors could access the sites and the likelihood that terrorists could use online gambling to launder money. Some pointed out that online gambling did not even exist when the United States signed a WTO agreement to open markets to various services. Eventually the WTO allowed Antigua to suspend its own WTO obligations to the United States, but these only amounted to $21 million a year. Antigua was also allowed to suspend its commitment to respect U.S. intellectual property rights, such as copyrights and patents. One commentator remarked that this was akin to legalizing product piracy.

The U.S. government confirmed that it had reached agreements with Canada, Japan, and the EU. The terms of those agreements remained secret for national security reasons. In the meantime, civil libertarians and the U.S. gambling industry were successful in introducing a bill to the U.S. Congress to allow the online gambling decision to be made at the state level instead of the national level. They argued that taxes assessed on the gambling sites could fund critical government programs.

Sources: Lorraine Woellert, "A Web Gambling Fight Could Harm Free Trade," *BusinessWeek,* August 13, 2007, p. 43; "Antigua PM Hopeful about Web Gambling Talks with US Lawmakers," *Dow Jones International News,* November 11, 2007; Marcia Coyle, "Small Island Places Legal Wager," *National Law Journal,* June 9, 2008, p. 1; and Kara Rowland, "Push Planned to Repeal Online Gambling Ban," *Washington Times,* May 6, 2009, p. 6.

appears to have been more advantageous to industrialized countries and the world's poorest countries. However, countries that comprise the economic middle—many of which are located in Asia and South America—have not fared as well. Real per-capita income grew by less than 20 percent in these countries in the last two decades of the 20th century. This was less than half the growth rate in upper-income countries and less than one-eighth the growth in the low-income countries.[43]

Middle-income countries appear to face the possibility of being squeezed out of the world economy. They do not have the political institutions or as educated a workforce to compete with the upper-income countries, so they are forced to compete with countries such as China and India in the production of more standardized products. However, this may be a losing battle as well, because these low-income countries have considerably lower wage rates. No wonder a garment worker in Mexico reported his boss threatening, "If you don't work harder, we are going to shut this plant down and move it to Central America."[44]

Thus, globalization remains controversial. Even countries such as South Korea that have benefitted substantially from trade liberalization express hostility towards it. South Korea's largest teachers' union has urged members to tell students that free trade can increase poverty, hurt the environment, and increase inequality. A survey of 8,000 respondents in ten Asian economies revealed South Koreans to be skeptical of globalization. Only 27 percent of Koreans viewed globalization positively compared to the Asian average of 38 percent.[45]

PUT THIS CHAPTER TO USE: Check out Country Market Report on the student companion website at http://www. cengage.com/ international.

CONCLUSION

The global economy is in a state of transition from a set of strong national economies to a set of inter-linked trading groups. This transition has accelerated over the past few years with the collapse of communism, the coalescing of the European trading nations into a single market, and the expansion of membership in the WTO. The investment by Europeans, Japanese, and Americans in one another's economies is unprecedented. In much of the developing world, trade and investment liberalization has accelerated as well.

There is no doubt that the world has been moving toward a single global economy. Information technology, telecommunications, and the Internet have made worldwide information on prices, products, and profits available globally and instantaneously. With markets more transparent, buyers, sellers, and investors can access better opportunities, lowering costs and ensuring that resources are allocated to their most efficient use. Past changes have helped some groups and hurt others, and it remains unclear what the future of globalization will be. Successful companies will be able to anticipate trends and respond to them quickly. Less successful companies will miss the changes going on around them and wake up one day to a different marketplace governed by new rules.

QUESTIONS FOR DISCUSSION

1. Suppose that Brazil can produce, with an equal amount of resources, either 100 units of steel or 10 computers. At the same time, Germany can produce either 150 units of steel or 10 computers. Explain which nation has a comparative advantage in the production of computers. Choose a mutually advantageous trading ratio and explain why this ratio increases the welfare of both nations.

2. What problems could export tariffs cause?

3. Do you agree with the protesters who claim that the WTO has excessive power over national governments? Will free trade widen the gap between rich and poor? Why or why not?

4. Should the WTO force Utah to accept gambling?

5. What makes regional integration more difficult for developing countries?

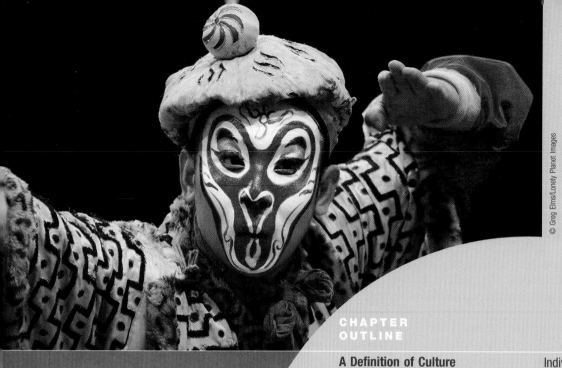

© Greg Elms/Lonely Planet Images

CHAPTER OUTLINE

© Inmagine/18439GNG

3
Cultural and Social Forces

WHEN DISNEY, THE U.S.-BASED ENTERTAINMENT GIANT, decided to open a theme park in Europe, it had almost no direct overseas experience. Tokyo Disneyland had proved successful, but it had been developed and run by a local Japanese partner. When EuroDisney opened in France, management had already incorporated changes in its successful models from California and Florida. To accommodate the cooler, damper climate in France, more indoor attractions were developed and more covered walkways were installed. Multilingual telephone operators and guides were hired to assist visitors from different European countries. Kennels were built for the many French families who would never think of going on vacation without the family dog. Estimates of restaurant traffic took into consideration the fact that Europeans like to linger over their food and are far less tolerant of standing in lines than are Americans.

Still, for the first year of operations, EuroDisney refused to sell alcohol on its premises because this practice clashed with its American idea of family entertainment. The management also refused to cut prices during off-season months, despite a time-honored European tradition of doing this at vacation destinations. The first year of operation was disappointing. Disney then bowed to cultural realities and adopted wine, beer, and differentiated prices. Adapting to European culture paid off. EuroDisney became Europe's top tourist attraction—even more popular than the Eiffel Tower.[1]

However, when Disney later opened a theme park in Hong Kong, the cultural challenges resumed. Originally Disney planned to serve the Chinese delicacy shark's fin soup—until Chinese conservationists objected. Disney also underestimated visitor demand during mainland China's weeklong Lunar New Year holiday. Hundreds of guests with valid tickets found themselves shut out of the park.[2] Learning from this early misstep, Disney later took advantage of China's special Lunar New Year celebrations to promote its mascot Mickey Mouse during the Chinese Year of the Rat.[3]

In Chapter 1 we noted that the complexities of international marketing are partially caused by societal and cultural forces. In Chapter 3 we describe some of these cultural and societal influences in more detail. However, because it is not possible to list all of them—or even to describe the major cultures of the world—only some of the more critical forces are highlighted. Figure 3.1 shows the components of culture that are described in this book. Rather than identifying all the cultural or societal factors that might affect international marketers, we concentrate on analytic processes that marketers can use to identify and monitor any of the numerous cultural influences they will encounter around the globe.

A DEFINITION OF CULTURE

Anthropology is the study of human behavior. Cultural anthropology examines all learned human behaviors, including social, linguistic, and family behaviors. **Culture** encompasses the entire heritage of a society transmitted orally, via literature, or in any other form. It includes all traditions, morals, habits, religion, art, and language. Children born anywhere in the world have the same essential needs for food, shelter, and clothing. But as they mature, children experience desires for nonessential things. *How these wants develop* and *what relative importance the individual assigns to them* are based on messages from families and peers. This socialization process reflects each person's culture.

For example, eating habits and tastes vary greatly around the world, but few of these variations reflect physiological differences among people. Instead, food is extremely culture-bound. One exception relates to milk products. Many people in China lack the enzymes to digest milk products. But like many things Western, milk is becoming increasingly popular in China among a new generation more socialized to Western products. To bridge the gap—in taste and enzymes—many dairy producers in China are selling yogurt-based drinks, which many Chinese find easier to digest.[4]

The role and influence of culture in modern society are evolving as more and more economies become interlinked. Samuel Huntington identifies the cultures of the world as Western (the United States, Western Europe, Australia), Orthodox (the

Culture all human knowledge, beliefs, behavior, and institutions transmitted from one generation to another

FIGURE 3.1
Cultural Analysis

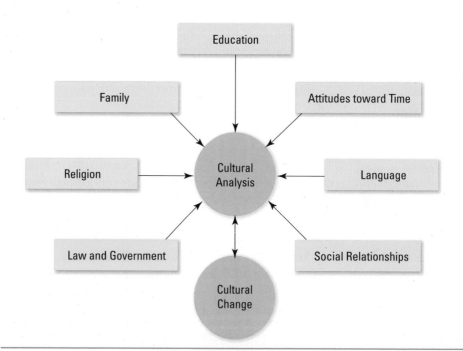

former Soviet republics, Central Europe), Confucian (China, Southeast Asia), Islamic (the Middle East), Buddhist (Thailand), Hindu (India), Latin American, African, and Japanese.[5] He argues that conflict in the post–Cold War era will occur between the major cultures of the world rather than between nations. Francis Fukuyama disagrees that cultural differences will necessarily be the source of conflict. Instead, he foresees that increasing interaction between cultures will lead to cross-stimulation and creative change.[6] In any case, understanding cultures helps marketers avoid costly mistakes in the marketplace today.

Cultural Influences on Marketing

The function of marketing is to earn profits from the satisfaction of human wants and needs. To understand and influence consumers' wants and needs, we must understand their culture. Cultural understanding is also necessary when international marketers interact with foreign competitors, distributors, suppliers, and government officials.

Figure 3.2 is a diagram of how culture affects human behavior. As the figure shows, culture is embedded in such elements of the society as religion, language, history, and education. These aspects of the society send direct and indirect messages to consumers regarding the selection of goods and services. The culture we live in answers such questions as the following: Is tea or coffee the preferred drink? Is black or white worn at a funeral? What type of food is eaten for breakfast?

Isolating Cultural Influences

One of the most difficult tasks for global marketers is assessing the cultural influences that affect their operations. In the actual marketplace, several factors are always working simultaneously, and it is extremely difficult to isolate any one factor. Frequently, cultural differences have been held accountable for any noticeable differences among countries. But do these differences result from underlying religious beliefs, from the prevailing social structure, or simply from different sets of laws? In this chapter we will examine the cultural influences of religion, the family, education, attitudes toward time, social interactions, and language. The cultural factors of government and law will be discussed in Chapter 4.

RELIGION

McDonald's operates in over a hundred countries and is the world's largest user of beef. The U.S.-based fast-food chain was drawn to India with its population of 1,000 million, even though the majority of Indians were Hindus and did not eat beef. At the McDonald's in Delhi a sign reads, "No beef or beef products sold at this restaurant." Pork is also omitted to avoid offending India's Muslims.

FIGURE 3.2
Cultural Influences on Buyer Behavior

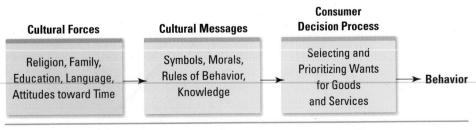

Cultural Forces	Cultural Messages	Consumer Decision Process	
Religion, Family, Education, Language, Attitudes toward Time	Symbols, Morals, Rules of Behavior, Knowledge	Selecting and Prioritizing Wants for Goods and Services	→ Behavior

McDonald's adapted to India's religious cultures by eliminating beef and pork from its menu. Differences in material culture—the physical objects used by society—can also affect global marketers. For example, the level of automobile ownership in India is lower than in the United States. Consequently, the drive-thru window is less common. On McDonald's Indian website, customers can learn how to navigate this cultural import—in four easy steps.

© 2009 H.R.P.L.

Many businesspeople ignore the influence religion may have on the marketing environment. Religion can have a profound impact on societies. It helps determine attitudes toward social structure and economic development. Its traditions and rules may dictate what goods and services are purchased, when they are purchased, and by whom. For example, the Shinto religion encourages the Japanese people to cultivate a strong patriotic attitude, which may in part account for Japan's excellent economic performance. Alcoholic beverages are banned in Saudi Arabia on religious principles, and Israeli airline El Al does not fly on Saturday, the Jewish Sabbath.

Table 3.1 lists the leading religions for selected countries. It is beyond the scope of this text to provide a complete description of all world religions and their implications for marketing. By briefly examining several of the world's major religions, however, we can illustrate their potential impact.

Marketing and Western Religions

Historically, the religious tradition in the United States, based on Christianity and Judaism, has emphasized hard work, thrift, and a simple lifestyle. These religious values have certainly evolved over time; many of our modern marketing activities would not exist if these older values had persisted. Thrift, for instance, presumes that a person will save hard-earned wages and use these savings for purchases later on. Today, Americans take full advantage of the ample credit facilities that are available to them. The credit card is such a vital part of the American lifestyle that saving before buying seems archaic. Most Americans feel no guilt in driving a big SUV or generously heating a large house.

Christmas is one Christian tradition that remains an important event for many consumer goods industries in all Christian countries. Retailers have their largest

TABLE 3.1 LEADING RELIGIONS OF SELECTED COUNTRIES

COUNTRY	RELIGION[a]		
Africa			
Cameroon	Muslim	Christian	Animist
Congo	Christian	Animist	Muslim
Ethiopia	Orthodox Christian	Muslim	Protestant
Ghana	Christian	Animist	Muslim
Kenya	Protestant	Catholic	Animist
Mauritius	Hindu	Christian	Muslim
Nigeria	Christian	Muslim	Animist
South Africa	Christian	Animist	Secular
Zambia	Christian	Hindu	Muslim
Zimbabwe	Christian	Animist	Secular
Asia			
China	Secular	Buddhist	Taoist
India	Hindu	Muslim	Christian
Indonesia	Muslim	Christian	Hindu
Japan	Shintoist	Buddhist	Christian
Malaysia	Muslim	Buddhist	Hindu
Pakistan	Muslim	Hindu	Christian
Philippines	Catholic	Muslim	—
Singapore	Buddhist	Muslim	Secular
South Korea	Christian	Buddhist	—
Thailand	Buddhist	Muslim	Traditional
Europe			
Denmark	Catholic	Protestant	Muslim
France	Catholic	Muslim	Jewish
Germany	Protestant	Catholic	Secular
Italy	Catholic	Protestant	Jewish
Netherlands	Catholic	Protestant	Muslim
Norway	Protestant	Secular	Catholic
Poland	Catholic	Secular	Orthodox Christian
Portugal	Catholic	Secular	Protestant
Russia	Orthodox Christian	Muslim	Secular
Spain	Catholic	Protestant	Secular
Switzerland	Catholic	Protestant	Secular
United Kingdom	Christian	Muslim	Sikh
Middle East/Central Asia			
Armenia	Orthodox	Muslim	Secular
Egypt	Muslim	Christian	—

continued

Table 3.1 continued

COUNTRY		RELIGION[a]	
Israel	Jewish	Muslim	Secular
Jordan	Muslim	Christian	Secular
Kazakhstan	Muslim	Orthodox Christian	Catholic
Morocco	Muslim	Jewish	Christian
Saudi Arabia	Muslim	—	—
Tunisian	Muslim	Jewish	Christian
Turkey	Muslim	Christian	Jewish
Turkmenistan	Secular	Muslim	Orthodox Christian
North America			
Canada	Catholic	Protestant	Orthodox Christian
United States	Protestant	Catholic	Secular
Latin America/Caribbean			
Brazil	Catholic	Traditional	Protestant
Chile	Catholic	Protestant	Jewish
Colombia	Catholic	Protestant	Secular
Cuba	Secular	Catholic	Protestant
Jamaica	Protestant	Traditional	Catholic
Mexico	Catholic	Protestant	Secular
Peru	Catholic	Protestant	Traditional
Uruguay	Catholic	Protestant	Jewish
Venezuela	Catholic	Jewish	Muslim

[a]As reported by countries and in descending order left to right.

Source: Adapted from *Cultural Practices and Heritage: Leading Religions,* UNESCO.

sales around that time. However, Christmas is a good illustration of the substantial differences that still exist among even predominantly Christian societies. A large U.S.-based retailer of consumer electronics discovered these differences the hard way when it opened its first retail outlet in the Netherlands. The company planned the opening to coincide with the start of the Christmas selling season and bought advertising space accordingly for late November and December, as retailers do in the United States. The results proved less than satisfactory. Major gift giving in Holland takes place not around December 25, Christmas Day, but on St. Nicholas Day, December 6. Therefore, the opening of the company's retail operation was late and missed the major buying season.

From a marketing point of view, Christmas has increasingly become a global phenomenon. For many young Chinese, Christmas is not regarded as a religious holiday but simply represents "fun." Fashionable bars charge up to $25 for entrance on Christmas Eve, and hotel restaurants charge $180 for a Christmas Eve function.[7] The week around Christmas is the top grossing week for movie theaters in China, as young Chinese head out to theaters together instead of watching pirated DVDs at home.[8] Santa Claus is increasing in popularity in the predominantly Sunni Muslim country of Turkey. In Istanbul shopping centers, children stand in line to sit on Santa's lap and ask for gifts. Stores sell Santa suits and statues.[9]

Another Christian holiday, Saint Valentine's Day, has become popular in Iran despite disapproval of conservative Muslim clerics who view the holiday dedicated to love as decadent and immoral. Its popularity is spawned by young people who hear about it via satellite television and the Internet and respond by throwing parties and buying Valentine's Day gifts. Stores note that sales in the week prior to Valentine's Day are now similar to those before *Norouz*, the traditional Iranian New Year's Day. Valentine paraphernalia is both imported (from China!) and produced locally.[10]

Kosher conforming to Jewish dietary laws

The **kosher** diets of Orthodox Jews present certain marketers with both challenges and opportunities. For example, eating pork is forbidden, and meat and milk may not be eaten together. Many processed foods containing meat products have come under increased scrutiny. These include cereals, such as Kellogg's Frosted Mini Wheats, that are traditionally eaten with milk.[11]

The rigorously Orthodox make up about 12 percent of Israel's 4.7 million Jews, but their numbers are growing more rapidly than those of the rest of the population. As a result, many companies are addressing this segment of the market. Israeli food manufacturers have expanded their lines of strictly kosher products and have employed packaging and advertising in keeping with the more traditional sensitivities of Israel's Orthodox communities. Elite, a chocolate manufacturer, ran a contest for Orthodox children in which chocolate wrappers could be exchanged for cards showing prominent rabbis or religious teachers. Coca-Cola ran a separate line of advertisements aimed at Orthodox consumers in Israel. These ads depicted Coke drinkers in conservative dress instead of the scantily clad young people used in advertisements aimed at the Israeli public in general.[12] In addition, a cell phone company in Israel sells phones stripped to basic voice service. This offering was in response to many orthodox Jews who did not want the distractions of the myriad of services and features offered on the typical cell phone.[13]

Marketing and Islam

Islam is the religion of nearly 20 percent of the world's population. It is an important cultural force not only in the Middle East but in Asia and Africa as well. In fact, some of the world's largest Muslim populations live in China, Indonesia, and Malaysia.

Koran the sacred text of Islam

Hadith an authoritative collection of the sayings and reported practices of Mohammed

Sunna a way of life prescribed for Muslims based on the practices of Mohammed and scholarly interpretations of the Koran

The prophet Mohammed established Islam in Mecca, located in modern-day Saudi Arabia, in the year 610. By the time of the prophet's death in 632, the holy book of Islam, the **Koran**, had been completely revealed. Muslims believe it contains God's own words. The Koran was supplemented by the **Hadith** and the **Sunna**, which contain the reported words and actions of the prophet Mohammed. These works are the primary sources of guidance for all Muslims on all aspects of life.

Islam affects marketers in a number of ways (see Table 3.2). For example, Islam prohibits the paying or collecting of interest. In most Muslim countries, commercial banks must compete with Islamic banks, which do not offer savings accounts that pay interest. Although these accounts are not attractive to all, many devout Muslims prefer to keep their money in these banks. Islamic banks have also developed a unique product to compete with interest-bearing accounts at other banks. The profit-loss account allows customers to invest their savings in businesses that the bank preselects. Annual profits from the businesses are distributed into the shareholders' accounts.

Greater awareness of these Islamic traditions can create new business opportunities. For example, Muslims are also required to pray five times daily in the

TABLE 3.2	MARKETING IN AN ISLAMIC FRAMEWORK
ELEMENTS	**IMPLICATIONS FOR MARKETING**
Fundamental Islamic Concepts	
A. *Unity*—Concept of centrality, oneness of God, harmony in life.	Product standardization, mass media techniques, central balance, unity in advertising copy and layout, strong brand loyalties, a smaller evoked size set, loyalty to company, opportunities for brand extension strategies.
B. *Legitimacy*—Fair dealings, reasonable level of profits.	Less formal product warranties, need for institutional advertising and/or advocacy advertising, especially by foreign firms, and a switch from a profit-maximizing to a profit-satisfying strategy.
C. *Zakat*—2.5 percent per annum compulsory tax binding on all classified as "not poor."	Use of "excessive" profits, if any, for charitable acts; corporate donations for charity, institutional advertising.
D. *Usury*—Cannot charge interest on loans. A general interpretation of this law defines "excessive interest" charged on loans as not permissible.	Avoid direct use of credit as a marketing tool; establish a consumer policy of paying cash for low-value products; for high-value products, offer discounts for cash payments and raise prices of products on an installment basis; sometimes possible to conduct interest transactions between local/foreign firms in other non-Islamic countries; banks in some Islamic countries take equity in financing ventures, sharing resultant profits (and losses).
E. *Supremacy of human life*—Compared with other forms of life, objects, human life is of supreme importance.	Pet food and/or products less important; avoid use of statues, busts—interpreted as forms of idolatry; symbols in advertising and/or promotion should reflect high human values; use floral designs and artwork in advertising as representation of aesthetic values.
F. *Community*—All Muslims should strive to achieve universal brotherhood—with allegiance to the "one God." One way of expressing community is the required pilgrimage to Mecca for all Muslims at least once in their lifetime, if able to do so.	Formation of an Islamic economic community—development of an "Islamic consumer" served with Islamic-oriented products and services ("kosher" meat packages, gifts exchanged at Muslim festivals, and so forth); development of community services—need for marketing of nonprofit organizations and skills.
G. *Equality of peoples*	Participative communication systems; roles and authority structures may be rigidly defined, but accessibility at any level relatively easy.
H. *Abstinence*—During the month of Ramadan, Muslims are required to fast without food or drink from the first streak of dawn to sunset—a reminder to those who are more fortunate to be kind to the less fortunate and as an exercise in self-control.	Products that are nutritious, cool, and digested easily can be formulated for *Sehr* and *Iftar* (beginning and end of the fast).
I. *Consumption of alcohol and pork is forbidden; so is gambling.*	Opportunities for developing nonalcoholic items and beverages (for example, soft drinks, ice cream, milk shakes, fruit juices) and nonchance social games, such as Scrabble; food products should use vegetable or beef shortening.
J. *Environmentalism*—The universe created by God was pure. Consequently, the land, air, and water should be held as sacred elements.	Anticipate environmental, antipollution acts; opportunities for companies involved in maintaining a clean environment; easier acceptance of pollution control devices in the community (for example, recent efforts in Turkey have been well received by the local communities).

continued

Table 3.2 continued

ELEMENTS	IMPLICATIONS FOR MARKETING
K. *Worship*—Five times a day; timing of prayers varies.	Need to take into account the variability and shift in prayer timings in planning sales calls, work schedules, business hours, customer traffic, and so forth.
Islamic Culture	
A. *Obligation to family and tribal traditions*	Importance of respected members in the family or tribe as opinion leaders; word-of-mouth communication, customer referrals may be critical; social or clan allegiances, affiliations, and associations may be possible surrogates for reference groups; advertising home-oriented products stressing family roles may be highly effective—for example, electronic games.
B. *Obligations toward parents are sacred*	The image of functional products should be enhanced with advertisements that stress parental advice or approval; even with children's products, there should be less emphasis on children as decision makers.
C. *Obligation to extend hospitality to both insiders and outsiders*	Product designs that are symbols of hospitality, outwardly open in expression; rate of new product acceptance may be accelerated and eased by appeals based on community.
D. *Obligation to conform to codes of sexual conduct and social interaction*—These may include the following:	
1. Modest dress for women in public.	More colorful clothing and accessories are worn by women at home, so promotion of products for use in private homes could be more intimate—such audiences could be reached effectively through women's magazines; avoid use of immodest exposure and sexual implications in public settings.
2. Separation of male and female audiences (in some cases).	Access to female consumers can often be gained only through women as selling agents, salespersons, catalogues, home demonstrations, and women's specialty shops.
E. *Obligations to religious occasions*—For example, two major religious observances are celebrated—*Eid-ul-Fitr, Eid-ul-Adha*.	Tied to purchase of new shoes, clothing, and sweets and preparation of food items for family reunions, Muslim gatherings. There has been a practice of giving money in place of gifts. Increasingly, however, a shift is taking place to more gift giving; because of lunar calendar, dates are not fixed.

Source: Mushtaq Luqmani, Zahir A. Quraeshi, and Linda Delene, "Marketing in Islamic Countries: A Viewpoint," *MSU Business Topics* (Summer 1980), pp. 20–21. Reprinted by permission.

direction of the holy city of Mecca. Dubai-based Ilkone Mobile Telecommunications launched a phone in the Middle East with an internal compass to identify the direction to Mecca and an alarm for prayer times. A complete version of the Koran in Arabic and English was also included.[14]

Islam also prescribes a number of rules concerning food consumption and personal cleanliness. Products that contain no forbidden ingredients such as pork and alcohol may be certified **halal** (acceptable under Islamic teaching). Halal not only affects food products but many other products as well, such as lipsticks and vaccines.[15]

Halal permitted under Islamic law

In Malaysia, a government agency certifies that products are halal. Products must be free of forbidden foods, and production facilities must meet standards of

A Dairy Queen in Bahrain offers a half-price Deluxe Double Cheeseburger as a special Ramadan promotion. During the month of Ramadan, observant Muslims abstain from eating or drinking between sunrise and sunset as part of a spiritual fast.

cleanliness and proper storage. Every product sold by Nestlé Malaysia is certified halal. Even Singapore, where only 14 percent of the 3 million population is Muslim, has established its own halal certification body. Indonesia has a Muslim population of nearly 200 million. In response to consumer demand, the Indonesian government also established halal certification. When it was discovered that the Japanese food company Ajinomoto was using a pork-based enzyme in its halal seasoning products in Indonesia, the company had to pull tons of product off the shelves. The company not only faced possible legal action but also suffered a loss of consumer trust.[16]

The world market for Muslim halal food alone is estimated at $580 billion. Nestlé, with halal sales of $3 billion, is the largest producer of halal foods, which it produces in 75 factories world wide.[17] Fast-food companies such as McDonald's and Kentucky Fried Chicken have also obtained halal certificates to serve the Muslim market. Even a Brazilian beef processor adapted some of its packing plants to meet halal certification after managers visited Egypt and realized the potential of the halal beef market.[18] In fact, the United Arab Emirates (UAE) imports 80 percent of its halal food from countries such as Brazil and Australia.[19]

In many Muslim countries such as Indonesia, Ramadan (the month in which Muslims fast from dawn to dusk) is the major annual shopping season. Following the evening meal, most families watch television with special Ramadan programming. Because of this, advertising slots in the evening during Ramadan command the highest prices of any time during the year.[20]

Many companies even adopt a religious message in their advertisements at this time. A Coca-Cola commercial, developed by McCann-Erickson Malaysia, featured a small boy and his mother going with gifts to an orphanage, the mother with a rug and basket of food, the boy with his cherished bottle of Coca-Cola. After sunset the little boy leaves his house to go back to the orphanage to break fast and share the Coca-Cola with his new friends. The ad ends with the slogan "Always in good spirit. Always Coca-Cola." It appealed to religious sentiment across national boundaries and was scheduled to air in 20 countries.[21]

Marketing and Eastern Religions

Asia is a major market today for many international firms, and global marketers must take into account the possible impact of the Eastern religious and philosophical traditions of Hinduism, Buddhism, Confucianism, and Shintoism. Hinduism and Buddhism are the two largest Eastern religions. Hinduism is professed by about 450 million people, most of whom live in India, where Hindus constitute nearly 85 percent of the population. Hindu theology varies among believers but is generally polytheistic, with different groups showing a preference for one or several gods. In India, October and November are full of traditional holidays. As such, the two months are the Indian equivalent of the Christmas shopping season in Europe and the United States—a time for gift giving and major purchases.[22]

Hinduism includes a doctrine of rebirth into conditions determined by a person's prior life. A person can be reborn as a human, an animal, or a celestial being. Hinduism also encompasses a hereditary caste system that requires Hindus to marry within their own caste. Many Hindus are vegetarian, and eating beef is particularly taboo. Buddhism also began in India but rejected many of Hinduism's hierarchical structures. Today it is influential predominantly in East and Southeast Asia.

In India, Hyundai respects local beliefs when it launches new car models on auspicious days selected from the Hindu calendar.[23] A Seattle-based company showed far less sensitivity when it launched a line of toilet seats. The Sacred Seat Collection depicted images of Hindu gods such as Ganesh, the elephant god of learning. Several Indian politicians joined members of the large U.S. Hindu population in condemning the company.[24]

Confucianism is not a religion, but its founder Confucius is regarded as the greatest of China's sages and his impact is still greatly felt. Confucius taught respect for one's parents and for education, values common among Chinese today. Confucius' name has also proved valuable to marketers in China. Kong Demao was one of the two surviving members of the 77th generation of the family of Confucius. Since the early 1990s she had been the nominal chair of three distillers in the Qufu region of China, the ancestral home of Confucius. When all three distillers took the Confucius family name for their products in the mid-1980s, sales soared. In the 1990s, two of the distillers went to court over who really owned the name. Although the case remained unsettled, all three distillers decided it would be wise to contact Kong and pay a stipend for the use of her name. She was also named "Lifetime Honorary President" of the Confucius International Travel Agency.[25]

Japan has been heavily influenced both by Buddhism from Korea and by Confucianism from China. In the late 19th century, Japan's earlier Shinto religion was revived as the patriotic symbol of Japan, the emperor being exalted as the descendant of the sun goddess. Shinto rituals were performed at state occasions. State Shinto was abolished after World War II, but popular cults persist. When the first Starbucks abroad opened in Tokyo, Shinto priests offered prayers at the opening ceremony.[26] One enterprising tour group brings foreign tourists to Japan to view Shinto processions during October, a festival month in a number of Japanese cities.[27]

Global marketers require a keen awareness of how religion can influence business. They need to search actively for influences that may not be readily apparent. Showing respect for local religious traditions is an important part of cultural sensitivity.

THE FAMILY

The role of the family varies greatly among cultures, as do the roles that the various family members play. Across cultures, we find differences in family size, in the employment of women, and in many other factors of interest to marketers. Companies familiar with family interactions in Western society cannot assume that they will find the same patterns elsewhere.

In the United States, there has been a trend toward the dissolution of the traditional nuclear family. With people marrying later and divorcing more often, the "typical" family of father, mother, and children living in one dwelling has become far less common than in the past. More recently, a similar trend in Western Europe has resulted in an increase in the number of households even in countries where the overall population is decreasing. This outcome has in turn increased demand for many consumer durables, such as washing machines and ovens, whose sales correlate with number of households rather than with population. Also, an increasing number of women are working outside the home (see Table 3.3), a situation that boosts demand for frozen dinners and child-care centers.

Marketers should not expect to find the same type of family structure in all countries. In many societies, particularly in Asia and Latin America, the role of the male as head of the household remains pronounced. Some cultures still encourage the bearing of male rather than female children. In most cultures, 105 boys are born for every 100 girls, but in China the figure for boys is 118.5 and in South Korea, 116. In some areas of South Korea, boy births outnumber girls 125 to 100, indicating that female fetuses may be being aborted.[28] This male dominance coincides with a lower rate of participation by women in the labor force outside the home. This situation results in a lower average family income. The number of children per family also varies substantially by country or culture. In many Eastern European countries and in Germany, one child per family is fast becoming the rule, whereas families in many developing countries are still large by Western standards.

Extended Families

So far we have discussed only the nuclear family. However, for many cultures, the extended family—including grandparents, in-laws, aunts, uncles, and so on—is of considerable importance. In the United States, older parents usually live alone, whether in individually owned housing, in multiple housing for the elderly, or in nursing homes (for those who can no longer care for themselves). In countries with lower income levels and in rural areas, the extended family still plays a major role, further increasing the size of the average household. In China, 67 percent of parents with grown children live with one of their children, and 80 percent of such parents have contact with their children at least once a week.[29]

TABLE 3.3 FAMILY STATISTICS OF SELECTED COUNTRIES (IN PERCENTAGES)

COUNTRY	POPULATION GROWTH RATES[a]	SHARE OF WOMEN IN ADULT LABOR FORCE	COUNTRY	POPULATION GROWTH RATES[a]	SHARE OF WOMEN IN ADULT LABOR FORCE
Australia	1.1	45	Malaysia	1.9	—
Austria	0.2	45	Mexico	1.3	36
Belgium	0.2	44	Netherlands	0.5	44
Brazil	1.4	43	Nigeria	2.2	37
Canada	1.0	47	Norway	0.5	47
Chile	1.1	36	Pakistan	2.0	—
China	0.6	52	Russian Federation	−0.5	49
Denmark	0.3	47	Singapore	1.5	40
Egypt	1.9	22	South Africa	0.8	44
France	0.4	46	Spain	1.1	41
Germany	0.1	45	Sweden	0.4	48
Greece	0.3	41	Switzerland	0.2	45
Hungary	−0.3	46	Thailand	0.2	45
India	1.6	28	Turkey	1.4	26
Indonesia	1.3	37	United Kingdom	0.3	46
Italy	0.1	40	United States	1.0	46
Japan	0.2	41	Venezuela	1.8	40

[a]Average annual population growth rate between 2000 and 2005.

Source: Adapted from *Statistics and Indicators on Women and Men*, United Nations Statistics Division (http://www.un.org), June 2007. © United Nations, 2007. Reproduced with permission.

Extended families or clans play an important role among overseas Chinese as well. Driven by poverty and political upheaval, waves of families fled China to other countries in Asia during the past 200 years. They developed dense networks of thrifty, self-reliant communities united by their Chinese ethnicity. These Chinese communities have flourished in both commerce and industry. For example, ethnic Chinese make up 1 percent of the population and 20 percent of the economy in Vietnam, 1 percent and 40 percent in the Philippines, 4 percent and 50 percent in Indonesia, and 32 percent and 60 percent in Malaysia.[30] Ironically, the Chinese homeland has followed a one-child policy during the past generation in an attempt to curb its population growth. This policy is having an immediate impact on the younger generation's ability to form the traditional Chinese family business. Young entrepreneurs in China report that they establish business relationships with fellow students from high school or university instead of with siblings and cousins.

Beyond the Family

Most societies appreciate and promote a strong family unit. However, Francis Fukuyama argues that a culture can suffer from too great an emphasis on family values. Some cultures, such as that of southern Italy, emphasize nuclear family

Low-trust society a society in which trust is extended only to immediate family members

relationships to the exclusion of all others. It has been said that adults are not persons in southern Italy; they're only parents. In this **low-trust society**, trust is extended only to immediate family members.[31]

Yet business relationships depend on trust. Even with contracts and law courts, businesses could not survive if managers spent all their time in litigation. If trust is not extended beyond the family, business dealings must stay within the family. This practice stymies the growth of modern large-scale enterprises and impedes development. For this reason, southern Italy remains one of the poorest regions in Western Europe. Most of the developing world qualifies as relatively low-trust, according to Fukuyama's paradigm. Comparatively few large corporations in the private sector evolved outside North America, Europe, and Japan. Those that did retained their family ties much longer than firms in developed countries.

High-trust society a society in which trust is extended to persons beyond the immediate family, encouraging the emergence of various voluntary organizations such as civic groups and modern corporations

Germany, Japan, and the United States are all very different in many aspects of culture. However, Fukuyama notes that these three countries are **high-trust societies**. They all share a history of voluntary associations—civic, religious, and business—that extend beyond the family. This history of associating with nonfamily members to accomplish common goals taught people that they could trust others who were not blood relations. This experience paved the way for large, publicly owned corporations to emerge, because family businesses could feel secure in raising money outside the family, and stockholders could eventually trust their investments in the hands of professional managers. Marketers who compete in high-trust countries usually must contend with these large corporate competitors. However, the history of associations can also be exploited by savvy marketers. Marketers of credit cards in Japan discovered that consumers took quickly to credit cards cobranded with associations and clubs, because the typical Japanese was proud to belong to civic groups.

In many countries, such as Turkey, the traditional and modern coexist—presenting marketers with both challenges and opportunities.

Courtesy of Dr. Liesl Riddle

WORLD BEAT 3.1

FLYING OR CLEANING?

SOME CONSIDER JAPAN'S RECORD on gender empowerment to be less than impressive. The country ranks 58th out of 108 countries. However the mass retirement of Japanese in the baby boom generation is opening new opportunities for Japanese women. Even airlines, who previously only hired male pilots, are beginning to hire women as well.

With more women working and flying, professional housecleaners are becoming more common in Japan. For decades, housecleaning was considered the job of the Japanese housewives, and even well-to-do families didn't hire strangers to clean their houses. But Japanese society is experiencing a redefinition of gender roles as women enter the workforce in record numbers.

Nonetheless, the industry faces a number of challenges—not least of which is the high cost of delivering services in

Japan. The country discourages immigration and labor costs remain high. The Duskin Company, a pioneer in Japan's housecleaning market, charges 15,000 yen ($113) to clean a single toilet bowl and a minimum of $420 to do spring cleaning of a two-bedroom apartment. Another company ran a half-price sale on weekdays promoting the idea that guilty housewives could keep their outsourcing secret from their husbands.

Cleaning entrepreneurs aren't discouraged. The Japan Housecleaning Organization, a volunteer group with 60 members, offers a ten-day training course for novices—mainly middle-aged men who have lost their corporate jobs during Japan's extended economic recession. Housecleaners even have their own section in the yellow pages. But they're listed under the English word *house-cleaning*, which is preferred over the Japanese word *soji*.

Sources: "Women's Dream of Becoming Airline Pilots No Longer Pie in the Sky," *Kyodo News*, December 23, 2008; Yumiko Ono, "Japan's Distress Prompts an Odd Career Transition," *Wall Street Journal,* April 1, 2002, p. B1; Anthony Faiola, "Japanese Women Live, and Like It, on Their Own," *Washington Post*, 31 August 2004, p. A01; and "Firms Fail to Recognize Economic Importance of Women at Own Peril," *Nikkei Weekly*, April 6, 2009.

EDUCATION

Education shapes people's outlooks, desires, and motivations. To the extent that educational systems differ among countries, we can expect differences among consumers. However, education not only affects potential consumers; it also shapes potential employees for foreign companies and for the business community at large.

In the United States, compulsory education ends at age 16. Virtually all students who obtain a high school diploma stay in school until age 18. In high school, about 25 percent take vocational training courses. After high school, students either attend college or find a job. About half of all high school graduates go on to some type of college. This pattern is not shared by all countries. Many students in Europe go to school only until age 16. Then they join an apprenticeship program. This is particularly the case in Germany, where formal apprenticeship programs exist for about 450 job categories.

The extent and quality of education in a society affect marketing on two levels: the consumer level and the employee level. In societies in which the average level of participation in the educational process is low, one typically finds a low level of literacy. Basic literacy levels can vary widely across countries (see Table 3.4). This variation in reading ability not only affects the earning potential of consumers, and thus the level of consumption, but also determines the communication options for marketing programs, as we will see in Chapters 14 and 15. Another concern is how much young people earn. In countries such as Germany, where many of its youth have considerable earnings by age 20, the value and potential of the youth market

TABLE 3.4	ADULT LITERACY RATES FOR SELECTED COUNTRIES (IN PERCENTAGES)								
COUNTRY	MALE	FEMALE	COUNTRY	MALE	FEMALE	COUNTRY	MALE	FEMALE
Algeria	80	60	China	95	87	Peru	93	82
Argentina	97	97	Egypt	83	59	Qatar	89	89
Armenia	100	99	Estonia	100	100	Russian Federation	100	99
Benin	48	23	Ghana	66	50	Saudi Arabia	87	69
Bolivia	93	81	Honduras	80	80	South Africa	84	81
Brazil	88	89	Indonesia	94	87	Thailand	95	91
Bulgaria	99	98	Iran	84	70	Turkey	95	80
Cambodia	85	64	Israel	98	96	Vietnam	94	87
Cameroon	77	60	Mexico	92	90			
Chile	96	96	Morocco	66	40			

Source: Adapted from *Indicators on Literacy*, United Nations Statistics Division (http://www.un.org), June, 2007. © United Nations, 2007. Reproduced with permission.

is quite different from those in the United States, where a substantial number of young people do not enter the job market until age 21 or 22.

The educational system also affects employee skills and executive talent. In the United States, the sales organizations of many large companies are staffed strictly with university graduates. In many other countries, sales as a profession has a lower status and attracts fewer university graduates. The typical career path of an American executive involves a four-year college program and, in many cases, a master's degree in business administration (MBA) program. This format for executive education is less common in other countries, despite the fact that MBA programs have proliferated around the world in the past 25 years. For example, large corporations in Korea hire fewer MBAs than their American counterparts, but they import top management educators to teach in their in-house executive programs.

Thus different countries have substantially different ideas about education in general and about management education in particular. Traditional European education emphasizes the mastery of a subject through knowledge acquisition. In contrast, the U.S. approach emphasizes analytic ability and an understanding of concepts. Students passing through the two educational systems probably develop different thinking patterns and attitudes. It requires a considerable amount of cultural sensitivity for an international manager to understand these differences and to make the best use of the human resources that are available.

ATTITUDES TOWARD TIME

In Poland, decisions are usually made quickly. In Kazakhstan, canceling a meeting at the last minute is common, whereas punctuality is strictly observed in Romania.[32] These are all examples of behaviors that reflect cultural attitudes toward time. In the United States, time is seen as having economic value. It is a commodity to be planned for and used wisely. Schedules are set and appointment times are interpreted precisely. If a meeting is scheduled at 3:00 p.m., participants are expected to arrive at 3:00 p.m. In many other countries, such as Costa Rica and Saudi

Arabia, meetings rarely begin on time. An American arriving at a meeting in Saudi Arabia can wait quite a while for others to show up. Faced with this phenomenon, the American is likely to be annoyed. Time is being wasted!

Monochronic versus Polychronic Cultures and Temporal Orientation

Monochronic culture a culture in which activities are undertaken one at a time and people respect schedules and agendas

The United States is basically a **monochronic culture**. Activities are undertaken one at a time. People respect schedules and agendas. However, Asian cultures are basically **polychronic cultures**, and expectations are different.[33] At any one time, a manager is expected to be managing multiple tasks. Schedules and agendas must bend to the needs of people, and interruptions are not the exception but the rule. It is not unusual for a high-ranking Indian manager to stop work to listen to an employee's family problems. Similarly, it would be impolite to abruptly cut off a conversation with one group to attend a prearranged meeting with another group. Salespeople from monochronic cultures who travel to polychronic cultures should expect to be kept waiting and should not interpret their clients' tardiness as lack of interest or disrespect.

Polychronic culture a culture in which multitasking is common, schedules and agendas bend to the needs of people, and interruptions are common

Latin culture sometimes appears to be more monochronic and sometimes more polychronic.[34] Managers from South America explain that a monochronic orientation is more appropriate for work situations but a polychronic orientation is more appropriate for private life and entertaining.

Temporal orientation a society's predominant time focus—either on the past, the present, or the future

Temporal orientations also vary by culture. Some cultures, such as Mexico and Brazil, are oriented to the present: Life is enjoyed for the moment. One Mexican ceramics manufacturer noted that as soon as his employees made enough money for the week, they stopped coming to work. The United States is a future-oriented culture, where efforts are focused more on working to achieve a future goal. European and Middle Eastern cultures are more oriented to the past, placing a greater

One Red Eye/Jason Alden

Young Peruvians enjoy socializing in this advertisement for Backus beer. Social life of Latin cultures remains polychronic even as work becomes more monochronic.

emphasis on historical achievements and relationships. When Israel and Egypt signed a peace treaty 30 years ago, it ended a war that had been going on for nearly 30 years. The U.S. government, which had assisted in the peace process, expected business relations to blossom between the two countries. Today, Israeli firms have barely begun to penetrate the Egyptian market. Egyptians—consumers, distributors, potential partners, and government officials—are still highly aware of the 30 years of war that preceded the peace.

Work and Leisure Time

Different societies have different views about the amounts of time it is appropriate to spend at work and in leisure pursuits. In most economically developed countries, leisure has become a major aspect of life. In such countries, the development of the leisure industries is an indication that play and relaxation can be as intensely consumed as any other products.

Society significantly influences work and leisure through statutory vacation allowances and public holidays. Traditionally, European statutes have required companies to give employees 25–30 days of vacation annually, whereas many workers in the United States, Japan, Mexico, and the Philippines enjoy only 5–10 vacation days. These differences result in lower working hours per year in Europe than in the United States, Japan, and Mexico.

Increasingly, globalization may force a convergence in work hours. For example, on average, German employees work about 25 percent fewer hours than their counterparts in the United States. For 25 years, German unions successfully pushed for a shorter workweek in hopes of creating more jobs. However, this resulted in German labor costs becoming the highest in the world, and German companies are now shifting jobs out of Germany in order to remain globally competitive. The recent addition of Eastern European countries to the European Union (EU) is expected to accelerate this trend. Facing the threat of job losses, French workers at a car components factory owned by Bosch voted to work longer hours for the same pay. Some saw this vote as the beginning of a de facto rollback of France's 35-hour legal workweek.[35]

THE HOFSTEDE MEASURES OF CULTURE

Geert Hofstede developed a four-dimensional framework by which to measure several key attributes of cultures. This framework emerged as a result of his research on IBM employees and has since attracted considerable interest among business scholars.[36] The research involved over 116,000 questionnaires and incorporated 72 different national subsidiaries, 20 languages, and 38 occupations. Hofstede's insights can be very useful to international marketers. The four dimensions are power distance, individualism-collectivism, masculinity-femininity, and uncertainty avoidance. The scores for 69 countries and regions are listed in Table 3.5. Although Hofstede's four dimensions do not, of course, fully describe national cultures, they are a useful place to begin.

Power Distance

Power distance is the extent to which the less powerful members within a society accept that power is distributed unevenly. Geert Hofstede tells the story of a clash

Power distance a measure of culture capturing the extent to which the less powerful members within a society accept that power is distributed unevenly

TABLE 3.5 VALUES OF HOFSTEDE'S CULTURAL DIMENSIONS FOR 69 COUNTRIES OR REGIONS

COUNTRY/REGION	POWER DISTANCE	INDIVIDUALISM	MASCULINITY	UNCERTAINTY AVOIDANCE
Arabic countries[a]	80	38	53	68
Argentina	49	46	56	86
Australia	36	90	61	51
Austria	11	55	79	70
Bangladesh	80	20	55	60
Belgium	65	75	54	94
Brazil	69	38	49	76
Bulgaria	70	30	40	85
Canada	39	80	52	48
Chile	63	23	28	86
China	80	20	66	30
Colombia	67	13	64	80
Costa Rica	35	15	21	86
Czech Republic	57	58	57	74
Denmark	18	74	16	23
East African region[b]	64	27	41	52
Ecuador	78	8	63	67
Estonia	40	60	30	60
Finland	33	63	26	59
France	68	71	43	86
Germany	35	67	66	65
Greece	60	35	57	112
Guatemala	95	6	37	101
Hong Kong	68	25	57	29
Hungary	46	80	88	82
India	77	48	56	40
Indonesia	78	14	46	48
Iran	58	41	43	59
Ireland	28	70	68	35
Israel	13	54	47	81
Italy	50	76	70	75
Jamaica	45	39	68	13
Japan	54	46	95	92
Luxembourg	40	60	50	70
Malaysia	104	26	50	36
Malta	56	59	47	96
Mexico	81	30	69	82

continued

Table 3.5 continued

COUNTRY/REGION	POWER DISTANCE	INDIVIDUALISM	MASCULINITY	UNCERTAINTY AVOIDANCE
Morocco	70	46	53	68
Netherlands	38	80	14	53
New Zealand	22	79	58	49
Norway	31	69	8	50
Pakistan	55	14	50	70
Panama	95	11	44	86
Peru	64	16	42	87
Philippines	94	32	64	44
Poland	68	60	64	93
Portugal	63	27	31	104
Romania	90	30	42	90
Russia	93	39	36	95
Salvador	66	19	40	94
Singapore	74	20	48	8
Slovakia	104	52	110	51
South Africa	49	65	63	49
South Korea	60	18	39	85
Spain	57	51	42	86
Surinam	85	47	37	92
Sweden	31	71	5	29
Switzerland	34	68	70	58
Taiwan	58	17	45	69
Thailand	64	20	34	64
Trinidad	47	16	58	55
Turkey	66	37	45	85
United Kingdom	35	89	66	35
United States	40	91	62	46
Uruguay	61	36	38	100
Venezuela	81	12	73	76
Vietnam	70	20	40	30
West African region[c]	77	20	46	54
Yugoslavia	76	27	21	88

[a]Egypt, Iraq, Kuwait, Lebanon, Libya, Saudi Arabia, and United Arab Emirates.
[b]Ethiopia, Kenya, Tanzania, and Zambia.
[c]Ghana, Nigeria, and Sierra Leone.

Sources: Geert Hofstede, *Cultures and Organizations: Software of the Mind* (New York: McGraw-Hill, 1991), pp. 53, 68, 84, and 113; and Geert Hofstede, *Culture's Consequences* (Thousand Oaks, CA: Sage, 2001), p. 502.

of cultures between the high-power-distance culture of France and the low-power-distance culture of Sweden:

The nobles of Sweden in 1809 deposed King Gustav IV, whom they considered incompetent, and surprisingly invited Jean Baptiste Bernadotte, a French general who had served under their enemy Napoleon, to become King of Sweden. Bernadotte accepted and he became King Charles XVI; his descendents occupy the Swedish throne to this day. When the new king was installed, he addressed the Swedish Parliament in their language. His broken Swedish amused the Swedes, and they roared with laughter. The Frenchman who had become king was so upset that he never tried to speak Swedish again.[37]

As a French general, Bernadotte was used to deference from those below him in the hierarchy. Members of Parliament would never laugh at a king in France or criticize him to his face. Even today, France has a high-power-distance score compared with other Western European countries. Nearly all the top jobs in the French public and private sectors are held by graduates of two elite institutions—the École Nationale d'Administration and the École Polytechnique.

Beginning in the family, children in high-power-distance cultures are expected to be obedient to their parents. Respect for parents and elders is considered a virtue. In low-power-distance countries, children learn to say no at a young age and are encouraged to attain personal independence from the family. In these societies, subordinates are less dependent on their bosses and are more comfortable approaching their bosses and contradicting them.

Individualism-Collectivism

Individualism-collectivism a measure of culture capturing the extent to which a society evaluates a person as an individual rather than as a member of group

Hofstede's second dimension of culture is the **individualism-collectivism** dimension. The United States rates very high on individualism. However, most of the world is far more collectivist. In collectivist societies, the good of the group prevails over the good of the individual. From birth, individuals are integrated into strong, cohesive groups. They are identified in terms of their group allegiance and their group role.

The collectivist world view tends to divide people into in-groups and out-groups. In other words, people do not simply choose which in-group to join. Often one has to be born into an in-group, such as a family, an ethnic group, or a nationality. Collectivist societies tend to be more suspicious of outsiders, whereas individualistic societies are more welcoming of them. For example, only one of an individual's parents needs to be an American for the individual to qualify as an American citizen. Furthermore, one can be an American citizen simply by virtue of having been born in the United States, even of foreign parents. And if one does not qualify by birth, immigration is a possibility. Each year hundreds of thousands of immigrants request and are granted American citizenship. More collectivist societies, on the other hand, do not bestow citizenship so freely. For one to qualify as an Egyptian citizen, both of one's parents should be Egyptian, and naturalization is virtually unknown in this country.

Individuals in collectivist societies are more dependent on their group and more loyal to it than members of individualistic societies. Group members are expected to take care of one another. In turn, they tend to follow group norms and to avoid deviating from the group in opinions or behavior. This group cohesiveness may transfer to groups joined later in life, such as friends from high school and college or corporate colleagues.

A difference between a collectivist and an individualist market is illustrated by the South Korean social networking site Cyworld. Cyworld differs from U.S. social sites that specialize in bringing strangers together. Cyworld emphasizes strengthening relationships between current friends, coworkers, and relatives. It creates a space to keep in contact from high school through parenthood.[38]

Outsiders may come to be trusted in collectivist societies, but only after they have invested much time and effort. Many firms relate a common experience in Saudi Arabia: A manager is sent to Saudi Arabia to establish business relations. After a long time, the potential Saudi client agrees to do business with the firm, but only if the manager who originally established the relationship stays and manages the relationship. In other words, the trusted outsider must be a person, not a firm.[39]

Masculinity-Femininity

Masculinity-femininity a measure of culture relating to assertiveness/modesty and competitiveness/nurturance

Hofstede's third dimension of culture is **masculinity-femininity**. This was (not surprisingly) the only dimension identified in the IBM study in which male and female respondents' scores were significantly different. Nonetheless, some countries were rated more masculine overall, including their women, and some more feminine overall, including their men. Masculinity is associated with assertiveness. Femininity is associated with modesty and nurturance. Masculine societies value ambition, competitiveness, and high earnings. Feminine societies are concerned with public welfare. For example, the percentage of gross national product (GNP) that a state allocates for aid to poor countries does not correlate with wealth but does correlate with femininity.

In Denmark, a feminine country, students tend to prepare a résumé that underplays their achievements. Interviewers know that they must ask probing questions to elicit an account of these achievements in the interview. Students in more masculine societies, such as the United States, tend to construct their résumés to broadcast any achievements. In this regard, Hofstede noted that Americans look like braggarts to Danes and that Danes look like "suckers" to Americans.

Uncertainty Avoidance

Uncertainty avoidance a measure of culture relating to general worry about the future

Uncertainty avoidance is the state of being uneasy or worried about what may happen in the future. It is not the same as being averse to risk. People who are risk-averse are afraid that something specific might happen—for example, that an inflated stock market might crash or that they might fail their final exams because they haven't studied hard. People who are uncertainty-avoidant are *anxious in general*. Exams always make them anxious, even if they have studied hard and have done well in the past. The future is uncertain for all of us. Typical persons from low-uncertainty-avoidance societies accept this fact and are confident that they can deal with whatever might arise. In other words, they are comfortable "rolling with the punches." Typical persons from high-uncertainty-avoidance societies try to control and minimize future uncertainty. They have a tendency to work hard or at least to feel more comfortable if they are busy doing something.

Uncertainty-avoidant cultures don't like ambiguity. Events should be clearly understandable and as predictable as possible. Teachers in these cultures are expected always to have the answers. In low-uncertainty-avoidance cultures, on the other hand, teachers are allowed to say, "I don't know." High-uncertainty-avoidance cultures have an emotional need for formal and informal rules. Low-uncertainty-avoidance cultures dislike rules. What rules they do employ, however, are generally more respected than are the many rules of uncertainty-avoidant cultures.

High-uncertainty-avoidance cultures tend to think that what is different is potentially dangerous. This fear may make such cultures less innovative than low-uncertainty-avoidance cultures, because radically new ideas are suspect to them.

At a private cram school outside of Seoul, Korean students retreat to a remote location to study unceasingly for their college entrance exams. South Korea scores high in uncertainty avoidance.

However, they can prove outstanding at implementing the ideas of others. As Hofstede noted, Britain (a low-uncertainty-avoidance culture) has produced more Nobel Prize winners than Japan (a high-uncertainty-avoidance culture), but Japan has brought more new products to the world market.[40]

Uses and Limitations of the Hofstede Measures

The Hofstede measures are an excellent way to identify quickly those areas where significant cultural differences exist. Americans dealing with distributors in Guatemala must remember that their agents come from a very different culture. Guatemala scores much higher on power distance and uncertainty avoidance. It is a very collectivist society, whereas the United States is a very individualistic one. If we send a young American manager to negotiate terms with Guatemalan distributors, our American manager must be careful to show proper respect and deference to any older distributors. Our manager should expect the distributors to ask for clear and detailed contracts. In turn, our manager should take care that the distributors belong to the right in-group. For example, do their group ties allow them to reach the right retailers and to access preferential financing? Have the potential distributors conformed to group norms, and have they established themselves as trustworthy within their group?

We must remember that all these scores are relative. Depending on the reference point, Japan can appear collectivist or individualistic. American culture is more individualistic than Japanese culture, but Japanese culture is more individualistic than South Korean culture. When a multinational company sends American managers to deal with Japanese customers, these managers must adjust to a more collectivist culture. When the multinational sends South Korean managers to deal with the same Japanese customers, they must adjust to a more individualistic culture.

Hofstede's framework is the culture framework that has received by far the most interest by business researchers.[41] Yet, the framework has a number of limitations. Not all countries were included in the original IBM study. Because IBM had no subsidiaries in Russia or Eastern Europe in the late 1970s, with the exception of Yugoslavia, we have no original scores for these markets. Luckily, new studies have added to the list. Still, for reasons of sample size, some countries in both Africa and the Middle East were grouped together despite probable cultural differences between them. We must also keep in mind that ethnic groups and regional populations within a country can vary significantly from the national average.[42] Also, the Hofstede measures should not be used for stereotyping people. They do present us with central tendencies or averages for a culture, but they cannot be used to describe any one person who might come from that culture. Some individual Swedes will behave in a more "masculine" manner than some Japanese, even though Sweden as a whole is a feminine culture and Japan as a whole is a masculine one.

Although the Hofstede measures are useful for identifying cultural differences and suggesting potential cross-cultural problems that international marketers may face, they do not capture or elucidate all aspects of a culture. Britain and the United States appear nearly similar across all the Hofstede measures. Still, they differ in many aspects of culture. For example, Britain exhibits greater class consciousness than is found in the United States, and the United States scores higher on religiosity, as exhibited, for example, in church attendance. People in the United States are more outgoing in expressing their emotions, whereas the British are more reserved.

In fact, the Hofstede scores sometimes fall prey to **cultural paradox**. In other words, they appear to argue *against* an observed cultural phenomenon. For example, Japanese score higher than Americans on uncertainty avoidance. Yet they intentionally use ambiguous clauses in business contracts, whereas Americans incorporate every contingency in their contracts.[43] We cannot hope to capture a complete culture in four numeric measures. They are a great place to start, but they are only a start.

> **Cultural paradox** a common behavioral norm in a culture that appears to contradict a prior conceptual model of that culture

Cultural Change

How quickly does culture change? Are the Hofstede measures valid after 30 years? Will they be valid 30 years from now? Culture does change, but most writers on culture agree that it changes very slowly. In the 1920s, the Ottoman Empire that ruled Turkey was ousted in a military uprising. A new charismatic leader, Ataturk, attempted in various ways to distance Turkey from its culture of the past and force Turks to adopt more European ways. A major assault was made on collectivism. Voluntary organizations such as political parties and business associations were required by law to be open to all. Ethnic affiliations that had played a major role in the politics of the Ottoman Empire were discouraged under Ataturk. Citizens were socialized to think of themselves simply as Turks. Physical emblems of religious affiliations, such as the veil worn by Muslim women and the fez worn by Muslim men, were outlawed. Eighty years later, much has changed in Turkey, and Ataturk enjoys hero status among nearly all Turks. Yet his attempt to defeat collectivism has failed. Modern Turkey struggles with the Kurdish ethnic question in the East, Islamic political parties win elections, and Turkey scores only 37 on Hofstede's individualism measure.

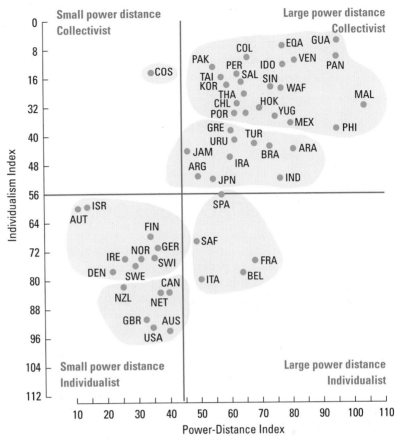

FIGURE 3.3
The Positions of 50 Countries and 3 Regions on Power Distance and Individualism-Collectivism Dimensions[a]

[a]ARA, Arabic-speaking countries (Egypt, Iraq, Kuwait, Lebanon, Libya, Saudi Arabia, United Arab Emirates); ARG, Argentina; AUS, Australia; AUT, Austria; BEL, Belgium; BRA, Brazil; CAN, Canada; CHL, Chile; COL, Colombia; COS, Costa Rica; DEN, Denmark; EAF, East Africa (Ethiopia, Kenya, Tanzania, Zambia); EQA, Ecuador; FIN, Finland; FRA, France; GBR, Great Britain; GER, Germany F.R.; GRE, Greece; GUA, Guatemala; HOK, Hong Kong; IDO, Indonesia; IND, India; IRA, Iran; IRE, Ireland (Republic of); ISR, Israel; ITA, Italy; JAM, Jamaica; JPN, Japan; KOR, South Korea; MAL, Malaysia; MEX, Mexico; NET, Netherlands; NOR, Norway; NZL, New Zealand; PAK, Pakistan; PAN, Panama; PER, Peru; PHI, Philippines; POR, Portugal; SAF, South Africa; SAL, Salvador; SIN, Singapore; SPA, Spain; SWE, Sweden; SWI, Switzerland; TAI, Taiwan; THA, Thailand; TUR, Turkey; URU, Uruguay; USA, United States; VEN, Venezuela; WAF, West Africa (Ghana, Nigeria, Sierra Leone); YUG, Yugoslavia.

Source: Geert Hofstede, *Cultures and Organizations* (McGraw-Hill, New York: 1991), pp. 23, 51, 83, and 111. Reprinted with permission of the author.

It is true that most developing countries rate high on power distance and collectivism (see Figure 3.3), and the average religiosity of a country's population tends to decline with increased economic development. These observations have led some to conclude that as economies develop, all societies will someday converge in a single, modern culture. Americans in particular tend to believe that this modern culture will resemble American culture. Yet, ironically, the United States remains an outlier regarding the religiosity rule. Despite enjoying one of the highest per-capita incomes in the world, Americans remain one of the world's most religious societies.[44] Also, Americans rate higher on the traditional value of national pride than do citizens in other developed countries. Based on these observed patterns of social development, Sweden and the Netherlands are arguably better examples of modernity than is the United States.[45]

It is important to remember that cultures in the world today vary greatly. With global media, Internet connection, and human migration, virtually all cultures are affected by other cultures. All societies are evolving. In a hundred years, Indonesia will undergo cultural change, but it won't become America. In a hundred years, America will undergo cultural change as well. Marketing managers from all nations will continue to deal with the cultural differences that make all nations unique.

LANGUAGE AND COMMUNICATION

Knowing the language of a society can become the key to understanding its culture. Language is not merely a collection of words or terms. Language expresses the thinking pattern of a culture—and to some extent even forms the thinking itself. Linguists have found that cultures with more primitive languages or a limited range of expression are more likely to be limited in their thought patterns. Some languages cannot accommodate modern technological or business concepts, forcing the cultural elite to work in a different language.

The French are particularly sensitive about their language as an embodiment of their culture and seek to protect it from outside influence. The French government has proposed legal action to limit further incursions by other languages, especially by English. For example, *le airbag* is called *coussin gonflable de protection* and *fast food* is *restauration rapide.* France persuaded the European community that 40 percent of TV programming should be produced domestically. Cinema tickets in France are taxed and the funds used to support the French film industry as protection against the U.S. film industry, which has come to dominate the European film market.

Table 3.6 lists the official languages of selected countries. Note that some countries have more than one official language. When Disney released its first animated film produced in India, it was available in three languages–Hindi, Tamil, and Telugu.[46] In fact, India has 19 official languages, although the most commonly spoken language is Hindi. South Africa has 11 official languages. A very few countries, such as the United States, do not designate an official language. African countries with diverse tribal languages often adopt a colonial European language as their official language. However, the use of this official language may be restricted to elites. Similarly, Spanish is one of the official languages of Bolivia, but 2 native Indian languages are also official. Certain languages are associated with certain regions of the world, but key markets in these regions may speak a different language. For example, Arabic is associated with the Middle East, but Persian (Farsi) is spoken in Iran, and Turkish in Turkey. Spanish is associated with Latin America, but Portuguese is spoken in Brazil.

Forms of Address

The English language has one form of address: All persons are addressed with the pronoun *you.* This is not the case in many other languages. The Germanic, Romance, and Slavic languages always have two forms of address, the personal

TABLE 3.6

OFFICIAL LANGUAGES OF SELECTED COUNTRIES

COUNTRY	LANGUAGE(S)	COUNTRY	LANGUAGE(S)	COUNTRY	LANGUAGE(S)
AFRICA		Russian Federation	Russian	**MIDDLE EAST**	
Angola	Portuguese	Spain	Spanish	Egypt	Arabic, English, French
Cameroon	French, English	Switzerland	French, German, Italian, Romansh	Iraq	Arabic
Chad	French, Arabic			Iran	Farsi
Ethiopia	Amharic	United Kingdom	English, Welsh	Israel	Hebrew, Arabic
Kenya	Swahili	**AMERICAS**		Lebanon	Arabic, French
Mozambique	Portuguese	Argentina	Spanish	Turkey	Turkish
Niger	French	Belize	English	**ASIA**	
Nigeria	English	Bolivia	Aymara, Quechua, Spanish	Pakistan	Urdu, English
Rwanda	French, Kinyarwanda			Sri Lanka	English, Sinhala, Tamil
Somalia	Somali	Brazil	Portuguese	Japan	Japanese
EUROPE		Canada	English, French	Malaysia	Malay
Belgium	Dutch, French, German	Chile	Spanish	Philippines	Tagalog, English
Finland	Finnish, Swedish	Haiti	French, Creole	Singapore	Chinese, English, Malay, Tamil
France	French	Jamaica	English		
Germany	German	Mexico	Spanish	South Korea	Korean
Italy	Italian	Peru	Spanish	Thailand	Thai
Netherlands	Dutch, Frisian	Venezuela	Spanish		

Source: Adapted from *Cultural Practices and Heritage: Leading Languages,* UNESCO Cultural Policy Resources (http://www.unesco.org).

and the formal. Japanese has three forms. A Japanese person will use a different form of address with a superior, a colleague, or a subordinate, and there are different forms for male and female in many expressions. These differences in language represent different ways of interacting. English, particularly as it is spoken in the United States, is much less formal than Japanese. Americans often address their bosses and customers by their first names. In Japan this practice could be considered rude. Consequently, knowing the Japanese language gives a foreigner a better understanding of cultural mores regarding social status and authority.

Low-context culture a culture in which communication is explicit and words tend to retain their meaning in all situations

High-context culture a culture in which communication is more implicit and the meanings of words change depending on who is speaking to whom, where that person is speaking, and under what circumstances he or she is speaking

The Context of Language

When an American executive says "yes" in a negotiation, this usually means "Yes, I accept the terms." However, *yes* in Asian countries can have a variety of meanings. It can mean that your hearers recognize that you are talking to them but not necessarily that they understand what you are saying. It can mean that they understood you but disagree with you. It can mean that they understand your proposal and will consult with others about it. Or, finally, it can indicate total agreement.

The simple term *yes* is a good example of how some languages can be affected by social milieu or context. In **low-context cultures** such as the United States, communication is explicit and words tend to retain their meaning in all situations. In Asian **high-context cultures**, meanings are more implicit. The meanings of words change depending on who is speaking to whom, where that person is speaking, and under what circumstances. These subtleties make communication all the more difficult for persons who were not born and raised in those cultures.[47] Not surprisingly, collectivist cultures tend to be high-context cultures.

Before beginning a conversation or a negotiation in high-context cultures, the parties involved need to take part in preliminary chats in order to place one another in the correct social context. For example, do both parties come from the same social background, or is one an outsider? Do both negotiators possess the status required to make a final decision on their own, or will they need to consult with others? In high-context cultures, these questions would never be asked or answered directly. Instead, people are socialized to pick up on the right cues, such as where someone went to school or how long that person has been employed with his or her company. "Placing each other" helps negotiators determine how they will interact and interpret each other's statements.

Also, *how* something is said may be considered as important, or even more important, than what is said. When U.S. Secretary of State James Baker told the Iraqis that the United States would attack Iraq if they did not get out of Kuwait, the high-context Iraqis understood that the Americans would not attack them. Baker spoke calmly and did not seem angry. Therefore, the Iraqis concluded that they needn't take the threat seriously.[48]

Body Language

Body language nonverbal communications, including touching, making arm and hand gestures, and keeping a proper distance between speakers

As important as understanding a verbal foreign language is, it is only part of the challenge. The use of nonverbal communications, or **body language**, is also important. Body language includes such elements as touching, making arm and hand gestures, and keeping the proper distance between speakers. Mexicans happily come within 16–18 inches of a stranger for a business discussion. For Latins, Arabs, and

Students at a Japanese smiling school.

Noboru Hashimoto

Africans, proximity is a sign of confidence. Asians, Nordics, Anglo-Saxons, and Germanic people consider space within 1 yard or meter as personal space. When a Mexican moves closer than this to an English person, the English person feels invaded and steps back, giving the Mexican the incorrect message that he or she does not want to do business.[49] The appropriateness of eye contact varies with culture as well. Americans consider making eye contact while speaking a sign of trustworthiness. Many Asian cultures, such as that of Korea, can consider it a sign of disrespect.

Showing Emotion

Affective culture a culture in which speakers are allowed—even expected—to express emotions

Neutral culture a culture that discourages a show of emotion

Another way in which cultures vary in their communication style is the degree to which they exhibit emotion. In **affective cultures**, such as Italy, the United States, and Arab countries, speakers are allowed—even expected—to express emotions more than in nonaffective or **neutral cultures**, such as China, Korea, and Japan. If upset or even excited, a speaker is allowed to speak louder and gesticulate. This is not to say that Americans and Italians feel emotions more strongly than Koreans but merely that Koreans are expected not to *show* emotions. Persons from affective cultures can unnerve those from neutral cultures with their displays of emotion. On the other hand, persons from neutral cultures can appear inscrutable to those from affective cultures.

Despite their nonaffective culture, Japanese marketers are reconsidering the power of a smile. Some retail and service businesses are sending employees to newly opened smile schools that consider "importing joviality" to be their corporate mission. Yoshihiko Kadokawa, author of *A Laughing Face*, believes that smiling at customers increases sales and boosts employee morale. However, teachers at Japan's smile schools concede that smiling excessively is still controversial in Japan, where it is thought to reflect suicidal tendencies, especially among males.[50]

OVERCOMING THE LANGUAGE BARRIER

International marketing communications are heavily affected by the existence of different languages. Advertising has to be adjusted to each language, and personal contacts are made difficult by the language barrier. To overcome this language barrier, businesspeople all over the world have relied on three approaches: the translation of written material, the use of interpreters, and the acquisition of foreign-language skills.

Translating and Translators

Translations are needed for a wide range of documents, including sales literature, catalogues, advertisements, and contracts. Some companies send all correspondence through a translation firm. For a company that does not have a local subsidiary in a foreign market, competent translation agencies are available in most countries. The largest translation staff in the world belongs to the EU, which has 1,500 people translating 1.2 million pages of text per year into its three working languages: English, French, and German. EU bureaucrats also use machine translation to provide rough translations used for e-mail and other less official communications.

Traveling with executives and attending meetings, personal translators can perform a very useful function when a complete language barrier exists. They are best used for a limited time only. Realistically, they cannot overcome long-term communication problems. When one is traveling in Asia, it is tempting to use senior subsidiary managers, who are usually bilingual, as translators. However, this practice should be avoided. Translators are considered low-level staff members in Asia, and senior managers employed in this manner would be looked down on.

Translation Problems

Both translation services and translators work by translating one language into another. In certain situations, however, it is almost impossible to translate a given meaning accurately and fully into a second language. When the original idea, or thought, is not part of the second culture, for example, the translation may be meaningless. When China first liberalized its economy after years of strict communism, Chinese translators had difficulty translating basic English business terms such as *profit* and *loss*, because these concepts were unknown in the communist-planned economy.

Translation problems abound with the use of brand names in various markets. Brand names can be particularly affected by language, because they are not normally translated but are merely transliterated. Consequently, a company may get into trouble using a product name in a foreign country, even though its advertising message is properly translated. Coca-Cola's launch in China was complicated by the fact that, when spoken aloud, its brand name sounds like "bite the wax tadpole" in Chinese.

Today, global companies tend to choose product names carefully and test them in advance to ensure that the meaning in all major languages is neutral and positive. They also make sure that the name can be easily pronounced. Language differences may have caused many blunders, but careful translations have now reduced the number of international marketing mistakes. Still, the language barrier remains, and companies that make a conscientious effort to overcome this barrier frequently achieve better results than those that do not.

Which Language to Learn?

One can draw two major conclusions about the impact of language on international marketing. First, a firm must adjust its communication program and design communications to include the languages used by its customers. Second, the firm must be aware that a foreign language may reflect different thinking patterns or indicate varying motivations on the part of prospective clients and partners. To the extent that such differences occur, the simple mechanical translation of messages will not suffice. Multinational firms require marketing managers with foreign-language abilities. Still, managers cannot be expected to speak all languages. Global marketers are increasingly united by the use of English as a global business language. Chile inaugurated a nationwide campaign to ensure that all high school students became fluent in English. The objective: to make Chile a world-class exporter.[51]

English has the advantage of being a noncontextual language that many consider relatively easy to learn. Its influence in international commerce was established first by the British Empire and later by the influence of the United States and U.S. multinational firms. According to a study by the Organisation for Economic Co-Operation and Development in Paris, 78 percent of all websites and 91 percent of secure websites are in English.[52]

The widespread use of English has even allowed U.S. firms to outsource customer service tasks to call centers based in India. These centers tap into a large pool of English-speaking labor to answer calls from U.S. consumers concerning anything from late credit card payments to problems with software. Indian service personnel call themselves by American names—Barbara, not Bhavana—and learn to speak with an American accent. Customers on the line have no idea they're talking to someone on the other side of the world.[53]

Many companies are adopting English as their primary language, even companies that operate largely outside the English-speaking world.[54] Matsushita, the world's largest seller of consumer electronics, issued a controversial directive: Managers must pass an English-competency test in order to be promoted. Other Japanese companies that have tied promotions to the ability to speak English include Toyota, NEC, Hitachi, Komatsu, and IBM Japan. In 2000, only students in Afghanistan, Laos, and Cambodia scored lower on English standardized tests than did students in Japan, despite a heavy emphasis on English-language learning in Japanese schools. Matsushita believes that its company's mentality has remained monocultural and monolingual even though half its revenues and half its employees are non-Japanese. It hopes to globalize the mindset of managers by requiring them to think occasionally in a foreign language.[55]

Although English has become the language of commerce and electronic communications, a marketing manager's personal relationships will often benefit from the manager's having achieved language skill in a customer's native tongue. Both Philips Electronics NV, the Dutch consumer giant, and U.S.-based General Electric have adopted English as their corporate language, and managers are not required to speak a local language to run a subsidiary. However, both companies appreciate multilingual managers and consider languages skills to be an advantage.[56] In fact, cultural empathy may best be developed by learning a foreign language, and learning any language will help develop cultural sensitivity. By learning even one foreign language, a student can gain a better appreciation of all different cultures.

ADAPTING TO CULTURAL DIFFERENCES

Some companies make special efforts to adapt their products or services to various cultural environments. One such celebrated case is McDonald's, the U.S. fast-food franchise operator. Sixty percent of McDonald's sales and all of its top ten restaurants, measured in terms of sales and profits, are now overseas. Still, there are some countries where the standard McDonald's hamburger menu does not do well. In Japan, McDonald's had to substantially adapt its original U.S.-style menu. It introduced McChao, a Chinese fried rice dish. This dish proved to be a good idea in a country where 90 percent of the population eats rice daily. The results were astounding. Sales climbed 30 percent after the McChao was introduced. McDonald's continues to innovate in Japan with the Teriyaki McBurger and Chicken Tatsuta.

Even when a firm tries hard to understand the culture of a new market, it is difficult to foresee every cultural surprise. When Big Boy, a U.S.-based hamburger chain, opened in Bangkok, the franchisee in Thailand also discovered that he needed to make adaptations to the menu to suit Thai tastes. However, those were not the only cultural surprises. Many Thai consumers were at a loss about what to make of the chain's giant statue of a boy in checkered overalls. Some Thais left bowls of rice and incense at the feet of the statue as though it were a religious icon. Other Thais said the statue spooked them.[57]

Cultural adaptation is not limited to better understanding and meeting the needs of consumers. Cultural differences also affect how marketers interact with employees in international markets. Big Boy discovered that its Thai employees would not eat on shifts but insisted on eating together, all at the same time.[58] Interbrew, the

WORLD BEAT 3.2

WHO'S THE BOSS?

IN TRADITIONALLY HIERARCHICAL INDIA, bosses were known for their autocratic ways. However, making employees happy has become a new priority for many Indian managers in the technology and call-center sectors, and this means introducing a more democratic workplace.

Rival companies constantly try to poach each other's best workers. At one point employee turnover in the call-center industry hit 50 percent a year. High turnover in the technology sector also makes life particularly difficult for managers in companies that increasingly win high-end multiple-year contracts. A first step to making employees happy is increased benefits, from training to health benefits for parents of employees. But changes go further than good pay and perks. In India's outsourcing industry it is common for workers to e-mail the company chairman and acceptable to go over the head of one's immediate boss. Employees even put suggestions in the corporate suggestion boxes. And managers take them seriously.

One reason for this change in management style may be the fact that more top managers no longer come from India's traditional elites. Top universities in India are no longer sure bets for heritage students. Children of alumni must compete for entrance slots just like other applicants. For example, the CEO of HCL Technologies lived in poverty after his father's death and took turns with his brothers working to put each other through school.

Today the CEO personally answers all e-mails from his employees, approximately 50 a week. HCL Industries has also introduced a 360-degree evaluation system that allows bosses, peers, and underlings to rate a manager. HCL even posts these reviews online. A number of major companies in the West have visited HCL to learn more about their management style. Too date, most have deemed it too democratic.

Sources: Jared Sandberg, "'It Says Press Any Key; Where's the Any Key?'—India's Call-Center Workers Get Pounded, Pampered," *Wall Street Journal*, February 20, 2007, p. B1; Jena McGregor and Manjeet Kripalani, "The Employee is Always Right," *BusinessWeek*, November 19, 2009, pp. 80–82; and Anand Giridharadas, "A Shift to Meritocracy Uproots the Old Elites," *International Herald Tribune*, January 30, 2009, p. 1.

Belgian brewing giant, entered the Korean market by purchasing 50 percent of Korea's Oriental Brewing Company. Both sides experienced a high degree of stress when managers from Belgium and the United States arrived in Korea. The Western managers insisted that the staff speak their minds. The Korean managers, on the other hand, were used to a hierarchical relationship based on respect and unswerving loyalty to the boss. Still, after a bumpy start, the blend of two cultures turned out to be a good thing for the company.[59]

Marketing managers who enter different cultures must learn to cope with a vast array of new cultural cues and expectations as well as to identify which old ones no longer work. Often they experience stress and tension as a result. This effect is commonly called **culture shock**. The authors of *Managing Cultural Differences* offer the following ten tips to deflate the stress and tension of cultural shock:

- Be culturally prepared.
- Be aware of local communication complexities.
- Mix with the host nationals.
- Be creative and experimental.
- Be culturally sensitive.
- Recognize complexities in host cultures.
- See yourself as a culture bearer.
- Be patient, understanding, and accepting of yourself and your hosts.
- Be realistic in your expectations.
- Accept the challenge of intercultural experiences.[60]

Culture shock stress and tension resulting from coping with new cultural cues and expectations

How do cultural considerations affect your marketing plans? Continue with your Country Market Report on the student companion website at http://www.cengage.com/international.

CONCLUSION

In this chapter, we explored a small sample of the wide variety of cultural and social influences that can affect international marketing operations.

It is essential for international marketers to avoid cultural bias in dealing with business operations in more than one culture. As the president of a large industrial company in Osaka, Japan, once noted, our cultures are 80 percent identical and 20 percent different. The successful businessperson is the one who can identify the differences and deal with them. Of course, this is a very difficult task, and few executives ever reach the stage where they can claim to be completely sensitive to cultural differences.

QUESTIONS FOR DISCUSSION

1. How might the educational systems of the United States and Germany affect the marketing of banking services to young adults aged 16 to 22?
2. You have been asked to attend a meeting with Belgian, Turkish, and Japanese colleagues to develop a global plan for a new aftershave. Using the Hofstede scores for these countries, discuss the challenges you would face in the meeting. Assume your native culture.
3. What effects might the Internet have on cultural differences?
4. Why do you think food is such a culturally sensitive product?
5. When a firm enters a new market, how can managers "learn" the culture?

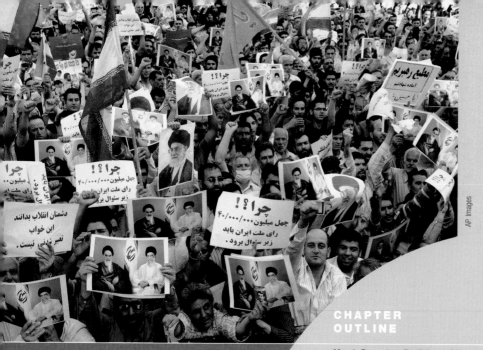

AP Images

© Imagine/18439GNG

4
Political and Regulatory Climate

LEARNING OBJECTIVES

After studying this chapter, you should be able to:

- List and explain the political motivations behind government actions that promote or restrict international marketing.

- Identify pressure groups that affect international marketing.

- Discuss specific government actions salient to international marketing, such as boycotts and takeovers.

- List and compare the four basic legal traditions that marketers encounter worldwide.

- Cite examples illustrating how national laws can vary and change.

- Differentiate between the steps involved in managing political risk and those involved in planning for regulatory change.

OIL-RICH VENEZUELA was once considered an attractive Latin American market. However, when Venezuelans elected Lieutenant Colonel Hugo Chavez president, he threatened to default on Venezuela's foreign debt and to reassert government control over much of the economy. The new president overhauled the country's constitution and judiciary, centralizing more power in the presidency. The response of foreign businesses was immediate. The next year foreign investment fell 40 percent. Eli Lilly and Honda were among the multinational firms that closed operations in Venezuela.[1] Conditions did not improve for companies that stayed. Several years later Venezuela announced that cement companies were to be nationalized. Mexico-based Cemex, the world's largest cement company, rejected a government offer of $500 million for its Venezuelan assets. Cemex estimated their worth to be three times as much.[2] Another major Mexican company, industrial baker Bimbo, was accused of funding anti-Chavez political groups—an accusation the company denied.[3]

This chapter identifies the political forces that influence global marketing operations. These forces include both the host and home governments of international firms. Governments both support and restrict business as they seek to achieve a variety of goals from self-preservation to protecting their nation's cultural identity. International marketers must also be aware of special-interest groups that exert pressure on governments with respect to an increasing number of issues from environmental concerns to human rights.

Dealing simultaneously with several political and regulatory systems makes the job of the global marketing executive a complex one. These factors often precipitate problems that increase the level of risk in the international marketplace. Global companies have learned to cope with such complexities by developing strategies that address the more predictable regulatory changes and the less predictable political risks. These strategies are explained at the end of the chapter.

HOST COUNTRY POLITICAL CLIMATE

The rapidly changing nature of the international political scene is evident to anyone who regularly reads, listens to, or watches the various news media. Political upheavals and changes in government policy occur daily and can have an enormous impact on international business. For the executive, this means constant adjustments to exploit new opportunities and minimize losses.

Besides the international company, the principal players in the political arena are the host country governments and the home country governments. Sometimes transnational bodies or agencies such as the European Union (EU) or the World Trade Organization (WTO) can be involved. Within a national market, the interactions of all these groups result in a political climate that may positively or negatively affect the operations of an international business. The difficulty for the global company stems from the firm being subject to all these forces at the same time. The situation is further complicated by the fact that companies maintain operations in many countries and hence must simultaneously manage many sets of political relationships.

In this section of the chapter, we discuss the political climate of host countries. Any country that contains an operational unit (marketing, sales, manufacturing, finance, or research and development) of an international company can be defined as a **host country**. International companies deal with many different host countries, each with its own political climate. These political climates are largely determined by the motivations and actions of host country governments and local interest groups.

Host country a country that contains an operational unit (marketing, sales, manufacturing, finance, or R&D) of an international company

Political Motivations

Businesses operate in a country at the discretion of its government, which can encourage or discourage foreign businesses through a variety of measures. The host government plays the principal role in host countries in initiating and implementing policies regarding the operation, conduct, and ownership of businesses. Today more than 190 nations have been accepted as members of the United Nations, a figure that gives some indication of the large number of independent countries that exist at this time. Although each government may give the impression of acting as a single and homogeneous force, governments in most countries represent a collection of various, and at times conflicting, interests. Governments are sharply influenced by the prevailing political philosophy, local pressure groups, and the government's own self-interest. All of these factors lead to government actions that international companies must recognize and actively incorporate into their marketing strategies. Of prime importance is the marketer's ability to understand the rationale behind government actions.

As many political scientists have pointed out, government actions usually arise from the government's interpretation of its own self-interest. This self-interest, often called national interest, may be expected to differ from nation to nation, but it typically includes the following goals:

- *Self-preservation.* This is the primary goal of any entity, including states and governments.
- *Security.* To the greatest extent possible, each government seeks to maximize its opportunity for continued existence and to minimize threats from the outside.

TABLE 4.1	HOST GOVERNMENT GOALS AND POLICY ACTIONS					
	GOAL					
ACTION	**SELF-PRESERVATION**	**SECURITY**	**PROSPERITY**	**PRESTIGE**	**IDEOLOGY**	**CULTURAL IDENTITY**
"Buy local"	X	X	X			
Nontariff barriers	X		X			
Subsidies	X		X	X		
Operating restrictions	X	X				X
Local content			X			
Ownership conditions		X			X	X
Boycotts					X	
Takeovers	X	X	X		X	

X = Likelihood of using given action to accomplish that goal.

- *Prosperity.* Improved living conditions for the country's citizens are an important and constant concern for any government. Even dictatorships base their claim to legitimacy in part on their ability to deliver enhanced prosperity.
- *Prestige.* Most governments or countries seek this either as an end in itself or as a means of reaching other objectives.
- *Ideology.* Governments frequently protect or promote an ideology in combination with other goals.
- *Cultural identity.* Governments often intervene to protect the country's cultural identity.[4]

The goals just cited are frequently the source of government actions either encouraging or limiting the business activities of international companies (see Table 4.1). Many executives erroneously believe that such limiting actions occur largely in developing countries. On the contrary, there are many examples of restrictive government actions in the most developed countries. Such restrictive behavior most often occurs when a government perceives the attainment of its own goals to be threatened by the activities or existence of a body beyond its total control, namely the foreign subsidiary of a multinational company.

National Sovereignty and the Goal of Self-Preservation

Sovereignty supremacy of authority or rule free from external control

A country's self-preservation is most threatened when its national sovereignty is at stake. **Sovereignty** is the complete control exercised within a given geographic area, including the ability to pass laws and regulations and the power to enforce them. Governments or countries frequently view the existence of sovereignty as critical to achieving the goal of self-preservation. Although sovereignty may be threatened by a number of factors, it is the relationship between a government's attempt to protect its sovereignty and a company's efforts to achieve its own goals that are of primary interest to us.

Subsidiaries or branch offices of international companies can be controlled or influenced by decisions made at headquarters, beyond the physical or legal control of the host government. Therefore, foreign companies are frequently viewed as a threat to the host country's national sovereignty. (It is important to recognize in this context that *perceptions* on the part of host countries are typically more important than actual facts.)

Many attempts at restricting foreign firms are now discouraged under agreements established by the WTO. Still, these agreements exclude a number of sensitive areas. Countries often limit foreign ownership of newspapers, television, and radio stations for reasons of preserving national sovereignty. They fear that if a foreign company controlled these media, it could influence public opinion and limit national sovereignty. Internet businesses can be especially vulnerable to government censorship. Google's YouTube has been banned or temporarily blocked in China, Turkey, and Thailand in response to postings deemed insulting or threatening by the national governments of those countries. Google concedes that balancing free expression and local laws is a delicate task.[5]

The Need for National Security

It is natural for a government to try to protect its country's borders from outside forces. The military typically becomes a country's principal tool to prevent outside interference. Consequently, many concerns about national security involve a country's armed forces or related agencies. Other areas sensitive to national security are aspects of a country's infrastructure, its essential resources, utilities, and the supply of crucial raw materials, particularly oil. To ensure their security, some host governments strive for greater control of these sensitive areas and resist any influence that foreign firms may gain over such industries.

A Chinese bid for a U.S. oil company was abandoned due to security concerns and political opposition in the United States. Soon after, Dubai Ports World, a company owned by the government of Dubai, acquired a British company with shipping-terminal operations at five U.S. ports. Faced with an almost certain veto from the U.S. congress, Dubai Ports World agreed to shed the U.S. port operations of the purchased company.[6]

However, the protection of national security interests through regulations requiring local sourcing is experiencing an overall decline in the defense and telecommunications industries. This trend has been influenced by two factors. First, it is not economical for each country to have its own defense and telecommunications industry. Second, the high cost of research and development means that in many cases, the small local defense supplier will have inferior technologies.

Fostering National Prosperity

Another key goal for governments is to ensure the material prosperity of their citizens. Prosperity is usually expressed in national income or gross national product (GNP), and comparisons between countries are frequently made in terms of per-capita income or GNP per capita. (Comparisons are also made on the basis of GNP adjusted by purchasing-power parity to reflect comparable standards of living.)

However prosperity is measured, most governments strive to provide full employment and an increasing standard of living. Part of this goal is to enact an economic policy that will stimulate the economic output of businesses active within their borders. International companies that set up production facilities in a host country can assume an important role, because they can add to a host country's GNP and thus enhance its income. Cognizant of this, Japanese auto company

To learn more about how the United States promotes exports, go to the export promotion link on the student companion website at http://www.cengage.com/international.

Toyota pledged to produce in North America at least two-thirds of the vehicles it sold in that region as a form of political insurance.[7]

Many host governments also try to improve the nation's prosperity by increasing its exports. Particularly in Europe, heads of governments often engage in state visits to encourage major export transactions. Political observers often note that both the French president and the German chancellor spend a substantial amount of their state visits on business and trade affairs, more so than is typically the case for the president of the United States. Attracting international companies with a high export potential to set up operations in their countries is of critical interest to host governments. Frequently, such companies can expect special treatment or subsidies, especially from governments in developing countries. For example, Egypt offered attractive tax holidays to foreign investors who undertook export-oriented projects, and Mexico exempted foreign investors from local-partner requirements if their projects were totally for export.

Enhancing Prestige

When Olusegun Obasanjo was elected president of Nigeria, he inherited a decision to host the next All-Africa Games. Nigeria had recently rescheduled its foreign debt. By hosting the games, the Nigerian government had accrued building costs for a new stadium that exceeded $340 million, twice what the government planned to spend on health care for one year.[8]

The pursuit of prestige has many faces. Whereas the governments of some countries choose to support team sports or host international events to enhance national prestige, other governments choose to influence the business climate for the same reason. Having a national airline may give rise to national prestige for a developing country. Other countries may support industries that achieve leadership in certain technologies, such as telecommunications, electronics, robotics, or aerospace.

Promoting Ideology

For nearly 50 years North and South Korea have been technically at war. In the 1950s, North Korea was the richer and more industrialized of the two Koreas. North Korea pursued the ideology of *juche,* or self-reliance.[9] Today it is South Korea that is by far the wealthier and more industrialized country.

Governments often attempt to promote ideology. In doing so, they affect business in a variety of ways. Throughout most of the 20th century, communist governments disallowed private enterprise. Trade with noncommunist Western countries was strongly discouraged. Like North Korea, the Soviet Union paid a high price for its desire to be free of the capitalist world. Rather than taking advantage of licensing technology that was developed in the West, the Soviets followed the more expensive route of attempting to develop their own parallel technologies.

The role that ideology plays in communist China seems ambiguous from the point of view of foreign firms doing business there today. China reopened trade and investment relations with the West in the early 1970s. Since then the country has undergone significant market liberalization. General Motors and Starbucks operate with and alongside China's traditional state-owned industries. Some state-owned enterprises have been privatized. In other words, they have been sold, wholly or in part, to private owners. Chinese firms must now generate profits or face the specter of new bankruptcy laws. Still the Chinese government insists that these changes do not compromise communist ideology.

Multinational firms from both Mexico and the United States saw their Venezuelan operations targeted by socialist president Hugo Chavez.

Thomas Coex/AFP/Getty Images

Protecting Cultural Identity

With the global village becoming a reality, one of the major effects on countries is in the area of culture. Governments can sometimes resist what they believe to be a foreign assault on their culture. For example, both Iran and Venezuela have at one time attempted to outlaw foreign brand names, requiring international marketers to establish names for their products in Persian and Spanish, respectively.

Whereas most countries once were able to determine broadcast policy on their own, control over broadcasting, and therefore culture, is now perceived to be in the hands of a few large, mostly U.S. firms. These firms are most visible in entertainment, the production and distribution of movies, TV programs, videos, and music recordings. Even more important have been the roles of TV companies through the use of satellite transmission. As we saw in Chapter 3, this massive invasion of foreign cultural products has prompted a negative reaction among certain European governments. France launched a campaign against Google's alleged encroachment on French culture when Google announced a plan to scan millions of books in the English language from libraries in Britain and the United States. The president of France's national library warned that English-language sources and the American view of history would dominate the Internet.[10] Led by France, several European countries established a counteroffensive—a book-scanning project dubbed the European Digital Library.[11]

Host Country Pressure Groups

Host country governments are not the only forces able to influence the political climate and affect the operations of foreign companies. Other groups have a stake in the treatment of companies and in political and economic decisions that indirectly affect foreign businesses. In most instances, they cannot act unilaterally. Thus they try to pressure either the host government or the foreign businesses to conform to their views. Such pressure groups exist in most countries and may be made up of either ad hoc groups or established associations. For example, the Beijing-based non-profit Institute of Public and Environment Affairs has released names of 70 multinational companies ([MNCs] and thousands of Chinese companies) that it alleges have violated China's environmental laws. MNCs include DuPont, Nestlé, PepsiCo, and Suzuki Motor Corporation. The institute's Green Choice initiative collects and posts environmental records on a publicly accessible online database. Some companies have since cleared their names or addressed the issues raised by the institute.[12]

Some of the most potent pressure groups are found within the local business community itself. These include local industry associations and occasionally local unions. When local companies are threatened by foreign competition, they frequently petition the government to help by placing restrictions on the foreign competitors. When Pakistan became a potentially critical U.S. ally in the Afghan war, the Pakistani government asked the United States to reduce tariffs on textiles from Pakistan. However, officials at the American Textile Manufacturing Institute moved immediately to stop any possible cuts in tariffs that could hurt U.S. textile firms.[13]

Blogging is an increasingly important tool for grassroots protests. China alone has over 20 million bloggers who could possibly target an MNC. In one case a 29-year-old TV news anchor in Hong Kong posted on his blog a condemnation of Starbuck's opening a store in Beijing's Forbidden City (the former residence of the country's emperors), stating that it marked an erosion of Chinese culture. Within a week the posting was viewed half a million times. Correspondents camped outside the controversial café and the authorities announced that they would review their decision to allow Starbuck's to locate there.[14]

HOST GOVERNMENT ACTIONS

Governments promulgate laws and take actions in a variety of ways to advance their agendas. In Chapter 2 we reviewed a number of government actions that affect a firm's ability to transfer products across borders. Many government actions, such as those affecting exchange rates, can indirectly affect international markets. Other actions can have a more direct impact on a firm's ability to access a foreign market and operate successfully. Some of these actions are discussed next.

Government Subsidies

Government subsidies represent free gifts that host governments dispense in the hope that the overall benefits to the economy will far exceed such grants. They are popular instruments used to attract foreign investment. Governments are especially inclined to use direct or indirect subsidies to encourage firms that will be major exporters. Exporters bring multiple benefits, providing employment and increasing national revenue through export sales.

An example of a direct subsidy is a government's paying $1 for each pair of shoes to help a local producer compete more effectively in foreign markets. An indirect subsidy is the result of a subsidy on a component of the exported product. For example, a government may provide a subsidy on the electricity used to manufacture tents that are then exported. Or it might subsidize research in the pharmaceutical industry. WTO agreements outlaw direct export subsidies as well as local-content subsidies that are contingent on the use of domestic over imported goods. Indirect subsidies are usually not prohibited. However, they remain a contentious issue between trading nations.

Ownership Restrictions

Host governments sometimes pursue the policy of requiring that local nationals become part owners of foreign subsidiaries operating within their borders. These governments believe that this guarantees that multinationals will contribute to the local economy. Restrictions can range from an outright prohibition of full foreign ownership to selective policies aimed at key industries.

India has used ownership conditions extensively. India's Foreign Exchange Regulation Act of 1973 stipulated that foreign ownership could not exceed 40 percent. International Business Machines Corporation (IBM) decided to leave rather than give up majority control over its subsidiary. Coca-Cola also decided to leave rather than share its secret formula with Indian partners. However, when changes in the government brought a softening of India's stance, the country tentatively began to court firms. Coke negotiated a return to India without revealing its cola formula.

In many ways, the Indian case reflects the patterns of many countries. The 1960s and 1970s saw a tightening of the control over foreign ownership. More recently, the trend has been toward investment liberalization. Most countries now recognize that foreign investment provides significant benefits to the nation, such as employment, technology, and marketing know-how. This new trend has brought the elimination of many prior restrictions, such as those related to ownership. Nonetheless, ownership restriction persists in some markets. In the wake of U.S. occupation, many Iraqi businesses feared that large corporate investors from abroad would take over whole sectors of the economy and crowd out local competition. Consequently, they called for investment rules similar to those in the United Arab Emirates, which require that domestic ventures be at least 51 percent locally owned.[15]

Operating Conditions

Governments establish and enforce many regulations that affect the environment in which businesses operate. Host countries control firms in the areas of product design and packaging, pricing, advertising, sales promotion, and distribution. Some of these restrictions, and strategies to deal with them, are included in later chapters that deal directly with the marketing mix. Where such operating restrictions apply to all firms, domestic and international, the competitive threat is lessened.

Companies may still find restrictions a problem when the way they have to operate varies from that to which they are accustomed. Furthermore, local restrictions may sometimes be peculiar to a certain market and thus hard to predict. For example, the province of Buenos Aires in Argentina passed a law requiring shops targeting female adolescents to stock clothing in sizes equivalent to sizes 6–16 in the United States. Brazilian shops usually cater only to the very thin. Officials believe this has contributed to Argentina experiencing one of the world's highest rates of anorexia and bulimia.[16]

An Egyptian girl drinks a bottle of Coke in downtown Cairo. Coca-Cola was once banned by the Arab boycott, giving rival Pepsi an advantage in the Middle East. Now both global competitors contend for the Arab market.

AP Images

What countries are the most dangerous and why? Check out the Current Travel Warnings on the student companion website at http://www. cengage.com/ international.

Where operating restrictions apply to foreign or international firms only, the result will be a lessening of competitiveness, and companies should seriously consider these constraints before entering a market. One such restriction involves work permits or visas for foreign managers or technicians whom multinational firms may wish to employ in their various national subsidiaries. Any citizen of an EU country is free to work in any other EU country, but visa constraints remain an operational hindrance in most of the world.

Local restrictions may also pose a problem to global marketers when they become unusually burdensome in certain markets. To sign up to be an Avon sales representative takes only minutes unless you are in China. There it takes two weeks, and potential saleswomen must take a written test and listen to a lecture on China's latest sales regulations. Although China lifted a prior ban on direct sales, the industry remains tightly regulated. The government caps sales commissions at 30 percent, and sales representatives can only make money by selling the products and not by recruiting other sales representatives.[17]

Sometimes operating conditions are affected by what governments fail to do. Kidnappings for ransom have risen in Latin America. For several years, Mexico City became particularly notorious for kidnappings by criminal gangs, and foreign companies found it difficult to recruit expatriate managers for their operations there. In any case, operating costs may increase in these countries as a result of the need to provide employees with heightened security.

Boycotts of Firms

Government boycotts can be directed at companies of certain origin or companies that have engaged in transactions with political enemies. Boycotts tend to shut some companies completely out of a given market. For example, the United States imposed a two-year ban on imports from Norinco, a major Chinese defense and industrial manufacturer, because of the company's alleged sale of ballistic-missile technology to Iran. The Norinco boycott made it illegal for U.S. companies to purchase products from the company or any of its many subsidiaries.[18]

One of the most publicized boycott campaigns was the 50-year boycott waged by Arab countries against firms that engaged in business activity with Israel. The boycott was administered by the Arab League. Ford Motor Company was one U.S. company placed on the Arab boycott list when it supplied an Israeli car assembler with flat-packed cars for local assembly. Xerox was placed on the list after financing a documentary on Israel, and the Coca-Cola Company was added to the boycott list for having licensed an Israeli bottler.

The Arab boycott became less relevant with the changing political situation in the Middle East. The last major fighting between Israel and the Arab states took place in 1973, and since then Egypt has signed a peace treaty with Israel. By the 1990s, many Arab countries only selectively enforced the boycott. After the Iraq conflict and Desert Storm, many more countries abandoned it. Coca-Cola returned to the Arab soft-drinks market, and Coca-Cola attained a 33 percent share of the Arab Gulf's $1.2 billion market.[19]

Takeovers

Takeover a host-government-initiated action that results in a loss of ownership or direct control by a foreign company

Expropriation the formal seizure of a business operation, with or without the payment of compensation

Confiscation expropriation without compensation

Domestication the limitation of certain economic activities to local citizens

Though relatively rare, no action a host government can take is more dramatic than a takeover. Broadly defined, **takeovers** are any host-government-initiated actions that result in a loss of ownership or direct control by the foreign company. There are several types of takeovers. **Expropriation** is a formal, or legal, seizure of an operation with or without the payment of compensation. Even when compensation is paid, there are often concerns about the adequacy of the amount, the timeliness of the payment, and the form of payment. **Confiscation** is expropriation without any compensation. The term **domestication** is used to describe the limiting of certain economic activities to local citizens. This can involve a takeover by compensated expropriation, confiscation, or forced sale. Governments may also domesticate an industry by merely requiring the transfer of partial ownership to nationals or by requiring that nationals be promoted to higher levels of management. If an international company cannot or will not meet these requirements, however, it may be forced to sell its operations in that country.

Today expropriations have virtually ceased. In fact, a reverse trend has emerged. In renewed attempts to encourage foreign investment, countries such as Algeria, Egypt, and Tanzania have considered returning companies to prior foreign owners, or at least allowing these former owners to repurchase them. The British bank Barclays International returned to Egypt, where it had been expropriated 15 years earlier. Like many oil-exporting countries, Saudi Arabia nationalized its energy sector in the 1970s. However, the Saudi government began to reopen the sector in the 21st century when it named Exxon, the world's largest publicly owned oil company, as operator of a major natural-gas project requiring an investment of $15 billion.[20]

WORLD BEAT 4.1

REVIVING THE ARAB BOYCOTT

OVER 60 YEARS HAVE PASSED since Arab countries inaugurated their boycott of Israel and firms sympathetic to Israel. Today many Arab governments no longer seriously enforce this boycott. However, if governments fail to enforce the formal boycott of Israel, this doesn't stop Arab consumers from organizing grass-roots boycotts. American firms are often targets because of perceived U.S. support of Israel. These impromptu consumer boycotts have been a way for Arab consumers, many living under non-democratic regimes, to vent their frustration with the slow progress of peace negotiations between Israel and the Palestinians. In addition, this informal boycott has extended to consumers in non-Arab Muslim states such as Malaysia.

In the United Arab Emirates, supporters of a boycott distributed a list of American brands and firms to avoid. In Egypt, boycott victims have included the perennial targets Starbuck's, McDonald's, and Coca-Cola. But even Pepsi—a longtime favorite in the Arab World from the days of the Arab boycott against Coke—failed to escape unscathed. A chain message circulated among Egyptian high school students claimed that Pepsi stood for Pay Every Penny to Support Israel and called for a ban on the soft drink. Fliers were also distributed asking consumers to stop eating at Pizza Hut and to reject American products such as Gillette razors, Nike shoes, and Marlboro cigarettes.

The sales of Americana Foods—an Egyptian company that owns franchises for Pizza Hut, KFC, Baskin-Robbins, Hardee's, TGI Friday's, and Subway—plunged 30 percent during one consumer boycott. Even U.K.-based Sainsbury's saw its supermarkets in Cairo subject to violent attacks as a consequence of the firm's alleged connections with Israel.

McDonald's responded to a consumer boycott in Egypt with leaflets stressing its local Egyptian ownership of outlets and its employment of 2,000 Egyptians. Sales soon recovered. Outlets of A&W, Chili's, and Radio Shack displayed Palestinian flags. Coca-Cola sponsored Egypt's most popular soccer team as well as the Palestinian national soccer team. Sainsbury's took to playing Koranic music in its supermarket aisles and published an advertisement signed by 4,800 Egyptian employees stating that the company did not support Israel.

Sources: "Is the Arab boycott Dead?" in Kate Gillespie, Jean-Pierre Jeannet, and David H. Hennessey, *Global Marketing* (New York: Houghton Mifflin: , 2007); "Israel Boycott Bureaus Underline Commitment to Arab Boycott," *BBC Monitoring Middle East*, October 21, 2008; "Malaysia Exercised over Gaza," *Inter Press News Service*, January 15, 2009; and "Boycotts: Peaceful Protest of Shooting Ourselves in the Foot?" *Daily News Egypt*, February 10, 2009.

HOME COUNTRY POLITICAL FORCES

Managers of international companies need to be concerned not only about political developments abroad; many developments that take place at home also have a great impact on what a company can do internationally. Political developments in a company's home country tend to affect either the role of the company in general or, more often, some particular aspects of its operations abroad. Consequently, restrictions can be placed on companies not only by host countries but by home countries as well. Therefore, an astute international marketer must be able to monitor political developments both at home and abroad. This section of the chapter explores home country policies and actions directed at international companies.

Home Country Actions

Home countries are essentially guided by the same six interests described earlier in this chapter: self-preservation, national security, prosperity, prestige, ideology, and cultural identity. For example, subsidies, offered by host governments to foreign investors, may also be offered by home governments as well. In general, a home government wishes to have its country's international companies accept its national priorities. As a result, home governments at times look toward international companies to help them achieve political goals.

In the past, home country governments have tried to prevent companies from doing business overseas on ideological, political, or national security grounds. In the extreme, this can result in an embargo on trade with a certain country. One long-running trade embargo imposed by the U.S. government involved Vietnam. Imposed in 1975, this embargo was lifted in 1994. More recently the United States banned the sale of luxury goods including iPods and plasma televisions to North Korea in what was called a novel effort to undermine the lavish lifestyle of that country's eccentric president and his political elite.[21] Organizations fined for allegedly breaking a U.S. embargo include Chevron Texaco, for trading with Iraq (fined $14,071); Wal-Mart and the New York Yankees, for trading with Cuba (fined $50,000 and $75,000, respectively); Exxon Mobil, for trading with Sudan (fined $50,000); and Fleet Bank, for trading with Iran (fined $41,000).[22] On the other hand, the United States, an ally of Israel, passed legislation forbidding U.S. firms from complying with the Arab boycott of Israel. The U.S. government did not want U.S.-based multinational firms to comply with someone else's embargo.

Unilateral restrictions, those imposed by one country only, put businesses from that country at a competitive disadvantage and are often fought by business interests. Because of this risk to the competitiveness of their businesses, governments prefer to take multilateral actions together with many other countries. Such actions may arise from a group of nations or, increasingly, from the United Nations. The trade embargo by the international community against South Africa was one of the first such actions. As a result of consumer group pressures, many companies had already left South Africa to protest its apartheid regime. However, the embargo affected a wider group of firms in the late 1980s when it was imposed by most countries. When the political situation in South Africa changed and apartheid was abolished, the United States, together with other nations, lifted the embargo. The United States has since been the largest foreign investor in South Africa, some of the largest firms being Dow Chemical, Ford, General Motors, Coca-Cola, and Hyatt.

Other multilateral actions by the international community are the trade sanctions enforced by the United Nations against Iraq as a result of the Gulf War. Another multilateral embargo was imposed against Serbia. Although this embargo was partially lifted in 2000, Serbia's access to international funds was still contingent on its continued transition to democracy.

For the latest information on unilateral U.S. actions, go to U.S. Trade Sanctions and Embargoes on the student companion website at http://www.cengage.com/international.

Home Country Pressure Groups

The kinds of pressures that international companies are subject to in their home countries are frequently different from the types of pressures brought to bear on them abroad. International companies have had to deal with special-interest groups abroad for a long time. The types of special-interest groups found domestically have come into existence only recently. Such groups are usually well organized and tend to get extensive media coverage. They have succeeded in catching many companies unprepared. These groups aim to garner support in order to pressure home governments to sponsor regulations favorable to their point of view. They also have managed to place companies directly in the line of fire.

International companies come under attack for two major reasons: (1) for their choice of markets and (2) for their methods of doing business. A constant source of controversy involves international companies' business practices in three areas: product strategies, promotion practices, and pricing policies. Product strategies include, for example, the decision to market potentially unsafe products such as pesticides. Promotional practices include the way products are advertised or pushed through distribution channels. Pricing policies include the possible charging of higher prices in one market than in another.

The infant formula controversy of the early 1980s involved participants from many countries and serves as a good example of the type of pressure that international companies sometimes face. Infant formula was being sold all over the world as a substitute for or supplement to breast-feeding. Although even the producers of infant formula agreed that breast-feeding was superior to bottle-feeding, changes that had started to take place in Western society decades before had caused infant breast-feeding to decline. Following World War II, several companies had expanded their infant formula production into developing countries, where birthrates were much higher than in the West. Companies that had intended their products to be helpful found themselves embroiled in controversy. Critics blasted the product as unsafe under Third World conditions. Because the formula had to be mixed with water, they maintained, poor sanitary conditions and contaminated water in developing countries led to many infant deaths. Poor mothers could also water down the formula to such an extent that babies were malnourished. As a result, these critics urged an immediate stop to all promotional activities related to infant formula, such as the distribution of free samples.

The Nestlé Company, as one of the leading infant formula manufacturers, became the target of a boycott by consumer action groups in the United States and elsewhere. Under the leadership of INFACT, the Infant Formula Action Coalition, a consumer boycott of all Nestlé products was organized to force the company to change its marketing practices. Constant public pressure resulted in the development of a code sponsored by the World Health Organization (WHO) that primarily covers the methods used to market infant formula. Under the code, producers and distributors may not give away any free samples. They must avoid contact with consumers and are forbidden to do any promotion geared toward the general public. The code is subject to voluntary participation by WHO member governments.

Boycotts have even been attempted at the state level in the United States. Massachusetts passed a state law denying state contracts to companies that did business in Myanmar (formerly Burma) because of that country's brutal dictatorship. Apple, Motorola, and Hewlett-Packard all cited the Massachusetts law when pulling out of Myanmar. A U.S. District Court judge subsequently ruled that the Massachusetts law interferes with the federal government's right to set foreign policy.[23] Despite this setback, global firms must contend with the growing influence of home country pressure groups.

What causes are global rights activists pursuing now? Check out the Public Citizen: Global Trade Watch home page from the student companion website at http://www.cengage.com/international.

LEGAL ENVIRONMENTS

In many ways, the legal framework of a nation reflects a particular political philosophy or ideology. Just as each country has its own political climate, so the legal system changes from country to country. Internationally active companies must understand and operate within these various legal systems. Most legal systems of the world are based on one of four traditions: common law, civil law, Islamic law, or socialist law.

Common Law

Common law is derived from English law found in the United Kingdom, the United States, Canada, and other countries previously part of the British Commonwealth. Common law acknowledges the preeminence of social norms. Law arises from what society acknowledges as right and from what has commonly been done and accepted. Laws passed in such countries are frequently interpreted in the courtroom, where a jury consisting of citizens often determines the outcome of a case. Lawyers in these countries are as likely to look to prior case decisions as to the law itself in order to argue their own cases.

Civil Law

Civil, or code, law is based on the Roman tradition of the preeminence of written laws. It is found in most European countries and in countries influenced by European colonialism, such as countries in Latin America. In these countries, laws may be more encompassing as well as precise. Judges play a far more important role in the civil-law system than under common law, whereas juries usually play a lesser role. A traditional difference between civil-law countries and common-law countries has been the way they have viewed trademark protection. The first to officially register a trademark in civil-law countries owned the trademark. However, in common-law countries, someone who actually used the trademark before another registered it could successfully challenge the registration.

Islamic Law

Islamic law is derived from the Koran as well as from other Islamic traditions. Islamic law dominates family law in most Muslim countries, but its application to business situations varies greatly from country to country. To begin with, there are four major schools of Islamic law, and countries differ as to which they follow. Furthermore, not all Muslim countries apply Islamic law to commercial transactions. Some do, of course. Saudi Arabia forbids the collection of interest on loans. An importer cannot go to a bank and pay interest to borrow money to import automobiles from overseas. However, an importer can borrow money and pay interest in many Muslim countries. In fact, during the 19th and 20th centuries, most Muslim countries adopted their commercial laws from one or more European countries. Because of this, business law in the Middle East often falls under the civil-law tradition.

Socialist Law

Socialist law arose from the Marxist ideological system established in China, Russia, and other former Eastern bloc countries during the twentieth century. Under Marxist rule, economic power was often centralized, and market economies were virtually unknown. Business laws as we know them were absent or underdeveloped. For example, Chinese citizens have only recently been allowed to bring lawsuits against foreign companies or Chinese government ministries. This has inspired activists in China to consider suing tobacco companies for targeting young people.[24]

As many socialist countries liberalize their economies, they are often forced to look outside for quick fixes for their lack of legal sophistication. For example, Russia turned to the United States and law professors in Houston to help develop laws pertaining to petroleum. When Russia joined the WTO, it agreed to adopt new laws concerning trademarks and patents. Unfortunately, many observers note that Russia today has difficulty enforcing these laws effectively. Even the judges have little experience with the new legislation.

When countries such as Russia opened to global trade and investment, they discovered that their socialist law needed to be amended or replaced to deal with new legal realities—such as profits and competition.

Image copyright Sailorr, 2009. Used under license from Shutterstock.com

China faces similar problems. The Chinese legal system has inspired little confidence from foreign investors. However, when China joined the WTO, the government began training judges to administer the new trade regulations. Legal teams were organized to ensure that city and provincial governments adhered to the new policies.[25] Still, China's current legal system is based on a very limited statutory code. In addition, it also lacks a recognized body of precedent case law.[26]

NATIONAL REGULATORY ENVIRONMENTS

Regulatory environments also vary among countries. Businesses face greater regulatory burdens in developing countries than they do in developed countries. It can take 153 days to establish a business in Mozambique compared with 3 days in Canada. It takes 21 steps to register a commercial property in Nigeria compared with only 3 steps in Finland. The World Bank estimates that the least regulated countries from a business point of view are New Zealand, the United States, and Singapore.[27]

Japan has had the most regulated business environment among the developed countries. Twenty years after Temple University established its Tokyo campus, it is the only U.S. university offering full-degree courses. Forty other U.S. universities pulled out of Japan due to a plethora of regulations. For example, to qualify as an official university, universities must own their own buildings, have their own sports field and gym, operate on less than a 25 percent debt-equity ratio, and get government approval for new programs. Even Temple doesn't meet all these criteria. Without official status, Temple operates at a competitive disadvantage when trying to recruit students.[28]

In recent years, however, Japan has experienced a trend toward deregulation and market liberalization. As a result of this shift, conflict has increased and corporate lawsuits are becoming more common. Japan now needs more lawyers as Japanese increasingly shun mediation and the number of court cases soars. Japan estimates that it will need to more than double its number of lawyers by 2018. In 2004 alone, nearly 70 new law schools opened within Japanese universities.[29]

Japan is not the only country where international marketers face ambiguous or evolving regulatory environment. In addition to dealing with many different legal systems' national laws, managers must constantly contend with changes. As the global marketplace becomes ever more interconnected, regulatory changes appear all the more regularly.

Legal Evolution

One area of law that has seen considerable evolution worldwide is product liability law. Regulations concerning product liability were first introduced in the United States. If a product is sold in a defective condition such that it becomes unreasonably dangerous to use, then both the manufacturer and the distributor can be held accountable under U.S. law. For a long time, product liability laws in Europe were lax by U.S. standards, but they have been expanded in the past 20 years. Still there are differences that result from the different legal and social systems. In the EU, trials are decided by judges, not common jurors, and the extensive welfare system automatically absorbs many of the medical costs that are subject to litigation in the United States. Traditionally, product liability suits seldom posed problems for international marketers in developing countries. However, when accidents attributable to Firestone tires on Ford Explorers occurred, plaintiffs appeared in Saudi Arabia and Venezuela as well as in the United States. Today, global publicity surrounding product crises no doubt prompts more consumers in more countries to seek redress for problems.

A second area of law that varies from country to country involves bankruptcy. In the United Kingdom, Canada, and France, the laws governing bankruptcy favor creditors. When a firm enters bankruptcy, an administrator is appointed. The administrator's job is to recover the creditors' money. In Germany and Japan, on the other hand, bankruptcies are often handled by banks behind closed doors. The emphasis is on protecting the company and helping it reestablish itself. In the United States, bankruptcy law also tends to protect the company. Management prepares a reorganization plan that is voted on by the creditors. Creditor preference varies by country as well. For example, Swiss law gives preference to Swiss creditors.

As with product liability, attitudes toward bankruptcy and regulations pertaining to it have not remained static. In China, bankruptcies were unheard of under the communist system until China drafted its first bankruptcy code in 1988. One proponent of the new law noted that nobody understood it and everybody was scared of it. A major case involving a trust and investment corporation revealed that many vagaries in the law still existed. Creditors settled out of court and experienced huge losses. Nonetheless, the number of bankruptcies in China has soared since 2000.[30]

Today the regulation of transactions in cyberspace is critical to the future of electronic commerce. WTO members have made a political commitment to maintain a duty-free cyberspace.[31] However, many other issues concerning the governance of the Internet have not been resolved, and it even remains unclear which country can claim territorial jurisdiction in this inherently international medium. What will be the future of Internet taxation, privacy safeguards, and censorship?

The complexity of the technology, as well as its rapid change, challenges traditional ideas of regulation.[32]

In the following chapters, we will be discussing other national and international laws that affect the management of products, pricing, distribution, and promotion. In many cases these laws are also evolving. Regional associations, especially the EU, are increasingly setting supranational laws that affect marketing within their member states. Attempts are also under way to set global standards of legal protection, such as in the area of patents and trademarks. In the future, this may help simplify the job of the international marketer.

Some moves to internationalize laws, however, are opposed by multinational firms. The Hague Conference on International Private Law has considered a global treaty for enforcement of legal judgments. This agreement would require U.S. courts to enforce judgments by foreign courts in exchange for similar treatment abroad for U.S. judgments. Internet providers were among the many U.S. firms that opposed the treaty. E-commerce businesses were especially concerned that the treaty would subject them to a plethora of lawsuits by allowing consumers to sue businesses under local law wherever their websites were accessible.[33] For the time being, however, national laws still prevail in the vast majority of cases, and even global standards, when established, will be administered through local legal systems.

Attitudes toward Rules

Egypt experiences 44 traffic deaths per 100 million kilometers of driving. This compares with 20 deaths in Turkey and only 1.1 in the United States. To try to decrease traffic fatalities, the Egyptian government began the new millennium by instituting tough new speeding and seat belt laws, complete with hefty fines. Seat belt sales soared at first and then precipitously declined. One auto parts dealer who once sold 250 seat belts a day saw his sales fall to only 2 or 3 a day. A year later, Egypt's fatality statistics remained the same. Many Egyptians had chosen to buy cheap seat belts that could fool the police but didn't really work. Furthermore, the police were deluged with complaints when they gave out tickets. Because the seat belts didn't work, why should the driver be fined for not buckling up? One Egyptian summed up the public's skepticism, "I think those laws are just so the government can make our lives more miserable than they already are. They want to imitate the West in everything."[34]

Jean-Claude Usunier notes that rules and laws can be established that are respected and implemented quite explicitly. On the other hand, there may be a discrepancy between rules and what people actually do. He suggests that attitudes toward rules are affected by two basic criteria—the level of power distance in a society and whether a society has a positive or a negative human nature orientation (HNO). **HNO-positive societies** assume people can be trusted to obey the rules, whereas **HNO-negative societies** assume just the opposite. The United States is an HNO-positive society with low power distance. This results in pragmatic rules that most people respect and obey. In countries such as Italy and France, HNO is also positive but power distance is high. Ordinary people view themselves as being better than their rulers. As a result, many feel that laws can be challenged to a certain degree. In Germany and Switzerland, power distance is low but HNO is negative. Laws are made democratically, but society still does not trust people to obey them. To ensure compliance, rules must be applied strictly and with very explicit sanctions. In many developing countries, power distance is high and HNO is

HNO (human nature orientation)-positive societies societies that assume people can be trusted to obey the rules

HNO (human nature orientation)-negative societies societies that assume people cannot be trusted to obey the rules

negative. Rules may often be strict, formal, and even unrealistic. In this atmosphere there is often a high discrepancy between the law and what people actually do or what is even enforced by the authorities.[35] Societies such as these can be especially confusing to international marketers who come from countries such as the United States.

Harry Triandis explains differences in attitudes toward rules by categorizing cultures as either tight or loose. In **tight cultures**, there are many rules, norms, and standards for correct behavior. In **loose cultures**, such rules are few. Tight cultures criticize and punish rule breakers more severely. Triandis proposes that tight cultures are likely to be more isolated and less influenced by other cultures, since agreement on norms is important. Afghanistan under the Taliban would be an extreme example of a tight culture. High population density may also contribute to tight cultures, since people might need tightness to interact more smoothly under close conditions.[36]

Tight cultures societies with many rules, norms, and standards for correct behavior

Loose cultures societies with few rules, norms, or standards for correct behavior

REGULATORY CHANGE

International marketers must understand the different political and regulatory climates in which they operate. This is a challenging job in itself because of the many national markets involved. They must also be prepared to deal with changes in those environments. These changes can be moderate or drastic, and they can be more or less predictable. The more moderate and predictable changes we call **regulatory change**. The more drastic and unpredictable changes we call political risk, which we discuss in the next section. Regulatory change encompasses many government actions, such as changes in tax rates, the introduction of price controls, and the revision of labeling requirements. Although less dramatic than the upheavals associated with political risk, regulatory changes are very common. International marketers lose far more money to regulatory change than to political risk.

Regulatory change moderate and relatively predictable change in laws and regulations

Predicting Regulatory Change

Whatever strategy a firm chooses to employ in the face of regulatory change, it is useful to be able to predict whether and when such change will occur. Nothing is certain, but most regulatory change affecting international marketers should not come as a total surprise. Many government actions have economic bases. By understanding the issues covered in Chapter 2, an international marketer can identify probable government responses to prevailing conditions. For example, if export earnings are depressed in a developing country and if foreign investment is low, the government may be forced to devalue the currency. No one may be able to predict what day this will occur, but contingency plans should be in place for when it does occur.

It is also very important that the international marketer listen for signals from the government or influential parties. For months before Egypt disallowed additional foreign investment in packaged foods, local business leaders could be heard in the local media calling for such restrictions. When foreign investors first returned to China, the Chinese government warned them concerning repatriation of profits. They were told that their ability to remove profits from China would be somehow contingent on their export sales. Many firms paid no attention to this warning and later discovered that they did not qualify to repatriate profits. Some even admitted that they thought China had been joking about the possible restriction.

Firms can find themselves caught in embarrassing situations if they fail to heed signals. On the other hand, if they take signals seriously, they can formulate plans for different contingencies. How should the firm respond to a currency devaluation, an increased tax, or new restrictions on advertising? Contingency planning enables marketing managers to avoid crises and to make deliberate and careful decisions about what strategy will be appropriate to employ in the face of regulatory change.

Managing Regulatory Change

James Austin suggests four strategic options for a company to consider when faced with regulatory change:

- *Alter.* The company can bargain to get the government to alter its policy or actions.
- *Avoid.* The company can make strategic moves that bypass the impact of a government's action.
- *Accede.* The company can adjust its operations to comply with a government requirement.
- *Ally.* The company can attempt to avoid some risks of government actions by seeking strategic alliances.[37]

Before deciding to try to alter a new regulation, the company should assess its bargaining power vis-à-vis the government. As depicted in Figure 4.1, a company is more likely to try to alter a new regulation when the regulation significantly affects its operations and the firm's bargaining power is high. If the firm's bargaining power is low, it will be more successful by seeking an appropriate ally or allies. If a policy is not very threatening and the firm's power is relatively low, the firm may be best served by acceding. After all, the firm should pick its battles with a government. It is too expensive and exhausting to fight every new regulation.

A firm's bargaining power is enhanced by its ability to pay taxes, employ citizens, and deliver exports to assist the national trade balance. During diplomatic tensions between the United States and France prior to the Iraq War, the South Carolina state legislature took up a resolution calling for a boycott of French products. The resolution passed the state House, 90–9. But suddenly the bill died and wasn't taken up by the state Senate. As it turned out, most of the tires sold in the United States by the French group Michelin were made in factories located in South Carolina.[38]

Political mapping the process of identifying all individuals involved in a regulatory decision—politicians, bureaucrats, key members of pressure groups—and understanding their various points of view

To bargain more successfully, a company should use political mapping of a government.[39] **Political mapping** consists of identifying all individuals involved in a regulatory decision—politicians, bureaucrats, pressure groups—and understanding their various points of view. This allows the firm to better address their concerns. However, it is not always easy to do this. Chinese companies estimated that billions of dollars in Chinese-Iraqi contracts were left in limbo after the United States invaded Iraq. They were particularly concerned because China did not support the U.S. invasion. Even more daunting was identifying who in Iraq could make a decision about the many contracts.[40] Similarly, multinational firms have noted that shifting power among bureaucrats in China makes it difficult to do political mapping in that country.[41]

Ravi Ramamurti argues that increasingly a company's bargaining power lies not in itself alone but in the motivation and power of its home government to influence the firm's host government.[42] For example, Motorola discovered after it had

FIGURE **4.1**
**Strategic
Approaches to
Regulatory Change**

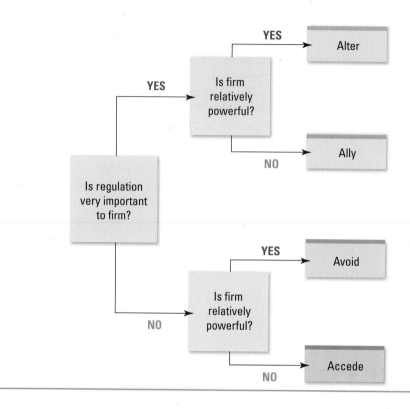

designed and test-marketed a new pager in Japan that the pager did not meet new industry standards. These standards were developed by Motorola's Japanese competitors and enforced by the Japanese government. Instead of redesigning its pager, Motorola first attempted to convince the Japanese government to alter its policy and allow the Motorola design to go to market. Redesigning the pager would prove costly, and Motorola believed its bargaining power was high, especially if the U.S. government would back it in its appeal.[43]

If a firm believes its bargaining power is relatively weak, an ally strategy may be employed. During the Firestone tires/Ford Explorer product-harm crisis, the government of Saudi Arabia impounded the affected vehicles as they arrived on the shipping dock. However, Saudi Ford dealers were able to help rescind this order by convincing the government that they were the ones being hurt and not the multinational companies.[44] Pepsi tried unsuccessfully for several years to enter the Indian market as a wholly owned subsidiary. Finally, the company found a powerful local partner in the Indian beverage industry with whom to enter into a joint venture. The joint venture was quickly approved.

Pepsi also employed the other strategy associated with low bargaining power—accede—when negotiating to enter the Indian market. At the time, India had strict foreign exchange regulations that would stop Pepsi from taking profits out of the country. Pepsi believed that any attempt to convince the Indian government to alter this policy on its behalf would prove futile. The firm also expected to reinvest all Indian profits in the local market for the foreseeable future. Therefore, Pepsi acceded to the government policy. This accession allowed the firm to save time on lengthy negotiations and enter a potentially lucrative market sooner.

Other companies find that they can avoid regulations by making relatively minor changes in their marketing mix. For example, Clearasil could sell its product in

Japanese supermarkets if it did not explicitly promote the product as an acne medicine. Otherwise, it was restricted to selling through pharmacies. For years Brazil's price control board allowed firms to set any price they wanted on newly introduced products. Current products or improved versions of current products, however, were subjected to a tedious and unpredictable appeal process before any increase in price was authorized. As a result, companies such as Gillette were inclined to introduce an improved product, such as a better razor blade, as a totally new product rather than as an improved version of an existing line.

POLITICAL RISK

Recently, the U.S. Securities and Exchange Commission (SEC) announced new disclosure rules for firms seeking to sell securities in the United States. Firms must now report their activities in countries subject to American government sanctions, such as Cuba, Iraq, and the Sudan. The SEC requires firms to disclose anything that could make their offering risky or speculative. In the past, this included environmental risks and impending lawsuits. Now it includes political risks as well.[45]

The presence of political risk means that a foreign company can lose part or all of its investment, market, or earnings in another country as a result of political actions on the part of a host government, the firm's home government, or pressure groups. As we have noted, the political climate of a country is hardly ever static. Sometimes, a firm is faced with sudden and radical changes in the political climate of a host country.

Political risk is the possibility that an unexpected and drastic change due to political forces will result in adverse circumstances for business operations. Sudden changes of power, especially when the new leadership is committed to a leftist

Political risk the possibility that an unexpected and drastic change due to political forces will result in adverse circumstances for business operations

WORLD BEAT 4.2

PORK POLITICS

THE UNITED STATES HAS A STRATEGIC OIL RESERVE, but China has a strategic pork reserve. With pork the favorite meat for most consumers in China, the Chinese government maintains a strategic frozen pork and live pig reserve to guard against severe shortages. Furthermore, in Chinese culture pigs are associated with prosperity and good fortune. Many prospective parents try to time the birth of a child to fall within the Year of the Pig to ensure their child has a lucky life.

However, the importance of pork in the Chinese diet and culture does not make pigs immune from politics. Shortly before China entered the last Year of the Pig in 2008, China Central Television banned all images or spoken references to pigs in advertisements. The reason: respect for Muslims.

who consider pigs unclean. Muslims constitute about 2 percent of the Chinese population. Some believe the ban was an attempt to ease ethnic tensions arising from an incident in which Chinese security forces killed 18 suspected Muslim terrorists. Others link it to the fact that China imports vast quantities of oil from Muslim countries.

Many foreign companies, including Nestlé and Disney, had already developed advertising campaigns featuring pigs to coincide with China's Year of the Pig. However, advertising agencies in China confessed that they were used to such surprise legislation. Despite the advertising ban on pigs, the Chinese post office launched a series of special issue stamps featuring Disney's cartoon pig, Piglet, to celebrate the New Year.

Sources: Gordon Fairclough and Geoffrey A. Fowler, "Pigs Get the Ax in China TV Ads," *Wall Street Journal,* January 25, 2007, p. A1; Rowan Callick, "Year of the Pig," *The Australian,* February 1, 2007, p. 8; and Christopher Bodeen, "Chinese Pork Prices Rattle Public, Politics," *Austin American Statesman,* May 31, 2007, p. A4.

Political unrest discourages foreign investment. This is one reason why African markets have received relatively low attention from many global marketers.

economic and political philosophy, have led to hostile political climates and takeovers. Such changes in government can happen as a result of unexpected coup d'états or revolutions. However, as occurred in Venezuela, it can sometimes result from a democratic election.

All political instability may not pose the possibility of negative consequences to every firm. Many businesses in the tiny emirate of Kuwait viewed the Iraq war and the toppling of the regime of Saddam Hussein as presenting potential business opportunities in the neighboring country of 20 million people.[46] The security industry is booming in Central America where gang-related crime is a serious problem. Guatemala's business community alone pays $335 million for protection from 250 licensed security firms. Who has the biggest market share in the region? Wackenhut, a Miami-based security firm, acquired by Denmark's Group 4 Flack.[47]

The fall of the Iranian shah in 1979 is a vivid example of a sudden change that caught many companies by surprise and did adversely impact their business interests. Unlike communist revolutions earlier in the century, Iran's revolution was centered on Islam. Still, anti-American sentiment resulted in the taking hostage of U.S. citizens at the American Embassy in Tehran. President Jimmy Carter retaliated by seizing Iranian assets under U.S. jurisdiction and ordered all U.S. companies to cease doing business with Iran. The impact on U.S. business alone involved around 4,000 firms whose claims against Iran were eventually settled by the International Tribunal at the Hague. One of the largest settlements outside the petroleum industry was $49.8 million paid to the tobacco company R.J. Reynolds.[48] And not only U.S. companies sustained damage. Many companies operating from Europe and Japan were forced, as a result of the revolution, to shut down either all or parts of their operations. The subsequent war between Iran and Iraq further limited the attractiveness of the Iranian market and inflicted additional losses on remaining foreign investors.

The Iranian experience taught international marketers an important lesson pertaining to political risk. For many years, firms believed political risk applied only

to capital investments in foreign countries. After all, expensive manufacturing plants could be seized. Surprisingly, the Reynolds case involved damage not to brick-and-mortar facilities but rather to unpaid accounts receivable for cigarettes exported to Iran. In fact, many companies that were simply exporting to Iran found themselves the victims of political risk. So did firms that were licensing their technology or brand names to local Iranian manufacturers. In many cases, the new government forbade importers and licensees from making payments to foreign businesses. However a firm chooses to enter a market, political risk may be a concern.

What can companies do? Internationally active companies have reacted on two fronts. First, they have started to perfect their own intelligence systems to avoid being caught unaware when changes disrupt operations. Second, they have developed several risk-reducing strategies that help limit their exposure, or the losses they would sustain, should a sudden change occur. The following sections will concentrate on these two solutions.

Political Risk Assessment

The business disruption in Iran inspired many companies to establish systems to systematically analyze political risk. To establish an effective political risk assessment (PRA) system, a company has to decide first on the objectives of the system. Another aspect concerns the internal organization, or the assignment of responsibility within the company. Finally, some agreement has to be reached on how the analysis is to be done.

Objectives of Political Risk Assessment.

Companies everywhere would like to know about impending government instabilities in order to avoid making new investments in those countries. Even more important is the monitoring of existing operations and their political environment. Particularly with existing operations, knowing in advance about potential changes in the political climate is of little value unless such advance knowledge can also be used for future action. As a result, PRA is slowly moving from predicting events to developing strategies that help companies cope with changes. But first, PRA has to deal with the potential political changes. Many questions must be answered: Should we enter a particular country? Should we stay in a particular country? What can we do with our operations in market X, given that development Y can occur? In undertaking PRA, companies are well advised to look for answers to six key questions:

- How stable is the host country's political system?
- How strong is the host government's commitment to specific rules of the game, such as ownership or contractual rights, given its ideology and power position?
- How long is the government likely to remain in power?
- If the present government is succeeded by another, how will the specific rules of the game change?
- What would be the effects on our business of any expected changes in the specific rules of the game?
- In light of those effects, what decisions and actions should we take now?

Organization and Analysis.

One survey of large U.S.-based international firms found that over half the firms had internal groups reviewing the political climate of both newly proposed and current operations. In companies that did not have formalized systems for PRA, top executives tended to obtain firsthand information through foreign travel and talking with other businesspeople.[49]

Rather than rely on a centralized corporate staff, some companies prefer to delegate PRA responsibility to executives or analysts located in a particular geographic region. Some use their subsidiary and regional managers as a major source of information. Other firms employ distinguished foreign-policy advisers or maintain outside advisory panels.

Several public or semipublic sources exist that regularly monitor political risk. The Economist Intelligence Unit (EIU), a sister company of the *Economist,* monitors some eighty countries on the basis of a variety of economic and political factors. These factors include debt, current account position, economic policy, and political stability. *Euromoney* publishes country risk ratings, including political risk evaluations (see Table 4.2).

Usually firms use several approaches and sources to assess political risk. What companies do with their assessment depends on the data they collect. Political risk assessment can help the firms stay out of risky countries.

However, go/no-go decisions can be difficult to make. Risk analysis is not fortunetelling. No one can predict with certainty when the next revolution or war will take place. Like Iran in the late 1970s, some politically risky countries possess very attractive markets. Therefore, political risk analysis is only one of the activities that must be undertaken in the course of deciding whether or not to enter or stay in a foreign market. Many companies integrate their political assessments into their overall financial assessments of projects. In cases where the firm expects higher political risk, the company may add anywhere from 1 to 5 percent to its required return on investment. In this manner the company balances political risk against market attractiveness.

Risk Reduction Strategies

Political risk assessment not only aids firms in market entry and exit decisions but can also alert them to the necessity of risk-reducing strategies. Such strategies can enable companies to enter or stay in riskier markets. A classic way to deal with politically risky countries is to seek higher and faster returns on investment. The average return on foreign direct investment in Africa is often higher than that for any other region of the world, according to an UNCTAD study. This is partially because firms invested in projects that promised quick returns.[50] Many companies have also experimented with different ownership and financing arrangements. Others use political risk insurance to reduce potential losses.

Local Partners. Relying on local partners who have excellent contacts among the host country's governing elite is a strategy that has been used effectively by many companies. This may range from placing local nationals on the boards of foreign subsidiaries to accepting a substantial capital participation from local investors. For example, General Motors joined forces with Shanghai Automotive Industry Corporation, a state-owned firm, in a 50-50 joint venture to make Buicks, minivans, and compact cars in China.

However, the use of local partners may not decrease the chance of expropriation, and such partners can become liabilities if governments change. General Motors entered into a joint venture in Iran with a partner closely connected with the shah. After the revolution ousted the shah, GM's partner's shares were expropriated. GM then found itself in partnership with the new Islamic government.

TABLE 4.2 SAFEST EMERGING MARKETS: POLITICAL RISK RATINGS

RANKING	COUNTRY	RANKING	COUNTRY	RANKING	COUNTRY
1	United Arab Emirates	39	Peru	77	Swaziland
2	Cyprus	40	Panama	78	Vanuatu
3	Bahrain	41	Egypt	79	Bosnia-Herzegovina
4	Malta	42	Kazakhstan	80	Zambia
5	Qatar	43	Costa Rica	81	Tanzania
6	Bermuda	44	Azerbaijan	82	Jamaica
7	Taiwan	45	Macau	83	Yemen
8	Israel	46	Colombia	84	Argentina
9	Bahamas	47	Antigua & Barbuda	85	Pakistan
10	Saudi Arabia	48	Jordan	86	Uganda
11	Czech Republic	49	Turkey	87	Algeria
12	Slovak Republic	50	Vietnam	88	Syria
13	Brunei	51	Indonesia	89	Fiji
14	South Korea	52	Philippines	90	Cambodia
15	Oman	53	Macedonia (FYR)	91	Paraguay
16	Poland	54	Ukraine	92	St. Vincent & the Grenadines
17	Chile	55	Guatemala	93	Tonga
18	Botswana	56	El Salvador	94	Bangladesh
19	Barbados	57	Albania	95	Seychelles
20	Estonia	58	Armenia	96	Madagascar
21	Hungary	59	Mongolia	97	Kenya
22	Malaysia	60	Dominican Republic	98	Benin
23	China	61	Georgia	99	Serbia
24	Mexico	62	Ghana	100	Grenada
25	Lithuania	63	Nigeria	101	Moldova
26	Russia	64	St Lucia	102	Mali
27	South Africa	65	Honduras	103	Equatorial Guinea
28	Mauritius	66	Angola	104	Bolivia
29	India	67	Uruguay	105	Belize
30	Croatia	68	Belarus	106	Rwanda
31	Romania	69	Maldives	107	Lebanon
32	Latvia	70	Papua New Guinea	108	Dominica
33	Brazil	71	Montenegro	109	Ethiopia
34	Thailand	72	Venezuela	110	Namibia
35	Bulgaria	73	Sri Lanka	111	Gabon
36	Morocco	74	Cape Verde	112	Ecuador
37	Tunisia	75	Lesotho	113	Suriname
38	Trinidad & Tobago	76	Mozambique	114	Nepal

continued

Table 4.2 continued

RANKING	COUNTRY	RANKING	COUNTRY	RANKING	COUNTRY
115	New Caledonia	130	Guyana	145	Liberia
116	Iran	131	Sierra Leone	146	Chad
117	Djibouti	132	Côte d'Ivoire	147	Guinea-Bissau
118	Senegal	133	Bhutan	148	Burundi
119	Solomon Islands	134	Uzbekistan	149	Myanmar
120	Turkmenistan	135	Tajikistan	150	Central African Republic
121	Cameroon	136	Burkina Faso	151	Eritrea
122	Kyrgyz Republic	137	Togo	152	Afghanistan
123	Niger	138	Mauritania	153	Somalia
124	Gambia	139	Laos	154	Micronesia
125	Sudan	140	Malawi	155	Cuba
126	Samoa	141	Haiti	156	Zimbabwe
127	Nicaragua	142	Dem. Rep. of the Congo	157	Marshall Islands
128	Congo	143	Sao Tome & Principe	158	North Korea
129	Libya	144	Guinea	159	Iraq

Source: Rankings from "Country Risk Survey Results," *Euromoney*, September 2008. Reprinted with permission.

Minimizing Assets at Risk. If a market is politically risky, international marketers may try to minimize assets that are at risk. For example, R.J. Reynolds could have refused to extend credit to its cigarette importer in Iran. Instead of accumulating accounts receivable that were at risk, the firm could have demanded payment before shipment. However, as we have mentioned before, some politically risky countries can be attractive markets. This was the case in Iran in the mid-1970s, when many foreign firms were vying for Iranian markets. In light of such intense competition, few companies could afford to be heavy-handed with their Iranian customers.

Another way to minimize assets at risk is to borrow locally. Financing local operations from indigenous banks and maintaining a high level of local accounts payable minimize assets at risk. These actions also maximize the negative effect on the local economy if adverse political actions are taken. Typically, host governments are reluctant to cause problems for their local financial institutions. Local borrowing is not always possible because restrictions may be imposed on foreign companies that might otherwise crowd local companies out of the credit markets. However, projects located in developing countries can sometimes qualify for loans from the World Bank. Pioneer, a major global firm in hybrid seeds, was offered such financing when it considered investing in Ethiopia. These arrangements not only reduce the capital at risk but also lend multilateral support for the venture.

Finally, larger multinational firms may attempt to diversify their assets and markets across many countries as a way to manage political risk. If losses are realized in one market, their impact does not prove devastating to the company as a whole. Of course, this is more difficult to do if a company is small. Several smaller U.S. firms faced bankruptcy as a result of losses ensuing from the Iranian Revolution.

Private insurers, such as Bellwood Prestbury, now offer kidnap and ransom insurance to firms involved in politically risky markets.

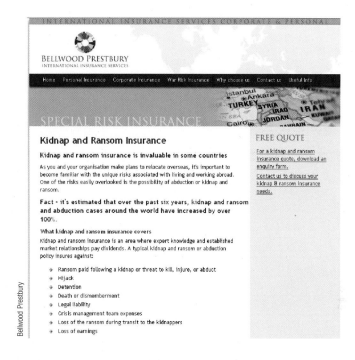

Bellwood Prestbury

Political Risk Insurance. As a final recourse, international companies can often purchase insurance to cover their political risk. With the political developments in Iran and Nicaragua occurring in rapid succession and the assassinations of President Park of Korea and President Sadat of Egypt all taking place between 1979 and 1981, many companies began to change their attitudes on risk insurance. Political risk insurance can be costly but can offset large potential losses. For example, as a result of the UN Security Council's worldwide embargo on Iraq, companies stood to collect $100–$200 million from private insurers and billions from government-owned insurers.[51]

For more information on OPIC, check out its home page from the student companion website at http://www.cengage.com/international.

Companies based in the United States can use the Overseas Private Investment Corporation (OPIC). OPIC was formed by the U.S. government to facilitate the participation of private U.S. firms in the development of less developed countries. Since the Islamic Revolution in Iran, OPIC has covered exporters as well as foreign investors. OPIC offers project financing and political risk insurance in one hundred developing countries. The agency covers losses caused by currency inconvertibility, expropriation, and bellicose actions such as war and revolution. Selected projects using OPIC are listed in Table 4.3. But even OPIC faces challenges from special-interest groups. A lawsuit was brought against OPIC by Friends of the Earth, Greenpeace, and others. They accused the agency of failing to conduct environmental reviews before financing projects that contributed to global warming.[52]

GLOBAL MARKETING AND TERRORISM

The Overseas Security Advisory Council is a public-private partnership that seeks to provide early warning of bombings or other attacks to corporate offices worldwide as terrorists look increasingly toward "soft targets." The council is overseen by the U.S. State Department and advises international companies such as Citigroup, Boeing, Dupont, and McDonald's. Its site gets about 1.8 million visits a month, and the council distributes about 10,000 e-mails daily. Jennifer Harris, 23,

| TABLE 4.3 | SELECTED 2008 OPIC PROJECTS | | |

COUNTRY	U.S. SPONSOR	PROJECT DESCRIPTION	LOAN/GUARANTY/ INSURANCE
Algeria	Ionics Incorporated of Watertown, MA	Potable water	Loan
Botswana	Kalahari Gas Corporation	Electricity production	Guaranty
Egypt	Apache Corporation	Natural gas production	Insurance
Gaza	Morganti Group, Inc.	Power project	Insurance
Guatemala	Colite Outdoor of West Columbia, SC	Construction of billboards	Insurance
Honduras	Colite Outdoor of West Columbia, SC	Construction of billboards	Insurance
Indonesia	Unocal Corporation and Pertamina	Offshore crude oil and natural gas production	Loan
Kenya	Living Water International	Potable water wells	Loan
Mexico	ICA-Fluor	Energy infrastructure development	Guaranty
Morocco	CMS Generation Company	Domestic electrical energy production	Loan
Nigeria	Deamar Group	Flour mill	Loan
	Hercules Lifeboat	Life boat services	Insurance
Pakistan	Sweetwater International of Salt Lake City	Advanced oil treatment technology to increase crop yields	Insurance
Philippines	Golden Cypress Water Company	Bottled water	Loan
Russia	International Scientific Products Corporation of New York	Optical components manufacturing facility	Loan
South Korea	Majestic Group Korea	Ruby Tuesday franchise restaurant	Loan
Zambia	Africa Mortgage Finance Zambia	Mortgage financing for 5,000 new homes	Loan

Source: http://www.opic.gov. 2008 Projects.

handled a call from a company whose chief executive officer was planning to meet with a regional governor in India. Ms. Harris's research revealed that there had been seven attempts on the governor's life in the past year. The CEO decided to telephone instead.[53]

The rise of international terrorism has affected global marketers in different ways. Some firms choose to avoid or leave certain markets because the local government has alleged ties to terrorists. General Electric was one of several companies that chose to stop seeking contracts in Iran when the company was criticized by a U.S. senator for taking "blood money" from a state that supported terrorists.[54] Other companies have found their marketing strategies affected by terrorism. Coca-Cola and Procter & Gamble once advertised on Al-Manar Television, a satellite news channel run by the militant Shiite group Hezbollah. However, the U.S. Treasury designated Al-Manar a terrorist entity, making it illegal for U.S. firms to continue to advertise on the channel.[55]

Multinational firms must consider a possible terrorist threat to their own operations. Businesses are the most common target of terrorist attacks, and bombings are the most common terrorist events.[56] Faced with the possibility of such an attack, Starbucks pulled out of Israel.[57] Terrorists have also been known to extort payments from multinationals. However, such payments may be deemed illegal by home governments. Chiquita pled guilty to breaking U.S. law and agreed to

$25 million in fines for paying a terrorist group in Colombia to assure the safety of its employees there.[58]

Whole industries have also been affected by the rise in terrorism. One of the immediate industries to feel the impact of global terrorism was tourism. With a high risk of terrorism, Americans spent more tourism dollars in Mexico instead of taking trans-Atlantic flights to Europe.[59] Tourists from the Middle East began to shun the United States where they faced new border checks and suspicion, favoring a new destination—Malaysia. In 2003, Middle East tourists to the United States dropped 36 percent from three years earlier.[60]

Another industry directly affected by global terrorism is international education. Tightened security in the United States has made acquiring student visas more difficult for foreign students planning to study there. Consequently, a battle for global market share of international students has emerged. Among the most aggressive countries are Malaysia, India, China, Sweden, and the Netherlands. Two other proactive competitors are the Middle East emirate of Dubai and Singapore. Dubai particularly targets students from the Middle East who face difficulties in obtaining U.S. visas. Both Dubai and Singapore follow the model of partnering with high-quality foreign universities to set up local programs. Among such universities participating in Dubai are the University of Southern Queensland, India's Mahatma Gandhi University, and Dublin Business School. Singapore has attracted Stanford and Cornell from the United States, French business school INSEAD, and the German Institute of Science and Technology. Singapore's goal is to attract 150,000 foreign students, resulting in a contribution of 5 percent to the national economy.[61]

Global terrorists may particularly target infrastructure such as ports, airlines, and other transportation and communication systems.[62] Such attacks threaten to wreak havoc as companies try to supply international buyers. Dow Corning makes over 10,000 deliveries a month to 20,000 customers in 50 countries. Its products are used in the manufacture of products from shampoos to textiles. September 11th and other terrorist attacks can disrupt the firm's ability to deliver products to customers. For example, Dow Cornings's team of planners met for months to discuss backup plans if the war in Iraq were to upset their global logistics. During the Persian Gulf War, one product destined for a cosmetics company in France ended up in Saudi Arabia. This held up production for two weeks and upset the French customer.

Similar to Dow, a number of large companies already had systems in place to respond to disruptions caused by situations other than terrorism. For example, DaimlerChrysler had control centers to deal with disruptions from hurricanes to industrial disputes.[63] However, Dow Corning's chief logistics officer for China estimates that most big companies could be better prepared with scenario planning. They would probably only have to invest $1.5 million in contingency plans.[64]

Corporate security has been heightened in a number of companies. PepsiCo, with over $500 billion in sales and over 143,000 employees worldwide, responded to the terrorist threat by creating a new position—vice president of global security. At Oracle, a corporate steering committee coordinates a number of departments, including security, information technology, product development, and human resources. At Marriott, crisis management has been centralized to ensure consistency across its different businesses. Seventy percent of respondents to a survey administered by the U.S. Chamber of Commerce reported that that their firms had reviewed their security policies in light of a terrorist threat, and 53 percent had acted on recommendations arising from those reviews.[65]

The U.S. government has made certain precautions mandatory by law. Companies that export agricultural products or processed foods to the United States must register with the U.S. Department of Agriculture and submit to increased scrutiny. The Treasury Department maintains a list of individuals and organizations believed to be linked with terrorism. To do business with anyone or any company on that list is a criminal offense for U.S. citizens or companies. Needless to say, these new regulations have vastly increased demand by companies for preemployment screening as well as background checks on clients, vendors, distributors, and business partners.[66]

How do political issues affect your marketing plans? Continue with your Country Market Report on the student companion website at http://www.cengage.com/international.

The direct and indirect costs associated with terrorism for the S&P 500 companies alone is estimated to be over $100 billion a year. This number includes insurance, redundant capacity, and lost revenues due to decreased purchases from fearful consumers.[67] Nonetheless, 90 percent of the respondents in the Chamber of Commerce survey reported that they did not believe their company would be a target of terrorists.[68] As the immediate threat fades, many midsize companies, in particular, may regard the expense of planning for terrorist attacks as too costly. In another survey, conducted by the Conference Board, 40 percent of top executives of midsize companies agreed that "security is an expense that ought to be minimized."[69] It is further estimated that 40 percent of very large U.S. companies do not have terrorism insurance.[70]

CONCLUSION

In this chapter, we have outlined major political and regulatory issues facing international companies. Our approach was not to identify and list all possible government actions that may have an impact on international marketing. Instead, we have provided a background to make it easier to understand these actions and the motivations behind them. It is up to executives with international responsibility to devise strategies and systems for dealing with these challenges posed by governments.

What is important is to recognize that companies can—to a degree—forecast and manage regulatory change. They can also adopt risk reduction strategies to compensate for some of the more unpredictable political risks. For effective global marketing management, executives must be forward looking, must anticipate potentially adverse or even positive changes in the environment, and must not merely wait until changes occur. To accomplish this, systematic monitoring procedures that encompass both political and regulatory developments must be implemented.

The past several years have brought enormous political changes to the world, changes that are affecting global marketing operations of international firms. On the one hand, these changes have resulted in the opening of many previously closed markets. On the other hand, global terrorism has emerged, presenting its own challenges. Regulatory change and political risk will continue to play a large role in global marketing. Firms must learn how to avoid disasters as well as how to identify and take advantage of opportunities.

QUESTIONS FOR DISCUSSION

1. The construction industry in Japan has traditionally been dominated by the domestic suppliers. Few foreign construction companies have won projects in Japan. What aspects of Japan's political forces may have influenced this local control over the Japanese construction market? What political or regulatory forces may lead to the opening of this market for foreign firms?

2. Do ownership restrictions such as local-partner requirements always ensure that multinational firms will contribute more to the local economy than they would otherwise?

3. What are the different methods a company can use to obtain and/or develop political risk assessment information? What do you think are the strengths and weaknesses of each?

4. John Deere has decided to enter the tractor market in Central America. What strategies

could it use to reduce the possible effects of political risk?

5. Choose a cause promoted by Public Citizen's Global Trade Watch. Do you agree with the cause? Why or why not? What firms are or could be involved in the controversy?

6. How is global terrorism similar to and different from prior political risk faced by global marketers?

Maps

© Photodisc/Getty Images

MAP **1** The World

GREENLAND
(DENMARK)

ICELAND

ALASKA
(U.S.)

60N

IRELAND

CANADA

40N

PORTUGAL

Azores

UNITED STATES

Bermuda ·

ATLANTIC OCEAN

MOR

Midway Is.

WESTERN
SAHARA
(MOROCCO)

BAHAMAS

DOMINICAN REP.

20N

MAURITAN

Hawaiian Is.

MEXICO

CUBA

Virgin Is.

JAMAICA   HAITI

ST. KITTS AND NEVIS
ANTIGUA AND BARBUDA
DOMINICA

BELIZE
HONDURAS

Puerto Rico

BARBADOS

CAPE
VERDE

SENEGAL

PACIFIC OCEAN

GUATEMALA
EL SALVADOR

NICARAGUA

ST. LUCIA
GRENADA

ST. VINCENT AND
THE GRENADINES

GAMBIA

GUINEA

GUINEA-BISSAU

COSTA RICA

TRINIDAD AND TOBAGO

SIERRA
LEONE

IV
CO

PANAMA

VENEZUELA

GUYANA

FR. GUIANA

LIBERIA

EQU

COLOMBIA

SURINAM

Equator

0

SÃO TOM

Galapagos Is.

ECUADOR

WESTERN
SAMOA

PERU

BRAZIL

TONGA

BOLIVIA

20S

Easter Is.

PARAGUAY

CHILE

URUGUAY

ARGENTINA

40S

Falkland Is.

160W   140W   120W   100W   80W   60W   40W   20W

60S

80S

MAP **2** Contemporary Europe

No longer divided by ideological competition and the cold war, today's Europe features a large number of independent states.

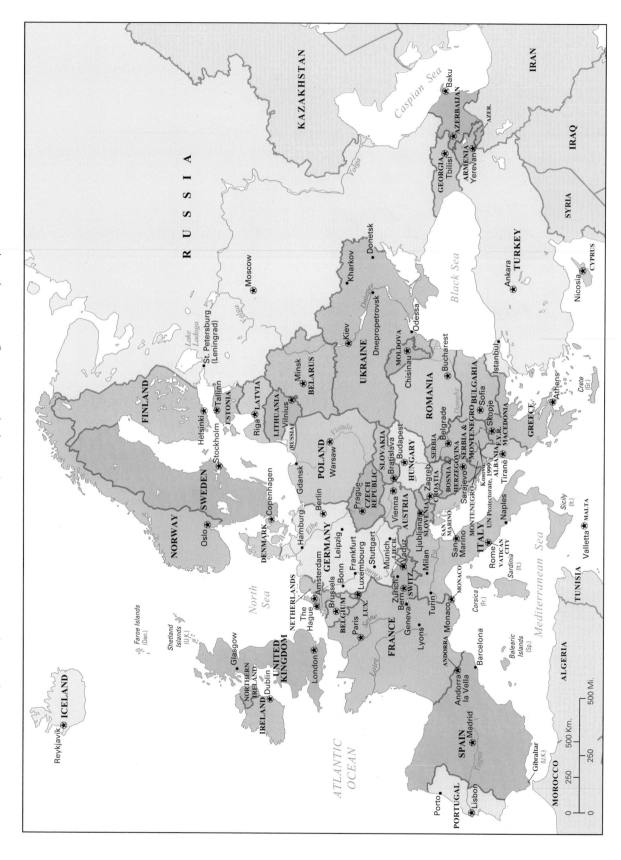

MAP **3** The End of the Soviet Union

When Communist hardliners failed to overthrow Gorbachev in 1991, popular anti-Communist sentiment swept the Soviet Union. Following Boris Yeltsin's lead in Russia, the republics that constituted the Soviet Union declared their independence.

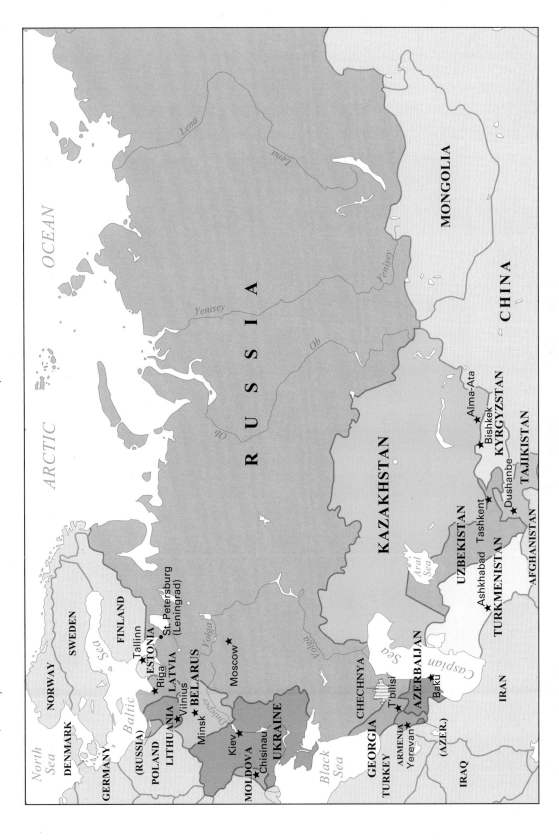

MAP **4** The End of Soviet Domination in Eastern Europe

The creation of new countries out of Yugoslavia and Czechoslovakia and the reunification of Germany marked the most complicated change of national borders since World War I. The Czech Republic and Slovakia separated peacefully, but Slovenia, Croatia, Macedonia, and Bosnia and Herzegovina achieved independence only after bitter fighting.

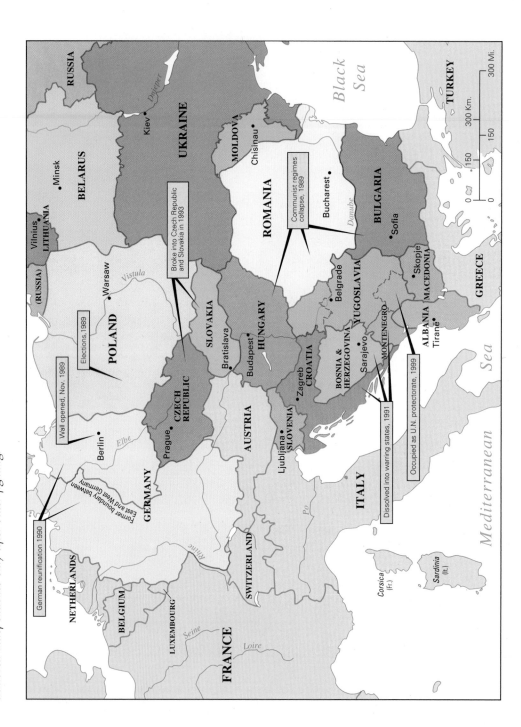

MAP **5**   Central America and the Caribbean

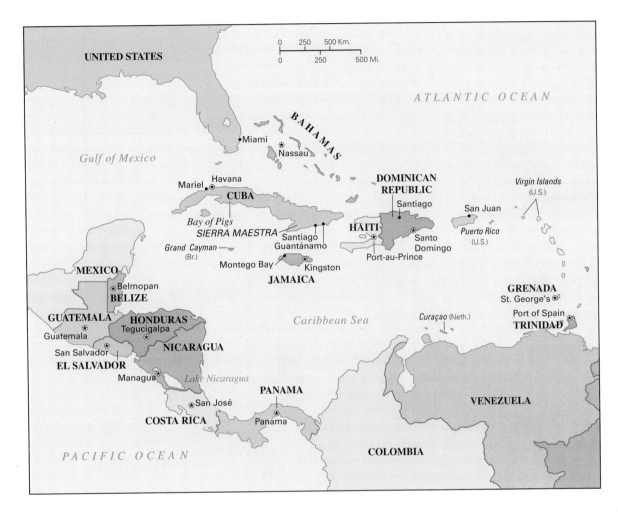

UNITED STATES

ATLANTIC OCEAN

Gulf of Mexico

•Miami

BAHAMAS

⊛ Nassau

DOMINICAN
REPUBLIC

Virgin Islands
(U.S.)

Mariel Havana
⊛

CUBA

Santiago
•

San Juan
⊛

Bay of Pigs

SIERRA MAESTRA

Santiago

HAITI

Puerto Rico
(U.S.)

Grand Cayman
(Br.)

Guantánamo

Santo
Domingo

Montego Bay

⊛
Kingston

Port-au-Prince

MEXICO

JAMAICA

⊛ Belmopan

GRENADA
St. George's ⊛

BELIZE

Caribbean Sea

Curaçao (Neth.)

Port of Spain
⊛

GUATEMALA

HONDURAS
Tegucigalpa
⊛

TRINIDAD

Guatemala
⊛

San Salvador
⊛

NICARAGUA

EL SALVADOR

Managua ⊛

Lake Nicaragua

PANAMA

VENEZUELA

⊛ San José

PACIFIC OCEAN

COSTA RICA

Panama

COLOMBIA

0   250   500 Km.

0   250   500 Mi.

MAP **6** Modern South America

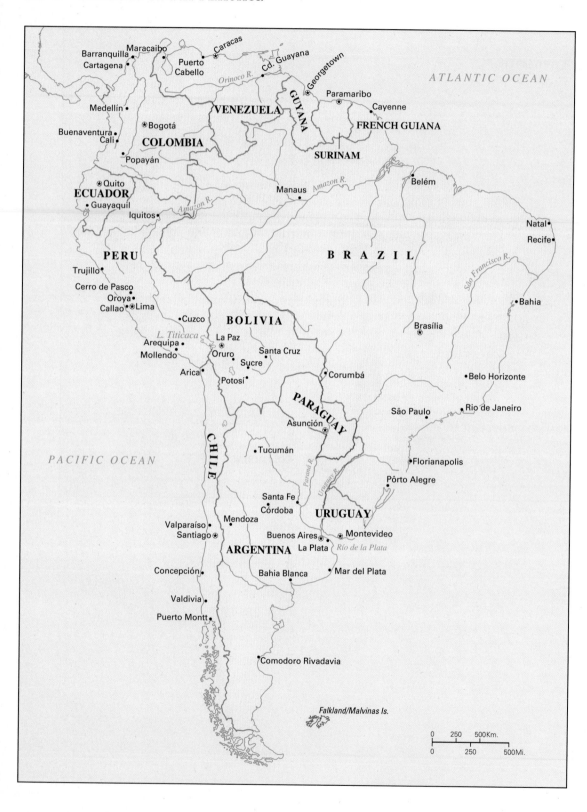

MAP **7** New States in Africa and Asia

Divided primarily along religious lines into two states, British India led the way to political independence in 1947. Most African territories achieved statehood by the mid-1960s, as European empires passed away, unlamented.

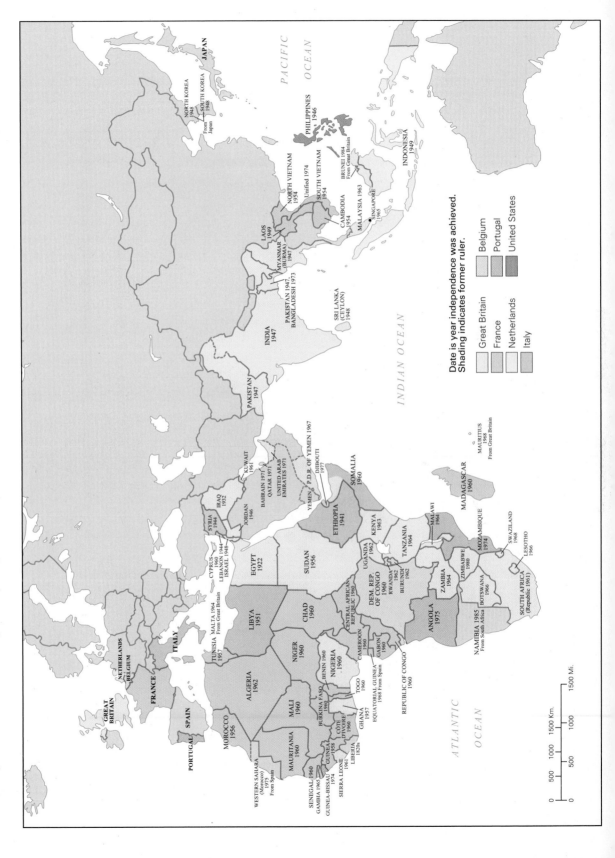

Date is year independence was achieved.
Shading indicates former ruler.

- Great Britain
- France
- Netherlands
- Italy
- Belgium
- Portugal
- United States

PACIFIC OCEAN

JAPAN

NORTH KOREA 1948
SOUTH KOREA 1948
From Japan

PHILIPPINES 1946

BRUNEI 1984 From Great Britain

INDONESIA 1949

NORTH VIETNAM 1954 Unified 1974
SOUTH VIETNAM 1954

CAMBODIA 1954
MALAYSIA 1963
SINGAPORE 1965

LAOS 1949

MYANMAR (BURMA) 1947

PAKISTAN 1947, BANGLADESH 1973

SRI LANKA (CEYLON) 1948

INDIA 1947

PAKISTAN 1947

INDIAN OCEAN

KUWAIT 1961

BAHRAIN 1971
QATAR 1971
UNITED ARAB EMIRATES 1971

YEMEN P.D.R. OF YEMEN 1967
DJIBOUTI 1977

SOMALIA 1960

MADAGASCAR 1960

MAURITIUS 1968 From Great Britain

IRAQ 1932

SYRIA 1944
JORDAN 1946

ETHIOPIA 1941

KENYA 1963

MALAWI 1964

SWAZILAND 1968

CYPRUS 1960
LEBANON 1944
ISRAEL 1948

EGYPT 1922

SUDAN 1956

UGANDA 1962
DEM. REP. OF CONGO 1960
RWANDA 1962
BURUNDI 1962

TANZANIA 1964

ZIMBABWE 1980

MOZAMBIQUE 1974

LESOTHO 1966

MALTA 1964 From Great Britain

TUNISIA 1957

LIBYA 1951

CHAD 1960

CENTRAL AFRICAN REPUBLIC 1960

ZAMBIA 1964

BOTSWANA 1966

NAMIBIA 1985 From South Africa

SOUTH AFRICA (Republic 1961)

NETHERLANDS
BELGIUM

ITALY

FRANCE

SPAIN

MOROCCO 1956

ALGERIA 1962

NIGER 1960

NIGERIA 1960

CAMEROON 1960
GABON 1960

ANGOLA 1975

GREAT BRITAIN

PORTUGAL

MAURITANIA 1960

MALI 1960

BURKINA FASO 1960
BENIN 1960

TOGO 1960

EQUATORIAL GUINEA 1968 From Spain

REPUBLIC OF CONGO 1960

WESTERN SAHARA (Morocco) 1975 From Spain

SENEGAL 1960
GAMBIA 1965
GUINEA-BISSAU 1974
GUINEA 1958
SIERRA LEONE 1961
LIBERIA 1820

GHANA 1957
COTE D'IVOIRE 1960

ATLANTIC OCEAN

0   500   1000   1500 Km.
0   500   1000   1500 Mi.

MAP **8** World Religions

Believers in Islam, Christianity, and Buddhism make up large percentages of the population in many countries. Differing forms of these religions seldom coincide with national boundaries. As religion revives as a source of social identity or a rationale for political assertion or mass mobilization, the possibility of religious activism spreading across broad geographic regions becomes greater, as does the likelihood of domestic discord in multireligious states.

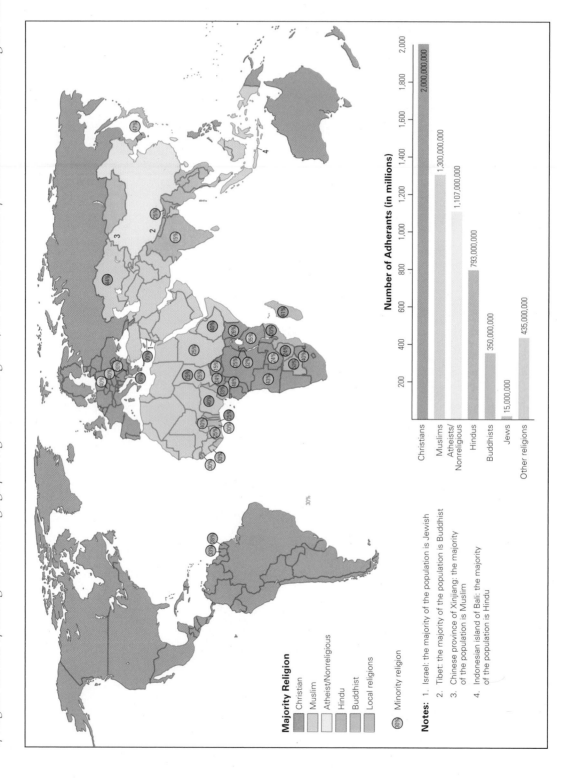

Majority Religion

Christian
Muslim
Atheist/Nonreligious
Hindu
Buddhist
Local religions

Minority religion

Notes: 1. Israel: the majority of the population is Jewish
2. Tibet: the majority of the population is Buddhist
3. Chinese province of Xinjiang: the majority of the population is Muslim
4. Indonesian island of Bali: the majority of the population is Hindu

Number of Adherants (in millions)

Religion	Number of Adherents
Christians	2,000,000,000
Muslims	1,300,000,000
Atheists/Nonreligious	1,107,000,000
Hindus	793,000,000
Buddhists	350,000,000
Jews	15,000,000
Other religions	435,000,000

MAP **9** Modern Islam

Although the Islamic heartland remains the Middle East and North Africa, Islam is growing steadily in Africa south of the Sahara and is the faith of heavily populated Indonesia.

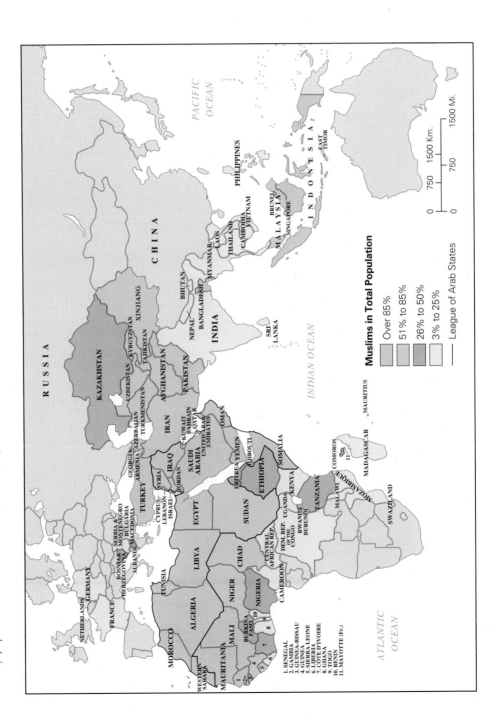

Muslims in Total Population

Over 85%
51% to 85%
26% to 50%
3% to 25%
League of Arab States

1. SENEGAL
2. GAMBIA
3. GUINEA-BISSAU
4. GUINEA
5. SIERRA LEONE
6. LIBERIA
7. CÔTE D'IVOIRE
8. GHANA
9. TOGO
10. BENIN
11. MAYOTTE (Fr.)

MAP **10** Water Supply Coverage

Environmental experts estimate that the current global population has about 80 percent of the water it needs and about 60 percent of sanitary water supplies. These maps show the differences between raw water supplies and sanitary water supplies, by national boundaries.

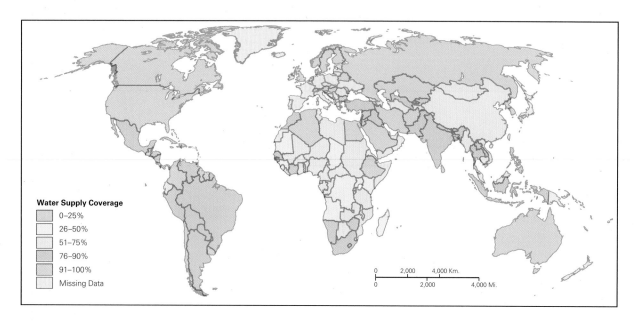

Water Supply Coverage
- 0–25%
- 26–50%
- 51–75%
- 76–90%
- 91–100%
- Missing Data

MAP **11** Sanitation Coverage

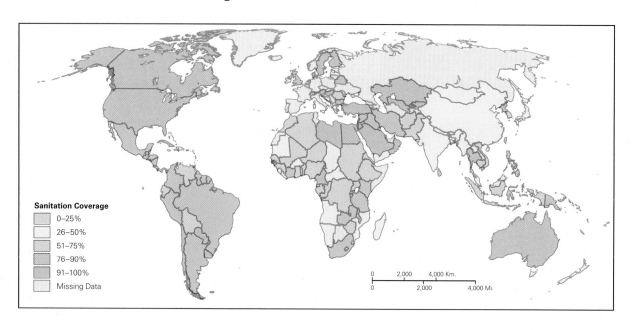

Sanitation Coverage
- 0–25%
- 26–50%
- 51–75%
- 76–90%
- 91–100%
- Missing Data

MAP **12** World Population Growth

At current rates of growth, every three years, the world's population will increase by the equivalent of a nation the size of the United States. Most of this population increase will be in some of the world's poorest nations. (NG Maps/National Geographic Society Image Collection. Reprinted with permission.)

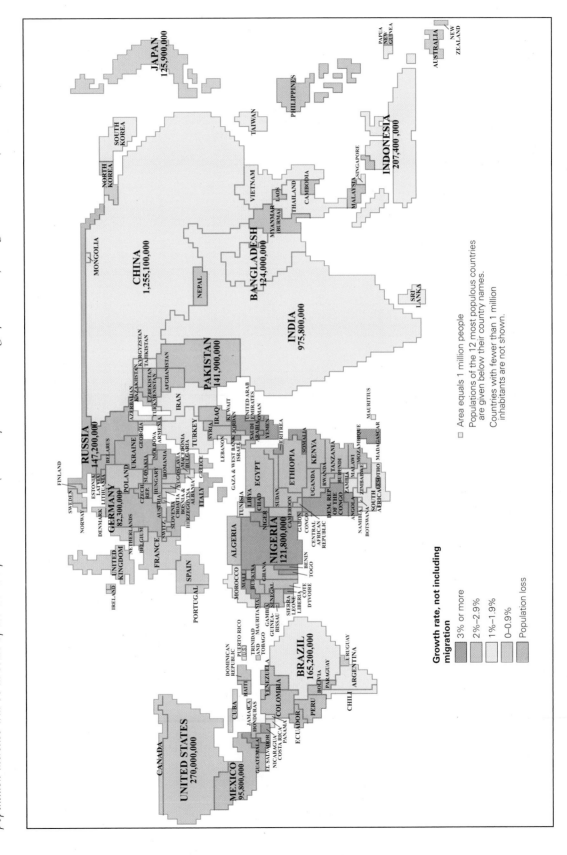

Growth rate, not including migration

- 3% or more
- 2%–2.9%
- 1%–1.9%
- 0–0.9%
- Population loss

☐ Area equals 1 million people

Populations of the 12 most populous countries are given below their country names.

Countries with fewer than 1 million inhabitants are not shown.

Analyzing Global Opportunities

© Tom Cockrem/Lonely Planet Images

© Inmagine/18439GNG

5
Global Markets

LEARNING OBJECTIVES

After studying this chapter, you should be able to:

- List the factors that influence consumers' abilities to buy and explain how these affect various national markets.

- Describe Maslow's hierarchy-of-needs model and apply it to consumers in different cultures.

- Give examples of how consumer behavior is similar across cultures and examples of how it may differ from one culture to another.

- Describe segmentation options for consumer markets abroad.

- Explain why business-to-business markets vary in buyer needs and behavior from one country to another.

- List the special qualities of national and multinational global buyers.

- Describe the five "screens" a foreign firm must pass through to win a government contract.

- Explain the role of bribery in international contracts.

SINCE THE SIGNING OF NAFTA many U.S.-based companies have eyed Mexico's market with great interest. Thanks in part to the rising purchasing power of women, Mary Kay, a Dallas-based manufacturer of cosmetics, has watched Mexico become one of its top foreign markets. Wal-Mart has become Mexico's number one retailer. But for latecomer Starbucks, Mexico presented an enigma. Mexico was the fifth-largest producer of coffee in the world, yet Mexicans rarely drank coffee. The average Mexican consumed less than 2 pounds of coffee a year, compared with the 10 pounds consumed by the average American and the 26 pounds consumed by the average Swede. Could Starbucks create a greater demand for coffee among Mexican consumers? Could its upscale coffee shop format offer a product that was attractive to customers in a developing country?[1]

To begin to develop an effective strategy for global markets, a firm must first consider the type of market in which it competes. Markets can comprise consumers, businesses, or governments.

In this chapter we explore issues that arise when targeting these different categories of markets in global markets. We address factors that make each category similar—and yet different—across cultures. Consumer markets may exhibit global segments whose needs and behaviors are relatively uniform across cultures. Business-to-business markets can produce global buyers with unique demands. Government buyers often have multiple agendas. Still, national differences affect all these markets, making the job of addressing their wants and needs all the more challenging for the global marketer.

UNDERSTANDING MARKETS AND BUYERS

In every marketing situation, it is important to understand potential buyers and the process they use to select one product over another. Most elements of a marketing program are designed to influence the buyer to choose one's product over competitors' products. In the case of each type of buyer—consumer, business, and government—the marketer must be able to identify who the buyers are and how they make a purchase decision.

When launching disposable diapers worldwide, Procter & Gamble established a global marketing team in Cincinnati, believing that babies' diaper needs would be the same around the globe. They later found out that, whereas mothers in most countries are concerned about keeping their babies' bottoms dry, Japanese mothers are not. In Japan, babies are changed so frequently that thick, ultra-absorbent diapers were not necessary and could be replaced by thin diapers that take up less space in the small Japanese home.[2] Similarly, many business supply firms have discovered that CEOs in developing countries make purchase decisions that are usually delegated to purchasing managers in developed countries.

The Consumer Market

Consumers around the world have many similar needs. There is even some evidence that global consumption patterns are converging. The traditionally wine-drinking French are drinking more beer, and beer-drinking Germans are drinking more wine. Japan, traditionally a fish-eating country, is consuming more beef, and many Swiss now prefer French cheese to their traditional Swiss varieties. However, to assume that buyers in different countries engage in exactly the same buying processes and apply exactly the same selection criteria can be disastrous. Buyers can differ in terms of who decides to buy, what they buy, why they buy, how they buy, when they buy, and where they buy.

All people must eat, drink, and be sheltered from the elements. Once these basic needs are met, consumers then seek to improve their standard of living with a more comfortable environment, more leisure time, and increased social status. Still, consumption patterns vary greatly from one country to another, because consumers vary widely in their ability and motivation to buy. For example, consumption patterns for wine vary tremendously from country to country. In France, the average annual consumption is 25.7 liters (6.8 gallons) per person, compared with 6.5 liters in the United States, 4.5 liters in Japan, and only .4 liters in Turkey. Consumption patterns of contact lenses vary by country as well. Americans per capita purchase nearly twice as many contact lenses as the Japanese purchase. Mexicans per capita purchase ten times as many contact lenses as the Chinese purchase.[3]

Basic needs and the desire for an improved standard of living are universal throughout the world, but unfortunately, not everyone can achieve these objectives. The economic, political, and social structure of the country in which consumers live affects their ability to fulfill their needs and the methods they use to do so. To understand a consumer market, we must examine the following three aspects:

- The consumer's ability to buy
- Consumer needs
- Consumer behavior

A vendor sells soap at a rural market in Kenya. Many small businesses in the developing world are part of the informal economy.

Image copyright Arnold John Labrentz, 2009. Used under license from Shutterstock.com

Ability to Buy

To purchase a product, consumers must have the ability to buy. The ability to buy a product may be affected by the amount of wealth a country possesses. A country accumulates wealth by the production and sale of goods within the country and the sale of goods to other countries (exports). The inflows of money from the latter are offset by the outflows of money to pay for necessary imports.

A very important indicator of total consumer potential is **gross national product (GNP)** because it reflects the generation of wealth in a country, which is an indicator of overall market size. The GNP per capita expresses this value per person, so it is a crude indicator of potential per consumer. GNP and **per-capita income (PCI)** can vary significantly from country to country. With a PCI of $38,095 in Japan and $54,499 in Sweden, one can expect the demand for automobiles to be greater in those countries than in Kenya or Vietnam, each with a PCI below $1,000. One of the main reasons why Starbucks was attracted to Mexico was its increasing income per capita. Despite some cultural differences among markets, Starbucks noticed a strong correlation between PCI and coffee consumption.

It is important to note, however, that PCI statistics have an inherent flaw that can undermine their comparability across all markets. The International Monetary Fund (IMF) recognizes that converting income denominated in local currencies into U.S. dollars at market rates can underestimate the true purchasing power of consumers in poor countries relative to those in rich countries. Because of this, the IMF suggests using statistics pertaining to **purchasing-power parity**, which take into account national differences in product prices. For example, assessed in terms of purchasing-power parity, Egypt's buying power increases from $2,015 (PCI) to $5,904.

Gross national product (GNP) the total market value of all goods and services produced within the borders of a country during a specific period

Per-capita income (PCI) a country's average income per person for a specific period

Purchasing-power parity a theory that prices of internationally traded commodities should be the same in every country and therefore that the true exchange rate is the ratio of these prices in any two countries

Table 5.1 shows purchasing-power parity for selected developed and developing countries.

Distribution of wealth also has implications for market potential. Income distribution across the population of a country can distort the market potential in a country. For example, over 80 percent of India's population and nearly 35 percent of China's population live on less than $2 a day.[4] If a few people possess nearly all the wealth and the remainder are poor, there will be few people in the middle. As a result, many products that depend on a middle-class market may fare poorly.

Surprisingly, lower-income segments of the population can be attractive markets for consumer goods. In many developing countries, the buying power of the poor may be underrepresented in official statistics. Much of the income earned by the poor in these countries is never reported to the authorities. Thus they are said to participate in the **informal economy**. Informal economies can be very large. In Mexico, 27 percent of the labor force is estimated to be in the informal sector.[5] However, this number is dwarfed by India's informal economy in which more than 90 percent of the country's 470 million workers are employed.[6] In addition, the relatively high cost of real estate in urban centers keeps many of the poor locked in slums. Any increase in their disposable income is spent not on relocating but on purchasing more upscale consumer products. For example, mothers in poor neighborhoods of Calcutta, India, often buy the most expensive brand of milk for their children.

Still, the market potential of the very poor in developing countries is hotly debated. C.K. Prahalad proposed that marketing to the very poor in developing countries could earn profits for companies while also alleviating poverty. He encouraged

Informal economy the totality of economic activity of individuals and businesses that operate without licenses, permits, or reporting procedures required by law

TABLE 5.1

PER-CAPITA INCOME AT MARKET EXCHANGE RATES AND PURCHASING-POWER PARITY IN SELECTED COUNTRIES

	MARKET EXCHANGE RATES	PURCHASING POWER PARITY		MARKET EXCHANGE RATES	PURCHASING POWER PARITY
Argentina	$8,146	14,354	Korea	20,582	26,340
Brazil	8,449	10,298	Mexico	8,914	14,581
Chile	10,125	14,688	Paraguay	1,962	4,767
Egypt	2,015	5,904	Philippines	1,915	3,539
Ethiopia	297	871	Poland	11,860	17,559
Germany	44,488	35,551	Romania	8,744	12,698
Hungary	15,461	19,829	Russia	12,012	16,160
India	1,081	2,786	Sweden	54,499	37,525
Indonesia	2,142	3,990	Switzerland	64,635	42,840
Iran, Islamic Republic of	5,042	11,209	Turkey	10,737	13,447
Japan	38,095	34,500	United Arab Emirates	50,383	39,076
Kazakhstan	8,835	11,563	United States	46,859	46,895
Kenya	860	1,734	Vietnam	937	2,774

Source: Data selected from "World Economic Outlook Database 2008," *International Monetary Fund,* http://www.imf.org.

firms to rethink a potential market of consumers who earned less than $2 a day.[7] By providing poor consumers with quality products at low prices, companies could help developing countries and build brand loyalty among consumers who would eventually earn more money. This proposal has garnered much attention from multinational firms. However, evidence suggests that bottom-of-the-pyramid marketing is not an easy proposition to put into practice.

Prahalad's original estimate of 4 billion consumers at the **bottom of the pyramid (BOP)** has been challenged by many who think the number may be as low as 600 million worldwide.[8] Others have noted that many BOP consumers live in rural areas that are hard to reach, causing distribution costs to eliminate possible profits. The characteristics of BOP markets can also vary greatly across cultures, limiting a firm's ability to transfer marketing know-how from one country to another. Furthermore, a number of BOP marketing initiatives, including ones undertaken by Nestlé and Unilever, have been eliminated or scaled back.[9] The interest in poor consumers in developing countries continues, but many suggest that these consumers must have resources above $2 a day.

Bottom of the pyramid (BOP) consumers in developing countries who earn less than $2 a day

Consumer Needs

Products and services are purchased to fulfill basic human needs. Abraham **Maslow's hierarchy of needs** divides human needs into four levels and proposes that humans will satisfy lower-level needs before seeking to satisfy higher-level needs. The lowest level of needs is physiological needs. These include the need for safety, food, and shelter. The second level encompasses the social needs of friendship and love. The third level consists of the need to receive respect from others, and the highest level of needs is related to self-actualization or developing one's personality. The structure of consumption for each country varies depending on the income per capita. A developing country, such as China, spends over 50 percent of the national income on food, whereas consumers in developed countries, such as France and the United States, spend less than 20 percent on food.

Maslow's hierarchy of needs a theory stating that human needs are divided into four levels and that humans satisfy lower-level needs before seeking to satisfy higher-level needs

Although it is possible to generalize about the order of consumer purchases on the basis of Maslow's hierarchy of needs, there is some debate about its cross-cultural applicability. Hindu cultures emphasize self-actualization before materialism. In developing countries, consumers may deprive themselves of food in order to buy refrigerators to establish their social status and fulfill their need for esteem.[10] Asian consumers often purchase luxury goods to enhance or maintain face even when their income is relatively low. Such consumers may be thrifty in everyday life yet splurge on luxury consumption.[11] Consumers from more individualistic countries such as the United States may attach less importance to purchases related to belonging to a group or enhancing face and more importance to hobby-related products that may enhance self-actualization. In Japan, on the other hand, great attention and expense are devoted to ritual gift-giving even among business associates, and Japanese children are socially obliged to hold lavish funerals for their parents.

Consumer Behavior

The ability to buy is influenced by a variety of economic elements, which are much easier to identify and quantify than elements related to consumers' motivations to buy. As we noted earlier, all consumers exhibit some similarities as members of the human race. However, buyer behavior is not uniform among all

WORLD BEAT 5.1

SEGMENTING CHINA

CHINESE ARE BUYING MORE and saving less. Chinese household savings have slipped to 16 percent of GDP from over 20 percent in the mid-1990s. They are now no higher than household savings in France and are lower than household savings in India, which total 22 percent of GDP. With the Chinese market appearing ever more attractive, global firms are seeking to expand their presence in the country. But a question remains: Which China to target?

China is an amalgam of many cultures and different buying behaviors. In big cities, shoppers are increasingly frequenting international retailers, such as Wal-Mart and Carrefour. In villages, consumers shop at small mom-and-pop stores. Many urban Chinese are sophisticated and experienced shoppers, whereas many villagers are still

first-time buyers of many products. Price makes a difference too. Urban Chinese pay more than a dollar for Crest toothpaste in exotic flavors such as Icy Mountain Spring or Morning Lotus Fragrance. In the villages, consumers appreciate a more basic formula with a price under 50 cents.

One emerging segment is of particular interest to some multinational firms. China's luxury segment is on the rise. In a single year, sales of locally produced luxury cars jumped 57 percent. General Motors has plans to make China the second largest Cadillac market. However, they will have to battle entrenched rivals, such as Audi, and more recent newcomers such as Toyota's Lexus. Diamonds are another growing market. Many young Chinese women have adopted the Western tradition of expecting a diamond ring from their fiancés.

Sources: Christina Passariello, "Style and Substance," *Wall Street Journal*, August 2, 2007, p. B1; Dexter Roberts, "Scrambling to Bring Crest to the Masses," *BusinessWeek*, June 25, 2007; Dexter Roberts, "Cadillac Floors It in China," *BusinessWeek*, June 3, 2007, p. 52; and James T. Areddy, "Spent Force," *Wall Street Journal*, May 2, 2006, p. A1.

humans. Buyer behavior is learned, primarily from the culture, and so it differs from one culture to another. Throughout this book many cultural differences in consumer behavior will be addressed.

To begin with, culture can directly affect product usage. For example, selling insurance in Muslim countries may prove more difficult because some religious leaders consider buying insurance gambling, which is prohibited under Islam. However, marketers of luxury goods find the Japanese to be excellent customers. Cramped living conditions in Japan combined with a heritage of aesthetic sensibility result in a desire for luxury designer items. A Japanese preoccupation with travel has helped promote a preference for foreign luxury brands in particular.[12]

All global marketers involved with product or packaging design should be aware of the impact of aesthetics on consumer purchasing decisions. One example of cross-cultural similarities and differences in this regard involves color preferences. A study of consumers in eight countries revealed that some universal color preferences do exist. Blue was either the first or the second favorite color in every country, and there was no difference in liking in respect to black, green, red, or white. However, there were differences in preferences for brown, gold, orange, purple, and yellow. Black and red signify happiness to the Chinese and are commonly chosen for wedding invitations. In India, Hindus consider orange the most sacred color. The color purple is associated with expensive products in Japan, China, and South Korea but with inexpensive products in the United States.[13]

The structure of the family and the roles assigned to each member also play an important part in determining what products are purchased and how the decision to purchase is made. Table 5.2 depicts the decision-making roles of husbands and wives in product purchases in five countries and suggests that there are similarities and differences across countries. Therefore, international marketers should be

TABLE 5.2	SUMMARY OF CROSS-CULTURE BUYING DECISION ACCORDING TO PURCHASE CATEGORIES & COUNTRY						

		DECISION MAKERS' PURCHASE CATEGORIES					
BUYING DECISION	COUNTRY	VACATION	FOOD	APPLIANCES	SAVINGS	FURNITURE	AUTO
		DECISION MAKERS					
What	Turkey	J	W	W	J	J	H
	Guatemala	J	W	W	J	J	H
	Vietnam	J	W	W	J	J	H
	United States	J	W	J	J	J	H
	Canada	J	W	W	J	J	H
When	Turkey	H	W	W	J	J	H
	Guatemala	H	W	W	J	J	H
	Vietnam	H	W	W	J	J	H
	United States	H	W	J	J	J	J
	Canada	H	W	J	J	J	J
Where	Turkey	J	W	W	J	J	H
	Guatemala	J	W	W	J	J	H
	Vietnam	J	W	W	J	J	H
	United States	J	W	J	J	J	H
	Canada	J	W	J	J	J	H
How	Turkey	J	W	J	J	J	H
	Guatemala	J	W	J	J	J	H
	Vietnam	J	W	J	J	J	H
	United States	J	W	J	J	J	J
	Canada	J	W	J	J	J	H

Key: J = Joint, W = Wife, H = Husband

Source: Talhar Harcar, John E. Spillan, and Orsay Kuchkemiroglo, "A Multi-National Study of Family Decision Making," *The Multinational Business Review* (13/2), 2007. p. 17.

aware that variations in family purchasing roles may exist in foreign markets as a result of social and cultural differences. Marketing strategy may need to change to take into account the respective roles of family members. In Saudi Arabia, house-wives primarily make decisions as to what packaged foods to buy even if a male servant or member of the family does the actual shopping.

Segmenting Markets

Once global marketers identify possible national markets to enter, they must remember that further **market segmentation** is important for three reasons:

- All residents of a country are not alike. Consequently, marketers cannot develop one marketing strategy that will adequately address the needs of everyone in a country. UPS discovered this when it surveyed Chinese consumers. Its

Market segmentation the aggregation of prospective buyers into groups (segments) that have common needs and will respond similarly to a particular marketing strategy

research concluded that China could not be viewed as a single market because Chinese consumers had "countless personal preferences."[14]

- You do not need every consumer in a country to buy your product in order to be successful in that market—you just need a large enough segment of the market to be willing and able to buy your product.
- How—and how much—you adapt your marketing mix (product, price, distribution, promotion) in a national market will depend on the segment you target in that market.

Most segmentation is done within a country. Should a Japanese cosmetics firm target French housewives or French working women? Should a U.S. soft-drink company develop a different marketing mix for Brazilian teens than the one it developed for Brazilian adults? Should a Bolivian furniture company enter the U.S. market by targeting the East Coast or the West Coast?

Segmenting by Region.   There are several reasons why global firms may decide to target a geographical region within a national market. In Chapter 3 we noted that some countries have multiple cultures that can vary by region. Certain regions may be richer or poorer than others. This can be particularly evident when comparing urban and rural populations in developing countries. Regions may even vary by their acceptance of foreign products. For many years Midwesterners in the United States resisted imported beer. Recently, imports have been making inroads there—but sales are still lower than along the coasts.[15] Some firms even choose to target by municipality: The Belgium beer Stella Artois entered the U.S. market by targeting key trend-setter cities.

Segmenting by Demographics.   Although we often think of culture as a geographic phenomenon, culture can vary to a certain degree by class and generation as well. Men and women are often socialized differently, resulting in certain cultural differences between the genders. Therefore, segmentation by demographics, such as income, gender, or age, is common domestically and useful in international markets as well. Often marketers segment by more than one demographic variable, such as age and gender. Table 5.3 presents a segmentation scheme for Chinese women of different ages. Targeting a market segment determined by the right combination of demographic considerations can result in an attractive marketing strategy. In India, young people, especially women, make up a small segment of the competitive automobile market. But with a growing middle class and rising salaries for young people, Suzuki has been successful in designing an attractive car for young, middle-class women—the Zen Estilo. It comes in eight fashion colors including purple fusion and virgin blue and sells for less than $8,000. When the car was first launched, consumers faced a six-week wait to purchase one in Mumbai.[16]

Segmenting by income is particularly salient in developing countries. Some companies target wealthy elites. A Dior phone, priced from $5,000, was created in response to the new luxury markets in China and Russia.[17] On the other hand, poorer segments are receiving increasing attention from global marketers. Cellphone giant Nokia claims a 66 percent market share in Africa, where sales are strong among poorer consumers.[18] As noted above, there has been increasing interest in lower-income markets in developing countries.[19] However, the definition of this segment varies. Definitions can range from consumers who make less than $6,000 a year to those who make $2 a day.[20] Therefore, marketers must be clear as to what income level they are actually envisaging when they target this segment.

TABLE 5.3	THREE FEMALE CONSUMER GROUPS IN MAINLAND CHINA		
	IDEOLOGUES	**TRADITIONALISTS**	**MODERNS**
	Born before or during the founding of New China (1949)	Born during the Cultural Revolution (1966-76)	Born after the open-door policy (1978)
	Focus: <ul><li>Communist philosophy</li><li>Democratic family system</li></ul>	*Focus:* <ul><li>Family-oriented</li><li>Confucianistic</li></ul>	*Focus:* <ul><li>Self-indulgent</li><li>Self-oriented</li></ul>
	Values: <ul><li>Serving country, promoting national welfare</li><li>Patriotic, societal, and instrumental</li><li>Devoted to community activities</li></ul>	*Values:* <ul><li>Devoted to traditional family values</li><li>Family responsibility</li><li>Belief in "face" and "reciprocity"</li><li>Concern with loyalty and harmony</li></ul>	*Values:* <ul><li>Social and economic independence</li><li>Materialism; modernism</li><li>Belief in Western ideas</li></ul>
	Consumer behavior: <ul><li>Active participation in environmental protection and political affairs; loyalty to indigenous and green products</li><li>Prefer local products to promote the nation's economy and employment</li></ul>	*Consumer behavior:* <ul><li>Influenced by family members and friends</li><li>Planned consumption</li><li>Aroused to buy by gift-giving situations</li><li>Concern with saving; price sensitivity</li></ul>	*Consumer behavior:* <ul><li>Concerned with self-giving</li><li>Favor beauty and health products</li><li>Overriding authority over allocation of household expenses</li><li>Favor foreign brands</li><li>Brand and quality key factors in purchase decisions</li><li>Less time to shop</li><li>Impulse buying</li><li>Get information through reading</li></ul>
	Marketing strategies: <ul><li>Promote national loyalty by forming JVs with local companies to localize product image</li><li>Get support from socially respected individuals or government figures</li><li>Promotion should emphasize societal rather than individual values</li></ul>	*Marketing strategies:* <ul><li>Emphasize family values</li><li>Promote occasions or events to stimulate gift buying</li><li>Promote sales through discounts and coupons</li><li>Encourage repeat buying by promoting brand loyalty</li><li>Design ads with light-hearted, humorous themes</li></ul>	*Marketing strategies* <ul><li>Create brand names for quick reference</li><li>Make buying and consumption more convenient</li><li>Design sales effort to stimulate impulse buying</li><li>Consider using in-store stimuli (attractive packaging, point-of-purchase)</li><li>Use magazine and direct-mail ads</li></ul>

Source: Lee, Jenny (S.Y.) et al., "Changing Roles and Values of Female Consumers in China," May–June 2004, p. 18. Copyright © 2004, with permission from Elsevier.

Choosing between rich and poor is not always necessary. Many companies target both richer and poorer segments in the same market, adapting their marketing strategies accordingly. L'Oréal sells its global brand Excellence Cream hair color in India for $11 a bottle. It has also introduced another hair dye priced below $3 targeted at the lower-income Indian consumer.[21] Similarly, Wal-Mart in Mexico targets different income segments with different store chains. Its flagship Wal-Mart Supercenter chain targets Mexicans ranging from the lower middle class to the elite, whereas its Sam's Club chain targets the upper middle class and elites only, and its Bodega Aurrera chain targets lower-income Mexicans.[22]

© Diego Azubel/epa/Corbis

Cosmopolitan teenagers in China participate in a costume play that originated in Japan but has grown in popularity with youth worldwide. The cosmopolitan phenomenon has motivated some global marketers to target global segments.

Segmenting by World View. Within any country there may be segments that are more open to the idea of buying foreign products as well as possessing the means to do so. Certain segments within a national market may be inclined to purchase global brands because they enhance their self-image of being cosmopolitan, sophisticated, and modern.[23] Such **cosmopolitans** arguably make easier targets for global marketers. Cosmopolitans have often been associated with younger, urban consumers. Urban populations in emerging markets have long been thought to be more accessible (physically and psychologically) than rural populations. Furthermore, they tend to be richer. Economists at the World Bank were startled to discover that the average family of four living in Hanoi spent the equivalent of $20,000 when calculated as purchasing-power parity—even though Vietnam is considered one of the poorest countries in the world.[24] Table 5.4 depicts the urban-rural distribution of population across selected countries.

> Cosmopolitans consumers who purchase global brands to enhance their self-image of being sophisticated and modern

Global Segments. The cosmopolitan phenomenon has motivated some global marketers to think in terms of **global segments**, transnational consumer segments based on age, social class, and lifestyle rather than on national culture. For example, social class is a grouping of consumers based on income, education, and occupation. Within a culture, consumers in the same social class tend to have similar purchase patterns. Even across cultures this may be the case, especially among young, affluent professionals. A study of young consumers with college educations living in Romania, Ukraine, Russia, and the United States revealed that these consumers possessed a strong preference for global brands.[25] A study of MBA students representing 38 nationalities revealed cross-cultural similarities in how these students evaluated product quality. The students were young, affluent, mobile, well educated, and fluent in English. Across nationalities and cultural groups, all rated brand names the highest as a cue to product quality. Similarly, all rated retailer reputation

> Global segments transnational consumer segments based on lifestyle or demographics such as age and social class rather than on nationality

TABLE 5.4 URBAN/RURAL POPULATION DISTRIBUTION (%)

COUNTRY	URBAN	RURAL	COUNTRY	URBAN	RURAL
Afghanistan	24	76	India	29	71
Bermuda	100	0	Japan	66	34
Bolivia	66	34	Mexico	77	23
Brazil	83	17	Nigeria	48	52
Burundi	10	90	Poland	61	39
Chile	86	14	Russian Federation	73	27
China	43	57	Saudi Arabia	82	18
Egypt	43	57	Singapore	100	0
France	77	23	South Korea	80	20
Germany	74	26	Turkey	69	31
Greece	61	39	United States	82	18

Source: Adapted from *Indicator of Human Settlements*, December 2008, Population Division of the United Nations Secretariat. © United Nations, 2008. Reproduced with permission.

the lowest and placed price between the other two cues. The importance of physical appearance of the product did vary some among cultures, however.[26] As this study shows, some—but not all—aspects of buyer behavior may converge across cultures when examining a transnational segment.

Technological changes in telecommunications have brought different nationalities in contact with one another—sometimes on a daily basis. Blogs, instant messaging, smartphones, and social networking sites, such as YouTube, allow young people to share ideas and can drive demand for fashion, food, consumer electronics, and entertainment.[27] However, for most products and segmentation schemes, persistent national differences continue to limit the usefulness of global segmentation.

Just-Like-Us Segmentation. Of course, some marketers simply decide that they will position their product in international markets exactly as it is positioned in the home market. Such a strategy appears easy. Marketers simply sell their product to anyone overseas who wants to buy it as is. They bet on attracting customers in foreign markets who are similar to those they already serve domestically.

Mobile consumers consumers who are aware of and purchase foreign products because of exposure to foreign markets from overseas work, study, or travel

One factor that supports a just-like-us strategy is the increase in world migration that has resulted in **mobile consumers**. While overseas, these mobile consumers can be good target markets for products from their homelands. When they return to their homelands, they can be good target markets for products from former host countries. Market researchers note that Central American consumers are faithful purchasers of American products. A large percentage of the population of Central America has lived in the United States at one time, thus increasing their familiarity with American brands.[28] Emigration from India has also spurred the international sales of Indian motion pictures. The hit Bollywood musical *Main Hoon Na* grossed $2.5 million in North America and the U.K. just ten days after its release.[29]

Nonetheless, there are dangers to relying on just-like-us segments. For example, the just-like-us strategy has sometimes been employed by producers of high-end luxury goods under the assumption that luxury buyers are relatively similar across national markets. However, regional differences can arise even among luxury buyers. Lexus sedans went from zero to luxury-class market leader in the United States in a ten-year period, but sales remained stymied in Europe. Europeans associated luxury with brand heritage and attention to detail, whereas Americans focused on comfort, size, and dependability. The biggest selling point of the Lexus in the U.S. market was its reliability; it didn't break down. For Europeans, that just wasn't enough from a luxury car.[30]

Furthermore, targeting the **just-like-us segment** overseas is likely to result in sales to fewer consumers worldwide and limits a firm's global profit potential. In addition, such a strategy blinds marketers to unique national opportunities. For example, toy stores in China discovered that some of their biggest buyers were adults shopping for themselves. The same proved true for comic books. For some adults it was an excuse to enjoy a childhood they missed first time around when China was much poorer and consumer products were practically nonexistent in the marketplace. For others, it was a way to escape and relax in the very competitive climate of reform-era China.[31] If toy manufacturers simply targeted children like they would in most countries, they could miss the adult-market opportunity in China.

Just-like-us segments market segments in foreign countries that closely resemble marketers' domestic buyers

BUSINESS MARKETS

It is commonly said that business buyers around the world are much more predictable and similar than consumers in their purchasing behavior. They are thought to be more influenced by the economic considerations of cost and product performance and less affected by social and cultural factors. After all, purchasing agents in Japan who are buying specialty steel for their companies will attempt to get the best possible products at the lowest cost, which is similar to how purchasing agents in the United States or Germany would act.

In fact, business-to-business marketing in the global arena is considerably influenced by variations across cultures. Take, for instance, the offer of a personal gift to a prospective buyer. In Latin America, Europe, and the Arab world, offering a gift at first meeting is usually considered inappropriate and may even be construed as a bribe. However, small gifts are often given at first meetings in Japan. In China a carefully chosen gift is interpreted as a sign that the giver values a business relationship.[32]

A number of cross-cultural differences can be observed in buyer motivation and behavior. Because business markets often encompass longer-term relationships between customer and supplier, cultural attitudes toward social relationships are especially important. Sales are often subject to negotiations, and negotiating encompasses many aspects of culture. In addition to dealing with cross-cultural differences, international marketers increasingly find themselves selling to multinational firms, whose buyer behavior presents its own set of challenges.

The Business Buyer's Needs

Cost-performance criterion the expected performance of industrial products or capital equipment relative to the costs to purchase and use such products or equipment

Industrial products, such as machinery, intermediate goods, and raw materials, are sold to businesses for use in a manufacturing process to produce other goods. If the objective of the manufacturer is to maximize profits, the critical buying criterion will reflect the performance of the product purchased relative to its cost. This **cost–performance criterion** is a key consideration for industrial buyers, along with such other buying criteria as the service and dependability of the selling company.

Headquartered in
St. Louis, Missouri,
Emerson has 250
manufacturing sites
worldwide. It is one
of many business-
to-business marketers
with a global presence.

Similar considerations arise in other business-to-business sales transactions. A study of how international companies chose foreign exchange suppliers revealed that price was an important factor in both the selection of a supplier and the volume of business allotted to a supplier. Also, large suppliers were generally preferred over smaller suppliers. Nonetheless, account management and service quality could outweigh price, and customers favored suppliers from their home markets.[33]

Because the cost–performance criterion is often critical, the economic situation in the purchasing country affects the decision process. This is particularly true for the purchase of new machinery. When buying machinery, a firm must weigh the advantages of adopting a capital-intensive technology against those of adopting a labor-intensive technology. Labor costs play a key role in this decision. Countries with a surplus of labor normally have lower labor costs because supply exceeds demand. These lower pay rates weigh heavily in favor of a labor-intensive method of manufacture. Therefore, these countries will be less apt to purchase sophisticated automatic machinery; the same job can be done with the cheaper labor.

Wage levels vary from country to country. Selling an industrial robot that replaces three workers in the manufacture of a product can be more easily justified in Norway or Germany, where average labor costs are 20 percent more than in the United States, than in Britain, where labor costs are less than 80 percent of the U.S. labor rate. Developed countries with a high labor rate are prime targets for automated manufacturing equipment. Companies that want to export to developing countries where labor is cheaper must be aware that labor-saving measures may not be appreciated or readily applied. For example, the Chinese government encourages the import of labor-intensive technology that can effectively employ its vast population.

Of course, there are exceptions to this rule. When international banks expanded into the Arab Gulf, they were faced with a decision concerning the level of technology for teller services. In other developing countries, the banks employed older, labor- and paper-intensive technology. However, labor in the Gulf was scarce and expensive as a consequence of the region's sudden oil wealth and its small population. In light of this, many banks chose to purchase the latest technology available from the United States.

The newly industrialized countries of Asia, such as South Korea, Taiwan, and Singapore, are becoming increasingly important markets for industrial products. For example, during the 1990s, Asia-Pacific overtook both North America and Europe as the major market for new elevator sales. Still, some differences can be observed in buyer needs and wants in these markets. Business buyers look for long-term commitment from their suppliers. They expect to see foreign firms adapt products to local needs and commit themselves to frequent contact with the buyer. A global competitor should expect to keep a well-stocked warehouse and to locate a technical staff and sales office in the local market. Because many of the industrial buyers in this region are medium-sized firms, they might expect more regular training to be provided over the life of the business relationship. Price can be a critical factor in the sales as well, because many of these businesses work on tight margins. Similarly, special product features that might appeal to buyers in more industrially developed markets are less important in these markets.[34]

Developing Business Relationships

Business-to-business sales usually involve ongoing relationships. The seller and buyer communicate more directly and establish a relationship that continues over time. For example, sales may involve the design and delivery of customized products, or after-sale service may be an important component of the product. These business relationships are based on mutual understanding, past experiences, and expectations for the future.

Building such a relationship involves a social exchange process. One firm (usually, but not always, the supplier) takes the initiative and suggests that the two firms do business. If the other firm responds, commitments gradually are made. The parties determine how to coordinate their activities, trust is established, and a commitment to a continued relationship arises. The firms may become increasingly interdependent, such as by agreeing to develop a new product together.[35] Because of this close working relationship, cultural sensitivity will be necessary in cases in which seller and buyer come from different cultures.

Although these business relationships have an overall informal character, specific transactions, many of which can be unique to the relationship, will need to be formalized. Because of this, negotiations are often involved in business-to-business sales. Negotiations encompass not only specifics concerning price and financing terms but also such issues as product design, training, and after-sale service.

Cross-cultural negotiations are a particular challenge to global marketers. To begin with, marketers may face the translation problems that we discussed in Chapter 3. Furthermore, whereas some cultures enter negotiations with a win-win attitude, other cultures envisage negotiations as a zero-sum game wherein one side is pitted against the other. Americans can be especially nonplused when they find themselves negotiating with Russians. Russian negotiators often begin with unreasonable requests in order to test their American counterparts and see how tough they really are. Russian negotiators can surprise Americans with emotional outbursts and anti-Western tirades. Russians also take advantage of Americans' sense of urgency and desire to use time effectively. They may ask the same question repeatedly, feign boredom, and even appear to fall asleep during negotiations![36]

Perhaps some of the toughest cross-cultural negotiations took place after China reopened to world trade. Many foreign firms were interested in the potential of the Chinese market. Americans wanted to negotiate clear, legal contracts with Chinese clients and partners. The Chinese, on the other hand, interpreted this approach as betraying a lack of trust on the part of Americans. They sought to establish close relationships with foreign firms based on mutual loyalty. To them a contract was far less important than these relationships. For their part, Americans found the Chinese as irreverent of time as the Russians. Unlike the Russians, the Chinese appeared passive in their demeanor. Any display of anger, frustration, or aggression on the part of American negotiators was likely to backfire, and mock tantrums were definitely taboo.[37] Furthermore, many Chinese would appear at the negotiating table, and American negotiators found it difficult to figure out who had real authority to agree to terms. Cross-cultural negotiations frustrated many Americans and discouraged, or at least delayed, their entry into this huge market. In the meantime, competitors from Japan and Asia's overseas Chinese community found the negotiations less culturally harrowing. As a result, many entered the Chinese market more rapidly.

Because negotiations involve many aspects of culture—social relationships, attitudes toward power, perceptions of time, and of course language—they must be undertaken with the greatest cultural sensitivity. In most business-to-business sales, negotiations do not end with the first purchase decision. They permeate the continuing relationship between global marketer and buyer. For this reason, global marketers must never assume that marketing industrial products or services remains the same worldwide.

Marketing to Global Buyers

Global buyers present marketers with new challenges. There are two kinds of global buyers: national global buyers and multinational global buyers.[38] **National global buyers** search the world for products that are used in a single country or market. Their job has been far easier since the introduction of the Internet. **Multinational global buyers** similarly search the world for products but use those products throughout their global operations. Such buyers are commonly multinational firms, but they also include organizations such as the World Health Organization. Because both national and multinational global buyers are relatively sophisticated about suppliers and prices, competition for their business tends to be intense.

National global buyers firms that search the world for products that are used in a single country or market

Multinational global buyers firms that search the world for products to be used throughout their global operations

Multinational global buyers in particular may represent large accounts. They use their market power to command better service and even lower prices. Finding cost-effective inputs is increasingly crucial for most multinational firms, because they too are often under pressure to deliver good products at a low price. Centralized purchasing is one way in which multinational corporations attempt to keep costs down. For example, General Motors and three Japanese automakers—Fuji Heavy Industries, Isuzu Motors, and Suzuki Motor—announced that they had unified their purchasing organizations for selected parts, components, and services in order to reduce costs. GM holds equity stakes in the three Japanese firms.[39]

Many Fortune 500 companies have recognized this strategic importance of purchasing and have elevated purchasing managers to the vice-president level within their organizations. Firms that sell to multinational global buyers often give them special attention. Practicing what is called **global account management**, they assign special account executives and service teams to these valuable but demanding global buyers. We will discuss this further in Chapter 14.

Global account management the assignment of special account executives and service teams to handle the needs of valuable but demanding global buyers

GOVERNMENT MARKETS

A large number of international business transactions involve governments. For example, 80 percent of all international trade in agricultural products is handled by governments. The U.S. government buys more goods and services than any other government, business, industry, or organization in the world.[40] Selling to governments can be both time-consuming and frustrating. However, governments are large purchasers, and selling to them can yield enormous returns.

The size of government purchases depends on the economic or political orientation of the country. In highly developed, free-market countries, the government plays less of a role than in other markets. The amount of government purchases is also a function of state-owned operations. For example, in the United States the only government-owned operation is the postal system, whereas in India the government owns not only the postal system but also much of the telecommunications, electric, gas, oil, coal, railway, airline, and shipbuilding industries.

The Buying Process

Governmental buying processes tend to be highly bureaucratic. To sell to the U.S. Department of Defense, for example, a firm has to get on a bidding list for each branch of the armed forces. These bidding lists are issued on an annual basis. A firm that is unable to get on the list must wait a full year to try again. Similarly, negotiating with other governments can be a very long and formal process. The World Trade Organization has attempted to make government contracts more transparent and open to foreign bidders. However, only 28 countries are signatories to this agreement, and the agreement only covers larger government contracts.

As we saw in Chapter 4, governments pursue several different agendas, which often complicate government purchasing. For example, a government might wish to promote its local industry as well as decrease its trade deficit. For these reasons, governments often discriminate against foreign suppliers and give preference to local suppliers. In some sophisticated industries such as aerospace, there may be no viable local competitor in many countries. Then the government might ask potential foreign suppliers to subcontract simpler project inputs to local firms. Alternatively, Saudi Arabia asks major foreign government contractors to invest some of their profits in local Saudi industries.

Fluor Corporation is one of the world's largest engineering, procurement, and construction organizations. It maintains offices in 25 countries across six continents. Fluor markets to governments as well as to businesses.

Global marketers pursuing government sales in high-tech fields may also run afoul of the national agendas of their home countries. The threat of compromising national security has prompted governments, especially that of the United States, to institute restrictions on the overseas sale of certain technologies, such as nuclear plants, computers, telecommunications, and military weapons.

Government procurement processes vary from country to country. Here are some strategies global firms might have to consider when bidding on government contracts overseas:

- **Source the proposed project with local manufacturing.** As noted above, many countries such as Russia and the United Arab Emirates still give preference to local suppliers if other things are equal. Governments rarely expect all sourcing to be local, but they can require or prefer that some is. Multinational contractors do not have to establish their own manufacturing facilities in-country if there are competent local suppliers from which to source.
- **Partner with a respected local firm or individual.** Even when local agents are not required to bid on a government contract, an esteemed local business partner may help a foreign firm maneuver through the local bureaucracy.
- **Commit to training locals.** Companies may be favored if they will employ and train local citizens.
- **Be flexible as to pricing.** Governments often appreciate favorable financing terms. Countertrade arrangements, in which a foreign supplier agrees to take partial payment in local goods or services, may be required for some contracts.
- **Use the appropriate language.** Although English is sometimes acceptable in bids, the local language may be required or preferred.
- **Be patient.** Many different decision makers may be involved in granting a government contract. This can slow the process.

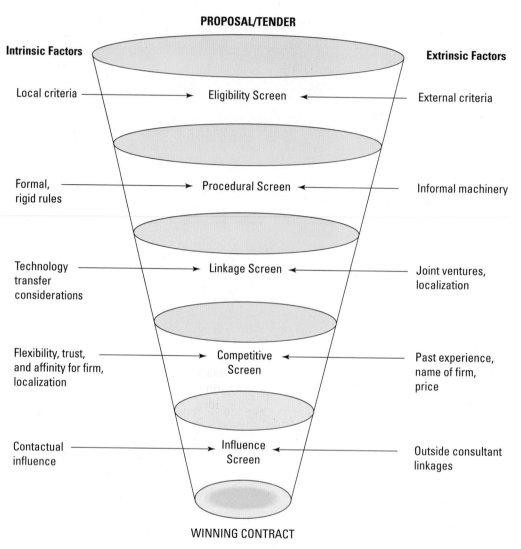

FIGURE 5.1
Marketing to Governments in Developing Countries

PROPOSAL/TENDER

Intrinsic Factors

Extrinsic Factors

Local criteria → Eligibility Screen ← External criteria

Formal, rigid rules → Procedural Screen ← Informal machinery

Technology transfer considerations → Linkage Screen ← Joint ventures, localization

Flexibility, trust, and affinity for firm, localization → Competitive Screen ← Past experience, name of firm, price

Contactual influence → Influence Screen ← Outside consultant linkages

WINNING CONTRACT

Source: Mushtaq Luqman, Ghazi M. Habib, and Sami Kassem, "Marketing to LDC Governments," *International Marketing Review* 5, no. 1 (Spring 1988), p. 59.

Government Contracts in Developing Countries

While the procedure for winning a major government contract can be lengthy, it can be particularly so in developing countries. Figure 5.1 depicts the various "screens" that global marketers must pass through to secure large government contracts in developing countries.[41] A foreign firm must first address the **eligibility screen**. To make the bidding process efficient and manageable, governments seek to weed out firms that are not serious or are too small to handle the contract. For example, Saudi Arabia may ask bidders on a contract to submit a $100,000 fee with their bid or to provide a bond for 1 percent of the tender value, and the Malaysian government expects top management to be actively involved in the process as a sign of the firm's long-term commitment to the market.[42] Alternatively, governments may simply restrict the bidding to several well-known international firms

Eligibility screen the initial requirement placed by governments on firms seeking to bid on government contracts in developing countries; firms must be judged to be serious in their intent and large enough to handle the contracts that are invited to bid on a particular project. This approach is common in the defense and civil aviation industries.

If the project is complicated or represents a new task for the purchasing government, outside consultants may be employed to design the project and oversee its implementation. For example, Bechtel, a large U.S. engineering firm, could be hired as a consultant for complex construction projects. As a result, Bechtel's designs are more likely to follow U.S. industry standards, and this gives U.S. firms a competitive advantage when bidding on the contract.

Political considerations can play a role at this stage as well. For example, China is now the world's largest arms importer, ahead of India, Turkey, Taiwan, and Saudi Arabia. Ninety percent of Chinese arms imports are from Russia.[43] Russian armament firms are considered to be more reliable than American ones. U.S. firms could at any time be forbidden by the U.S. government to enter into or fulfill a contract with China.

After passing the eligibility screen, the foreign firm encounters the **procedural screen**. At this point, numerous bureaucratic procedures must be followed and numerous forms properly filled out. This can be all the more difficult because the process may not be overt. In Mexico bids may be disqualified if they fail to address minute technical details.[44] It is suggested that firms seeking government contracts in Brazil be patient, establish significant in-country presence, and budget considerable financial resources in order to respond to legal challenges and bureaucratic delays.[45] The firm may need to take special care to discover who is actually in charge and to understand exactly what needs to be done. Laws and procedures can and often do change. Hiring local consultants who have had experience with the process is often a good idea.

The firm must then negotiate the **linkage screen**. It must address and implement the various government requirements related to assisting local businesses. This can include finding a local partner with whom to establish a joint venture. Alternatively, it might involve finding local suppliers to outsource a portion of the contract. For example, Abu Dhabi and Dubai, two oil-rich Arab Gulf emirates, have asked Airbus and Boeing for commitments to outsource some of parts production to the Arab Gulf in return for billions of dollars worth of jetliner sales.[46]

After passing through these three screens, the firm must still face the **competitive screen**. Passing this screen involves bidding a competitive price. In most cases, competitive bids will be determined not only by the profit each firm seeks to capture but the different product-service offerings proposed by each competitor. In some cases, governments will pay more for higher quality and elite features. In other cases, governments may focus more on low price. For example, the U.S. Commercial Service alerts U.S. firms that the Egyptian government may not always want the best quality products or services because superior features suggest too high a price.[47] In addition to price, the firm's reputation, its past experience in developing countries, and its cultural sensitivity are also important. Because large projects can take several years to negotiate and many years to implement, the firm must exhibit an ability to be flexible as situations evolve and change.

Firms may even be asked to help finance the project they bid on. A good example of how governments seek creative financing from firms involves India's highway improvement plans. The World Bank estimates that India's annual highway spending will soon quadruple to $4 billion a year, making India very attractive to international road-building firms. But how India will finance road construction remains uncertain. One Indian state sought builders that would agree to operate the roads as private concerns before turning them over to the

Procedural screen a requirement that firms bidding on government contracts in developing countries follow numerous bureaucratic procedures

Linkage screen a common requirement that international firms bidding on government contracts in developing countries identify ways in which specific local businesses will participate in or otherwise benefit by the proposed contracts

Competitive screen a requirement that firms bidding on government contracts in developing countries be competitive in experience, reputation, and cultural sensitivity as well as in price

state. In lieu of direct payment from the government, the builders could collect tolls for ten years.[48]

The final hurdle, the **influence screen**, requires a firm to identify the ultimate decision makers and to be sure it meets their needs. For example, selling radar to the Taiwanese may involve high officers in the air force who are pursuing a defense agenda. However, the ministry of industry may be involved as well. It may be pursuing an agenda of technology transfer and local outsourcing. The firm must be sure to address all these concerns. Managing this process is challenging for global marketers, but winning a large and attractive contract can make it all worthwhile.

Influence screen a requirement that firms bidding on government contracts in developing countries identify key decision makers and assure their proposals meet the needs of all parties

Bribery and Government Markets

Bribery is the giving of something of value to an individual in a position of trust to influence their judgment or behavior. Bribes can be offered to purchasing agents or other decision makers within companies to induce them to favor one supplier over another. Most bribery scandals in international marketing, however, involve government contracts. Government employees are in a particular position of trust because they are hired to work for the public good. If a government is awarding an aerospace contract, the government employees responsible for choosing the supplier should consider the value of the supplier to the country as a whole. If a key decision maker influences the decision for his or her personal gain, then public trust is betrayed. Bribes offered to win contracts are most common in industries where contracts are large and where few public employees are involved in the award decision.

Bribery giving something of value to an individual in a position of trust to influence his or her judgment or behavior

Bribery is more endemic in less developed countries. A recent study confirmed that a country's GNP per capita is the best barometer of the level of government bribery (corruption) in that country. The same study also showed that bribery is more prevalent in countries that score higher on the Hofstede power-distance dimension.[49] Table 5.5 lists ratings by country on an index of perceived corruption.

TABLE 5.5 CORRUPTION PERCEPTIONS INDEX (CPI)

COUNTRY RANK	COUNTRY	CPI SCORE[a]	COUNTRY RANK	COUNTRY	CPI SCORE[a]	COUNTRY RANK	COUNTRY	CPI SCORE[a]
1	Denmark	9.3	14	Germany	7.9	27	Estonia	6.6
1	Sweden	9.3	14	Norway	7.9	28	Spain	6.5
1	New Zealand	9.3	16	Ireland	7.7	28	Qatar	6.5
4	Singapore	9.2	16	United Kingdom	7.7	28	Saint Vincent	6.5
5	Finland	9.0	18	United States	7.3	31	Cyprus	6.4
5	Switzerland	9.0	18	Japan	7.3	32	Portugal	6.1
7	Iceland	8.9	18	Belgium	7.3	33	Israel	6.0
7	Netherlands	8.9	21	Saint Lucia	7.2	33	Dominica	6.0
9	Australia	8.7	22	Barbados	7.0	35	UAE	5.9
9	Canada	8.7	23	France	6.9	36	Botswana	5.8
11	Luxembourg	8.3	23	Chile	6.9	36	Puerto Rico	5.8
12	Austria	8.1	23	Uruguay	6.9	36	Malta	5.8
12	Hong Kong	8.1	26	Slovenia	6.7	39	Taiwan	5.7

continued

Table 5.5 continued

COUNTRY RANK	COUNTRY	CPI SCORE[a]	COUNTRY RANK	COUNTRY	CPI SCORE[a]	COUNTRY RANK	COUNTRY	CPI SCORE[a]
40	South Korea	5.6	72	Swaziland	3.6	115	Maldives	2.8
41	Mauritius	5.5	80	Burkina Faso	3.5	115	Niger	2.8
41	Oman	5.5	80	Brazil	3.5	115	Malawi	2.8
43	Macao	5.4	80	Saudi Arabia	3.5	115	Zambia	2.8
43	Bahrain	5.4	80	Thailand	3.5	115	Egypt	2.8
45	Bhutan	5.2	80	Morocco	3.5	121	Togo	2.7
45	Czech Republic	5.2	85	Senegal	3.4	121	Vietnam	2.7
47	Malaysia	5.1	85	Panama	3.4	121	Nigeria	2.7
47	Costa Rica	5.1	85	Serbia	3.4	121	Sao Tome	2.7
47	Hungary	5.1	85	Montenegro	3.4	121	Nepal	2.7
47	Jordan	5.1	85	Madagascar	3.4	126	Indonesia	2.6
47	Cape Verde	5.1	85	Albania	3.4	126	Honduras	2.6
52	Slovakia	5.0	85	India	3.4	126	Ethiopia	2.6
52	Latvia	5.0	92	Algeria	3.2	126	Uganda	2.6
54	South Africa	4.9	92	Bosnia	3.2	126	Guyana	2.6
55	Seychelles	4.8	92	Sri Lanka	3.2	126	Libya	2.6
55	Italy	4.8	92	Lesotho	3.2	126	Eritrea	2.6
57	Greece	4.7	96	Gabon	3.1	126	Mozambique	2.6
58	Turkey	4.6	96	Mali	3.1	134	Nicaragua	2.5
58	Lithuania	4.6	96	Jamaica	3.1	134	Pakistan	2.5
58	Poland	4.6	96	Guatemala	3.1	134	Comoros	2.5
61	Namibia	4.5	96	Benin	3.1	134	Ukraine	2.5
62	Samoa	4.4	96	Kiribati	3.1	138	Paraguay	2.4
62	Croatia	4.4	102	Tanzania	3.0	138	Liberia	2.4
62	Tunisia	4.4	102	Lebanon	3.0	138	Tonga	2.4
65	Kuwait	4.3	102	Rwanda	3.0	141	Yemen	2.3
65	Cuba	4.3	102	Dominican Republic	3.0	141	Cameroon	2.3
67	El Salvador	3.9	102	Bolivia	3.0	141	Iran	2.3
70	Romania	3.8	102	Djibouti	3.0	141	Philippines	2.3
70	Colombia	3.8	102	Mongolia	3.0	145	Kazakhstan	2.2
72	Bulgaria	3.6	109	Armenia	2.9	145	Timor-Leste	2.2
72	FYR Macedonia	3.6	109	Belize	2.9	147	Syria	2.1
72	Peru	3.6	109	Argentina	2.9	147	Bangladesh	2.1
72	Mexico	3.6	109	Vanuatu	2.9	147	Russia	2.1
72	China	3.6	109	Solomon Islands	2.9	147	Kenya	2.1
72	Suriname	3.6	109	Moldova	2.9	151	Laos	2.0
72	Trinidad	3.6	115	Mauritania	2.8	151	Ecuador	2.0

[a]10 = highly clean and 0 = highly corrupt.

Source: 2008 Transparency International, http://www.transparency.org.

Although most developing countries seek foreign investment for economic growth, several studies have found that governmental corruption is a serious obstacle to foreign investment in a country. The difference in corruption levels between host and home countries affects investment as well: Corruption significantly reduces investment from less corrupt countries.[50] Another study found that foreign entrants into national markets chose joint ventures more often than wholly owned subsidiaries as the level of corruption increased.[51]

U.S. Foreign Corrupt Practices Act.   Virtually all countries outlaw the bribing of their own government officials. In the late 1970s, the United States went a step further and outlawed the bribing of foreign officials. Until then, American firms that bribed foreign officials were not prosecuted under U.S. law, even though U.S. law disallowed claiming foreign bribes as tax deductions. This resulted in many multinationals keeping records of these bribes for their tax accountants. When government investigators were searching for illegal contributions to President Nixon's reelection fund, they discovered many such entries in company books.

The American public was dismayed. Despite heavy business lobbying against its passage, the U.S. Foreign Corrupt Practices Act (FCPA) was passed in 1977. This law forbids U.S. citizens to bribe foreign government employees and politicians. U.S. citizens are also forbidden to pay money to agents or other individuals who in turn pass money on to government employees. In short, American companies are held accountable for agents that bribe. Titan Corporation paid a record $28.5 million in fines for failing to properly supervise and control 120 agents working in 60 countries.[52] In addition, U.S. citizens are required to report any bribery occurring within their organizations and must not cover it up. The firm itself is required to keep good records. If audited, it must be able to account for all payments overseas. Fines are assessed for noncompliance.

Most important, perhaps, managers involved face jail sentences. A former chairman of Kellogg, Brown & Root received a seven-year prison sentence, the longest to date.[53]Although originally envisaged as a deterrent to U.S. citizens, the U.S. FCPA has been increasingly interpreted in such a way as to prosecute non-U.S. citizens as well. For example, a Swiss lawyer was indicted in the United States for conspiring to bribe foreign officials in connection with a failed $450 million Caspian Sea oil deal. The lawyer was charged with one count of conspiracy to violate the U.S. FCPA.[54]

Expediting payments small bribes paid to civil servants to perform their duties in a timely manner

U.S. firms are allowed to make expediting payments, however. **Expediting payments** are small sums paid to civil servants to do their jobs. For example, if office computers were sitting at customs and not being processed, an expediting payment might speed up the paperwork. Two multinational companies, Unilever and BP Amoco, admitted in parliamentary hearings in London that their managers did make facilitating payments in developing countries. The counsel for Unilever said that although these payments were not encouraged, they were tolerated as long as they were small and were used to expedite something that would have happened eventually anyway. The general auditor of BP Amoco said the payments were made to avoid delays and not to gain an unfair advantage over competitors.[55] However, some firms have refused to participate in facilitating payments. Procter & Gamble refused to do so when entering Brazil, despite the prevalence of such payments there. One P&G manager recalls that government employees soon learned not even to ask the firm for such payments.

Many U.S. businesses feared that the U.S. FCPA would put them at a competitive disadvantage overseas, especially in emerging markets, because other

WORLD BEAT 5.2

CLEANING UP RUSSIA

GOVERNMENT CORRUPTION presents a major impediment to doing business in Russia. An estimated 9 percent of Russia's procurement budget is lost to corrupt practices, and as high as US$30 billion a year finds its way into the pockets of corrupt officials.

Such corruption has had a negative impact on both foreign and local investment in the country. To alleviate the situation, President Vladimir Putin spearheaded reforms such as increasing judges' low salaries fivefold to counter courtroom bribes. A new law also bans the intervention of state prosecutors in private litigation between contending business parties, and new rules sharply restrict the discounts that railroad regulators can offer shippers. These discounts often rewarded customers who paid the biggest bribes. Another law reduced the number of business activities that required a license from 2,000 to 100. Fewer licenses reduce the opportunity for a bureaucrat to receive a bribe. The need to receive—and pay for—official signatures has stifled the creation of new businesses.

Yet five years into Putin's cleanup, most Russians remained pessimistic about the government's ability to curb corruption. Only 15 percent of respondents in a poll administered by Gallup International expected that conditions would improve soon. Forty percent expected conditions to remain the same, and 45 percent believed corruption in Russia would only get worse.

Sources: "Vicious Circle of Corruption," WPS Russian Media Monitoring Agency, December 7, 2007; Natalia Leshchenko, "Watchdog Names Scale of Corruption in Russia's Public Procurement," Global Insight Daily Analysis, December 12, 2007; and Paul Starobin and Catherine Belton, "Cleanup Time," *BusinessWeek*, January 14, 2002, pp. 46–47.

competitor nations had not adopted a similar law. The law no doubt has been a handicap in some cases, but overall it does not appear to have undermined U.S. exports to bribe-prone countries. The law may have helped U.S. managers in one respect: It has kept them out of jail overseas. A study of bribery scandals in the Middle East over a period of nearly 20 years revealed no American having been imprisoned for bribing a government official. This was in contrast to the experiences of Asians and Europeans.[56]

Check out the student companion website for the latest country corruption scores (http://www.cengage.com/international).

Other Antibribery Conventions. In 1997, 34 nations signed an antibribery pact. These included the 29 members of the Organisation for Economic Co-operation and Development (OECD), as well as Argentina, Brazil, Chile, Bulgaria, and Slovakia. Under the agreement, the member countries agreed to propose to their parliaments national laws designed to combat overseas bribery.[57] Similarly, the United Nations Convention Against Corruption was signed in December 2003. Signatories include the United States, Russia, China, Japan, and much of Europe. National governments must still ratify the law and put in place regulations to support it. The convention aims at encouraging the recovery of funds moved overseas by corrupt officials and was prompted by developing countries anxious to recover such funds.[58]

Which buyers will you target? Continue with your Country Market Report on the companion website (http://www.cengage.com/international).

The efficacy of these multilateral agreements has been controversial. Germany embarked on a number of overseas bribery investigations of its multinationals, including one of engineering conglomerate Siemens AG, after years of allowing German companies to write off international bribes as expenses. However, watchdog organization Transparency International published a report concluding that only one-third of OECD member states had taken significant action to enforce antibribery laws. It identified Britain, Canada, Italy, Japan, and the Netherlands as falling particularly short.[59] Some non-U.S. executives have complained that they are now targeted in FCPA investigations because Washington believes that their home countries are not seriously combating corruption despite the new antibribery conventions.[60]

TABLE 5.6 — BRIBE PAYERS INDEX

RANK	COUNTRY	SCORE[a]	RANK	COUNTRY	SCORE[a]
1	Belgium	8.8	12	Spain	7.9
1	Canada	8.8	13	Hong Kong	7.6
3	Netherlands	8.7	14	South Africa	7.5
3	Switzerland	8.7	14	South Korea	7.5
5	Germany	8.6	14	Taiwan	7.5
5	Japan	8.6	17	Brazil	7.4
5	United Kingdom	8.6	17	Italy	7.4
8	Australia	8.5	19	India	6.8
9	France	8.1	20	Mexico	6.6
9	Singapore	8.1	21	China	6.5
9	United States	8.1			

[a]0 = very high level of bribery; 10 = negligible bribery.

Source: Transparancy International, *Bribe Payers Index 2008.*

Table 5.6 ranks 21 leading exporting countries in terms of perceptions of the propensity of their firms to bribe in developing countries. Transparency International noted in its 2002 Bribe Payers Index that domestic companies in the countries surveyed are seen to be more likely to pay or offer bribes than multinational firms, receiving a score of 1.9 on average (where 0 represents the highest likelihood of bribery and 10 represents the lowest).

CONCLUSION

In this chapter we introduced some basic issues of buyer behavior across cultures. We showed that buyers in various national markets can exhibit similar needs, wants, and even behaviors. In many ways, however, buyers differ from one culture to another. This is true whether the buyer is a consumer, a business, or a government. The challenge to the global marketer is to understand when it is possible to exploit similar needs and behaviors and when it is important to adapt to different buyer conditions. In addition, we observed that many buyers increasingly search the world for products. This intensifies competition and makes it all the more imperative that global marketers understand their markets and address the needs of their buyers.

QUESTIONS FOR DISCUSSION

1. What critical factors influence a consumer's ability to purchase a product such as a stereo system?
2. How might segmenting by country be useful to global marketers of cosmetics? What could limit the usefulness of such segmentation?
3. Will the buying process be more similar from country to country for deodorant or delivery vans? Why?
4. If you were selling a product that is purchased mostly by governments, such as a nuclear power plant, how would you prepare to sell to Belgium, Egypt, and Mexico? What means would you use to understand the government buying process in each of these countries?
5. Why do you think that the U.S. Foreign Corrupt Practices Act allows expediting payments? Why are these payments seen as less reprehensible than other forms of bribery?

© John Neubauer/Lonely Planet Images

© Inmagine/18439GNG

6
Global Competitors

LEARNING OBJECTIVES

After studying this chapter, you should be able to:

- Describe ways in which one global competitor can address another.

- List and explain four basic strategic options that local firms can employ in the face of competition from multinational firms.

- Explain how attitudes toward competition have evolved differently in different cultures, and cite examples from both developed and developing countries.

- Note examples of how home governments can still support the global competitiveness of their firms despite the trend toward trade liberalization.

- Discuss the major competitors from developing countries— state-owned enterprises and business groups— and explain how they differ from multinational companies.

- Describe how a firm's country of origin can help or hurt it in the global marketplace.

PROCTER & GAMBLE largely created the market for shampoo in China. Previously, many Chinese still washed their hair with bar soap. Slick Western-style commercials launched P&G's Head and Shoulders brand, and its success encouraged other multinationals to develop the Chinese market further. These multinationals included Japan's Kao Corporation, France's L'Oréal, and Anglo-Dutch Unilever, as well as U.S.-based Colgate-Palmolive and Bristol-Myers Squibb. For ten years, big global brands such as Coke and Head and Shoulders killed local brands in China. Then things changed. Chinese brands recaptured two-thirds of the shampoo market and strongly reasserted themselves in other consumer nondurables such as soap, laundry detergent, and skin moisturizer. A state-owned company even produced one of China's largest-selling brands of toothpaste.

Local brands competed first on price but were learning to develop other selling points as well. One Chinese shampoo, Olive, successfully advertised that it made black hair glossier, an attribute that appealed to local consumers. Procter & Gamble took note and introduced a new shampoo that included traditional medicinal elements to add sheen to black hair. The general manager of P&G's shampoo business summed up the new environment: "These days new local brands are always coming at you. And we take them very seriously."[1]

Multinationals who entered the Chinese market later often found tough local competitors had upgraded their products and services in order to preempt any new foreign competitors. When Disney opened a theme park in Hong Kong, many visitors from the Chinese provinces complained that it was smaller than their locally owned theme parks. In addition, Chinese firms are no longer satisfied to stay in China.[2] A survey of the top 100 Chinese companies revealed that 70 percent had already entered foreign markets and most others were considering doing so.[3]

To begin to develop an effective strategy for global markets, a firm must consider not only buyers but competitors as well. Understanding global buyers is only half the job. Global marketers must compete for those buyers. Potential competitors include both global competitors and local competitors. Each presents unique challenges. Furthermore, the national origin and cultural heritage of firms can determine their organization, their sources of competitive advantage, and the tactics they employ to compete.

In this chapter we address issues of global competition. We begin by noting ways in which competitors can engage each other globally—global firm versus global firm, and local firm versus global firm. We explore why cultures developed different attitudes toward competition and look at differences among competitors from different parts of the world. The chapter concludes by examining how buyers respond to firms from different countries.

THE GLOBALIZATION OF COMPETITION

To be successful in global markets, firms must not only understand their potential buyers but also learn to compete effectively against other firms from many different countries. International firms have both advantages and disadvantages when they encounter local competition in foreign markets. Multinational corporations may be larger than local firms and may have better access to sources of finance. They may enjoy greater experience worldwide in product development and marketing. This experience can be brought to play in the new market. However, local competitors may better understand the local culture and hence operate more effectively not only in addressing consumer needs but in dealing with local distributors and governments as well. Today many local competitors, even those in less developed markets, have built up popular brands that a foreign newcomer can find difficult to dislodge.

Global Firm versus Global Firm

Some industries are becoming increasingly global. In these industries, the same global competitors hold significant global market share and face each other in virtually every key market. Major global competitors such as Kodak and Fuji Film consider each other carefully on a worldwide basis. They watch each other's moves in various markets around the world in order to respond to, or even preempt, any actions that will give the competitor a market advantage. Unilever, a European-based firm, and Procter & Gamble of the United States clash in many markets, particularly in laundry products. The two firms compete with each other in most world markets, and action in one market easily spills over into others. The same phenomenon occurs in the aerospace industry. Buyers are global, and research and development (R&D) costs are high. Competitors are few, and they keep close tabs on one another. In fact, the industry is largely defined by just two firms—Airbus and Boeing.

George Yip suggests several ways in which one global competitor can address another.[4]

Cross-country subsidization the use of profits from one country in which a business operates to subsidize competitive actions in another country

- **Cross-country subsidization**. Using profits from one country in which a business operates to subsidize competitive actions in another country. Bic was one of the first companies to do this effectively. Bic used profits made in France to attack competitor Scripto's pen business in Britain. Then Bic used profits made in Europe to attack Scripto in its U.S. home market. Because Scripto's national subsidiaries were largely independent of each other, the firm didn't see Bic coming.

Counterparry a counterattack against a competitor in one country in response to a prior attack by that competitor in another country

- **Counterparry**. Defending against a competitive attack in one country by counterattacking in another country. Fuji successfully entered the United States and gained 25 percent of the film market. Kodak counterattacked in Japan, exerting great efforts to strike back at Fuji in its home market.

- **Globally coordinated moves**. Mounting a coordinated assault in which competitive moves are made in different countries. For example, some multinational firms now choose global rollouts for products. By introducing new products in all major national markets simultaneously, a firm ensures that its global competitors have no time to learn from one market in order to respond in another.
- **Targeting of global competitors**. Identifying actual and potential global competitors and selecting an overall posture—attack, avoidance, cooperation, or acquisition. We will have more to say about cooperating with potential competitors in Chapter 9.

One of the longest-running battles in global competition has been the fight for market dominance between Coca-Cola and PepsiCo, the world's largest soft-drink companies. Traditionally, the two firms have been relatively close in the U.S. market, but Coca-Cola has long been the leader in international markets. In terms of worldwide market share, Coke leads Pepsi by better than a two-to-one margin. However, the battle for global market share is an ongoing one that erupts simultaneously on several fronts. Key battleground markets are the emerging markets of Russia, China, and India.

Despite entering the Russian market over 30 years after Pepsi did, Coke was able to pull ahead of its global rival in that market.[5] However, the market shares of the two brands are very close in China. In an attempt to overtake Pepsi, Coke paid $80 million for four-year sponsorship rights for the Beijing Olympics. While Pepsi was not an actual sponsor, some Chinese bottlers handed out Pepsi shirts to onlookers along the Olympic torch route. As a result, 10 percent of Chinese consumers thought Pepsi was an Olympics sponsor.[6]

In India, Coca-Cola had previously relinquished its market position when the Indian government passed a law that would require the company to share its secret cola formula with local partners. Although the law was later repealed, Coke delayed returning to India whereas rival Pepsi made India a priority market. When

Globally coordinated move the employing of simultaneous actions across countries to gain competitive advantage over global or local rivals

Targeting of global competitors the process of identifying actual and potential global competitors, planning how to compete against each of them, and implementing those plans

In a remote city in Bolivia, Coke and Pepsi wage their global cola war.

Paul Panayiotou/Alamy

Coke finally returned, it found Pepsi well established in the market. The Coke brand still trails Pepsi, but the competition between the two brands is fierce. Pepsi accused Coke of hoarding over five million returnable Pepsi bottles collected from recyclers in order to disrupt Pepsi production. Pepsi called the police, and a court ordered Coke to return the bottles. The two companies subsequently agreed to a regular exchange of bottles.[7]

As can be expected in true global competition, Coke and Pepsi square off in all important markets. Both firms coordinate their strategies across markets, leverage knowledge and experience gained in many national markets, and employ vast global resources as they battle for global market share.

Global Firm versus Local Firm

Local firms can compete effectively against much larger international companies if they act wisely. When Wal-Mart entered Britain, many expected it to dominate the market despite the presence of Tesco, a local retail giant. However, Tesco held its own while Wal-Mart struggled. Tesco's secret was information on its consumers. Tesco signed up 12 million customers for its Clubcard program. In exchange for offering consumer discounts, Tesco gained access to tracking consumer purchases.[8] By knowing its customers well and developing a relationship with them, Tesco captured a local advantage. In other markets, local competitors have also kept global competitors at bay. In Brazil, Grupo Positivo commands a larger market share of personal computers than does Dell or Hewlett-Packard, and in Russia a local producer of dairy products is larger than multinational Danone.[9]

Strategies for Local Firms

Although global firms may have superior resources, they often become inflexible after several successful market entries and tend to stay with standard approaches when flexibility is needed. Often the global firm's strongest local competitors are those who watch global firms carefully and learn from their moves in other countries. Recently several top Indian retailers decided to invest over $1 billion each to upgrade their operations to world-class standards before global competitors like Wal-Mart entered the Indian market.[10] These local competitors don't simply respond to the entry of global competitors into their markets. They prepare for it.

Niraj Dawar and Tony Frost suggest four successful strategies for smaller local firms that suddenly find themselves competing with more powerful multinationals. Depending on the type of industry they are in, local firms can choose to be defenders, extenders, contenders, or dodgers. In industries where customization to local markets remains a competitive asset, defender and extender strategies can be successful. Other industries, such as telecommunications and automobiles, are by nature more global—buyer needs vary relatively little from one market to another, and both economies of scale in production and high R&D costs favor enterprises with global reach and vast resources. In such global industries, local firms must consider contender or dodger strategies.[11]

Defender Strategy. A defender strategy focuses on leveraging local assets in market segments where multinational firms may be weak. Local assets often include knowledge of local tastes and customs, as well as good relationships with local distributors and suppliers. A good example of a defender strategy is the trend in Turkey for restaurants to bring back regional cuisines to compete with multinational fast-food chains. Ibrahim Tatlises, a Turkish pop music and television star, successfully created a fast-food chain based on *lahmacun*, a thin pizza-like dough with meat and spices.[12] Similarly, Chinese competitors in Internet businesses have proven very competitive against invading multinational companies (MNCs) by being market saavy. Dangdang, China's largest online retailer allows consumers to pay with postal money orders or cash-on-delivery because credit cards are not commonly used in China.[13] Despite their local assets, local firms may need to seek out new efficiencies to defend their home markets. Chilean banks chose to outsource check processing to a single service supplier in order for all to achieve the necessary economies of scale to compete with the multinationals.[14]

Extender Strategy.   Sometimes local firms find that the assets that worked well for a defender strategy can also work in certain foreign markets. Extenders focus on expanding into foreign markets similar to their own, using successful practices and competencies that they have already developed in their home market. SAB's (South African Breweries, now SABMiller PLC) earlier experience in African countries with primitive distribution channels and antiquated production facilities proved useful when the company entered Eastern Europe.[15] Televisa, Mexico's largest media company, has extended to become one of the world's largest producers of Spanish-language soap operas.[16] Its impact is felt in the United States as well as in Latin America. In some local markets, such as Los Angeles and Houston, Spanish-language Univision is the most-watched network.[17] However, when Mexican packaged-foods giant Bimbo moved into the United States, it faced more difficulties. Like Televisa, Bimbo knew the Mexican consumer and was well poised to target the Mexican market in the United States. However, like SAB, one of Bimbo's key competencies—the ability to deal with small mom-and-pop stores—did not extend well into the U.S. market.[18]

Before going global, South African Breweries (SAB) was a successful regional extender.

One Red Eye/Philip Meech

Contender Strategy. Competing in more global industries can be difficult for smaller local firms faced with established global competitors. Yet some have succeeded by upgrading their capabilities to take on the multinational companies. This usually means expanding their resources to invest in the necessary R&D expenditures and larger-scale production that these industries can demand. Many privately held local companies find that they need to go public to raise more money through a stock offering. Because their resources may still be limited compared to those of entrenched multinational firms, contenders may seek out niches—at least at first—that are underserved by their competitors. Arçelik is a top competitor in the Turkish market for appliances such as refrigerators, washing machines, and dishwashers. At home Arçelik enjoys a renowned brand name and vast distribution. It first entered the British market by targeting consumers who wanted small, tabletop refrigerators, a segment that U.S. and European competitors ignored. However, Arçelik moved beyond its initial niche by investing heavily in R&D. The Japan Institute of Product Maintenance chose Arçelik's washing-machine factory in Turkey for the first award for excellence given any such plant outside Japan.[19]

Dodger Strategy. If local firms in more global industries lack the resources or managerial vision to become contenders, they can find themselves edged out even in their home market by multinational firms offering better and cheaper products. To survive, a local firm can avoid, or dodge, competition by finding a way to cooperate with its more powerful competitors. It can focus on being a locally oriented link in the value chain, becoming, for instance, a contract manufacturer or local distributor for a multinational firm. Many dodgers just sell out to a multinational firm that wishes to acquire them. Many such acquisitions have occurred in Europe and the United States as well as in developing countries.

When a multinational firm buys a local competitor, it can change the competitive dynamics of a market practically overnight. For many years, Heinz in Indonesia faced little competition to its ABC brand from local soy sauce manufacturers. Then global rival Unilever bought the local Bango brand and added it to its extensive distribution system. Bango's market share tripled while Heinz's ABC brand fell 20 percent in only four years. Heinz was forced to re-formulate the ABC recipe because many Indonesians said they preferred the less salty taste of Bango. It also introduced the first package upgrade in 15 years.[20]

CULTURAL ATTITUDES TOWARD COMPETITION

Table 6.1 lists the top 25 companies in the world and their nations of origin. Not surprisingly, understanding and responding appropriately to competitors is much more difficult if competitors come from different countries and cultures. Cultures vary in their attitudes toward competition and in their histories of industrial development. These attitudes affect the rules of the competitive game—both written and unwritten—in societies. Understanding these attitudes and histories can help marketers better understand both local competitors in host markets and global competitors that come from different home markets.

Is competition good or bad? Most Americans would agree that competition is good. It encourages new ideas and keeps prices down. However, this is not a universal attitude. In the late 19th and early 20th centuries, the United States

TABLE 6.1	TOP 25 GLOBAL COMPANIES				
RANK	**COMPANY**	**COUNTRY**	**RANK**	**COMPANY**	**COUNTRY**
1	HSBC Holdings	United Kingdom	14	Allianz	Germany
2	General Electric	United States	15	Total	France
3	Bank of America	United States	16	Wal-Mart Stores	United States
4	JPMorgan Chase	United States	17	Chevron	United States
5	ExxonMobil	United States	18	American Intl Group	United States
6	Royal Dutch Shell	Netherlands	19	Gazprom	Russia
7	BP	United Kingdom	20	AXA Group	France
8	Toyota Motor	Japan	21	Banco Santander Centarl Hispano	Spain
9	ING Group	Netherlands	22	ConocoPhillips	United States
10	Berkshire Hathaway	United States	23	Goldman Sachs Group	United States
11	Royal Bank of Scotland Group	Britain	24	Citigroup	United States
12	AT & T	United States	25	Barclays	United Kingdom
13	BNP Paribas	France			

Source: Data from "The Global 2000," *Forbes*, April 2, 2008. Reprinted by permission of Forbes.com © 2009 Forbes LLC.

established antitrust laws to discourage monopolies and encourage competition. Shortly before, Americans watched powerful firms cut prices to drive competitors out of the market. Afterward, these firms or trusts took advantage of their monopolist positions to raise prices to consumers. Newspapers roused citizens across the country, and the U.S. government received a mandate to trust-bust. Even years later, General Motors was forced to operate divisions as separate firms to help dissipate its strong market power in the United States. Other countries have experienced different histories relating to competition and have therefore developed different attitudes toward it.

Competition in Europe

Europe, like the United States, is a major source of multinational corporations. However, industry structure and attitudes toward competition have traditionally differed between these two regions. In most European countries, family-owned businesses play a greater role in the economy than they do in the United States. In Germany, family-owned businesses employing fewer than 500 persons account for almost 80 percent of all employment. Even among publicly traded companies, it is not uncommon to find the board dominated by the founding family and their friends. Many Europeans remain suspicious of the pressures caused by stock markets, believing they force management toward short-term goals to the detriment of longer-term goals. Some also believe that the corporate governance associated with publicly traded companies is a burden that is more about policing than adding value.[21]

Despite European Union (EU) integration, emotional ties to national champions still persist in Europe. In fact, a recent survey suggests that barriers to integration within the EU may be emotional rather than regulatory. A corporate-reputation survey undertaken in the largest EU countries revealed a significant bias toward national heritage companies. Thirteen of the 15 "most visible" companies cited by respondents in Germany and France were based in the respondents' home countries. Among British respondents, 11 of 15 were U.K.-based companies.[22]

For many years, European governments allowed their firms to engage in cartel behavior that was outlawed in the United States. Even as late as the 1970s, European airlines met openly to discuss and later establish the mutual dropping of first-class services on trans-European flights. In fact, Europe rarely enforced antitrust laws until the 1980s. However, the EU has surprised many with a new vigilance in enforcing antitrust laws.

Although Europe imported much of its antitrust law from the United States, it has evolved differently. In the United States, the laws aim to protect consumers from monopolists. In the EU, they exist to guarantee fairness among competitors in the unified market. For example, Microsoft was fined over $2 billion for "abusing its near-monopoly position" in the EU. Microsoft had been found guilty of illegally bundling Windows Microsoft Player inside its Windows operating system, thereby hurting independent producers of media-player software. The director of the U.S. Department of Justice disagreed with this ruling, noting that Europe's stance would harm consumers by discouraging corporate innovation.[23]

Furthermore, under U.S. law, if a merger helps enable two companies to offer a broad portfolio of related products, this is seen as creating efficiencies that could in turn benefit consumers. In the EU, however, this would be seen as having the potential of blocking competitors out of the market. Consequently, the EU objected to a merger between two EU firms, Grand Metropolitan and Guinness, that would have created the world's largest liquor company. The EU feared that the new firm, by combining their portfolios of products from champagne to whiskey, could pressure distributors to shut out competitors. The EU also blocked a merger under their jurisdiction of General Electric and Honeywell International, two U.S.-based multinationals in the aerospace industry, despite the fact that the United States had approved the merger. This decision prompted allegations that European takeover rulings were biased against U.S. firms. However, an independent inquiry found no evidence of systematic bias.[24]

Historically, European governments have intervened more than the U.S. government to save their failing companies. Recently this may be changing. After September 11th devastated the airlines industry, the U.S. government offered its airlines a $5 billion bailout with an additional $10 billion in loan guarantees. But European antitrust legislation refused to allow European governments to bail out airlines. European carriers had to respond immediately—cutting costs and reducing debts. This has left them leaner and meaner than U.S. rivals.[25] Similarly, during the global economic downturn of 2009, European governments were more reluctant to interfere to save failing companies than was the U.S. government.

Competition in Japan

In the last three decades, Japanese markets have experienced more intense competition than markets in the United States and Europe. Whereas IBM enjoyed dominance in the computer mainframe market in the United States, four major competitors—Fujitsu, Hitachi, NEC, and IBM Japan—fought for market share in Japan. In fact, four to eight strong contenders can be found in virtually every industry. Japanese firms are rarely seen to leave mature industries through acquisition, bankruptcy, or voluntary exit.[26]

Horizontal keiretsus large and diverse industrial groups in Japan

Largely contributing to this phenomenon are the **horizontal keiretsus**. *Keiretsu* means "order or system." In Japan, six large industrial groups, or keiretsus, have evolved, and each keiretsu is involved in nearly all major industries. Group companies are technically independent and publicly owned. However, they are loosely coordinated by minority cross-shareholdings and personal relationships. A major player in these groups is the keiretsu bank. Group companies and especially the group bank will help members out in times of trouble. When Mazda faced bankruptcy, the Sumitomo Bank provided the car company with generous financing and encouraged employees of group companies to buy Mazdas. Banks retain shares of group companies despite low returns and have been effective in preventing takeovers by competitors.[27]

For decades Japanese managers never worried about stock prices, and postwar Japan never experienced a hostile takeover of a major business. Despite increased competition, weak companies were not forced out of the Japanese market. However, the poor economic environment in Japan during the late 1990s began to show cracks in the system. The Japanese government made it clear that it would allow banks to fail, which caused Japanese banks to be more wary about propping up group companies. In fact, Japan is experiencing one of the biggest transfers of corporate ownership in 50 years, with many U.S. companies now buying into Japanese firms. Despite these recent trends, a study of Japanese keiretsus revealed that the system appeared to be very much intact.[28]

Competition in Emerging Markets

Developing countries have traditionally been wary of competition. In the mid-twentieth century, many of these countries were still dependent on commodities and were attempting to industrialize rapidly. However, the moneyed segments of society preferred to keep to the businesses they knew best—agriculture, commerce, and the military. The few who ventured into industry and were successful discovered that others quickly followed them into the same business. Soon there were far too many competitors vying for market share in a small market. New ventures failed. As a consequence, potential industrialists became even harder to find. To encourage local investment in industry and the building of factories, governments often limited foreign competition by raising tariffs or imposing quotas on imports. In addition, many governments licensed local production. For example, the Iranian government refused to issue further licenses for new factories once producers could establish that they were capable of supplying the entire Iranian market.

Market liberalization the encouragement of competition where monopolies or strict entry controls previously existed

More recently, most developing countries, as well as the transitional economies of the former Soviet bloc, have embraced market liberalization. **Market liberalization** is the encouraging of competition where prior monopolies or strict entry controls previously existed. It takes a variety of forms. Production licensing is often relinquished and import controls relaxed. Host governments may further competition by encouraging multinational corporations to invest in their markets. India liberalized its market and encouraged foreign investment by granting multinational firms freer access to foreign exchange, the right to hold majority equity stakes in their Indian investments, and permission to use foreign brand names where these were previously not permitted. Other countries, such as Egypt, courted foreign investors with tax holidays for up to ten years.

There are several reasons for this change in attitude toward competition in the emerging world. Some of the pressure to liberalize markets is external. Many countries in the emerging world have joined the WTO and needed to remove barriers to imports in order to comply with WTO regulations. For example, India dismantled the last of its major import quotas in response to a ruling from the WTO. Until then, manufacturers of consumer goods faced virtually no import competition in India. Other countries are under pressure to liberalize from bilateral partners such as the United States.

Much of the pressure to liberalize is internal, however. After 50 years of protection, local competitors have often failed to deliver quality products for reasonable prices. Part of this failure is due to conditions outside their control, such as limited financing available for businesses in developing countries. Still, consumers in the emerging world, along with their governments, have begun to think that protecting infant industries contributes to their failure ever to grow up. A study of 3,000 Indian firms revealed that productivity grew more slowly in the 1990s than in the 1980s.[29] Furthermore, many governments are setting their sights on competing in export markets. Allowing more competition in the national market forces local companies to be more globally competitive. Multinational corporations in particular, with their higher technology, more extensive financial resources, and global market know-how, are expected to help fuel export expansion.

As developing countries liberalize their markets, governments are also cracking down on what they deem to be improper competitive behavior. Many actions that have been accepted for many years are now outlawed. In Mexico, a new antitrust commission acts as both judge and jury on complaints of anticompetitive behavior brought against firms. The commission has the authority to investigate allegations and impose fines. It can block any corporate acquisition in Mexico and can prevent the creation of a private monopoly in cases where the government decides to sell prior state-owned monopolies to the private sector.

Mexico's antitrust commission found Coca-Cola and its bottlers guilty of abusing their dominant position in Coke's largest market outside the United States. Needless to say, Pepsi initiated the investigation. Coke had a 72 percent share of the Mexican carbonated soft-drink market, and most of its sales came from small mom-and-pop stores located across the country. Coke was ordered by the commission to stop using its exclusivity agreements that forbade the small retailers from carrying competitors' products. Pepsi has similar agreements with its retailers in Mexico. But the ruling doesn't apply to Pepsi, because Pepsi doesn't occupy the dominant position in the market.[30]

HOME COUNTRY ACTIONS AND GLOBAL COMPETITIVENESS

In Chapter 4, we discussed how the home governments of firms can affect these firms' international marketing—in particular, how home governments might possibly harm their firms and in so doing create political risk. However, most home governments are eager for their firms to prove competitive in the global marketplace, and many seek out specific ways to improve the competitiveness of their firms. The WTO discourages direct government subsidies to firms and restricts, in most cases, the ability of member states to protect home markets with quotas and high tariffs.

Still, many other government policies exist that can affect global competitiveness. Governments can offer export assistance in the form of export promotion organizations that help educate local firms about foreign markets. Home governments may also assist in negotiations for major contracts with foreign governments. The competition between aerospace giants Airbus and Boeing also involves government assistance for R&D. Furthermore, some analysts judge the competition between the two companies to be so intense that no new player could enter the market without significant government support. However, both the Chinese and Russian governments have signaled that they are ready to supply such support to ensure a national presence in this industry.

Governments can also pursue economic and competition policies at home that enhance the ability of their firms to compete in foreign markets. These policies can include tax rates, labor laws, and the extent to which home governments tolerate monopolistic or oligopolistic behavior in the home market.

The heads of state of the EU met in Barcelona and determined that Europe should try to become the world's most competitive economy. The Barcelona summit resolved to liberalize labor markets by lowering labor taxes and reducing benefits to the unemployed. It also took steps to deregulate energy markets, giving businesses the freedom to choose their gas and electricity suppliers. It was hoped that these measures would decrease the costs of European-based businesses, allowing them to compete more effectively internationally.[31]

WORLD BEAT 6.1

WATER WARS

WHEN COCA-COLA INTRODUCED its bottled water brand, Dasani, to the United Kingdom, many considered it one of the worst marketing blunders ever. At the time, bottled water was the fastest growing market in the drinks industry, and the Danone Group held the highest market share. Entering the British market for bottled water appeared to be a good way for Coca-Cola to expand its presence in this growing market. To adhere to British health regulations, calcium chloride was added to the water. However this resulted in increasing the level of bromate in the water that could increase the risk of cancer. A public outcry arose, and Dasani was withdrawn from the market. Plans to launch it in other European markets were abandoned. Nonetheless, Dasani became the number two bottled water in the U.S. market and was launched in a number of international markets including Canada, Japan, South Korea, and several African markets.

However, Coca-Cola claimed that two months after launching Dasani in Argentina, Danone, in partnership with its advertising agency, sent anonymous emails to journalists and non-governmental organizations (NGOs) accusing Coca-Cola of exploiting weaker regulations in Latin America in order to sell its "cancer water" there. It took Coca-Cola two years to trace the e-mails back to Danone. In the meantime, Coca-Cola Argentina researched the effect the e-mails had on consumers. Thirty percent of consumers surveyed reported that they were aware of the rumor that Dasani caused cancer. Sixty percent of that group believed the rumor. Furthermore, the rumor was not contained to Argentina. Consumers across Latin America had heard it as well.

Coca-Cola concluded that sales of Dasani in Argentina were only half what market research had predicted and consequently brought a law suit against Danone for spreading the cancer rumor and damaging the Dasani brand. An Argentine judge acknowledged Danone's complicity in spreading the rumor but dismissed the suit nonetheless. The reason: Since Dasani had barely entered the Argentine market at the time of the rumor attack, the rumor could not have influenced many consumers. Coke appealed the ruling and subsequently won the lawsuit.

Sources: Serena Saitto, "Argentine Judge Rejects Coke's Complaint Against Danone," *Wall Street Journal*, August 13, 2007, p. B2; Serena Saitto, "Past Mistakes Haunt Coca-Cola Water Business in Latin America," *Dow Jones Newswires*, August 14, 2007; "Danone Concerned by Dasani Advances," *BMI Industry Insights*, December 18, 2007; and Jonathan Prynn, "Coca-Cola Tries to Tap into the Bottled Water Market Again," *London Lite*, May 22, 2008, p. 21.

One ongoing controversy concerning home government policy and competitiveness involves the cement industry. Mexico's Cemex grew from a regional player to the world's third-largest cement supplier and the leading brand in the United States. U.S. rivals accused Cemex of using its dominance in Mexico to finance its expansion overseas unfairly and to cut prices in the U.S. market. Cemex's position in the Mexican market, where it held a 60 percent share of the market, allowed it to charge unusually high prices. Profits in Mexico were an extraordinary 46 percent before taxes—nearly double what they were in the more competitive U.S. market. Such profits at home enabled Cemex to buy competitors abroad as well as to decrease prices in foreign markets. An investigation by Mexico's competition commission found Cemex innocent of monopolistic behavior. Unsatisfied with the commission's decision, the U.S. government decided to impose antidumping duties on cement imported from Mexico. In some years, these have amounted to more than 100 percent for Cemex.[32]

COMPETITORS FROM EMERGING MARKETS

Until recently, most global strategists focused on the multinational companies from the United States, Europe, and Japan. But as we saw in the cases of Procter & Gamble in China and Arçelik in Britain, multinational companies increasingly find themselves competing with firms from developing countries. Table 6.2 lists the largest global firms from key Asian markets. Major firms in developing countries are usually quite different from those in the United States. Large firms that have evolved locally in emerging markets are usually one of two types—state-owned enterprises and business groups. With the trend toward market liberalization, both face strong challenges at home from foreign multinationals. Nonetheless, these local firms can still prove quite competitive both in their own national markets and, increasingly, in global markets. Furthermore, new entrepreneurial ventures from developing countries are evolving and targeting overseas markets.

State-Owned Enterprises

State-owned enterprises (SOEs) sometimes appear in the developed world, but their scope and impact have been significantly greater in developing countries. In the second half of the 20th century, many governments in developing countries

TABLE 6.2	ASIA'S TEN LARGEST COMPANIES		
COMPANY	**COUNTRY**	**COMPANY**	**COUNTRY**
LG CORP	South Korea	Woolworths Ltd	Australia
BHP Billiton	Australia	Reliance Industries-RIL	India
Hon Hai Precision Industry	Taiwan	Tata Steel	India
China Mobile	China	Rio Tinto	Australia
China Construction Bank	China	Noble Group	Hong Kong

Source: Adapted from "Asia's Fab 50 Companies," *Forbes.com*, September 3, 2008. Reprinted by permission of Forbes.com © 2009 Forbes LLC.

were trying to end their dependence on commodity exports by rapidly industrializing their economies. Often the private sector failed to meet government expectations in this regard. Most shied away from investing in factories and production, areas they knew little about. To meet their goals, governments increasingly fell back on doing the job themselves and established SOEs that operated not only in the manufacturing sector but sometimes in wholesaling and retailing as well. For example, SOEs in Egypt came to account for 25 percent of nonagricultural employment in the country.

Being state owned can provide firms certain competitive advantages over firms in the private sector, but some disadvantages are also involved. State-owned firms may receive priority access to financing that is scarce in the developing world. They may be protected from bankruptcy and may be granted monopoly positions in their home markets. They may even derive trade protection by virtue of their government ownership. Some believe that Chinese petroleum SOEs may be immune from U.S. sanctions for cooperating with countries the United States considers to be supporters of terrorism because such actions could be interpreted as direct economic warfare against the Chinese government.[33]

However, these advantages may be offset by the many ancillary agendas SOEs are forced to accept. For example, Sri Lanka's state-owned timber company was expected to sell timber below market prices to subsidize housing in the country. Egyptian college graduates were guaranteed jobs in SOEs, and the Venezuelan government could commandeer the earnings of its state-owned oil company to help with a fiscal shortfall.

In the 1980s and 1990s, many SOEs in developing countries, as well as those in the former Soviet Union and Eastern Europe, underwent privatization. **Privatization** occurs when SOEs or their assets are sold to private firms or individuals. Rather than investing the money necessary to revamp these enterprises, governments choose to sell them. Part of the impetus to do so involves a change in ideology. Many governments have lost faith in continued government-led industrialization. Privatizations have swept through more than 100 countries and have involved over 75,000 SOEs. In many cases, multinational corporations have purchased these firms. For example, Philip Morris, the U.S.-based food and tobacco company, was able to acquire a stake in Czechia's Tabak, previously the Czech monopolist in tobacco.

However, the global impact of SOEs in the oil industry continues despite the trend toward privatization. The state-owned oil companies of Kuwait and Venezuela have ventured out of their countries and have invested in Europe and the United States. The Kuwaiti company purchased refinery capacity in Europe as well as an extensive network of retail outlets from former Gulf Oil. Both of these SOEs are considered serious global competitors. In Russia, a major source of future oil supplies, the state has moved to increase its ownership in the previously privatized sectors of oil and natural gas.

Although the era of SOEs is waning, their importance in the Chinese market is still largely intact. For example, private express shipping companies, including U.S.-based FedEx, UPS, and DHL, were directed not to deliver letters or packages under 1.1 pounds and not to charge prices below those of the China Post. In addition, they could not deliver any mail to private homes or to offices of the Chinese government. The industry estimated that the new restrictions could amount to a loss of 60 percent of the Chinese market just as business was soaring. Industry executives claimed that the order violated commitments China made when it entered the WTO. However, the Chinese government maintained the action was legal

Privatization the practice of selling state-owned enterprises or their assets to private firms or individuals

and noted that China Post had to deliver mail to all locations in China, including places where it could not make a profit. Private companies were under no such obligation. China also invoked an antiterrorism rationale for the move. The government needed to ensure that all deliveries were subjected to screening for anthrax and other poisons.[34]

Hybrid a firm in which a government holds a partial, though usually significant, equity position

Chinese SOEs or **hybrids** dominate many sectors of the Chinese economy. Incidents such as the one involving the express shipping carriers have led to concerns that China's new antitrust laws—based on European laws—may target foreign multinationals while sidestepping reforms to China's powerful SOEs. The Chinese government is also encouraging SOEs, such as those in the auto industry, to combine forces to become bigger and stronger global competitors.[35] Chinese hybrid and computer giant, Lenovo, even acquired the personal computer business of U.S.-based IBM. While Chinese SOEs are proving worthy adversaries to foreign firms, they are increasingly open to hiring foreign managers, particularly in middle management positions. Lenevo hired an American as its chief executive.[36]

Business Groups

Business groups large business organizations consisting of firms in diverse industries interlinked by both formal and informal ties

In the private sector of developing countries, business groups have emerged as the major competitors. **Business groups** differ from large corporations in developed countries in several key ways. Business groups have been exclusively or almost exclusively concentrated in their home markets. Most striking is their diversity. Business groups participate in many industries. It would not be uncommon to find a business group involved in steel, insurance, packaged goods, automobile distribution, and textiles. For example, Arçelik is part of the larger Koç Group in Turkey. This group participates in industries as diverse as consumer goods, energy, mining, finance, and construction. Group businesses are often interlinked, with group companies owning partial shares of each other. The true bond, however, is not one of equity ownership but is a fiduciary bond or bond of trust. It is the culture of businesses in the group to work for the good of the whole. Managers often move between these companies, and personal bonds are forged. In the difficult business environments of developing countries, all eventually benefit from mutual aid.[37]

Similar to Japanese keiretsus, most groups have a financial core—a business with access to cash to finance the other businesses. This is commonly a bank or an insurance company. In the case of Arab Contractors in Egypt, it was the parent company's own extensive retirement fund. This financial core proved a key competitive advantage in an environment where financing was scarce. Because these groups evolved in highly controlled economies, another competitive advantage was their adroit handling of government relations. For example, the Tata Group established India's first steel mill and attempted to address seriously the industrial policy goals of India. Dynastic marriages between business group families and politically connected families were not uncommon. For example, the son of the head of Arab Contractors married the daughter of Egyptian president Anwar Sadat.

Like virtually all firms in developing countries, business groups began as family-owned enterprises, and today the original families still play an important role in most cases. However, as these firms expanded, more professional management was introduced. Other changes have swept through business groups as well. Perhaps the most important of these has been the new competition that business groups face from multinational corporations. Many more multinational corporations have entered emerging markets in the wake of trade and investment liberalization. With

Headquartered in Istanbul, Koç Holding is one of the most esteemed business groups in Turkey. It operates in four core sectors: energy, automotive, consumer durables, and finance. Koç ranks among the top 50 public companies in Europe and among the top 200 in the world.

the lifting of protectionist policies that once protected local firms by excluding imports and even discouraging foreign investment, multinationals now threaten business groups with new technology, quality products at competitive prices, global brands, and strong financial resources. They also compete for the best management talent in the country, something that was once the domain of the business groups. Also, as governments loosen their hold over their economies, the groups' competitive advantage in managing government relations has become less important.

In response to these new threats, many business groups are rethinking the strategies that have served them well in the past. Some argue that the diversity of the past should be abandoned. Instead, the firm should restructure itself around its strongest business or businesses and expand these into foreign markets. In other words, business groups are considering becoming more like multinational firms. Tata, India's largest business group, refocused itself at home by cutting back participation in low-margin businesses. Still the group remained in such varied industries as tea, cars, power, and phone networks. With global ambitions, it purchased Britain's Tetley Tea as well as automakers Jaguar and Land Rover to gain immediate access to international brands.

Anticipating an alignment with Europe and a subsequent loss of protection for local industries, Turkey's business groups have also been adapting to changing times. One of the largest of these groups, Haci Omer Sabanci Holding, is streamlining its activities by focusing on core areas such as energy, the Internet, and telecommunications, while planning to sell its interest in areas such as textiles and plastics. The Turkish group, like many groups in Latin America, is also actively seeking out foreign multinational firms as joint venture partners.[38]

Even so, some still argue that it is premature to expect that business groups will disband in developing countries. The political and economic environments in these countries remain tumultuous, and the strategic value of rendering mutual assistance and forming strong government ties is as real today as before. In fact, many SOEs in Vietnam are themselves aligning into business groups.[39] This suggests that the benefits of business groups may not be restricted to the private sector. Whatever their future, business groups currently represent the strongest local competition in many developing countries.

New Global Players

Recently, firms from developing countries have appeared as major regional and even global competitors in a number of industries. These firms increasingly challenge the established positions of multinationals from the United States, Europe, and Japan. Some, like Arçelik, are outstanding units of older, restructuring business groups. Others are firms that have been established more recently. Acer, the Taiwanese computer giant rose to a strong position in the Asian consumer PC market.[40] Hikma Pharmaceuticals was established in Jordan and carved out a niche for itself as a respected producer of generic drugs with operations in the United States, Europe, and several developing countries. A number of firms, such as Mexico's Cemex and South African Breweries, have used a strong cash flow from their dominant position in one of the larger emerging markets to fund the purchase of established companies abroad. This has helped catapult such companies into positions among the top-ranked global competitors of their industries. The success of companies from newly emerging markets requires a rethinking of the impact that competitors from the emerging world may have on global markets in the future.

THE COUNTRY-OF-ORIGIN ADVANTAGE

Does an international company enjoy a market advantage—or disadvantage—because of the reputation of its home market? When Arçelik entered the European market, the firm was concerned that its home country, Turkey, would diminish its brand in the eyes of European consumers. Consumer response to the country of origin of products has been studied for 30 years. The findings are mixed, but certain trends can be observed. Although certain biases persist, consumers seem to change their minds over time, reflecting a dynamic environment for global competition.

Country of origin the country with which a firm is associated—typically its home country

Country of origin denotes the country with which a firm is associated—typically its home country. For example, IBM is associated with the United States and Sony with Japan. Several studies have concluded that consumers usually favor products from developed countries over those from less developed countries. The reputation of some countries appears to enhance the credibility of competitors in product groups for which the country is well known, such as wines and perfumes for France, video recorders for South Korea, and Persian carpets for Iran. A positive or negative effect of country of origin can sometimes be product-specific. Russian automobiles may evoke a negative image in the minds of consumers, but Russian vodka may evoke a positive response.[41] In a few cases, country of origin can

WORLD BEAT 6.2

CHILEAN GROCERY STORES DEFEND, EXTEND, AND DODGE

ALTHOUGH CHILE is one of the smallest of the South American markets, its retail sector is one of the most advanced, and per capita purchasing power in the country is high by regional standards. Local competitors have fiercely defended their home market, whereas foreign entrants such as Home Depot, J.C. Penny, and Sears have lost money and left. Grocery retailing in Chile has long been dominated by two strong local competitors, Cencosud and D&S. These two grocery chains successfully drove global competitors Carrefour and Ahold out of the Chilean market. D&S even hired a former manager of Carrefour Spain and studied Carrefour operations in Argentina to better understand this rival.

Furthermore, Cencosud has turned its sights to international markets. It became the second largest retailer in Argentina and acquired two local Brazilian grocery chains to give it immediate access to a market much larger than Chile. The company is also interested in expanding into Colombia, Mexico, and Peru. However, back home in Chile, the two local grocery giants entered a price war. D&S gained market share by promoting everyday low prices while accepting lower margins and cutting expenses in logistics and inventory handling. This caught the eye of U.S.-based Wal-Mart. Wal-Mart eventually purchased a majority share of D&S.

Sources: Constanza C. Bianchi and Carolina Reyes, "Defensive Strategies of Local Companies Against Foreign Multinationals: Evidence from Chilean Retailers," *Latin American Business Review*, vol. 6, no, 2, 2005, pp. 67–85; "Retailers Expand International Operations," *BMI Industry Insights*, December 10, 2007; and "Chile Retail: Bigger and Better," *Economist Intelligence Unit-Business Latin America*, April 13, 2009, p. 4.

connote more general product attributes. Germany is known for engineering quality and Italy for design quality.

Nonetheless, country of origin can be confusing. A study of American college students found that they associated famous brands with Germany, Japan, or the United States. The vast majority of student respondents (over 90 percent) failed to associate Nokia with Finland, Lego with Denmark, or Samsung with South Korea. Over half of respondents thought Nokia and Samsung were Japanese and Lego was American.[42]

A country-of-origin bias is not limited to products or to consumer markets. Country-of-origin biases toward services appear to be similar to those toward products.[43] They have been observed among industrial buyers as well. Buyers of industrial products in South Korea rated Japanese, German, and American suppliers higher than suppliers from their own country.[44] Another study revealed that U.S. buyers were more willing to purchase from established industrialized countries than from newly industrialized ones, with the exception of Mexico.[45]

The issue of country of origin is increasingly complicated by the fact that multinational companies produce products in various countries. Which matters most to consumers—the home country associated with the brand or the country where the product is actually manufactured or assembled? Research on this question is inconclusive. A strong global brand may sometimes offset a negative **country of manufacture**. However, this is not always the case. For example, a study of Nigerian consumers of high-technology products revealed that where a product was produced was considered more important than the company name or brand of the product.[46] Globalization has also resulted in products whose inputs come from a number of countries. One study confirmed that **country of parts** affected perceptions of both manufacturing quality and overall quality of products.[47]

Country of manufacture the country in which a product is manufactured or assembled

Country of parts the country in which an input to a final product is produced

In spite of estranged relations between Iran and the United States, the appeal of American products persists in Iran. On a billboard in Tehran, a local candy manufacturer mimics American soft drink Coca-Cola.

Managing Country-of-Origin Perceptions

Buyer attitudes toward certain countries can change, and this has important implications for global competitors. Both Japan and South Korea saw their products rise in esteem over a relatively short period of time.[48] Now Japanese products score higher than U.S. or German products in some countries, including China and Saudi Arabia.[49] In recent years, a number of countries, including Portugal, Estonia, and Poland, have employed branding experts to help them project a better image. Finland even undertook a campaign to enhance its image as a center of high-tech innovation, hoping that a better national image would help its high-tech companies in the U.S. market. But countries must realize branding is more than hype, it must be backed by reality. Consequently, major changes in country brand image can take 20 years to achieve.[50]

Firms that suffer from a negative country of origin commonly settle for lower prices to offset perceptions of lower quality. However, there are a number of strategies that can improve buyer perception of the quality of products that suffer from a negative country-of-origin effect:

- Production may be moved to a country with a positive country-of-origin effect. If this is too difficult, key parts can be sourced from such countries. Kia's Sorento is assembled in Korea but relies on high-profile brand-name components from European and U.S. suppliers to boost its image overseas.[51]
- A negative country-of-origin bias may be offset by using a channel that distributes already accepted complimentary products. A study determined that consumers dining in a Mexican-themed restaurant were significantly more likely to buy Mexican wine than were consumers in other restaurants.[52]
- Communication and persistence can eventually pay off. When Arçelik attempted to introduce its Beko brand washing machines to the French furniture chain Conforama, the French sales staff objected to displaying the Turkish product. Then Valerie Lubineau, Beko's head of marketing in France, revealed that the firm had been manufacturing Conforama's respected in-house brand for years.

Eight months later, the new Beko machines were outselling their European rivals.[53] Firms that consistently provide good products and service can even change buyers' attitudes toward their country of origin. A study showed industrial buyers who were experienced with suppliers from Latin America rated these countries higher than buyers who had had no such business dealings.[54]

MY ACCOUNT   MY SHOPPING BAG   CHECKOUT   HELP   **SHANGHAI TANG**
上海滩

WHAT'S NEW   WOMEN   MEN   CHILDREN   ACCESSORIES   HOME GOODS   GIFTS

AUTHENTIC range

Velvet Tang Jacket with "Double Fish" Embroiderey Lining
USD 915.00

Women's Velvet and Two-Tone Silk Reversible Tang Jacket
USD 835.00

Silk "Double Fish" Reversible Mein Lap
USD 800.00

Velvet Tang Jacket
USD 915.00

Silk "Double Fish" Coolie Jacket
USD 315.00

"Double Fish" Two-Tone Cap Sleeve Qi Pao
USD 415.00

"Double Fish" cap sleeve qi pao
USD 400.00

Silk "Double Fish" Cap Sleeve Long Qi Pao
USD 465.00

Shanghai Tang is a luxury brand originating in China. To counter a poor image of products labeled "Made in China," the company labeled its products "Made by Chinese."

Beyond Quality

Up until now we have been discussing how country of origin can affect perceptions of quality. However, country of origin can affect purchase behavior in other ways. Some consumers are disinclined to purchase foreign products altogether. They believe that buying imported products results in job loss, and consequently hardship, at home. This phenomenon is called **consumer ethnocentrism**. Russian consumers often rate high on ethnocentrism despite their belief that imported products surpass the quality of domestic goods.[55] Within a national population, some segments will exhibit higher levels of consumer ethnocentrism than others. Research has not revealed consistent results as to who is more likely to be ethnocentric. However, several studies suggest that women and older consumers may be more ethnocentric.

Other buyers harbor political objections to purchasing products from a specific foreign country. This phenomenon is called **consumer animosity**. Consumer animosity can be stable or situational. **Stable animosity** arises from difficult historical relations between two countries.[56] For example, Chinese rate Japanese products high in quality. However, many Chinese harbor animosity toward the Japanese because of Japan's occupation of China during World War II. This animosity can negatively affect purchase of Japanese products independent of judgments concerning product quality.[57]

Situational animosity is a response to a current economic or political event.[58] Such animosity surfaced in response to the Iraq War, particularly pitting Britain and the United States against Canada, France, and Germany. Activist websites in Germany urged consumers not to purchase 250 British and American products and suggested local alternatives.[59] But it was the U.S. consumer population that exhibited the greatest consumer animosity. An American backlash against French products arose when France objected to America's invasion of Iraq. Exports of French wine to the United States dropped nearly 18 percent, and overall French exports decreased by more than 17 percent, suggesting that Americans responded to calls to boycott French products.[60] Even some U.S.-based firms were vulnerable. A poll determined that many Americans thought U.S. firms Grey Poupon and Yoplait were French.[61]

French businesses became very concerned about consumer animosity in the United States. The president of France's principal employer's association called upon U.S. consumers not to take out their antagonism out on French businesses, but to send telegrams to the French embassy.[62] Similarly, the president of Canada's Automotive Parts Manufacturers Association reported that members had noticed a chilly response from purchasing agents for U.S. automakers. Although most Canadians agreed with their government's refusal to join the U.S.-led war in Iraq, Canadian business leaders also worried that deteriorating relations with the United States could imperil the $1 billion in daily trade between the neighboring countries.[63]

Sometimes situational consumer animosity proves short-lived. Once besieged by angry farmers who believed their livelihoods were threatened by the American fast-food chain, KFC retreated to a single store in India. However, three years later the company had expanded to 30 stores.[64] Nonetheless, the disruptions caused from consumer animosity can linger. Many Americans, upon abandoning French wine, discovered that they preferred wine from America, Australia, and Chile. Arla Foods, along with all Danish firms, experienced consumer animosity in the Arab World when a Danish newspaper published cartoons of the Prophet Mohammed. Some Muslim consumers believed the insult to their religion was so great

Consumer ethnocentrism the belief that purchasing imported products results in job loss and consequently hardship for a buyer's home country

Consumer animosity political objection to purchasing products from a specific foreign country

Stable animosity consumer animosity arising from difficult historical relations between two countries

Situational animosity consumer animosity as a response to a current economic or political event

What competitive environment will you encounter? Continue with your Country Market Report on the companion website at http://www. cengage.com/ international.

that it could never be forgiven.[65] Arla also experienced difficulty returning to the limited space available on grocery store shelves in Saudi Arabia after competition had replaced Arla during the height of the consumer boycott against the firm.

CONCLUSION

This chapter has introduced some basic issues of global competition. We have explored ways by which global competitors engage each other and strategies that local firms employ to survive in an increasingly global marketplace.

We also saw that the cultural challenge in the global marketplace is not limited to buyers. The rules of the competitive game will vary from country to country. Both local and global competitors may possess strengths and weaknesses that reflect to some extent the environment and history of their home countries. Strategic global marketers must not only target appropriate buyers worldwide but also understand and successfully engage the competition that exists for those buyers.

QUESTIONS FOR DISCUSSION

1. What advantages might a Japanese competitor have in the Japanese market over an American firm attempting to enter that market?
2. What do you think governments should be allowed to do to help their home firms be more globally competitive? What do you think constitutes unfair assistance?
3. Are business groups doomed?
4. Nearly all studies of the country-of-origin effect focus on how buyers evaluate products and on their intention to purchase products. How might the country-of-origin effect manifest itself in other situations?

© Mark Hemmings/Lonely Planet Images

© Inmagine/18439GNG

7
Global Marketing Research

After studying this chapter, you should be able to:

- List and describe the four steps involved in the research process.
- Differentiate between the challenges posed by secondary data collection and those posed by primary data collection.
- Note cultural differences in marketing research, and explain ways in which market researchers can adjust to them.
- Describe problems related to comparability of studies undertaken in different national markets.
- Explain the value of analysis by inference to global marketers.
- Note ways to monitor global competitors.
- Explain the requirements for a global marketing information system.

SPANISH RETAILER ZARA takes only four or five weeks to design a new fashion collection, compared with the six months it takes its major competitors. Zara's designers frequent fashion shows and talk to customers. One designer remarks, "We're like sponges. We soak up information about fashion trends from all over the world." The firm sent out new khaki skirts during the night to some of its 449 stores worldwide. From their desks at headquarters, Zara managers can check real-time sales on computers to see where the skirts are selling. They keep in constant contact with store managers in order to spot and react to trends quickly. After selling well in Asia earlier in the year, camouflage motifs are now popular in France and Lebanon. But stripes outsell camouflage in Spain. Long plaid skirts are big in Kuwait.[1] Understanding the market allows Zara to thrive even during global recessions.[2]

Our purpose in Chapter 7 is to explore methods for collecting appropriate data to better understand potential markets. Our emphasis is managerial rather than technical. Throughout the chapter, we focus on how companies can obtain useful and accurate information that will help them make more informed strategic decisions, such as decisions related to market choice and to the marketing mix that will be discussed in later chapters. This chapter begins by examining the scope and challenges of international research. We then describe the research process, with particular emphasis on data collection. The chapter concludes with a discussion of global information systems.

THE SCOPE OF GLOBAL MARKETING RESEARCH

Global marketing research is meant to provide adequate data and cogent analysis for effective decision making on a global scale. The analytic research techniques practiced by domestic businesses can be applied to international marketing projects. The key difference is in the complexity of assignments because of the additional variables that international researchers must take into account. Global marketers have to judge the comparability of their data across a number of markets and are frequently faced with making decisions based on the basis of limited data. Because of this, the researcher must approach the research task with flexibility, resourcefulness, and ingenuity.

Traditionally, marketing research has been charged with the following three broad areas of responsibility:

- *Environmental studies.* Given the added environmental complexity of global marketing, managers need timely input on various national environments.
- *Market studies.* One of the tasks that researchers most frequently face is to determine the size of a market and the needs of potential customers.
- *Competitive studies.* Another important task for the international marketing researcher is to provide insights about competitors, both domestic and foreign.

In earlier chapters we have covered many issues involved in an environmental study. Of particular interest are the economic, physical, sociocultural, and political environments of a market. Studies focusing on a national market are frequently undertaken when a major decision regarding that market has to be made. This could include a move to enter the country or an effort to increase significantly the firm's presence in that market through large new investments. As a company gains experience in any given country, its staff and local organization accumulate considerable data on the social and cultural situation, and this store of information can be tapped whenever needed. Therefore, a full study of these environmental variables is most useful when the company does not already have a base in that country and its relevant experience is limited.

Nonetheless, managers should carefully monitor changes in their markets. They may also find it useful to keep informed about the latest regulations governing their industry in other countries, even if they do not conduct any business there. Policies in one country often spread to others. This is particularly true within regional blocs. And on an even larger scale, the trade and investment policies of a country have been shown to be influenced by the country's trading partners.[3]

Global marketing research also is used to make both strategic and tactical decisions. Strategic decisions include deciding what markets to enter, how to enter them (exporting, licensing, joint venture), where to locate production facilities, and how to position products vis-à-vis competitors. Tactical decisions are decisions about the specific marketing mix to be used in a country and are made on an ongoing basis. Decisions about advertising, sales promotions, and sales forces all require data derived from testing in the local market. The type of information required is often the same as that required in domestic marketing research, but the process is made more complex by the variety of cultures and environments. Table 7.1 shows the various types of tactical marketing decisions needed and the kinds of research used to collect the necessary data.

The complexity of the international marketplace, the extreme differences that exist from country to country, and the company's frequent lack of familiarity

TABLE 7.1 INTERNATIONAL MARKETING DECISIONS REQUIRING MARKETING RESEARCH

MARKETING MIX DECISION	TYPE OF RESEARCH
Product policy decisions	Focus groups and qualitative research to generate ideas for new products
	Survey research to evaluate new product ideas
	Concept testing, test marketing
	Product benefit and attitude research
	Product formulation and feature testing
	Price sensitivity studies
Pricing decisions	Survey of shopping patterns and behavior
Distribution decisions	Survey of shopping patterns and behavior
	Consumer attitudes toward different store types
	Survey of distributor attitudes and policies
Advertising decisions	Advertising pretesting
	Advertising post-testing/recall scores
	Surveys of media habits
Sales promotion decisions	Surveys of response to alternative types of promotion
Sales force decisions	Tests of alternative sales presentations

Source: C. Samuel Craig and Susan P. Douglas, International Marketing Research, © 2005, p. 35. Reprinted by permission of John Wiley & Sons, Ltd., Chichester, West Sussex, U.K.

with foreign markets accentuate the importance of international marketing research. Before making market entry, product positioning, or marketing mix decisions, a marketer must have accurate information about the market size, customer needs, competition, and relevant government regulations. Marketing research provides the information the firm needs to avoid the costly mistakes of poor strategies or lost opportunities.

The lack of proper marketing research can sabotage product development for a foreign market. On the strength of a research study conducted in the United States, one U.S. firm introduced a new cake mix in England. Believing that homemakers wanted to feel that they participated in the preparation of the cake, the U.S. marketers devised a mix that required homemakers to add an egg. Given its success in the U.S. market, the marketers confidently introduced the product in England. The product failed, however, because the British did not like fancy American cakes. They preferred cakes that were tough and spongy and could accompany afternoon tea. The ploy of having homemakers add an egg to the mix did not eliminate basic differences in taste and style.[4]

On the other hand, well-conceived market research can provide insights that promote success. To better fine tune their services at Hong Kong Disneyland, Disney employed researchers with stopwatches to time how long Chinese guests took to eat. They discovered that the Chinese took an average of ten minutes longer than Americans. As a result, Disney added 700 extra seats to the park's dining areas.[5]

CHALLENGES IN PLANNING INTERNATIONAL RESEARCH

After determining what key variables to investigate, international marketers still face a number of challenges. Whereas domestic research is limited to one country, international research includes many. The international market researcher must choose which countries and market segments to investigate. For many countries, secondary information may be limited or expensive. Primary research can prove culturally challenging. In addition, the comparison of research results from one national study to another is hindered by the general difficulty of establishing comparability and equivalence among various research data. Definitions of socioeconomic status, income, and education can vary widely among countries, which makes even the simplest demographic comparisons between markets challenging.

THE RESEARCH PROCESS

Although conducting marketing research internationally adds to the complexity of the research task, the basic approach remains the same for domestic and international assignments. Either type of research is a four-step process:

1. Problem definition and development of research objectives
2. Determination of the sources of information
3. Collection and analysis of the data from primary and secondary sources
4. Analysis of the data

These four steps may be the same for both international and domestic research, but problems in implementation may occur because of cultural and economic differences from country to country.

WORLD BEAT 7.1

SELLING THE CENSUS

UNDERTAKING A CENSUS in a developing country is a daunting task. The first Indian census occurred in 1872. The census involves interviewing every citizen in order to gather information on the social, demographic, economic, and cultural characteristics of each individual. The upcoming census expects to employ more than 2.5 million enumerators, mostly school teachers, who will travel from house to house to conduct these interviews.

During China's economic census, millions of surveyors questioned business owners about production, sales, and profits. The government sought to better understand its own economy and to improve the dismal reputation of Chinese statistics. In the past, government officials have felt pressured to report growth rates that neither exceeded

nor fell short of official targets. As a result, these reports were unreliable. The government also promised not to use any information from the census to pursue tax evaders.

In the sub-Saharan country of Liberia, respondents are also wary of the census, believing it is undertaken for the purpose of tax collection. Some even worry that it could be part of a military recruitment drive. In recent memory, boys as young as age five have been conscripted to fight. To address these concerns, the Liberian government used billboards to remind villagers to stay home during the three-day counting period. The government even employed a pop star to write a song about the census. Translated into the country's 16 languages, the song played daily on the radio.

Sources: Rama Rao, "Switching Over to a Register-Based Census," *The Hindu*, May 11, 2008, p. 16; Rukmini Callimachi, "Wary Liberians a Challenge for Census-Takers," Associated Press, March 21, 2008; and Brian Bremner and Dexter Roberts, "Fuzzy Numbers No More?" *BusinessWeek*, February 14, 2005, p. 7.

Problem Definition and Development of Research Objectives

In any market research project, the most important tasks are to define the problem and, subsequently, to determine what information is needed. This process can take weeks or months. It eventually determines the choice of methodologies, the types of people to survey, and the appropriate time frame in which to conduct the research.

In determining the research question, managers must decide on an *etic* or an *emic* approach. The **etic approach** assumes that a research question developed in one culture can be more or less translated for use in another cultural context. Etic research is useful in that it allows comparisons across countries but can miss important differences between countries. In contrast to the etic approach, the **emic approach** focuses on understanding each local context from its own cultural frame of reference. The emic approach assumes that cultures are so different that mere translation of a concept across cultures is dangerous to truly insightful research. For example, bicycles in a developed country may be competing with other recreational goods, such as skis, baseball gloves, and exercise equipment. In a developing country, however, they provide basic transportation and hence compete with small cars, mopeds, and scooters. A global firm could fail to understand why growth in bicycles was declining in Malaysia if it asked questions only about the consumer's purchase and use of other recreational products.

Etic approach concepts and measures of concepts developed in one cultural context are translated and used in other cultural contexts

Emic approach separate research studies are developed to capture the uniqueness of each cultural context

Data Collection

For each assignment, researchers may choose to base their analyses on **primary data** (data collected specifically for this assignment), **secondary data** (previously collected and available data), or a combination of both secondary and primary sources. Because costs tend to be higher for research based on primary data, researchers usually exhaust secondary data first. Often called desk research or library research, this approach depends on the availability and reliability of material. Secondary sources may include government publications, trade journals, and data from international agencies or service establishments such as banks, ad agencies, and marketing research companies.

Primary data data collected for a specific research purpose and obtained by direct observation or by direct contact with sources of information

Secondary data data already in existence that was collected for some purpose other than the current study

UTILIZING SECONDARY DATA

For any marketing research problem, the location and analysis of secondary data should be a first step. Although secondary data are not available for all variables, data can often be obtained from public and private sources at a fraction of the cost of obtaining primary data. Increasingly, these sources are disseminating or selling their data over the Internet.

Sources of Secondary Data

A good approach to locating secondary sources is to ask yourself who would know about most sources of information on a specific market. For example, if you wanted to locate secondary information on fibers used for tires in Europe, you might consider asking the editor of a trade magazine on the tire industry or the executive director of the tire manufacturing association or the company librarian for Akzo Nobel, a Dutch company that manufactures fibers.

Check out the student companion website (http://www.cengage. com/international) for ideas and links to online sources of secondary data.

Sources of secondary data for international markets include Web search engines, banks, consulates, embassies, foreign chambers of commerce, libraries with foreign information sections, foreign magazines, public accounting firms, security brokers, and state development offices in foreign countries. Marketers can also "eavesdrop" on the Internet. Every day customers comment online concerning products and services. By monitoring chatrooms, newsgroups, and listserves, marketers can analyze comments to learn what their customers and their competitors are thinking.[6] For-pay subscription sources for secondary research, such a Factiva or Euromonitor, can often be accessed via a university or corporate library.

Many governments collect and disseminate information concerning foreign markets to encourage their national firms to export. To make access to information easier and more streamlined, the U.S. government combined the foreign market research of its various embassies, departments, and bureaus into a single export portal located at http://www.export.gov. Although designed for exporters, the site is useful to foreign investors as well.

Problems with Secondary Data

There are problems associated with the use of secondary data. They include (1) the fact that not all the necessary data may be available, (2) uncertainty about the accuracy of the data, (3) the lack of comparability of the data, and (4) the questionable timeliness of some data. In some cases, no data have been collected. For exam-

A census taker collects information in India.

ple, many countries have little data on the number of retailers, wholesalers, and distributors. In Ethiopia and Chad, population statistics were unavailable for many years.

The quality of government statistics is definitely variable. For example, Germany reported that industrial production was up by 0.5 percent in one month but later revised this figure, reporting that production actually declined by 0.5 percent, an error of 100 percent in the opposite direction. An *Economist* survey of 20 international statisticians rated the quality of statistics from thirteen developed countries on the criteria of objectivity, reliability, methodology, and timeliness. The leading countries were Canada, Australia, Holland, and France; the worst were Belgium, Spain, and Italy.[7]

Although a substantial body of data exists from the most advanced industrial nations, secondary data are less likely to be available for developing countries. Not every country publishes a census, and some published data are not considered reliable. In Nigeria, for example, population size is of such political sensitivity that published census data are generally believed to be highly suspect. A study by the International Labor Organization found actual unemployment to be 10.4 million people in Russia, compared with the official figure of 1.7 million people unemployed![8] However, income remains the most problematic demographic category of all state statistics in developing countries. For example, in Central Asia a significant share of family income comes from the informal economy such as black markets, street vending, and bribery. Since respondents won't admit these sources of income, Central Asian governments estimate incomes based on questions relating to household expenditures.[9]

According to a report by the U.S. Foreign Commercial Service in Beijing, Chinese government statistics are often riddled with *shuifen* or "water content." China has begun to crack down on fraudulent statistics, however, using new laws to discipline local officials who exaggerate their successes. Still, data reliability remains a problem in many developing countries. For this reason, companies sometimes have to proceed with the collection of primary data in developing countries at a much earlier stage than in the most industrialized nations.

The entry of private-sector data collectors into major emerging markets may help ameliorate the shortcomings of government statistics. Since the late 1990s the Gallup Organization has collected data on the Chinese. Gallup interviewers poll 4,000 randomly selected respondents from both rural and urban China. Questions cover a wide range of topics: How much money do you make? What do you buy? What are your dreams? The results of these surveys are compiled in Gallup publications of consumer attitudes and lifestyles in modern China.[10]

Another problem is that secondary data may not be directly comparable from country to country. The population statistics in the United States are collected every 10 years, whereas population statistics in Bolivia are collected every 25 years. Also, countries may calculate the same statistic but do so in different ways. Gross domestic product (GDP) is the value of all goods and services produced in a country and is often used in place of GNP. GDP per capita is a common measure of market size, suggesting the economic wealth of a country per person. As we noted in Chapter 5, the International Monetary Fund (IMF) has decided that the normal practice of converting expressions of GDP in local currencies into dollars at market exchange rates understates the true size of developing economies relative to rich ones. Therefore, the IMF has decided to use purchasing-power parity, which takes into account differences in prices among nations.

Finally, age of the data is a constant problem. Population statistics are usually between two and five years old at best. Industrial production statistics can be from one to two years old. With different markets exhibiting different growth rates, it may be unwise to use older data to make decisions among markets. Market surveys previously undertaken by governments or private research firms are seldom as timely as a marketing manager truly needs.

ANALYSIS BY INFERENCE

Data available from secondary sources are frequently of an aggregate nature and fail to satisfy the specific information needs of a firm. A company must often assess market size on the basis of very limited data on foreign markets. In such cases, market assessment by inference is a possibility. This technique uses available facts about related products or other foreign markets as a basis for inferring the necessary information for the market under analysis. Market assessment by inference is a low-cost activity that should take place before a company engages in the collection of any primary data, which can be quite costly. Inferences can be made on the basis of related products, relative market size, and analysis of demand patterns.

Related Products

Proxy a product the demand for which varies in relationship with the demand for another product being investigated

Few products are consumed or used "in a vacuum"—that is, without any ties to prior purchases or to products in use. If actual consumption statistics are not available for a product category, proxies can prove useful. A **proxy** is a related product that indicates demand for the product under study. Relationships exist, for example, between replacement tires and automobiles on the road and between electricity consumption and the use of appliances. In some situations, it may be possible to obtain data on related products and their uses as a basis for inferring usage of the product to be marketed. From experience in other, similar markets, the analyst is able to apply usage ratios that can provide for low-cost estimates. For example, the analyst can determine the number of replacement tires needed by looking at the number of automobiles on the road. Radio audiences also tend to increase with the number of automobiles in a country. This was observed in China, prompting more interest in radio advertising among firms operating there.[11]

Relative Market Size

Quite frequently, if data on market size are available for other countries, this information can be used to derive estimates for the particular country under investigation. For example, say that market size is known for the United States and that estimates are required for Canada, a country with a reasonably comparable economic system and consumption patterns. Statistics for the United States can be scaled down, by the relative size of GNP, population, or other factors, to about one-tenth of U.S. figures. Similar relationships exist in Europe, where the known market size of one country can provide a basis for inferences about a related country. Of course, the results are not exact, but they provide a basis for further analysis.

Analysis of Demand Patterns

By analyzing industrial growth patterns for various countries, researchers can gain insights into the relationship of consumption patterns to industrial growth.

© Kal Müller

Electricity consumption can be used as an indicator of demand for electrical appliances in developing countries.

Relationships can be plotted between GDP per capita and the percentage of total manufacturing production accounted for by major industries.

During earlier growth stages with corresponding low per-capita incomes, manufacturing tends to center on necessities such as food, beverages, textiles, and light manufacturing. With growing incomes, the role of these industries tends to decline, and heavy industry assumes greater importance. By analyzing such manufacturing patterns, it is possible to make forecasts for various product groups for countries at lower income levels, because they often repeat the growth patterns of more developed economies.

Similar trends can be observed for a country's import composition. With increasing industrialization, countries develop similar patterns modified only by each country's natural resources. Energy-poor countries must import increasing quantities of energy as industrialization proceeds, whereas energy-rich countries can embark on an industrialization path without significant energy imports. Industrialized countries import relatively more food products and industrial materials than manufactured goods, which are more important for the less industrialized countries. Understanding these relationships can help the analyst determine future trends for a country's economy and may help determine future market potential and sales prospects.

COLLECTING PRIMARY DATA

Often, in addition to secondary data or when secondary data are not available or usable, the marketer will need to collect primary data. Researchers can design studies to collect primary data that will meet the information requirements for making a specific marketing decision. Primary sources frequently reveal data that are simply not available from secondary sources. For example, Siar Research International undertook a survey on shaving habits in Central Asia and discovered that over 50 percent of Kazakhstan men shave every day, whereas most Azerbaijan men shave only once a week.[12]

For the global marketer, collecting primary data involves developing a research instrument, selecting a sample, collecting the data, and (often) comparing results across cultures.

Observation

Observation is a valued methodology in international market research and increasingly attracts top management participation. For example, the new head of Wal-Mart International spent a few days in India in order to better understand Indian consumers. He looked in kitchens and bathrooms and noted that one family had three televisions but no refrigerator.[13] Similarly, the new chief marketing and corporate-affairs officer for McDonald's in China began his job with a ten-day trip, living with families across China, in order to become familiar with their eating and spending habits.[14]

Observation is particularly useful for revealing new ideas about consumer behavior that are free from the biases that researchers may bring to a study. Thus, it lends itself well to the emic approach. Observation can be a powerful research tool in developing countries where other techniques may be taboo or difficult to administer. In Cuba, where administering questionnaires on the street is strictly forbidden, foreign marketers can explore how Cubans behave by unobtrusively watching them shop. However, this approach should be used with caution. Unless a researcher is very familiar with the culture, observations can prove difficult to interpret and can lead to wrong research conclusions.[15]

Carefully crafted observational studies designed to understand subtle nuances in consumer behavior are sometimes referred to as **consumer ethnographies** and can prove useful in an increasingly complex global marketplace. Often these studies are administered by trained anthropologists. Visual cues are used to supplement field notes. Such cues are collected via photographs or videotape (when culturally acceptable) and capture elements of décor, design aesthetics, color, fashion, architecture, and icons.[16]

Consumer ethnographies carefully crafted observational studies designed to capture nuances in consumer behavior

A European furniture manufacturer commissioned a visual survey that created a database of nearly 13,000 photos from 30 countries. The visual survey revealed that Indians liked products that were both simple and practical. There was little decoration or storage space in the Indian kitchen. Windows rarely had curtains or blinds. In Sweden, however, the kitchen was the heart of the home. Utensils were prominently displayed, and small plants and candles were commonly used to give kitchens a cozy feel.[17]

To better understand consumers overseas, Procter & Gamble has introduced videotape to learn about the lifestyles and local habits of consumers in different countries. Videotaping one household in Thailand revealed that a mother engaged in multiple tasks, from watching television to cooking a meal, while feeding her baby. P&G believes that the behaviors that consumers don't talk about—such as multitasking while feeding a baby—could inspire product and package design in ways that could give the company a competitive edge over its rivals.[18]

Focus Groups

Another technique that can be used for collecting marketing research data is focus groups. The focus group can be particularly useful at an early stage in the

Parisians at an outdoor café. The French are among the slowest eaters in the world. Global marketers, such as Disney, often observe the time it takes for clients to finish a meal. This tells them how much seating must be provided at their restaurants.

development of a new product concept to gain valuable insights from potential consumers. The researcher assembles a small group of carefully selected respondents to discuss a product. The number may vary by culture. The norm is seven in Europe and eight to ten in the United States. A focus group of six or less may be more appropriate in Asia, where respondents may have more difficulty opening up in front of others.[19] The research company assembles the participants and leads the discussion; this avoids the bias that the active presence of a company representative might introduce. Of course, the discussion leader must speak in the native language of the participants. Representatives of the company can observe the focus group via videotaping or audiotaping, through a one-way mirror, or by sitting in the room.

Focus groups may face government regulation in certain countries. Communist Vietnam has only recently opened to Western businesses, yet marketing researchers find that the Vietnamese are enthusiastic about joining focus groups. Participation rates can range between 35 and 50 percent. But similar to China, the government of Vietnam restricts what can be asked in these groups and bans topics it considers too sensitive.[20]

Focus groups are also subject to a number of cross-cultural challenges:

- In certain Central Asian countries such as Kazakhstan, Turkmenistan, and Uzbekistan, men and women should not be present in the same focus group.[21] In some Muslim countries, it can even be difficult to find women who will agree to participate at all.
- In other countries, such as Japan, it may be difficult to get participants to criticize a potential product due to courtesy bias.
- Expect participants in polychronic cultures, such as Thailand, Malaysia, and Indonesia, to show up late—or not at all—for the focus group. Plan on inviting

a few extra participants to be sure you have enough for your group to continue.[22]

- In high-power-distance countries (most developing countries) young participants might not contradict older ones.
- A focus group in Brazil consisting of eight women can take an hour longer than a similar focus group in the United States due to the considerable time participants invest up front getting to know one another.[23] After all, introductory chats are the norm in high-context cultures.

Given these many cultural challenges, focus group leaders must be resourceful at using a questioning technique—and even interpreting body language—to get full value from this research approach.

Surveys

Survey research is extensively used in international marketing research. It lends itself to the etic approach but is also useful for testing emic insights developed via observation or focus groups. Survey research involves developing a research instrument, determining a sampling methodology, and then collecting the data. Each of these tasks is more complex in the global context.

Developing a Research Instrument. The process of developing a research instrument such as a survey questionnaire must often be done with multiple markets in mind, and every effort should be made to capture the appropriate environmental variables. Even research aimed at a single market might be compared, at a later date, with the results of research in another country. Nonetheless translation of a questionnaire is prone to difficulties. For instance, a surprising problem arises when translating questionnaires from English (an alphabetic-based language) into Japanese (a character-based language): They become longer! Since most respondents around the world prefer shorter questionnaires to longer ones, this presents market researchers with yet another cross-cultural obstacle.[24]

Indeed, a major challenge of instrument design involves translation from one language to another. Accurate translation equivalence is important, first to ensure that the respondents understand the question and second to ensure that the researcher understands the response. **Back translation** is commonly used. That is, first the questionnaire is translated from the home language into the language of the country where it will be used; this is done by a bilingual speaker who is a native speaker of the foreign country. Next a bilingual person who is a native speaker of the home language translates this version back into the home language. This translation is then compared to the original wording. Another translation technique is **parallel translation**, in which two or more translators translate the questionnaire. The results are compared, and any differences are discussed and resolved.

Idiomatic expressions and colloquialisms are often translated incorrectly. One international market research firm discovered this when working with a camera manufacturer. The client proposed to use in an advertisement a direct translation into Spanish of the English sentence "I get a good shot every time I use it." Unfortunately, this translated into "I get a good *gunshot* every time."[25] To avoid these translation errors, experts suggest the technique of back translation be used even in the local dialect, so that *ji xuan ji*, which means "computers" to Chinese speakers in China and Taiwan, does not become "calculators" to Chinese speakers in Singapore.[26] Similarly, the translation of "retail outlet" works in Mexican Spanish but not in Venezuelan Spanish. Venezuelans could interpret the translation to mean

Back translation a technique in which a questionnaire is translated from one language into a second language, translated back from the second language into the first language, and then compared with the original text

Parallel translation a technique in which two or more translators translate a questionnaire, compare their translations, and resolve any differences between the translations

"electrical outlet."[27] Even within the same city, differences in social class can result in different idioms. In one study of the adoption of new products, interviewers in Mexico City were selected from among the same social class as respondents.[28]

Translation problems also arise with measurement scales. U.S. respondents may readily recognize and understand the "school-grade" scale of A–F. However, such a scale would be meaningless elsewhere.[29] Similarly, researchers who employ scales with concepts such as "satisfied," "happy," and "delighted" may discover that some cultures fail to determine sufficient differences between such terms. In general, unless a researcher is very familiar with a culture, it is best to employ a numeric, or Likert, scale.

Finally, even with the best of translations, research can suffer if a concept is not readily understood. For example, Western researchers discovered that the Vietnamese tend to be very literal in their understanding of ideas. If a company asks for an opinion on a new package design concept, Vietnamese consumers may say they never saw it before, so it can't be done. Researchers must instead explain that the new packaging is available in other countries and then ask what consumers think of it.[30]

Selecting a Sample.   After developing the instrument and translating it into the appropriate language, the researcher must determine the appropriate sample design. What population is under investigation? Is it housewives between 20 and 40 years old or manufacturing directors at textile plants? When investigating buyer behavior, researchers must remember that the purchase decision maker can vary by country. For example, the key decision maker for purchasing diagnostic equipment in the United States is often a laboratory director. In Europe, where medical testing is more decentralized, the decision maker could be a department director or nurse manager.[31] The international market researcher must adjust the target population accordingly.

Researchers prefer using a probability sample in order to have greater assurance that sample results can be extrapolated to the population under investigation. To have a probability sample, potential respondents must be randomly selected from frames, or lists, of the population. In many developing countries such lists are difficult to find.[32] Instead, probability samples may need to be derived from neighborhood maps. In Saudi Arabia researchers commonly construct sampling frames based on residences located by city blocks in major cities.[33] Even where sampling frames are available, they are often out of date. Some market researchers use telephone directories. However, in Mexico, for example, the telephone directory may not correspond with those who currently possess the phone numbers. Further difficulties arise from inadequate transportation, which may prevent fieldworkers from reaching selected census tracts in some areas of the country.

Nonprobablistic sampling assumes no prior list of names (or residences) and may be employed when sampling frames are unavailable. Nonprobablistic sampling includes convenience, judgment, snowball, and quota sampling. Convenience sampling includes any respondent who is easily available. Judgment sampling chooses available respondents who are better informed or particularly appropriate for the study. When developing a light sport-utility vehicle for the Brazilian youth market, Ford polled young upper-class Brazilians at trendy nightclubs.[34] Snowball sampling asks initial respondents to identify other respondents who are appropriate for the study. Quota sampling specifies a certain number of respondents from each of several different demographic categories. Quota sampling is particularly appropriate in countries where populations are not homogenous. This is less of a problem in countries such as Japan or South Korea. However, Hong Kong and

Indonesia have culturally diverse populations. Population migration also poses a challenge. Approximately two-fifths of the residents of the Arab Gulf states are expatriate males who are temporarily working in the region.[35] Quota sampling is also appropriate when consumer behavior is known or suspected to differ greatly among groups. For example, in the Arab Gulf there are significant differences by nationality and income regarding brand preferences and loyalty for cigarettes.[36]

Collecting Data.   The next task of the international market researcher is to collect the data. An immediate problem may involve finding the right people to undertake the data collection. Finding the proper personnel in developing countries can be particularly challenging because most people may not even understand the concept of marketing research. To overcome this problem in South Africa, the managing director of one research firm guest lectures at tecknicons (schools where students who do not attend universities go to earn diplomas) in order to generate interest in marketing research. She reports that interest in this new profession is high, and she encourages students to volunteer at market research firms in order to gain experience.[37]

Another problem in developing countries can be the fact that many data collectors are poorly paid and are often paid by the response. This can lead to collectors simply filling out questionnaires themselves. Some of the safeguards against this in developed countries cannot be easily replicated in developing ones. To ensure quality, supervisors can call back respondents on a random basis to confirm their responses. Alternatively, supervisors can randomly listen in on telephone interviews. However, phone interviews are rare in developing countries, and collectors must often intercept respondents on the streets. This can make it more difficult for supervisors to check responses.

Collection Methods. Data can be collected by mail, by telephone, electronically, or face-to-face. In developed countries, telephone interviews have often been the method of choice. However, as noted, interviews by telephone are more difficult in developing countries where landline phones have less penetration and (as also noted earlier) telephone directories may be nonexistent or woefully out of date. For example, in the Central Asian nation of Kazakhstan, only 70–80 percent of households in large cities have telephones. In smaller cities, telephone connection is extremely low.[38]

Face-to-face interviews may be necessary in developing countries, but researchers may encounter challenges in approaching respondents in these traditional collectivist societies. Face-to-face interviews are decreasing in some developed countries, such as Holland, and being replaced by more Internet-based research. In Scandinavia, where Internet access is high, Internet research has become increasingly popular. Even so, market researchers suggest supplementing such research with telephone or face-to-face interviews in order to ensure a representative sample from the population. While developing countries lag behind developed ones in Internet access, market researchers are planning for the future. The number of consumers with Internet connection is rising in developing countries, where access is increasingly possible via mobile phones as well as via computers.

Participation and Response. A major issue in primary research, of course, is the willingness of the potential respondent to participate in the study. For example, in many cultures a man will consider it inappropriate to discuss his shaving habits with anyone, especially with a female interviewer. Respondents in the Netherlands or Germany are notoriously reluctant to divulge information about their personal financial habits. The Dutch are more willing to discuss sex than money.[39]

The preferred research medium also varies by country. Online research accounts for about 16 percent of surveys worldwide. However, online surveys are more common in Australia (30 percent) and Japan (28 percent). In contrast, they only account for about 2 percent of surveys in Russia. Russians prefer face-to-face interviews (40 percent) and telephone polls (28 percent).[40]

Developing countries can present additional problems to market researchers, including poor infrastructure, lower literacy levels, and disinclination to share information with strangers. In Mexico, unreliable mail service makes mail surveys impractical.[41] Mexican respondents prefer shorter questionnaires administered face to face but may be less forthcoming if interviewed at home than they would be if intercepted on the street. This is particularly true regarding information about personal income, because respondents may believe that the researchers are the tax authorities in disguise.[42] Convincing business buyers to participate in research studies is also difficult in many developing countries. Potential respondents are often concerned that the information they provide will be released to competitors or to the authorities.

Government Regulation of Data Collection.

Survey design, sampling, and data collection can all be affected by national legislation. For example, market researchers in the United States, where telephone interviews are common, now face state and national no-call lists that restrict their access to potential respondents. In Germany, street and mall interviews have become less common because researchers must have a license from local authorities to approach respondents.[43] Opinion polls in China are subject to government screening; in addition, questions about politics and sex are often disallowed.[44]

Data collection and privacy concerns being raised in the European Union (EU) may affect marketing research globally. The EU Data Privacy Directive requires unambiguous consent from a person for each use of his or her personal data.[45] This limits both the use of telephone interviews and how data over the Internet is collected and used. All EU nations have data privacy legislation and a government privacy commission to enforce the EU policy. This legislation stipulates that data cannot be sent to a country that is not a member of the EU unless that country has an adequate level of privacy protection. The U.S. Department of Commerce has worked with EU officials to develop the Safe Harbor framework. This framework provides a streamlined way for individual U.S. firms to comply with the European standards and thus continue to receive data from Europe. More recently, Japan has exhibited concerns about privacy similar to those in the EU and passed legislation forbidding market research companies from using secondhand lists to contact individuals without first acquiring the consent of those individuals.[46]

Comparing Studies Across Cultures.

A researcher must deal with problems of comparability when research is undertaken in more than one country to compare buyer attitudes or behavior in different markets. Were the samples similar in all markets? A study comparing software adoption among small-business owners in Brazil with that among managers in large U.S. corporations may identify differences based more on firm size than on nationality. Are measures comparable cross-culturally? For example, measures of affluence such as size of residence or number of vacations may prove problematic because Europeans live in smaller homes and receive more vacation days than Americans do.[47] Needless to say, issues of comparability should be addressed at the beginning—not the end—of the research process.

Another issue of comparability that arises concerns the response to scales commonly used in survey research. Some cultures express themselves comfortably in extremes, whereas responses in other cultures hover more centrally, making it difficult to determine whether consumers in that country are indeed more neutral about products or whether these tepid responses are an artifact of culture. When interpreting surveys in particular, researchers should be concerned with **scalar equivalence**. What does it mean to rate a product "7" or "8" on a 10-point scale? In Latin America, an "8" would indicate lack of enthusiasm, whereas in Asia it would be a very good score.[48] One study of respondents in Australia, France, Singapore, and the United States suggests that the use of a 5- or 7-point scale (as opposed to a 10-point scale) minimizes such cross-cultural differences without sacrificing much research insight.[49]

Another issue that affects comparability is **courtesy bias**. Courtesy bias arises when respondents attempt to guess what answer the interviewer wants to hear and reply accordingly. For example, a taste test could result in respondents saying they liked the product even if they didn't. The level of courtesy bias varies among cultures. It can be a particular problem in Mexico as well as in many Middle Eastern and Asian countries.

Scalar equivalence the similarity among respondents in their interpretation of calibrations along a continuum

Courtesy bias a phenomenon in which respondents fail to reply honestly but instead supply the answer they believe an interviewer wishes to hear

WORLD BEAT 7.2

MIDDLE EAST RESEARCH

MARKETING RESEARCH PROFESSIONALS working in Middle Eastern nations with predominantly Muslim populations say that the area's already limited acceptance of Western marketing research methods was not undermined by the terrorist attacks in September 2001 and their military aftermath—but neither is there any reason to expect tremendous growth in the region.

According to an industry newsletter, the international marketing research industry's total research revenues derived from studies done in Muslim nations amount to no more than about $25 million annually, a tiny slice of the $4.3 billion in non-U.S. research revenues posted by the 25 largest international marketing research firms alone. The most significant new trend in the research industry—the Internet interview—is not even an option in the Middle East because of the small number of consumers with home Internet service.

In the Middle East, one distinct social boundary exists between men and women in nearly all endeavors, including, for example, most research focus groups. In conservative Saudi Arabia, where strict interpretation of Islam demands segregation of the sexes, mixed-gender groups are flatly prohibited. But even in more liberal Muslim nations, such as Egypt, mixed-gender groups are usually not recommended. Muslim women often defer to men,

letting males dominate the conversation, which skews the results of a focus group. Segregation still is the best way to get Muslim women to open up. Yet the idea of females caught on tape and possibly observed by strangers also conflicts with cultural norms.

In rural areas of Saudi Arabia, mail is delivered not to homes or P.O. boxes, but only to businesses, so researchers can't use the postal system for consumer recruitment. Mall intercept is not common or widely understood by consumers, and this makes it difficult to approach strangers in Middle Eastern shopping malls. Western researchers are left to recruit via word of mouth (so-called *snowballing*). Typically, they partner with a local research company or use other local contacts willing to inquire among their own social circles for participants. But, although a native can better explain the project's concept and more effectively recruit fellow citizens, each "seed contact" can be allowed to generate only a small number of referrals, lest the information be collected from within too narrow a circle of acquaintances. A few weeks of recruitment fieldwork in the United Kingdom could translate into many more weeks for the same study in a Muslim country. As a result, research projects typically take much longer to complete in Muslim countries.

Source: Reprinted with permission from Steve Jarvis, "Western-Style Research in the Middle East," *Marketing News,* April 29, 2002, pp. 37–38, published by the American Marketing Association.

STUDYING THE COMPETITION

Results in the marketplace do not depend solely on researching buyer characteristics and meeting buyer needs. To a considerable extent, success in the marketplace is influenced by a firm's understanding of and response to its competition. Firms may investigate competitors in order to **benchmark**. Benchmarking involves identifying best practices in an industry in order to copy those practices and achieve greater efficiency. For example, when the pharmaceutical firm Merck decided to rejuvenate its subsidiary (Merck Banyu) in the important Japanese market, it looked into what competitors, including world leader Pfizer, were doing. As a result, Banyu salespersons were told to focus on a smaller number of drugs in order to achieve increased efficiencies.[50]

Keeping track of a firm's competitors is also an important strategic function. Kodak learned through competitive intelligence that Fuji was planning a new camera for the U.S. market. Kodak launched a competing model just one day before Fuji. Motorola discovered through one of its intelligence staff who was fluent in Japanese that the Japanese electronics firms planned to build new semiconductor plants in Europe. Motorola changed its strategy to build market share in Europe before the new capacity was built. This type of strategic intelligence can be critical to a firm.[51]

To undertake effective research about its competition, a company must first determine who its competitors are. The domestic market will certainly provide some input here. However, it is important to include any foreign company that either currently is a competitor or may become one in the future. The monitoring should not be restricted to activity in the competitors' domestic market but, rather, should include competitors' moves anywhere in the world. Many foreign firms first

Benchmarking the act of identifying best practices in an industry in order to adopt those practices and achieve greater efficiency

AP Images

The major player in its Mexican home market, Bimbo now competes in the United States. One reason for Bimbo's entering the U.S. market was to better understand its potential American competition.

innovate in their home markets, expanding abroad only when the initial debugging of the product has been completed. Therefore, a U.S. firm would lose valuable time if it began monitoring a Japanese competitor's activities only upon that competitor's entry into the U.S. market. Any monitoring system needs to be structured in such a way as to ensure that competitors' actions will be spotted wherever they occur first. Komatsu, Caterpillar's major competitor worldwide in the earth-moving industry, subscribed to the *Journal Star*, the major daily newspaper in Caterpillar's hometown, Peoria, Illinois. Also important are the actions taken by competitors in their foreign subsidiaries. These actions may signal future moves elsewhere in a company's global network of subsidiaries.

Table 7.2 lists the types of information a company may wish to collect on its competitors. Aside from general business statistics, a competitor's profitability may shed some light on its capacity to pursue new business in the future. Learning about others' marketing operations may enable a company to assess, among other things, the market share to be gained in any given market. Whenever major actions are planned, it is extremely helpful to anticipate the reactions of competitive firms and include them in the company's contingency planning. Of course, monitoring a competitor's new products or expansion programs may give early hints of future competitive threats.

Analysis that focuses solely on studying the products of key competitors can often miss the real strength of the competitor. To understand an industry and where it is headed over the next five years, it is important to study the core competencies in the industry. For example, Chaparral Steel, a profitable U.S. steel maker, sends its managers and engineers to visit competitors, customers, and suppliers' factories to identify the trends and skills that will lead steel making in the future. Chaparral also visits university research departments to spot new competencies that may offer an opportunity or pose a threat.[52]

There are numerous ways to monitor competitors' activities. Thorough study of trade or industry journals is a starting point. Also, frequent visits can be made to major trade fairs where competitors exhibit their products. At one such fair in

TABLE 7.2	MONITORING COMPETITION: FACTS TO BE COLLECTED
Overall Company Statistics Sales, market share, and profits Balance sheet Capital expenditures Number of employees Production capacity Research and development capability	Distribution system (includes entry strategy) Delivery schedules (also spare parts) Sales territory (geographic) **Future Intentions** New product developments Current test markets Scheduled plant capacity expansions Planned capital expenditures Planned entry into new markets/countries
Marketing Operations Types of products (quality, performance, features) Service and/or warranty granted Prices and pricing strategy Advertising strategy and budgets Size and type of sales force	**Competitive Behavior** Pricing behavior Reaction to competitive moves, past and expected

Texas, Caterpillar engineers were seen measuring Komatsu equipment.[53] In fact, the high level of competitive espionage that goes on at trade fairs can sometimes discourage participation. When one manufacturer exhibited a new toy at the famous Hong Kong Toy Fair, within three days retailers were being offered a duplicate toy. Some toy makers such as Mattel stopped exhibiting at the show. Instead, they decided to invite perspective buyers to their own in-house presentations.[54]

Important information can also be gathered from foreign subsidiaries located in the home markets of major competitors. The Italian office equipment manufacturer Olivetti assigned a major intelligence function to its U.S. subsidiary because of that unit's direct access to competitive products in the U.S. marketplace. A different approach was adopted by the Japanese pharmaceutical company Esei, which opened a liaison office in Switzerland, home base to several of the world's leading pharmaceutical companies.

Governments may also develop market reports (see, for example, the U.S. Export Portal). Some of these reports are free and others are provided for a fee. Private research organizations, such as PriceWaterhouseCoopers Industry Reports and Hoover's Online, also provide reports on particular companies or industries. These reports are easier to find on developed countries but are increasingly available for developing countries as well. In some cases, however, there may be no research report covering a specific country or product category. And be aware that reports from private sources can sell for hundreds or even thousands of dollars.

OUTSOURCING RESEARCH

The global firm can either attempt to collect and analyze all data itself or outsource some of its marketing research by using marketing research companies. Today all major national markets have local marketing research firms that can assist the international marketer. The early marketing research industry in China was strongly supported by Procter & Gamble—in fact, some believe that it wouldn't have survived without P&G.[55]

The development of an independent marketing research industry in some countries is constrained by culture and economic conditions. In much of Latin America, market volatility leads many local firms to believe they do not have the resources to pay for outside research. Poor enforcement of intellectual property laws makes market research firms wary of developing then trying to sell secondary research. A customer could legally buy a copy of the report then illegally sell it to others.[56] Nonetheless, the demand for quality multicountry research has spurred the marketing research industry to expand beyond traditional national boundaries and become increasingly global. The top 25 marketing/advertising/public opinion research conglomerates by 2003 already accounted for 66 percent of world spending. In 2002 alone, the top 25 acquired 36 research firms around the world.[57] Table 7.3 lists the world's top research companies.

DEVELOPING A GLOBAL INFORMATION SYSTEM

Companies that already have become global marketers, as well as those that plan to do so, must look at the world marketplace to identify global opportunities. The forces that affect an industry must also be analyzed to determine the firm's competitiveness. To evaluate the full range of opportunities requires a global

The Brazilian Institute of Public Opinion and Statistics (IBOPE) is among the top 25 global research organizations. It has operations in 14 countries in North and South America.

© Grupo IBOPE 2005

perspective for market research. Researchers must provide more than data on strictly local factors within each country. All firms that market their products in overseas markets require information that makes it possible to perform analysis across several countries or markets. However, leaving each local subsidiary or market to develop its own database will not result in an integrated marketing information system (MIS). Instead, authority to develop a centrally managed MIS must be assigned to a central location, and market reports need to be sent directly to the firm's chief international marketing officer.

For example, Coca-Cola has joined forces with its bottling partners around the world to share information and best practices. In a planned seven-year rollout, Coca-Cola plans to boost revenue by sharing sales information and communicating more effectively with partners. The new system will upgrade and expand data warehouses, decision support systems, and a worldwide Intranet to improve communications.[58] Similarly, Wal-Mart has pioneered an MIS that opens its computer system to its suppliers across the globe. Suppliers can track how well their products are selling worldwide or at one particular store.[59]

A principal requirement for a worldwide MIS is a standardized set of data collected from each market or country. The actual data collection can be left to a firm's local units, but they must proceed according to central and uniform specifications. By assessing buyer needs on a worldwide basis, the company ensures that products and services are designed with the global marketplace in mind.

It's time to consider the sources for your own research. What are their strengths and weaknesses? What are some possible sources and costs for some customized primary research? Continue with Country Market Report on the companion website (http://www.cengage.com/international).

TABLE 7.3   TOP 25 GLOBAL RESEARCH ORGANIZATIONS

RANK	ORGANIZATION	PARENT COUNTRY	WEBSITE	NO. OF COUNTRIES WITH SUBSIDIARIES/ BRANCH OFFICES[a]	GLOBAL RESEARCH REVENUES (US$ IN MILLIONS)	PERCENT OF GLOBAL REVENUES FROM OUTSIDE HOME COUNTRY
1	The Nielsen Co.	United States	www.nielsen.com	108	$4,220.0	48.5%
2	IMS Health Inc.	United States	www.imshealth.com	76	2,192.6	63.5
3	Taylor Nelson Sofres plc	U.K.	www.tnsglobal.com	80	2,137.2	82.1
4	GfK AG	Germany	www.gfk.com	63	1,593.2	75.0
5	The Kantar Group	U.K.	www.kantargroup.com	61	1,551.4	66.0
6	Ipsos Group SA	France	www.ipsos.com	56	1,270.3	88.6
7	Synovate	U.K.	www.synovate.com	57	867.0	93.8
8	IRI	United States	www.infores.com	8	702.0	37.2
9	Westat Inc.	United States	www.westat.com	1	467.8	–
10	Arbitron Inc.	United States	www.arbitron.com	2	352.1	3.9
11	INTAGE Inc.	Japan	www.intage.co.jp	2	281.1	0.9
12	J.D. Power and Associates	United States	www.jdpa.com	8	260.5	29.2
13	Harris Interactive	United States	www.harrisinteractive.com	7	226.8	29.1
14	Maritz Research	United States	www.maritzresearch.com	4	223.3	16.1
15	The NPD Group Inc.	United States	www.npd.com	13	211.1	24.0
16	Opinion Research/Guideline Group	United States	www.infousa.com	7	202.2	43.1
17	Video Research Ltd.	Japan	www.videor.co.jp	3	169.6	0.1
18	IBOPE Group	Brazil	www.ibope.com.br	16	116.5	21.5
19	Lieberman Research Worldwide	United States	www.lrwonline.com	4	87.5	18.7
20	comScore Inc.	United States	www.comscore.com	5	87.2	11.6
21	Cello Research & Consulting	U.K.	www.cellogroup.co.uk	2	79.9	48.6
22	Market Strategies Intl.	United States	www.marketstrategies.com	2	61.8	9.7
23	BVA Group	France	www.bva.fr	4	55.6	4.9
24	OTX	United States	www.otxresearch.com	2	54.5	6.8
25	Dentsu Research Inc.	Japan	www.dentsuresearch.co.jp	1	54.2	–
	TOTAL				$17,525.4	57.3%

[a]Includes countries that have subsidiaries with an equity interest or branch offices or both.

Source: Adapted with permission from *Marketing News*, published by the American Marketing Association, "Top 25 Global Research Organizations," August 15, 2008.

CONCLUSION

In this chapter, we discussed some major challenges and difficulties that companies encounter in securing data necessary for international marketing. Major difficulties include the lack of basic data on many markets and the likelihood that research methods will have to be adapted to local environments. A final goal of global marketing research is to provide managers with a uniform database covering all the firm's present and potential markets. This will allow for cross-country comparisons and analysis, as well as the incorporation of worldwide consumer needs into the initial product design process. Given the difficulties in data collection, achieving this international comparability of data is indeed a challenge for even the most experienced professionals.

Still, the world has changed greatly in the past 25 years. At that time, market information around the world was sparse and unreliable, especially in developing and undeveloped countries. Now, through the efforts of governments, transnational organizations, and global marketing research companies, information is available for virtually every market in the world from Canada and Mexico to Uzbekistan and Mongolia. As a revolutionary communications tool, the Internet is also pushing research horizons. Today global marketers can use more widely available information to make better market decisions and devise more effective marketing strategies.

QUESTIONS FOR DISCUSSION

1. Why is it so difficult to do marketing research in multicountry settings?
2. What are the challenges of using a marketing research questionnaire that is developed in the United States but will be used in Japan and Mexico as well?
3. If you were estimating the demand for vacuum cleaners, what type of inference analysis would you use? Give a specific example.
4. Note various ways in which the Internet could assist international marketing researchers.
5. List ways in which Kodak might monitor Fuji Film. Why is such surveillance important?

PART **3**

Developing Global Participation Strategies

Competence Level		Decision Area
ENVIRONMENTAL *Competence*	**1**	Understanding the Global Marketing Environment
	2	The Global Economy
	3	Cultural and Social Forces
	4	Political and Regulatory Climate
ANALYTIC *Competence*	**2**	Analyzing Global Opportunities
	5	Global Markets
	6	Global Competitors
	7	Global Marketing Research
STRATEGIC *Competence*	**3**	Developing Global Participation Strategies
	8	**Global Market Participation**
	9	**Global Market Entry Strategies**
FUNCTIONAL *Competence*	**4**	Designing Global Marketing Programs
	10	Global Product Strategies
	11	Global Strategies for Services, Brands, and Social Marketing
	12	Pricing for International and Global Markets
	13	Managing Global Distribution Channels
	14	Global Promotion Strategies
	15	Managing Global Advertising
MANAGERIAL *Competence*	**5**	Managing the Global Marketing Effort
	16	Organizing for Global Marketing

© Photodisc/Getty Images

HOBBS/Alamy

© Inmagine/18439GNG

8
Global Market Participation

LEARNING OBJECTIVES

After studying this chapter, you should be able to:

- List and describe five reasons why firms internationalize.

- Differentiate between born-global firms and other companies.

- Explain the difference between a standalone attractive market and a globally strategic one.

- Cite the advantages and disadvantages of targeting developed countries, developing countries, or transitional economies.

- List and describe the filters used for screening national markets.

- Explain the pros and cons of choosing markets on the basis of market similarity.

KRAFT IS THE LARGEST packaged-foods company in North America. In the United States, it has dominated grocery store shelves for years, with such famous brands as Jell-O, Kool-Aid, Life Savers, Oreo cookies, and Philadelphia cream cheese. However, Kraft is stuck in a slow-growth industry in the United States. Despite careful cost cutting and imaginative marketing, sales dropped 16 percent over a seven-year period. Furthermore, Kraft's strongest overseas market is Western Europe, a market that is nearly saturated as well. Kraft now plans to expand into emerging markets. The company has identified China, Russia, Brazil, and Southeast Asia as the growth engines of the international market.[1] Unfortunately, major global competitors such as Unilever and Nestlé entered these markets much earlier. Also, Kraft's strongest products—convenience foods—don't sell as well in developing countries, where consumers have less disposable income. In contrast, Unilever offers such basics as fortified rice in India.[2]

In this chapter, we introduce key issues that companies face as they pursue global market participation. Historically, internationalization patterns of firms range from opportunistic, or unplanned, responses to overseas opportunities to carefully constructed expansion. Increasingly, firms must determine whether going international is merely an option or a necessity for survival in the global marketplace. Firms must be more proactive in selecting an appropriate course for market expansion. Entering new foreign markets can be expensive and can place heavy demands on management time. Firms must decide which regions and specifically which foreign markets will receive priority.

INTERNATIONALIZING MARKETING OPERATIONS

Internationalization the expansion of a firm beyond its domestic market into foreign markets

Internationalization is the term we use for a firm's expansion from its domestic market into foreign markets. Whether to internationalize is a strategic decision that will fundamentally affect any firm, including its operations and its management. Today, most large companies operate outside their home markets. Nonetheless, it is still useful for these companies to consider their motivations for continued international expansion. For many smaller or newer companies, the decision to internationalize remains an important and difficult one. There can be several possible motives behind a company's decision to begin to compete in foreign markets. These motives range from the opportunistic to the strategic.

Opportunistic Expansion

Many companies promote their products on the Internet or in trade journals to their domestic customers. These media are also read by foreign business executives or distributors, who place orders that are initially unsolicited. Such foreign transactions are usually more complicated and more involved than a routine shipment to a domestic customer. Therefore, the firm must decide whether to respond to these unsolicited orders. Some companies adopt an aggressive policy and begin to pursue these foreign customers actively. Many have built sizable foreign businesses by first responding to orders and then adopting a more proactive approach later. Most large, internationally active companies began their internationalization in this opportunistic manner.

Social networking site Friendster.com exemplifies opportunistic internationalization. Though it was among the first to launch during America's social networking phenomenon, technical difficulties on Friendster eventually caused many domestic users to switch to competitors such as MySpace. However, Friendster had a strong customer base among Asian-Americans with family in Asia, and the site caught on, managing to survive on the other side of the globe. Despite being an English-language site, 70 percent of its traffic now comes from Southeast Asia, where Friendster holds the number two ranking among social networking sites in Malaysia, Indonesia, and Singapore.[3]

Pursuing Potential Abroad and Diversifying Risk

Perhaps the most common reason for a company to expand internationally is the lure of increasing sales and profits from entering new markets. Expanding a firm's product lines abroad can be an attractive alternative to launching new products. For example, Coca-Cola's push to develop new products, such as bottled water, only came after the company had taken its original cola into virtually every country in the world.

Sometimes tough competition at home makes the overseas sales appear all the more alluring. This is one reason why Ford, then number two in the U.S. car market, internationalized faster in the 20th century than then-dominant General Motors. More recently, a survey of Chinese firms—both state-owned and private—discovered that a growing number of Chinese companies are seeking to market abroad in order to escape the intense competition that now exists in the Chinese market.[4]

Courtesy of DHL Corporation

DHL follows customers abroad—even to the gates of China's Forbidden City.

Another major reason to internationalize is the possibility of avoiding risks inherent to operating in only one market. Having alternative sources of sales can also offset negative results from political risk or economic downturns in the domestic market. A year into a major U.S. recession that devastated sales in its home market, Starbucks' corporate earnings were bolstered by growing overseas sales. Diminishing the impact of macroeconomic risk at home has also been forwarded as a major reason why Latin American firms seek foreign markets.

Exploiting Different Market Growth Rates

Companies seeking growth abroad often pay particular attention to market growth rates, which are subject to wide variations among countries. A company based in a low-growth country may wish to expand into faster-growing countries to take advantage of growth opportunities. Table 8.1 demonstrates how the growth rate of soft drinks varies by region. Some beverages, such as carbonated drinks and juices, are in the decline stage of the product life cycle in North America but still experience strong growth elsewhere. On the other hand, North America is one of the best growth markets for bottled water.

The area of the Pacific Rim (which includes Japan, South Korea, Taiwan, China, Hong Kong, Thailand, Singapore, Malaysia, and Indonesia) experienced above-average economic growth rates in the past generation. This prompted many international firms to invest heavily in that region. On the other hand, many Japanese pharmaceutical companies look to the United States for their future growth. For years these firms concentrated solely on Japan, the world's second-largest pharmaceutical market. Recent growth in the Japanese market has been relatively flat, partly because of a crackdown on high pharmaceutical prices by the Japanese government's national health insurance company. However, the U.S. market continues to climb and is now nearly four times the size of the Japanese market.[5]

TABLE 8.1	EXPLOITING DIFFERENT MARKET GROWTH RATES PERCENTAGE GROWTH IN SOFT DRINK SALES BY REGION		
REGION	**CARBONATES**	**FRUIT/VEGETABLE JUICE**	**BOTTLED WATER**
World	12.2	30.2	58.0
Asia Pacific	19.6	97.3	78.7
Eastern Europe	26.1	67.5	66.0
Latin America	23.9	39.4	68.3
Middle East and Africa	20.3	34.3	52.0
North America	−4.8	−13.2	80.2
Western Europe	14.1	14.0	29.5

Source: Soft Drinks, *Euromonitor International*, 2008. © 2008 Euromonitor International. Reprinted with permission.

When the domestic market for a firm's product becomes mature, a company can open new opportunities by entering foreign markets where the product may not be very well known. Among firms following this strategy are many packaged-goods marketers such as Procter & Gamble. These companies often target markets where the per-capita consumption of their products is still relatively low. With economic expansion and the resulting improvement in personal incomes in these new markets, these companies can experience substantial growth over time—even though operations in the United States and Europe show little growth.

Following Customers Abroad

For other companies the decision to internationalize may occur when one of its key customers moves abroad to pursue international opportunities. The establishment of international networks of major professional accounting and consulting firms was motivated by a desire to service key domestic clients overseas. Similarly, express shipper DHL probably became the first Western firm to reenter war-torn Afghanistan. Its rationale: The U.S. military was one of its biggest customers.[6] Sometimes a customer will specifically request that a supplier follow them to an international market. Gruma, Mexico's largest flour producer, has been a major supplier of tortillas to KFC's Taco Bell for years. At KFC's request, Gruma expanded into China.[7]

Following current customers into foreign countries can help to minimize the risk associated with entering a new market. Foods firm McCormick & Company entered China by supplying McDonald's and other Western fast-food chains that it first supplied in the United States. This allowed the company to establish a solid base in China from which to pursue new Chinese restaurant customers and retail chains.[8]

Globalizing for Defensive Reasons

Sometimes companies are not particularly interested in pursuing new growth or potential abroad but decide to enter the international business arena for purely defensive reasons. When a domestic company sees its markets invaded by foreign firms, that company may react by entering the foreign competitor's home market in return. As a result, the company can learn valuable information about the competitor that will help in its operations at home. The company can also slow down a competitor by denying it some of the cash flow from its profitable domestic operation—cash that could otherwise be invested in expansion abroad.

Many U.S. companies opened operations in Japan to be closer to their most important competitors. Major companies such as Xerox and IBM use their local subsidiaries in Japan to learn new ways to compete with the major Japanese firms in their field. Similarly, Kao, the Japanese packaged-goods giant, opened an office in Cincinnati to be close to the headquarters of Procter & Gamble.

Cemex is the largest cement producer in the Western Hemisphere. The Mexican company began its drive to internationalize by expanding across its border into the United States. Cemex then acquired two large cement plants in Spain, taking the company into Europe. Cemex's entry into international markets occurred partly in response to the invasion of its market by Holderbank, a Swiss-based company and the world's largest cement producer. Cemex has since expanded its international operations into 50 countries.

Check out the Japanese links on the student companion website at http://www.cengage.com/international.

Mexican firm CEMEX entered international markets when foreign firms began entering the Mexican market. CEMEX has since evolved into a global leader in the cement industry.

Born Globals

Most large global corporations have followed a similar sequence of internationalization. Typically, these companies develop their domestic markets and then tentatively enter international markets, usually by exporting. As their international sales grow, these companies gradually establish marketing and production operations in many foreign markets. This traditional pattern seems to be followed by most firms. However, some newer firms are jumping into global markets without going through the various stages of development. Such firms are termed **born global**.

Born-global firms recognize from the beginning that their customers and competition are international. This is particularly true of many high-tech startup companies. Logitech, the maker of computer input devices, is one such company. Logitech's market coverage and its marketing strategy were global virtually from its inception. The company not only opened sales offices rapidly throughout the world but also established factories in China, Taiwan, the United States, Switzerland, and Ireland. As a result Logitech has become a major PC mouse producer, operating in 100 countries worldwide.

Born global term referring to a firm that establishes marketing and other business operations abroad upon formation of the firm or immediately thereafter

Is There a First-Mover Advantage?

Even when a new company isn't technically born global, most firms today begin internationalizing earlier and faster than they did in the past. This is due in part to the advantages of internationalization discussed earlier in this chapter. However, a fast move overseas can be taxing even for the most successful domestic companies because developing each new national market can entail significant start-up costs. Starbucks is a case in point. Starbucks only projected to see its first profit for its international business five years after it began its overseas expansion.[9]

First-mover advantage a market advantage relating to brand awareness, sales, and profits that accrues to the first significant competitor to enter a new market

One reason to internationalize quickly and to enter foreign markets early may be a desire to capture a **first-mover advantage**. Volkswagen and General Motors forecasted slowing growth in their home markets and were among the first foreign automobile manufacturers to enter China. The two companies have been rewarded for their foresight with significantly stronger brand recognition in one of the fastest growing auto markets.[10] However, a first-mover advantage is not guaranteed to all early entrants. An analysis of 4,500 foreign investors in China revealed that market pioneers enjoyed a small advantage in market share but not in profitability. Also, large firms in high-growth industries appeared to be best positioned to realize a first-mover advantage.

EVALUATING NATIONAL MARKETS

Whether a domestic firm is first internationalizing or an established multinational is looking to extend its global reach, deciding which markets to enter, and prioritizing those markets, is a major requirement for successful global marketing strategy. The most common way to assess a national market is to evaluate its standalone attractiveness. However, George Yip suggests that global marketers should further assess national markets on global strategic importance as well.[11] (See Table 8.2.)

Standalone Attractive Markets

A national market can appear attractive in a number of ways. First, the potential primary market needs to be assessed. Two key considerations are the size of market and its growth rate. Then the firm must consider its possible competitive

TABLE 8.2	EVALUATING NATIONAL MARKETS	
STANDALONE ATTRACTIVE MARKETS	**GLOBALLY STRATEGIC MARKETS**
Large markets	Potential source of major profits
Significant potential for growth	Important foreign market for key competitors
Less competitive market	Home market of major customers
Government incentives	Lead market

position. What share of market could it reasonably attain? The less competitive a national market, the better chance to attain a larger market share. A government may also increase the standalone attractiveness of its national market by offering potential market entrants a variety of incentives. A low level of taxation and regulation will increase market attractiveness.

Governments can also grant tax or other incentives to individual firms that choose to invest in their countries. Such incentives are not as common as they once were. However, they still play a role in certain countries and in certain industries. The government of Singapore, for example, has offered foreign universities incentives to open branches and offer degrees in Singapore. The incentives include preferential real-estate terms and tax-free status. The University of Chicago and French business school INSEAD have each opened small campuses, whereas other schools, including Cornell's School of Hotel Admisinistration, have set up joint ventures with local academic institutions. The Singapore government hopes these incentives will eventually attract 150,000 foreign students a year.[12] And they are not alone. The United Arab Emirates are also attempting to attract private investment in higher education and offering incentives to overseas institutions.

Globally Strategic Markets

Some standalone attractive markets are also globally strategic markets. However, certain standalone *unattractive* markets might also be judged to be globally strategic. Globally strategic markets are the current and future battlegrounds where global competitors engage one another.

As global marketers eye the array of countries available, they soon become aware that not all countries are of equal importance on the path to global leadership. Markets that are defined as crucial to global market leadership, markets that can determine the global winners among all competitors, markets that companies can ill afford to avoid or neglect—such markets are **must-win markets**. Typically, these markets show potential for major profits. A market that delivers large profits can subsidize competitive battles elsewhere in the world. In the past, the United States has been the largest single market for many industries, making it globally strategic to many firms. Similarly, the larger developed countries often qualify as must-win markets because of their relative wealth and purchasing power. More recently, China has emerged as another country that many global firms consider to be a must-win market. China is a very competitive market, and for many foreign companies, current profits in this market are dismal. However, many firms are afraid to leave this potentially large market for their competitors to exploit unchallenged.

Other globally strategic markets are the home countries of global customers. As multinational business buyers become more centralized in their purchasing

Must-win markets markets crucial to a firm's global market leadership

WORLD BEAT 8.1

SAY GOODBYE TO THE WORLD'S BEST MARKET

THE NEW PRESIDENT of Japanese car manufacturer Mitsubishi Motors traveled to Detroit to begin talks with potential buyers of Mitsubishi's U.S. operations. Weak sales by the U.S. subsidiary were compounded by losses due to extending credit to young car buyers, many of whom had poor credit ratings and later defaulted on their loans. The company had sustained losses in the United States for the past three years. Losses in the last year totaled $2 billion.

For most global competitors, a presence in the U.S. market would seem like a no-brainer. But all companies do not agree. For example, European car manufacturer Peugot chose to bypass the U.S. market for a faster-growing developing market—China. Peugot left the U.S. market in 1991, when its sales there were dwindling. Although Peugot's CEO recognizes that the firm must some day reenter the United States, it had no plans to do so in the immediate future.

Carlsberg agrees. The U.S. beer market is the largest in the world, but the Danish brewer puts Serbia higher than the United States on its list of new markets to investigate. Carlsberg is the world's fifth-largest brewer, and its chief executive thinks the company can be successful without the U.S. market. Instead, he wants the company to focus on faster-growing markets in Eastern Europe, Russia, and Asia.

But is America phobia a good idea? One beer analyst in Amsterdam estimates that Carlsberg's shares trade in Denmark at about 10 percent lower than rival global brands that are active in the U.S. market. As for Mitsubishi, a new CEO and a new commitment to dealers and customers alike finally led to an 8 percent increase in vehicle sales and a small operating profit in North America.

Sources: Neal E. Boudette, "Road Less Travelled," *Wall Street Journal*, August 4, 2003, p. A1; Dan Bilefsky, "Not on Tap," *Wall Street Journal*, October 7, 2003, p. B1; Norihiko Shirouzu and Jathon Sapsford "An Ailing Mitsubishi Motors Seeks Buyer for U.S. Operations," *Wall Street Journal*, February 18, 2005, p. B1; and Amy Chozick, "A CEO's Personal Touch Revs Up Mitsubishi in the U.S.," *Wall Street Journal*, July 10, 2007, p. B1.

decision making, having a presence close to their headquarters can give a global supplier an advantage. Many multinationals also have major sales in their home markets and consequently want global suppliers to understand—and supply—their needs in those markets.

The home markets and important foreign markets of global competitors are also globally strategic markets. This is where innovations are likely to first appear. As noted in Chapter 6, a presence in such markets allows a firm to undertake counterparries against its global competitors in markets where such actions will deliver the most harm. The home markets of major global competitors in an industry are usually lead markets as well.

Lead markets countries or regions that possess major research and development sites for an industry or are recognized for being trendsetters

Lead markets include major research and development sites and vary by industry. Such markets are characterized as having demanding customers who push for quality and innovation. For example, Japan is a lead country for many industries, but Toray Industries, a major Japanese company in a number of plastic and textile industries, chose to run its artificial-leather affiliate, Alcantara, from Italy. Alcantara's success can be attributed largely to the design of its leather products. Toray's management considered Italy the world leader in design, and Italy is a recognized lead market for high-end textiles and clothing.[13]

Lead markets may also be global or regional trendsetters. Cold Stone Creamery, an ice cream company based in Arizona, entered the Asian market with the strategy of targeting sophisticated urbanites. Japan was chosen as the first country to enter because of its role as lead fashion and fad market of Asia. What becomes "cool" in Japan often spreads to Korea, China, and other Asian countries.[14]

GEOGRAPHIC MARKET CHOICES

Although evaluating national markets one by one has its advantages, at any one time, a company may decide to target the developed nations of Europe, Japan, and North America. Alternatively, it may prefer to pursue less developed countries in Latin America, Africa, Asia, or the former Soviet bloc. Each of these options presents its own challenges and opportunities, as depicted in Table 8.3.

Targeting Developed Economies

Developed economies account for a disproportionately large share of world gross national product (GNP) and thus tend to attract many companies. Ten developed countries (the United States, Canada, the United Kingdom, Germany, France, the Netherlands, Sweden, Switzerland, Japan, and Australia) account for both a large proportion of the world's international trade and most of its foreign direct investment. As a result, companies that see themselves as world-class marketers cannot afford to neglect these pivotal markets. Firms with technology-intensive products have especially concentrated their activities in the developed world. Although competition from both international firms and local companies is usually more intense in these markets, developed countries are often deemed to be more standalone attractive than are most developing countries. This is primarily because the business environment is more predictable and the trade and investment climate is more favorable. Also, developed countries are usually more globally strategic as they are most often the home countries or major markets of global competitors as well as lead research markets.

Developed countries are located in North America (the United States and Canada), Western Europe, and Asia (Japan, Australia, and New Zealand). Although some global firms such as IBM operate in all of these countries, many others may be represented in only one or two areas. U.S. multinational companies established strong business bases in Europe very early in their development but only more recently in Japan. Japanese firms tend to start their overseas operations in the United States and Canada and then move to Europe.

TABLE 8.3   **MARKETING ATTRACTIVENESS BY COUNTRY CATEGORY**

DEVELOPED COUNTRIES	DEVELOPING COUNTRIES	TRANSITIONAL ECONOMIES
Richest markets	Poorer markets	Many close to Western Europe
Potential sources of major profits	Great variation in size of national markets	Some members are of European Union
Lead markets	Generally higher growth potential	Educated population
Major markets of key competitors	Poorer markets are usually less competitive	Cultural distance from West varies across countries
Home markets of many global customers	Cultural distance is higher for triad firms but lower for regional competitors	High growth potential, especially for Russian Federation
Lower political risk	Government incentives may be available for less attractive markets	Less developed legal infrastructure relating to business and marketing
	Higher political risk	Higher political risk
	Some developing countries emerging as lead markets and home markets of global competitors	

Kenichi Ohmae first articulated the importance of developing a competitive position in the major developed markets. Ohmae maintained that for most industries, it was important to compete effectively in all three parts of the **triad** of the United States, Europe, and Japan. The three areas of this strategic triad account for about 80 percent of sales for many industries. In these cases, the position of competitors in triad markets can determine the outcome of the global competitive battle. Companies need to be strong in at least two areas and at least to be represented in the third. Real global competitors are advised to have strong positions in all three areas.[15]

Because of the importance of the triad countries in international trade, global companies go to great lengths to balance their presence such that their sales begin to mirror the relative size of the three regions. A company under-represented in one area or another will undertake considerable investment, often in the form of acquisitions, to balance its triad portfolio. Alcatel, a leading European manufacturer of telecommunications equipment, realized that 50 percent of the global opportunity for its market was located in the United States. In response, the company began a major investment drive into the LAN (local area network) switching business, acquiring Xylan Corporation and Assured Access Technology, two California-based firms.[16]

Though the more mature markets of developed countries are arguably more difficult to enter, these markets may still hold potential for a late entrant who is determined and creative—as Toyota discovered. Whereas the European auto market shrank in the mid-2000s, Toyota's European sales soared. What contributed to this surge in sales? A design studio in France that turned out models that looked distinctively Mediterranean. Products were well received and deemed to match the avant-garde styling of the Europeans while ranking first in quality surveys across Europe.[17]

Procter & Gamble is well represented in the developed world and is expanding in developing countries.

Targeting Developing Countries

Developing countries differ substantially from developed countries in terms of both geographic region and level of economic development. Markets in Latin America, Africa, the Middle East, and some parts of Asia are characterized by a higher degree of risk than markets in developed countries. The past experience of international firms doing business in developing countries has not always been positive. Trade restrictions often forced companies to build local factories in order to access the local market. Many firms believed that such an investment was not justified, given the market size and the perceived risk of the venture. However, with the present trend toward global trade liberalization, many formerly closed countries have opened their borders to imports. This has encouraged many more firms to consider emerging markets. However, political and economic risks are still higher in developing countries than in the triad.

Because of the less stable economic climates in those areas, a company's operation can be expected to be subject to greater uncertainty and fluctuation. Furthermore, the frequently changing political situations in developing countries often affect operating results negatively. As a result, some markets that have experienced high growth for some years may suddenly experience drastic reductions in growth. For example, Whirlpool's sales in Brazil, measured in U.S. dollars, declined by $200 million as a result of a devaluation of the Brazilian currency.[18] And Exxon, the world's largest publicly traded company, stood by virtually helpless when Hugo Chavez's Venezuelan government expropriated significant company assets present in the country in 2007.[19] Despite the difficulties associated with operating in these emerging markets, the average market value of multinational firms with operations in developing countries has been shown to be significantly higher than that of multinationals that are not present in such countries.[20]

Developing countries may appear to be attractive markets for several reasons. Market growth in developing countries can sometimes be higher than in the triad, often as a result of higher population growth. Middle-class consumers are appearing in markets once seen as consisting of a small elite and a large impoverished underclass. India now boasts the world's largest middle-class market in absolute numbers. In very poor developing countries, governments may still offer multinational companies government incentives such as tax breaks for bringing manufacturing jobs to the country.

With a substantial increase in global migration, remittances sent home from emigrant workers overseas has significantly increased the buying power in many developing countries—including Turkey, Pakistan, and the Philippines. In Latin America, Mexico receives over $10 billion annually in remittances, and Brazil receives over $4.5 billion. Even smaller countries, such as Colombia, El Salvador, and the Dominican Republic, each receive over $2 billion in remittances. Although many of the overseas workers who send remittances home work in the United States, this is in no way the sole destination of workers. At least 500,000 Latin Americans work in Spain, and Brazil receives half its remittances from Brazilians of Japanese descent who work in Japan.[21]

In many situations, the higher risks in these markets are compensated for by higher returns, because competition can be less intense in developing markets. Hyundai, the largest of Korea's major car manufacturers, has expanded by acquiring or building car plants in Turkey, India, Egypt, Botswana, and Eastern Europe. Hyundai was particularly attracted to these markets by the lack of intense competition there.[22] However, not all developing countries exhibit low levels of competition. As noted earlier, China is one of the most competitive markets in the world.

When evaluating developing countries, most firms focus on standalone attractiveness. However, some developing countries are becoming increasingly globally strategic. The growth potential of markets in China and India put them into this category. As the second-largest beer market in the world, China has attracted as many as 60 foreign brewers. Carlsberg of Denmark, a brewer with a large international business, predicts that China will be the world's largest beer market in the near future, usurping that distinction from the United States. Because of this, Carlsbad planned to invest as much as $1 billion in the country.[23] Coke considered India a problematic market and had withdrawn from India, but as soon as Pepsi invested there, Coke committed itself to reentering India. At the time, Coke still considered India to be unattractive on a standalone basis but was afraid it could lose its permanent global position to Pepsi if Pepsi captured the Indian market unopposed.

Thus firms should watch for rapidly changing competitive situations in major emerging markets and adapt accordingly. Citibank had long been a favorite bank among the Brazilian elite. However, it became distracted by a merger with Travelers Group and failed to pursue the Brazilian market aggressively just as other foreign banks were rapidly making headway through acquisitions. Because of this, Citibank dropped to 14th place in the market.[24]

In addition, as we saw in Chapter 6, competitors from certain emerging markets, such as China, India, Mexico, and South Korea, are now global contenders. Multinationals may need to establish a presence in the home countries of key competitors from the emerging markets just as they have done in the home markets of their more traditional triad competition. For example, Taiwanese electronics companies have become world leaders in several important product categories. Elitegroup and First International became the world's largest independent manufacturers of printed circuit boards. GVC, another Taiwanese company, rose to the leading position as modem producer, surpassing Hayes of the United States.[25] In certain industries, international firms must be present in Taiwan if they intend to keep abreast of product development changes.

Targeting Transitional Economies

Table 8.4 lists the top 20 emerging markets. While most of these are traditional developing countries, two—Russia and Poland—are transitional economies from the former Soviet bloc. The economic liberalization of such countries opened a large new market for many international firms. This market typically represents about 15 percent of the worldwide demand in a given industry. Under Soviet rule, transitional economies experienced a generation without free enterprise or commercial law. Because of this, even new laws to protect companies—such as laws pertaining to patent and trademark protection as well as minority shareholder rights—have sometimes proven difficult to enforce. Yet unlike in most developing countries, the education and literacy levels of the transitional economies are among the highest in the world.

The recent economic performance of these different national markets has varied. Many Eastern European states have joined the European Union (EU), but they remain among the poorest members. Nonetheless, the transitional economies of Eastern Europe enjoy the location advantage of being next to the triad region of Western Europe. And as more firms enter these markets, other firms appear eager to follow. One reason for this phenomenon is the fear of losing a new market to a competitor. However, another reason is that the presence in these markets of more and more international players reassures other firms and lowers the perceived unpredictability associated with Eastern Europe. French retailer Auchon cited the presence of rivals Leclerc and Casino as a key driver behind their decision to enter the Polish market.[26]

TABLE 8.4   **LARGEST EMERGING MARKETS**

COUNTRY	RANK		COUNTRY	RANK	
	SIZE	GROWTH RATE		SIZE	GROWTH RATE
China	1	1	Taiwan	11	20
India	2	3	Philippines	12	13
Russia	3	19	Argentina	13	6
Brazil	4	26	Saudi Arabia	14	17
Indonesia	5	12	Poland	15	21
South Korea	6	24	Egypt	16	7
Mexico	7	16	Thailand	17	10
South Africa	8	11	Venezuela	18	5
Turkey	9	8	Colombia	19	15
Pakistan	10	18	Malaysia	20	14

Source: Adapted from *Market Potential Indicators* 2008, globalEDGE, Michigan State University (http://www.globaledge.msu.edu). Copyright © 2008 by Michigan State University. All rights reserved. Reprinted with permission.

A billboard in Moscow promotes the global brand L'Oréal. Many consider Russia to be a strategic market.

© Jeremy Nicholl/Alamy

The Russian market has proved to be more problematic than most markets in Eastern Europe and is sometimes viewed by firms as less attractive on a standalone basis. Liberalization has been slower, and markets have often been plagued by a greater lack of regulation and by the presence of organized crime. The year after Cadbury opened its first chocolate plant in Russia, the Russian ruble underwent a significant devaluation. Cadbury's Russian operation took years to recover from that shock.[27] Although the Russian market may present auto manufacturers with one of their best potential growth markets, bureaucratic impediments and political uncertainties have made most global automotive companies cautious of the Russian market. Nonetheless, because of its size and abundant natural resources, Russia has the most potential to become a globally strategic market among the transitional economies.

Targeting BRIC

BRIC Brazil, Russia, India, and China

The term **BRIC** designates Brazil, Russia, India, and China. These four countries represent very large emerging markets. The growth rates of their economies increased from 3 percent in the early 1990s to about 7 percent in 2009. Because of this, some firms believe that these countries represent the strategic growth markets of the near future. (Others add South Korea and thus focus on **BRICK**.) Given the large number of emerging markets, both developing countries and transitional economies, focusing on four or five reduces the complexity of market entry choices. However, firms should be cautious of oversimplification and ignoring opportunities in other national markets.

BRICK Brazil, Russia, India, China, and South Korea

COUNTRY SELECTION

After determining what type of foreign markets it wishes to pursue, the firm must choose which countries in particular to target. There are more than 200 countries and territories, but very few firms compete in all of these. Adding another country to a company's portfolio requires additional investment in management time and effort, as well as in capital. Each additional country also represents a new business risk. It takes time to build up business in a country where the firm has not previously been represented, and profits may not be realized until much later on. Consequently, companies need to perform a careful analysis before they decide to move ahead.

The Screening Process

The assessment of country markets usually begins with gathering relevant information on each country and screening out the less desirable countries. A model for selecting foreign markets is shown in Figure 8.1.

The model includes a series of filters to screen out countries. The overwhelming number of market opportunities makes it necessary to break the selection process down into a series of steps. Although a firm does not want to miss a potential opportunity, it cannot conduct extensive marketing research studies in every country of the world. The screening process is used to identify good prospects. Two common errors that companies make in screening countries are (1) ignoring countries that offer good potential for the company's products and (2) spending too much time investigating countries that are poor prospects.

Macroindicators data useful in estimating the total market size of a country or region

The first stage of the selection process is to use macroindicators to discriminate between countries that represent basic opportunities and those that either offer little or no opportunity or involve excessive risk. **Macroindicators** describe the total market in terms of economic, social, geographic, and political information. The

FIGURE 8.1
Screening Foreign Markets

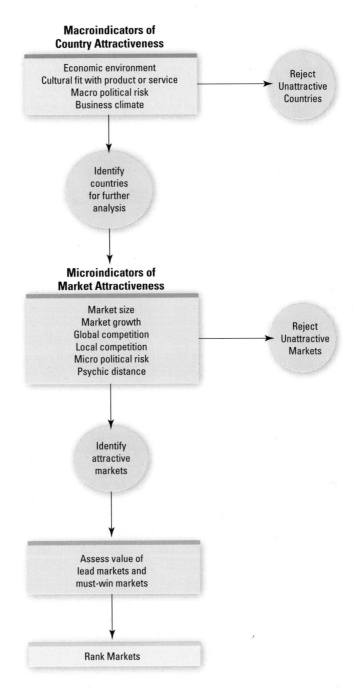

Macroindicators of Country Attractiveness

Economic environment
Cultural fit with product or service
Macro political risk
Business climate

Reject Unattractive Countries

Identify countries for further analysis

Microindicators of Market Attractiveness

Market size
Market growth
Global competition
Local competition
Micro political risk
Psychic distance

Reject Unattractive Markets

Identify attractive markets

Assess value of lead markets and must-win markets

Rank Markets

Source: R. Wayne Walvoord, "Export Market Research," *Global Trade Magazine*, May 1980, p. 83. Reprinted by permission.

variables that are included reflect the potential market size and the market's acceptance of the product or similar products. The second stage of the screening process focuses on microlevel considerations, such as competitors, ease of entry, cost of entry, and profit potential. The focus of the screening process switches from total market size to profitability. The final stage of the screening process is an evaluation and rank-ordering of the potential target countries on the basis of corporate resources, objectives, and strategies. Lead markets and must-win markets receive extra consideration.

Criteria for Selecting Target Countries

The process of selecting target countries through the screening process requires that the companies decide what criteria to use to differentiate desirable countries from less desirable countries. In this section, we explain several key factors and their uses in the market selection process.

Market Size and Growth.   The greater the potential demand for a product in a country, the more attractive that market will be to a company. Measures of market size and growth can be made on both a macro and a micro basis. On a macro basis, it may be determined that the country needs a minimum set of potential resources to be worth further consideration. The macroindicators of market potential and growth are generally used in the first stage of the screening process because the data are readily available and can be used to eliminate quickly those countries with little or no potential demand. Table 8.5 summarizes the potential macroindicators of market size.

A variety of readily available statistics can serve as macroindicators of market size. A company that sells microwave ovens may decide not to consider any country with a personal disposable income per household of less than $10,000 a year. The rationale for this criterion is that if the average household has less than $10,000, the potential market for a luxury item such as a microwave oven will not be great. However, a single statistic can sometimes be deceptive. For example, a country may have an average household income of $8,000, but there may still be a million households with an income of over $10,000. These million households will be potential buyers of microwaves.

Because the macroindicators of market size are general and crude, they do not necessarily indicate a perceived need for the product. For example, a country such as Iran may have the population and income to suggest a large potential market for razors, but the male consumers, many of whom are Muslims and wear beards, may not feel a need for the product. In the next stage of the screening process, it is recommended that microindicators of market potential be used. **Microindicators** usually indicate actual consumption of a company's product or a similar product,

Microindicators data useful in estimating the consumption of a certain product in a country or region

---

TABLE 8.5   MACROINDICATORS OF MARKET SIZE

Geographic Indicators	Economic Characteristics
Size of country, in terms of geographic area	Total gross national product
Climatic conditions	Per-capita income
Topographical characteristics	Income growth rate
Demographic Characteristics	Personal or household disposable income
Total population	Income distribution
Population growth rate	
Age distribution of the population	
Degree of population density	

Margaret Gowan/Stone/Getty Images

Global marketers are increasingly interested in rural markets in developing countries, but a lack of adequate distribution to these regions can pose problems.

therefore signaling a perceived need. Table 8.6 lists several examples of microindicators of market size.

These microindicators can be used to estimate market size further. The number of households with televisions indicates the potential market size for televisions if every household purchased a new television. Depending on the life of the average television in use, one can estimate the annual demand. As we noted in Chapter 7, consumption figures for similar or substitute products can be used as proxies if actual consumption statistics are not available for a certain product category. For example, if a firm is trying to measure the potential market size and receptivity for a palm-held communicator, it might choose as a proxy the number of telephone lines

TABLE 8.6	MICROINDICATORS OF MARKET SIZE	
Radios		Hotel beds
Televisions		Telephones
Cinema seats		Tourist arrivals
Scientists and engineers		Passenger cars
Hospitals		Civil airline passengers
Hospital beds		Steel production
Physicians		Rice production
Alcohol consumption		Number of farms
Coffee consumption		Land under cultivation
Gasoline consumption		Electricity consumption

TABLE 8.7	INDICATORS OF POLITICAL RISK	
Probability of nationalization		Percentage of voters who are Communist
Bureaucratic delays		Restrictions on capital movement
Number of expropriations		Government intervention
Number of riots or assassinations		Limits on foreign ownership
Political executions		Soldier/civilian ratio
Number of Socialist seats in the legislature		

per person, the number of personal computers per person, or cellular telephone usage. Similarly, in determining the market size for surgical sutures, marketers might use the number of hospital beds or the number of doctors as a proxy. The number of farms might indicate the potential demand for tractors, just as the number of cars is likely to indicate the number of tires needed.

Political Conditions.   The influence of the host country's political environment was described in detail in Chapter 4. Although political risk tends to be more subjective than the quantitative indicators of market size, it is equally important. Any company can be hurt by political risk, which can result in anything from limitations on the number of foreign company officials and on the amount of profits paid to the parent company, to refusal to issue a business license. Though less radical than invasions, industrial disputes such as strikes can be a major disruption to business. The incidence of such events varies greatly from country to country. The most "strike-prone" among the developed countries are Italy, Belgium, and the Netherlands.[28] Table 8.7 shows some indicators of political risk that may be used in country selection.

Competition.   In general, it is more difficult to determine the competitive structure of foreign countries than to determine the market size or political risk. Because of the difficulty of obtaining information, competitive analysis is usually done in the last stages of the screening process, when a small number of countries are being considered. However, when firms seek to identify globally strategic markets (as opposed to simply standalone attractive markets) competitive analysis will be undertaken earlier in the screening process.

   As noted in Chapter 7, there are various sources of information on competition, though availability varies widely, depending on the size of the country and the product. Many of the larger countries have chambers of commerce or other in-country organizations that may be able to assist potential investors. For example, if a firm is investigating the Japanese market for electronic measuring devices, the following groups could help it determine the competitive structure of the market in Japan:

- U.S. Chamber of Commerce in Japan
- Japan External Trade Organization (JETRO)
- American Electronics Association in Japan
- Japan Electronic Industry Development Association
- Electronic Industries Association of Japan
- Japan Electronic Measuring Instrument Manufacturers Association

WORLD BEAT 8.2

THE LURE OF RURAL MARKETS

WHEN MULTINATIONAL FIRMS enter developing countries, they usually target urban markets. In some developing countries, this can be just one or two major cities, such as Tehran in Iran or Santiago in Chile. Urban markets have the most sophisticated and richest consumers as well as the most developed distribution systems. For these reasons, many multinational firms, such as Nestlé in India, still focus on the urban market. However, some global marketers are awakening to the potential of long overlooked rural markets in developing countries and transition economies. But the decision to expand to the rural market may be as complex as a decision to enter a different national market, and new marketing strategies involving adaptations to products, price, distribution channels, and promotion may be needed to succeed in the rural markets.

Coca-Cola actively pursues rural consumers in two of the developing world's largest markets—China and India.

Its strategy is to provide extremely cheap sodas to populations once considered too poor or difficult to reach. This decision came as Coke watched a considerable decline in its growth rate in the major Chinese and Indian cities. But rural markets are not free from competition. Local Chinese soda companies have already achieved a first-mover advantage in China's countryside. Ironically, they targeted rural China to avoid competing head-on with Coca-Cola.

Brewer SABMiller also looks to rural markets to develop its presence in China. The company claims to have captured the largest national market share at a fraction of the cost of its big-city competitors. But expanding distribution to rural customers in developing countries is not so simple for all products. Tyson Foods' presence in China is limited to major metropolitan areas where the infrastructure is sufficient to safely sell the company's refrigerated and frozen products.

Sources: "Coca-Cola to Focus on Indian Rural Areas for Growth," *Asia Pulse*, May 13, 2004; "Why Nestle India Does Not Want a Revolution," *Financial Express*, May 18, 2003; Dexter Roberts, "China's Power Brands," *BusinessWeek*, November 8, 2004, p. 50; Adrienne Carter, "It's Miller Time in China," *BusinessWeek*, November 27, 2006, p. 66; and Jane Lanhee Lee, "China Hurdle: Lack of Refrigeration," *Wall Street Journal*, August 20, 2007, p. A7.

Market Similarity.   The concept of market similarity is simple. Managers believe that their success in the home market is more easily transferrable to markets similar to the one in which they already compete. This idea is sometimes called **psychic distance**. Therefore, when a company decides to enter foreign markets, it will first tend to enter markets that are psychically close or more similar to its home market. For example, a U.S. firm usually enters Canada, Australia, and the United Kingdom before entering less similar markets such as Egypt, South Korea, and India. The premise behind the selection of similar markets is the desire of a company to minimize risk in the face of uncertainty. For example, entering a market that has the same language, a similar distribution system, and similar customers is less difficult than entering a market in which all these variables are different.

Strong evidence exists that market similarity can be used for country selection. A study of 954 product introductions by 57 U.S. multinational firms found a significant correlation between market selection and market similarity.[29] Born-global firms also exhibit a propensity to first enter national markets that are more similar to their home markets.[30] As shown in Table 8.8, the selection of foreign markets by Australian exporters correlates closely with psychic distance. Of the ten major markets closest to Australia in psychic distance, only one is not among the country's top ten export destinations.

There are two dangers of choosing markets on the basis of similarity. First, the benefits of similarity need to be balanced against the market size. Australia may be similar to the United States but may have relatively little demand compared with China or Indonesia. Air France flies to more African cities than any non-African

Psychic distance the perceived degree of similarity between markets

| TABLE 8.8 | IMPACT OF PSYCHIC DISTANCE ON EXPORT MARKETS OF AUSTRALIAN EXPORTERS | | | | | |

COUNTRY	PSYCHIC DISTANCE RANK	EXPORTER RANK	COUNTRY	PSYCHIC DISTANCE RANK	EXPORTER RANK
United Kingdom	1	4	Indonesia	14	11
New Zealand	2	1	Philippines	15	18
United States	3	2	Sweden	16	19
Singapore	4	3	Germany	17	13
Hong Kong	5	5	China	18	9
Japan	6	6	Chile	19	23
Canada	7	16	Taiwan	20	12
Papua New Guinea	8	8	United Arab Emirates	21	20
Fiji	9	10	Kuwait	22	24
Malaysia	10	7	Kenya	23	25
South Africa	11	17	Thailand	24	15
India	12	19	South Korea	25	14
Italy	13	21			

Note: Psychic distance calculated from 15 variables including culture, immigration, trade agreements, language, colonial ties, and development level.

Source: Adapted with permission from *Journal of International Marketing*, published by the American Marketing Association, Paul Brewer, "Operationalizing Psychic Distance: A Revised Approach," Vol. 15, No. 2, 2007, pp. 44–66.

airline. France's colonial history arguably gives Air France (and other French companies) a competitive advantage in its former African empire, which includes Cameroon, Chad, Gabon, Guinea, Ivory Coast, Mali, Senegal, and other countries, because of linguistic, economic, and cultural ties.[31] However, some have argued that French firms have sometimes lost out on bigger growth markets in the Pacific Rim because of their emphasis on markets in Africa.

A second problem associated with selecting national markets based on perceived similarity is the fact that firms can overestimate the degree of similarity between markets. When Starbucks internationalized, it discovered that just because foreign consumers spoke English didn't mean that the markets operated the same. For example, in the United States, the firm's strategy was to find the best corners in the best markets to locate its stores. That approach proved too expensive in Britain, where real estate prices were higher.[32] When Canadian retail chains entered the United States, managers assumed that the United States was just like Canada only bigger. They believed that the retail concepts that worked in Canada would work in the United States. Instead, U.S. consumers proved very different from Canadian consumers. They demanded more service, shopped harder for bargains, and were far less loyal to national chains than were their Canadian counterparts. In addition, competition proved far more intense in the United States. As a result, familiarity bred carelessness, and the chains struggled to survive in what proved to be a very alien market.[33]

Psychic-distance paradox a phenomenon in which a market thought to be similar to another market turns out to be dissimilar

This culture shock experienced by managers entering foreign markets that they had perceived to be similar to their own is sometimes called the **psychic-distance paradox**. A study of firms from Denmark, Sweden, and New Zealand suggests that this shock effect may be more common among producers of customized products than among producers of more standardized products.[34]

Listing Selection Criteria

A good way to screen countries is to develop a set of criteria that serve as minimum standards that a country must meet in order to move through the stages of the screening process. The minimum cutoff number for each criterion will be established by management. As one moves through the screening process, the selection criteria become more specific. The screening process that could be used by a manufacturer of kidney dialysis equipment is depicted in Table 8.9.

The analysis begins by looking at gross national products. Introduction of dialysis equipment in a new market requires a significant support function, including salespeople, service people, replacement parts inventory, and an ensured continuous supply of dialysate fluid, needles, tubing, and so on. Some countries lack the technical infrastructure to support such high-level technology. Therefore, management may decide to consider only countries that have a minimum size of $15 billion GNP, a criterion that excludes many of the developing economies of the world from consideration.

The selection process continues by examining the concentration of medical services in the remaining countries. Hemodialysis is a sophisticated procedure that requires medical personnel with advanced training to perform it. For a country to support advanced medical equipment, it requires a high level of medical specialization. Higher levels of medical concentration allow doctors the luxury of specializing in a field such as nephrology (the study of kidneys). Management may determine that a population of less than 1,000 per doctor and a population of less than

TABLE 8.9   SCREENING PROCESS EXAMPLE: TARGETING COUNTRIES FOR KIDNEY DIALYSIS EQUIPMENT

FILTER NUMBER	TYPE OF SCREENING	SPECIFIC CRITERIA
1	Macrolevel research	GDP over $15 billion GDP per capita over $1,500
2	General market factors related to the product	Fewer than 200 people per hospital bed Fewer than 1,000 people per doctor Government expenditures over $100 million for health care Government expenditures over $20 per capita for health care
3	Microlevel factors specific to the product	Kidney-related deaths over 1,000 Patient use of dialysis equipment—over 40 percent annual growth in treated population
4	Final screening of target markets	Numbers of competitors Political stability

200 per hospital bed indicate that medical personnel will be able to achieve the level of specialization needed to support a hemodialysis program.

Public health expenditures reflect the government's contribution to the medical care of its citizens—a factor of obvious importance with respect to hemodialysis. Management may believe that countries that do not invest substantially in the health care of their populations generally are not interested in making an even more substantial investment in a hemodialysis program. Thus, countries that do not have a minimum of $20 in public health expenditure per capita or $100 million in total expenditures for health care would be eliminated from consideration.

Then management may decide that there are two microlevel factors to consider: the number of kidney-related deaths and the growth rate of the treated patient population. The number of deaths resulting from kidney failure is a good indicator of the number of people in each country who could have used dialysis equipment. The company will be interested only in countries with a minimum of 1,000 deaths per year due to kidney-related causes. Analysis of the growth rate of the population requiring kidney treatment demonstrates a growth in potential demand.

Finally, management must consider political risk and competition. Newly opened markets with the greatest growth potential may be the best targets for a new supplier of dialysis equipment, because competition is not so entrenched as it would be in a mature market. Alternatively, management may decide to enter a lead market where a major competitor is strong in order to monitor technology development and possibly block that competitor. The weighting of these microlevel factors will determine the primary target market.

Grouping International Markets

A final consideration in selecting national markets is the option of entering a group of countries in a single geographic region, be they the developed countries of Western Europe or the less developed countries in South America or the Middle East. It is often necessary to group countries together so that they can be considered as a single market or as a group of similar markets. Two principles that often drive the need for larger market groupings are critical mass and economies of scale. **Critical mass**, a term used in physics and military strategy, embodies the idea that a certain minimum amount of effort is necessary before any impact will be achieved. **Economies of scale** is a term used in production situations; it means that greater levels of production result in lower costs per unit, which obviously increases profitability.

The costs of marketing products within a group of countries are lower than the costs of marketing products to the same number of disparate countries for four reasons. First, the potential volume to be sold in a group of countries is sufficient to support a full marketing effort. Second, geographic proximity makes it easy to travel from one country to another, often in two hours or less. Third, the barriers to entry are frequently the same in countries within an economic group—for example, the EU. Finally, in pursuing countries with similar markets, a company gains leverage with marketing programs.

There is some debate over the long-term role of market groups. The EU has become a strong group with a single currency, but many economic groups may become subordinate to the role of the World Trade Organization (WTO). Also, given the broad membership of the WTO and its strong enforcement powers, the regional market group will generally need to conform to the rules and practices of the WTO when dealing with all other WTO countries.

Critical mass the minimal effort and investment needed to compete effectively in a market

Economies of scale profitability gained through the phenomenon that as the size of a production run increases, per-unit costs decrease

Which countries belong to which regional groups? Check out Regional Groups on the student companion website at http://www.cengage.com/international.

How standalone attractive or strategically important is your market choice? Continue with your Country Market Report on the student companion website at http://www.cengage.com/international.

It is also important to remember that just being neighbors isn't enough to make countries into a viable market group. Take, for example, the countries in the Caucasus region. Armenia and Azerbaijan are technically at war. Turkey blockades Armenia in sympathy with Azerbaijan. Relations between Georgia and Armenia remain strained, as do relations between Iran and Azerbaijan. Travel and shipping among the countries are poor as well. Roads are bad, and the easiest flight connections in the region are all via Moscow or Istanbul.[35] Clearly these countries do not present themselves as a likely group to the global marketer.

Neither does geographic distance necessarily preclude countries from being grouped together. For example, the so-called "Anglo cluster," consisting of Australia, Canada, England, Ireland, New Zealand, South Africa, and the United States, is a collection of countries that were once a part of the British empire and are today relatively wealthy. In addition, most of their populations speak English and have many cultural values in common.[36] For some firms, it makes sense to target part or all the Anglo cluster when considering market entry. For example, when Australian winemaker BRL Hardy launched their Banrock Station brand they chose Australia, New Zealand, the United Kingdom, and the United States as their key markets.

CONCLUSION

Any company that wishes to engage in global marketing must make a number of very important strategic decisions concerning global market participation. At the outset, the company must commit itself to some level of internationalization. Increasingly, firms are finding that an international presence must be pursued for competitive reasons. It is a necessity, not simply an option. Once committed, the company needs to decide where to go, both in terms of geographic regions and specific countries. Standalone attractiveness of markets must be balanced with their global strategic importance. Firms must determine what participation they want and need in developed, developing, and transitional economies. Being in the right international markets establishes the groundwork for the firm's global marketing strategy.

QUESTIONS FOR DISCUSSION

1. Why might a firm in packaged goods choose to enter a globally strategic market rather than a market that is more standalone attractive? In what way would your answer differ for a firm manufacturing and marketing medical diagnostic equipment?

2. What advantages might a Korean-based company such as Hyundai have entering markets in developing countries?

3. Discuss the pros and cons of packaged-goods manufacturers targeting Eastern Europe and Russia.

4. What could be the advantages and disadvantages of being a born-global firm?

5. Unlike firms early in their internationalization, MNCs (multinational corporations) do not appear to favor entering new markets that are similar to their home markets over entering those that are dissimilar. Why do you think that is?

Gavin Hellier / Alamy

© Inmagine/18439GNG

9
Global Market Entry Strategies

LEARNING OBJECTIVES

After studying this chapter, you should be able to:

- Differentiate among market entry options—indirect exporting, direct exporting, licensing, franchising, contract manufacturing, assembly, and full-scale integrated manufacturing—and note the conditions under which each is an appropriate strategy.

- Explain the role of export management companies, export agents, and export consortiums.

- Note the ways in which the Internet has affected the international entry strategies employed by firms.

- List the pros and cons of establishing wholly owned subsidiaries and the pros and cons of establishing joint ventures.

- Compare and contrast technology-based, production-based, and distribution-based strategic alliances.

- Explain when entering a market by acquisition is desirable.

- Define entry strategy configuration, bundling, and unbundling, and explain their significance to market entry strategies.

- Explain why market exit—and possibly reentry—strategies might be necessary.

EVEN THE ARTS are going global. Russia's Bolshoi Ballet has actively sought overseas expansion since the collapse of the Soviet Union left the world-famous dance troupe strapped for funds. The Guggenheim art museum in New York, concerned with its limited endowment, has also expanded into foreign markets. But what is the best way for ballet companies and art museums to enter foreign markets? Traditionally, they exported their product by taking their dancers or art exhibits on tour. Today other market entry options are being employed. The Bolshoi has licensed its name to schools in Brazil and Japan. The Guggenheim has established subsidiary branches in Bilbao, Venice, and Berlin. Even the Vatican is considering ways to enter world markets by licensing the images from its repository of manuscripts, prints, coins, and artwork to interested companies in the fields of collectibles, giftware, apparel, and décor.

Any enterprise, whether a for-profit company or a not-for-profit museum, that pursues a global strategy must determine the type of presence it expects to maintain in every market where it competes. A company may choose to export to the new market, or it may decide to produce locally. It may prefer full ownership of a local operation, or it may seek partners. Once a commitment has been made, changes can be difficult and costly. Therefore, it is important to approach these decisions with the utmost care. Not only is the financial return to the company at stake, but the extent to which the company can implement its global marketing strategy also depends on these decisions. In this chapter, we concentrate on the major entry strategies by explaining each alternative in detail and citing relevant company experiences. An overview of possible entry strategies appears in Figure 9.1.

FIGURE 9.1
Market Entry
Strategies

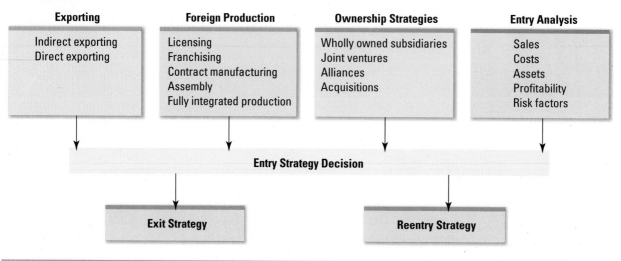

EXPORTING AS AN ENTRY STRATEGY

Exporting to a foreign market is a strategy that many companies follow for at least some of their markets. Few countries offer a large enough market to justify local production. Exporting allows a company to manufacture its products for several markets centrally and thus achieve economies of scale. When this occurs, a firm can realize more profits, lower its prices, or sometimes do both. In addition, both transportation costs and government tariffs have fallen considerably in the past 25 years. These conditions make exporting all the more cost-effective. Therefore, many firms use exporting as a way to grow their business while limiting risk and avoiding large investments.

Home governments often assist firms by providing information on export markets. As a result there is a great deal of information available on export markets. Much is available online. For example, Table 9.1 lists a number of services offered by the U.S. Export Portal.

However, a study of 992 export decision makers from the United Kingdom, Austria, Germany, New Zealand, and the United States found that firms serving a few countries used less information than firms serving many countries. The study also identified that the sheer volume of export information could be a problem for both large and small exporters without sufficient staff to understand and interpret the available information.[1]

A firm has two basic options for carrying out its export operations. Markets can be contacted through an intermediary located in the exporter's home country—an approach called **indirect exporting**. Alternatively, markets can be reached directly or through an intermediary located in the foreign market—an approach termed **direct exporting**.

Indirect Exporting

Several types of intermediaries located in the home market are ready to assist a manufacturer in contacting international markets or buyers. A major advantage of using a domestic intermediary lies in its knowledge of foreign market conditions.

Indirect exporting exporting through an intermediary located in the exporter's home country

Direct exporting exporting through an intermediary located in a foreign market

TABLE 9.1	TYPICAL SERVICES PROVIDED BY THE U.S. EXPORT PORTAL (http://www.export.gov)

- Basic guide to exporting
- Country market reports
- Industry-specific trade data and analysis
- Trade lead database
- Information on trade fair and other promotional events
- Foreign standards and certification information
- Assistance with export financing
- Information on economic sanctions and export licenses
- Advocacy and dispute resolution
- Assistance finding freight forwarders
- Best methods for handling orders and shipments
- Assistance locating foreign agents and distributors
- Advice on pricing and methods of payment
- Personalized counseling
- Online course for exporters

Particularly for companies with little or no experience in exporting, the use of a domestic intermediary provides the exporter with readily available expertise.

Export Management Company. An export management company (EMC) is a firm that handles all aspects of export operations under a contractual agreement. The EMC normally takes responsibility for the marketing research, patent protection, channel credit, and shipping and logistics, as well as for the actual marketing of products in a foreign market or markets. An EMC can operate either as a merchant that takes title to the products or as an agent that does not take title but provides services for a fee or commission. Arrangements between an EMC and a manufacturer will vary, depending on the services offered and the volume expected. The advantages of an EMC include the following: (1) little or no investment is required to enter the international marketplace, (2) no in-house personnel are required, and (3) the EMC offers an established network of sales offices as well as international marketing and distribution knowledge. The main disadvantage is that the manufacturer gives up direct control of the international sales and marketing effort.

Export Agents. Export agents are individuals or firms that also assist manufacturers in exporting goods. They are similar to EMCs, except that they tend to provide more limited services and to focus on one country or one part of the world. Export agents understand all the requirements for moving goods through international channels, but they do not provide all the services that an EMC provides. These agents focus more on the sale and handling of goods. The advantage of using an export agent is that the manufacturer does not need to have an export manager to handle all the documentation and shipping tasks. The main disadvantage is the export agent's limited market coverage. To cover different parts of the world, a firm would need the services of numerous export agents.

Direct Exporting

A company engages in direct exporting when it exports directly to customers or solely through intermediaries located in foreign markets. In other words, no domestic intermediary is involved. In direct exporting, an exporter must deal with a large number of foreign contacts, possibly one or more for each country the company enters. A direct exporting operation requires more expertise, management time, and financial resources than does indirect exporting, but it gives the company a greater degree of control over its distribution channels. Most firms interested in exporting can seek assistance online from their home governments for basic training and advice.

Independent Distributor versus Marketing Subsidiary.   To handle the marketing of its products within its target market, the company must choose between relying solely on local independent distributors and establishing its own marketing subsidiary. In making this choice, the company must consider costs, control, and legal restrictions.

An independent distributor earns a margin on the selling price of the products. Although using an independent distributor entails no direct cost to the exporter, the margin the distributor earns represents an opportunity that is lost to the exporter. By switching to a sales subsidiary to carry out the distributor's tasks, the exporter can keep the margin previously paid to the distributor. For example, say a manufacturer of electronic machinery exports products priced at $7,500 each (at the factory in Boston). With airfreight, tariffs, and taxes added, the product's landed costs amount to $9,000. An independent distributor will have to price the products at $13,500 to earn a desired gross margin of $33^1/_3$ percent, or $4,500 per machine.

Alternatively, the exporter can set up a wholly owned marketing subsidiary, in this case consisting of a manager, a sales manager, several sales agents, clerical staff, a warehousing operation, and the rental of both an office and a warehouse

The U.S. Export Portal offers assistance to U.S. exporters in finding distributors overseas. Many governments offer similar services to their own exporters.

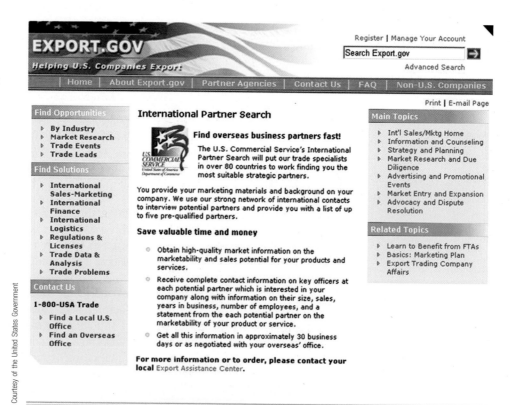

Courtesy of the United States Government

location. If the total estimated cost of these arrangements is $450,000 annually, the firm can break even at sales of one hundred machines.

With increasing volume, the incentive to start a marketing subsidiary grows. On the other hand, if the anticipated sales volume is small, using the independent distributor will be more efficient because sales are channeled through a distributor who is maintaining the necessary staff for several product lines.

Firms marketing products that require the development of special skills or special working relationships with customers tend to have their own marketing subsidiaries. This way the company may better control the delivery of after-sale service. If the firm has definite ideas about the correct way to price and promote its products, it may wish to establish a marketing subsidiary as well. The subsidiary could then implement the full strategy for the marketing mix, such as setting prices, developing advertising programs, and choosing media.

Still, a commitment to a marketing subsidiary should not be made without careful evaluation of all the costs involved. The operation of a subsidiary adds a new dimension to a company's international marketing operation. It requires a financial commitment in a foreign country, primarily for the financing of accounts receivable and inventory. Also, the operation of a marketing subsidiary entails a number of general administrative expenses that are essentially fixed in nature. The size of the available market in a country will often determine the appropriate market entry strategy. For example, Duckworth and Kent, the world's leading manufacturer of titanium ophthalmic surgery instruments, located in the United Kingdom, has a marketing subsidiary in the United States, its largest market, but uses distributors in most other markets.[2]

Firms may also face government restrictions on the use of wholly owned marketing subsidiaries. Although these constraints are declining with trade liberalization, they persist in some developing countries such as Saudi Arabia. Exporters to Saudi Arabia have traditionally been required to use Saudi agents or establish a marketing subsidiary with a Saudi partner.

Cooperating for Export.   Companies that compete against each other in their domestic market may sometimes unite to address export markets. Brazil's Ministry of Development, Industry and Foreign Trade promotes such **export consortiums** wherein companies unite to share the logistical and promotion costs of entering foreign markets. Brazil's two largest frozen meat processors formed a consortium to target Russia and selected countries in Africa, the Middle East, and the Caribbean. It is very unlikely that Brazilian antitrust law would allow such cooperation in the domestic market, but governments often encourage it in export markets.

Export cooperation can also occur among small and medium-sized enterprises (SMEs). One study of exporter SMEs in the Jutland peninsula of Denmark revealed that 83 percent cooperated with other firms in the same industrial sector. For example, a manufacturer of windmills exported to California purchased the motors from another local SME. Firms in the textile and clothing sector mounted mutual exhibits at trade fairs. Manufacturers of wooden furniture might contribute different products—a desk, chair, or bookshelf—to a commonly marketed export suite. The success of these smaller ventures in competitive export markets can be attributed in part to this sort of cooperation.[3]

Exporting and the Internet.   The Internet has greatly increased the ability of firms to export directly. A company that establishes a server on the Internet and opens up a web page can be contacted from anywhere in the world. Consumers

TABLE 9.2	WEBSITES OF TOP 25 GLOBAL BRANDS		
BRAND	**WEBSITE**	**BRAND**	**WEBSITE**
Coca-Cola	www.coca-cola.com	Marlboro	www.marlboro.com
Microsoft	www.microsoft.com	American Express	www.americanexpress.com
IBM	www.ibm.com	Gillette	www.gillette.com
GE	www.ge.com	Louis Vuitton	www.louisvuitton.com
Nokia	www.nokia.com	Cisco	www.cisco.com
Toyota	www.toyota.com	Honda	www.honda.com
Intel	www.intel.com	Google	www.google.com
McDonald's	www.mcdonalds.com	Samsung	www.samsung.com
Disney	www.disneygo.com	Merrill Lynch	www.ml.com
Mercedes-Benz	www.mercedes.com	HSBC	www.hsbc.com
Citi	www.Citibank.com	Nescafé	www.Nescafe.com
HP	www.hp.com	Sony	www.sony.com
BMW	www.bmw.com		

Source: Reprinted from "The 100 Top Brands," *BusinessWeek*, August 6, 2007, by special permission, copyright © 2008 by The McGraw-Hill Companies, Inc.

and industrial buyers who use modern Internet browsers can search for products, services, or companies and, in many instances, can make purchases online. Table 9.2 lists the websites of the top 25 global brands.

The impact of the Internet has been felt by SMEs as well as larger multinationals. Prior to the Internet, SMEs accounted for about one-quarter of total U.S. exports. With the advent of the Internet, this figure rose quickly to about one-third. SMEs can take advantage of virtual trade missions, videoconferencing, and online ordering. They can reach markets with daily communication and advertising without the need to send full-time salespeople into the field or to employ traditional export management companies. In fact, web-based startups in Europe often plan globally from their inception.[4]

Exporters using the Internet as an entry option do face several challenges. They may need to communicate in different languages, conform to different privacy regulations, and adapt to different cultures. Cultural factors, such as the need to touch and see products (common in Egypt and Mexico), can inhibit consumer purchasing online.[5] Also, Internet penetration varies greatly from 74 percent in North America to under 6 percent in Africa.[6] Table 9.3 lists the top 50 national markets with the best potential for Internet marketing.

Internet exporters must also overcome a number of fulfillment challenges. These challenges include cross-border issues involved with completing a sale, such as shipping the product, paying tariffs, collecting funds, and providing after-sale service to customers all over the world. Export management consultants have arisen to help with a number of these problems. One such company, Next Linx, was founded by Rajiv Uppal, an Indian-born engineer working in the United States. Uppal realized that new e-exporters still needed to know that their product could be hit with an education tax in Pakistan or that the same product could be subject

TABLE 9.3	TOP 50 MARKETS FOR ONLINE OPERATIONS		
RANK	COUNTRY	OVERALL SCORE	CONSUMER & BUSINESS ADOPTION
1	United States	8.95	9.50
2	Hong Kong	8.91	9.50
3	Sweden	8.85	9.05
4	Australia	8.83	8.70
4	Denmark	8.83	8.60
6	Singapore	8.74	9.70
6	Netherlands	8.74	8.60
8	United Kingdom	8.68	9.20
9	Switzerland	8.67	8.40
10	Austria	8.63	9.35
11	Norway	8.60	9.15
12	Canada	8.49	8.85
13	Finland	8.42	8.60
14	Germany	8.39	8.95
15	South Korea	8.34	9.05
16	New Zealand	8.28	8.50
17	Bermuda	8.22	8.80
18	Japan	8.08	8.65
19	Taiwan	8.05	8.39
20	Belgium	8.04	8.20
21	Ireland	8.03	8.50
22	France	7.92	8.15
23	Malta	7.78	8.90
24	Israel	7.61	7.70
25	Italy	7.55	7.60
26	Spain	7.46	7.35
27	Portugal	7.38	7.85
28	Estonia	7.10	7.60
29	Slovenia	6.93	7.70
30	Greece	6.72	6.95
31	Czech Republic	6.68	7.20
32	Chile	6.57	6.40
33	Hungary	6.30	6.75
34	Malaysia	6.16	6.60
35	United Arab Emirates	6.09	6.00
36	Slovakia	6.06	6.05
37	Latvia	6.03	6.10

continued

Table 9.3 continued

RANK	COUNTRY	OVERALL SCORE	CONSUMER & BUSINESS ADOPTION
37	Lithuania	6.03	6.35
39	South Africa	5.95	6.35
40	Mexico	5.88	5.90
41	Poland	5.83	5.80
42	Brazil	5.65	5.20
43	Turkey	5.64	5.75
44	Argentina	5.56	5.20
45	Romania	5.46	5.20
46	Saudi Arabia	5.23	4.55
47	Thailand	5.22	5.10
48	Bulgaria	5.19	4.70
49	Jamaica	5.17	4.90
50	Trinidad & Tobago	5.07	4.60

Source: Adapted from Economist Intelligence Unit, *The 2008 E-Readiness Rankings,* pp. 24–25. Copyright © 2008 by Economist Intelligence Unit. Reprinted by permission and author's calculations.

to state tariffs as well as a national tariff in Brazil. And exporters of wine to the European Union (EU) would need to navigate the EU's 132 different categories of wine, each with its own tariff schedule.[7] Clearly, online exporters must stay alert to the constant regulatory and logistics changes that affect their businesses.

FOREIGN PRODUCTION AS AN ENTRY STRATEGY

Licensing

With licensing, a company assigns the right to a copyright or patent (which protects a product, technology, or process) and/or a trademark (which protects a product name) to another company for a fee or royalty. Proprietary information, or trade secrets not protected by patents, can also be licensed. The foreign company, or licensee, gains the right to exploit the patent or trademark commercially on either an exclusive (the sole right to sell in a certain geographic region) or a nonexclusive basis.

Sometimes the licensee initiates the contract. Infopro, the largest information-technology media group in Taiwan, specializes in publishing Chinese-language editions of American publications under license. The group entered a licensing agreement with the Harvard Business School to produce a Chinese version of the prestigious management journal *Harvard Business Review. Infopro Harvard Business Review* was designed to have about 70 percent of its content translated from the original American text, supplemented with locally researched articles on business and management techniques.[8]

Licenses are signed for a variety of time periods. Depending on the investment needed to enter the market, the foreign licensee may insist on a longer licensing period to recover the initial investment. Typically, the licensee makes all the necessary capital investments (machinery, inventory, etc.) and markets the products in the assigned sales territories, which may consist of one or several countries. Licensing agreements are subject to negotiation and tend to vary considerably from company to company and from industry to industry.

Reasons for Licensing. Licensing can be very attractive for some companies such as Everlast Worldwide Inc. Since 1910 Everlast has been the preeminent brand in the world of boxing equipment. Its products have been used for training and professional fights by leading figures in the sport. The company's licensed products generate over $200 million in retail sales each year. In fact, licensing at Everlast is so successful that the company created a new management position: senior vice president of global licensing.[9]

Companies use licensing for many reasons. A company may not have the knowledge or the time to engage more actively in international marketing. If so, it can still realize income from foreign markets by using licensees. Licensing may also be employed for less attractive foreign markets, allowing the firm's scarce managerial resources to be concentrated on more lucrative markets. The market potential of the target country may be too small to support a new manufacturing or marketing operation. A licensee may have the option of adding the licensed product to an ongoing operation, thereby reducing the need for a large investment in new fixed assets. Finally, a company may not have sufficient capital to be able to expand into multiple markets. Using licensing as a method of market entry, a company can gain market presence without making an equity investment.

In some countries where the political or economic situation appears uncertain, a licensing agreement may avoid the potential risk associated with investing in fixed facilities. Both commercial and political risks are absorbed by the licensee. In other countries, governments favor the granting of licenses to independent local manufacturers as a means of building up a local industry. In such cases, a foreign manufacturer may prefer to team up with a capable licensee despite a large market size, because other forms of entry may not be possible.

Licensing can also help global firms enter difficult markets. Roche continues to expand in the Japanese pharmaceutical market through licensing its products with Chugai Pharmaceuticals. The Japanese market is difficult to penetrate without knowledge of the drug approval process and access to the distribution channels. Chugai Pharmaceuticals has licensed two cancer drugs and a hepatitis drug from Roche. The licensing approach for Roche also speeds up the market entry process for Roche, giving them fast access to the second-largest pharmaceutical market in the world.

Disadvantages of Licensing. A major disadvantage of licensing is the company's substantial dependence on the local licensee to produce revenues and thus royalties. **Royalties** are usually paid based on a percentage of sales volume. Once a license is granted, royalties are paid only if the licensee is capable of performing an effective marketing job. Because the local company's marketing skills may be less developed, revenues from licensing may suffer accordingly. Although there is a great variation from one industry to another, licensing fees in general are substantially lower than the profits that can be made through exporting or local manufacturing. Depending on the product, licensing fees may range anywhere between 1 percent and 20 percent of sales, 3 to 5 percent being more typical for industrial products.

Royalties payments by a licensee to a licensor in exchange for the right to produce and market the licensor's product or service within a certain region

Ironically, if a local licensee is too successful, an international firm may reconsider the wisdom of licensing. More direct participation in a successful market can reap higher rewards in profits than mere licensing fees. Some licensing contracts even include provisions for the licenser to increase its participation if it eventually wishes to do so. Hutchinson Whampoa Ltd. of Hong Kong announced that it was forming a company that would license Priceline's patented bidding system to allow Asian consumers to purchase tickets online. As part of the arrangement, Priceline would be given the option of eventually buying up to 50 percent of the new company.[11]

Another potential disadvantage of licensing is the uncertainty of product quality. A foreign company's image may suffer if a local licensee markets a product of substandard quality. For this reason, firms often seek licensees based on their production knowledge and reputation for quality. New Zealand–based Fonterra Co-Operative Group signed a licensing agreement with Arab Dairy to produce and sell Fonterra's products in Egypt and other Middle East countries. The two companies had worked together on projects before, and Fonterra was convinced of the quality standards of its new licensee. Fonterra had a partner in China, however, who went bankrupt as the result of producing and selling melamine-tainted baby products. These products may have been responsible for several deaths and the hospitalization of thousands of infants.[12] Even when a quality licensee is located, however, ensuring uniform quality requires the licenser to provide additional resources that may reduce the profitability of the licensing activity.

Licensing will also require a certain commitment of management time and resources. Licensees may need to be trained. Appropriate records must be kept, and licenser audits must be conducted. Serious consideration must be given to problems that could arise. In case of disagreements between licenser and licensee, there must be provisions for dispute resolution. In the context of which national law will the contract be interpreted? How and in which country will arbitration take place? What are the conditions for termination of the licensing contract?

The possibility of nurturing a potential competitor is viewed by many companies as a final disadvantage of licensing. Licenses are usually limited to a specific time period. Licensees can use similar technology independently after the license has expired and can, therefore, turn into a competitor. This is less of a concern if the licensed technology changes quickly or if a valuable brand name is involved. Of course, firms must be careful that they—and not their licensee—hold the trademark to their brand in each national market.

Franchising

Franchising is a special form of licensing in which the franchiser makes a total marketing program available, including the brand name, logo, products, and method of operation. Usually, the franchise agreement is more comprehensive than a regular licensing agreement, inasmuch as the total operation of the franchisee is prescribed.

Numerous companies that successfully exploited franchising in their home market are exploiting opportunities abroad. Among these companies are McDonald's, Kentucky Fried Chicken (KFC), Burger King, and other U.S. fast-food chains with operations in Latin America, Asia, Europe, and the Middle East. Service companies such as Holiday Inn, Hertz, and Manpower have also successfully used franchising to enter foreign markets. The United States is home to the greatest number of franchisers. However, franchising is increasingly important in many non-U.S. markets, where growth potential is higher than in the more mature U.S. market.

WORLD BEAT 9.1

THE MIDDLE EAST FRANCHISE

PAYLESS HAS 600 stores in the United States, Canada, the Caribbean, Central and South America, Guam, and Saipan. Now the U.S.-based discount shoe retailer has set its sights on the Middle East. A partnership between Payless and master franchisee M.H. Alshaya aims to open 200 stores in the region, including in Bahrain, Egypt, Qatar, Jordan, Kuwait, Lebanon, Saudi Arabia, and the United Arab Emirates (UAE). These will be the company's first stores developed through franchising. The use of Middle East franchisees with regional reach is not uncommon. Figaro's Pizza chose Sense Gourmet as its master franchisee. The first Figaro store opened in Abu Dhabi, and Sense Gourmet plans to open other stores across nine Arab countries. Similarly, the master licensee of Uno Chicago Grill expects to open 20 stores in nine Arab countries as well.

Franchising is booming across the Arab World. Australian-owned Ecowash offers a waterless car-washing franchise and identifies the Middle East as its fastest growing market. Local franchisors are as enthusiastic as foreign firms. Mashawi Lebanese Restaurant is looking to franchise its brand across the Middle East. If successful there, the company will franchise in Europe, Asia, and the United States. Even the African Development Bank is enthusiastic about franchising. It has funded a $40 million Franchising Sector Support Program for Egypt.

However, franchising can have its surprises. Cairo's luxury Grand Hyatt Hotel was banned from selling alcohol by its owner and franchisee, a pious Saudi sheikh. The Hyatt parent company objected. Despite Islamic conservatism in Egypt, the Egyptian government had not banned alcohol for fear of hurting its important tourist industry. An agreement was struck between franchisor and franchisee: Alcohol could be sold in one restaurant within the hotel.

Sources: David Twiddy, "Payless Shoe Source Opens in Middle East," *Associated Press Newswires*, March 31, 2009; "Sense Gourmet Opens First Middle East Figaro's Pizza Outlet in Abu Dhabi," *Al-Bawaba News*, January 20, 2008; "USA's Uno Chicago Grill to Open 20 New Restaurants in Middle East," *Middle East and North Africa Today*, May 23, 2008; "Cairo's Grand Hyatt Brings Back Booze after Compromise with Saudi Owner over Alcohol Ban," *Associated Press Newswire*, August 26, 2008; "Middle East Franchise Market to Grow by 25%," *Al-Bawaba News*, May 14, 2008; and "AFDB Lends $40 Million to Local Franchising Sector," *IPR Strategic Information Database*, June 1, 2009.

For example, Mexico is the world's seventh largest franchise market with about 750 different franchises operating in 70 different industries with 55,000 points of sale. Franchising has grown consistently in Mexico at a rate of 14 to 17 percent annually and now accounts for 6 percent of gross domestic product (GDP).[13] Similarly, franchising accounts for 5 percent of the Philippines' GDP.[14]

U.S.-based franchisors dominate among foreign franchisors in Mexico. In Morocco, however, French firms are most common and account for 42 percent of all franchisors. In comparison, U.S. franchises only account for 12 percent of the Moroccan franchise market.[15] In fact, franchisers of many national origins have entered international markets. Singapore-based Informatics Holdings Inc. franchises computer training schools in Asia. Interbrew franchises its Belgium Beer Café. The Japanese company Yoshinoya D&C has opened 91 stores in California that sell *gydun*, a seasoned beef and rice dish. Even an Egyptian college student who began exporting hookahs, Egypt's traditional water pipes, to the United States branched into franchising, supplying 50 accounts with a complete hookah system for a water pipe café, including equipment, staff training, and management advice.[16]

Finding the right franchisee is critical for successful franchising. The United States Commercial Service offers an array of services to help U.S. franchisors identify qualified franchisees. Its offices in 80 countries provide trade specialists to screen potential franchisees, network with local franchise associations, and arrange meetings for U.S. franchising executives.[17] Whereas many franchisees worldwide

Master franchises are common in countries such as Kazakhstan in Central Asia.

ITPhoto/Alamy

Master franchises franchises that include exclusive rights to market within a whole city or country

The International Franchise Association gives tips on how to avoid franchising pitfalls. The U.S. Federal Trade Commission's website lists complaints against franchisers. Check out these and other franchise links on the student companion website at http://www.cengage.com/international.

are individual entrepreneurs, in some countries, companies or wealthy individuals buy **master franchises** that give them exclusive rights to a whole city, a whole country, or even a whole region of the world. In the Central Asian state of Kazakhstan, most franchising operations are supervised by master franchisees operating out of Turkey or Russia.[18] Master franchises have traditionally been sophisticated partners of established multinational franchise chains. U.S.-based Gold's Gym operates in 28 countries and uses master franchises outside its home market.[19]

With its rapid global growth, however, the franchising industry has been hit with numerous complaints and has even been plagued by fraud in the past few years. One individual on the Internet actually claimed his government had privatized its Consumer Protection Agency, for which he was selling local franchises.[20] As a result of the surge in complaints, many countries are tightening their franchising laws to help protect franchisees.

Local Manufacturing

Another widely practiced form of market entry is the local manufacturing of a company's products. Many companies find it advantageous to manufacture in the host market instead of supplying that market with products made elsewhere. Sometimes local production represents a greater commitment to a market. Numerous factors, such as local costs, market size, tariffs, labor laws, and political considerations, may affect a choice to manufacture locally. The actual type of local production depends on the arrangements made. It may be contract manufacturing, assembly, or fully integrated production.

Contract Manufacturing.   Under contract manufacturing, a company arranges to have its products manufactured by an independent local company on a contractual basis. The local manufacturer's responsibility is restricted to production. The local producer manufactures in accordance with orders from the international firm. The products are then turned over to the international company, which assumes the marketing responsibility for sales, promotion, and distribution. In a way, the international company "rents" the production capacity of the local firm to avoid establishing its own plant and to circumvent barriers that prevent the import of its products. For example, Finnish tire manufacturer Nokian Tyres contracted with Matador AS of Slovakia to produce up to 500,000 tires a year, tires that Nokian would in turn sell to the European car market.[21]

Sometimes contract manufacturing is chosen for countries with a low-volume market potential combined with high tariff protection. In such situations, local production appears advantageous to avoid high tariffs, but the local market does not support the volume necessary to justify the building of a single plant. These conditions tend to exist in the smaller countries of Central America, Africa, and Asia. Contract manufacturing is also employed where the production technology involved is widely available. Otherwise, contract manufacturers would not have the necessary know-how. If research and development and/or marketing are of crucial importance in the success of the product, then contract manufacturing can be an attractive option, especially when excess capacity in an industry makes manufacturing the least profitable part of the product's value chain. However, contract manufacturing is viable only when an appropriate local manufacturer can be located.

Assembly.   By moving to an assembly operation, the international firm locates a portion of the manufacturing process in the foreign country. Typically, assembly consists only of the last stages of manufacturing and depends on a ready supply of components or manufactured parts to be shipped in from another country. (In the chemical and pharmaceutical industry, this latter stage is referred to as **compounding**.) Assembly usually involves the heavy use of labor rather than extensive investment in capital outlays or equipment. Sometimes host governments force firms to establish assembly operations either by banning the import of fully assembled products or by charging excessive tariffs on them.

Motor vehicle manufacturers have made extensive use of assembly operations in numerous countries. General Motors has maintained major integrated production units only in major markets. In many other countries, disassembled vehicles arrive at assembly operations that produce the final product on the spot. BMW operates assembly plants in Indonesia, Malaysia, Thailand, the Philippines, and Vietnam. BMW reports that a demand of 1,500 cars per year can justify the cost of a local assembly plant. Local assembly plants let BMW test the waters and expand into markets where tariffs and other local hurdles cannot be overcome with an export strategy of shipping completed cars to these markets.[22]

Full-Scale Integrated Production.   Establishing a fully integrated local production unit is the greatest commitment a company can make for a foreign market. Building a plant involves a substantial capital outlay. Companies do so only where demand appears ensured. International companies can have any number of reasons for establishing factories in foreign countries. These reasons are related primarily to market demand or cost considerations. Often, the main reason is to take advantage of lower costs in a country, thus providing a better basis for competing with local

Compounding a term referring to the last stages of manufacturing in the chemical and pharmaceutical industries

firms or other foreign companies already present. Also, high transportation costs and tariffs may make imported goods non-competitive.

Although most manufacturing tends to shift from developed to developing countries, Mexican firms are moving production to the United States. The DuPont Company sold three plants to Alfa SA. Alfa is refitting the former textile plants to produce plastics used in beverage containers and frozen-food trays. Over a period of only ten years, Mexico has moved from number 33 to the sixth-largest investor in the United States. The Alfa case illustrates reasons why U.S. manufacturing looks good to Mexican firms:

- Though production costs are higher in the United States, production in Mexico would result in longer delivery times to the U.S. market.
- The plants were available relatively cheap as U.S. firms withdrew from older, lower technology industries.
- Local governments offered tax and job-creation credits—in this case, $1 million.
- Alfa was able to renegotiate contracts with the workforce, decreasing wages by up to 25 percent in some cases.[23]

Establishing Local Operations to Gain or Defend Market Position.
Some companies build a plant to gain new business and customers. Local production can represent a strong commitment to a market and is often the only way to convince clients to switch suppliers. This is of particular importance in industrial markets, where service and reliability of supply are main factors in the choice of product or supplier. In some developing countries, establishing local operations may be the only way to enter a local market, although this requirement is becoming more rare with the spread of trade liberalization and the impact of the World Trade Organization.

At other times, companies establish production abroad to protect markets already built through exporting. Such markets can be threatened by protectionist government policies or by relative changes in currency exchange rates. Following an established customer abroad can also be a reason for setting up international operations. When customers move into new markets, suppliers of both products and services move too. Deutsch Advertising, a North America advertising firm, had worked with Novartis on the antifungal drug Lamisil in the United States. Deutsch later announced that it would be following Novartis into Italy, Germany, the United Kingdom, and Switzerland.[24]

Shifting Production Abroad to Save Costs. Firms may also shift production abroad to save costs and remain competitive. In order to continue to compete with American and Japanese carmakers in the important U.S. market, German-based Mercedes-Benz opened a factory in the United States, where total labor, components, and shipping costs were among the lowest in the developed world.

Some products may be too costly to transport long distances, and this makes them poor candidates for export. Fresh orange juice is one such product. Brazil is currently the top producer of orange juice in the world, whereas the United States consumes 40 percent of all orange juice. The U.S. market has a strong demand for fresh, not-from-concentrate orange juice that sells for higher prices. This fresh product is particularly costly to ship because it consists mainly of water.[25] Brazilian orange juice firms bought land to develop orange groves in Florida and multinationals with Brazilian ties soon accounted for about half of Florida's orange juice industry.[26]

Sometimes, international firms with plants in Taiwan, Malaysia, Thailand, and other foreign countries may have little intention of penetrating these markets with the help of their new factories. Instead, they locate abroad to take advantage of favorable conditions that reduce the manufacturing costs of products that are sold elsewhere. This strategy has been employed by many U.S. companies and has more recently been adopted by Japanese and European firms as well. Morinaga, Japan's leading dairy company, built a new powdered-milk plant in China not so much to enter the Chinese market as to establish a low-cost base from which to capture share in other Asian markets. Such decisions of a sourcing or production nature are not necessarily tied to a company's market entry strategy but may have important implications for its global competitiveness.

Manufacturing and Intrafirm Licensing.   Although international licensing arrangements were originally designed as an alternative for firms manufacturing abroad, today they are sometimes used in conjunction with a firm's own manufacturing operations. A firm may license its trademark or technology to its own manufacturing subsidiary if taxes on royalties are less than taxes on repatriated profits. Such an arrangement might also be employed when a subsidiary is not wholly owned but, rather, shared with a local partner. A licensing contract with its own joint venture can give an international firm a greater and more guaranteed payback on its contribution to the venture.

OWNERSHIP STRATEGIES

As we have noted, companies investing in foreign markets also face ownership decisions. Do they want to establish a wholly owned subsidiary or a joint venture? Alternatively, they may decide to explore longer-term contractual relationships, or alliances. There are advantages and disadvantages to each of these options. For this reason, most firms employ a combination of ownership strategies. For example, the Strauss Group, based in Israel, has ambitions to become a major player in the global coffee market. Its first venture overseas was to Brazil, where it acquired 50 percent ownership in a leading coffee producer. However, in Eastern Europe, Strauss chose to establish its own coffee production and marketing facilities.[27]

Wholly Owned Subsidiaries

Wholly owned subsidiaries are operations in a host country that are fully owned by a foreign parent firm. They can involve marketing, assembly, or full-scale integrated production operations. Firms must have the necessary capital investment to undertake this ownership option. There are, of course, advantages to wholly owned subsidiaries. The firm has a free hand to establish the strategy for the subsidiary. It is also able to keep all the profits of the subsidiary and need not share them with partners. For these reasons, national markets that are more strategically important may be good candidates for a wholly owned subsidiary. Such a subsidiary can also be more easily integrated into a global network. For example, a parent can allot the U.S. export market to its wholly owned subsidiary in Taiwan. If relative production and transportation costs change, however, the firm can take the U.S. market away from the Taiwanese subsidiary and give that market to its wholly owned Mexican subsidiary. There would be no local Taiwanese partner to oppose this move.

 Nonetheless, global marketers should be wary of equating ownership of a foreign subsidiary with control of that subsidiary. A study of firms that had shut down wholly owned subsidiaries overseas revealed that local management at these subsidiaries often became involved in activities that undermined the marketing strategy of the multinational firm. These activities included stealing cash, equipment, and inventory; misusing expense accounts; registering brand names to third parties; and even selling proprietary information to the competition.[28] Wholly owned subsidiaries are only controlled by headquarters when headquarters exerts the effort and oversight necessary to establish such control. Therefore, in addition to committing greater financial resources to wholly owned subsidiaries, firms must also commit to devoting the considerable management time necessary to establish and run a successful overseas operation.

Joint Ventures

If firms do not have the resources to invest in a wholly owned subsidiary, or if host government restrictions disallow them, companies can consider entering a market with a joint venture partner. Under a joint venture arrangement, the foreign company invites an outside partner to share stock ownership in the new unit. Traditionally, the other partner has been a local firm or individual located in the host market. The particular equity participation of the partners may vary, with some companies accepting either a minority or a majority position.

One study of multinational firms revealed that respondent firms had no fewer than four joint ventures in foreign markets and one firm was involved in 385 international joint ventures. However, joint ventures may not be as popular as they once were.[29] Joint ventures once represented 29 percent of U.S. overseas investments. Evidence suggests that this percentage has now declined to 20 percent.[30] Even in developing countries, where joint ventures once accounted for 60 percent of foreign investments, the number of new joint ventures has dropped significantly and many current joint ventures are being terminated.[31]

There are several reasons why joint ventures have fallen from favor. International firms often prefer wholly owned subsidiaries for reasons of control; once a joint venture partner secures part of the operation, the international firm can no longer function independently. This sometimes leads to inefficiencies and disputes over responsibility for the venture. If an international firm has strictly defined operating procedures for budgeting, planning, manufacturing, and marketing, getting the joint venture to accept the same methods of operation may be difficult. Problems may also arise when the partner wants to maximize dividend payout instead of reinvestment, or when the capital of the venture has to be increased and one side is unable to raise the required funds.

There has also been a disturbing trend toward local partners competing with their foreign partner. This can occur because technology transfer to a joint venture can easily be adopted by the local parent firm and used in other businesses outside the joint venture. General Motors (GM) formed a 50-50 joint venture with Shanghai Automotive Industry Corporation to produce Buicks, Cadillacs, and Chevrolets for the Chinese market. This joint venture has been highly successful. However, Shanghai Automotive is increasingly competing with GM as it introduces its own lines after benefiting from GM technology.[32]

Parallel firm a firm established by local partners or managers of a joint venture to illegally compete with the joint venture by using the joint venture's technology, market knowledge, and brand

Just as worrying is the phenomenon of **parallel firms**. Parallel firms are established independently by local partners or managers of a joint venture for the purpose of using the foreign firm's technology, market information, and even its brand name. Such firms are theoretically illegal but often compete effectively against the joint venture because of lax enforcement of laws. For example, one well-known producer of condiments discovered that a manager in its Chinese joint venture was using bottles and labels of its brand to sell his own product manufactured in a separate factory. The company tried to shut down the parallel firm through legal means but failed. It had to resort to making a deal with the manager to stop production.[33]

Reasons for Entering into Joint Ventures. Despite the potential for problems, joint ventures can offer important advantages to the foreign firm. In markets where host governments disallow wholly owned investments, joint ventures with a local partner may be the only alternative. When China first opened to foreign investment, the Chinese government required foreigners to partner with local companies, usually state-owned enterprises. More recently, the Vietnamese government has steered a number of multinational companies into joint ventures with local partners, many of whom do not provide capital contributions equal to their equity shares in these ventures.[34]

If a firm is trying to enter many foreign markets quickly, joint ventures may help leverage scarce capital and managerial resources. In some cases, the partner may provide local manufacturing or excellent government or distribution contacts. By bringing in a partner, the company can share the business and political risks for a new venture. Furthermore, the partner may have important skills or market knowledge of value to the international firm. This is particularly important in difficult markets. Virtually every Internet company that attempted to enter the Chinese market faced significant regulatory and competitive challenges. Both Yahoo! and eBay finally resorted to joint venturing in this important market.[35]

Of course, to enter into a joint venture, an international firm must find an available partner. Table 9.4 gives some indication why local partners seek to establish joint ventures with international firms. A survey of Mexican companies identified access to technology and association with recognized international brands as the two most often cited reasons why local firms sought U.S. partners. In certain instances, local firms seek international ties to become more competitive and thus block new competitors from entering their home markets. Others go so far as to try to coopt potential competitors by directly partnering with them.

Joint Venture Divorce: A Constant Danger. Not all joint ventures are successful or fulfill their partners' expectations. Various studies have placed the instability rates of joint ventures at between 25 and 75 percent.[36] There are a number of reasons for ending a joint venture. Sometimes the regulations that force foreign firms to take local partners are rescinded. This occurred in China. As a result, joint ventures are no longer the most common mode of entry into China,[37] and many foreign partners who entered China early now seek exclusive ownership of their Chinese joint ventures. Unilever gradually bought out its partners in all of its original 14 joint ventures in China. Similarly, Procter & Gamble has also bought out partners in many of their Chinese ventures.[38] Starbucks also began to buy back the equity of local Chinese partners as soon as China revoked its joint venture requirement.[39]

When joint ventures are used to enter many international markets relatively cheaply and quickly, a parent firm may wish later to increase its stake in the venture or even reclaim full control when financial resources are more readily available. Starbucks undertook rapid international expansion, establishing almost 5,000 coffeehouses overseas in just 12 years. In some international markets, Starbucks stores operate under joint venture agreements. However, the company later

TABLE 9.4 WHAT MOTIVATES MEXICAN FIRMS TO SEEK U.S. PARTNERS?	
MOTIVATION	**PERCENTAGE OF RESPONDENTS**
Access to technology	71
Access to recognized brand	56
Product/service knowledge of partner	47
Access to products and services	40
Supplier access	33
Access to new products/market areas	27
Short-term credit	24
Access to raw materials	22
Customer access	22
Reduce costs	22
Block competitors	20
Capital access	18
Access to marketing infrastructure	16
Geographic market access	16
Reduce risks	13
Co-opt competitor	13
Geographic market knowledge of partner	13
Access to long-term credit	11

Source: Reprinted from *The Columbia Journal of World Business*, Winter 1995, Kate Gillespie and Hildy J. Teegen, "Market Liberalization and International Alliance Formation: The Mexican Paradigm," p. 63. Copyright © 1995, with permission from Elsevier.

increased its stake in some of its joint ventures, and this trend is expected to continue.[40]

Sometimes the choice of partner turns out to be less than ideal. Cristal, a U.K.-based food hygiene consultancy, advises hotels, food processing plants, and restaurants around the world. Joint ventures have played an important part in the firm's international expansion. In Egypt, however, Cristal chose a well-established partner with expertise in engineering rather than in tourism. Trying to learn the tourism industry and the food hygiene industry in a short time proved overwhelming. Cristal had to buy back shares from the partner and take over management of the venture.[41]

At times, problems can arise between parents over the strategic direction of the joint venture. Brasil Telecom is a joint venture between Telecom Italia and Opportunity, a local Brazilian investment company. Despite being one of Brazil's largest fixed-line telecommunications companies, Brasil Telecom found itself headed for arbitration in London when its two parents became deadlocked over expansion options. The Italian parent wanted to move quickly into mobile telephone operations. Opportunity wanted the joint venture to pursue what it thought were more profitable businesses, such as acting as an Internet service provider. The relationship

WORLD BEAT 9.2

DANONE'S WAHAHA WOES

FRANCE'S GROUPE DANONE SA has often depended on joint venture partners to enter foreign markets quickly. This strategy appeared to be a success in China, where Danone partnered with multimillionaire Zong Quinghou. Danone's Wahaha joint venture claimed 23 percent of China's bottled water market, helping to make Danone the country's largest soft drinks company—bigger even than Coca-Cola, a company that chose to enter the Chinese market alone.

Mr. Zhong had run the joint venture since its inception, although he only owned 49 percent of it. However, a decade into the venture, Danone accused its partner of cutting it out of more than $100 million in revenue, stating that Mr. Zong had run parallel businesses that produced and sold products the same as or similar to those of the Danone venture. The disagreement soon turned nasty. Danone sued Mr. Zong's wife and daughter, assisted U.S.

tax authorities in investigating its partner, and got a court to back its request to freeze Zong-family off-shore accounts.

After three years and more than 30 lawsuits in seven countries, Danone had yet to win a case. Mr. Zong announced that the joint venture was heading for a divorce and stated that Danone should sell its share in the venture to him or to a third party. However, each side was billions of dollars apart in its valuation of the venture.

In the meantime, Danone announced that future investment in India, another Asian mega-market, would be done independently and without partners. Its 13-year joint venture with India's Wadia Group had turned sour over a disagreement concerning Danone's use of the Tiger biscuit brand. Danone sold its share to Wadia and declared that it would compete in India with its own brands in the future.

Sources: James T. Areddy and Deborah Ball, "Danone's China Strategy Is Set Back," *Wall Street Journal,* June 15, 2007, p. A10; James T. Areddy, "Partners Fight over Wahaha in China," *Wall Street Journal,* July 28, 2008, p. B1; Jenny Wiggins, "Danone and Wadia Part Ways," *Financial Times,* April 15, 2009, p. 17; and "Court Quashes Wahaha Appeal," *South China Morning Post,* May 19, 2009, p. 2.

between the parent companies became increasingly hostile, and both wished to take full control of the joint venture.[42]

In some cases, however, joint venture divorce can be amiable. Teijin of Japan dissolved its joint venture with U.S.-based Molecular Simulations (MSI), a major global player in computerized chemistry. The negotiated settlement specified that Teijin would receive $10 million from Pharmacopeia, the company that had since acquired MSI. Teijin was willing to sell its share in the joint venture because it had already accomplished its objective—gaining adequate expertise in computerized chemistry through the venture.[43] Still, buying out partners can be expensive and is further complicated if the two partners vary greatly on their assessment of a venture's worth.

It is always wise to have a "prenuptial agreement." Yet a surprising number of joint venture agreements fail to acknowledge the possibility of joint venture dissolution. AT&T and British Telecom formed a joint venture, Concert, to serve large multinational business customers. A former AT&T executive involved in the negotiations claims that the absence of an exit agreement was deliberate. It was intended to make sure both companies remained committed to the partnership. Two years later, however, the venture was losing $210 million a quarter and was judged a failure by both parents. Without an exit agreement, there was no simple way to determine how Concert's assets—including 75,000 kilometers of fiber optic cable—would be divided.[44]

Strategic Alliances

A more recent phenomenon is the development of a range of strategic alliances. Alliances encompass any relationship between firms that exceeds a simple sales transaction but stops short of a full-scale merger. Thus, the traditional joint venture between a multinational corporation (MNC) and a local company is a form of alliance. So is a contract manufacturing or licensing agreement. However, the term **strategic alliance** is commonly used to denote an alliance involving two or more firms in which each partner brings a particular skill or resource—usually, they are complementary. By joining forces, each firm expects to profit from the other's experience. Typically, strategic alliances involve technology development, production, or distribution. The number of strategic alliances has been driven by the increased globalization of firms. As firms expand into multiple countries, they often use strategic alliances to speed up entry into multiple markets as well as to gain access to assets and technologies that may be specific to certain countries.[45]

Strategic alliance an alliance involving two or more firms in which each partner contributes a particular skill or resource—usually complementary—to a venture

Technology-Based Alliances. Many alliances are focused on technology and the sharing of research and development expertise and findings. The most commonly cited reasons for entering these technology-based alliances are access to markets, exploitation of complementary technology, and a need to reduce the time it takes to bring an innovation to market.

One of the companies most experienced with technological alliances is Toshiba, a major Japanese electronics company. The company's first technological tie-ups go back to the beginning of last century, when it contracted to make lightbulb filaments for U.S.-based General Electric. The company has since engaged in alliances with many leading international companies, many of whom are competitors. For example, IBM, Sony, and Toshiba joined forces to create the Cell Alliance, which created the Cell chip to compete with chips by Intel. Sony will use the chip in PlayStation 3, Toshiba will use it in digital television sets, and IBM will use it in computer servers and workstations.[46]

French carmaker Peugot has bucked the industrywide trend toward global mergers and has become one of the most profitable carmakers outside Japan. Management contends that the key to its success has been producing innovative cars in quick succession and that mergers can slow down innovation if managers are struggling to integrate two companies. Instead, Peugot has relied on alliance partners to cut costs of developing new components—such as an alliance with Ford to develop diesel engines.[47]

Production-Based Alliances. A large number of production-based alliances have been formed, particularly in the automobile industry, where firms seek increased efficiency through component linkages. A production-based alliance also made sense for coffee retailer Starbucks. Starbucks joint ventured with Pepsi to produce bottled frappuccino for sale in the United States and China.[48] Even service providers may reap advantages from production-based alliances. International alliances focused on operations allow airlines to offer fuller services and more extensive routes as well as providing cost savings to the participating firms. For example, the Star Alliance of 13 airlines has agreed to a standard set of specifications for either the Airbus A350 or the Boeing 7E7, which will result in a significant reduction in the inventory costs for replacement engines, brakes, avionics, and other replacement parts, which the Star Alliance member will share.[49]

Distribution-Based Alliances. Alliances with a special emphasis on distribution are becoming increasingly common. General Mills, a U.S.-based company marketing breakfast cereals, had long been number two in the United States, with some 27 percent market share, compared to Kellogg's 40 to 45 percent share. With no effective position outside the United States, the company entered into a global alliance with Nestlé of Switzerland. Forming Cereal Partners Worldwide (CPW), owned equally by the two companies, General Mills gained access to the local distribution and marketing skills of Nestlé in Europe, the Far East, and Latin America. In return, General Mills provided product technology and the experience it had acquired competing against Kellogg's. CPW was formed as a full business unit with responsibility for the entire world except the United States. Today, CPW has sales of $1.4 billion and operates in over 130 countries.[50]

The Future of Alliances. Although many older alliances were spawned by technology exchange and were contracted among manufacturing companies, some of the most innovative arrangements are signed by service firms. Many of these, however, have proved to be short-lived in a never-ending rearrangement between the world's leading players. This is particularly true of large telecommunications carriers. One alliance was WorldPartner, which included AT&T, the Japanese KDD, Singapore Telecom, and Unisource of Europe, itself a combination of several European firms. The alliance served about 700 international clients, in 35 countries. However, the alliance was effectively dissolved as a result of AT&T's move to link up with British Telecommunications.

Although many alliances have been forged in a large number of industries worldwide, it is not yet clear whether these alliances will actually become successful business ventures. Experience suggests that alliances with two equal partners are more difficult to manage than those with a dominant partner. Furthermore, many observers question the value of entering alliances with technological competitors. The challenge in making an alliance work lies in the creation of multiple layers of connections, or webs, that reach across the partner organizations.

Many strategic alliances fail. Perhaps more surprisingly, strategic alliances may continue in effect for years even after they have proven unviable. For example, Deutsche Telekom, France Telecom, and Sprint created a three-way alliance, Global One. Only after six years of higher than expected losses and internal conflicts did the partners dissolve the alliance. Research indicates that the high cost of terminating an alliance, high sunk costs, and high alliance visibility all contribute to a delay in dissolving failing alliances.[51]

ENTERING MARKETS THROUGH MERGERS AND ACQUISITIONS

International firms have always made acquisitions. However, the need to enter markets more quickly has made the acquisition route extremely attractive. This trend has probably been aided by the opening of many financial markets, making the acquisition of publicly traded companies much easier. Even unfriendly takeovers in foreign markets are now becoming increasingly common.

By purchasing an established business, the firm eliminates the need to build manufacturing and distribution capabilities from scratch. Buying an established brand gives the firm immediate market presence and market share. South Africa Breweries (SAB) purchased Miller Beer from Philip Morris for $3.4 billion. The acquisition gave SAB instant access to the U.S. market as well as the well-known brands of Miller Lite, Miller High Life, Miller Genuine Draft, and Milwaukee's Best. The acquisition also gave SAB a strong foothold as the second-largest brewer in the world to battle Anheuser Busch. SAB continued its expansion strategy with acquisitions in Italy, China, and Colombia.[52]

Wal-Mart internationalized by using different ownership strategies in different countries. Market entry by acquisition has increasingly become the most common mode of entry, however.

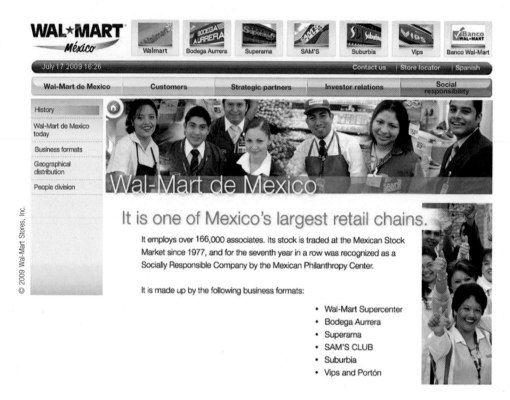

© 2009 Wal-Mart Stores, Inc.

Acquisition is also an attractive strategy when a market is already dominated by established brands and saturated with competitors. New entrants would find such a market difficult to break into, and the addition of a totally new player might make the market even more competitive and unprofitable for all. eBay has spent more than $1.6 billion on acquisitions, including $150 million to take full control of Eachnet in China.[53] In some extreme cases, the government might allow entry only by acquisition in order to protect a depressed industry from new entrants. Such was the case with the Egyptian banking industry in 2001, when the government would allow international banks only to buy existing Egyptian banks and refused to grant them licenses to start new businesses.[54]

Because they are often late movers into international markets, firms from developing countries frequently opt for acquisitions as a route to enter markets, including more mature markets such as the United States. Mexico's Bimbo is a bakery with a virtual monopoly at home. It expanded into the United States with the purchase of Texas-based Mrs. Baird's Bakeries for $300 million. Later purchases of several other bakeries in Canada and the United States elevated Bimbo to third-largest bakery in the world. A number of Indian companies—in industries as diverse as telecommunications, auto parts, and pharmaceuticals—are also entering developed countries via acquisition. In fact, after India removed government regulations limiting access to foreign capital, Indian companies spent $3.7 billion on foreign acquisitions in a single year.[55]

Despite their advantages, overseas acquisitions can pose challenges to global marketers. Businesses for sale often have big problems. As late movers to international markets, a number of Chinese firms chose to acquire companies overseas, especially in the competitive markets of the developed world. Chinese computer manufacturer

Lenevo bought the PC division of IBM for $1.25 billion, but only after that division had accumulated losses of nearly $1 billion for the four years prior to the sale. China's largest auto-parts manufacturer acquired a 21 percent share in a U.S. company that went bankrupt a year later, and Chinese consumer electronics–maker TCL Corporation bought the RCA and Thomson brands only to discover that their plans of lean manufacturing went only so far. The company failed to keep up with technological changes in the market. Three years after the purchase TCL stock prices had fallen 75 percent.[56]

Increasingly, as companies try to grab market share abroad via acquisitions, competitors are trying to block them from employing this market entry strategy. U.S. white goods company Whirlpool Corporation agreed to pay the high price of $2.8 billion for U.S. competitor Maytag Corporation in order to assure that China's Haier would not acquire Maytag and thus gain an immediate advantage in the U.S. market.[57]

ENTRY STRATEGY SELECTION AND CONFIGURATION

This chapter has explained the various entry strategies available to international and global firms. A number of variables influence the choice of entry strategy. A meta-analysis of more than 600 articles found that the mode of entry chosen by a firm was significantly influenced by country risk, cultural distance, company assets, international experience, and advertising intensity in the potential country.[58] In reality, however, most entry strategies consist of a combination of different formats. We refer to the process of deciding on the best possible entry strategy mix as **entry strategy configuration**.

Rarely do companies employ a single entry mode per country. A company may open up a subsidiary that produces some products locally and imports others to round out its product line. The same foreign subsidiary may even export to other foreign subsidiaries. In many cases, companies have bundled such entry forms into a single legal unit, in effect layering several entry strategy options on top of each other.

Bundling of entry strategies is the process of providing just one legal unit in a given country or market. In other words, the foreign company sets up a single company in one country and uses that company as a legal umbrella for all its entry activities. However, such strategies have become less typical—particularly in larger markets—and many firms have begun to unbundle their operations.

When a company **unbundles**, it essentially divides its operations in a country into different companies. The local manufacturing plant may be incorporated separately from the sales subsidiary. When this occurs, companies may select different ownership strategies, for instance allowing a joint venture in one operation while retaining full ownership in another part. Such unbundling becomes possible in the larger markets, such as the United States, Germany, and Japan. It also enables the firm to run several companies or product lines in parallel. ICI, the large U.K. chemicals company, operates several subsidiaries in the United States that report to different product line companies back in the United Kingdom and are independently operated. Global firms that grant such independence to their product divisions will find that each division will need to develop its own entry strategy for key markets.

EXIT STRATEGIES

Circumstances may make companies want to leave a country or market. Failure to achieve marketing objectives may be the reason. German DHL ceased domestic

Entry strategy configuration the process by which a firm determines the best possible entry strategy for a country or region

Bundling the act in which a firm combines all its operations in a certain country or region into a single legal unit

Unbundling the act in which a firm divides its operations in a certain country or region into different legal units

pickups and deliveries of express mail within the United States when the economy soured in 2008, though it continued to deliver international shipments.[59] Nonetheless, international companies have to be aware of the high costs attached to the liquidation of national operations. Substantial amounts of severance pay may have to be dispensed to employees, and the firm may lose credibility in other markets.

Consolidation

Sometimes an international firm may need to consolidate its operations. This may mean a consolidation of factories from many to fewer such plants. Production consolidation, when not combined with an actual market withdrawal, is not really what we are concerned with here. Rather, our concern is a company's actual abandonment of its plan to serve a certain market or country.

Consolidation can be an option if a firm fails to establish itself in a particularly competitive market. European retailer Carrefour left the Mexican market in the face of strong local competition.[60] Similarly, Yahoo! announced its retreat from five European markets—the United Kingdom, Ireland, France, Germany, and Spain—when it found itself a distant third in these markets. Auctions have proved to be well suited to the Internet, but sellers and buyers tend to gravitate to the largest sites, leading to natural monopolies in online auction markets. eBay, the auction leader in the United States and most of Europe, agreed to pay exiting Yahoo! to promote eBay's European auction sites through banner ads and text links.[61]

Market consolidation often occurs when an international firm acquires more debt than it can handle. To service the debt, poorly performing markets must be abandoned. Even successful operations may be sold to raise cash. Avon Products sold 60 percent of its successful Japanese company for about $400 million to reduce Avon's debt in the United States. Dutch retailing giant Ahold had to exit the Latin American market when an accounting scandal back home in Europe prompted creditors to call in the company's 11 billion euro debt.[62]

Political Considerations

Changing government regulations can at times pose problems that induce some companies to leave a country. Political risk can also motivate firms to leave a market. Sainsbury is a U.K.-based supermarket chain that employs 100,000 people worldwide. It entered the Egyptian market by purchasing 80 percent interest in a state-owned retailer. The subsidiary posted a significant loss the next year, partly as a result of problems with goods clearing customs and difficulty in obtaining building permits. These losses were exacerbated by an organized campaign against the company orchestrated by anti-Israel protesters who generally targeted Western companies operating in Egypt.[63] Three years after entering the market, Sainsbury announced that it would pull out of Egypt, selling its stake to its Egyptian partner and incurring a loss of $140 to $175 million.[64]

Reentry Options

Sometimes companies reverse their exit decision and enter markets a second time. This can occur when the political environment improves. DHL Worldwide Express returned to Afghanistan after exiting 15 years earlier when market prospects looked bleak.[65] It can also occur when market conditions change. Burger King left the Japanese market after a price war with McDonald's. However, six years later,

Private security officers stand guard outside a KFC restaurant in Rawalpindi, Pakistan, after the United States led attacks on neighboring Afghanistan. As icons of American culture, U.S.-based fast-food chains are sometimes targets of politically motivated mobs. One such mob burned a KFC restaurant in Karachi, Pakistan. Mob violence in India encouraged KFC to leave that market.

AP Images

What could be an appropriate entry strategy for your target market? Continue with your Country Market Report on the student companion website at http://www.cengage.com/international.

after the Japanese began eating more U.S. fast food, Burger King reentered the market.[66]

Sometimes firms simply realize that their first attempt at market entry was ill conceived. Dunkin' Donuts exited the Chinese market after only a few years. Its sweets were too sweet for Chinese tastes. It underestimated the difficulty of selling coffee to a nation of tea drinkers, and it partnered, oddly and unsuccessfully, with an aerospace company. Ten years after leaving the Chinese market, Dunkin' was ready to try again. Success in other Asian markets, including Taiwan, had given the company more confidence. This time Dunkin' partnered with a Chinese company that specialized in operating shopping centers and restaurants. Dunkin' performed extensive local testing of its products and lowered the level of sugar in its pastries. The company also invested in finding prime real estate for its locations. Even the choice of the company's local Chinese name, "Everybody Is Happy," was determined only after months of debate.[67] China, a market once abandoned, had clearly become a new priority.

CONCLUSION

Market entry strategies can have a profound impact on a firm's global strategy. They determine the number of foreign markets a firm can enter and the speed at which a firm can internationalize. They affect the profits the firm will make in each national market and the risk it will assume. They can even obligate a firm to local partners, thus constraining its power to act solely in its global self-interest. Despite the importance of the market entry decision, surprisingly few multinationals appear to recognize its strategic significance. A study of 105 firms in four European countries found that only 36 percent of managers even reviewed alternative entry options.[68] Choosing the best entry strategy is complex and involves many considerations. The relative importance of these considerations varies by industry and by the strategic goals of each firm. It also varies according to the strategic importance of each national market. Table 9.5 presents some key considerations and their impact on the potential appropriateness of different entry options. Clearly, no one option is ideal under all conditions.

For example, speed of market entry may be an important consideration in some cases. If a firm is in an industry where products face high development costs, it will want to sell in many countries.

If it is not already present in many markets, it will need to expand rapidly to keep up with global competitors. This is all the more true if products have a short life cycle, as is the case with many high-technology products. Often the need to be in many markets quickly requires a firm to take partners, because it simply doesn't have enough money or managerial depth to take on the task itself. Licensing, joint venturing, or entering distribution alliances becomes attractive.

In all cases, managers must decide how many resources they can and want to commit to a market. Resources include investments necessary for increasing or relocating manufacturing, as well as investments related to product research and development and to the implementation of marketing strategy. Exporting or licensing might require no new capital investment or very little incremental investment to increase current production. Wholly owned manufacturing facilities require significant capital investments. Joint ventures and other alliances can cut capital costs in research and development, manufacturing, and distribution. Another important resource is management time. Direct exporting may not require additional capital investment but will require a greater commitment of

TABLE 9.5	APPROPRIATENESS OF MARKET ENTRY STRATEGIES MODE OF ENTRY					
STRATEGIC CONSIDERATION	INDIRECT EXPORTING	DIRECT EXPORTING- MARKETING SUBSIDIARY	LICENSING	WHOLLY OWNED PRODUCTION	JOINT VENTURE	ACQUISITION
Speed of entry	High	High	High	Low	Low	High
Ease of exit	High	Moderate	Moderate	Low	Low	Low
Rapidly changing technologies	Low	High	High	Moderate	Moderate	Moderate
Resource demands	Low	Moderate	Moderate	High	High	High
Profit potential	Low	High	Low	High	Moderate	Moderate
Competitive intensity of market	Low	Moderate	Moderate	Moderate	Moderate	High
Integration into global network	Low	High	Low	High	Low	Moderate
Strategically important country	Low	High	Low	High	Moderate	Moderate
Unimportant market	High	Low	Moderate	Low	Low	Low
Cultural distance	High	Low	Moderate	Low	Moderate	Low
Congruence with host government's goals	Low	Low	Moderate	High	High	Moderate

management time than indirect exporting. Joint ventures and alliances can help ease the demands on this critical resource.

Other concerns include profitability and flexibility. Will exporting to a market produce higher returns than producing there? Economies of scale in global or regional production may or may not offset the costs of transportation and tariffs. Licensing and joint ventures require that profits be shared. If the political environment or the business prospects of a country are uncertain, the flexibility involved with an entry strategy becomes a consideration. How quickly and at what cost can the firm expand in the market or retreat from it? Redirecting exports is easier than closing an overseas plant. Partnership or licensing agreements can limit future actions both within the market and globally.

Firms must also consider different entry strategies for different countries. Establishing a sales subsidiary may be the best alternative for entering some countries, whereas joint ventures may be necessary to enter others. Firms should allot their greatest efforts and resources to the most strategic global markets. They should always consider how an entry strategy will later affect their ability to integrate operations in that country into the global whole.

Firms must balance the advantages and disadvantages of different entry strategies. Even when a firm is clear about its strategic goals, rarely does an entry option present no drawbacks whatsoever. Governments may disallow the ideal market entry choice, forcing a company to fall back on a less desirable option or to avoid the market altogether. Compromises must often be made. Marketers should expect to manage a variety of entry strategies, and still other types of entry strategies may be devised in the future, presenting global marketers with new opportunities and challenges.

QUESTIONS FOR DISCUSSION

1. Why might entry strategies differ for companies entering the United States, those entering China, and those entering Costa Rica?
2. How might the entry strategy of a born-global firm (see Chapter 1) differ from that of a mature multinational company?
3. Why would licensing sometimes be appropriate—and sometimes inappropriate—for a strategically important country?
4. Is there such a thing as a "no-fault" joint venture divorce? Or is joint venture dissolution always the result of some sort of failure?
5. If a company exits a market and then wishes to return ten years later, what peculiar challenges might it face?

Alain Nogues/Corbis

CHAPTER OUTLINE

© Immagine/18439GNG

10
Global Product Strategies

LEARNING OBJECTIVES

After studying this chapter, you should be able to:

- List the advantages of product standardization and product adaptation.

- Differentiate between mandatory and discretionary product adaptations.

- Explain the concepts of global product standards and generic management system standards.

- Explain why product lines can vary from country to country.

- Define modularity and explain its impact on global product development.

- Compare and contrast the product development roles played by a multinational firm's headquarters and the roles played by its subsidiaries.

- Explain the importance of lead markets and note their importance to product development.

- Describe how companies may access new products by purchasing research and development or by importing products from other firms.

- Discuss the use of acquisitions, joint ventures, and alliances for the purpose of product development.

- [Explai]n the process of [introdu]cing new products [in globa]l markets, [including] concept testing, [test mar]keting, and the [rate of n]ew product [adoptio]n.

ONCE A HOLLYWOOD BLOCKBUSTER MOVIE could take seven months to arrive in some countries. Now this time is cut to 60 days. The Internet is one reason for this new speed. Foreign consumers are using Web retailers such as Amazon.com to buy films on DVD as soon as they are available in the United States. In many cases, these films have not yet opened in all national markets. Furthermore, movie fans around the world can access movie promotions on the Web. These promotions appear even before the domestic launch. Waiting months to see these movies frustrates foreign consumers.

But creating a global motion picture for a global launch isn't easy. When Universal developed the film Dr. Seuss's *How the Grinch Stole Christmas*, it realized prior to production that the movie would be translated into 30 languages. However, Dr. Seuss's works present peculiar problems because of the tricky language that makes it difficult to translate. Local writers were given leeway to adjust the translated verse if they thought it didn't make sense. In some cases, the translators were able to preserve rhymes partly by making up their own words to go with Dr. Seuss's made-up words. In Spanish, the "Pontoos" mountains where the Grinch lives were replaced by the "Pontienes" range—a word concocted to rhyme with "*los quienes*," meaning "the Whos" in Spanish. Furthermore, the translation problem was avoided somewhat in the film by a decision to modify the original English-speaking version of the movie. The Seussian metered narration was left out of long stretches of the movie and replaced by new dialogue.[1]

This chapter examines issues pertaining to the adaptation of products to global markets. In this chapter we begin by exploring the many environmental factors that can prevent the marketing of uniform or standardized products across a multitude of markets. Subsequent sections focus on packaging and labeling, product warranties, and product-line management across countries. The chapter concludes with a discussion of global product development.

PRODUCT DESIGN IN A GLOBAL ENVIRONMENT

One of the principal questions in global marketing is whether a firm's products can be sold in their present form or whether they need to be adapted to foreign market requirements. The benefits of adaptation are compared with those of standardization in Table 10.1. Standardizing products across markets has certain advantages. Standardization can help firms realize economies of scale and increases speed to market. In some cases standardization even serves to better satisfy global customers. Adapting products, on the other hand, can better address buyer needs and may even be necessary to legally sell a product in certain national markets.

Benefits of Product Standardization

If a standardized product can be sold in many countries, economies of scale in manufacturing may be realized. Economies of scale vary by industry, but to the extent they exist, they allow products to be produced more cheaply. As a result, a firm can sell its product at a cheaper price, likely increasing its share of market. Alternatively, a firm can keep the price the same but realize a greater profit margin, which in turn can support higher investment in promotion or research and development.

Product life cycle the market stages a product experiences over time: introduction, growth, maturity, decline, and withdrawal

If a product requires high development costs but has a short **product life cycle**, as is the case for many high-technology products, it may need to enter global markets very rapidly. In other words, firms must sell high volumes in many markets to recoup their investment before the product becomes obsolete. Adapting such a product to different national markets may simply take too long.

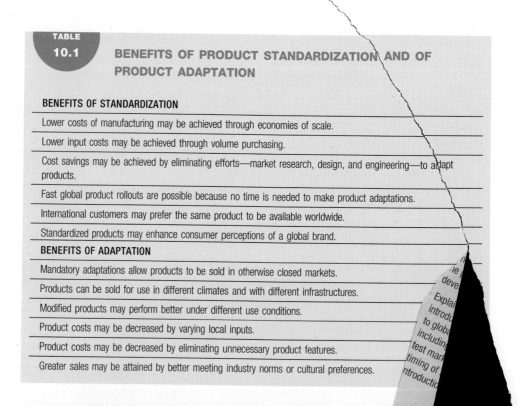

TABLE 10.1	BENEFITS OF PRODUCT STANDARDIZATION AND OF PRODUCT ADAPTATION

BENEFITS OF STANDARDIZATION

Lower costs of manufacturing may be achieved through economies of scale.

Lower input costs may be achieved through volume purchasing.

Cost savings may be achieved by eliminating efforts—market research, design, and engineering—to adapt products.

Fast global product rollouts are possible because no time is needed to make product adaptations.

International customers may prefer the same product to be available worldwide.

Standardized products may enhance consumer perceptions of a global brand.

BENEFITS OF ADAPTATION

Mandatory adaptations allow products to be sold in otherwise closed markets.

Products can be sold for use in different climates and with different infrastructures.

Modified products may perform better under different use conditions.

Product costs may be decreased by varying local inputs.

Product costs may be decreased by eliminating unnecessary product features.

Greater sales may be attained by better meeting industry norms or cultural preferences.

Furthermore, if buyers themselves are international firms, they may prefer a standardized product that is available worldwide. This preference for a standardized product is sometimes observed in consumer markets as well. When an Arabized version of the television series *The Simpsons* debuted on Arab television, Homer (or "Omar") still worked at the nuclear power plant in Springfield where he lived with his dysfunctional family, including his disrespectful son. However, Omar did not hang out at bars or eat bacon, and he drank soft drinks instead of beer. Despite the cultural sensitivity of these adaptations, some Arabs who had watched *The Simpsons* in the United States thought the various cultural adaptations ruined the show.[2] In contrast, when Cold Stone Creamery entered Japan it eschewed culturally sensitive adaptations such as offering green tea ice cream. Instead it kept to American iconic flavors, such as cotton candy and cake batter, in order to stand out from the local competition.[3]

Benefits of Product Adaptation

Despite the advantages of standardization, many products need to be adapted for different national markets. Even marketers who have long resisted product adaptation now acknowledge its necessity. After years of insisting that foreign buyers adapt to the taste of French wine, wine growers in France's Bordeaux region abandoned tradition and began to develop wines that the global consumer preferred—lighter and more fruity. The strategy reversed a five-year decline in sales, and wine exports from the region increased 26 percent in a single year.[4]

The need for adaptation is true even for Internet firms that only virtually enter international markets. Simply translating the text of a website may not be enough. Do people read from right to left or from left to right, from top to bottom or from bottom to top? What colors and shapes do they like? The answers to these questions will strongly influence the graphic layout of the site and its use of icons.[5] What standards—governmental or societal—could affect the content of the site? U.S. Internet firms routinely alter the content of their sites in Asia, self-censoring to avoid offending local governments, especially those in China, Singapore, and Malaysia, which have clamped down on Internet access.

Many adaptations are **discretionary**; that is, firms may choose to make certain adaptations or not to do so. In some cases, however, adaptations are **mandatory**. They are necessary for the product to be sold in a local market. Some mandatory adaptations are responses to differing physical realities. For example, consumer electronics must be adapted to work with different voltages, alternating currents, and electric plug designs, each of which varies from country to country.

Most mandatory adaptations, however, are made to adhere to national legal requirements. For example, a French court required Yahoo! to block French users from accessing Nazi memorabilia on its U.S.-based website, thereby setting a precedent and suggesting that Web companies operating on the global Internet could be required to conform to standards of individual countries. The judge gave Yahoo! three months to comply with the ruling by installing a key-word-based filtering system to block French citizens from viewing Yahoo! sites where Nazi items were being sold—or else be subject to fines of nearly $13,000 a day.[6]

Sometimes discretionary adaptations can become mandatory. Originally, Microsoft declined to translate its software into Icelandic, a language spoken by only 270,000 people. Customers in Iceland were apparently able to manage without it. However, when Iceland's government demanded that Microsoft translate its program, the firm agreed rather than face leaving the market.[7]

Discretionary adaptation a product adaptation that is optional but possibly desirable for a certain market

Mandatory adaptation a product adaptation that a firm must make to sell a product in a certain country or region

Selecting the most desirable product features for each market is an involved decision for global marketers. The approach taken should include a thorough review of a number of factors that could determine both mandatory and discretionary adaptations. These include climatic, infrastructure, and use conditions; cultural preferences; size and cost considerations; and performance and quality standards.

Climatic, Infrastructure, and Use Conditions

International marketers often adapt products to conform to physical realities such as regional variations in climate and infrastructure. Air conditioners in Saudi Arabia must be able to operate under conditions that are hotter and dustier than those in most U.S. locations. Paint must be adapted to various climatic conditions, such as heat, cold, moisture, and wind. Automobile manufacturers must consider which side of the street cars are driven on—the left or the right—and adjust the steering wheel accordingly. For instance, drivers in Britain and Japan drive on the left. Marketers of packaged foods must consider the distribution infrastructure of the country. How long will the product be in the distribution channels? Are warehouses air-conditioned and trucks refrigerated? Most chocolate is easily damaged if not kept cool. One worldwide manufacturer of industrial abrasives even had to adjust products to differing availability of raw materials. The firm responded by varying the raw-materials input from one country to another, while maintaining exacting performance standards.

Products may also need to be adapted to different use conditions in various markets. Procter & Gamble was forced to adapt the formulation of its Cheer laundry detergent to accommodate different use conditions in the Japanese market. Cheer was initially promoted as an all-temperature detergent. However, many Japanese consumers washed their clothes in cold tap water or used leftover bath water. The Japanese also liked to add fabric softeners that decreased the suds produced by detergent. Procter & Gamble reformulated Cheer to work more effectively in cold water with fabric softeners added and changed its positioning to superior cleaning in cold water.

In some local markets, customers may even expect a product to perform a function different from the one for which it was originally intended. One U.S. exporter of gardening tools found that its battery-operated trimmers were used by the Japanese as lawn mowers on their small lawns. As a result, the batteries and motors did not last as long as they would have under the intended use. Because of the different function desired by Japanese customers, a design change was eventually required.

Adapting Products to Cultural Preferences

Cultural adaptations are usually discretionary adaptations. Yet understanding cultural preferences and adapting products accordingly can be extremely important to success in local markets. To the extent that fashion and tastes differ by country, companies often change their styling. Color, for example, should reflect the aesthetic values of each country. For Japan, red and white have happy associations, whereas black and white indicate mourning. Green is an unpopular color in Malaysia, where it is associated with the jungle and illness. Textile manufacturers in the United States who have started to expand their export businesses have consciously used color to suit local needs. For example, the Lowenstein Corporation has successfully used brighter colors for fabrics exported to Africa.

© Charles Gupton

The typical Japanese home is smaller than its U.S. counterpart, creating a demand for smaller appliances.

The scent and sounds of a product may also have to be changed from one country to another. Strawberry-scented shampoo failed to sell in China, where consumers shun nonedible items that smell like foods.[8] Word processing engineers had to change programs destined for Japan that "pinged" when users tried to do something that was not possible. Japanese office workers complained that they were mortified that co-workers could hear when they made mistakes. The "ping" was deleted.[9]

As we saw in Chapter 3, food is one of the most culturally distinct product areas. In China, Nestlé snack wafers are sold in flavors, such as sesame and red bean, to appeal to local tastes.[10] Nestlé's popular instant coffee, Nescafé, is produced in more than 200 variations—more variations than the number of countries where it is sold. Product adaptations are even necessary within some national markets. In Switzerland, the French-speaking Swiss like strong, black coffee. The German-speaking Swiss prefer light coffee with milk.[11]

Cultural differences relating to food can extend beyond mere taste. As we discussed in Chapter 3, religion can dictate what people will and will not eat. Other traditional beliefs may require product adaptations as well. Frito-Lay wondered why its potato chips didn't sell in China in the summertime. Research revealed that Chinese consumers associated fried foods like potato chips with *yang*, which according to Chinese traditional medicine generates body heat and should be avoided in hot weather. The company then introduced a "cool lemon" variety packaged in pastel shades. The new lemon chips became Frito-Lay's best-selling item in China.[12] In general, a branded food product in the United States is likely to be considerably higher in fat, sodium, and added sweeteners than the same branded product sold in the Chinese, Japanese, and European markets.[13]

Even factual knowledge is not immune to a little cultural tweaking. Microsoft's online encyclopedia, *Encarta*, lists the height of Europe's highest mountain, Mont Blanc, as 4,808 meters (15,770 feet) in its French version. In the Dutch version, this height is listed as 4,807 meters. The Italians believe the correct height to be 4,810 meters, so that's what the Italian version says.[14]

Product Size and Dimensions

Within three years of entering the U.S. market, IKEA, the Swedish furniture and household products company, decided to abandon its smaller European sizes in furniture and bed linens and developed bigger sizes for the new market. American homes are 1,800 square feet on average—twice the size of the average European home. Larger furniture just looked better in American homes. Even drinking glasses had to be made bigger to accommodate ice, which is rarely used in Europe.[15]

When other design features require no modification, product size and dimensions may need adaptation. Product size can be affected by physical surroundings and available space. In many countries, limited living space necessitates home appliances that are substantially smaller than those found in a country such as the United States, where people live in larger dwellings. Recently, U.S.-made major appliances have been imported into Japan by discount chains. Although the volume is still small by international standards, certain wealthier Japanese consumers favor these large appliances. However, some customers have had to return them after purchase because they could not get the refrigerators through their apartment doors.

The different physical characteristics of consumers can also influence product design. Swiss watch manufacturers learned over the years to adapt their watchbands to different wrist sizes. For example, Japanese have smaller wrists than Americans. A leading Italian shoe manufacturer had a similar experience exporting shoes to the United States. The company learned that Americans have thicker ankles and narrower, flatter feet. To produce a properly fitting shoe, the Italian company decided to make appropriate changes in its design to achieve the necessary comfort for U.S. customers.

Another important decision, particularly for U.S. firms, is whether to select a metric or a nonmetric scale for the sale of their products abroad. With most of the world operating on the metric standard, the United States is one of the few remaining major nonmetric markets. The firm must often go beyond a single translation of nonmetric into metric sizes (or vice versa) to help consumers understand the design of its products. In some cases, companies may be required to change the physical sizes of their products to conform to legal standards based on the metric scale.

Cost and Price Considerations

In markets where many potential consumers have little disposable income, packaged-goods manufacturers often determine that smaller sizes are necessary to offer the customer a lower-priced, accessible product. In Latin America, where 25 percent of the population lives on less than $2 a day, sales of Nestlé Brazil's Bono cookies jumped 40 percent in a single year when the company decreased the package size from 200 grams to 149 grams.[16] In India, Hindustan Lever Ltd., a subsidiary of Unilever, sells Sunsilk shampoo in bottles for the upper classes and in sachets, good for one use, to consumers who cannot afford to buy a bottle.[17] Similarly, Unilever introduced a mini deodorant stick in several Asian countries, because many consumers in developing countries can afford deodorant only for special occasions.[18]

Another way to decrease costs is to develop products that can be sold in more than one national market. Unilever created a research team to develop a product called Cubitos—miniature bouillon cubes—to appeal to consumers in developing countries. The cubes were designed to be crumbled over food as a flavor enhancer and to cost about 2 cents apiece. After determining that the flavors that would appeal to consumers in most countries were meat, garlic, and onion, the company then rolled out the new Cubitos in 25 countries.[19]

To keep prices low, companies can also adapt the physical qualities of the product as well as the size. Procter & Gamble considers what price consumers can afford to pay in developing countries. Then they design products to meet these price targets. To keep costs down for its Ace handwashing detergent, P&G omitted enzymes from its formula.[20] However, global marketers should be aware that consumers in developing countries may demand bigger and better products as their incomes increase. In China, the world's second largest automobile market, consumers are increasingly purchasing more upscale models.[21]

Adapting to Performance and Quality Expectations

Manufacturers typically design products to meet domestic performance expectations. Such expectations do not always apply in other countries, and product changes are required in some circumstances. Some companies go to great lengths to meet different quality standards in foreign markets. German automaker BMW found that its customers in Japan expected the very finest quality. Typically, cars shipped to Japan had to be completely repainted. Even very small mistakes were not tolerated by customers. When service was required, the car was picked up at the customer's home and returned when the work was completed.

The necessity to increase product quality or performance for a foreign market tends, if the need exists, to be readily apparent. Opportunities for product simplification are frequently less obvious to the firm. Products designed in highly

Decreasing the size of a product to make it more affordable is a successful strategy in developing countries. In Brazil, sales of Nestlé's Bono cookies soared when the company cut the package size from 200 grams to 149 grams.

developed countries often exceed the performance needed in developing countries. Customers in these markets may prefer products of greater simplicity, not only to save costs but also to ensure better service over the products' lifetime. Companies have been criticized for selling excess performance where simpler products will do. Some multinational firms are addressing this issue. For example, when Philips created a product line for consumers in rural India, it focused on scaling back features in order to deliver inexpensive products such as a wind-up radio and a back-to-basics television set.[22] Also ready to fill this market gap are companies from less developed countries whose present levels of technology are more in line with consumer needs. For example, local Egyptian firms that produce consumer products invest very little in elaborate features or attractive packaging in order to deliver products at very low prices.

Of course, manufacturers from developing countries can face the opposite challenge when attempting to sell overseas. They must increase the performance of their products to meet the standards of industrialized countries. Producing quality products that are competitive on export markets has become something of a national obsession in Mexico. Major companies such as the Alfa business group and Cemex have joined forces with universities to establish programs to supply Mexican industry with top-flight engineers. And the effort has paid off. Fifteen years after the country joined NAFTA (the North American Free Trade Agreement), Mexico's exports had more than doubled.[23]

Global Standards

Incompatible national standards both help and hinder global competitors. Incompatible technologies in the mobile phone industry mean that it is very difficult for a single make of handset to compete worldwide. A lack of international standards also impacts the movie industry. The ultra-grisly movie *Hannibal* grossed more than $230 million worldwide, but its scenes of cannibalism and dismemberment caused an outcry in Italy, where its rating suggested it was appropriate for all audiences. In the United States, no one under 17 was supposed to be admitted without an adult, but children as young as 8 were seen entering with their parents. In Western Europe, viewers had to be at least 15—with or without accompanying adults. But in Portugal and Uruguay, they only had to be 12 years old.[24]

Given the growth in international commerce, there are benefits to having international standards for items such as credit cards, screw threads, car tires, paper sizes, and speed codes for 35 mm film. And country-to-country differences become immediately obvious when you try to plug in a hair dryer in various countries. Although national standards institutes ensure consistency within countries, an international agency is necessary to coordinate across countries.

Voluntary Standards.   Many countries have organizations that set voluntary standards for products and business practices. Groups such as the Canadian Standards Association and the British Standards Institute (BSI) formulate standards for product design and testing. If producers adhere to these standards, buyers are assured of the stated level of product quality.

The unification of Europe has forced Europeans to recognize the need for multi-country standards. In areas where a European standard has been developed, manufacturers who meet the standard are allowed to include the European Union (EU) Certification Symbol, CE. Firms both in and out of the EU are eligible to use the CE symbol, but they must be able to demonstrate their compliance with the standards.

The U.S. standard-setting process is much more fragmented than Europe's. In the United States, there are over 450 different standard-setting groups, loosely coordinated by the American National Standards Institute (ANSI). After a standard is set by one of the 450 groups, ANSI certifies that it is an "American National Standard," of which there are over 11,000 on the books.

The International Standards Organization (ISO), located in Geneva, was founded in 1947 to coordinate the setting of global standards. The ISO is a nongovernmental organization, a federation of national standards bodies from some 140 countries. Each member of the ISO is the firm "most representative of standardization in its country"; only one such member is allowed per country. Most standards set by the ISO are highly specific, such as standards for film speed codes or formats for telephone and banking cards. ISO standards for components of freight containers have made it possible for shipping costs around the world to be lowered substantially.[25]

To set an international standard, representatives from various countries meet and attempt to agree on a common standard. Sometimes they adopt the standard set by a particular country. For example, the British standard for quality assurance (BS5750) was adopted internationally as ISO 9000 in 1987. This standard was revolutionary in that it was a **generic management system standard**. As the first such international standard, ISO 9000 ensured that an organization could consistently deliver a product or service that satisfied the customer's requirements because the company followed a state-of-the art management system. In other words, the company possessed quality management. ISO 9000 can be applied to any organization,

Generic management system standard an international standard covering a particular set of corporate behaviors to which companies can choose to comply and consequently become certified as to their compliance

WORLD BEAT 10.1

ROLLING OVER

WHEREAS THE EUROPEANS build car roofs to withstand being dropped upside down or flipped off a moving dolly, their U.S. counterparts employ a less rigorous safety test that hasn't been changed in 50 years. U.S. automakers say their roofs match the Europeans' in safety. However, the National Highway Traffic Safety Administration (NHTSA) test, developed by General Motors in the late 1960s, calls for vehicles to be tested with their windshields intact. In a rollover, the windshield commonly breaks when the roof first hits the ground, and vehicle roofs lose between 10 percent and 40 percent of their structural strength without the windshield. Some of the most popular SUVs in the United States have a significant chance of rolling over in a one-vehicle accident, and a quarter of the 42,000 road deaths in the United States are caused by rollovers.

Europe has no roof-strength standards, but all three of the U.S. automakers' affiliates—GM's Saab, Ford's Volvo, and DaimlerChrysler's Mercedes-Benz—choose to subject their vehicles to tougher roof tests. Saab tests vehicles by ramming them into a bundle of electrical cable to simulate hitting a moose. In the past 20 years, the number of German traffic deaths has dropped 70 percent, whereas in the United States it has only dropped 20 percent.

Increasingly competing on price, U.S. automakers claim to have trouble pricing in safety innovations. Nonetheless, the U.S. government has doubled the standard for roof strength. By 2017 roofs on new vehicles must comply with this new standard, which will add to the weight of vehicles. Ironically, the added weight will make it more difficult for automobile manufacturers to comply with fuel economy standards also set by the U.S. government.

Sources: Aaron Bragman, "U.S. NHTSA Roof Crash Standards Improvement to Cost US$1.4 Billion Annually," *Global Insight Daily Analysis*, May 5, 2009; "U.S. will Require Stronger Roofs," *Globe and Mail*, May 7, 2009; David Welch, "Stability Shouldn't Be Optional," *BusinessWeek*, August 30, 2004, p. 50; and House Energy and Commerce Subcommittee on Commerce, Trade and Consumer Protection Hearing, *Auto Safety: Current Mandates and Emerging Issues*, Congressional Documents and Publications, May 18, 2009.

Visit the ISO and the ANSI links on the student companion website at http://www.cengage.com/international.

large or small, whatever its product or service. ISO 14000 is a similar generic management system standard that is primarily concerned with environmental management. Companies that meet this standard must show that they do minimal damage to the environment.

Mandatory Standards. Sometimes product standards are not voluntary but regulated by law. In these cases, adaptation is mandatory, not discretionary, for market entry. Most often these mandatory standards involve product quality and safety, hygiene, and environmental concerns. Meeting these standards can add costs to the product, but failing to comply may keep a firm out of an important market. For example, Kinder Eggs, made by Italian candy giant Ferrero SpA, are popular in one hundred countries and are ranked on the ACNielsen list of top global brands. But they are illegal in the United States. Wrapped in orange and white foil, the hollow chocolate eggs contain intricate plastic or wooden toy prizes. These represent a choking hazard according to the U.S. Consumer Product Safety Commission.[26]

Many believe that Europe has come to dominate the creation of international standards through its influence at the ISO and its proactive stance toward setting mandatory standards. Already the standards established by the European Commission have become effective standards for firms in Asia and Latin America that aspire to export to Europe. EU standards concerning consumer safety are generally tougher than their U.S. counterparts—forcing U.S. companies to take note and conform. For example, the EU ordered manufacturers to eliminate or drastically curtail six toxic substances (such as lead and mercury) or face fines, prison, and a ban on their products. One company, Coherent Inc., estimated that changes to comply with the new code would cost the company $10 million. Other countries such as China, Taiwan, Korea, Canada, and Australia announced plans to adopt similar restrictions.[27]

The EU also has greater authority to recall products and impose emergency bans when products are thought to be unsafe. The EU's precautionary principle allows regulators to ban products based on a lower burden of proof of their danger than can regulators in the United States. For example, the EU banned cheap Chinese cigarette lighters that were also deemed unsafe in Canada and Mexico. The same lighters remained available in the U.S. market despite three years of government testing.[28]

Despite attempts to make product standards uniform across Europe, many mandatory product standards remain far from standardized. For example, size requirements for license-plate holders on the backs of vehicles vary by country, sometimes only by a few centimeters.

PACKAGING AND LABELING FOR GLOBAL MARKETS

Differences in the marketing environment may require special adaptations in product packaging. Different climatic conditions often demand a change in the package to ensure sufficient protection or shelf life. The role a package assumes in promotion also depends on the market's retailing structure. In countries with a substantial degree of self-service merchandising, firms should choose a package with strong promotional appeal for consumer products. In addition, distribution handling requirements are not identical the world over. In the high-wage countries of the developed world, products tend to be packaged in such a way as to reduce further handling by retail employees. For consumer products, all mass merchandisers have to do is place products on shelves. In countries with lower wages and less elaborate retailing structures, individual orders may be filled from larger packaged units, a process that entails extra labor on the part of the retailer.

Specific packaging decisions that may be affected include size, shape, materials, color, and text. Size may differ by custom or in terms of existing standards, such as metric and nonmetric requirements. As noted earlier, higher-income countries tend to require larger unit sizes; these populations shop less frequently and can afford to buy larger quantities each time.

Packages can assume almost any shape, largely depending on the customs and traditions prevailing in each market. Materials used for packaging can also differ widely. Whereas Americans prefer to buy mayonnaise and mustard in clear plastic containers, consumers in Germany and Switzerland buy these same products in tubes. Cans are the customary material in which to package beer in the United States, whereas most European consumers prefer glass bottles.

The package color and text have to be integrated into a company's promotional strategy and therefore may be subject to specific tailoring that differs from one country to another. The promotional effect is of great importance for consumer goods and has led some companies to attempt to standardize their packaging in color and layout. In areas such as Europe and Latin America, where consumers frequently travel to other countries, standardized colors help them identify a product quickly. This strategy depends on devising a set of colors or a layout with an appeal beyond one single culture or market. An example of a product with a standardized package color is Procter & Gamble's leading detergent, Tide. The orange and white box familiar to millions of U.S. consumers can be found in many foreign markets, even though the package text may appear in the language of the given country.

Cultural implications of packaging and labeling can sometimes create problems in unexpected ways. One exporter of software to Saudi Arabia identified its CD-ROMs for the Saudi market by putting the Saudi flag on the box. The flag bears the word *Allah*, the Arabic word for "God." For many devout Muslims, to discard the box would imply disrespect for God. As a result, the local distributor was left with lots of boxes that both customers and employees declined to throw away.[29]

Packaging can even face legal restrictions. A British law cut the number of pills that could be sold in packages of aspirin and acetaminophen to reduce overdoses leading to death and liver failure caused by impulsive self-poisoning. Tablets were also required to be blister-wrapped to make swallowing large quantities impulsively even more difficult. Three years later, deaths by overdoses of these pills had decreased dramatically in the United Kingdom.[30]

Labeling is another concern for international marketers. Labeling helps consumers understand better the products they are buying and can convey rudimentary instructions for their use. What languages must the labels be in? What government requirements are involved?

Increasingly, packaged-foods companies must adhere to government requirements concerning labeling, but many other products are affected as well. China is home to two-thirds of the world's cashmere goats. When the country began exporting cashmere sweaters and other garments, many manufacturers exaggerated the amount of cashmere in their products. This brought them into collision with the United States' 60-year-old Wool Products Labeling Act, which requires that fabrics and garments made out of wool and other fine animal hairs be accurately labeled to reflect their true content. The Federal Trade Commission can seek penalties in federal court as high as $11,000 for each violation.[31]

GLOBAL WARRANTY AND SERVICE POLICIES

Buyers around the world purchase products with certain performance expectations and further expect companies to back their promises concerning product performance. As a result, warranties and service policies can become an integral aspect of a company's international product strategy. Companies interested in doing business abroad frequently find themselves at a disadvantage, relative to local competitors, in the area of warranties and service. With the supplier's plant often thousands of miles away, foreign buyers sometimes want extra assurance that the supplier will back the product. Thus, a comprehensive warranty and service policy can become a very important marketing tool for international companies.

Product Warranties

A company must address its warranty policy for international markets either by declaring its domestic warranty valid worldwide or by tailoring warranties to specific countries or markets. Although declaring a worldwide warranty with uniform performance standards would be administratively simple, local market conditions often dictate a differentiated approach. In the United States, many computers are sold with a 90-day warranty, whereas 12 months is more typical in Europe and Japan.

Companies are well advised to consider actual product use. If buyers in a foreign market subject the product to more stress or abuse, some shortening of the warranty period may become necessary. In developing countries, where technical sophistication is below North American and European standards, maintenance may not be adequate, causing more frequent equipment breakdowns. Another important factor is local competition. Because an attractive warranty policy can be helpful in obtaining sales, a firm's warranty policy should be in line with those of other firms competing in the local market.

Still, failure to maintain quality, service, or performance in one country can rapidly have a negative impact in other countries. Perrier, the French bottled-water company, had to withdraw its Perrier water from U.S. retail stores after the product was found to contain benzene in concentrations above the legal limit. This U.S. test result triggered similar tests by health authorities in other countries. Soon Perrier had to withdraw its products in other countries, eventually resulting in a worldwide brand recall. Nearly ten years later, Coca-Cola experienced a similar problem with bottling plants in Belgium, leading to a recall of many products not only in Belgium but also in France and Poland. Some 200 consumers complained of illness after drinking Coca-Cola products. This prompted the largest product recall in the firm's history.[32]

Global Product Service

For some products, no warranty will be believable unless backed with an effective service organization. Although service is important to the consumer, it is even more crucial to the industrial buyer, because any breakdown of equipment or product is apt to cause substantial economic loss. This risk has led industrial buyers to be conservative in their choice of products, always carefully analyzing the supplier's ability to provide service in the event of need.

To provide the required level of service outside the company's home base poses special problems for global marketers. The selection of an organization to perform the service is an important decision. Ideally, company personnel are preferable because they tend to be better trained. However, this approach can be organized economically only if the installed base of the market is large enough to justify such an investment. In cases in which a company does not maintain its own sales subsidiary, it is generally more efficient to turn to an independent service company or a local distributor. To provide adequate service via independent distributors requires extra training for the service technicians, usually at the manufacturer's expense. In any case, the selection of an appropriate service organization should be made in such a way that fully trained service personnel are readily available within the customary time frame for the particular market.

Closely related to any satisfactory service policy is an adequate inventory for spare parts. Because service often means replacing some parts, the company must store sufficient inventory of spare parts within reach of its markets. Whether this inventory is maintained in regional warehouses or through sales subsidiaries and distributors depends on the volume and the required reaction time for service calls. Industrial buyers will generally want to know, before placing substantial orders, how the manufacturer plans to organize service.

Firms that demonstrate serious interest in a market by committing themselves to setting up their own sales subsidiaries are often at an advantage over firms that use distributors. One German truck manufacturer that entered the U.S. market advertised the fact that "97 percent of all spare parts are kept in local inventory," thus assuring prospective buyers that they could get spares readily. Difficulty in establishing service outlets may even influence a company's market entry strategy. This was the case with Fujitsu, a Japanese manufacturer of electronic office equipment. By combining forces with TRW, a U.S.-based company, Fujitsu was able to sell its office equipment in the U.S. market backed by the extensive service organization of TRW.

Because the guarantee of reliable and efficient service can be such an important aspect of a firm's entire product strategy, investment in service centers sometimes must be made before any sales can take place. In this case, service costs must be viewed as an investment in future volume rather than merely as a recurring expense.

MANAGING A GLOBAL PRODUCT LINE

In early sections of this chapter, we discussed issues concerning individual products. Most companies, however, manufacture or sell a multitude of products. Starbucks doesn't vary its product formulations from country to country, but the product line can vary. For example, local product development produced a Strawberries and Cream Frappuccino specifically for the British market. Green Tea Frappuccino was the largest-selling Frappuccino in Taiwan and Japan before the product was offered elsewhere.[33] Pronto Cafes, one of Starbucks's competitor chains in Japan, sold coffee by day and liquor at night. So a Starbucks outlet in the Japanese city of Kobe quietly began selling beer and wine. Selling alcohol in Starbucks USA would be far more difficult because of the stricter alcohol licensing laws in the United States.[34]

As with each individual product decision, the firm can either offer exactly the same line in its home market and abroad or, if circumstances demand, make appropriate changes. In some cases, product lines overseas may be broader than those at home. When discount shoe retailer Payless entered the Middle East market, it extended its line of men's sandals by 100 percent.[35] However, product lines abroad

McDonald's adapts to the
Asian market by offering
rice-based dishes.
Multistory restaurants,
such as this one in China,
are more common in Asia
as well.

Geoff A Howard/Alamy

are commonly characterized by a narrower width than those found in a company's
domestic market. Table 10.2 reveals significant regional variability in the availability of many Procter & Gamble products. Some, such as detergents and disposable
diapers, are sold in all regions, whereas heartburn medicine Prilosec OTC is only
sold in North America.

The circumstances that can lead to deletions from product lines vary, but some
reasons dominate. Lack of sufficient market size is a frequently mentioned reason.
Companies with their home base in large markets such as the United States, Japan,
or Germany will find sufficient demand in their home markets for even the smallest market segments, justifying additional product variations and greater depth in
their lines. Abroad, opportunities for such segmentation strategies may not exist,
because the individual segments may be too small to warrant commercial exploitation. Lack of market sophistication is another factor in product-line variation.
Poorer developing countries may not demand some of the most advanced items
in a product line. Finally, new-product introduction strategies can affect product
lines abroad. For most companies, new products are first introduced in their home
markets and are introduced abroad only after the product has been successful at
home. As a result, the lag in extending new products to foreign markets also contributes to a product-line configuration that differs from that of the firm's domestic
market.

TABLE 10.2 REGIONAL AVAILABILITY OF SELECTED PROCTER & GAMBLE PRODUCTS

	NORTH AMERICA	EUROPE, MIDDLE EAST, AFRICA	LATIN AMERICA	ASIA
A Touch of Sun	X			X
Ace	X	X	X	
Actonel	X	X		
Alomatik		X		X
Always	X	X	X	X
Attento				X
Ayudin			X	
Bold	X	X	X	X
Bounty	X	X	X	X
Camay	X	X	X	X
Cover Girl	X		X	X
Crest	X	X	X	X
Dawn	X		X	
Daz		X		
Fairy		X		X
Frost & Tip	X			
Gillette	X	X	X	X
Gleem	X			
Iams	X	X		
Ivory	X	X	X	X
Lenor		X		X
Loreto			X	X
Luvs	X		X	X
Muse				X
Olay	X	X	X	X
Pampers	X	X	X	X
Prilosec OTC	X			
Salvo	X		X	
Senior			X	
SK-II	X	X		X
Tide	X	X	X	X
Vizir		X		
Whisper				X
Yes		X		
Zest	X	X	X	X

Source: Corporate website http://www.pg.com (viewed July 20, 2009).

Firms confronted with deletions in their product lines sometimes develop country-specific offerings to fill the gap in the line. In China, where an estimated 300 million people are studying English, Disney has added English instruction to its clothing and entertainment product lines.[36] However, such a strategy can be pursued only by a firm with adequate research and development (R&D) strength in its foreign subsidiaries.

Exploiting Product Life Cycles

Experience has shown that products do not always occupy the same position on the product life cycle curve in different countries. As Figure 10.1 shows, it is possible for a product to be in different stages of the product life cycle in different countries. A firm can extend product growth by expanding into new markets to compensate for declining growth rates in mature markets. On the other hand, a company can enter new national markets too rapidly, before the local market is ready to absorb the new product. To avoid such pitfalls and to take advantage of long-term opportunities, international companies may pursue the following strategies.

During the introductory phase in a product's life cycle, the product may have to be debugged and refined. This job can best be handled in the original market or in a country close to company R&D centers. Also, the marketing approach will have to be refined. At this stage, the market in even the more advanced countries is relatively small, and demand in countries with lower levels of economic development will hardly be commercially exploitable. Therefore, the introductory stage is usually limited to the advanced markets, often the company's domestic market.

When a product faces life cycle maturity or decline in one market, it may still be marketed successfully in others. Volkswagen originally introduced its famous Beetle car in the 1930s but later withdrew it from production everywhere except Mexico. It should be remembered, however, that for some high-technology products, life cycles are very short. In these cases, products are likely to be sold worldwide—or at least in all viable markets—soon after their introduction in the domestic market.

FIGURE 10.1
Possible Product Life Cycle for a Product in Different Countries

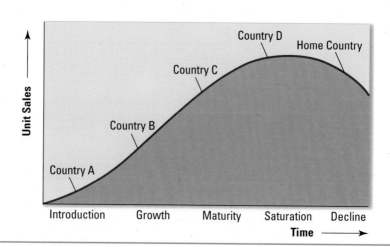

DEVELOPING A GLOBAL PRODUCT

Firms increasingly experience pressure for cost reduction in order to remain competitive. Yet there are relatively few opportunities for producing completely standardized products. As a result, many firms now employ a new strategy, global product development. With **global products**, a portion of the final design is standardized. However, the design retains some flexibility so that the end product can be tailored to the needs of individual markets. This represents a move to standardize as much as possible those areas involving common components or parts.

One of the most significant changes in product development strategy is the move toward **modularity**. This process involves the development of standard components that can easily be connected with other standard components to increase the variety of products. By doing this, global firms can realize significant cost savings from standardization while providing some customization for different markets.

This modularized approach has come to be especially important in the automobile industry, in which both U.S. and European manufacturers are increasingly creating world components to combat growing Japanese competitiveness. For example, General Motors has established a modular product architecture for all its global automobile projects. Future GM cars will be designed using combinations of components from seventy different body modules and about a hundred major mechanical components, such as engines, power trains, and suspension systems. GM aims to save 40 percent in radio costs alone by reducing the 270 types of car radios it uses worldwide to only 50.[37]

The challenge faced by GM and other automobile manufacturers is similar to that faced by manufacturers and marketers of both industrial and consumer products all over the world. Cost pressures force them to standardize, whereas market pressures require more customization of products. Conceptually, these companies can gain from increasing the standardized components in their products while maintaining the ability to customize the product "at the end" for each market segment.

Most international firms must take advantage of economies of scale on the standardized portion, or core, of their products. Different firms achieve different levels of standardization, but rarely is a firm able to standardize its product 100 percent. For one company, even moving from a global core representing 15 percent of the total product to 20 percent of the total product may result in a considerable cost improvement and represent the maximum level of standardization desirable. For another firm, the core may have to represent 80 percent of the total product to achieve the same effect. These levels depend on the characteristics of the market that the company or industry faces.

NEW PRODUCT DEVELOPMENT PROCESSES FOR GLOBAL MARKETS

Many firms now develop new products with global markets in mind. These global products are based on cores and derivatives. The product core might be the same for all products in all regions. An extended core might apply for each region but differ across regions. Each region might launch product derivatives specific to the regional conditions. This core strategy allows for maximizing the appeal of different configurations, while maintaining a stable product base and thus reducing basic development costs.

Global product a product for which a portion of the final design is standardized and a portion can be adapted to individual markets

Modularity a process involving the development of standard components that can easily be connected with other standard components to increase the variety of final products

The shift from local to global development requires that the company consider the unique or special concerns for major markets from the outset, rather than later attempting to make various adaptations to the initial model or prototype. The example at the beginning of this chapter, Universal's film *How the Grinch Stole Christmas*, is a perfect example of global product development. A global product, then, is not identical in all countries. Instead, a global product is designed from the outset with the goal of maximizing the percentage of identical parts to the point where local needs can be met quickly with a minimum of additional costs.

The Organization of Head-Office-Sponsored Research and Development

Most companies that currently engage in R&D on a global scale originally conducted their development efforts strictly in centralized facilities in the firm's domestic market. Even today, the largest portion of R&D monies spent by international firms goes to support efforts in domestically located facilities. As a result, most new product ideas are first developed in the context of the domestic market. Initial introduction at home is followed by a phase-in introduction to the company's foreign markets.

There are several reasons for this traditional approach. First, R&D must be integrated into a firm's overall marketing strategy. This requires frequent contacts and interfacing between R&D facilities and the company's main offices. Such contacts are maintained more easily with close proximity. Many companies centralize R&D because they are concerned that duplication of efforts will result if this responsibility is spread over several subsidiaries. Centralized R&D is thought to maximize results from scarce research funds. A final important reason for centralization is the company's experience in its domestic market. Typically, the domestic market is very important to the company, and in the case of international companies based

---

WORLD BEAT 10.2

THE GLOBAL PICTURE

THE TELEVISION SHOW *Law & Order: Criminal Intent* was a hit in the United States, so what would have to be done to adapt it for a French audience? The detectives' desks in *Paris Enquetes Criminelles* are still cluttered, but the background reflects the sleek modern architecture of Parisian police stations. Mention of the mob is omitted, and the plots must account for France's Napoleonic legal code.

Although adaptation is often necessary for TV's $110 billion export industry, speed to market is important as well. Once Europeans had to wait months or years to find out what happened on popular U.S. television shows. However, the Internet now has viewers sharing plot summaries online. Simulcast may be ideal, but is sometimes difficult. Still the

delay is decreasing. Episodes of *Lost* can appear in Britain just days after they air in the United States.

Technological change and the need to cut costs have pushed the motion picture industry toward global products and global launches. Motion picture producers are also looking for ways to cut costs on new product development by avoiding developing a new film from scratch. To do so, they are looking overseas for ideas. DreamWorks has led the Hollywood movement to remake Asian films. It spent $1 million for the rights to the Japanese horror flick *Ringu*, which was selling to packed theaters in Asia. Hollywood's version, *The Ring*, netted $200 million worldwide and $129 million in the United States.

Sources: Karen Mazurkewich, "Hollywood Sees Starry Remakes in Asian Films," *Wall Street Journal*, July 11, 2003, p. B1; Brooks Barnes, "New Accent," *Wall Street Journal*, March 1, 2007, p. A1; and Aaron O. Patrick, "The Race to Get TV Shows Overseas," *Wall Street Journal*, March 28, 2007, p. B1.

in the United States, Germany, and Japan, it is often the largest market as well. As a result, new products are developed with special emphasis on the domestic market, and R&D facilities, therefore, should be close by.

There are many good reasons for centralizing product development at the company's head office, but it remains a challenge for a centralized engineering and development staff of the firm to keep all relevant product modifications in mind before the design is frozen. Experience shows that later changes or modifications can be expensive. To keep a product acceptable in many or all relevant markets from the outset requires the product development staff to become globalized early in the creation process. Only a "globally thinking" product development staff will ensure the global acceptability of a product by incorporating the maximum possible number of variations in the original product.

International Lead Markets and Research and Development

As we noted in Chapter 8, participation in lead markets can be an important part of global strategy. In general, a **lead market** is a market whose level of development exceeds that of the markets in other countries worldwide and whose developments tend to set a pattern for other countries. Lead markets are not restricted to technological developments as embodied in product hardware. The concept covers developments in design, production processes, patterns in consumer demand, and methods of marketing. Therefore, virtually every phase of a company's operation is subject to lead market influences, although those focusing on technological developments are of special importance.

In the middle of the 20th century, the United States achieved a position of virtual dominance as a lead market. Not only were U.S. products the most advanced with respect to features, function, and quality, but they also tended to be marketed to the most sophisticated and advanced consumers and industrial buyers. This U.S. advantage was partially based on superior production methods, especially the pioneering of mass production in the form of the assembly line. The U.S. advantage extended to management methods in general, and particularly to access to new consumers. The rapid development of U.S.-based multinational firms was to a considerable degree based on the exploitation of these advantages in applying new U.S. developments abroad and in creating extensive networks of subsidiaries across a large number of countries. But the overwhelming lead of the United States over other countries did not last. Foreign competitors from Europe and Japan eroded the U.S. firms' advantages. As a result, no single country or market now unilaterally dominates the world economy.

The fragmentation of lead markets has led to a proliferation of product development centers, substantially complicating the task of keeping abreast of the latest developments in market demands, product design, and production techniques. Even formerly developing countries, such as South Korea, have achieved lead-market status in some categories. Korea's Samsung Electronics tied for third place in *BusinessWeek*'s Industrial Design Excellence Awards.[38]

To prosper in today's increasingly internationalized business climate, corporations must keep track of evolving lead markets as major sources for new product ideas and production techniques. New product ideas can stem from influences in buyer demand, manufacturing processes, and scientific discoveries. No single country may play a lead role in all facets of a firm's business. This means that any corporate R&D effort must look for new developments abroad rather than solely in the domestic market.

Lead market a national or regional market whose level of development exceeds that of other markets and whose experience sets the pattern for other markets

The Role of Foreign Subsidiaries in Research and Development

Each year General Motors gives what it calls Kettering Awards to employees whose ideas help GM retain technology leadership, improve customer service, or save production time and costs. Kettering Awards have recognized researchers and engineers not only from the United States, Canada, and Germany but from Brazil and India as well.[39]

Foreign subsidiaries may assume certain R&D functions if products require some adaptation to the local market. In larger markets, subsidiaries may even be responsible for developing products specifically for local consumption. Disney committed to shooting Russian-language films in Russia after box office sales soared in that country.[40]

Subsidiaries may assume a more global role when they are located in a lead market. A subsidiary located in a lead market is usually in a better position to observe developments and to accommodate new demands. Consequently, international firms with subsidiaries in lead markets have an opportunity to turn such units into effective "listening posts." Global firms may also take a more proactive stance toward subsidiary research in lead markets. Kodak's Pocket Camera was conceived and developed in the company's Japanese subsidiary before it was launched in the United States.

Increasingly, multinational firms are investing in research facilities abroad in order to obtain input from key markets. To globalize their own research, Japanese companies have made heavy investments in U.S.-based research facilities. Hundreds of Japanese scientists already work side by side with Americans in research laboratories on exchange programs. This investment aims at accessing scientific talent in other countries. Companies chasing such talent around the world are

Yahoo! acquired BharatMatrimony as a quick way to enter the marriage website market in India.

Copyright © 2009 Consim Info Pvt Ltd

opening development centers wherever talent can be found. China now ranks number five globally in patent applications, and many Western firms have opened development facilities there.[41] Among those firms are Intel and Microsoft, which have opened research centers near Beijing, where many of China's leading universities are clustered. Many companies are no longer using these centers only to adapt products to the Chinese market. P&G used its Chinese research center as a lead site for developing a new grease-fighting formula for the Tide detergent that the company markets in Asia, Eastern Europe, and Latin America.[42]

To develop a global product also requires a different organizational setup. Changes instituted by General Motors are indicative of actions taken by other international firms. With the advent of world cars, GM realized that the company needed closer coordination between its domestic units and its overseas subsidiaries. Therefore, GM moved its international staff from New York to Detroit in order to speed up communication between domestic and international staffs, and it adopted the "project center" concept to manage its engineering effort. Each division or foreign subsidiary involved in a new car design lends engineers to a centrally organized project center, which designs, develops, and introduces the new model. Upon introduction of the model, the project center is disbanded. Of course, not every firm will find a project center approach feasible. Other alternatives include assigning primary responsibility to a subsidiary that has special capability in the new product field.

In the future, international companies will have to make better use of the talents of local subsidiaries in the development of new products. Increasingly, the role of the subsidiary as simply a selling or production arm of the company will have to be abandoned, and companies will have to find innovative ways to involve their foreign affiliates in the product development process. This involvement can be patterned after several role models. The **strategic leader** role, with responsibility for developing a new range of products to be used by the entire company, may be assigned to a highly competent subsidiary in a market of strategic importance. Another subsidiary with competence in a distinct area may be assigned the role of **contributor**, adapting some products in smaller but still important markets. Most subsidiaries, being smaller and located in less strategic markets, will be expected to be **implementers** of the overall strategy, without making a major contribution either technologically or strategically.[43]

Strategic leader the home base or major subsidiary of a multinational firm, responsible for developing products used by the entire company

Contributor a subsidiary responsible for adapting some products for smaller markets

Implementer a subsidiary the primary role of which is to implement a firm's global strategy

Purchasing Research and Development from Foreign Countries

Instead of developing new products through its own R&D personnel, a company may acquire products from independent outside sources. This can be accomplished by licensing, purchasing products, or acquiring other firms.

Licensing has been the traditional approach to gaining access to new developments from lead markets. Licensing can be a boon to entrepreneurs who have few funds for R&D. One Spanish entrepreneur who originally organized study-abroad programs for Spanish university students decided to bring U.S. universities to Spain via the Internet. Building on his relationships with three prestigious American universities—Columbia University, the University of Chicago, and the University of California at Berkeley—he secured the Spanish-language rights to their online courses. The company translates courses and contracts with banks and with small and medium-sized businesses interested in outsourcing corporate education. The company is investigating expansion in Mexico, Chile, and Argentina as well.[44]

Importing as a Source of New Products

Some corporations decide to forgo internally sponsored R&D, instead importing finished products directly from a foreign firm to supplement their product lines. For example, Dutch brewing giant Heineken NV formed an alliance with Mexico's Fomento Economico Mexicano SA (Femsa) to become the sole U.S. importer for three years of two popular Mexican beer brands. The alliance is expected to help the company break into the Hispanic market and boost Heineken's volume by 28 percent in the competitive U.S. beer market.[45] Such a strategy should be pursued with great care, because firms may establish or expand a market position for competitors who may choose to pursue the market on their own in the future. This strategy may best apply in areas that do not represent the core of the firm's business and technology.

Acquisitions as a Route to New Products

International acquisitions in order to gain new technology or unique products are increasingly common in global markets. Yahoo! purchased BharatMatrimony in order to add a marriage site to its online business in India.[46] Conversely, Indian software companies have been acquiring software companies in the United States. These acquisitions are partially motivated by a desire to access more value-added products.

Acquisitions can be a way to move more quickly into a national market already dominated by competitors. The same holds true for adding a new product to a firm's product line. Madame Kin Wo Chong established the Wanchai Ferry brand in Hong Kong. The firm was later acquired by General Mills and used to introduce a line of frozen Chinese dinner kits into an already competitive U.S. market.[47]

Alliances for New Product Development

As noted in Chapter 9, many companies are finding alliances an effective way to share technology and R&D for competitive advantage. To share the huge cost of developing new products, some companies have established joint ventures or joined consortia to share in new product development. Under the **consortium approach**, member firms join in a working relationship without forming a new entity. On completion of the assigned task, member firms are free to seek other relationships with different firms. There is a shift toward such nonequity forms of R&D agreements occurring more or less uniformly across countries. This is most likely due to improved protection for contracts and intellectual property.[48]

Because the development of new aircraft is particularly expensive, the aircraft industry offers several examples of the consortium approach to product development. The high development costs require that large passenger aircraft be built and sold in series of 200 or 300 units to break even. Under these circumstances, several companies form a consortium to share the risk. One of the first highly successful efforts was the European Airbus, developed and produced by French, British, and German manufacturers.

The consortium approach can be employed by global buyers as well as manufacturers. Several global airlines that have alliances to sell tickets and buy fuel together are considering joint purchases of jetliners. One such group comprises Air Canada, Austrian Airlines, Lufthansa, and SAS. Joint purchases will require an alignment of normally diverse tastes for options such as cabin interiors, seating configurations, and flight kitchens. In return for agreeing to standard features,

Consortium approach an approach involving firms united in a working relationship without the formation of a new legal entity

manufacturers have agreed to pass some of the cost savings from standardization on to the customers.[49]

INTRODUCING NEW PRODUCTS TO GLOBAL MARKETS

Once a product has been developed for commercial introduction, a number of complex decisions still need to be made. Aside from the question of whether to introduce the product abroad, the firm has to decide on a desirable test-marketing procedure, select target countries for product introduction, and determine the timing or sequence of the introduction. Given the large number of possible markets, decisions surrounding new product introduction often have strategic significance.

Determining which product to introduce abroad depends, of course, on sales potential. Following a careful analysis, a marketer develops a list of target countries. The company then can choose from among several paths leading to actual introduction in the target countries.

Concept Tests

Once a prototype or sample product has been developed, a company may decide to subject its new creation to a series of tests to determine its commercial feasibility. It is particularly important to subject a new product to actual use conditions. When the development process takes place outside the country of actual use, a practical field test can be crucial. The test must include all necessary usage steps to provide complete information. In a classic case, CPC International tested the U.S. market for dehydrated soups made by its newly acquired Knorr subsidiary. The company concentrated primarily on taste tests to ensure that the final product suited U.S. consumers. Extensive testing led to different soup formulations from those sold in Europe. CPC, however, had neglected to have consumers actually try out the product at home as part of their regular cooking activities. Such a test would have revealed consumers' discontent with the Knorr dehydrated soups' relatively long cooking time—up to 20 minutes, compared with 3 minutes for comparable canned soups. The company recognized these difficulties only after a national introduction had been completed and sales fell short of expectations.

The concept-testing stage would be incomplete if the products were tested only in the company's domestic market. A full test in several major markets is essential so that any shortcomings can be addressed at an early stage before costly adaptations for individual countries are made. Such an approach is particularly important in cases in which product development occurs on a multinational basis with simultaneous inputs from several foreign subsidiaries. When Volkswagen tested its original Rabbit models, test vehicles were made available to all principal subsidiaries to ensure that each market's requirements were met by the otherwise standardized car.

Test Marketing

Just as there are good reasons to test-market a product in a domestic market, an international test can give the firm valuable insights into the launch of global products. A common approach to international test marketing is to use a single country as a proving ground before other markets are entered. In Europe, smaller markets such as the Netherlands, Belgium, Austria, and Switzerland may be used to launch a new product. Because of these countries' small size, a test would

Fifteen hundred multinational firms operate in Ontario, Canada. Canada has also proven to be a good test market for products later launched in the United States.

include national introduction, and the results would be assumed to be applicable in other countries.

Sometimes, however, a test market takes place in a country other than the country of the initial launch. IBM tested a new branding campaign for its Global Services line in Canada but launched it in the United States, and Carewell Industries test-marketed a toothbrush in Singapore before its U.S. launch.[50] Similarly, Microsoft and Motorola sometimes test-market in South Korea—where nearly three out of four homes have broadband Internet access—before launching products in the U.S. market.[51]

Circumstances are never exactly the same from one national market to another, and extrapolating results from a test market in one country to other countries must be done with caution. However, the selection of countries for new product launches is increasingly based on test marketing in one or two countries, with a rapid move toward a global rollout. Heinz tested its new teenager-oriented ketchup campaign in Canada and then rolled it out worldwide with minor modifications. Clearly, global marketing is moving rapidly toward the time when testing and test interpretation will be done on the basis of data from different—and sometimes distant—markets, and the time when each local market was tested locally before launch is rapidly passing.

Timing of New Product Introductions

Eventually, a company will be faced with establishing the sequence and the timing of its introduction of a new product in its home market and foreign markets. When should the product be introduced in each market? Should the firm use a phased-entry or a simultaneous-entry approach?

As we have noted, firms usually introduce new products first in their domestic markets to gain experience in production, marketing, and service. However, a foreign market may prove the better choice for a product launch. DaimlerChrysler of Germany, the largest truck company in the world, traditionally launches new innovations in its home market of Germany because of its large size and sophisticated buyers. However, German buyers are relatively slow to adopt service innovations. Analysis undertaken when the company was considering a launch of a remote diagnosis system (RDS) revealed that Japan would be a better market for an initial product launch.[52]

Although Japan was deemed an attractive market for the RDS launch, Toyota bypassed the Japanese market when launching the Lexus, its upscale automobile. Although Toyota holds almost half of the Japanese market, it is weak in the high-end segment in Japan, where wealthy consumers tend to favor German imports. Therefore, the upscale brand was launched in the United States instead, where it quickly became a status symbol. Sixteen years later, Japan finally introduced the Lexus to its home market.[53]

Increasingly, companies have to invest ever larger amounts for developing new technologies or products. As these investments rise, the time required to bring new generations of products to the market has increased, leaving less time for the commercialization of products before patents expire or new competitors come out with similar products. Companies have been forced to introduce new products rapidly to virtually all markets, including those in major developing countries. As a result, today the average lagtime between domestic introduction and foreign introductions has diminished considerably. One year after being introduced in the United States, Vanilla Coke was expanded to more than 30 countries.[54]

Technological advances sometimes aid in promoting global launches. Madonna's children's book *The English Roses* hit bookstores in 100 countries in 30 languages simultaneously. An alliance of co-publishers in different countries worked together utilizing new digital printing technology that allowed plants to switch quickly among languages. The alliance was also able to garner cost advantages from their greater bargaining power with paper suppliers as well as the ability to save costs on illustrations. The simultaneous launch also took advantage of the ability to create global buzz via Internet discussion sites.[55]

Global launches are not without their challenges. When DHL Worldwide Express rolled out a new supply-chain solution for its high-tech customers, thirty staff members from around the world engaged in what was described as a grueling process.[56] When Avon planned a worldwide launch of a new lipstick on a single day, the plan was later abandoned for fear that the product would not be available in all the markets by the appointed day.[57]

Do you need to adapt your product for your target country? Continue with your Country Market Report on the student companion website at http://www.cengage.com/international.

CONCLUSION

To be successful in global markets, companies often need to be flexible in product and service offerings. Although a given product may be very successful in a firm's home market, environmental differences between markets can often force a company to make unexpected or costly changes. A small group of products may be marketed worldwide without significant changes, but most companies will find that global success depends on a willingness to adapt to local market requirements. For companies that successfully master these additional international difficulties while showing a commitment to foreign customers, global success can lead to increased profits and to more secure market positions both domestically and globally.

The challenge for global marketers is to find the best balance between the standardizing of products and services and adapting them to specific markets. Adaptations are frequently expensive when done after the fact. In the future, companies will increasingly consider international opportunities early in the development cycle of a new product. Understanding different national markets and planning early for necessary adaptations to these markets will enable firms to develop new products that are usable immediately in many markets. Such a move toward international integration of product development will result in the creation of more successful global products.

Another increasingly influential factor in new product development is speed. For competitive reasons, companies want to be among the first to enter with a new product or service, because early entrants tend to obtain the biggest market share. To increase speed to market, companies may work on collaborative development processes. They can opt to reduce the time between first domestic introduction and worldwide launch. In the end, many firms will undertake multicountry launches or simultaneous global product rollouts. Still, the risk increases with such global launches, because less time is available to test the product, ensure that it meets the market performance needs, and sufficiently tailor it to any given country.

QUESTIONS FOR DISCUSSION

1. Compare probable product adaptations for consumer products versus high-technology industrial products. What differences exist? Why?

2. American fast food, music, and movies have become popular around the world with little product adaptation, whereas U.S. retailers, banks, and beer companies have had to adapt their products more to global markets. Why?

3. What, in your opinion, will be the future for global products?

4. What is the impact of a loss of lead-market position in several industries for U.S.-based corporations?

5. If you were to test-market a new consumer product today for worldwide introduction, how would you select test countries for Europe, for Asia, and for Latin America?

11

Global Strategies for Services, Brands, and Social Marketing

HEWLETT-PACKARD CORPORATION wins a $3 billion contract to manage Procter & Gamble's global information technology services.[1] The head of Microsoft's Russian operations lectures her employees on the value of intellectual property and exhorts them not to buy counterfeit products.[2] In Kenya, a local office of Care International promotes behavioral changes that will decrease diarrheal diseases.[3]

In Chapter 10 we discussed the global implications of product development. In this chapter we examine issues related specifically to service marketing, global brands, and brand protection. In addition, we explore the role of social marketing in the international arena. Although many of the issues covered in Chapter 10 apply to services as well, we begin this chapter by discussing what makes services different from physical products. We then illustrate how culture can affect a number of issues associated with services marketing. We continue with a discussion of the various implications of selecting brand names for international markets and present the pros and cons associated with global branding. The following section focuses on brand protection. We conclude by examining how global marketing can be extended to many aspects of social marketing.

LEARNING OBJECTIVES

After studying this chapter, you should be able to:

- Describe ways in which marketing services differs from the international marketing of physical products.

- Explain how culture can affect key aspects of services marketing.

- Compare the advantages and disadvantages of using global brand names and using single-country brand names.

- Differentiate between a global brand name and a global brand strategy.

- Identify the strengths and weaknesses of global brands versus local brands.

- Define private branding and explain why it is used by some international firms.

- Differentiate among trademark preemption, counterfeiting, and product piracy, and suggest ways in which firms can seek to minimize each of these.

- Explain how global social marketing is similar to—and different from—the international marketing of products and services.

MARKETING SERVICES GLOBALLY

More than half of Fortune 500 companies are primarily service providers.[4] The value of services produced in the world today now exceeds that of manufactured physical products,[5] and international trade in services represents about 25 percent of total world trade.

One of the largest categories of service exports is business services. These services are provided to firms, governments, or other organizations and include communication services, financial services, software development, database management, construction, computer support, accounting, advertising, consulting, and legal services. Many services are now aimed at multinational companies themselves. For example, IBM's Global Services supplies multinational firms with a variety of information technology services, from running a customer's information technology department to consulting on system upgrades and building global supply-chain management applications.

Services aimed at business buyers that are most likely to be exported are those that have already met with success domestically. The experience of U.S.-based service companies can be used as an example. Some of the services that have been most successfully marketed abroad are financial services. Commercial banks such as Citibank, Chase, and Bank of America have built such extensive branch networks around the world that foreign deposits and profits make up nearly half of business volume. Advertising agencies have also expanded overseas either by building branch networks or by merging with local agencies. Similarly, many U.S.-based marketing research firms have expanded into foreign countries.

International accounting services have experienced tremendous growth as well. Overseas expansion is important to U.S.-based accounting firms for several reasons. Among the leading accounting firms, international revenue typically exceeds domestic revenue. Revenue is growing more rapidly abroad, and margins are also better for international operations. Many of the firms' accounting clients have gone through globalization themselves and demand that their accountants have a global presence as well. Also, the liberalization of trade in Europe and elsewhere has boosted cross-national business, increasing demand for international accountants.

The legal profession is also finding numerous opportunities overseas. Many U.S. law firms have opened up overseas branch locations, primarily in London, to capture business from investment banks and other financial services firms that must have a presence in both New York and London, major capital market centers. U.S. and British law firms have targeted the Japanese market since 2005, when Japan first allowed foreign law firms to hire Japanese lawyers, merge with Japanese firms, and practice Japanese law.[6]

Trade in business services has traditionally taken place primarily among developed economies such as the United States, the Netherlands, France, Japan, the United Kingdom, Germany, and Italy. However, service providers from developing countries are increasingly visible on the global stage. Forty-three of the top 225 international construction companies are now Chinese. These firms operate projects in 180 countries and account for 17.5 percent of construction projects in Asia, 9.5 percent in the Middle East, and 7.4 percent in Africa. China's largest construction company, China State, has even entered developed markets, winning a contract to build a Marriott Hotel in New York and three schools in South Carolina.[7]

Marketing services to consumers abroad—such as gyms, cleaning services, restaurant chains, and insurance policies—has also expanded. Even healthcare has internationalized. Johns Hopkins, a premier American healthcare research hospital and service provider, has opened medical facilities in Dubai and Singapore.

However, marketing services to consumers may turn out to be more difficult than selling to businesses. Because consumer behavior and usage patterns usually differ more between countries than business usage patterns do, many services have to be adapted even more to local conditions to make them successful.

Because services have commonly been considered more culture bound than physical products, they have usually been located close to the consumer. Technological advances, however, have allowed many services, such as customer-support call centers, to be outsourced. Still, culture matters. When a consultant investigated Monterrey, Mexico, as a possible call center location for the U.S. market, he went to a local shopping mall to test the service culture. He discovered short lines and friendly sales clerks who approached customers. Both signified high expectations of service. English speakers, American movies showing at the mall, and sales clerks who spent their spring vacations in Texas further suggested that local employees would understand U.S. culture and service expectations.[8]

Services differ from physical products in four key ways. They are *intangible*. They cannot be stored or readily displayed or communicated. Production and consumption of services are *simultaneous*. Services cannot be inventoried, and production lines do not exist to deliver standardized products of consistent quality. Therefore, delivered services are *heterogeneous* in nature. Finally, because services cannot be stored, they assume a *perishable* nature.[9]

The Mexican affiliate of Ernst & Young places an advertisement in English. Many service providers in fields such as accounting and consulting have followed multinational clients abroad.

**Without the right piece,
it is hard to put the puzzle together.**

At Mancera Ernst & Young, we are always concerned about providing the service that best suits your needs to help you meet your goals.

Team up with us and consolidate your business.

www.ey.com/mx

AUDIT • TAX • LEGAL • TRANSACTION ADVISORY SERVICES (TAS)

MANCERA
ERNST & YOUNG
Quality In Everything We Do

Mancera Ernst & Young

These unique qualities of services affect their international marketing. Guaranteeing service quality worldwide is more difficult, and there are fewer opportunities to realize economies of scale with services than with physical products. **Back-stage elements of services** (planning and implementation aspects of services invisible to the customer) are easier to standardize cross-culturally than **front-stage elements of services** (aspects of service encounters visible to the customer).[10] For example, a fast-food provider such as McDonald's might standardize purchasing and inventory procedures, but its counter personnel in Saudi Arabia would still need to speak Arabic, and its seating design would need to accommodate separate areas for men and women.

Back-stage elements of services the planning and implementation aspects of services, invisible to the customer

Front-stage elements of services the aspects of service encounters that are visible to the customer

Culture and the Service Experience

Culture affects a number of aspects of the service experience, including customer expectations, customer satisfaction and loyalty, the waiting experience, and the recruitment and behavior of service personnel.

Customer Expectations. Customers may exhibit different expectations concerning service levels. Department stores in Japan still employ women in kimonos to bow and greet customers as they arrive at the store. Service personnel are available and solicitous. In the United States, consumers tend to be willing to forgo high levels of service in favor of low prices. They are more accustomed to self-service and may even feel nervous in the presence of hovering salespeople. Consumers in Switzerland are delighted when their local grocer chooses the best produce for them. As regular customers from the neighborhood, they deserve the best. Of course, this means that new customers are given the poorer produce. This would seem discriminatory and unfair to American customers. If residing in Switzerland, they would prefer to drive to a hypermarket where produce is prepackaged and the service encounter can be avoided altogether.

Asian cultures traditionally expect and deliver high levels of service. Whereas an American saying purports that "the consumer is always right," a similar saying in Japan states that "the customer is God."[11] Despite higher expectations of service, Asian business customers complain less when they receive poor service than do customers in the West.[12] One possible explanation is that customers in more collectivist cultures may tend to self-sacrifice and maintain self-discipline in order not to harm the relationship with the service provider. Alternatively, lack of complaining may be attributed to an attempt not to embarrass the service provider or cause a loss of face. However, dissatisfied customers are likely to voice dissatisfaction to other members in their reference group.[13] Customers in collectivist cultures may exhibit more loyalty and stay with a poor service provider longer than customers in a more individualistic culture, but their loyalty is not absolute. Given a lack of complaints, service providers can be caught unaware when these dissatisfied customers eventually leave.

The Waiting Experience. Time is always an aspect of services, and attitudes toward the time it takes to be served vary across cultures. For example, waiters in European restaurants take care not to hurry patrons. Eating a meal is supposed to be an enjoyable experience most often shared with friends. Servers also wait to be asked to deliver the bill for the meal; diners may wish to sit for hours. Americans would wonder what had happened to their waiter. Americans expect fast service at restaurants and like the bill to be dropped promptly on the table. What would be a good service experience for a European diner would be a bad one for an American.

Attitudes toward waiting in line vary as well. The English are famous for their orderly and patient waits in lines, or queues. In the French-speaking part of Switzerland, members of this otherwise polite population are likely to become a jostling mob when caused to wait at an entrance. Americans introduced the idea of establishing a single line leading to multiple service points instead of having separate lines for each point. This invention addressed the common American complaint that one inevitably ended up standing in the slowest-moving line. Americans have difficulty understanding why the rest of the world hasn't adopted this idea.

In certain parts of the world, social norms may require that men and women stand in different lines. This can be observed at metro stops in Mexico City during rush hours. In Egypt the imported design of having an "in" line leading to a service point and an exit leading away from it was reinterpreted as one line for men and one for women, with each line alternately taking its turn at the service point.

Service Personnel. When the local manager of a U.S.-based hotel chain was preparing to open a new hotel in Egypt, he was faced with a dilemma. American tourists would expect waitresses who could take their order in English. Egyptian women who spoke English almost invariably came from the upper classes. No young lady from those classes would be caught in public serving food to strangers. In a panic, the manager called friends and family and finally borrowed enough sisters, daughters, and nieces to staff the restaurant in time for opening day. Within a week, one waitress met and married a Saudi multimillionaire who came to eat at the restaurant. Whether apocryphal or not, the story spread like wildfire, and the manager never again had trouble recruiting waitresses!

In many cultures, such as the Middle East, working in a service occupation is commonly considered akin to being a servant. This social stigma can make it hard to recruit qualified personnel for some positions, especially those that require

Peter Titmuss/Alamy

Customers wait their turn in Russia. Cultural attitudes toward standing in line vary across countries. Global marketers must understand such cultural differences in order to successfully address service expectations.

higher levels of education as well as technical and interpersonal skills. Until relatively recently, flight attendants for many airlines from the Middle East had to be imported from Europe, and nursing has never achieved the status in the Middle East as it has in the West. Men as well as women feel the stigma. It is not uncommon for well-paid technical repairmen, such as those who work in the air-conditioning industry, to dress in a suit and tie and carry their tools in a briefcase.

Therefore, companies can experience difficulties in hiring employees who share core organizational values when they leave their home country. Disney had no trouble recreating the "Happiest Place on Earth" when transferring its Disneyland concept to Tokyo. Japanese cultural norms of safety, cleanliness, and customer service are a natural fit with Disney's company ethos. Meanwhile, success at Disneyland Paris proved far more elusive. French citizens and potential employees highly value individuality and freedom of expression and have found Disney's human resource policies to be restrictive and invasive.[14]

Service personnel are critical for the delivery of services. Because properly trained professionals may be difficult to find in some countries, multinational service firms may need to exert greater effort to recruit and train employees. However, many multinationals gain a recruiting advantage by offering salaries in excess of local competition.

BRANDING DECISIONS

Whether marketing products or services, global firms must manage and defend the value of their brands. Brands provide a name or symbol that gives a product (or service) credibility and helps the consumer identify the product. A brand that consumers know and trust helps them make choices faster and more easily. A globally recognized brand name can be a huge asset even when a firm enters new markets. For example, when McDonald's opened its doors in Johannesburg, South Africa, thousands of people stood in line. When Coke entered Poland, its red and white delivery trucks drew applause at traffic lights.[15]

BusinessWeek ranks the top global brands using a methodology developed by Interbrand Corporation. This methodology estimates the net present value of future sales of the brand taking into consideration factors such as market leadership, stability, and global reach—the brand's ability to cross geographical and cultural borders. Furthermore, all brands must be global in nature—at least a third of brand revenues must be derived outside the firm's domestic market. As Table 11.1 shows, the top global brands are dominated by U.S. brands, followed by European brands, although a number of Asian companies, such as Toyota, Honda, Sony, and Samsung, have built strong global brands.

Selecting Brand Names

Selecting appropriate brand names on an international basis is substantially more complex than deciding on a brand name for just one country. Typically, a brand name is rooted in a given language and, if used elsewhere, may have either a different meaning or none at all. Ideally, marketers look for brand names that evoke similar emotions or images around the world.

Brand name and symbol selection is critical. International marketers must carefully evaluate the meanings and word references in the languages of their target audiences. Can the name be pronounced easily, or will it be distorted in the local language? A good example of brand adaptation is the name choice for Coca-Cola,

TABLE 11.1 TOP 30 GLOBAL BRANDS		
RANK	**BRAND**	**HOME COUNTRY**
1	Coca-Cola	U.S.
2	IBM	U.S.
3	Microsoft	U.S.
4	GE	U.S.
5	Nokia	Finland
6	Toyota	Japan
7	Intel	U.S.
8	McDonald's	U.S.
9	Disney	U.S.
10	Google	U.S.
11	Mercedes-Benz	Germany
12	Hewlett-Packard	U.S.
13	BMW	Germany
14	Gillette	U.S.
15	American Express	U.S.
16	Louis Vuitton	France
17	Cisco	U.S.
18	Marlboro	U.S.
19	Citi	U.S.
20	Honda	Japan
21	Samsung	S. Korea
22	H&M	Sweden
23	Oracle	U.S.
24	Apple	U.S.
25	Sony	Japan
26	Pepsi	U.S.
27	HSBC	Britain
28	Nescafé	Switzerland
29	Nike	U.S.
30	UPS	U.S.

Source: Adapted from "Best Global Brands," *Business Week*, September 29, 2008, by special permission, copyright © 2008 by The McGraw-Hill Companies, Inc.

which means "tasty and happy" in Chinese. Mercedes-Benz's Chinese name means "striving forward fast," and Sharp's means "the treasure of sound." However, branding in Asia, and especially in China, may rely even more on the visual appeal of logos than on brand names. The simple graphical logos of Volkswagen, Mercedes-Benz, and Lexus are rated high, whereas the icons of Cadillac, General Motors, and Fiat are less appealing.[16]

Single-Country versus Global Brand Names.   Global marketers are constantly confronted with the decision of whether the brand name needs to be universal. Brands such as Coca-Cola and Kodak have universal use and lend themselves to an integrated international marketing strategy. With worldwide travel so common, many companies do not think they should accept a brand name unless it can be used universally.

Of course, using the same name elsewhere is not always possible. In such instances, different names have to be found. Procter & Gamble had successfully marketed its household cleaner, Mr. Clean, in the United States for some time. This name, however, had no meaning except in countries using the English language. This prompted the company to arrive at several adaptations abroad, such as *Monsieur Propre* in France and *Meister Proper* in Germany. In all cases, however, the symbol of the genie with gleaming eyes was retained because it evoked similar responses abroad and in the United States. Google also opted for a local name for the Chinese market. Its new name, *Gu Ge*, means "Harvest Song" in Chinese. Before the change, some Chinese citizens had dubbed the company Gougou ("doggy") or Gugou ("old hound").[17]

Selecting a Global Name

As noted above, a good brand name should be easy to read and pronounce while suggesting product benefits. However, it should not convey negative images in any market where it might be sold. There are dozens of stories about companies using a global name with negative or offensive meanings in another language. For example, a global construction equipment company marketed one piece of equipment as the "Grab Bucket" to describe its use in English. The company was surprised to discover that in Germany the name was interpreted to mean the sale of cemetery flowers because *grab* was interpreted as "grave" and *bucket* as "bouquet."[18]

Given the almost unlimited possibilities for names and the restricted opportunities to find and register a desirable one, international companies devote considerable effort to the selection process. Some consulting companies specialize in finding brand names with worldwide application. These companies bring citizens of many countries together and, under the guidance of a specialist, they are asked to state names in their particular language that would combine well with the product to be named. Speakers of other languages can immediately react if a name comes up that sounds unpleasant or has distasteful connotations in their language. After a few such sessions, the consultants may accumulate as many as 1,000 names that will later be reduced to 500 by a company linguist. The client company then is asked to select 50 to 100 names for further consideration. At this point, the names are subjected to a search procedure to determine which have not been registered in any of the countries under consideration. In the end, only about ten names may survive this process. From these, the company will have to make the final selection. Although this process may be expensive, the cost is generally considered negligible compared with the advertising expenditures invested in the brand name over many years.

When confronted with the need to search for a brand name with global applications, a company can consider the following:

* An arbitrary or invented word not to be found in any dictionary of standard English (or other language), such as Toyota's Lexus.

- A recognizable English (or other-language) word, but one totally unrelated to the product in question, such as the detergent Cheer.
- An English (or other-language) word that merely suggests some characteristic or purpose of the product, such as Mr. Clean.
- A word that is evidently descriptive of the product, although the word may have no meaning to persons unacquainted with English (or the other language), such as the diaper brand Pampers.
- A geographic place or a common surname, such as Kentucky Fried Chicken.
- A device, design, number, or some other element that is not a word or a combination of words, such as the 3M Company.[19]

Changing Brand Names

At times, firms may choose to change the name of a brand in local markets or even worldwide. This is not an easy choice. If a product has substantial market share in one or more markets, changing its name can confuse or even alienate consumers. Colgate-Palmolive, the large U.S.-based toiletries manufacturer, purchased the leading toothpaste brand in Southeast Asia, "Darkie." With a minstrel in blackface as its logo, the product had been marketed by a local company since 1920. After the acquisition, however, Colgate-Palmolive came under pressure from many groups in the United States to use a less offensive brand name. The company sponsored a large amount of research to find both a brand name and a logo that were racially inoffensive and yet close enough to the original to be recognized quickly by consumers. The company changed the name to "Darlie" after an exhaustive search. Still, in some markets where the "Darkie" brand had as much as 50 percent market share, it was a substantial marketing challenge to convert brand loyalty, intact, from the old to the new name.[20]

More recently, China's Lenevo saw its global market share shrink after it bought the PC division of IBM and proceeded to substitute the Lenevo brand for the IBM

Kraft's Lacta brand, popular across Europe, evokes the alpine image of Swiss chocolate.

brand. The company had successfully negotiated for the rights to use the IBM name for five years after the acquisition. However, Lenovo's later decision to drop the IBM name prematurely hurt sales outside China.[21]

Today some multinational companies are reconsidering earlier decisions concerning brand names. Unilever launched Jif household cleaner in the United Kingdom in 1974. Twenty-five years later, the product held a 74 percent share of the market. Despite Jif's market dominance and name recognition, Unilever decided to change its name to correspond to the name under which it was sold in other major markets. When the product was first rolled out, it received different names based in part on ease of pronunciation in each local language. This resulted in Jif becoming Cif in France and 39 other countries. It was Viss in Germany and Vim in Canada. The product wasn't introduced in the United States, where the name was already associated with a peanut butter marketed by competitor Procter & Gamble. Unilever undertook extensive market research to ensure that consumers would not be upset by the change and also supported the new name with substantial promotion to reassure the customer that Cif was actually Jif.[22]

Federal Express launched its courier business in the United States in the 1970s. The Federal Express name reflected the U.S. overnight delivery service. As Federal Express opened its international operations, however, the name was a problem. In Latin America *federal* connoted corrupt police, and in Europe the name was linked to the former Federal Republic of Germany. Therefore, Federal Express changed its name to FedEx, which in some cases is used as a verb meaning "to ship overnight."[23] Because FedEx dealt with many multinational companies as clients, it wanted a single name to use globally.

Global Brand Strategies

McDonald's is the world's largest fast-food restaurant and operates in 119 countries. It is ranked among the top ten on Interbrand's list of best global brands. But the positioning of the brand (and how it is perceived) varies across the globe. In the United States, McDonald's represents convenience in a family-friendly environment. In India, where adaptations make McDonald's offerings affordable to even the lower classes, the brand connotes value for money. In other parts of Asia, the chain is viewed as a trendy rendezvous for teenagers and young adults.[24]

The concept of global branding goes beyond simply establishing a global brand name. Yet experts disagree on what exactly makes a global brand. Is it global presence or global name recognition? There are certainly brand names such as Coca-Cola that are well known in most countries of the world. Does the name connote similar attributes worldwide? Is the product the same? Is the brand a powerful player in all major markets? Heineken qualifies on the first two conditions, but not on the third. It has positioned itself as a quality imported beer in its many export markets. The beer and the bottle remain the same across markets. However, its lack of adaptation has kept it a well-known but minor player in the various national markets.

As we have noted, *BusinessWeek* defines a global brand as one with at least a third of sales outside the firm's domestic market. Other definitions are less encompassing, describing global brands as brands whose positioning, advertising strategy, personality, look, and feel are in most respects the same in all countries.[25] Firms that develop global brands with these characteristics are said to follow a **global brand strategy**.

Global brand strategy a strategy in which the positioning, advertising, look, and personality of a brand remain constant across markets

Several steps are involved in developing and administering a global brand strategy:

1. A firm must identify common customer needs worldwide and determine how the global brand can deliver both functional and emotional benefits to these customers.
2. A process must be established to communicate the brand's identity to consumers, channels, and the firm's own employees.
3. There should be a way to track the success of the global identity of the brand, such as the customer opinion surveys employed by Pepsi.
4. The firm must determine whether it will follow a more centralized, top-down approach to global branding or a more gradual, bottom-up approach. Sony and Mobil take **top-down approaches**, wherein a global management team determines the global brand strategy and then country strategies are derived from it. In a **bottom-up approach**, country strategies are grouped by similarities in such variables as the level of economic development and the competitive situation (whether or not the brand is dominant in the market). Common elements are first identified within these groupings. Over time, a more global strategy emerges as subsidiaries share experiences and best practices.[26]

Top-down approach an approach to global branding in which a global team determines the global brand strategy and country strategies are derived from this strategy

Bottom-up approach an approach to global branding in which brand strategy emerges from shared experiences and best practices among the firm's subsidiaries

Brand champion a manager or group within a firm charged with the responsibility for building and managing a global brand

In any case, a **brand champion** should be given the responsibility for building and managing a global brand. This should include monitoring the brand across markets, as well as authorizing the use of the brand on other products and businesses (brand extensions). The brand champion can be a senior manager at corporate headquarters, a product development group, or the manager of a lead country or one with major market share for the brand. For example, Unilever at one time gave its French subsidiary custody over its Lipton brand.[27]

For many multinational firms, global branding offers a way to cut costs and present a consistent customer communication about the brand. Global branding became popular as a strategy among transnational companies as early as the

---

WORLD BEAT 11.1

REPOSITIONING BEER

BELGIAN BREWER INTERBREW NV decided that its financial future lay in snob appeal. So it decided to sell its Stella Artois brand—a beer known in Belgium as "fit for an old peasant"—as a premium label elsewhere. The strategy began in London where the beer was advertised as "reassuringly expensive." Stella soon became the top imported beer in the United Kingdom. Then Interbrew chose the New York market to put its strategy seriously to the test. The company hired a team of young partygoers to identify the 20 most exclusive bars in the city. Stella, priced at a premium $100 a keg, was supplied to those 20 bars. Sales doubled from the year before.

SABMiller PLC also announced its plans to introduce plebian Miller Genuine Draft as a sophisticated international premium brew in Hungary, Slovakia, Romania, the Czech Republic, Poland, and Italy. The firm hoped that a new European branding would create a "global buzz" for the struggling U.S. icon, especially in markets where beer consumption was on the rise. The beer would be priced similar to other export beers such as Heineken and would be targeted at hip bars. The only problem: Europeans tend to think U.S. beers are too light and watery.

Sources: Dan Bilefsky, "U.S. Beer Has Euro-Puzzle," *Wall Street Journal Europe*, July 21, 2004, p. A5; David Kesmodel, "SABMiller Profit Climbs," *Wall Street Journal Europe*, May 16, 2008, p. 7; and "Polish Beer Consumers Loyal to Domestic Brands," *Polish News Bulletin*, July 1, 2008.

mid-1980s. Today Unilever claims that three-fourths of its business comes from 20 global brands.[28] Some of the original enthusiasm with global branding has abated, however, as consumers in different countries reject brands they judge as resulting from least-common-denominator thinking. Multinational firms have responded with more hybrid **global strategies**, through which they attempt to combine the quality improvements and cost savings of backstage activities, such as technology, production, and organization, with elements more tailored to local tastes, such as adapting product features, distribution, and promotion.[29]

Some propose that the term **international brands** be used to differentiate brands that follow such a global strategy from other global brands that maintain a more standardized marketing strategy and mix across national markets.[30] However, the term *global brand* continues to be commonly used for both.

Consumer Response to Global Brands.

To better understand what consumers worldwide thought of global brands, Douglas Holt, John Quelch, and Earl Taylor conducted the Global Brands Study. This study used both qualitative and quantitative research design and incorporated responses from 3,300 consumers in 41 countries.[31] The researchers concluded that consumers evaluate global brands on three key dimensions:

- *Quality signal.* Consumers observe the fierce competitive battles among global brands over quality. Global brands become a cue for quality. Forty-four percent of brand preference is explained by this dimension.
- *Global myth.* Global brands are symbols of cultural ideals relating to modernity and a cosmopolitan identity. A focus-group participant in the Global Brands Study opined, "Local brands show what we are; global brands show what we want to be." Another participant remarked, "Global brands make us feel like citizens of the world."[32] Twelve percent of brand preference is explained by this dimension.
- *Social responsibility.* Because the firms behind global brands are perceived to have extraordinary power and influence, consumers expect these companies to address social problems—a demand that local firms can more easily dodge. For example, local companies would not be asked to address global warming, but multinational energy companies such as BP and Shell would be. Eight percent of brand preference is explained by this dimension.

The research team goes on to identify four global segments based on these three dimensions of global brands:

- **Global citizens**. These consumers rely on the success of a global brand to identify products of quality and innovation. However, they also expect transnational firms to behave responsibly on issues such as workers' rights and the environment. This segment was the largest in the study and accounted for 55 percent of consumers. Global citizens were relatively rare in Britain and the United States but more common in Brazil, China, and Indonesia.
- **Global dreamers**. This segment was the second-largest in the study—23 percent of consumers. These consumers both equate global brands with quality and are attracted by the lifestyle they portray. However, these consumers are less concerned with social issues relating to transnational firms. Another study confirmed the importance of the global dreamer segment. It reported that many young consumers in Romania, Russia, the Ukraine, and the United States viewed themselves as part of the global world and therefore preferred global brands across product categories.[33]

Global strategy a strategy that captures the quality improvements and cost savings of standardized backstage activities but adapts key elements of the marketing mix, such as product features, distribution, and promotion to local tastes

International brand a brand that follows a global strategy but does not maintain a strict standardized marketing strategy and mix across all national markets

Global citizens consumers who associate global brands with quality and innovation and expect transnational firms to behave responsibly regarding workers' rights and the environment

Global dreamers consumers who equate global brands with quality and are attracted by the lifestyle they portray

Antiglobals consumers who are skeptical of the quality of global brands and of the transnational companies who own them

- **Antiglobals**. This segment—about 13 percent of consumers—is skeptical of the quality of global brands as well as the transnational companies who own them. They prefer to buy local and avoid global brands. This segment is relatively more common in Britain and China and relatively less common in Egypt and South Africa.

Global agnostics consumers who judge global brands and local brands by the same criteria and are neither impressed nor alienated by the fact that a brand is global

- **Global agnostics**. This segment judges global brands and local brands by the same criteria and is neither impressed nor alienated by the fact that a brand is global. Estimated at about 8 percent of consumers, global agnostics' numbers are relatively high in the United States and South Africa and low in Japan, Indonesia, China, and Turkey.

Despite the existence of antiglobals and global agnostics, a later study found that global brands tend to evoke positive feelings overall. This positive halo effect was present among both pro-global and antiglobal respondents. The researchers conclude that despite the fact that some people voice negative attitudes toward global brands, there may still be something emotionally appealing about a brand that is widely recognized and available and is basically the same across markets.[34]

Pan-Regional Branding

Although there may be few genuinely global brands, pan-regional branding is increasing in importance. In Latin America, Brazil's Varig Airlines undertook a design and logo change to broaden its regional appeal. The revamped Varig logo looks modern and imparts warmth, which supports an advertising program that features well-rested passengers getting off their flights.[35] Similarly, the Shangri-La Hotel chain has built a strong regional brand across Asia. Shangri-La offers all the amenities of a luxury hotel, along with Asian hospitality. The staff uniforms reflect the local costumes. Shangri-La uses its advertising to appeal to executives in Asia, who are often judged by the hotels they choose. The tag line on Shangri-La ads is "It must be Shangri-La."[36]

To create Asian brands, managers suggest employing a mix of cultural symbols from different Asian countries, which is what the travel portal Zuji did. *Zuji* means "footprint'" in Mandarin Chinese. However, consumer research revealed that the name was perceived to be Japanese, evoking feelings of quality and trust. The colors chosen for the site were bright blue and green, typically Thai colors.[37]

Furthermore, a study of Asian branding concluded that firms seeking to create successful regional brands should capitalize on a newfound Asian pride and confidence. For example, younger Asian women consider Japan and Korea to be more fashionable than France or America in terms of fashion or music. The study also suggested that Asian consumers feel more affinity to brands. Still, using a Western connection can help Asian brands overcome any negative country-of-origin associations that may persist. Such Western connections can range from a brand history of success overseas to shooting part of a brand commercial in New York City.[38]

Eurobrands regional brands in Europe

In Europe, regional brands are called **Eurobrands**. In a survey of more than 200 European brand managers in 13 countries, 81 percent indicated that they were aiming for standardization and homogenization of brands, whereas only 13 percent said they were leaving each country free to decide its own strategy.[39] The survey clearly indicates a strong preference for a Eurobrand strategy for most companies. Examples of Eurobrands—products marketed across Europe with the same brand name, formula, and packaging as well as the same positioning and advertising strategy—include Procter & Gamble's Pampers and Head & Shoulders shampoo, Michelin tires, and Rolex watches.

An advertisement for Haevichi Hotel, a well-known brand in Asia.

Global Brands versus Local Brands

The findings from the Global Brands Study raise questions as to the intrinsic value of global or regional brands compared with local brands. Despite a significant trend towards multinational brands, local brands still survive. In Belgium, Procter & Gamble tried to replace its leading local detergent Dash with its European-wide brand Ariel; it discontinued advertising for Dash. However, P&G soon saw its sales in detergents plummet and it was forced to renew its support for Dash.[40]

A study of consumers in France, Germany, Italy, and the United Kingdom further highlights what might be the countervailing power of local brands. Consumers reported that local brands possessed the same quality as that of global brands. Furthermore, local brands were deemed more reliable and thought to deliver more value for money.[41] In fact, the global reach of a multinational's major brands will vary by brand. Some brands may be sold in only one or two countries, whereas others are sold in many more. Table 11.2 illustrates the global reach of selected Kraft brands.

Although evidence indicates that local brands remain powerful in the United States and Europe, there is also evidence that local brands can be competitive in developing countries as well. Global brands were especially attractive to consumers

TABLE 11.2	GLOBAL REACH OF SELECTED KRAFT BRANDS
BRAND	**MARKETS**
Alpen Gold	Poland, Russia, Ukraine
Capri Sun	Puerto Rico, United States
Grand Mere	France
Honey Maid	Canada, United States
Jacobs	Austria, Baltics, Czech Republic, Germany, Greece, Hungary, Poland, Romania, Russia, Slovakia, Switzerland, Turkey, Ukraine
Jell-O	Canada, Mexico, Puerto Rico, United States
Kenco	Ireland, United Kingdom
Kool-Aid	Canada, Mexico, Philippines, Puerto Rico, United States
Lacta	Brazil, Italy
Lunchables	United States
Marabou	Denmark, Finland, Sweden
Maxwell House	Canada, China, France, Germany, Ireland, Middle East, Poland, Russia, Taiwan, Ukraine, United Kingdom, United States
Milka	Argentina, Austria, Belgium, Bulgaria, Croatia, Czech Republic, France, Germany, Hungary, Italy, Netherlands, Poland, Romania, Russia, Spain, Turkey
Miracle Whip	Australia, Canada, Denmark, Germany, Philippines, United States
Oreo	Argentina, Australia, Canada, China, Indonesia, Mexico, Netherlands, Peru, Poland, Puerto Rico, Romania, Russia, Spain, Taiwan, Thailand, United States, Venezuela
Ritz	Australia, Canada, China, Ecuador, Hong Kong, Indonesia, Mexico, Peru, Puerto Rico, Taiwan, Thailand, United Kingdom, United States
Royal	Argentina, Brazil, Columbia, Ecuador, Peru, Portugal, South Africa, Spain, Venezuela
Simmenthal	Italy
South Beach Living	United States
Stove Top	Canada, United States

Source: Selected data from brand pages "Kraft: Largest Brands," http://www.kraftfoods.company.com.

in Russia and former Soviet satellite states during the late 1990s. More recently there appears to be a backlash against global brands, as many consumers possibly become disenchanted with their higher prices and the sometimes monopolization of markets by such brands. Nostalgia for local brands has motivated multinational firms to resurrect local brands. Kraft bought the traditional Hungarian candy bar, Sport Szelet, and marketed it complete with its 50-year-old package design. Unilever followed suit with the traditional Baba personal-care brand.[42]

When asked whether they preferred a local or a global brand for products of identical price and quality, Chinese consumers overwhelmingly preferred local brands for food, toiletries, and household items, although they preferred global brands for home electronics. Consumers were evenly split between local and global brands when it came to clothes. Therefore, it is understandable that when France's packaged-foods company Danone buys Chinese companies, it continues to sell products under their original Chinese brands. Overall, 80 percent of Danone's sales in China are credited to these Chinese brands. The company was even asked by the Chinese government to create a Chinese cola to compete with Coke and Pepsi. Future Cola holds the number three spot in China and is known as "the Chinese people's own cola."[43]

Still, it is not all bad news for global brands. Surveys conducted in various developing countries suggest that across product categories, a well-known Western brand name increases perceived quality of the product or service. For specific product categories, global brands associated with a Western country of origin enjoy an additional benefit, as customers in developing countries relate their product with an enhanced social status.[44] Thus, the controversy surrounding local and global brands continues.

Private Branding

The practice of private branding, or supplying products to another party for sale under that party's brand name, has become quite common in many markets. The Japanese company Ricoh (now a global leader in small personal copiers and fax machines) once operated as a contract manufacturer for more established firms and used private branding to gain market access in Europe and the United States. Today many Chinese companies employ this strategy as a means to enter export markets.[45]

In addition, powerful retailers in international markets are developing their own in-house private brands and outsourcing the manufacture of these products. Such brands can represent significant competition for global brands. For example, Mahindra & Mahindra in India decided to launch its own private label brands at its newly launched Mom & Me stores. The private brands will be sold alongside global brands such as Mattel.[46]

Private branding offers particular advantages to a company with strong manufacturing skills but little access to or experience with foreign markets. Arranging for distribution of the firm's product through local distributors or companies with existing distribution networks reduces the risk of failure and provides for rapid volume growth via instant market access.

Private-branding contracts are not without drawbacks for the manufacturing firm. With control over marketing in the hands of another manufacturer or distributor, the firm remains dependent and can only indirectly influence marketing. For long-term profitability, companies often find that they need to spend the money to create brand equity, which requires promoting and selling products under their own brands. Changing from a supplier to a global brand power-house is not easy, however. In the 40 years since Asia emerged as a major manufacturing center, only a few companies have been successful in establishing world-class brands—among them Sony and Canon from Japan and Samsung from South Korea. Many Asian manufacturers still lack marketing departments and suffer from a lack of experience in direct selling to overseas retailers.[47]

Trademarks the names, words, and symbols that enable customers to distinguish among brands

Preemption the legal hijacking or registration of a brand name when the brand is not yet registered

TRADEMARKS AND BRAND PROTECTION

Violations of **trademarks**—the names, words, and symbols that enable customers to distinguish among brands—have been an inescapable problem for global marketers. These violations can involve the legal hijacking or local **preemption** of a brand name. For example, someone could register the Gucci brand name in a country where Gucci had yet to register its brands. If Gucci wanted to enter that market, it would have to buy back its brand name or sell under another. Trademark pre-emption is especially easy in countries that do not require that the brand be sold in the market after registration.

International treaties to protect well-known international brands from being pre-empted in local markets go back to the Paris Convention of 1883. However, problems can arise even in signatory countries. Claiming its rights under the Paris Convention, Gucci fought two cases in Mexico against infringing firms. It won one case but lost the other. In the latter case, the Mexican judge was not convinced that the Mexican government had even ratified the Paris Convention more than 100 years before.

Today, the Paris Convention has been superseded by trademark protection rules under the World Trade Organization. Countries that join the WTO must establish national laws that protect global brands. These laws must encompass a procedure by which the owners of famous international brands can successfully oppose the registration of their brands by local preemptors. Local laws must be adequate to deter counterfeiters, and countries must not discriminate between local and foreign firms who apply for trademark protection. Depending on a country's level of economic development, it may be allowed up to 11 years to bring its local laws into compliance.

Holding countries to these requirements is somewhat ambitious, however, given the fact that the signatory countries of the WTO exhibited very different levels of trademark protection at the time they joined. A study of national trademark protection in the years prior to establishment of the WTO shows distinct patterns across country categories. Developed countries provided the best overall protection. Less developed countries and the transition economies of Russia and Eastern Europe exhibited much weaker local laws, and processing times for foreign trademark applications were exceptionally slow in the transition economies. Many newly industrialized countries, including Taiwan and South Korea, had already established local laws on a par with those of developed countries. However, a lack of resources undermined the ability of such countries to enforce these laws adequately.[48]

The norms established by the WTO are no doubt a step in the right direction, but problems still persist. Although the countries of the former Soviet bloc have adopted trademark protection laws in accordance with WTO guidelines, the enforcement of these laws remains problematic. There have been concerns that Russian judges and prosecutors don't understand the nature of Russia's newly adopted trademark laws—although the laws look good on paper. The U.S.-based tobacco company Philip Morris lost a case it brought in an effort to stop a Russian company from producing cigarettes whose packaging closely resembled that of two of Philip Morris's best-selling brands. Grupo Modelo, the Mexican beer company that makes Corona, also lost a trademark dispute with a Russian brewery that Modelo accused of stealing its brand name.[49] Still, some headway is being made in Asia. Starbucks won a lawsuit in China against a coffee-shop chain whose Chinese name was nearly identical to Starbucks. Similarly, Honda won a case against a motorcycle manufacturer calling itself Hongda.[50]

Significant differences also persist in national trademark regimes despite moves to unify brand protection worldwide. In the United States, trademark rights usually extend to related goods and services. In China this is not the case, and multiple registrations may be necessary to cover a firm's full product line.[51] Many, but not all, governments require that a trademark be used in their markets if it is to receive continued protection there. Starbucks registered its trademark in Russia but then let the trademark expire without using it in the

WORLD BEAT 11.2

BRAND PREEMPTION IN INDONESIA

BRITAIN'S IMPERIAL TOBACCO GROUP PLC, the world's fourth-largest cigarette maker, was planning to build a $70 million factory in Indonesia to produce its premier Davidoff cigarettes. But a local company, Sumatra Tobacco, that specialized in claiming famous trademarks, already owned the Davidoff name in Indonesia. In total, this local company had registered 201 famous trademarks in Indonesia, including Chanel and Remy Martin. Sumatra Tobacco not only made products associated with the famous brands but applied the brands to product extensions as well—such as their Rolex cigarettes, which Sumatra Tobacco sold in China.

Imperial Tobacco is not the only firm that has faced brand preemption in Indonesia. Intel, the world's largest manufacturer of microprocessors, has lost battles against the Indonesian maker of Intel jeans and the Indonesian maker of Intel home electronics. Originally the problem was Indonesia's trademark law dating from 1961, which stated that the first party to register a trademark in Indonesia was the owner of that trademark in the country. Indonesia's new trademark law was supposed to stop such preemption of famous international brands, but the courts don't always appear to be enforcing the law. In fact, the U.S. commercial guide for Indonesia notes that the local court system can be frustrating and unpredictable.

Imperial appealed its case to Indonesia's Supreme Court. In the meantime, the company began looking for other sites for a Southeast Asian manufacturing center. Eventually the Supreme Court ruled in favor of Imperial Tobacco. Still, Sumatra Tobacco contested the decision, causing Imperial to further delay its planned investment in Indonesia. Some observers expect that other investment in Indonesia will be hampered until Indonesian judges are given adequate training in intellectual property rights.

Sources: Timothy Mapes, "Big Cigarette Firm Fumes at Jakarta Over a Trademark," *Wall Street Journal*, May 22, 2003; Gunawan Suryomurcito, "Intellectual Property Laws Still Weak," *Jakarta Post*, January 31, 2005, p. 6; Frans H. Winarta, "Protection of Popular Brands," *Jakarta Post*, April 4, 2008, p. 8; and *Doing Business in Indonesia*, U.S. and Foreign Commercial Service and U.S. State Department, 2009.

Russian market. A local preemptor then registered the brand, because it was considered to be abandoned by its original owner. Starbucks retrieved the brand only after a prolonged legal battle.[52]

Counterfeits and Piracy

Counterfeiting the illegal use of a registered trademark

Today, the biggest problem international marketers face in trying to protect their brands is counterfeiting. **Counterfeiting** is the illegal use of a registered trademark. A counterfeiter copies a branded product, cashing in on its brand equity. Thus counterfeiters injure legitimate businesses by stealing their brand equity. The World Customs Organization estimates that counterfeits account for 6 percent of global merchandise trade or more than $600 billion a year.[53] It is estimated that many *Fortune* 500 firms spend from $2 to $10 million annually to combat counterfeit products.[54]

Consumers can be injured as well when they unwittingly buy counterfeits believing that they are buying the real product. Because counterfeits usually do not mimic the quality or safety of the original product, they can fail to perform as expected. Counterfeit AC Delco brake pads last only half as long as the real thing. Mitsubishi Elevator Company received a complaint from a customer whose new elevator kept stopping between floors. The elevator turned out to be a counterfeit. One of the greatest consumer threats posed by global counterfeiting is the growth in counterfeit pharmaceuticals. The World Health Organization notes that up to 10 percent of medicines worldwide are counterfeits.[55]

Piracy the counterfeit production of copyrighted material

The term **piracy** is commonly applied to the counterfeit production of copyrighted material such as books and computer software. Because illegal production—or more aptly, reproduction—of these products is relatively simple and inexpensive, they become easy targets. Recorded music has long suffered from piracy, and counterfeit music is believed to outsell legitimate music in many countries. In China nearly all downloaded music is believed to be stolen. Chinese Internet search engines, such as Baidu.com, propagate this phenomenon by facilitating convenient downloads of pirated music.[56] Google China does not offer this service.[57] Some experts suggest they have paid dearly for these decisions, controlling just 23 percent of the search market, compared with 58 percent commanded by Baidu.com.[58]

DVDs are also a major target of pirates. Just a few years ago, pirating DVDs required a factory with disc-pressing equipment costing $1 million. As a result, the major players were Asian crime syndicates that could afford such an investment. Now the same technology that allows home-video buffs to "burn" their own DVDs is reshaping the competitive landscape of piracy—and threatening to make it even more costly to the motion picture industry. Piracy has now gone small and mobile, making counterfeiters harder for authorities to locate and crack down on. Hong Kong's authorities have shifted from looking for producers of counterfeits to shutting down the retailers that sell them. In a five-year period, such stores were cut from 1,000 to only 80.[59]

Counterfeiting of trademark-protected products flourishes in countries where legal protection of such trademarks is weak. China accounts for the production of about two-thirds of all counterfeits. Other problem countries include the Philippines, Russia, Ukraine, Brazil, Pakistan, Paraguay, and Vietnam.[60] In Vietnam, counterfeits thrive because the government has few resources to enforce existing laws effectively or control the borders. Some international consumer goods companies doing business in Vietnam claim their sales are reduced by as much as 50 percent by the ready availability of illegal, and cheaper, products. Procter & Gamble is believed to have lost sales of up to 25 percent as illegal operators collected its

© 2009 Microsoft Corporation

For Microsoft, fighting piracy is a global effort.

containers and refilled them with counterfeit products. The same happened to brand-name cognac and whiskies. Reused bottles were filled with sugar rum.[61]

The emergence of e-business has contributed to the further growth of counterfeit global trade. Total online counterfeit business volume is estimated at $25 billion, a tenth of the total counterfeit volume. Internet counterfeiters are scattered across an estimated 5,000 websites. They include both international operators and local teenagers operating out of a basement. Rolex, the Swiss-based producer of luxury watches, regularly checks eBay auctions where, on any given day, hundreds of counterfeit Rolex watches may be up for bids. The manufacturers of many other luxury items do the same. Louis Vuitton regularly checks eBay and acts on counterfeit products. By early 2001, eBay, concerned that it could be held liable for frauds or other illegal sales, began screening and removing from its site items that clearly infringed on copyrights.[62] Still, many luxury goods manufacturers believe eBay the company has not done enough to curb the flow of counterfeit goods. In 2008, Louis Vuitton and other luxury brands filed and won a $64 million lawsuit against the Internet retailer, which profits from each item sold through its site, authentic or not.[63]

Fighting Counterfeits

Multinational companies can try to stop the counterfeiting of their products in a number of ways.[64]

- ● *Do Nothing.* Firms may ignore counterfeits if they are not significantly threatening their brand. Stopping counterfeiters can become an expensive and time-consuming project for a firm. Unfortunately, most firms now realize that doing nothing is no longer an option.
- ● *Co-Opt the Offenders.* One manufacturer of hardware products discovered that a counterfeiter from Asia was producing an excellent copy of its product. The counterfeiter was asked to become the firm's legitimate contract manufacturer. Distributors of counterfeits may also be recruited to be legitimate distributors of the brand. However, this option has a downside: Many legitimate contract manufacturers, licensees, and distributors participate in the counterfeit market as well. Their legitimate status can help hide their more nefarious operations. Unilever discovered that one of its suppliers in Shanghai was making excess cases of soap and selling them directly to retailers. Procter & Gamble discovered that a Chinese supplier was selling empty P&G shampoo bottles to another company, which filled them with counterfeit shampoo.[65] When New Balance discovered a licensee selling "unauthorized" shoes in international markets, they decided their best option was to buy the shoes back from the licensee at $10 per pair, rather than risk brand dilution by allowing the shoes to be sold at a discount in the market.[66]
- ● *Educate Governments.* Firms can take steps to educate governments about the social and political implications of counterfeits and solicit their assistance in shutting down counterfeiters. Some governments, particularly those in developing countries, have long been unsympathetic to multinational pleas to address counterfeits. Counterfeits often provide employment opportunities in developing countries, and some governments believe that the price consumers in poor countries pay for global brand equity is unnecessary and extreme.

However, there are signs that even governments in developing countries are changing their minds about the value of counterfeits due to several factors:

- As already noted, counterfeits can sometimes hurt consumers. In Africa, counterfeit drugs account for as much as 40 percent of the market.[67]
- Many governments are increasingly concerned about the downside of their large informal economies (including counterfeiters and their distributors) because participants in the informal economy do not pay taxes or adhere to labor codes.[68] One exception to this rule is North Korea, whose government is purported to earn $100 million a year from counterfeits produced there.[69]
- Counterfeits increasingly harm firms from developing countries, not just foreign multinationals. Countries such as Brazil, Korea, and Taiwan now realize that their own domestic brands are being counterfeited. Even Chinese brands such as Tsingtao beer and Li-Ning shoes have become targets of counterfeiters.[70] This has motivated local governments to become more serious about addressing the problem.
- Counterfeiting is increasing the domain of organized crime and even terrorists, the latter of which use proceeds from counterfeits to finance their terrorist activities. Both groups threaten the sovereignty of legitimate governments.

- ***Advertise.*** Multinationals can attempt to communicate the advantages of buying the authentic product rather than counterfeits. Additionally, campaigns may be devised to educate consumers about the ethical issues relating to counterfeits. When the Harry Potter series was launched in China, the publisher arranged for the books to be printed on a light green paper and planned a media blitz to explain to consumers how to tell the real thing from the counterfeit.[71]

  Disney also selected this option in Hong Kong when it ran a promotion encouraging consumers to enter a contest for DVDs, television sets, and trips to Hong Kong Disney. The entry form required that consumers attached an official red hologram-covered sticker available only on legitimate Disney products. The contest also employed the Chinese lucky number 88, selling coupons for legitimate Disney products at a price of 88 yuan (about $11). The promotion was advertised on Disney's variety and cartoon show in China—Dragon Club—and children were encouraged to look for the authentic holograms. The company claimed that 250,000 entries arrived in the first three weeks alone and the promotion had already paid for itself. Some are skeptical however, noting that counterfeiters have been known to counterfeit holograms successfully.[72]

- ***Participate Directly in Investigation and Surveillance.*** Governments cannot always be relied on to shut down counterfeiting. Increasingly, firms have begun to take over investigatory roles usually played by police. The Motion Picture Association hires its own private police to establish spy networks in Asia, track down pirates of DVDs, and assist customs agents to raid illegal operations.[73] Louis Vuitton is reported to employ twenty full-time staff to work with teams of investigators and lawyers to protect its brand from counterfeiters. However, such activities are not without peril. One executive of a major European alcoholic beverage company was shot at twice and wounded once while trying to help curtail counterfeiters in Thailand.[74]

- ***Change Aspects of the Product.*** Firms can continuously change aspects of their products and employ high-tech labeling and packaging. For instance, AstraZeneca's ulcer medication, Nexium, employs holograms, molecular tags, and tamper-proof seals. Other approaches include invisible marking devices or inks, nanotracers, laser etchings, and sophisticated bar codes that contain the date and location of production. However, many counterfeiters are very adept at countering these changes and employ state-of-the-art manufacturing facilities.
- ***Push for Better Legislation Against Counterfeits.*** The United States passed the Trademark Counterfeiting Act of 1984, which makes counterfeiting punishable by fines of up to $250,000 and prison terms of up to five years. China lowered its threshold for criminal prosecution of counterfeiters in 2004. Now an individual need only be caught with $6,000 worth of counterfeit goods to face prosecution versus $12,000 previously.[75] Many other countries are strengthening their laws and increasing penalties for counterfeiting. This is even true of many newly industrialized countries that were once major offenders. Still, new legislation is only the beginning. The enforcement of new legislation may remain weak in most developing countries for many years in the future.
- ***Employ Coalitions.*** Global firms may achieve better results if they work together to lobby governments for improvements in laws and enforcement. This can be true for home governments as well. The Chinese government appears to have begun to respond to complaints about counterfeiting more seriously since the United States, Europe, and Japan have appeared to speak with a single voice.
- ***Reconsider More Aggressive Pricing.*** In some cases, brand owners may choose to forgo some brand equity and lower prices to address counterfeits. Yamaha decided to lower prices in order to fight counterfeits in China. Its cheapest bike was reduced to $725 from $1,800. Counterfeiters who previously charged $1,000 had to respond by charging only $500.[76] Similarly, Mexican film and video distributors Videomax and Quality Films, in cooperation with the Motion Picture Association of America, decided to drop prices in the Mexican market and sell legitimate movies through the same street vendors who traditionally sold pirated copies of films. The distributors slashed prices enough that they matched or fell below those of pirated copies.[77]
- ***Exit or Avoid a Market.*** When Microsoft entered the Russian market, it faced a piracy rate for its software of 99 percent. The firm decided that targeting the consumer market was futile. Instead it focused solely on the business market, offering after-sales technology support as an inducement to purchase software legally.[78]

Although international firms continue to devise methods to stop counterfeits, they will remain a problem that global marketers will have to deal with for the foreseeable future. And the longer governments fail to address the problem, the stronger organized crime becomes as a result of its participation in this lucrative industry.

Check out our website at http://www.cengage.com/international for anticounterfeiting links.

SOCIAL MARKETING IN THE GLOBAL CONTEXT

Social marketing is the adaptation of marketing practices to programs designed to influence the voluntary behavior of target groups in order to improve their personal welfare and that of the society to which they belong.[79] The targets of social marketing might not believe—at least in the beginning—that they suffer from or are contributing to a problem. Such might be the case with teenagers who abuse

When developing a social marketing campaign in rural Kenya, Care International used market research techniques, such as focus groups and surveys, to better understand their target markets.

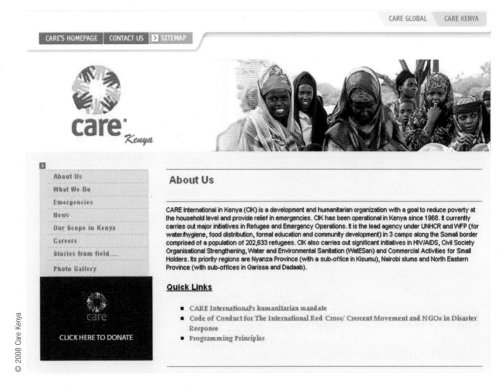

alcohol or drugs or fathers in Bangladesh who do not believe that their daughters should receive an education.[80]

Similar to marketing in the commercial sphere, social marketing has gone global. The global reach of nongovernmental organizations (NGOs) undertaking philanthropic and educational projects has never been greater. And whether they are local or transnational, public or private, organizations involved in social marketing are increasingly interested in exploring best practices from other countries.

As is the case with global products, social marketing programs employed across countries may exhibit standardized features as well as features adapted to various local conditions and cultures. For example, research demonstrates that high-risk behavior relating to the spread of AIDS can be reduced when popular opinion leaders (POLs) within a community are trained to introduce AIDS prevention endorsements into conversations with their peers. A team of social marketers from Wisconsin chose the POL model for international dissemination. The team identified leading AIDS prevention NGOs in 78 countries in Africa, Eastern Europe/Russia, Central Asia, Latin America, and the Caribbean. Each NGO was paired with a behavioral science consultant who was very familiar with the culture of the region the NGO served. Consequently, the NGO received assistance in adapting the POL model to best fit local cultural demands. Fifty-five percent of the NGOs incorporated the POL model into their programs. In addition, these NGOs networked with other organizations in their countries to promote the model. In 26 percent of targeted countries, the government also adopted the model into its official AIDS prevention programs.[81]

As noted earlier, marketing practices developed for commercial enterprises are often readily applicable to social marketing. When the global consulting firm McKinsey developed a program to improve the welfare of coffee growers in developing countries, it first segmented its market. Some growers could reasonably switch to growing specialty coffees in order to realize greater profits. However, others would need to abandon coffee growing altogether in order to survive. Social marketing recommendations were then developed for two different segments.[82] Similarly, social marketers associated with international NGO Care targeted farming and fishing communities in rural Kenya in a campaign to improve water cleanliness and decrease diarrheal diseases. Careful attention was paid to market research that used both focus-group and survey methodologies.[83]

Social marketing has benefited from the growth of global networks such as Facebook, Tweeter, MySpace, and others. For example, a group of young people in Colombia started "One Million Voices Against FARC." FARC is a paramilitary group that has terrorized Colombians for over 40 years. Aided by social networks, the organization inspired 12 million people in 190 cities around the world to rally in the streets against FARC. Within weeks of the protest, FARC witnessed massive desertions from their forces.[84]

Still, certain aspects of social marketing differentiate it from commercial marketing:

- Social marketing is not concerned with the profitability of a project the way commercial marketing is. Nonetheless, when people buy into a behavioral change being promoted by a social marketer, they must pay some kind of price. That price may involve a monetary payment or it may involve extra effort or the forgoing of something pleasurable. In some cases it may require a difficult decision to abandon long-held cultural beliefs. For example, as developing countries become more affluent, they face an increase in alcohol abuse. To combat this, some governments are attempting to alter traditional consumption patterns. One social marketing intervention in Thailand has successfully convinced villagers to forego serving alcohol at funerals.[85]

    To make the price of change more acceptable, social marketers may be called upon to offer incentives. The Care project in Kenya offered chemical tablets and water storage pots at subsidized prices to households willing to adopt new water quality procedures. The McKinsey report on coffee farming in developing countries suggested that NGOs and governments provide interim loans for farmers transitioning to new crops.

- Despite a lack of profit focus, social marketers must still seek monetary compensation to cover expenses and consequently stay in business. However, their funding comes from sources other than their target markets. These sources comprise governments as well as private donors. Additional marketing aimed at these sources of funds is also necessary. Social marketers must understand the motivations and values of these donors, and they must often compete with other social marketers for funding.

- Although NGOs may compete for funding, they often work together— formally or informally—to accomplish a common goal. Such **lateral partnerships** help facilitate efficiency savings.[86] They can also assist in the development of better, more effective practices. In the international context they can be especially useful. Multinational social marketers can offer additional funding and experience to local social marketers who provide cultural understanding and community access.

- Social marketers, especially in the international context, must consider how governments—both host and home—view the product they are marketing. Sometimes social marketers undertake jobs that fall under the usual auspices of governments. Some governments welcome the help. Others may be embarrassed by it. Also, what constitutes the public good—and the actions needed to accomplish it—can be politically charged subjects.

Lateral partnerships formal or informal agreements between NGOs to work toward a common goal and to facilitate efficiency

Do you need to adapt your service or social marketing for your target country? How would you register and protect your brand? Continue with your Country Market Report on our website at http://www.cengage.com/international.

CONCLUSION

In this chapter we see that social marketing and the marketing of services internationally have much in common with the global marketing of products. However, they each present unique challenges. Whether marketing products or services, additional efforts are required if a company wishes to develop global brands and to police counterfeits. For companies that successfully master these additional international difficulties while showing a commitment to foreign customers, global success can lead to increased profits and to more secure market positions both domestically and globally.

QUESTIONS FOR DISCUSSION

1. Why is it more difficult to pursue product standardization when marketing services?
2. Why do you think Poles already recognized the Coke name and logo when the product was first introduced in Poland?
3. Why is it difficult to decide whether to change a local brand name to a global brand name?
4. What are the pros and cons of a top-down approach to global branding? What are the pros and cons of a bottom-up approach?
5. How might a global brand be valuable to a social marketer?
6. How can social networks such as Facebook and MySpace affect social marketing in different countries? Give specific examples.

12

Pricing for International and Global Markets

LEARNING OBJECTIVES

After studying this chapter, you should be able to:

- Differentiate between full-cost pricing and marginal-cost pricing and explain the implications of both to global marketers.

- Note how international transportation costs, tariffs, taxes, local production costs, and channel costs all affect pricing decisions.

- Explain how different income levels, cultures, buyer power, and competitive situations in national markets can require different pricing strategies across these markets.

- Compare and contrast the ways in which exchange rate fluctuations and inflation rates complicate global pricing.

- List various examples of government price controls that global marketers might encounter.

- Define dumping and describe how it can constrain pricing strategies.

- Understand how the credit and collection infrastructure of a country can affect pricing decisions in that country.

- Describe how global marketers can manage export price escalation, determine transfer prices, and effectively quote prices in foreign currencies.

- Define parallel imports, explain their causes, and list ways in which they may be controlled.

- Differentiate among various forms of countertrade and balance the risk and opportunities of dealing with noncash exchanges.

IN RECENT YEARS the U.S. Justice Department has brought some of America's largest criminal cases to trial. The defendants are global managers from Belgium, Britain, Canada, France, Germany, Italy, Japan, Mexico, the Netherlands, South Korea, and Switzerland as well as from the United States. The charge is collusion with competitors to fix global prices. The penalty is a hefty fine for the company and a jail sentence for the manager. One price-fixing case involved vitamins. Multinational pharmaceutical firms reached production and price agreements that raised prices to packaged-foods companies such as General Mills, Kellogg's, Coca-Cola, and Procter & Gamble. These higher prices were of course passed on to consumers who took vitamins, drank milk, or ate cereal. Similarly, investigators uncovered a 17-year price-fixing conspiracy among American, German, and Japanese producers of sorbates, a food preservative. This cartel is estimated to have affected over a billion dollars in sales in the United States alone. Global cartels have raised prices on such diverse products as soft drinks, dynamite, and offshore oil and gas drilling platforms. Increasingly, governments in Europe and Asia are joining the United States in investigating the pricing policies of global firms.[1]

What would make a manager risk a jail sentence to fix a global price? The globalization of markets offers several possible explanations. Competition has intensified. Firms not only compete in foreign markets but also face foreign competition in their home markets. Consolidation in many industries has created fewer but bigger competitors. Demanding consumers want better products at lower prices. Pressures to lower prices abound. But pricing is the part of the marketing mix that delivers potential profits to the firm. For some companies, the temptation to bring order and certainty to a global market must seem overwhelming.

Managing global pricing is indeed more complex than establishing national pricing strategies. This chapter provides an overview of the key factors that affect pricing policies in an international environment (see Figure 12.1). First we look at how cost considerations affect international pricing decisions. We next explore the impact of market and environmental factors. Then we examine managerial pricing issues such as transfer pricing, global pricing, and countertrade.

FIGURE 12.1
Global Pricing Strategies

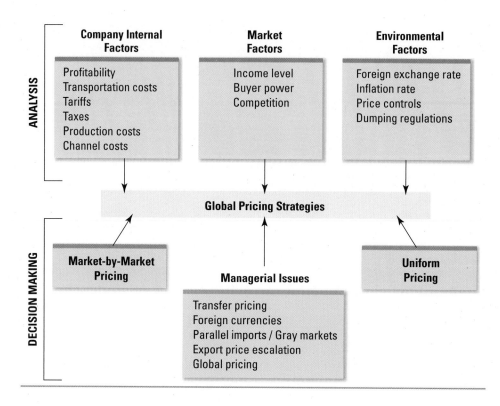

PROFIT AND COST FACTORS THAT AFFECT PRICING

American International Group introduced an insurance policy in rural India allowing farmers to insure a cow for only $10 a year.[2] Lower costs in India support this pricing strategy. Replacing a cow is cheaper in India than it is in the United States, and costs of employing service personnel in the insurance industry are lower in India as well. Most companies begin pricing deliberations on the basis of their own internal cost structure and their profit targets. Any effective pricing policy starts with a clear understanding of these cost and profit variables. Therefore, understanding the various cost elements is a prerequisite for a successful international pricing strategy.

According to standard accounting practice, costs are divided into two categories: fixed costs and variable costs. **Fixed costs** do not change over a given range of output, whereas **variable costs** vary directly with output. The relationship of these variables is shown in Table 12.1 for a fictitious company, Western Machine Tool, Inc., a manufacturer of machine tools that sell for $60,000 per unit in the U.S. market.

The total cost of a machine tool is $54,000. Selling it at $60,000, the company will make a profit of $6,000 before taxes from the sale of each unit. However, if one additional unit is sold (or not sold), the marginal impact amounts to more than an additional profit (or loss) of $6,000, because the extra cost of an additional unit will be limited to its variable costs only, or $26,000, as shown in Table 12.2. For any additional units sold, the **marginal profit** is $34,000, the amount in excess of the variable costs.

Let's say Western Machine Tool has a chance to export a unit to a foreign country, but the maximum price the foreign buyer is willing to pay is $50,000. Machine

Fixed costs costs that do not vary with changes in production levels

Variable costs costs that vary with changes in production levels

Marginal profit the change in total profit resulting from the sale of one additional unit of a product

TABLE 12.1	PROFIT AND COST CALCULATION FOR WESTERN MACHINE TOOL, INC.		
Selling price (per unit)			$60,000
Direct manufacturing costs			
Labor	$10,000		
Materials	15,000		
Energy	1,000	$26,000	
Indirect manufacturing costs			
Supervision	5,000		
Research and development	3,000		
Factory overhead	5,000	13,000	
General administrative cost	10,000		
Sales and marketing overhead	5,000	15,000	
Full costs			54,000
Net profit before tax			$ 6,000

TABLE 12.2	MARGINAL PROFIT CALCULATION FOR WESTERN MACHINE TOOL, INC.		
Selling price (per unit)			$60,000
Variable costs			
Direct manufacturing costs			
Labor	$10,000		
Materials	15,000		
Energy	1,000	$26,000	
Total variable costs			26,000
Contribution margin (selling price minus variable costs)			$34,000

Tool, using full-cost pricing, argues that the company will incur a loss of $4,000 if the deal is accepted. However, only $26,000 of additional variable cost will be incurred for a new machine, because all fixed costs are incurred anyway and are covered by all prior units sold. The company can in fact go ahead with the sale and claim a marginal profit of $24,000. In such a situation, a profitable sale may easily be turned down unless a company is fully informed about its cost composition.

Cost components are subject to change. For example, if growing export volume adds new output to a plant, a company may achieve economies of scale that result in overall reductions in unit cost. This consideration further supports the use of a marginal-pricing strategy. Marketers should beware, however, if marginal pricing significantly hurts domestic competition in the export markets. As we will see later in the chapter, this can lead to charges of dumping and consequent legal action against the exporters.

Transportation Costs

Spanish fashion chain Zara is one of the most important fashion chains in Europe and is known for responding quickly to fashion trends and for delivering new stock quickly to its foreign operations. But with distribution centered in Spain, prices increase the farther a store is from home base. For example, Zara prices in the United States can be 65 percent higher than they are in Spain.[3]

International marketing often requires the shipment of products over long distances. The cost of shipping can become an important part of the international pricing policy of some firms. A study of how U.S. and Korean companies set overseas prices suggests that companies that charge higher prices in foreign markets than in domestic markets do so because of transportation costs. In other words, these companies, both American and Korean, appear to use a cost-plus model for setting prices overseas, consciously adding in transportation costs to establish the price they eventually charge in foreign markets.[4]

For commodities in particular, low transportation costs can determine who gets an order. For more expensive and differentiated products, such as computers or sophisticated electronic instruments, transportation costs usually represent only a small fraction of total costs and have less influence on pricing decisions. For products between the two extremes, companies can substantially affect unit transportation costs by selecting appropriate transportation methods. For example, the introduction of container ocean vessels has made cost-effective shipment of many products possible. Roll-on, roll-off ships (ro-ro carriers) have reduced ocean freight costs for cars and trucks to very low levels, making exporters more competitive vis-à-vis local manufacturers. Still, because all modes of transportation, including rail, truck, air, and ocean, depend on a considerable amount of energy, the total cost is of growing concern to international companies and can be sensitive to the world price of oil.

On the website for FTD you can arrange to send flowers to friends in a number of different countries. The price will vary for each market. Florists in the network have different labor and rent costs in different regions. The average distance for a floral delivery varies across regions as well, resulting in different fuel costs.

Tariffs

When products are transported across national borders, tariffs may have to be paid. Tariffs are usually levied on the landed costs of a product, which include shipping costs to the importing country. Tariffs are normally assessed as a percentage of the landed value. The World Trade Organization (WTO), like its predecessor, the General Agreement on Tariffs and Trade (GATT), has gone a long way in reducing tariffs. However, they can still prove significant for certain products in certain markets. Tariff costs can have a ripple effect and increase prices considerably for the end user. Intermediaries, whether they are sales subsidiaries or independent distributors, tend to include any tariff costs in their costs of goods sold and to calculate operating margins on the basis of this amount. As a result, the impact on the final end-user price can be substantial whenever tariff rates are high.

Sometimes international firms attempt to avoid or lessen the cost effects of tariffs by having their products reclassified. When the U.S. tariffs for trucks were temporarily increased from 2.5 to 25 percent in an effort to stem imports, Land Rover of the United Kingdom complained that its $40,000 four-wheel-drive vehicle should not be classified as a truck, pointing out that the utility vehicle had four doors, not just two like the typical light truck. The vehicle was reclassified, and the higher duty was avoided.

Go to the student companion website (http://www.cengage. com/international) for links to information on national tariffs.

Taxes

A variety of local taxes also affect the final cost of products. For example, different national taxes contribute to the different prices charged in different national markets for luxury Hermès products. A Hermès beach towel, including taxes, can cost $553 in New York, $599 in Paris, $631 in Frankfurt, and $720 in Tokyo.[5]

One of the most common is the **value-added tax (VAT)** used by member countries of the European Union (EU). This tax is similar to the sales tax collected by state governments in the United States but involves more complicated assessment and collection procedures based on the value added to the product at any given stage.

Each EU country sets its own VAT structure. However, common to all is a zero tax rate (or exemption) on exported goods. A company exporting from the Netherlands to Belgium does not have to pay any tax on the value added in the Netherlands. However, Belgian authorities do collect a tax, at the Belgium rate, on products shipped from the Netherlands. Merchandise shipped to any EU member country from a nonmember country, such as the United States or Japan, is assessed the VAT rate on landed costs, in addition to any customs duties that may be applied to those products.

Different countries also assess different **sin taxes**. These are taxes assessed on products that are legal but are discouraged by the society. Cigarettes and alcoholic beverages commonly fall into this category. For example, Sweden countered a history of massive alcohol abuse by enacting Europe's highest taxes on alcoholic beverages. These taxes increased prices to consumers, who in turn reduced their consumption. Sweden's alcohol-related deaths and illnesses fell to among the lowest in the developed world. However, Sweden's membership in the EU threatened to undermine these gains. Swedes in the southern part of the country can now drive across a bridge to buy alcohol in Denmark at a far lower price and bring it back into Sweden.

Value-added tax (VAT) a tax that is levied at each stage in the production and distribution of a product or service based on the value added by that stage; the tax is ultimately passed on to the buyer

Sin taxes taxes assessed on products that are legal but discouraged by society

Local Production Costs

Up to this point, we have assumed that a company has only one producing location, from which it exports to all other markets. However, most international firms manufacture products in several countries. In such cases, operating costs for raw materials, wages, energy, and/or financing may differ widely from country to country, allowing a firm to ship from a particularly advantageous location in order to reduce prices by taking advantage of lower costs. Companies increasingly choose production locations that give them advantages in production costs as well as freight, tariffs, or other transfer costs.

Consequently, judicious management of sourcing points may reduce product costs and result in added pricing flexibility. Mexico has attracted many U.S. candy manufacturers. Part of the attraction is the youthful Mexican market known for its sweet tooth. However, Mexico is also being used as a platform to export candy back to the U.S. market. Mexican workers earn as little as one-tenth the pay of U.S. factory workers. Even more important is the lower cost of sugar in Mexico—about half the federally supported U.S. cost.[6]

Rarely do consumers themselves cross borders in search of lower prices in lower cost countries. However, this is relatively common in Poland where prices are among the highest in Europe.[7] It is also increasingly common for patients seeking relief from costly medical procedures. One patient flew 22 hours to Madras, India, to receive a hip replacement at the Apollo Hospital. The operation, which cost $4,000 in Madras, would have cost $30,000 in the United States or Europe.[8] Because of lower production costs, medical tourism is a growing industry in India.

Channel Costs

Channel costs are a function of channel length, distribution margins, and logistics. Many countries operate with longer distribution channels than those in the United States, causing higher total costs and end-user prices because of additional layers of intermediaries. Also, gross margins at the retail level tend to be higher outside the United States. Because the logistics system in a large number of countries is also less developed than that in the United States, logistics costs, too, are higher on a per-unit basis. All these factors add extra costs to a product that is marketed internationally.

Campbell Soup Company, a U.S.-based firm, found that its retailers in the United Kingdom purchased soup in small quantities of 24 cans per case of assorted soups, requiring each can to be handpicked for shipment. In the United States, the company could sell one variety of soup to retailers in cases of 48 cans per case. To handle the smaller purchase lots in England, the company had to add another level of distribution and new facilities. As a result, distribution costs were 30 percent higher in England than in the United States.[9]

MARKET FACTORS THAT AFFECT PRICING

Companies cannot establish pricing policies in a vacuum. Although cost information is essential, prices must also reflect the realities of the marketplace. International markets are particularly challenging because of the large number of local economic situations to be considered. Four factors in particular stand out and must be analyzed in greater detail: income level, buyer power, competition, and culture.

Income Level

As we have discussed in previous chapters, the income level of a country's population determines the amount and type of goods and services bought, especially in consumer markets. When detailed income data are not available, incomes are expressed by gross domestic product (GDP) or gross national product (GNP) divided by the total population. GDP is the total value of goods and services produced in a country. GNP includes this plus any income that residents receive from abroad. The new measures, GNP per capita and GDP per capita, are surrogate measures for personal income and are used to compare income levels among countries. To do so, all GNPs and GDPs have to be converted into the same currency. As we also noted earlier, converting GNP or GDP per capita into dollars on the basis of market exchange rates may understate the true purchasing power of a country's consumers. It is more accurate to look at developing countries' GNP or GDP per capita converted into dollars on the basis of relative purchasing power.

Discretionary income income remaining after the basic necessities of food, shelter, and clothing have been acquired

Furthermore, **discretionary income**—the amount left after the basic necessities of food, shelter, and clothing have been acquired—can vary from country to country. In much of Southeast Asia, children in their 20s still live with their parents. Virtually all the income they earn is discretionary, which makes them an attractive target market. In China, employees of state organizations often receive lucrative housing benefits, a practice that markedly increases their discretionary income.

As a result of widely differing income and price levels, elasticity of demand for any given product can be expected to vary greatly. Countries with high income levels often display lower price elasticities for necessities such as food, shelter, and medical care. These lower elasticities in part reflect a lack of alternatives such as "doing it yourself" that forces buyers in these countries to purchase such goods even at higher prices. By contrast, in many countries with lower income levels, a considerable part of the population has the additional alternatives of providing their own food or building their own shelters should they not have enough money to purchase products or services on a cash basis. The availability of such options increases price elasticity, because these consumers can more easily opt out of the cash economy than can consumers in developed economies.

Of course, in any country there will be a mix of different consumers with different income levels and potentially different price elasticities. In a study of the price elasticities of business-to-business (B2B) buyers of information technology system support, it was determined that in each country studied different sets of customers existed, with different price elasticities and different needs. The researchers determined that price elasticities could be used to segment across countries and therefore develop different regional or global offers to appeal to the different segments.[10]

Many multinational firms can realistically target only a select segment of the population in poorer countries, even when they adjust their prices downward. To accommodate a lower income level in China, a Big Mac costs the equivalent of $1.83, which is significantly below the cost of $3.54 for a Big Mac in the United States. McDonald's has typically resorted to introductory pricing that attracts more customers. Still, a McDonald's meal remains expensive in the Chinese context. A Chinese family of three can pay about 10 percent of a typical monthly urban salary, to eat one meal out.

Firms should regularly reassess their pricing policy in developing countries, especially if they are charging relatively high prices and targeting the elite. The growing middle classes in these countries can become a more attractive segment to target

Two Burmese monks walk past a billboard advertising Apple Macintosh computers in Myanmar. The appeal of a low price is appropriate in this Asian country where only about one person in a thousand owns a personal computer.

than a small upper class. For example, General Motors announced its development of a Farmers Car for China's 800 million rural inhabitants, whose incomes are even lower than those of city dwellers, in an attempt to tap a market segment hitherto ignored by multinational car manufacturers. The proposed price of the car was $7,000, down from the $40,000 charged for Buicks then sold to Chinese city dwellers.[11] Soon cars sold in the city were also becoming more affordable, as many manufacturers began to lower automobile prices. As a result of an increase in the incomes of Chinese consumers, competitively priced cars, and availability of consumer credit, China soon became the world's second largest automobile market.

Culture and Consumer Behavior

Culture can also affect consumer behavior, which in turn affects pricing. Local traditions can play a role in surprising ways. In China, the number 8 is associated with prosperity and good luck, whereas the number 4 is associated with death. A research study confirmed that marketers in China avoided prices that ended in 4, whereas prices ending in 8 were advertised four times more often than prices ending in other numerals.[12]

One aspect that can vary by culture is the role that high prices play in the purchasing decision. For example, Japanese are observed to pay unusually high prices for status products, and status cars command higher prices in Japan than they do in the United States. Some observers refer to this phenomenon as the "special Japanese price." A BMW 545i that lists for about $56,000 in the United States will sell for $84,000 in Japan. Similarly, an E500 Mercedes that sells for $57,000 in the United States will cost over $85,000 in Japan.[13] High prices can also be a cue for quality, but this can vary by culture as well. A study of American and Thai consumers concluded that the Thai consumers perceived themselves to lack product knowledge compared to the perceptions of the U.S. consumers. This caused the Thais to be more likely to infer product quality from price.[14]

Bargaining for a better price is another aspect of consumer behavior that is more common in some cultures than in others. In many emerging markets, such as Turkey, bargaining is acceptable—even expected—in the more traditional markets. Chinese consumers, who are also accustomed to bargaining, are using the Internet to increase their bargaining advantage. Websites encourage Chinese to get together and form buying teams to visit retail outlets and ask for quantity discounts. Hundreds of thousands of consumers registered on just one such site in a single year. In Shanghai, such a buying team negotiated discount prices from a General Motors dealership. However, some international retailers have refused to bargain.[15]

Buyer Power

Just as discretionary income is an important consideration in consumer markets, buyer power is crucial in B2B markets. In the recent recession in Europe, a major grocery chain removed about 300 Unilever products from its Belgium stores, claiming the prices were too high.[16] Large buyers, whether they be in retailing, services, or manufacturing, can become important to supplier firms, and in turn these buyers can demand lower prices from suppliers. If there are only a few buyers in a national industry, prices may be lower than in markets where there are many smaller buyers. In some global industries, such as aerospace, suppliers face the challenge of increasing buyer power at the international level.

Competition

The intensity and power of competition can also significantly affect price levels in any given market. A firm acting as the sole supplier of a product in a given market enjoys greater pricing flexibility. The opposite is true if that same company has to compete against several other local or international firms. Therefore, the number and type of competitors greatly influence pricing strategy in any market. As noted above, China has become the world's second largest car market. It is also one of the most competitive. Price cuts, by both domestic and global automobile companies, cut profit margins for all competitors. It is not unusual to see as much as 27 percent discounted off a list price in China.[17]

Cartel a group of companies acting together to control the price of certain goods or services

Occasionally, price levels are manipulated by **cartels**, or pricing agreements among competitors. Cartels in the United States are forbidden by law. Furthermore, U.S. companies may find themselves in violation of U.S. laws if they actively participate in any foreign cartel. Although many other foreign governments allow cartels provided that they do not injure the consumer, the EU is becoming stricter toward cartels. The European Commission charged 18 chemical companies with fixing the price of hydrogen peroxide, which included Akzo Nobel, Arkema, Degussa, Kemira, and Solvay. The companies can be fined up to 10 percent of their annual revenue if found guilty.[18]

Similarly, non-U.S. companies can be fined if their price fixing activity affects the U.S. market. As part of a plea agreement in U.S. court, British Airways and Korean Air each agreed to pay nearly $300 million in fines for colluding with competitors to fix fuel surcharges on passenger tickets and cargo.[19]

WORLD BEAT 12.1

ORDERED TO CARTEL?

AS CHINA BECOMES more dominant as a world manufacturer, its ability to set world prices increases as well—especially as many Chinese firms apparently see no reason to avoid collaborating on pricing. The Chinese manufacturers call it "self-regulation." Of course, such collaboration has made them the targets of recent antitrust investigations in the United States. Vitamin C is a case in point. After an agreement among China's four largest vitamin C producers caused prices to triple, a lawsuit was filed by a U.S. customer. Chinese defendants put forth two lines of defense: First, the companies asserted that they had raised prices to avoid accusations of dumping. Second, the companies claimed they were acting as agents of the Chinese government and were therefore not subject to U.S. antitrust laws. The latter claim was based on the fact that the

Chinese Ministry of Commerce had ordered the four companies to fix the higher price, and an act of state is rarely prosecuted in a foreign court. For example, the member countries of the oil cartel OPEC (Organization of Petroleum Exporting Countries) are not prosecuted for price fixing.

A U.S. district judge found the Chinese defense to be "unprecedented" and dismissed the claim to sovereign immunity. Many others were equally unsympathetic. One observer noted that Chinese companies priced their products low until they drove other competitors out of the market. Then they raised prices. In fact, when Chinese saccharine manufacturers raised prices, they admitted as much. Because they had overtaken U.S. and South Korean competitors, it no longer made sense to charge low prices.

Sources: John R. Wilke and Kathy Chen, "Planned Economy," *Wall Street Journal,* February 10, 2006, p. A1; John R. Wilke, "China Defends Price Fixing by Vitamin Makers," *Wall Street Journal,* November 25, 2008, p. B1; and "US Anti-Trust Ruling Impacts Magnesite Case," *Industrial Minerals,* January 1, 2009.

ENVIRONMENTAL FACTORS THAT AFFECT PRICING

We have thus far treated pricing as a matter of cost and market factors. A number of environmental factors also influence pricing at the international level. These external variables, which are not subject to control by any individual company, include foreign exchange rates, inflation, and government price controls. These factors restrict company decision-making authority and can become major concerns for country managers.

Exchange Rate Fluctuations

As discussed in Chapter 2, one of the most unpredictable factors affecting prices is the movement of foreign exchange rates. As the exchange rate moves up and down, it particularly affects exporters. When a company's costs are in its domestic currency, as this currency weakens, the firm's costs appear lower in another currency. For example, when the euro was first launched, each euro was valued at $1.20. Six months later, the euro had dropped to $1.00. As a result, products manufactured in Europe were cheaper in dollar terms and more attractive in the U.S. market, as well as in other national markets where governments pegged their currencies to the U.S. dollar.[20]

Foreign exchange fluctuations can also present difficulties for companies that export from countries with appreciating currencies. These firms are forced to accept decreased margins on sales denominated in foreign currencies or else raise prices to maintain their prior margins. The latter option could, of course, cause a drop in export demand. This was clear when the Russian ruble fell 22 percent over a period of a few months. Exports to Russia fell 50 percent. Faced with the option of buying

Check out our website (http://www.cengage. com/international) for links to national currency information.

a tube of locally produced toothpaste for 7 rubles or a tube of imported Colgate for 24 rubles, fewer Russian consumers chose the Colgate.[21]

Inflation Rates

The rate of inflation can affect product costs and may force a company to take specific action. Inflation rates have traditionally fluctuated over time and, more important, have differed from country to country. The United States and Europe have successfully managed inflation by raising interest rates whenever the economy starts to heat up, keeping inflation at 0 to 3 percent. Historically, inflation has been more of a problem in developing countries. In some cases, inflation rates have risen to several hundred percent. Argentina, Bolivia, Brazil, and Nicaragua have all experienced four-digit hyperinflation in the past. A country can be particularly susceptible to inflation if its currency devalues. This causes most imported goods to rise in cost almost immediately, adding to inflationary pressures.

A company can usually protect itself from rapid inflation if it maintains constant operating margins by constantly adjusting prices. However, consumer incomes often lag behind inflation, and many consumers may decide that higher prices simply price products out of their reach. Also, this strategy can be undermined if governments decide to enact price controls.

Price Controls

Despite the official claim that 96 percent of all prices are set by the market, the Chinese government enforces price controls on such key products as fertilizers, fuel, medicines, and transport services.[22] Price controls are most common in developing countries and may be applied to an entire economy to combat inflation. Alternatively, regulations may be applied selectively to specific industries. As a result of market liberalization, across-the-board price controls are now uncommon. Industry-specific controls are more common. For example, in response to rising prices, the Thai government threatened cement producers with price controls if they failed to cap their prices voluntarily. Furthermore, the cement producers agreed to cut off distributors who attracted complaints of overcharging.[23]

Pharmaceuticals are subject to price controls in many countries, including Canada, Japan, and European states. In the EU, where many aspects of the countries' economies are coordinated, methods of controlling prices for drugs can vary considerably. In India, pharmaceutical manufacturers who apply for patent protection must report the price of similar products available within India as well as the price of the drug in every country in which the drug is sold. The Indian government then assesses the therapeutic advantage of the drug and sets a limit on the premium that can be charged for the drug.[24]

Governments may allow a firm to raise prices if the firm produces evidence that the costs of producing its product have increased, which is often the case. This procedure requires significant management time, and the outcome is uncertain. Even if the price increase is ultimately approved, profit margins are likely to have deteriorated in the meantime. Alternatively, or additionally, a firm might address price controls by seeking product modifications that result in lower input costs and thus maintain or increase margins. Companies can also decide to leave a market because of price controls. However, price controls are usually temporary. Firms often discover that disappearing from a market can hurt a brand should they ever decide to reenter the market when price controls are retracted.

One of the best strategies to survive price controls is to have diversified markets. When corn prices shot up 67 percent during the ethanol craze, Mexico imposed price controls on tortillas and corn flour. Gruma, the country's largest flour manufacturer, supplied 75 percent of the corn flour used to make tortillas in Mexico. Luckily, the company had diversified internationally, and two-thirds of its sales were outside Mexico.[25]

Dumping Regulations

Dumping the practice of exporting a product at an "unfair" price and consequently damaging competition in the export market

The practice of exporting a product at an "unfair" price and consequently damaging local competition is referred to as **dumping**. Because of potential injuries to domestic manufacturers, most governments have adopted regulations against dumping. Antidumping actions are allowed under provisions of the WTO as long as two criteria are met: prices are set at less than "normal value" and this results in "material injury" to a domestic industry. The first criterion is usually interpreted to mean selling abroad at prices below those in the country of origin, although there are some exceptions. Subsequently, a complainant government may be required to establish that prices in its country are indeed set below full costs of manufacture, transport, and marketing. The WTO rules prohibit assessment of retroactive punitive duties and require all procedures to be open.

In the 1980s and early 1990s, 80 percent of antidumping charges were brought by the United States, Canada, the EU, and Australia—often against Asian countries. However, many of the new antidumping cases have been brought to the WTO by developing countries such as South Africa, India, Brazil, Indonesia, and Mexico. International marketers have to be aware of antidumping legislation that sets a floor under export prices, limiting pricing flexibility even in the event of overcapacity or an industry slowdown. On the other hand, antidumping legislation can work to a company's advantage, protecting it from foreign competition. In South Korea, the Korean Trade Commission found that Japanese industrial robots were sold at unfair prices in Korea, thereby harming the Korean robot industry. The Ministry of Commerce, Industry and Energy has asked that antidumping duties of 9 to 19 percent be put on Japanese products.[26]

Anti-dumping

If a company exports a product at a price lower than the price it normally charges on its own home not pass judgement. Its focus is on how governments can or cannot react to dumping – it disciplines

News back to top

- 7 May 2009: <u>WTO Secretariat reports increase in new anti-dumping investigations</u>

- 19 December 2008: <u>Rules Chair issues new negotiating texts</u>

- 20 October 2008: <u>WTO Secretariat reports surge in new anti-dumping investigations</u>

> <u>More news on anti-dumping</u>

CASE STUDIES

> <u>The Indian Shrimp Industry Organizes to Fight the Threat of Anti-Dumping Action</u>

> <u>The Reform of South Africa's Anti-Dumping Regime</u>

Introduction back to top

<u>Introduction to anti-dumping in the WTO</u> Links to anti-dumping section of the WTO guide "Understanding the WTO".

<u>Technical information about anti-dumping</u>

The WTO is increasingly hearing dumping complaints brought by developing countries.

Credit and Collection Infrastructure

Pricing can also be affected by the availability of credit in a country and the ability to collect payment if credit is extended to consumers. In India, most rural cell phone customers use prepaid cards instead of signing up for a monthly payment plan.[27] One reason for this is the need for poorer consumers to buy service in affordable amounts. However, the simple act of billing for cell phone service is undermined if a bill cannot be sent because mail service is unreliable. Internet billing is equally untenable if consumers are unlikely to have access to the Internet to pay their bills online.

In China, use of credit cards has lagged behind Internet shopping, posing a problem for online marketing. Online marketers rely instead on expensive cash-on-delivery systems or online payment options similar to the U.S. service PayPal. Either of these options increases costs, which have to be born by either the seller or the buyer.

MANAGERIAL ISSUES IN GLOBAL PRICING

Now that we have given you a general overview of the context of international pricing, we turn to managerial issues—matters that require constant management attention and are never really resolved. These issues include export price escalation, transfer pricing, quoting prices in foreign currencies, responding to parallel markets, setting global prices, and managing countertrade.

Managing Export Price Escalation

Export price escalation the phenomenon in which the costs of export documentation, overseas transportation, insurance, and tariffs raise the price of products abroad to a level above that of the price in the domestic market

As Table 12.3 illustrates, there are additional costs described earlier that can raise the price of an exported product substantially above its domestic price. This phenomenon is called **export price escalation**, and it raises both tactical and strategic questions. Tactically, an exporter must decide who pays for the different costs involved in exporting, whether or not to reengineer the product to keep costs down, and whether or not to explore a cheaper locale from which to export the product. The main strategic question is whether or not to reposition the product overseas.

If a firm employs a foreign distributor or sells directly to a customer abroad, it must clarify which of the various export costs are borne by the exporting firm and which are borne by the foreign distributor or customer. There are many terms used in export pricing that help clarify this issue. Lists of these terms are often available

TABLE 12.3	EXPORT PRICE ESCALATION: AN EXAMPLE	
DELIVERED COST OF PRODUCT	DOMESTIC MARKET	EXPORT MARKET
Factory Price	$10.00	$10.00
Domestic Transportation	1.00	0.75
Export Documentation		0.75
Overseas Freight		1.75
Insurance		0.25
Tariffs		0.75
Final Price	$11.00	$14.00

at national export portals, including the U.S. export portal at http://www.export.gov. However, among the more common terms are:

- **CIF (cost, insurance, freight)** is a term commonly used for ocean shipments and designates that the price quoted by the exporter includes the price for the goods and their transportation, including insurance, to the foreign port of debarkation.
- **CFR (cost and freight)** is similar to CIF in that it covers the cost of goods and transportation. However, the distributor or customer is responsible for paying to insure the goods in transit.
- **FOB (free on board)** designates that the exporter only pays for the cost of delivering the goods to the port of export. The buyer is responsible for the costs of loading, shipping, and insuring the products.

No matter who pays these different costs, export price escalation is likely to make the product more expensive overseas unless the exporter, the distributor, or both accept low margins. Instead of accepting low margins, a company may seek ways to decrease the costs of exported products such as reengineering its products to be less costly. Also, export sales may generate greater economies of scale in production, eventually allowing for a lower export price. Global marketers should also be careful in export pricing not to attribute costs to exports that only apply to products sold domestically such as the cost of advertising in the domestic market. Finally, an exporting firm may seek a cheaper production locale. If tariffs are high and the export market attractive, the firm might decide to produce, or assemble, in the foreign market itself. Ford was able to sell the cars it assembled in Russia at a much lower price than the imported cars of competitors, even though Ford imported 80 percent of the parts its used to make its Russian cars.[28]

Alternatively, a company may make the strategic decision to adjust the marketing mix to promote a more upscale status. This was a strategy adopted by California's My Dollarstore Inc. when the company entered India. The dollar stores offered middle class Indians, many of whom had studied or worked in the United States, a sense of being back in America with offerings such as Hershey's chocolate syrup and the latest flavor of Pringles potato chips. In the United States, dollar stores targeted bargain shoppers and were located in lower-rent strip malls. All products were priced at a dollar. In India, where transportation costs and tariffs had to be considered, products had to be priced at about $2. Consequently, dollar stores were opened in upscale malls and targeted the affluent.[29]

Determining Transfer Prices

A substantial amount of international market transactions take place between subsidiaries of the same company. It has been estimated that in-house trading between subsidiaries accounts for one-third of the volume among the world's 800 largest multinationals. An **international transfer price** is the price paid by the importing or buying unit of a firm to the exporting unit of the same firm. For example, the U.S. marketing subsidiary of a Taiwanese manufacturer of personal computers will pay a transfer price for the machines it receives from Taiwan. The actual transfer price may be negotiated by the units involved or may be set centrally by the international firm. How these prices are set continues to be a major issue for international companies and governments alike.

Because negotiations of transfer prices do not represent arm's-length negotiations between independent participants, the resulting prices frequently differ from

International transfer price the price paid by one unit of a firm to import a product or service supplied by another unit of the same firm

free-market prices. Companies may deviate from arm's-length prices to maximize profits or to minimize risk and uncertainty. To pursue a strategy of profit maximization, a company may lower transfer prices for products shipped from some subsidiaries, while increasing prices for products shipped to others, in order to accumulate profits in countries where it is advantageous, while keeping profits low elsewhere.

Different tax, tariff, or subsidy structures among countries frequently invite such practices. By accumulating more profits in a low-tax country, a company lowers its overall tax bill and thus increases profit. Likewise, tariff duties can be reduced by quoting low transfer prices to countries with high tariffs. In cases in which countries use a different exchange rate for the transfer of goods from that used for the transfer of capital or profits, a firm may attempt to use transfer prices to remove money from the country, rather than transferring profits at less advantageous rates. The same is true for countries with limits on profit repatriation. Furthermore, a company may want to accumulate profits in a wholly owned subsidiary rather than in one in which it has minority ownership. By using the transfer price mechanism, it can decrease the profits it shares with local partners.

Companies may also use the transfer price mechanism to minimize risk or uncertainty by moving profits or assets out of a country with chronic balance-of-payment problems and frequent devaluations. Because regular profit remittances may be strictly controlled in such countries, many firms see high transfer prices as the only way to repatriate funds and thereby reduce the amount of assets at risk. The same practice may be employed if a company anticipates political or social disturbances or a direct threat to profits through government intervention.

In actual practice, companies choose a number of approaches to transfer pricing. Market-based prices are equal to those negotiated by independent companies or at arm's length. Of 30 U.S.-based firms, 46 percent were reported to use market-based systems.[30] Another 35 percent used cost-based systems to determine the transfer price. Costs were based on a predetermined formula that could include a standard markup for profits.

Internal Considerations. Rigorous use of the transfer pricing mechanism to reduce a company's income taxes and duties or to maximize profits in strong currency areas can create difficulties for subsidiary managers whose profits are artificially reduced. It may be hard to motivate managers when the direct profit incentive is removed. Furthermore, company resource allocation may become inefficient, because funds are appropriated to units whose profits are artificially increased. Conversely, resources may be denied to subsidiaries whose income statements were subject to transfer-price-induced reductions. It is generally agreed that a transfer pricing mechanism should not be used for resource allocations; the gains incurred through tax savings may easily be lost through other inefficiencies.

External Problems. Governments do not look favorably on transfer pricing mechanisms aimed at reducing their tax revenues. U.S. government policy on transfer pricing is governed by tax law, particularly Section 482 of the Revenue Act of 1962. The act is designed to provide an accurate allocation of costs, income, and capital among related enterprises to protect U.S. tax revenue. Market prices are generally preferred by the Internal Revenue Service (IRS). The IRS will accept cost-plus markups if market prices are not available and economic circumstances warrant such use. Not acceptable, however, are transfer prices that attribute no profit to the U.S. unit. Other methods, such as negotiated prices, are acceptable as long as the transfer price is comparable to a price charged to an unrelated party. In addition, the IRS requires all companies to maintain detailed explanations of the rationale and analysis supporting their transfer pricing policy. The IRS developed the Advanced Pricing Agreement Program (APA), which became effective on December 31, 1993. Under this program, a company can obtain approval from the IRS for their transfer pricing procedures.

Australia, Japan, and Korea all have formal transfer pricing arrangements, and China, India, and New Zealand all have informal programs.[31] However, the strengthening of government regulations all around the world makes it necessary for global businesses to document and defend their transfer pricing methods. According to a study of 280 multinational companies operating in Europe, 85 percent had been audited on transfer pricing over a three-year period.[32] Audits of transfer pricing policies can result in billions of dollars of tax liability. The U.S. Internal Revenue Service (IRS) issued GlaxoSmithKline a tax bill of $5 billion as a result of an IRS audit that had begun more than 12 years earlier. The IRS argued that the company transferred costs to the United States from other countries at inflated prices to reduce their U.S. tax burden.[33]

Quoting Prices in a Foreign Currency

For many international marketing transactions, it is not always feasible to quote in a company's domestic currency when selling or purchasing merchandise. Although the majority of U.S. exporters quote prices in dollars, there are situations in which customers may prefer quotes in their own national currency. In fact, a research study of 671 companies in the United States, Finland, and Sweden found that companies that respond to customers' requests for prices quoted in their local currencies benefit from a larger volume of export business.[34]

When two currencies are involved in a market transaction, there is the risk that a change in exchange rates may occur between the invoicing date and the settlement date for the sale. This **transaction risk** is an inherent factor in international marketing and clearly separates domestic from international business. Fortunately, alternatives are available to protect the seller from transaction risk.

For most major currencies, international foreign exchange dealers located at major banks quote a spot price and a forward price. The **spot price** determines the number of dollars to be paid for a particular foreign currency purchased or sold today. The **forward price** quotes the number of dollars to be paid for a foreign currency bought or sold 30, 90, or 180 days from today. The forward price, however, is not necessarily speculation about what the spot price will be in the future. Instead, the forward price reflects interest rate differentials between two currencies for maturities of 30, 90, or 180 days. Consequently, there are no firm indications of what the spot price will be for any given currency in the future.

A company quoting in foreign currency for purchase or sale can simply leave settlement until the due date and pay whatever spot price prevails at the time. Such an **uncovered position** may be chosen when exchange rates are not expected to shift or when any shift in the near future will result in a gain for the company. With exchange rates fluctuating widely on a daily basis, even among major trading nations such as the United States, Japan, Germany, and the United Kingdom, a company can expose itself to substantial foreign exchange risks. Because many international firms are in business to make a profit from the sale of goods rather than from speculation in the foreign exchange markets, managers generally protect themselves from unexpected fluctuations.

Transaction risk the risk that a change in exchange rate that will prove unfavorable to either the seller or the buyer will occur between invoicing and settlement dates

Spot price/spot rate the rate of exchange between two currencies for delivery, one for the other, within one or two business days

Forward price/forward rate the price agreed upon by two parties for one to deliver to the other a set amount of currency at a fixed future date

Uncovered position a strategy in which a firm chooses not to take any action that would alleviate transaction risk

Hedging the act of contracting through financial intermediaries for the future exchange of one currency for another at a set rate

One such protection lies in **hedging**. Instead of accepting whatever spot market rate exists on the settlement in 30 or 90 days, a company can opt to contract through financial intermediaries for future delivery of foreign currency at a set price, regardless of the spot price at that time. This allows the seller to incorporate a firm exchange rate into the price determination. Of course, if a company wishes to predict the spot price in 90 days and is reasonably certain about the accuracy of its prediction, it may attempt to choose the more advantageous of the two: the expected spot or the present forward rate. However, such predictions should only be made under the guidance of experts familiar with foreign exchange rates.

To illustrate the selection of a hedging procedure, assume that a U.S. exporter of corporate jets sells a jet valued at $24 million to a client in Germany (see Table 12.4). The client will pay in euros quoted at the current (spot) rate on March 3 of $1.31, or €18,320,610. This amount will be paid in three months (90 days). As a result, the U.S. exporter will have to determine how to protect such an incoming amount against foreign exchange risk. Although uncertain about the outcome, the exporter's bank indicates that there is equal chance for the euro spot rate to remain at $1.31 (scenario C), to devalue to $1.20 (scenario A), or to appreciate to $1.45 (scenario B). As a result, the exporter has the option of selling the amount forward in the 90-days forward market, at $1.3213.[35]

An alternative available to the exporter is to sell forward the invoice amount to obtain a sure $23,947,980 at a cost of $52,020 on the transaction. In anticipation of a devaluation of the euro, such a hedging strategy would be advisable. Consequently, the $52,020 represents a premium to ensure against any larger loss such as the one predicted under scenario A. However, a company would also forgo any gain as indicated under scenario B.

Sometimes hedging is not an option when a firm is dealing with soft currencies or currencies undergoing upheaval. Prior to an expected devaluation of the ruble, nearly all exporters to Russia were seeking hedging contracts. Hedging contracts for rubles became increasingly hard to find and then disappeared from the market altogether. Once, when the Turkish government allowed the pegged lira to float, the lira collapsed nearly 40 percent over a few days. In the immediate disarray that ensued, hedging opportunities for the lira were similarly difficult to locate.

An alternative to hedging is covering through the money market. This involves borrowing funds in the currency at risk for the time until settlement. For example, a U.S. exporter that is holding accounts receivable in euros and is unwilling to absorb the related currency risk may borrow euros and exchange them for dollars for working-capital purposes. When the customer eventually pays in euros, the U.S. exporter uses these euros to pay off the loan. Any currency fluctuations will be canceled, resulting in neither loss nor gain.

TABLE 12.4	HEDGING SCENARIOS		
	A	B	C
Spot rate of March 3	$1.31	$1.31	$1.31
Spot rate as of June 3 (estimate)	1.20	1.45	1.31
U.S. dollar equivalent of €18,320,610 at spot rates on June 3	21,984,735	26,564,884	24,000,000
Exchange gain (loss)	(2,015,265)	2,564,884	0

Dealing with Parallel Imports or Gray Markets

As a result of different market and competitive factors, international marketers often choose to sell the same product at different prices in different national markets. When such price differences become large enough, entrepreneurs may step in and buy products in low-price countries to reexport to high-price countries, profiting from the price differential. This arbitrage behavior creates what is commonly called **parallel imports** or the **gray market**, because these imports take place outside of the official distribution channels established by the trademark owner.

Gray markets have never been more robust. Parallel imports within the EU have been encouraged by the introduction of the euro, which allows easy price comparisons from country to country. Similarly, gray markets have soared in response to the Internet, which enables buyers to compare prices easily across markets. In some cases, intermediaries are not even necessary to fuel parallel imports. Many older Americans buy their prescription drugs through one of many online and mail order Canadian pharmacies where prices are considerably cheaper. Although it is technically illegal for individuals to import pharmaceuticals into the United States, the law is not enforced.

Companies deplore gray markets because they hurt relationships with authorized dealers and especially because they undermine a company's ability to charge different prices in different markets in order to maximize global profits. Parallel imports are even credited with adding to Coca-Cola's public relations difficulties subsequent to a product-harm crisis in Europe. The company began a product recall after hundreds of Coke drinkers in Belgium complained of getting sick. Unfortunately, tracking down the questionable Belgium-produced Coke was complicated; it began showing up in places it shouldn't have been, such as Spain, Germany, and the United Kingdom. But this should have come as no surprise. The gray market for soft drinks is substantial in Europe.

Parallel imports/gray market imports that enter a market outside the official distribution channels established by the trademark owner

A pharmacy in Tijuana, Mexico. Medicine sold here can cost much more just across the border in the United States. Such discrepancies in prices encourage gray markets.

Seeking Legal Redress. Global firms would like governments to forbid parallel imports from entering their countries. But legal attempts to stop parallel imports have been stymied by the fact that governments around the world have taken different stands on gray markets. At issue is the right of a trademark owner to manage the sale of a trademarked product versus the ability of consumers to enjoy the lower prices usually provided by parallel imports. Most countries adopt some variation of the **exhaustion principle** that establishes the conditions under which a trademark owner relinquishes its right to control the resale of its product.

National exhaustion provides that once a firm has sold its trademarked product in a specific country, it cannot restrict the further distribution of that product in that particular country. However, the firm retains the legal right to stop its products sold elsewhere from entering the country as parallel imports. Unfortunately for global marketers, few countries adopt this principle, and when they do it often has limited application. For example, the United States recognizes national exhaustion for ethical pharmaceuticals. However, even this limited restriction of parallel imports is constantly under political attack by those who promote lower pharmaceutical prices in the U.S. market.

Regional exhaustion provides that once a firm has sold a trademarked product anywhere in a region it cannot restrict the resale of that product within that region. The EU follows the principle of regional exhaustion. Once a trademarked product is sold anywhere in the EU, the trademark owner cannot restrict its resale within the EU. However, the EU does allow trademark owners to stop parallel imports from coming into the EU from countries outside it. For example, Nintendo, the Japanese video game firm, was found in violation of European antitrust laws for working with distributors to illegally prevent sales from one EU country to another in order to keep prices high.[36] But the European Court of Justice upheld the right of Levi Strauss to stop parallel imports of its jeans coming into the United Kingdom from the United States at lower prices.

Many developed countries and most developing countries have adopted the principle of **international exhaustion**.[37] When a country adopts this principle it is virtually impossible to legally stop parallel imports from entering that national market. These countries welcome parallel imports into their country in order to encourage lower prices. In addition, developing countries are less concerned with the rights of trademark owners, because relatively few of their local firms hold valuable trademarks.

Regardless of which exhaustion principle is adopted by a country, national laws concerning parallel imports are, in fact, very complex. For example, Japan recognizes international exhaustion unless otherwise agreed by contract or if the original sale is subject to price controls.

U.S. laws concerning parallel imports are among the most confusing, possibly because they have evolved within the case law system. Essentially, the United States asserts that a firm exhausts its rights to restrict the resale of a product into the United States once that product is sold anywhere in the world. However, similar to Japan, the United States recognizes certain exceptions. Some of these exceptions have had little effect on gray markets. The one exception that companies have found useful in stopping parallel imports into the United States allows trademark owners to stop parallel imports from entering the U.S. market when those products are materially different from those being officially sold in the United States. For example, in the case of Perugina chocolate made in Venezuela under license from the Italian trademark owner, the court ruled the parallel imported chocolate made in Venezuela was different from the chocolate produced in Italy. The quality level, fat content, ingredients, and packaging varied and were likely to cause

Exhaustion principle a legal principle that establishes the conditions under which a trademark owner relinquishes its right to control the resale of its product

National exhaustion an exhaustion principle that states that once a firm has sold a trademarked product in a specific country, it cannot restrict the further distribution of that product in that country

Regional exhaustion an exhaustion principle that states that once a firm has sold a trademarked product anywhere in a region (such as the EU), it cannot restrict the resale of that product within that region

International exhaustion an exhaustion principle that states that once a firm has sold a product anywhere in the world, it cannot restrict its resale into a particular country

WORLD BEAT 12.2

CARS FOR KOREA

IMPORTED CARS WERE once a luxury in South Korea, commanding high prices. Those days are over. Parallel importers of high-end automobiles are discovering a new, more price-conscious Korean consumer. Worldwide, gray markets have long been associated with small and medium-sized firms. However, among the gray marketers in the Korean automobile market is one surprising new entrant—SK Group, one of Korea's large business groups.

Many wonder why such a large concern would deal in parallel imports. SK is already the authorized importer of luxury brands Jaguar and Infinity, and its price-cutting tactics with parallel imports have shaken the market. One SK official even admitted that the group didn't care if they made a profit on imports. Industry observers suspect that SK is looking for a customer base to which to sell its related lines of auto repairs and car insurance.

Ironically, it isn't only foreign cars that enter Korea though parallel markets. When South Korean Hyundai Motors launched its premium sports sedan Genesis in the United States, the price was set at $33,000. In Korea, the Genesis sold for over $48,000. One of the reasons for such a large difference in price was a Korean tax of 24.3 percent levied on vehicles that are both made and sold in Korea. In addition, the Korean version of the Genesis offered more than 20 optional features not available in the United States. The company also admitted that the Genesis was positioned as a relatively high-end car at home but was considered a more basic model overseas. Not all Koreans were happy about the higher price, and a number of gray marketers moved quickly to re-import the exported cars.

Sources: "Low-Price Parallel Imports Shake Up South Korea Auto Market," *Nikkei Report*, March 21, 2008; "Parallel Imports Underprice High-end Models," *Nikkei Weekly*, April, 21, 2008; "Why Is a Car That's Made in Korea Cheaper in the U.S.?" September 2, 2008, Joins.com.

confusion to the American consumer.[38] Therefore, the Italian trademark owner could restrict the import of the Venezuelan product into the U.S. market.

Other Corporate Responses to Gray Markets.   Research involving U.S. exporters identified three factors that significantly discouraged parallel imports.[39] First, firms that customize products more for local markets experience fewer problems with parallel imports. Even if the physical product stays the same, warranty customization may be employed. An authorized Porsche distributor in Singapore offered five years of free maintenance as a way to deter competition from parallel imports of the luxury automobile.[40] Second, firms experience fewer problems with gray markets if they own or maintain greater control over their distribution systems. Third, parallel imports are less likely to occur if an international firm maintains greater centralized control than if it allows national subsidiaries greater autonomy. One reason for this last observation is the fact that some local subsidiaries knowingly participate in parallel markets. For example, certain national managers at Bausch and Lomb cooperated with gray marketers in order to raise their own local sales figures, even though the parallel imports they helped fuel in other countries hurt the company overall.[41]

A fourth option is to alert consumers to the benefits of purchasing products through legitimate channels. This can be effective when product warranties, only available through authorized dealers, are important to buyers. In fact, a law in South Africa requires parallel importers to alert consumers to the fact that the South African authorized dealer is under no obligation to honor a manufacturer guaranty or warranty. This alert is required for all product displays and in-store promotions as well as for all advertisements and websites.[42]

A fifth, if somewhat controversial, option to stop gray markets is to limit supplies to distributors in lower-priced markets. The Bayer Group attempted to stop the parallel imports into the United Kingdom of a Bayer cardiovascular medicine, Adalat, from France and Spain, where the price of the drug was 40 percent lower. Bayer limited the amount wholesalers in these two countries could receive to the estimated demand of their own markets. The wholesalers complained, and the European Commission fined Bayer for what it considered anticompetitive agreements to limit parallel imports. However, the European Court of Justice reversed the earlier ruling of the European Commission, therefore allowing pharmaceutical manufacturers to limit supply to countries that are involved in parallel trade.

Finally, strategic pricing may be used to keep prices within range of each other, thus destroying opportunities for arbitrage. Such a strategy usually requires cutting prices in higher-priced markets and thus foregoing prior profits. It may also require raising prices in lower-priced markets and consequently losing sales. However, given limited legal redress and increasingly sophisticated parallel importers, firms realize that this is perhaps a necessary strategy to effectively address gray markets.

Setting Global Prices

To maximize a company's revenues, it would appear logical to set prices on a market-by-market basis, seeking in each market the best combination of price and expected volume to yield the maximum profit. This strategy was common for many firms in the early part of their international development. For many consumer products, there are still significant price differences across many countries. For example, Table 12.5 illustrates how McDonald's Big Mac prices can vary by country.

With the advent of global branding, international firms have become more concerned about issues of global pricing. They rarely dictate uniform prices in every country but do establish a particular pricing policy across countries—relatively higher prices for premium brands and relatively lower prices for value brands. In a study of global pricing policies among multinational companies from developed countries, the likelihood that a subsidiary would follow a pricing policy similar to that of the parent company in the home market was found to be influenced by market similarity in economic conditions, legal environment, customer characteristics, and stage in the product life cycle.[43]

Uniform pricing strategy a pricing strategy in which a firm charges the same price everywhere when that price is translated into a base currency

However, for products that are similar in many markets and for which transportation costs are not significant, substantial price differences quickly result in the emergence of parallel imports. This has led some firms to consider a policy of more uniform pricing worldwide. Employing a **uniform pricing strategy** on a global scale requires that a company charges the same price everywhere when that price is translated into a base currency. For example, in India, LVMH sells the Tag Heuer sports watch at prices of Rs 18,000 to Rs 40,000, which is on a par with the international prices that would be paid for the same watch in Dubai.[44]

Furthermore, global firms need to be careful about presenting varying prices to business customers with international operations. Oracle Corporation began standardizing prices for its software in response to business customers who questioned why the price in their country was higher than the price in other countries. In fact, global customers usually pressure for lower prices as well as for uniform prices. In a research study done with more than 50 executives responsible for global account management in the Americas, Europe, and Asia, global customers reported that they believed global procurement was a way to receive lower prices.[45]

TABLE 12.5	BIG MAC PRICES	

	PRICE	
	IN U.S. DOLLARS	PERCENTAGE DIFFERENCE OF LOCAL VS. U.S. PRICE
United States	$3.54	0%
Argentina	3.30	−7
Australia	2.19	−38
Brazil	3.45	−2
Britain	3.30	−7
Canada	3.36	−5
Chile	2.51	−29
China	1.83	−48
Egypt	2.34	−34
Euro Area	4.38	+24
Hungary	2.92	−18
Indonesia	1.74	−51
Israel	3.69	+4
Japan	3.23	−9
Malaysia	1.52	−57
Mexico	2.30	−35
New Zealand	2.48	−30
Poland	2.01	−43
Russia	1.73	−51
Singapore	2.61	−26
South Africa	1.66	−53
South Korea	2.39	−32
Sweden	4.58	+29
Switzerland	5.60	+58
Taiwan	2.23	−37
Turkey	3.13	−12

Source: Adapted from "Big Mac Index," *Economist*, Economist.com. © The Economist Newspaper Limited, London, July 10, 2009. Reprinted with permission.

Modified uniform pricing a pricing strategy in which a firm monitors price levels in different countries to close large price differentials and discourage gray markets

In reality, a uniform pricing strategy becomes very difficult to achieve whenever different taxes, trade margins, and customs duties are involved. Furthermore, firms that start out with identical prices in various countries soon find that prices have to change to stay in line with often substantial currency fluctuations. Although it is becoming increasingly clear that market-by-market pricing strategies will cause difficulties, many firms have found that changing to a uniform pricing policy is rather like pursuing a moving target. However, a company can employ **modified uniform pricing** by carefully monitoring price levels in each country and avoiding large gaps that encourage gray marketers to move in and take advantage of large price differentials.

Noncash Pricing: Countertrade

Sometimes international marketers come across situations in which an interested customer in an emerging market will not be able to arrange hard-currency financing. In such circumstances, the customer might offer a product or commodity in return. The supplier must then turn the product offered into hard currency. Such transactions, known as **countertrade**, were once estimated at 15 to 25 percent of world trade, although with the collapse of the former Soviet Union the volume of countertrade has declined significantly. Still, many countries have some form of countertrade requirement as part of their public procurement program. For example, in the Philippines, the Department of Agriculture requires that half the value of imports of agricultural equipment and machinery be paid with agricultural or fishery products.[46]

There are a number of different forms of countertrade, including compensation transactions, offset deals, and cooperation agreements.

Compensation Transactions. One usually speaks of a compensation transaction when the value of an export delivery is at least partially offset by an import transaction, or vice versa. Compensation transactions are typical for large government purchases, such as for defense projects, when a country wants to obtain some additional exports in exchange for the awarding of a contract. The government of Indonesia has required winners of major government contracts to take part of their payment in Indonesian commodities apart from oil and gas.

Compensation transactions fall into two categories: full compensation and partial compensation. Under full compensation the exporter commits to purchasing products or services at an amount equal to that specified in the export contract. Under partial compensation, the exporter receives a portion of the purchase price in hard currency and the remainder in merchandise.

In either case, the exporter will not be able to convert such merchandise into cash until a buyer can be found, and even then must usually do so at a discount. An option exists to sell such a commitment to a third party who may take over the commitment from the exporter for a fee. Therefore, when deciding whether to accept products for compensation, global marketers should differentiate between **hard goods** (easily salable merchandise) or **soft goods** (heavily discounted merchandise that may prove more difficult to resell).

Offset Deals. One of the most rapidly growing types of countertrade is the offset transaction. In an offset transaction, the selling company guarantees to use some products or services from the buying country in the final product. These transactions are particularly common when large government purchases are involved, such as purchases of public utilities or defense-related equipment. Governments are motivated to require offset deals because they can assist local businesses. For example, the South African government used offset deals very effectively to stimulate local industrial development in exchange for purchasing military equipment.

Cooperation Agreements. **Cooperation agreements**, or **buybacks**, are special types of countertrade deals extending over longer periods of time. Cooperation agreements usually involve related goods, such as payment for new textile machinery by the output produced by these machines. Although the sale of large equipment or of a whole factory can sometimes be clinched only by a cooperation agreement involving buyback of plant output, long-term negative effects must be

Countertrade a transaction in which goods are exchanged for other goods

Hard goods countertraded merchandise that is easy to resell

Soft goods countertraded merchandise that is difficult to resell

Cooperation agreements/buybacks countertrade arrangements extending over years and usually involving capital equipment in exchange for output of that equipment

considered before any deal is concluded. In industries such as steel or chemicals, the effect of high-volume buyback arrangements between Western exporters of manufacturing technology and Eastern European importers has sometimes been devastating. Western countries, especially Europe, have been flooded with surplus products, and the EU has established a general policy on cooperation arrangements to avoid further disruption of its domestic industries.

Managing Countertrade. The participants in a survey of 196 firms in Australia agreed that countertrade was of great importance (71 percent) and that it increased sales potential (67 percent), strengthened the firms' competitive position (61 percent), and fulfilled their buyers' requirements (53 percent).[47] Nonetheless, countertrade agreements can be complex and time-consuming. Thus they can be surprisingly demanding of corporate resources. Many larger firms have established specialized units whose single purpose is to engage in countertrade. Smaller companies can also take advantage of countertrade by using independent trading companies or specialist brokers.

Another challenge of countertrade arrangements is the difficulty in finding a buyer for the merchandise accepted as part of the transaction. Sometimes such transactions are concluded with organizations in countries where industry is protected. The merchandise, not easily salable on its own merits, may be of low quality. As a result, the exporter may have to sell the merchandise at a discount. The size of these discounts can vary considerably and can even run as high as a third of product value.

At the conclusion of the sales agreement, the exporter should obtain a very clear understanding of the merchandise offered for countertrade. The origin, quality, quantity, and delivery schedules for the merchandise should all be spelled out. Given such a detailed description, a specialized trader can provide an estimate of the appropriate discount. The astute exporter will raise the price of the export contract to cover such potential discounts. Therefore, it is paramount that the exporter not agree on any price before this other information is in hand. Maintaining flexibility in negotiation requires skill and patience but can spell the difference between making a profit and incurring a loss on a countertrade transaction.

Check out our website (http://www.cengage.com/international) for countertrade links.

What should you consider when setting prices in your target country? Continue with Country Market Report on our website (http://www.cengage.com/international).

CONCLUSION

Managing pricing policies for an international firm is an especially daunting task. The global marketer is confronted with a number of uncontrollable factors deriving from the economic, legal, and regulatory environment, all of which have an impact on how prices are established in various countries. In addition, coordinating pricing across countries is increasingly critical. Managing price differences across countries and keeping them within tolerable limits are major tasks in global pricing.

One of the most important factors affecting price levels remains foreign exchange fluctuation. Today, managers find currencies moving both up and down, and the swings have assumed magnitudes that may substantially affect the competitiveness of a company. Understanding the factors that influence the foreign exchange market and mastering the technical tools that protect firms against large swings have become required skills for the global marketer. To the extent that a company can make itself less vulnerable to exchange rate movements than its competitors are, it stands to gain additional competitive advantage.

Because the factors that affect price levels on an international scale are always fluctuating, the global pricing task is a never-ending process in which each day may bring new problems to be resolved. Competitors and arbiters are quick to exploit any weaknesses whenever a company is slow to adapt or makes a wrong judgment. Therefore, the pricing strategies of any firm selling abroad, whether a new exporter or an established multinational company, should remain under constant review.

QUESTIONS FOR DISCUSSION

1. Discuss the difficulties involved in having a standardized price for a company's products across all countries. What advantages does charging a standardized price offer?

2. You are an exporter of industrial installations and have received a $100,000 order from a Japanese customer. The job will take six months to complete and will be paid in full at that time. Now your Japanese customer has called you to request a price quote in yen. What will you quote in yen? Why?

3. What factors may influence McDonald's to price their Big Mac differently throughout Latin America?

4. What should be the government's position on the issue of parallel imports? Should the government take any particular actions?

Welcome to
Carrefour ⟨C⟩ يرحب بكم كــارفــور

Peter Bowater/Alamy

© Inmagine/18439GNG

13
Managing Global Distribution Channels

SHOPPERS IN CARACAS habitually patronize the small corner store. Venezuela's retail sector essentially consists of family-owned shops, modest-size supermarkets, and a few specialty chains. Even the modern malls are amalgams of boutiques. When hypermarket Tiendas Exito opened in an eastern suburb of Caracas, the new joint venture of French, Colombian, and Venezuelan partners was met with some skepticism in the press. Would Venezuelans really abandon the social ritual of shopping at the small local store?

Undaunted, the new hypermarket presented itself as resolved to help its customers curtail their expenses by undercutting competitors' prices by 8 percent. Volume purchasing, centralized warehousing and shipping, and computerized inventory control—all revolutionary in the local context—would be employed to deliver on this promise. And such a promise could be appealing to the Caracas public. An international study placed Caracas as the world's eighth most expensive city to live in, more expensive than Paris, Los Angeles, or Geneva. Yet for salaries, it rated thirteenth lowest of the 58 cities studied. One month after Tiendas Exito opened, sales were running 35 percent above expectations.[1]

Distribution systems have traditionally been shaped by a variety of factors—level of economic development, disposable income of consumers, the quality of infrastructure such as roads and telecommunications, as well as culture, physical environment, and the legal and political system. Global marketers need to understand how environmental influences may affect distribution policies and options. Using this knowledge, they must establish efficient channels for products on a country-by-country basis. They must also consider how the emergence of regional and global distributors and changes in global logistics can affect their operations at the transnational level.

In this chapter, we discuss the structure of global distribution systems and methods for selecting, locating, and managing channel members. We explore how the international firm gains access to local channels and manages international logistics. We conclude with a look at global trends in retailing and the managerial implications of international smuggling.

THE STRUCTURE OF THE GLOBAL DISTRIBUTION SYSTEM

Marketers who develop distribution strategies must decide how to transport products from manufacturing locations to the consumer. Although distribution can be handled completely by the manufacturer, often products are moved through intermediaries, such as agents, wholesalers, distributors, and retailers. An understanding of the structure of available distribution systems is extremely important in the development of a marketing strategy. The various channels available to a manufacturer are shown in Figure 13.1. Home-country channel members were discussed in Chapter 9. Host-country channel members are discussed below.

FOREIGN-MARKET CHANNEL MEMBERS

As shown in Figure 13.1, once products have left the home market, there are a variety of channel alternatives in the global marketplace: import intermediaries, local wholesalers or agents, and retailers. Even with local manufacturing, the company will still need to get its products from the factory to the consumers.

Import Intermediaries

Import intermediaries identify consumer needs in their local market and search the world to satisfy those needs. They normally purchase goods in their own name and act independently of manufacturers. As independents, these channel members use their own marketing strategies and keep in close contact with the markets they

FIGURE 13.1
International Marketing Channel Alternatives

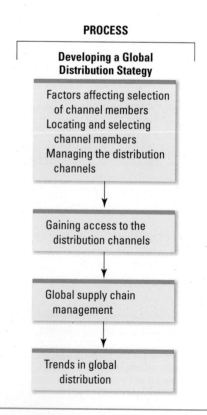

serve. A manufacturer that wants to distribute in an independent intermediary's market area should investigate this channel partner as one way to reach wholesalers and retailers in that area.

Local Wholesalers or Agents

In each country, there will be a series of possible channel members who move manufacturers' products to retailers, to industrial firms, or in some cases to other wholesalers. Local wholesalers will take title to the products, whereas local agents will not take title. Local wholesalers are also called distributors or dealers. In some cases, a local wholesaler receives exclusive distribution rights for a specific geographic area or country.

The functions of wholesalers can also vary by country. In some countries, wholesalers provide a warehousing function, taking orders from retailers and shipping them appropriate quantities of merchandise. Wholesalers in Japan perform basic wholesale functions but also share risk with retailers by providing them with financing, product development, and even occasional managerial and marketing skills.

WORLD BEAT 13.1

RETAIL REVOLUTION IN INDIA?

IT'S NO WONDER THAT INDIA is one of the most attractive retail markets on the globe right now. The market was recently valued at $370 billion. With a rapidly growing middle class, that number is expected to grow to $650 billion by the year 2015. Currently, retail demand is served predominantly by small, independent stores. Supermarkets and department stores make up only 5 percent of the retail industry. But large retailers are hoping to change that, and many have strategies in place to grab their slice of the expanding pie.

Foreign firms must tread lightly, however, when trying to establish a presence in India. Current regulations restrict non-Indian firms to minority investments in most retail ventures. This has led to a flurry of joint ventures by major international retailers, including German Metro AG, French giant Carrefour, and British retailer Tesco. However, many expect the government to eventually loosen current restrictions on foreign investment in the retail sector.

Still, government regulations may be the least of the obstacles facing big retailers. The increasing shift from small stores to large chains has prompted passionate, sometimes violent, resistance. Protests and demonstrations bordering on riots have swept the country as village traders, farmers, and small shopkeepers fear for their livelihoods. Retail accounts for 7 to 9 percent of employment, and some suggest that upwards of 40 million Indian jobs could be lost with the introduction of Western-style retailing to the country. To assuage concerns from small retailers and left-wing political parties, the government ordered new entry Wal-Mart to sell only to wholesalers, businesses, and their families and friends.

The resentment has not been reserved for foreign retailers. Indian firm Reliance Industries is arguably facing the brunt of the backlash. Government authorities have ordered several of Reliance's stores to close due to security concerns. Not surprisingly, the uproar has caused some foreign companies to put investment plans on hold. What the future holds for this attractive but problematic market remains to be seen.

Sources: Steve Hamm and Nandini Lakshman, "Widening Aisles for Indian Shoppers," *BusinessWeek,* April 30, 2007, p. 44; Vibhuti Agarwal and Krishna Pokharel, "India's Populists Resist Big Retail," *Wall Street Journal,* October 9, 2007, p. A6; John Elliott, "India's Shaky FDI Rules Need Clarification," *Financial Times,* July 9, 2009; and Emily Wax, "India's First Wal-Mart Draws Excitement, Not Protest," *Washington Post,* July 13, 2009, p. A8.

Retailers

Retailers, the final members of the consumer distribution channel, purchase products for resale to consumers. The size and accessibility of retail channels vary greatly by country. The population per retailer in Europe varies from lows of only 52 people in the Ukraine, 61 in Portugal, 65 in Hungary, and 66 in Spain to highs of to 292 people in Russia, 236 in Germany, and 203 in Austria.[2]

Retailing is exploding in many parts of Asia, where a large portion of the population is crossing the income threshold at which they start to buy entirely new categories of goods, such as packaged foods, televisions, or mopeds. This phenomenon, called **magic moments**, has hit Taiwan, Indonesia, Thailand, Malaysia, and China. When a country crosses the magic-moments threshold, distribution systems start to improve with the emergence of modern stores.[3] Furthermore, China has seen a significant shift from state-owned to private distribution. There has been a significant decline in state-owned retail and wholesale enterprises and a surge in privately owned retail and wholesale enterprises. The global marketer must evaluate the available retailers in a country and develop a strategy around the existing— and sometimes evolving—retail structure.

Magic moments a term designating the point at which modern retailing emerges within a country

Business-to-Business Channels

When the firm is selling to businesses instead of consumers, channels may still resemble those we have described. Small businesses in particular may purchase supplies from retail outlets that have been supplied by wholesalers. Many business-to-business sales go through shorter channels, however. Export agents, import intermediaries, or the manufacturer itself often contact business customers directly without the use of further intermediaries.

ANALYZING NATIONAL CHANNELS

A distribution strategy is one part of the marketing mix, and it needs to be consistent with other aspects of the marketing strategy: product policies, pricing strategy, and communication strategy. Figure 13.2 depicts important factors to consider when developing a distribution strategy. Before deciding on distribution strategies, global marketers must understand the nature of channels in their various markets. Of particular interest are the following variables:

1. *Distribution density.* Density is the amount of exposure or coverage desired for a product, particularly the number of sales outlets necessary to provide for adequate coverage of the entire market.
2. *Channel length.* The concept of channel length involves the number of intermediaries involved in bringing a given product from the firm to the consumer.
3. *Channel alignment and leadership.* Alignment is the structure of the chosen channel members to achieve a unified strategy.
4. *Distribution logistics.* Logistics involves the physical flow of products as they move through the channel.

The decisions involved in the first three of these areas cannot be approached independently. The decisions are interrelated, and they need to be consistent with other aspects of the marketing strategy. Although it is important to evaluate the distribution strategy logically, marketing managers often must work with an international distribution structure established under previous managers. That existing

FIGURE 13.2
Distribution Policies

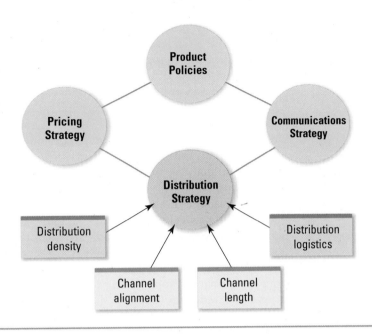

system may limit a company's flexibility to change and grow. Nevertheless, a creative marketer can usually find opportunities for circumventing the current arrangement. For example, Nordica of Italy had been selling in Japan for 25 years when the company decided it wanted more direct control over distribution. Nordica reached a financial agreement with its exclusive distributor, Daiwa Sports, and hired the 85 employees who had been handling its line. This allowed Nordica, which was later acquired by Tecnica, to take control without losing the experience and contacts developed by its distributor.[4] The following sections illustrate how company policies must adapt to distribution density, channel length, and channel alignment.

Distribution Density

The number of sales outlets or distribution points required for the efficient marketing of a firm's products is referred to as the **density of distribution**. The density is dependent on the shopping or buying habits of the average customer. Choosing the optimum distribution network requires the marketer to examine how customers select dealers and retail outlets by product category. For many consumer goods, an **extensive**, or wide, distribution is required if the consumer is not likely to exert much shopping effort. Such products, which are called convenience goods, are bought frequently and in nearby outlets. For other products, such as appliances or clothing, consumers may visit two or more stores. These products require a more limited, or **selective**, distribution, with fewer outlets per market area. For specialty goods, products that inspire consumer loyalty to specific brands, a very limited, or **exclusive**, distribution is required. It is assumed that the customer will search for the desired product and will not accept substitutes.

The key to distribution density, then, is the consumer's shopping behavior, in particular the effort expended to locate a desired item. This behavior, however, may vary greatly from country to country. In the United States, for example, where per-capita income is high, consumers shop for many regular-use items in supermarkets and other widely accessible outlets, such as drugstores. In other countries,

Density of distribution the number of sales outlets or distribution points utilized for a given geographic market

Extensive distribution a distribution strategy that employs many sales outlets per market area

Selective distribution a distribution strategy that employs few sales outlets per market area

Exclusive distribution a distribution strategy in which a product is available through only one outlet in a relatively large geographic area

particularly some with a much lower per-capita income, the purchase of such items is likely to be a less routine affair, and consumers may be willing to exert more effort to locate such items. This makes possible a less extensive distribution of products.

Where consumers buy certain products also varies a great deal from country to country. In Germany, contact lens solution is found only in stores that sell eyeglasses, but in France, it is also found in most drugstores. Whereas many magazines are sold in grocery stores in the United States, in the United Kingdom they are sold mainly through news agents. It is important to find out, early in your distribution analysis, where consumers buy the types of products you plan to market.

In the business-to-business sector as well, differences in buyer behavior or in the use of a particular product may require changes in distribution outlets and density. In the United States, for instance, radiology supply products are sold directly to hospitals and radiology departments through hospital supply distributors. In France, however, patients must pick up radiology supplies by prescription from a pharmacy before visiting the radiology department at the hospital. In this latter case, radiology supplies have to be promoted to physicians and then stocked at pharmacies to be successful. The distribution necessary in France is much more extensive than in the United States, where only hospitals are channel members.[5]

Channel Length

Channel length the number of intermediaries directly involved in the physical or ownership path of a product from the manufacturer to the buyer

The number of intermediaries directly involved in the physical or ownership path of a product from the manufacturer to the customer is indicative of the **channel length**. Long channels have several intermediaries. Short or direct channels have few or no intermediaries. Channel length is usually influenced by three factors: (1) a product's distribution density, (2) the average order quantity, and (3) the availability of channel members. Products with extensive distribution, or large numbers of final sales points, tend to have longer channels of distribution. Similarly, as the average order quantity decreases, products move through longer channels to enhance the efficiency of distribution.

Because distribution density affects channel length, it is clear that the same factors that influence distribution density influence channel length; foremost among these is the shopping behavior of consumers. The average order quantity often depends on the purchasing power or income level of a given customer group. In countries with lower income levels, people often buy food on a daily basis at nearby small stores. This contrasts sharply with more affluent consumers, who can afford to buy enough food or staples for a week or even a month and who don't mind traveling some distance to do more infrequent shopping.

Wholesale channels in Japan are the longest in the developed world, with most products moving through as many as six intermediaries. This lengthy distribution channel is more reminiscent of distribution systems in developing countries than of those in developed countries. However, the Japanese distribution system is responding to consumer demands for change. Following the lead of Dell Computer, Japan's Seiko Epson bypassed traditional Japanese channel members and began a direct sales effort to sell its personal computers. In doing so, the company was able to attract consumers by offering significant savings through its direct-marketing effort.[6] This change is not limited to personal computers. Japan now ranks second in the world in overall dollar volume of direct sales.[7]

AP Images

Global firms, such as Pepsi, are increasingly targeting rural markets in developing countries, but establishing distribution to such markets can be challenging.

Channel Alignment

Channel alignment the coordination of various channel members to the end of providing a unified approach to the marketing of a product or service

Channel alignment can be one of the most difficult tasks of marketing. The longer the channel, the more difficult it becomes to ensure that various channel members coordinate their actions so that a unified approach to the marketing of a product or service can be achieved. On an international level, the coordinating task is made all the more difficult because the company organizing the channel may be far away from the distribution system, with little influence over the local scene. The international company will find it much easier to control the distribution channel if a local subsidiary with a strong sales force exists. In countries where the company has no local presence and depends on independent distributors, control is likely to slip to the independent distributor. This loss of control may be further aggravated if the international company's sales volume represents only a small fraction of the local distributor's business. Of course, the opposite will be true when a high percentage of the volume consists of the international corporation's products.

Channel captain the dominant channel participant; dictates terms of pricing, delivery, and sometimes product design

Often, one participant emerges as the **channel captain** or dominant member. The channel captain frequently dictates terms of pricing, delivery, and sometimes even product design that affect other channel members. As a general rule, wholesalers are relatively powerful in developing countries. When countries develop, power shifts from wholesalers to either retailers or manufacturers. This can be seen in the United States where once-strong wholesalers have become less influential, and manufacturers or large retailers (such as Home Depot and Wal-Mart) have become channel captains. There remains one major exception to this rule: Wholesalers continue to dominate channels in Japan.

Global marketers must be aware of national differences that can significantly affect a firm's bargaining power in channel negotiations, and they must be prepared to respond to changes that affect bargaining power within national channels. For example, shopping in India has traditionally evoked images of small retail shops and crowded sidewalks. However, shopping centers are now popping up to cater to India's growing middle class, and organized selling outside India's estimated 12 million mom-and-pop outlets is rapidly expanding.

In China, wholesalers capture about 80 percent of the revenues from distributing consumer products, while retailers only realize 20 percent. (In the United States, these numbers are nearly reversed. Wholesalers get about 30 percent, with the rest going to retailers.) The Chinese government has protected wholesalers, many of whom are government owned. However, joining the World Trade Organization (WTO) is forcing change in China. Three trends are expected to significantly change wholesaling in China in the next ten years:

- Foreign companies will enter wholesaling, originally as joint ventures.
- Larger, more modernized retailers may increasingly bypass wholesalers.
- Manufacturers will increasingly use third-party logistics providers to cut out traditional wholesalers. This will occur as the consumer goods industry consolidates, making the economics of direct delivery more attractive.[8]

Distribution Logistics

Distribution logistics focuses on the physical movement of goods through the channels. An extremely important part of the distribution system, logistics is discussed in detail later in the chapter.

FACTORS INFLUENCING THE SELECTION OF CHANNEL MEMBERS

A marketer needs to identify and select appropriate distribution partners in various national markets. This selection of distribution partners is an extremely important decision, because the partner often will assume a portion of the marketing responsibility, or even all of it. Also, the distribution partner usually is involved in the physical movement (logistics) of products to the customers. A poor decision can lead to lackluster performance. Changing a distribution partner can be expensive or sometimes impossible because of local laws. Vulcan Chemical was fined $23 million for unfairly terminating the rights of Phillip J. Barker, which had a contract to market and distribute sodium chlorine and chlorine dioxide in Japan, China, South Korea, and Taiwan. Vulcan reported that its sales had fallen to less than $2 million per year, therefore warranting termination of the distribution contract.[9] The very success of a firm's international efforts depends on the partners it selects. Several factors influence the selection of distribution partners. These include costs, the nature of the product and product line, the desired level of control and coverage, and the potential synergy between the international firm and its channels.

Costs

Channel costs fall into three categories: initial costs, maintenance costs, and logistics costs. The **initial costs** include all the costs of locating and setting up the channel, such as executive time and travel to locate and select channel members, the costs of negotiating an agreement with channel members, and the capital costs of setting up the channel. Capital costs include the costs for inventories, goods in transit, accounts receivable, and inventories on consignment. The establishment of a direct-sales channel often requires the maximum investment, whereas use of

Initial channel costs the costs of locating or establishing a channel

distributors generally reduces the investment required. Firms can expect these costs to be higher in certain countries due to the necessity of selecting the proper channel members. Japan is one example of a country where it makes sense to spend more time and money up front, as the social and economic costs of dissolving a relationship can be unacceptably high.[10]

Channel maintenance costs the costs of managing and auditing channel operations

Logistics costs the costs of transporting and storing products and processing those products through customs

The **maintenance costs** of the channel include the costs of the company's salespeople, sales managers, and travel expenses. They also include the costs of auditing and controlling channel operations and the profit margin given to channel intermediaries. The **logistics costs** comprise the transportation expenses, storage costs, the cost of breaking bulk shipments into smaller lot sizes, and the cost for customs paperwork.

Predicting all of these various costs when selecting different channel members is often difficult, but it is necessary in order to estimate the cost of various alternatives. High distribution costs usually result in higher prices at the consumer level, which may hamper entry into a new market. Companies often establish direct channels, hoping to reduce distribution costs. Unfortunately, however, most of the functions of the channel cannot be eliminated, so these costs eventually show up anyway.

Product and Product Line

The nature of a product can affect channel selection. If the product is perishable or has a short shelf life, then the manufacturer is forced to use shorter channels to get the product to the consumer more rapidly. ProFlowers.com, an online flower portal, developed a distribution network that gets flowers from farmer to consumer in half the time it takes traditional florists. The delivery system's success has led to its adoption in selling meats, fruit, and other perishables online.[11] Through its affiliate company, Flowerfarm, delivery is available in nearly 80 countries.

A technical product often requires direct sales or highly technical channel partners. For example, Index Technology of Cambridge, Massachusetts, sold a sophisticated software product to automate the development of software systems called computer-aided systems engineering. The company entered the United Kingdom and Australia with a direct-sales effort, but to limit initial costs, it decided on distributors for France, Germany, and Scandinavia. However, insufficient revenues from these distributors led the company to set up its own sales efforts in France and Germany and to purchase its distributor in Scandinavia. The highly technical nature of the product required Index to invest more time and money in distribution than would be necessary if the firm sold a generic or unsophisticated product.

The size of the product line also affects the selection of channel members. A broader product line is more desirable for channel members. A distributor or dealer is more likely to stock a broad product line than a single item. Similarly, if a manufacturer has a very broad, complete line, it is easier to justify the cost of a more direct channel. With more products to sell, it is easier to generate a high average order on each sales call. With a limited product line, an agent or distributor will group a firm's product together with products from other companies to increase the average order size.

Control, Coverage, and Synergy

Each type of channel arrangement offers the manufacturer a different level of control. With direct sales, a manufacturer can control price, promotion, amount of effort, and type of retail outlet used. If these are important, then the increased level of control may offset the increased cost of a direct-sales force. Longer channels, particularly with distributors who take title to goods, often result in little or no control. In many cases, a company may not know who is ultimately buying the product.

Coverage is reaching the geographic area that a manufacturer wants to cover. Although coverage is usually easy to get in major metropolitan areas, gaining adequate coverage of smaller cities or sparsely populated areas can be difficult. Selection of one channel member over another may be influenced by the market coverage that the respective agents or distributors offer. To assess an agent's or distributor's coverage, the following must be determined: (1) location of sales offices, (2) salespersons' home base, and (3) previous year's sales by geographic location. The location of sales offices indicates where efforts are focused. Salespeople generally have the best penetration near their homes, and past sales clearly indicate the level of the channel member's success in each geographic area.

The choice of channel members or partners can sometimes be influenced by the existence of complementary skills that can increase the total output of the distribution system. This synergy normally occurs when a potential distributor has some skill or expertise that will allow quicker access to the market. For example, when Compaq entered the international personal computer market, it decided to sell only through a network of strong authorized dealers. While Compaq focused on developing market applications such as sales force automation, computer-aided design, and office productivity, it used the dealers to penetrate the marketplace. By the time of its merger with Hewlett-Packard, Compaq held market shares outside its domestic market of 3.7 percent in Japan, 6 percent in other Asian markets, 17.3 percent in Western Europe, and 14.6 percent in the rest of the world—compared with 13.8 percent in the United States.

LOCATING AND SELECTING CHANNEL PARTNERS

Building an international distribution system normally takes one to three years. The process involves the series of steps shown in Table 13.1. The critical aspect of developing a successful system is locating and selecting channel partners.

The development of an international distribution strategy in terms of distribution density, channel length, and channel alignment will establish a framework for the "ideal" distribution partners. The company's preference regarding key factors that influence selection of channel partners (costs, products, control, coverage, and

TABLE 13.1 PROCESS OF ESTABLISHING AN INTERNATIONAL DISTRIBUTION SYSTEM

1. Develop a distribution strategy.
2. Establish criteria for selecting distribution partners.
3. Locate potential distribution partners.
4. Solicit the interest of distributors.
5. Screen and select distribution partners.
6. Negotiate agreements.

In developing countries, consumers still shop at traditional markets such as this one in Rajasthan, India. But traditional retailers increasingly face global competition from firms such as Wal-Mart.

Nicholas DeVore/Stone/Getty Images

synergy) will be used with the distribution strategy to establish criteria for the selection of partners. Selection criteria include geographic coverage, managerial ability, financial stability, annual volume, and reputation. Several sources are useful in locating possible distribution partners. They include:

- *National export portals.* For example, the U.S. export portal, http://www.export.gov, assists U.S. exporters in locating distributors and agents overseas.
- *Banks.* If the firm's bank has foreign branches, they may be happy to help locate distributors.
- *Directories.* Country directories of distributors or specialized directories, such as those listing computer distributors, can be helpful.
- *Trade shows.* Exhibiting at an international trade show, or just attending one, exposes managers to a large number of distributors and their salespeople.
- *Competitors' distribution partners.* Sometimes a competitor's distributor may be interested in switching product lines.

Find links to distributor information on the student companion website at http://www.cengage.com/international.

- *Consultants.* Some international marketing consultants specialize in locating distributors.
- *Associations.* There are associations of international intermediaries or country associations of intermediaries; for example, a firm looking for a representative or agent in the United States could contact the following: Manufacturer's Agents National Association or http://www.manaonline.org; Manufacturer's Agents Association for the Food Service Industry.
- *Foreign consulates.* Most countries post commercial attachés at their embassies or at separate consulates. These individuals can be helpful in locating agents or distributors in their country.

After compiling a list of possible distribution partners, the firm may contact each, providing product literature and distribution requirements. Prospective distributors with an interest in the firm's product line can be asked to supply such information as lines currently carried, annual volume, number of salespeople, geographic territory covered, credit and bank references, physical facilities, relationship with local government, and knowledge of English or other relevant languages. Firms that respond should be checked against the selection criteria. Before making a final decision, a manufacturer's representative should go to the country and talk to retailers or the industrial end users to narrow the field down to the strongest two or three contenders. While in the country, the manufacturer's representative should meet and evaluate the distribution partner candidates.

MANAGING GLOBAL DISTRIBUTION

Selecting the most suitable channel participants and gaining access to the market are extremely important steps in achieving an integrated and responsive distribution channel. However, without proper motivation of and control over that channel, sales may remain unsatisfactory. This section discusses the steps that must be taken to ensure the flow of the firm's products through the channel by gaining the full cooperation of all channel members.

Motivating Channel Participants

Keeping channel participants motivated is an important aspect of international distribution policies. Financial incentives in the form of higher-than-average gross margins can be a very powerful inducement, particularly for the management of independent distributors, wholesalers, and retailers. The expected gross margins are influenced by the cultural history of that channel. For example, if a certain type of retailer usually gets a 50 percent margin and the firm offers 40 percent, the effort the retailer makes may be less than desired. Inviting channel members to annual conferences and introductions of new products is also effective. By extending help to the management of distributorships in areas such as inventory control, accounts collection, and advertising, the international firm can cultivate goodwill that will later stand it in good stead. Special programs may also be instituted to train or motivate the channel members' sales forces.

Programs to motivate foreign independent intermediaries are likely to succeed if monetary incentives are considered along with efforts that help make the channel members more efficient and competitive. To have prosperous intermediaries is, of course, also in the interest of the international firm. These programs or policies are particularly important in the case of independents that distribute products of other manufacturers as well. Often they are beleaguered by the principals of the other products they carry. Each is attempting to get the greatest possible attention and service from the distributor. Therefore, the international firm must find ways to ensure that the channel members devote sufficient effort to its products.

More intense contact between the export manufacturer and the distributor will usually result in better performance by the distributor. The amount of effort an international firm needs to expend depends on the marketing strategy for that market. For example, if the firm is using extensive advertising to pull products through a channel, the intermediary may be expected only to take orders and deliver the product; there is no need for it to contribute to the sales effort. If, on the other hand, the marketing strategy depends on the channel members' developing the market or pushing the product through the channel, then a significant sales effort will be required. As much as possible, the manufacturer should send product news and public relations releases to encourage attention to its product line and to support its distributors' efforts on its behalf.

Periodic visits to distribution partners can have a positive effect on their motivation and control. Often it is helpful to travel with a channel member salesperson to gain knowledge of the marketplace and to evaluate the skills of the salesperson. The most important benefit of a visit to the channel member is that it gives a clear message that the member's performance is important to the firm. Visits strengthen the personal relationship between the manufacturer and the channel member. A research study on the performance of international distribution partners found that using output controls such as how much volume the partner sold is actually less effective than social controls. Social controls refer to the patterns of interpersonal interactions between the partners, which highlights the need for in-depth relationships with mutual respect and trust.[12]

Changing channel strategies can be costly but necessary, especially as national markets evolve. However, until an international firm decides to eliminate a channel member, it should beware of strategies that cause conflict between manufacturers and channel members. Channel conflicts between a manufacturer and an independent distributor most often arise due to competition for sales between the distributor and the manufacturer's own direct sales force or competition between multiple distributors in the same channel and market.[13] Opening new discount channels that offer the same goods at lower prices is also problematic.

Controlling Channel Participants

An international company will want to exert enough control over channel members to help guarantee that they accurately interpret and appropriately execute the company's marketing strategies. The firm wants to be sure that the local intermediaries price the products according to the company's policies. The same could be said for sales, advertising, and service policies. Because the company's reputation in a local market can be tarnished when independent intermediaries handle local distribution ineffectively or inefficiently, international companies closely monitor the performance of local channel members. One way to exert influence over the international channel members is to spell out the specific responsibilities of each, such as minimum annual sales, in the distribution agreement. Attainment of the sales goal can be required for renewal of the contract.

Many international companies grant distribution rights only for short time periods, with regular renewal reviews. Caution is advised, however, because cancellation of distribution rights is frequently subject to both social norms and local laws that prohibit sudden termination. Although termination of a distributor or agent for nonperformance is a relatively simple action in the United States, termination of international channel members can be very costly in many parts of the world. In Japan, foreign firms must be especially careful in their selection of a local distributor, because firms are expected to commit themselves to a long-term relationship. When a firm terminates a distributor, it reflects poorly on that firm.[14] Finding another distributor could prove difficult under those circumstances.

In some countries, the international firm may have to pay a multiple of its local agent's annual gross profits in order to terminate the agent. In other countries, termination compensation for agents and distributors can include the value of any goodwill that the agent or distributor has built up for the brand, in addition to expenses incurred in developing the business. The international firm may also be liable for any compensation claimed by discharged employees who worked on the product line. As a result, termination of a channel member can be a costly, painful process, governed in nearly all cases by local laws that may tend to protect and compensate the local channel member.

Nonetheless, research suggests that multinational corporations operating in developing countries commonly buy or fire their local distributors or develop their own marketing and sales subsidiaries. These firms complain that distributors in emerging markets often fail to invest in business growth and aren't ambitious enough.[15]

GAINING ACCESS TO DISTRIBUTION CHANNELS

Entry into a market can be accomplished through a variety of channel members. However, the channel member whom it seems most logical to approach may already have a relationship with one of the firm's competitors. This poses some special challenges to international marketers. This section is aimed at illustrating alternatives that companies may employ when they encounter difficulties in convincing channel members to carry their products.

The "Locked-Up" Channel

A channel is considered locked up when a newcomer cannot easily convince any channel member to participate, despite the fact that both market and economic considerations suggest otherwise. Channel members customarily decide on a case-by-case basis what products they should add to or drop from their lines. Retailers typically select products that they expect to sell easily and in volume, and they can be expected to switch sources when better opportunities arise. Similarly, wholesalers and distributors compete for retail accounts or industrial users on economic terms. They can entice a prospective client to switch by buying from a new source that can offer a better deal. Likewise, manufacturers compete for wholesale accounts with the expectation that channel members can be convinced to purchase from any given manufacturer if the offer improves on the offers made by competitors.

Yet there are barriers that limit a wholesaler's flexibility to add or drop a particular line. The distributor may have an agreement not to sell competitive products, or its business may include a significant volume from one manufacturer that it does not want to risk upsetting. In Japan, relationships among manufacturers, wholesalers, and retailers are long-standing in nature and do not allow channel participants to shift their allegiance quickly to another source even when offered a superior product or price. Japanese channel members develop strong personal ties that make it very difficult for any participant to break a long-standing relationship. When Kodak entered the Japanese market, it had difficulty gaining access to the smaller retail outlets because Japan's Fuji Film dominated the four major wholesalers. Kodak worked for years to gain access to these large wholesalers, but it had little success. So when Kodak entered the digital camera market, it decided to acquire Chinon, a Japanese precision instrument company, to ensure better access to the market.[16]

Cultural forces may not be the only impediments blocking access to a channel of distribution. The members of a channel may not be willing to take any risks by pioneering unknown products. Competitors, domestic or foreign, may try to obstruct the entry of a new company. To respond to these challenges, global marketers should think creatively. When American Standard, the world's largest supplier of plumbing fixtures, tried to enter the Korean market, it found itself locked out of the normal plumbing distributors, which were controlled by local manufacturers. American Standard looked for an alternative distribution channel that served the building trade. It found Home Center, one of the largest suppliers of homebuilding materials and appliances, and thus successfully circumvented the locked channels.[17]

Kodak faced a similar challenge in China. When it first entered the market, Kodak was a distant fourth, facing stronger rivals, such as Fuji Film, and a locked-up distribution channel. Kodak took a gamble, recruiting Chinese entrepreneurs to open Kodak photo stores. The gamble paid off. Ten years later, its market share had soared to 63 percent while Fuji's had shrunk to only 25 percent. With nearly 8,000 photo stores across China, the company succeeded by tapping into the desire of many Chinese to run their own businesses.[18]

Alternative Entry Approaches

International marketers have developed several approaches to the difficult task of gaining access to locked-up distribution channels. These include piggybacking, joint ventures, and acquisitions.

Piggybacking.   When a company does not find any channel partners interested in pioneering new products, the practice of piggybacking may offer a way out of the situation. **Piggybacking** is an arrangement whereby another company that sells to the same customer segment takes on the new products. The products retain the name of the true manufacturer, and both partners normally sign a multiyear contract to provide for continuity. The new company is, in essence, "piggybacking" its products on the shoulders of the established company's sales force.

Under a piggyback arrangement, the manufacturer retains control over marketing strategy, particularly pricing, positioning, and advertising. The partner acts as a rented sales force only. Of course, this is quite different from the private-label strategy, whereby the manufacturer supplies a marketer, which then places its own brand name on the product. The piggybacking approach has become quite common in the pharmaceutical industry, where companies involve competitor firms in the launch of a particular new drug. Warner-Lambert, a major pharmaceutical company, launched its leading cholesterol-lowering drug Lipitor in the United States with the help of Pfizer. The drug was one of the most successful introductions ever.

Coca-Cola initiated a new twist on the piggyback arrangement when it offered its extensive distribution system across Africa to assist UNAIDS, a United Nations

Piggyback arrangement an arrangement in which one company agrees to distribute through its established channels the products of another company

agency fighting AIDS. Coke's distribution reaches every country in Africa except Sudan and Libya, and its products find their way even to the poorest villages. The company will be contributing warehouse and truck space, as well as logistics assistance, to help charities find the best routes for their literature and testing kits. However, Coca-Cola can't help distribute AIDS drugs that have to be kept cool, because its trucks are not refrigerated.[19]

Joint Ventures.   As we noted in Chapter 9, when two companies agree to form a new legal entity, it is called a joint venture. Such operations have been quite common in the area of joint production. Our interest here is restricted to joint ventures in which distribution is the primary objective. Normally, such companies are formed between a local firm with existing market access and a foreign firm that would like to market its products in a country where it has no existing market access. For example, two domestic beer producers had tied up retail outlets in Mexico with exclusivity contracts. As a result, Anheuser-Busch decided to enter Mexico through a joint venture with Mexican beer giant Modelo rather than trying to build a distribution system from scratch.

Acquisitions.   Acquiring an existing company can give a foreign entrant immediate access to a distribution system. For example, to gain access to pharmaceutical distribution channels in Japan, Merck purchased Japan's Banyu pharmaceutical company. Similarly, Roche Pharmaceutical of Switzerland purchased a controlling stake in Chugai Pharmaceutical.[20] Although it requires a substantial amount of capital, operating results tend to be better than those of new ventures, which usually entail initial losses. It is often less important to find an acquisition candidate with a healthy financial outlook or top products than to find one that has good relationships with wholesale and retail outlets.

GLOBAL LOGISTICS

The logistics system, including the physical distribution of manufactured products, is also an important part of international distribution. It involves planning, implementing, and controlling the physical flow of materials and finished products from points of origin to points of use. A capital-intensive and labor-intensive function outside of the core business of most companies, logistics has become increasingly complicated to manage. It is also costly, representing 15 to 35 percent of total revenues for most firms.

On a global scale, the task becomes more complex, because so many external variables have an impact on the flow of materials or products. As geographic distances to foreign markets grow, competitive advantages are often derived from a more effective structuring of the logistics system either to save time or costs or to increase a firm's reliability. The emergence of logistics as a means of achieving competitive advantage is leading companies to focus increased attention on this vital area. Many manufacturers and retailers are restructuring their logistics efforts and divesting themselves of their in-house distribution divisions in favor of outside logistics specialists.

Logistics Decision Areas

In this section, we describe the objectives of an international logistics system and the various operations that have to be managed and integrated into an efficient system. The total task of logistics management consists of five separate though

Shipping products by sea is popular with exporters. However, when time is critical, exporters choose air freight.

© iStockphoto.com/Dan Barnes

interrelated jobs: (1) traffic or transportation management, (2) inventory control, (3) order processing, (4) materials handling and warehousing, and (5) fixed-facilities location management. In what follows, we examine each of these decision areas in more detail.

Traffic or Transportation Management. Traffic management deals primarily with the modes of transportation for delivering products. Principal choices are air, sea, rail, and truck, or some combination thereof. Transportation expenses contribute substantially to the costs of marketing products internationally, so special attention must be paid to selecting the transportation mode. Such choices are made by considering three principal factors: lead time, transit time, and cost. Companies operating with long lead times tend to use slower and therefore lower-cost transportation modes, such as sea and freight. When a short lead time is called for, faster modes of transportation such as air and truck are used. Long transit times require higher financial costs because payments arrive later and because higher average inventories are stocked at either the point of origin or the destination. Here again, the modes of transportation appropriate for long transit times are sea and rail, whereas air and truck transportation can result in much shorter transit times. Transportation costs are the third factor to consider when selecting a mode of transport. Typically, air or truck transportation is more expensive than either sea or rail for any given distance.

Local laws and restrictions can have a significant impact on transport costs. For example, conflicting regulations at the national and local level make transport in

Indonesia notoriously expensive and inefficient. In addition, illicit payments to corrupt police officials and criminal organizations make moving goods to and from Indonesia even more burdensome.[21] Similarly, managing logistics in China continues to be difficult because of corruption and provincial protectionism that often allows only local companies to deliver within many cities. The American Chamber of Commerce in Shanghai estimates that logistics costs are four times higher in China than in many developed economies.[22]

Inventory Control. The level of inventory on hand significantly affects the service level of a firm's logistics system. In international operations, adequate inventories are needed as insurance against unexpected breakdowns in the logistics system. However, to avoid the substantial costs of tied-up capital, inventory is ideally reduced to the minimum needed. To reduce inventory levels, a number of companies have adopted the Japanese system of just-in-time (JIT) deliveries of parts and components. For example, many firms kept 30 to 40 days of buffer stocks of parts and components before instituting JIT. After JIT was implemented, buffer stocks could be lowered to 1 to 2 days. For companies that are moving manufacturing to China, JIT can become challenging. Shipments from China to the United States take 22 to 24 days and can sometimes be delayed due to power outages or floods; therefore, instituting JIT with components or parts from China can be problematic.[23]

Order Processing. Because rapid processing of orders shortens the order cycle and allows for lower safety stocks on the part of the client, this area becomes a central concern for logistics management. The available communications technology greatly influences the time it takes to process an order, and the Internet has vastly improved our ability in this regard. It is still true, however, that to offer an efficient order-processing system worldwide represents a considerable challenge to any company today. Doing this can be turned to competitive advantage; customers reap added benefits from such a system, and satisfied customers mean repeat business.

Swisscom, Switzerland's largest telecommunications provider, had been plagued with an opaque and inefficient ordering process that could take as long as 40 days to complete. The company installed new order processing software, enabling it to cut that figure to less than 10 days. This not only improved satisfaction ratings by employees and customers alike, it also increased the speed of customer payments.[24]

Materials Handling and Warehousing. Throughout the logistics cycle, materials and products will have to be stored and prepared for moving or transportation. How products are stored or moved is the principal concern of materials handling management. For international shipments, the shipping technology or quantities may be different, requiring firms to adjust domestic policies to these new circumstances. Warehousing in foreign countries involves dealing with different climatic conditions. Longer average storage periods may make it necessary to change warehousing practices. In general, international shipments move through different transportation modes than domestic shipments. Substantial logistics costs can be saved if the firm adjusts its shipping arrangements to the prevalent handling procedures abroad.

Automated warehousing is a relatively new concept for the handling, storage, and shipping of goods. Warehouses are often adjacent to the factory, and all goods are stored automatically in bins up to twelve stories high. The delivery and retrieval of all goods are controlled by a computer system. Even though automated warehouses require significant up-front capital and technology, they ultimately reduce warehousing costs significantly.

Radio Frequency Identification Development (RFID) technology involves small identity chips that can be put on pallets, boxes, or individual items. RFID is being used by Wal-Mart, Tesco, Metro, and many other firms to speed up material handling as products move from warehouses to trucks to customers' warehouses. For example, Kimberly-Clark ships cases and pallets from its factory in Germany to Metro, Tesco, and other retailers. It is expected that many suppliers to large retailers will be required to use RFID technology.[25]

Fixed-Facilities Location Management.   The facilities crucial to the logistics flow are production facilities and warehouses. To serve customers worldwide and to maximize the efficiency of the total logistics system, production facilities may have to be placed in several countries. This often entails a tradeoff between economies of scale and savings in logistics costs.

The location of warehousing facilities can greatly affect the company's ability to respond to orders once they are received or processed. It can also support the company's warranty policy, particularly its ability to deliver replacement products and parts on a timely basis. A company with warehouses in every country where it does business would have a natural advantage in delivery, but such a system increases the costs of warehousing and, most likely, the required level of inventory systemwide.

Therefore, the international firm should seek a balance that satisfies the customer's requirements for timely delivery and also reduces overall logistics costs. Microsoft opened a single warehouse and distribution center in Dublin, Ireland, to serve Europe. The new distribution center allowed the company to serve all European markets effectively and made it unnecessary for Microsoft to keep a warehouse and inventory in each country.

Global Supply Chain Management

Global supply chain management is a term increasingly used to encompass the many interrelated jobs involved in global logistics. **Global supply chain management** is the collective managerial behavior and decisions essential to the development of a functioning global supply chain. Its areas of responsibility include system integration, business process management, and supplier and customer relationship management. Whereas often used interchangeably with global logistics, global supply chain management covers several items often not considered part of logistics, including marketing relationships, product development and rollout, and the management of returns or goods flowing backwards in the supply chain. Its goal is to seamlessly integrate supply and demand management across companies and across borders.[26]

Management of a global supply chain will no doubt need tailoring to company-specific and country-specific needs. A study of supply chain relationships between the United States and Brazil revealed that the high-context Brazilians preferred more personal forms of contact, such as visits and phone calls rather than e-mails.[27] However, a survey of firms operating in North America, Europe, and the Pacific Basin confirmed several commonalities crucial to supply chain success. Delivery reliability and customer service were ranked as most important, followed by cost containment, delivery flexibility, and speed of delivery.[28]

Global supply chain management the collective managerial behavior and decisions essential to the development of a functioning global supply chain

GLOBAL TRENDS IN RETAILING

Retail systems throughout the world are continually evolving in response to economic and social changes. A manager developing a worldwide distribution strategy must consider not only the state of retail today but also the expected state of retail systems in the future. Table 13.2 illustrates how store category—small retailers, discounters, and hypermarkets—vary by region.

Larger-Scale Retailers

The entry of Wal-Mart into the United Kingdom, via its acquisition of Asda's 260 stores, offered consumers decreased prices and a growth in superstores, or hypermarkets. Wal-Mart has grown faster than any other retailer in the United Kingdom, and it is adding photo centers, jewelry centers, vision centers, and pharmacies.

There is a trend toward fewer but larger-scale retailers. As countries become more economically developed, the retail scene comes to be dominated by fewer, larger stores. This is particularly apparent in grocery retail, in which the number of smaller retailers throughout the world has decreased or remained constant,

TABLE 13.2   RETAIL OUTLETS BY REGION

	2003	2004	2005	2006	2007	2008
SMALL GROCERY RETAILERS						
Asia Pacific	10,895,328	11,173,097	11,390,213	11,608,601	11,798,846	11,968,247
Eastern Europe	487,341	485,521	484,369	483,484	482,553	480,192
Latin America	1,111,417	1,101,568	1,128,163	1,134,060	1,134,360	1,143,710
Middle East and Africa	822,276	819,109	804,469	796,502	790,980	797,051
North America	216,061	216,792	215,444	215,518	214,158	211,311
Western Europe	437,823	431,644	422,391	420,037	415,761	413,065
DISCOUNTERS						
Asia Pacific	673	1,176	1,488	1,743	1,944	2,166
Eastern Europe	4,165	4,799	6,196	7,587	8,941	10,020
Latin America	3,262	12,716	25,310	26,974	27,152	28,607
Middle East and Africa	1,789	1,931	2,037	2,163	2,285	2,512
North America	3,116	3,173	3,256	3,174	3,262	3,300
Western Europe	34,400	35,491	37,049	39,224	41,413	43,710
HYPERMARKETS						
Asia Pacific	1,293	1,721	2,029	2,485	2,872	3,337
Eastern Europe	687	830	990	1,207	1,391	1,556
Latin America	1,151	1,223	1,315	1,450	1,666	1,758
Middle East and Africa	270	289	342	341	379	431
North America	2,419	2,808	3,107	3,431	3,695	3,921
Western Europe	5,427	5,586	5,838	6,223	6,404	6,547

Source: Euromonitor.

whereas larger discount outlets and hypermarkets have increased in number. Three factors contribute to this trend: an increase in car ownership, an increase in the number of households with refrigerators and freezers, and an increase in the number of working wives. Whereas the European housewife of 25 years ago may have shopped two or three times a day in local stores, the increase in transportation capacity, refrigerator capacity, and family cash flow, along with the reduction in available shopping time, has increased the practice of one-stop shopping in supermarkets. As retailers become bigger and more sophisticated, they often become more powerful relative to both producers and wholesalers.

IKEA, the Scandinavian retailer, has been very successful in Europe, Asia, and the United States in luring customers into its 200,000-square-foot stores. The IKEA strategy of offering a narrow range of low-cost furniture that the customers themselves select, deliver, and assemble results in a lower price to the consumer. Once in the store, customers are given tape measures, catalogs, paper, and pencils. Child-care strollers are available, as well as free diapers. Each store has a restaurant with Scandinavian delicacies such as smoked salmon and Swedish meatballs. Customers can also borrow roof racks to help them bring furniture home. IKEA has created a fun shopping experience that encourages people to enjoy themselves and make purchases. Sales per square foot are three times higher than in traditional furniture stores. IKEA has more than 200 such stores in 37 countries.

Renewed Interest in Smaller Scale Retailers

While larger-sized retail outlets are increasing in number, independent stores are the dominant players in many markets and will be for some time to come. In Latin America, for example, small mom-and-pop stores continue to contribute 60 percent of total in-store sales.[29] This reality has not escaped many global players who have recently refocused attention specifically on how to work with these smaller concerns.

Procter & Gamble (P&G) is one such company. Disappointed with its percentage of sales coming from developing nations (26 percent compared to 40 percent for Colgate-Palmolive), the company is hoping to add one billion additional customers in the next few years, specifically women in developing countries. They plan to do so by getting their products into so-called "high-frequency stores," tiny, locally owned shops, often run inside of someone's house. P&G estimates there are 20 million such stores worldwide, only 2.5 million of which currently carry P&G products. The company is lobbying for shelf space in these stores, often one at a time, and selling more single-use products because space is very limited.[30] P&G has even entered an agreement with the Chinese government to improve existing retail outlets, to build new ones, and to provide retailing training to locals from 10,000 villages. The Chinese government supports the idea because of its potential to increase rural consumption and spur economic growth.[31]

Interest in smaller retailers is not restricted to developing countries. German Stihl refuses to sell its bright orange power tools through Lowe's or Home Depot in the United States. The company ran an add posing the question: What makes this handheld blower too powerful to be sold at Lowe's or Home Depot? The answer in smaller print: The power of 8,000 independent dealers who supply advice and service not available at big chain stores. Big retailers demand low prices from manufacturers to pass on to consumers. Some exporters believe this is a bad strategy to establish the reputation of a premium brand in a new market.[32]

International retailer IKEA is based in Sweden but has locations worldwide. In Saudi Arabia the store targets not only locals, but also the many expatriate workers resident in the country. Its website is in Arabic and English.

International Retailers

The number of international retailers is rising. Most originate in advanced industrial countries and spread to both the developed and the developing countries of the world. The trend was started by a number of large retailers in mature domestic markets that saw limited growth opportunities at home compared to the potential opportunities overseas. Among the most successful international retailers have been franchises, such as McDonald's and KFC, and discount retailers, such as Wal-Mart.

Similar to other multinational companies, retailers that seek markets abroad face many cultural factors that affect their marketing strategies and business operations. For example, in the Middle East, shopping is a major pastime of many Arab women, most of whom do not work outside the home. Some visit the same store several times a week to look for new merchandise. Dressing rooms are large, and family and friends often shop together. Service demands are high, and Arab women like to be pampered.[33] Understanding these cultural demands often gives local retailers an edge over foreign competition.

International retailers can also face unique regulatory hurdles. German authorities ordered Wal-Mart to raise prices on a number of products. The stores were accused of selling below cost, on a regular basis, products such as milk, sugar, and flour. This endangered small and medium-sized retailers and violated German anti-trust law.[34] Potential saleswomen for Avon in China must take a written test and listen to a lecture on China's latest sales regulations. Although China lifted a prior ban on direct sales, the industry is tightly regulated. The government caps sales commissions at 30 percent and sales representatives can only make money selling the product, not recruiting other sales representatives. In addition, just a short time after China liberalized its retail industry, new rules were being considered that could curtail the growth of foreign retailers. The proposed regulations included a requirement that big retailers file detailed blueprints for proposed new outlets and hold public hearings on their impact on communities.[35]

Despite the challenges of entering foreign markets, the internationalization of retailing has been facilitated by a number of factors, such as enhanced data communications, new forms of international financing, and lower governmental barriers to entry. The single European market has also motivated European retailers to expand abroad, as they see a number of new international retailers entering their domestic markets. Retailers are attracted to international markets such as China and India, which often offer higher growth rates than their home markets. As retail growth slows in more mature markets, many retailers search for future growth in emerging markets. Table 13.3 presents the rankings of 30 emerging markets considered most attractive to international marketers.

Overall, American retailers have entered foreign markets later than European and Japanese retailers. However, Wal-Mart's entry into its first foreign market, Mexico, met with phenomenal success. Ten years after first entering the Mexican market, Wal-Mart dominated the country's retail sector. The U.S. retailer joint-ventured with Cifra, the leading Mexican retailer and pioneer of discount stores in Mexico. In its early years, the venture faced several problems. Tariffs inflated the prices of products imported from the United States, and Wal-Mart faced considerable red tape in obtaining import permits. Delivery schedules were unreliable because of poor road systems. With the inauguration of NAFTA, tariffs tumbled, paperwork diminished, and road construction and improvement soared. Wal-Mart buys directly from U.S. suppliers and consolidates orders in its own distribution center in Laredo, Texas. Trucks hired from Wal-Mart deliver products to its Mexican stores the next day. As a large-volume buyer, Wal-Mart can require suppliers to label in Spanish. Most important, it can demand lower prices. The company passes these cost savings on to the Mexican customer, offering prices that the traditional small retailers can't match.

Despite its success in Mexico, other markets have proved more difficult. When first entering the Brazilian market, Wal-Mart failed to note that most target families owned only one car and did all their shopping on weekends. Car parks and store aisles at their superstores were unable to accommodate the weekend rush. Relationships with suppliers were strained, as meetings in this Portuguese speaking nation were always held in English. Wal-Mart has since adapted its practices to the local market by making small but significant operating changes, such as increasing the space devoted to selling food and building just one entrance to the store to reduce confusion.[36]

Sometimes international retailers have decided to abandon difficult markets. Wal-Mart retreated from the German and South Korean markets, and Home Depot pulled out of Chile. Despite the many obstacles abroad, successful international retailers tend to fall into three distinct categories: replicators, performance managers, and reinventors.[37]

<table>
<tr><td>TABLE 13.3</td><td colspan="3">RETAIL POTENTIAL OF EMERGING MARKETS</td></tr>
</table>

COUNTRY	RETAIL POTENTIAL RANK	MARKET ATTRACTIVENESS RANK	TIME PRESSURE RANK
India	1	21	2
Russia	2	7	1
China	3	14	5
United Arab Emirates	4	2	29
Saudi Arabia	5	13	13
Vietnam	6	30	2
Chile	7	7	20
Brazil	8	6	23
Slovenia	9	3	20
Malaysia	10	12	10
Algeria	11	29	6
Mexico	12	11	14
Latvia	13	1	20
Tunisia	14	19	27
Egypt	15	28	14
Lithuania	16	3	16
Ukraine	17	22	4
Peru	18	22	12
Morocco	19	27	11
Turkey	20	7	18
Bulgaria	21	16	8
Indonesia	22	18	16
Romania	23	16	7
Croatia	24	7	9
Philippines	25	25	24
Thailand	26	24	18
Hungary	27	5	28
Colombia	28	20	26
El Salvador	29	25	30
Argentina	30	14	24

Source: Selected data from 2009 Global Retail Development Index, A.T. Kearney, and author's calculations.

Replicators.   Replicators such as Benneton, Zara, and Starbucks develop a simple retail model, identify markets where that model will work, then export the model virtually unchanged. This strategy allows for fast international expansion, and economies of scale can be reaped from standardization even if local variations are accommodated by making minor adaptations to retail format or product

WORLD BEAT 13.2

RETREAT FROM GERMANY

GERMANS HAVE A SPECIFIC TYPE of shopping behavior, which differs from that of many other shoppers. To Germans, a sales clerk meeting them at the door to say hello or helping them pick out a suit is offensive and is interpreted as aggressive sales techniques. Therefore, when Wal-Mart started rolling out its supersized stores with "U.S. hospitality," it ran straight into culture shock. Customers wanted to pack their own purchases and do their shopping without interruptions. So, companies like Wal-Mart that built their success partially on service had to change their approach.

The German market offered Wal-Mart 84 million consumers with high average incomes and 99 percent literacy. The market presented challenges as well. In Germany, no-frills discounters, such as Aldi, have existed for years and dominate the market. Aldi carries only 700 items in a store versus 150,000 at a Wal-Mart Supercenter. In fact, Wal-Mart seems quite luxurious compared to Aldi, where

cases of goods are placed on pallets for the consumer to sort through. According to McKinsey & Company, Aldi's operating margins in Germany are 9.3 percent, making them more efficient than Wal-Mart, which struggled to make a profit in Germany.

To build store traffic, Wal-Mart has tried innovative promotions. Most of the company's 91 stores in Germany sponsored a singles' night on Friday nights. Single men and women registered for a raffle, left their information on a bulletin board, and received a small bow for their shopping carriage. The bow signalled their availability to others whom they might meet at the meat counter or while selecting fruit.

In the end, Wal-Mart simply could not find the appropriate mix to meet the unusual demands of the German market. The company elected to abandon its efforts, taking an $863 million loss. Wal-Mart sold its German assets to Metro, a global competitor based in Germany.

Sources: Cecilie Rohwedder, "Metro's Wal-Mart Deal Helps Boost Profit," *Wall Street Journal*, March 22, 2007, p. B4; Marcus Walker, "House of Discards," *Wall Street Journal Europe*, October 22, 2007, p. 30; "Culture Shock in Germany," in Kate Gillespie, David H. Hennessey, and Jean-Pierre Jeannet, *Global Marketing*, Houghton-Mifflin, New York, 2007; and Elizabeth Rigby and Gerrit Wiesmann, "Closing Time for Old Stores in Germany," *Financial Times*, June 10, 2009, p. 14.

offerings. Home and overseas businesses can be globally (or at last regionally) centralized, leading to easier coordination of markets and management of global brands.

Performance Managers. Performance managers such as Ahold and Kingfisher expand globally by acquiring existing retail businesses that they then develop as independent entities. These international retailers add value to these acquisitions in the form of their expertise in corporate finance, postmerger management, and management systems. Acquisitions can be a fast way to enter foreign markets, but transferring expertise and upgrading acquisitions can be time-consuming. Once expertise is transferred, however, performance mangers tend to relinquish autonomy to local management.

Reinventors. Reinventors such as Carrefour and Tesco employ standardized back-end systems and processes while creating a largely tailored retail format for each overseas market. For example, a Tesco supermarket in London will appear vastly different from one in Bangkok or Warsaw. However, a recent study reveals competence in retail logistics to be a major determinant of success for large retailers that move abroad. This competence allows these retailers to contain costs, shorten procurement times, and respond more quickly to customer needs.[38]

Every national market is a potential market for reinventors. But understanding the different markets and adapting to them takes time and can slow the process of internationalization. Finding the proper balance between centralized and local control can also prove challenging.

A Mary Kay advertisement for the Chinese market. Direct marketers often find developing countries to be attractive markets.

Courtesy of Mary Kay, Inc.

Direct Marketing

Although the United States is the global leader in direct marketing, the market is also growing elsewhere. As noted earlier, the complex, multilayered Japanese distribution system encouraged some foreign and local companies to go directly to consumers. The growth in direct marketing in Japan is supported by a number of demographic and technical factors. The dramatic increase in employed women from 50 percent to 75 percent has resulted in fewer available shopping hours. The introduction of toll-free telephone and cable has also made it easier to shop at home.

Direct marketing plays a role in emerging markets as well but faces a number of challenges. In certain countries, including Russia, direct marketing tends to be viewed negatively as one of those newfangled Western business concepts. Bertelsmann, the German-based media company, put its planned Book Club India project on hold after realizing that a segmentation exercise on India's 23 largest urban markets yielded a total of only 297,000 potential club members, which was too small to pursue the opportunity.[39] The infrastructure in most developing countries in terms of delivery and telecommunications also lags behind markets in the developed world. Telemarketing is hampered by a lack of phones. For example, only one in ten Brazilians has a phone. Still, Brazil is a large market and tends to be ahead of the rest of Latin America in direct marketing. Urban consumers in Brazil receive an average of ten direct-mail pieces a month.

Direct-sales firms such as Amway, Avon, and Mary Kay have proven highly successful in many emerging markets. For Avon, Brazil is second only to the United States in volume sales. The success of these companies was due in large part to their ability to recruit independent salespersons to promote their products. Many people in developing countries saw this as an opportunity to supplement meager incomes. In addition, direct sales appeals to collectivist cultures where people often mix business and personal relationships. Many Brazilian customers admit they will pay more to buy from someone they know rather than purchase the product cheaper at a store.[40] As a result, many local clones have emerged and flourished. Brazil's own Natura is seen as more upscale than Avon and has experienced phenomenal growth.

Online Retailing

The Internet has opened an entirely new channel for retailers and manufacturers to sell their products. U.S.-based online retailers, such as Amazon.com, have expanded abroad with specific "stores" in the United Kingdom and Germany. Most online retailing, however, crosses borders; consumers can reach any store anywhere with a legitimate Internet address.

Some parts of the world have reached near 100 percent adoption rates of e-commerce. The most active online purchasers come from South Korea, where 99 percent of Internet users shop online.[41] Other countries have not been such eager adopters. In Latin America, online sales are severely limited due to the lack of penetration of credit cards among the general public. However, credit card usage is expected to grow 20 percent annually across Latin America and should ease this constraint in the future.[42] Companies must also consider where their product is located in the product life cycle when trying to sell electronically in a foreign country. When Dell learned that over 90 million people in China had access to the Internet, it hurriedly implemented its famous American e-tailing strategy in the country with few modifications.[43] The strategy was unpopular with Chinese customers, who were often buying their first personal computer and simply unwilling to make a significant purchase sight-unseen.[44] Acknowledging its miscalculation, Dell signed a deal with Gome, China's largest electronics retailer, to sell its computers through the brick-and-mortar channel.[45]

In some cases, the ancient and modern worlds are meeting via the Internet. New websites are selling home furnishings, accessories, and toys made by traditional craftspeople in developing countries. By giving artisans direct access to a global marketplace, the Internet has the potential to improve the lot of poor families from Asia to the Americas. Specific success stories include Himalayan artists selling handmade copper jugs and pots, originally thought to be a dying art, on a site called Worldtomarket.com.[46] Elsewhere, Ugandan women are earning four times their country average by making sparkling jewelry to be sold by Bead for Life, a Colorado company.[47]

Online retailing requires a large connected population. As many e-commerce executives know, online retailing also depends on a solid fulfillment cycle that delivers the ordered merchandise quickly into the hands of the consumer. When this is to take place across borders, issues of taxation and tariffs may still remain, slowing down delivery systems. Many foreign markets do not yet offer reliable fulfillment centers for use by small online retailers. However, the trend is clearly in the direction of resolving this problem. Once this has occurred, many more consumers will reach into online stores in faraway places, potentially turning every online marketer into an international retailer.

SMUGGLING

Smuggling has recently emerged as a serious challenge to many international marketers.[48] Indian customs has credited the smuggling of gold, silver, and consumer durables into India with supporting a black-market economy equivalent to 20 percent of the national gross domestic product (GDP). In a single year, about half of all computer sales in Brazil involved smuggled computers. Today, smuggling accounts for an estimated one-third of all cigarettes sold worldwide.

Smuggling is the illegal transport of products across national borders and may involve the distribution of illicit products such as illegal drugs and arms. It also encompasses the illegal distribution of products that are legal to sell and use, such as computers, cosmetics, and VCRs. Prior to trade liberalization, the products most commonly smuggled into Mexico were consumer electronics, food and alcohol, clothing, automobiles and auto parts, and toys and games. It is the smuggling of legal products that concerns us here.

Smuggling is most prevalent in developing countries and in the transitional economies of the former Soviet bloc. It arose in response to traditionally high tariffs and low quotas placed on imported goods. For example, a smuggled VCR in Mexico could sell for $200, whereas its legally imported equivalent would sell for $600. With the move toward trade liberalization in the emerging world, we would expect smuggling to fade as tariffs and quotas decline.

Although smuggling has decreased in some countries, it hasn't been eradicated. There are several reasons for this. To begin with, trade liberalization is not universal or complete. The tariff levels on many products in many countries still promote smuggling. Governments may also restrict the inflow of products for reasons other than protecting local industries. For example, the Malaysian government banned beef byproducts from Australia and New Zealand when 40 cattle ranches in those countries were accused of failing to meet Islamic halal standards. This resulted in a surge of smuggled beef byproducts entering Malaysia.[49] Furthermore, tariffs are not the only taxes that smugglers can avoid. They can also avoid sales taxes and value-added taxes. If smugglers are to become legitimate importers, they must declare themselves to customs. This enables governments to identify them and demand income taxes from them. Therefore, the lowering of tariffs decreases the cost advantage that smugglers previously enjoyed but doesn't completely remove it. Finally, as many countries heighten surveillance at customs in order to stop and seize counterfeits entering their markets, counterfeiters are increasingly turning to smuggling. In a single incident, the U.S. government broke up a smuggling ring of counterfeit Nike shoes and seized $16 million worth of merchandise.[50]

For many years, international marketers viewed smuggling as a benign and even positive phenomenon. In some cases, smugglers distributed products to otherwise inaccessible markets. In other cases, smugglers delivered products to consumers at a considerably lower price, supporting greater sales and market growth. In either case, the international firm stood to gain by realizing greater sales revenue as the result of the smuggling of its products.

Smuggling the illegal transport of products across national borders

A recent analysis of the records of major international cigarette companies reveals that many executives in these firms knew that certain international distributors were involved in large-scale smuggling operations and cooperated in some ways to assist them. Three managers of British American Tobacco pleaded guilty to or were convicted of smuggling.[51] Several countries in Europe and the developing world have initiated lawsuits against cigarette companies to recover taxes lost as a result of smuggling, although these suits have largely been dismissed on jurisdictional grounds. Still, the behavior of the international cigarette industry is likely to make governments all the more skeptical of other international firms that claim ignorance of smuggling operations.[52]

Nevertheless, governments have sometimes exhibited ambivalent attitudes toward smuggling. Prior to Poland's joining the European Union (EU), 25 percent of liquor and 15 percent of cigarettes consumed in Poland were smuggled in from Russian, Belarus, or Ukraine. But patrolling the Polish border was stymied by a lack of money and agents, and custom inspectors often turned a blind eye to contraband. Officials who caught Russian smugglers just sent them back home. The Polish government also recognized that smuggling provided a livelihood to many in Poland's depressed eastern border economy where unemployment reached 35 percent.[53] But once Poland joined the EU, Brussels, afraid that the EU could be flooded with contraband goods smuggled in through Poland, moved to shut down the contraband trade. The EU insisted that fines be levied on smugglers and their cars impounded and Polish visas revoked. In addition, the EU assigned funds to ensure that Poland's customs department had the latest in detection equipment, such as state-of-the-art X-ray scanners.[54]

Furthermore, the darker side of smuggling is becoming apparent. In the past ten years, smuggling has evolved along lines of traditional organized crime. It has become more centralized and violent. As margins are squeezed by trade liberalization, smugglers have sought ways to protect their cost advantage, such as counterfeiting the products they previously bought. Some smugglers who transport consumer goods into developing countries have allied themselves with drug cartels to launder drug money. This phenomenon has caused firms such as Hewlett-Packard, Ford, General Motors, Sony, Westinghouse, Whirlpool, and General Electric to be invited by the U.S. Attorney General to answer questions about how the distribution of their products may have become involved in the laundering of drug money.[55] In the future, both host and home governments may require international marketers to take more precautions to ensure that their products are not distributed through these illegal channels.

To assess distribution strategies for your product and explore local channels, continue with the Country Market Report on the student companion website (http://www.cengage.com/international).

CONCLUSION

To be successful in the global marketplace, a company needs market acceptance among buyers and market access via distribution channels. To achieve access, the firm must select the most suitable channel members, keeping in mind that substantial differences exist among countries on both the wholesale and the retail levels. There are major differences among countries in distribution. Local habits and cultures, legal restrictions, and infrastructure can all affect the success of distribution in a new country.

Proper distribution policies have to allow for the local market's buying and shopping habits. A company should not expect the same distribution density, channel alignment, or channel length in all its markets. The logistics system must reflect both local market situations and the difficulties inherent in moving products longer distances. Finding willing and suitable channel members may prove extremely difficult. Access may be achieved only by forging special alliances with present channel members or local companies that have access to them. Once the distribution system has been designed, participants still need to be motivated and controlled to ensure that the firm's marketing strategy is properly executed. Increasingly, governments may hold international firms liable for smuggled products, forcing marketers to control their channels better.

A major technological revolution is taking place with online retailing and the widespread use of the Internet by consumers. These trends are likely to reshape the global distribution system and the way companies tap into markets all over the world. Access to the Internet makes it easier for business or household customers to tap into foreign suppliers. This has far-reaching consequences for all global marketers and needs to be considered as the new world economy adapts to the Internet challenge.

QUESTIONS FOR DISCUSSION

1. You have been assigned the task of selecting distributors in Malaysia to handle your firm's line of car batteries. What criteria will you use to select among the 12 possible distributors?

2. The performance of your agents and distributors in South America has been poor over the past three years. List possible ways in which to improve the management of these agents and distributors.

3. Given the trends in global retailing, what distribution strategies should a worldwide manufacturer of women's clothing consider?

4. Your firm has just entered the Polish market for bottled water. The major distributor is owned by a competitive producer of bottled water. What strategies can you use to gain access to this market?

5. Compare and contrast, from the manufacturer's point of view, the problems that parallel imports cause (Chapter 12) with those caused by smuggling. If governments increasingly restrict international marketers from stopping parallel imports, can these same marketers be held responsible for products' being smuggled? Explain your reasoning.

Alain Nogues/Corbis

© Imagine/18439GNG

14
Global Promotion Strategies

LEARNING OBJECTIVES

After studying this chapter, you should be able to:

- List the major factors that determine a firm's ability to use a push or a pull promotion strategy in different national markets.

- Contrast the benefits to the international marketer of using an international sales force with those of using local sales forces.

- Describe the impact that different purchasing behaviors, buying criteria, languages, and negotiation styles can have on international selling.

- Explain the importance of global account management.

- Describe how global marketers can successfully utilize international trade fairs and consortia as well as manage the international bidding process.

- Cite examples of how sales promotions vary across cultures, and suggest reasons for these differences.

- Note recent international trends in sales promotions, sports sponsorships, telemarketing, product placement, and managing word of mouth.

- Give examples of international public relations disasters, and suggest ways in which global marketers can promote the goodwill of their firms.

EACH YEAR, THE GOLIATHS of the civil aircraft industry face off at the Paris Air Show. America's Boeing Company and Europe's Airbus Industrie attempt not only to make sales, but also to capture the imaginations of potential clients. Company representatives meet with major customers to discuss current products and establish the leads that will eventually result in sales of these big-ticket items. But promoting current products is not enough. The Paris Air Show is a time to unveil new ideas and present the company's vision of the future of flight. This vision, as well as actual products, will help establish the image of each company. In this global industry, corporate image is very important. Can the firm deliver on its promises of speed, economy in-cabin amenities, and innovative ideas?[1] International marketers in civil aircraft must communicate to potential customers that the answer is yes.

Global promotion strategies encompass a firm's marketing communications and include personal selling, sales promotion, public relations, and advertising. Managing the communications process for a single market is no easy task. And the task is even more difficult for global marketers, who must communicate to prospective customers in many national markets. In the process, they struggle with different cultures, habits, and languages.

We begin this chapter by examining the cross-cultural implications of push strategies and pull strategies. We proceed to the challenge of developing a personal-selling effort on both the international and the local level, discussing differing sales practices as well as issues of recruitment and compensation of sales forces. Other promotion issues involving business-to-business and government sales are then discussed. We continue by exploring other aspects of global promotion such as sales promotions, sports sponsorships, spam, product placements, buzz, and public relations.

Advertising, another key element of the promotion mix, will be covered in detail in Chapter 15.

GLOBAL PROMOTION STRATEGIES

How to manage the promotion mix globally is a critical question for many companies. Some firms do business in a certain way and do not rethink their promotion decisions when they internationalize. However, many companies find themselves in countries or situations that require an adjustment or a substantial change in their promotion mix. This section and the ones that follow are devoted to understanding how different international environments affect promotion mix decisions.

Pull Versus Push Strategies

Pull strategy a promotional strategy directed at the final buyer or end user of a product or service

A **pull strategy** is characterized by a relatively greater dependence on promotion, including sales promotions and advertising, directed at the final buyer or end user for a product or service. Pull campaigns are typical for consumer-goods firms that target a large number of consumers. Pull campaigns are usually advisable when the product is widely used by consumers, when the channel is long, when the product is not very complex, and when self-service is the predominant shopping behavior. Increased or decreased reliance on pull campaigns for global markets depends on a number of factors. Most important are access to advertising media, channel length, and the leverage the company has with the distribution channel.

Marketers accustomed to having a large number of media available may find the choices limited in overseas markets. For many products, pull campaigns that rely heavily on advertising work only if access to electronic media, particularly television, is available. In some other countries, access to those media is restricted through time limits imposed by governments. Consequently, companies find it difficult to duplicate their promotional strategies when moving from an unregulated environment to more restricted environments.

Channel length is another major determinant of the feasibility of a pull campaign. Companies in consumer markets often face long channels. As a result, they try to overcome channel inertia by aiming their promotion directly at end users. When a company markets overseas, it may face an even longer channel because local distribution arrangements are different. Such is the case in Japan, where channels tend to be much longer than those in the United States. As a result, a greater reliance on a pull strategy may be advisable or necessary.

Distribution leverage is also different for each company from market to market. Gaining cooperation from local selling points, particularly in the retail sector, may be more difficult than in the domestic market. The fight for shelf space can be very intensive; shelf space in most markets is limited. Under these more competitive situations, reliance on a pull campaign becomes more important. If consumers are demanding the company's product, retailers will make every effort to carry it.

Push strategy a promotional strategy directed at the distributors of a product

In contrast to a pull strategy, a **push strategy** focuses on the distributors of a product rather than on the end user or ultimate buyer. Incentives are offered to wholesalers or retailers to carry and promote a product. A company may have to resort to a push strategy when lack of access to advertising media makes a pull strategy less effective. Limited ability to transfer a pull strategy from a company's home market has other effects on the company's performance in foreign markets. Reduced advertising tends to slow the product adoption process in new markets, forcing the firm to accept slower growth. In markets crowded with existing competitors, newcomers may find it difficult to establish themselves when avenues for pull campaigns are blocked.

WORLD BEAT 14.1

HINDU FESTIVALS ATTRACT MARKETERS

THE HINDU FESTIVAL OF DIWALI is associated with sweets. In India, companies like Cadbury, PepsiCo, and Pantaloon develop special promotions for the festival, which include special gift packs and festival-specific advertising campaigns. In Great Britain, Indian companies, such as Patak's, sponsor parades and musical events targeted at the country's ethnic Indian population.

India has many annual festivals, offering promotion opportunities to global and local marketers. However, the Kumbh Mela festival, which occurs only once every 12 years, set off a promotion war between Coca-Cola and Pepsi in the increasingly important Indian market. This Hindu festival draws 30 million participants to a ritual cleansing at the confluence of the Ganges and Yamuna rivers. Many participants come from rural villages and small towns where 80 percent of India's one billion people live. Many of these potential consumers are beyond the reach of most modern media. Getting them to try a product while at the festival could be the start of potentially extensive word-of-mouth advertising. At the latest Kumbh Mela festival, PepsiCo's Indian unit teamed up with the state tourism department to sell Pepsi at stalls and restaurants in addition to its own 20 exclusive vendors. Rival Coca-Cola was selling at 115 stalls. Coke also had 15,000 posters as well as billboards, banners, and police assistance booths painted red with the famous logo.

Some Indians criticize the commercialization of ancient religious traditions and particularly abhor the role of global marketers. Many nationalist Indians object to foreign products as symbols of economic imperialism. Still, the festival promotions appear to be successful. Car sales rise in India during many religious festivals. It is considered auspicious to purchase expensive items at those times, and car dealers offer attractive purchase plans to further promote this belief. As for the Kumbh Mela festival, after one rural participant treated himself to his fifth bottle of Pepsi in three days, he told Pepsi what the company wanted to hear—*I like it.*

Sources: From Rasul Bailay, "A Hindu Festival Attracts the Faithful and U.S. Marketers," *Wall Street Journal*, February 12, 2001; Ashok Bhattacharjee, "Indian Car Buyers Pause for Breath," *Bloomberg News*, December 14, 2005; "Big Brands Make a Splash as Sweet Prices Soar," Press Trust of India Limited, November 7, 2007; and Rasul Bailay and livemint, "Pantaloon to Launch Its Own Chocolate Brand," June 10, 2008.

Consequently, a company entering a new market may want to consider such situations in its planning and to adjust its expected results accordingly. A company accustomed to a given type of communications mix usually develops an expertise or a distinctive competence in the methods commonly used. When the firm is suddenly faced with a situation in which that competence cannot be fully applied, the risk of failure or underachievement multiplies. Such constraints can even affect entry strategies and the market selection process.

PERSONAL SELLING

Personal selling communication between a potential buyer and a salesperson to the end of understanding buyer needs, matching those needs to the supplier's products or services, and ultimately achieving a sale

Personal selling takes place whenever a customer is met in person by a representative of the marketing company. When doing business globally, companies must meet customers from different countries. These individuals may be used to different business customs and will often speak a different language. That is why personal selling is extremely complex and demands some very special skills on the part of the salesperson.

The complexity of a product usually influences how extensively personal selling is used. The level of complexity has to be compared with the product knowledge of the clients. A company selling the same products abroad as those sold domestically may find that more personal selling is necessary abroad if foreign clients are less sophisticated than domestic clients. A U.S. company may use the same amount of personal selling in Europe as it does in the United States but may need to put forth a greater personal-selling effort in developing countries if the product is new to those markets.

Although very effective as a promotion tool, personal selling requires the intensive use of a sales force and can be costly. Costs vary across countries. In the United States, a typical sales call is estimated to cost in excess of $300. This has motivated some companies to investigate other forms of promotion. Dell Computer considered sales calls to be too expensive in Brazil and instead mailed brochures to potential small-business clients. It took the company over a year to put together a list of names and addresses, because these were not readily available in Brazil. However, the mail campaign was a success in the end.

In this section, we differentiate between **international selling** and local selling. When a company's sales force travels across countries and meets directly with clients abroad, it is practicing international selling. This type of selling requires the special skill of being able to manage within several cultures. Much more often, however, companies engage in **local selling**: They organize and staff a local sales force made up of local nationals to do the selling in only one country. Different problems arise in managing and operating a local sales force than in managing multicountry salespersons.

International selling selling that crosses national boundaries and utilizes salespersons who travel to different countries

Local selling selling that targets a single country

International Selling (Multicountry Sales Force)

The job of the international salesperson seems glamorous. One imagines a professional who frequently travels abroad, visiting a large number of countries and meeting with businesspeople of various backgrounds. However, this type of work is quite demanding and requires a special set of skills.

International salespersons are needed only when companies deal directly with their clients abroad. This is usually the case for industrial equipment or business services but is rarely required for consumer products or services. Consequently, for our purposes, international sales will be described in the context of business-to-business selling.

Purchasing Behavior. In business-to-business selling, one of the most important parts of the job consists of identifying the buying unit in the client company. The buying unit consists of all persons who have input into the buying decision. The seller must locate and access the actual decision makers, who may hold different positions from company to company or from country to country. In different countries, the purchasing manager may have different responsibilities, and engineers may play a greater or a lesser role. Buying decisions are more centralized in many Asian and Latin American firms, and often the owner of the firm will make the final buying decision. Gaining access to top management may not be easy and may cause delays. Even in Europe, the time between a first sales call and a purchase can be 50 percent longer than in the United States. Sales times in Japan can also be longer because of the Japanese emphasis on consensus in the buying unit. The members of the buying unit will want to explore and debate alternatives, while striving for a sense of unity and collegiality among themselves.

Buying Criteria. In addition to different purchasing patterns, the international salesperson may have to deal with different decision criteria or objectives on the part of the purchaser. Buyers or users of industrial products in different countries may expect to maximize different goals. For example, Sealed Air had difficulty convincing businesses in Taiwan to purchase more expensive packaging systems to protect their products during shipping, even though these systems had proved cost-effective in avoiding breakage. Unlike buyers in other markets, Taiwanese manufacturers focused almost exclusively on the purchase price of the packaging.[2]

Language.   Overcoming the language barrier is an especially difficult task for the international salesperson. In Chapter 3, we discussed several issues related to culture and language that can affect international marketing in general and personal selling in particular. Different societies apply different forms of address, use or avoid certain body language, and feel differently about the appropriateness of showing emotion. Certain societies are low-context cultures, wherein the meanings of words are explicit. Other societies are high-context cultures, wherein the meanings of words are implicit and change according to who speaks them as well as when and where they are spoken. It is very difficult for a non-native speaker to become fluent in the language of a high-context culture.

Of course, the personal-selling effort is markedly enhanced if the salesperson speaks the language of the customer, but for many industries, dependence on the local language is not so strong today as it was just one or two decades ago. For many new and highly sophisticated products, such as electronics and aerospace, English is the language spoken by most customers. Consequently, with more and more executives speaking English in many countries, many firms can market their products directly without local intermediaries.

English is widely spoken in Europe, and it is the leading second language in Asia and Latin America. Consequently, the ability to speak a number of foreign languages is less of a necessity. Still, learning a foreign language can be an excellent way to understand a foreign culture, and language proficiency continues to have a very favorable impact on the sales process. Local customers often appreciate a sales representative who speaks their language; it indicates the company's commitment to their market as well as its appreciation of their people and culture.

In industries where knowledge of the local language is important, companies tend to assign sales territories to salespersons on the basis of language skills. A European multinational manufacturer of textile equipment assigns countries to its sales staff according to the languages they speak. This is more important in traditional industries, such as textile manufacturing, where businesses are more local in orientation and where managers may not speak English well.

Even executives who speak English fairly well may not understand all the details of product descriptions or specifications. As a result, a company can make an excellent impression by having its sales brochures translated into some of the key languages. European companies routinely produce company publications in several languages. Translations from English may not be needed for Scandinavia, where English proficiency is common. However, they may be valuable for other parts of the world where the level of English-language skills is not high.

Business Etiquette.   Global marketers selling to many markets are likely to encounter a diverse set of business practices as they move from one country to another. Because interpersonal behavior is intensely culture-bound, this part of the salesperson's job will vary by country. Many differences exist in how an appointment is made, how (and whether) an introduction is made, and in how much lead time is needed for making appointments. Whereas it is acceptable for visitors to arrive late in China, India, or Indonesia, arriving late in Hong Kong is not acceptable. Lateness causes the visitor to "lose face," which is an extremely serious matter among Hong Kong businesspeople. In Switzerland, where punctuality is also highly valued, clients may be favorably impressed if the salesperson arrives 10 or 15 minutes early for an appointment.

The salesperson must also know whether or not gifts are expected or desired. In most Chinese cultures, gift giving is viewed as a sign that the vendor is committed to establishing or sustaining a relationship with the client.[3] Exchanging business gifts is popular in Taiwan but less common in Saudi Arabia. In Switzerland, it is better to wait until the sale is finalized before offering a gift to a client. Even then the gift should not be too expensive, or it may be construed as a bribe and thus give offense. In short, what is expected or tolerated in some markets may be taboo in others.

No manager can be expected to know the business customs of every country, so important information must be obtained from special sources. A company's own foreign market representatives or sales subsidiary can provide key information or suggestions. Also, governments tend to collect data on business practices through their commercial officers posted abroad. Some business service companies, such as global accounting firms or global banks, also provide customers with profiles of business practices in foreign countries.

Foreign businesspersons receiving visitors from the United States or any other foreign country rarely expect the foreign visitor to be familiar with all local customs. However, it is always appreciated when the visitor can exhibit familiarity with the most common practices and some willingness to try to conform. Learning some foreign customs helps to generate goodwill toward the company and can increase the chances of making a sale.

Check out our website (http://www.cengage.com/international) for links to business etiquette sources.

International Sales Negotiations

It is the ultimate job of most sales forces to make a sale. As we mentioned in Chapter 5, negotiations can play an important role in selling, especially to businesses and governments. The terms of a sale—price, delivery terms, and financing options—can all be negotiable. Negotiations in the global arena are complicated because the negotiating partners frequently come from different cultural backgrounds. As a result, misunderstandings or misjudgments can occur among them. To maximize their effectiveness in these often difficult and protracted negotiations, international sales personnel must be attuned to cultural differences. Careful background preparation on the cultural norms prevalent in the foreign country is the starting point in successful negotiations and selling.

For example, the time it takes to negotiate sales can vary between countries. In some countries, such as China, negotiations tend to take much more time than in the United States or some other Western countries. One European company that operated a joint venture in China observed that during one negotiation, two weeks were spent in a discussion that elsewhere might have taken only a few hours. In this situation, much of the time was used for interdepartmental negotiations among the Chinese themselves rather than for face-to-face negotiations with the European company. However, in Pakistan, many international sales negotiations occur between the seller and the client's CEO, or a team including the CEO. Authority is centralized and decisions are relatively quick.[4]

Another difference between cultures is their attitude toward the final negotiated contract. Managers from the United States like to "get it all in writing." Contracts often spell out many contingencies and establish the position of both sides in light of these contingencies. Americans believe that the business relationship will proceed more smoothly if this is all worked out ahead of time. Other cultures consider

Global sales negotiations require cultural sensitivity. Increasingly, both buyers and sellers are exhibiting greater cross-cultural understanding.

this insistence on elaborate written contracts a sign of inflexibility or even lack of trust on the part of Americans. In Brazil, even a written contract may not be regarded as binding but, rather, as open for continued renegotiation. In any case, an understanding of the prevailing cultural attitudes is necessary to successfully negotiate the final sale.

A recent study suggests, however, that these cultural differences toward contracts should not be overemphasized. The study found that business people from relationship-oriented countries, such as Mexico and Turkey, did, in fact, appreciate written contracts, and Americans approved of broad contracts that allowed for good working relationships to develop. This apparent cultural convergence may be the result of increased global marketing.[5]

Local Selling (Single-Country Sales Force)

When a company is able to maintain a local sales force in the countries where it does business, many of the difficulties of bridging the cultural gap with clients are minimized. The local sales force can be expected to understand local customs, and the global company typically gains additional acceptance in the market. This is primarily because local sales forces are usually staffed with local nationals. However, many challenges remain, and managing a local sales force often requires different strategies from those used in running a sales force in the company's domestic market.

Role of Local Sales Force.   For firms that still use distributor sales forces to a large extent, a missionary sales force with limited responsibilities may suffice. A **missionary sales force** concentrates on visiting clients together with the local distributor's sales force. Its focus is on promoting the product rather than distributing the product or even finalizing the sale. If the global company's sales force needs

Missionary sales force salespersons who promote a firm and its products or services but do not close a sale to do the entire job, a much larger sales force will be necessary. The size of the local sales force depends, to a large extent, on the number of clients and the desired frequency of visits. This frequency may differ from country to country, which means that the size of the sales force will differ accordingly.

Control over a firm's sales activities is a frequently cited advantage of operating a company-owned local sales force. With its own sales force, the company can emphasize the products it wants to market at any time and can maintain better control over the way it is represented. In many cases, price negotiations, in the form of discounts or rebates, are handled uniformly rather than leaving these decisions to an independent distributor with different interests. Having a company sales force helps ensure that the personnel have the necessary training and qualifications. Control over all of these parameters usually means higher sales than those achieved with a distributor sales force.

Also, the local sales force can represent an important bridge to the local business community. For industries in which the buying process is local rather than global, the sales force speaks the language of the local customer. It can be expected to understand the local business customs and to bring the international firm closer to its end users. In many instances, local customers, although they may not object to buying from a foreign firm, may prefer to deal with local representatives of that firm.

The role of the local sales force needs to be coordinated with the promotion mix selected for each market. As many companies have learned, advertising and other forms of promotion can be used to make the function of the sales force more efficient. In many consumer-goods industries, companies prefer a pull strategy, concentrating their promotion budget on the final consumer. In such cases, the role of the sales force is restricted to gaining distribution access. However, as we have noted before, there are countries in which access to communications media is severely restricted. As a result, companies may place greater emphasis on a push strategy, relying heavily on the local sales force. This will affect both the role and the size of the firm's sales force.

Furthermore, cultural differences can affect how much time a local sales force must allot to attracting new customers versus retaining current ones. A study comparing buyer-seller relationships in Latin America and the United States concluded that Latin American buyers felt a stronger sense of loyalty to their current suppliers and were more willing to tolerate problems.[6] In such markets, a sales force would need to spend more time and exert more effort to attract new customers away from their current suppliers.

Foreign Sales Practices.   Although sales forces are employed virtually everywhere, the nature of their interaction with the local customer is unique to each market and may affect local sales operations. For most Westerners, Japanese practices seem substantially different. Here is an example reported by Masaaki Imai, president of Cambridge Corporation, a Tokyo management consulting and recruiting firm.

When Bausch & Lomb first introduced its then-new soft-lens line into Japan, the company targeted influential eye doctors in each sales territory for its introductory launch. The firm assumed that once these leading practitioners signed up for the new product, marketing to the majority of eye doctors would be easier. However, a key customer quickly dismissed one salesperson. The doctor said that he thought very highly of Bausch & Lomb equipment but preferred regular lenses for his patients. The salesperson did not even have a chance to respond. He decided, because it was his first visit to this clinic, to wait around for a while. He talked to several assistants at the clinic and to the doctor's wife, who was handling the administration of the practice.

The next morning, the salesperson returned to the clinic and observed that the doctor was very busy. He talked again with the assistants and joined the doctor's wife when she was cooking and talked with her about food. When the couple's young son returned from kindergarten, the salesperson played with him and even went out to buy him a toy. The wife was very pleased with the well-intentioned babysitter. She later explained to the salesperson that her husband had very little time to listen to any sales presentations during the day, so she invited him to come to their home in the evening. The doctor, obviously primed by his wife, received the man very warmly, and they enjoyed *sake* together. The doctor listened patiently to the sales presentation and responded that he did not want to use the soft lenses on his patients right away. However, he suggested that the salesperson try them on his assistants the next day. Therefore, on the third day, the salesperson returned to the clinic and fitted several of the clinic's assistants to soft lenses. The reaction was very favorable, and the doctor placed an order on the third day of the sales call.

Japanese customers often judge whether a company really wants to do business by the frequency of the sales calls they receive. Salespeople who make more frequent calls to a potential customer than the competition makes may be regarded as more sincere. This means that companies doing business in Japan have to make frequent sales calls to their top customers, even if only for courtesy reasons. Although this contact may occasionally be just a telephone call, the need to make frequent visits significantly affects the staffing levels of the company-owned sales force.

Recruiting a Sales Force. Companies have often found recruiting sales professionals quite challenging in many global markets. Although the availability of qualified sales personnel is a problem even in developed countries, the scarcity of skilled personnel is even more acute in developing countries. Global companies, accustomed to having sales staff with certain standard qualifications, may not find it easy to locate the necessary salespeople in a short period of time. One factor that limits their availability in many countries is the local economic situation. A good economic climate will limit the number of people a company can expect to hire away from existing firms unless a substantial increase over their present compensation is offered.

Furthermore, sales positions don't enjoy uniformly high esteem from country to country. Typically, sales as an occupation or career has generally positive associations in the United States. This allows companies to recruit excellent talent, usually fresh from universities, for sales careers. These university recruits often regard sales as a relatively high-paying career or as a path to middle management. Such an image of selling is rare elsewhere in the world. In Europe, many companies continue to find it difficult to recruit university graduates into their sales forces, except in such highly technical fields as computers, where the recruits are typically engineers. When selling is a less desirable occupation, the quality of the sales force may suffer. The time it takes to fill sales positions can be expected to increase dramatically if the company wants to insist on top-quality recruits.

Compensation. In their home markets where they usually employ large sales forces, global companies become accustomed to handling and motivating their sales forces in a given way. In the United States, typical motivation programs include some form of commission or bonus for meeting volume or budget projections, as well as vacation prizes for top performers. When a global company manages local sales forces in various countries, the company must determine the best way to motivate them. Salespersons from different cultures may not all respond the same way. Motivating practices may need to differ from country to country.

Jorge Vergara joined U.S.-based Herbalife when it first entered the Mexican market, and he soon became a star salesman. Then he left to start his own nutritional supplements company, Omnilife. Breaking with Herbalife's sales practices, Mr. Vergara modified his compensation system. Instead of rewarding on the basis of sales volume, he rewarded salespersons who sold consistently. He also paid them every two weeks, which is customary in Latin America, instead of monthly. After only eight years, Omnilife became one of Latin America's largest sellers of nutritional supplements, ahead of both Herbalife and Amway Corporation.[7]

One of the frequently discussed topics in the area of motivating sales-people is the value of the commission or bonus structure. In countries that rate high on uncertainty avoidance, sales representatives may prefer to receive guaranteed salaries. U.S. companies, on the other hand, have tended to use some form of commission structure for their sales forces. Although this may fluctuate from industry to industry, U.S. firms tend to use a more flexible and volume-dependent compensation structure than European firms do. Japanese firms more often use a straight-salary type of compensation. To motivate the sales force to achieve superior performance, the global company may be faced with using different compensation practices depending on local customs.

GLOBAL ACCOUNT MANAGEMENT

Traditionally, account management has been performed on a country-by-country basis. This practice invariably leads, even in large global firms, to a country-specific sales force. However, as we noted in Chapter 5, some companies organize their sales force into global account teams. The **global account team** services an entire customer globally or in all countries where a customer relationship exists. Global account teams may comprise members in different parts of the world, all serving segments of a global account and coordinated through a global account management structure.

Global accounts arose in response to more centralized purchasing within global firms. Companies that purchase similar components, raw materials, or services in many parts of the world realized that by combining the purchasing function and managing it centrally, they could demand better prices and service from suppliers. Today, many companies search the globe for the best buy.

Siemens's Automotive Systems Division has tailored its sales structure to these new realities. The company maintains global account teams for key customers such as Volkswagen and Ford. The teams are in charge of the firm's entire business, regardless of where the components are sourced or used. From the customer's perspective, the advantage stems from the clear designation of a counterpart who will handle all aspects of their business relationship.[8] The system of global account management is also practiced widely in the professional-service sectors. Globally active banks such as Citibank have maintained global account structures for years. Likewise, advertising agencies offer global clients global account management with seamless coordination across many countries. The world's leading accounting

Global account team a team dedicated to servicing a multinational global buyer

firms, such as Deloitte Touche Tohmatsu International, have long-standing traditions of managing international clients from a single unit.[9]

Global account management is greatly enhanced by sophisticated information technology (IT). With members of the team dispersed around the globe, it becomes essential to coordinate all actions meticulously. The development and rapid spread of such tools as videoconferencing and e-mail have greatly extended the reach of a management team beyond the typical one-location office.

Nonetheless, global account management can present challenges to global marketers. A study of 16 large multinational companies revealed that prices quoted to global accounts were more likely to fall than to rise. In 27 percent of cases, prices were assessed as becoming much lower within three years. Although global account management has been shown to be very effective in certain situations, it is a difficult and expensive structure to implement. Because of these concerns, many vendors set clear criteria as to which customers qualify as **worthwhile global accounts**. Potential global accounts may need to meet minimum revenue levels that will support the additional overhead required by global account management. Marriott International requires that potential global accounts purchase over $25 million, annually, in hotel services. While customers often desire to become a global account to obtain volume price discounts, vendors should expect a global account client to differentiate them as a vendor, resulting in increased sales volume.[10]

> **Worthwhile global account** an account that meets minimum revenue levels that support the additional overhead required by global account management

Implementing Successful Global Account Programs[11]

To implement a successful global account program, vendor companies should be as global and as coordinated as their customers—or problems can arise. One firm was surprised to receive a call from a global customer demanding service for a plant in Indonesia. The vendor had no sales or service operation in Indonesia but felt obliged to respond. Someone was flown out from a neighboring country at considerable expense.[12] Senior management commitment is essential. Global customers will expect to meet with senior managers from their key vendors on a regular basis. Top management must also authorize the allocation of essential people and resources to global account teams. This may require moving personnel and resources from countries and regions to a unit located at central headquarters.

Global account management requires a robust IT system. Global IT systems can track the progress of a global account in such areas as orders, back orders, shipments, accounts payable, complaints, and returns. They can also create value for the customer as well as for the vendor. For example, at Marriott International, the global account manager for IBM was able to track IBM's conference cancellations globally. These were costing IBM over one million dollars, annually. Marriott International's account managers created an internal electronic bulletin board for IBM employees to purchase cancelled space, thereby reducing IBM cancellation fees and substantially reducing IBM's cost.

Finally, global account managers must possess special skills. Many national account managers may not have sufficient cross-cultural skills or the broader business acumen required for the job. Required skills of global account managers are more aligned with those of a general manager than a senior salesperson. Global account managers may be called upon to analyze an industry, understand competitive strategies, and identify new ways in which their firm can contribute to a customer's strategy. Many companies with global account management programs will find that additional training may be necessary to managers assigned this task.

SELLING TO BUSINESSES AND GOVERNMENTS

Promotion methods that are oriented largely toward business or government markets can be important to international firms operating in those markets. In particular, the use of international trade fairs, bidding procedures for international projects, and consortium selling all need to be understood in their international context.

International Trade Fairs

Participation in international trade fairs has become an important aspect of business-to-business marketing abroad. Trade fairs are ideal for exposing new customers and potential distributors to a company's product range and have been used extensively by both newcomers and established firms. In the United States, business customers can be reached through a wide range of media, such as specialized magazines with a particular industry focus. In many overseas countries, the markets are too small to allow for the publication of such trade magazines for only one country. As a result, prospective customers usually attend these trade fairs on a regular basis. Trade fairs also offer companies a chance to meet with prospective customers in a less formal atmosphere. For a company that is new to a certain market and does not yet have any established contacts, participating in a trade fair may be the only way to reach potential customers.

There are an estimated 600 trade shows in 70 countries every year. Germany's Hannover Fair is considered the largest industrial fair in the world, attracting approximately 6,000 exhibitors in engineering and technology from over 60 countries. Other large general fairs include the Canton Fair in China and the Milan Fair in Italy. Germany hosts the most trade fairs, drawing in a total of about ten million visitors a year.[13] In addition to general trade fairs, specialized trade fairs concentrate on a certain segment of an industry or user group. Such fairs usually attract limited participation in terms of both exhibitors and visitors. Typically, they are more technical in nature. Some of the specialized trade fairs do not take place every year. One of the leading specialized fairs for the chemical industry is the Achema, which is held in Frankfurt, Germany, every three years. Other specialized fairs that enjoy an international reputation include the air shows of Paris and of Farnborough, England, where aerospace products are displayed.

Participation in trade fairs can save both time and effort for a company that wants to break into a new market and does not yet have any contacts. For new product announcements or demonstrations, the trade fair offers an ideal showcase. Trade fairs are also used by competitors to check out one another's most recent developments. They can give a newcomer an idea of the potential competition in some foreign markets. Consequently, trade fairs are a means of both selling products and gathering important and useful market intelligence. Therefore, marketers with global aspirations will do well to seek out the trade fairs directed at their industry or customer segment and to schedule regular attendance.

International exhibiting may require more planning than is necessary for domestic shows. First, begin planning 12 to 18 months in advance, taking into account the fact that international shipping may involve delays. Second, check show attendance. Many shows allow the general public to attend, in which case you may want to arrange for a private area for meeting with viable prospects. Third, in the United States, a show may be staffed by salespeople and middle managers. At many international shows, however, customers expect to see the CEO and senior management. Finally, use a local distributor, consultant, or sales representative to help with the local logistics and acquaint you with the local culture.[14]

The Paris Air Show is a major trade fair for the aeronautics industry. Established in 1909, it is now more than 100 years old.

Selling Through a Bidding Process

Global marketers of industrial products may become involved in a bidding process, particularly when major capital equipment is involved. Companies competing for such major projects must take a number of steps before negotiations for a specific purchase can begin. Typically, companies actively seek new projects and then move on to prequalify for the particular project(s) they locate before a formal project bid or tender is submitted. Each phase requires careful management and the appropriate allocation of resources.

During the **search phase**, companies want to make sure that they are informed of any project meriting their interest that is related to their product lines. For particularly large projects that are government sponsored, full-page advertisements may appear in leading international newspapers or may be posted on government websites. Companies can also utilize their networks of agents, contacts, or former customers to inform them of any project being considered.

In the **prequalifying phase**, the purchaser frequently asks for documentation from interested companies that wish to make a formal tender. No formal bidding or tender documents are submitted. Instead, the buyer is more interested in general company background and is likely to ask the firm to describe similar projects it has completed in the past. At this stage, the company will have to sell itself and its capabilities. A large number of companies may be expected to pursue prequalification.

In the next phase, the customer selects the companies—usually only three or four—to be invited to submit a **formal bid**. Formal bids consist of a written proposal of how to solve the specific client problem and the price the firm would charge for the project. For industrial equipment, this usually requires personal visits on location, special design of some components, and the preparation of full documentation, including engineering drawings, for the client. The bid preparation costs can

Search phase a phase in the bidding process in which potential suppliers identify projects of interest to them

Prequalifying phase a phase in the bidding process in which prospective buyers ask for documentation from interested suppliers to verify that bidders are trustworthy and capable of handling the proposed project

Formal bid a phase in the bidding process in which a potential supplier states the price it will charge a client for a project and details the terms of the project

be enormous, running as high as several million dollars for some very large projects. The customer will select the winner from among those submitting formal proposals. Rarely is it simply the lowest bidder who obtains the order. Technology, the type of solution proposed, the financing arrangements, and the reputation and experience of the firm all play a role.

Performance bond money supplied by a supplier and held in escrow to guarantee that a buyer will be reimbursed if a project is not completed in accordance with agreed-upon specifications

Once an order is obtained, the supplier company may be expected to insure its own performance. For that purpose, the company may be asked to post a **performance bond**, which is a guarantee that the company will pay certain specified damages to the customer if the job is not completed in accordance with the agreed-upon specifications. Performance bonds are usually issued by banks on behalf of the supplier. The entire process, from finding out about a new prospect until the order is actually in hand, may take from several months to several years, depending on the project size or industry.

Consortium Selling

Consortium a group of firms that participate in a project on a pre–agreed-on basis but act as one company toward the buyer

Turnkey project a project in which the supplier provides the buyer with a complete solution for immediate use, occupation, or operation

Because of the high stakes involved in marketing equipment or large projects, companies frequently band together to form a consortium. A **consortium** is a group of firms that share in a certain contract or project on a pre–agreed-on basis but act as one company toward the customer. Joining together in a consortium can help companies share the risk in some very large projects. A consortium can also enhance the competitiveness of the members if they are involved in turnkey projects. A **turnkey project** is one in which the supplier offers the buyer a complete solution so that the entire operation can commence "at the turn of a key."

Most consortia are formed on an ad hoc basis. For the job of creating a major steel mill, for example, companies supplying individual components might combine into a group and offer a single tender to the customer. The consortium members have agreed to share all marketing costs and can help one another with design and engineering questions. Similarly, a consortium could form to deliver a turnkey hospital to the Saudi Arabian government. This would involve building the physical facilities, installing medical equipment, recruiting doctors, and training staff—among other things. In either case, the customer gets a chance to deal with one supplier only, which substantially simplifies the process. Ad hoc consortia can be formed for very large projects that require unique skills from their members. In situations where the same set of skills or products is in frequent demand, companies may form a permanent consortium. Whenever an appropriate opportunity arises, the consortium members will immediately prepare to qualify for the bidding.

Consortium members frequently come from the same country. However, telecommunications consortia often combine a local firm, whose local connections are of great value, with one or two international telephone operating companies, which offer expertise in running a network. On occasion, these consortia include equipment suppliers that join to ensure that their equipment will be included in any eventual contract.

OTHER FORMS OF PROMOTION

So far, our discussion has focused on personal and industrial selling as key elements of a promotion mix. However, forms of promotion other than selling and advertising can play a key role in marketing. As we discussed in Chapter 13, direct sales is not only a distribution strategy, but a promotion strategy as well, because it involves communicating directly with the consumer. Another form of global promotion is sales promotion, which can include such elements as in-store retail promotions and coupons. Many of these tools are consumer-goods-oriented and are used less often in the marketing of industrial goods. In this section, we look at sales promotions, sports sponsorships, promotional aspects of direct sales, product placements, and management of word of mouth.

Sales Promotion

Sales promotion encompasses marketing activities that generate sales by adding value to products in order to stimulate consumer purchasing and/or channel cooperation. Sales promotions such as coupons, gifts, and various types of reduced-priced labels are used in most countries. In some countries, free goods, double-pack promotions, and in-store displays are also important. Government regulations and different retailing practices, however, tend to limit the options for global firms.

The area of sales promotion is largely local in focus. For example, in Mexico, 85 percent of cement sales are to individuals. Millions of do-it-yourselfers buy bags of cement to build their own homes. Cemex, the market leader in cement sales, sometimes buys food for a block party when a house is finished. And the company's 5,000 distributors can earn points toward vacations by increasing sales.[15]

Couponing—where consumers bring product coupons to a retail store and obtain a reduced price for a product—varies significantly from country to country. In the United States, coupons are the leading form of sales promotion. Coupon distribution is popular and growing in Italy, while in the United Kingdom and Spain, couponing is declining. Couponing is relatively new in Japan, where newspaper coupons were once outlawed.

An example of a sales promotion aimed at distributors is the slotting allowance. This is a payment made to retailers in return for their agreeing to take a new product. A slotting allowance helps compensate them for the time and effort expended in finding a space for the new product on their shelves. As products proliferate, finding shelf space is increasingly difficult, and firms must compete for access to that space. Slotting allowances in Europe's increasingly concentrated supermarket industry have become quite costly. Similarly, slotting allowances are expensive in Saudi Arabia, where shelf space in supermarkets is limited.

Although most sales promotions are relatively short-term, some may continue indefinitely. Promotions that encourage customer loyalty and repeat purchases are being used increasingly worldwide. Loyalty programs, such as frequent-flyer awards, have proliferated in the former Soviet bloc since the 1990s. Not all frequent-flyer programs were well managed. Polish Airlines established three levels of awards and service for frequent flyers (blue, silver, and gold) but actually treated all customers the same. This resulted in customer dissatisfaction with the program and a large defection of frequent flyers to competitor British Airways.[16]

Most countries impose restrictions on some forms of promotions. Games of chance are commonly regulated. Japan, for instance, limits the value of a promotional gift attached to a product to a maximum of 10 percent of the product's price. Japan also restricts the value of prizes awarded through lotteries. In the United States, American Express offered free trips from New York to London as prizes to qualifying customers. The company was unable to offer similar promotions to its Japanese customers, however, because Japan further restricted the values of such awards.

Historically, Germany has been among the most restrictive countries as far as most sales promotions are concerned. Laws enacted in the 1930s drastically restricted the use of discounts, rebates, and free offers that the Nazi government regarded as products of Marxist consumer cooperatives. Only a few years ago, a German court stopped a drugstore from giving away free shopping bags to celebrate the store's birthday. A large retailer was blocked from donating a small sum to AIDS research for each customer transaction using a Visa card. A court declared that this promotion unfairly exploited the emotions of customers.

A European directive on e-commerce finally necessitated the repeal of Germany's 70-year-old laws against promotions. The directive required that the rules of the country in which a vendor was based be applied to promotions throughout the European Union (EU). At the time, fewer than one in ten Germans had ever made a purchase over the Internet. Still, the German government feared that this directive would eventually put German competitors at a disadvantage by preventing them from offering promotions similar to those allowed in neighboring countries. Despite the repeal of the antipromotion laws, a broad law against unfair competition remains on the books in Germany. Some fear that certain competitors could still attempt to use it to block the promotions of others.[17]

Because global firms will encounter a series of regulations and restrictions on promotions that differ among countries, there is little opportunity to standardize sales promotion techniques across many markets. Sales promotion can also be influenced by local culture, as well as by the competitiveness of the marketplace. A study of consumer attitudes regarding sales promotions found significant differences even among Taiwan, Thailand, and Malaysia. The Taiwanese consumer preferred coupons to sweepstakes. The Malaysians and Thais both preferred sweepstakes to coupons.[18] In Europe, McDonald's discovered that children were content with a simple word puzzle on a menu tray or a small stuffed animal and did not require the more expensive Happy Meal promotions that the company used in the United States.[19] This variation among markets has caused most companies to make sales promotions the responsibility of local managers, who are expected to understand the local preferences and restrictions.

Nonetheless, a firm should make certain that there is adequate communication among its subsidiaries to ensure that the best practices and new promotion ideas are disseminated throughout the firm. Sometimes it is even critical to communicate problems associated with promotions so that they will not be repeated in other national markets. A Pepsi promotion in the Philippines that was intended to award $37,000 to one lucky winner fell victim to a computer error that produced thousands of winners. When Pepsi refused to honor the claims of all these winners, 30 Pepsi delivery trucks were burned, and company officials were threatened. Tragically, a woman and child were killed when a grenade tossed at a Pepsi truck rolled into a nearby store.[20]

Sports Promotions and Sponsorships

Major sports events are increasingly being covered by the mass media worldwide. The commercial value of these events has soared over the last decade. Today, large sports events, such as the Olympics and world championships in specific sports, cannot exist in their present form without funding by companies.

For some events, companies can purchase space for signs along the stadiums or arenas where sports events take place. When the event is covered on television, the cameras automatically take in the signs as part of the regular coverage. Aside from purchasing advertising spots or signage space in broadcast programs, individual companies can also engage in sponsorship. Sports sponsorship is common in

AP Images

Soccer's FIFA is increasingly alarmed by "ambushers," such as Chinese fans who showed up at the World Cup in South Korea wearing Samsung caps. Samsung was not an official sponsor of the games, but thanks to the caps, the company enjoyed free publicity from the television coverage of the games.

Europe and the United States, and its popularity is growing fast in certain parts of East Asia, the Middle East, Brazil, and India.[21]

To take advantage of global sports events, a company should have a logo or brand name that is worth exposing to a global audience. It is not surprising to find that the most common sponsors are companies that produce consumer goods with global appeal, such as soft-drink manufacturers, makers of consumer electronics products, and film companies. More recent global players, such as Samsung and Hyundai from Korea, often make extensive use of sports sponsorship abroad, especially in the emerging markets of Africa, East Europe, and Latin America.

A firm must consider the popularity of certain sports. Few sports have global appeal. Baseball and American football have little appeal in Europe or parts of Asia and Africa. However, football (soccer) is the number one spectator sport in much of the world. Nike spends an estimated 40 percent of its global sports advertising budget on soccer. The company entered into a multi-year, $429 million contract to outfit England's Manchester United football club. Nike has also sponsored the national soccer teams of six countries, including Brazil and the United States.

Through the intensive coverage of sports in the news media all over the world, many companies continue to use the sponsorship of sporting events as an important element in their global communications programs. Successful companies must exhibit both flexibility and ingenuity in the selection of available events or participants. In some parts of the world, sports sponsorship may continue to be the only available way to reach large numbers of prospective customers. However, in some cultures, global marketers must beware the backlash associated with a losing team. For example, fans called for a boycott of products such as Pepsi that were endorsed by the Indian cricket team following a humiliating loss against Australia.[22] Chinese fans are also fickle. When their teams lose, they stay at home—to the dismay of sponsors. Consequently, multinational firms in China are increasingly focusing on grass-roots programs. Pepsi sponsors teen soccer, Adidas funds soccer camps, and Nike has started a high school basketball league.[23]

Attempts by competition to hijack sports sponsorships also occur on a regular basis. In addition to its own legitimate sponsorships, Nike has been known to hijack promotion at major global sports events—such as buying up massive billboard space in Olympic cities when the company does not partake in official sponsorship. For the World Cup in 2006, such tactics proved more difficult. FIFA turned to local German courts to protect its marketing rights and asked cities to give preferential treatment to official sponsors when selling billboard space.[24]

WORLD BEAT 14.2

THE OLYMPICS VERSUS THE WORLD CUP

DURING THE OLYMPIC GAMES, teams from over 200 countries compete in almost every imaginable sport, hoping to bring home the gold, silver, or bronze medal. The Seoul Games are credited with transforming Samsung from a regional to a global brand, and Chinese computer giant Lenevo was among the top 12 global firms that spent at least $60 million each to be a sponsor of the Beijing Olympics. Despite a global economic downturn, Adidas, BP, EDF Energy, British Airways, and Lloyds have all signed on for the 2012 Summer Games in London.

The World Cup of football (referred to as soccer in the United States) is one sports event that challenges the Olympics as a promotional platform for global brands. In the United States, soccer does not have the viewership of other major league sports such as baseball, American football, basketball, and hockey, but the United States is not representative of the rest of the world. Football (soccer) reigns as the favorite TV sport in most countries, and the World Cup is a major media event around the world.

Adidas has a global market share of about 34 percent in soccer products. The German firm extended its 40-year relationship with the World Cup, agreeing to sponsor the World Cup in 2010 and 2014. In a deal estimated to cost $350 million, Adidas will also sponsor all Federation Internationale of Football Association (FIFA) tournaments taking place from 2010 to 2014, including the Men's World Cup, the Women's World Cup, and the World Youth Championship—at a cost to the company of $35 million. World Cup sponsors get two on-field advertising boards in all 20 stadiums. MasterCard, which tracks its exposure, receives 10 minutes to 13 minutes of visibility per 90-minute World Cup match, which is seen by billions of spectators worldwide as well as many of the 250 million soccer players.

Both the Olympics and World Cup are plagued by ambush marketers, nonsponsoring brands that pirate an association with the games. There have been around 400 cases of ambush marketing since the technique first emerged at the Los Angeles Olympics in 1984. When Budweiser was the official sponsor for the 2006 World Cup, Dutch fans came to the stadium wearing outfits with the name of rival beer brand Bavaria. Officials asked them to remove the outfits, and the fans were forced to watch the match in their underwear. The incident generated widespread buzz for Bavaria.

Sources: George Frey, "Leadership in Soccer Products Means Profitable World Cup Year in 2010," *Associated Press Newswires*, June 10, 2009; Roger Blitz, "'Ambush Marketing' Threat to 2012 Olympics," *Financial Times*, July 3, 2009, p. 4; Brian Mukisa, "Beware of Ambush Marketers at World Cup," *All Africa*, July 21, 2009; Robert Orr, "Financial Glue that Binds Olympic Rings Holding Firm," *Financial Times*, July 27, 2009; "Slim Pickings for Olympic Sponsors," *South China Morning Post*, July 27, 2009, p. 5; and "Ahead of the Games," *Marketing*, July 29, 2009, p. 14.

Telemarketing, Direct Mail, and Spam

Telemarketing can be used both to solicit sales and to offer enhanced customer service to current and potential customers. To make telemarketing effective, however, an efficient telephone system is required. Telephone sales for individual households may become practical when many subscribers exist and when their telephone numbers can be easily obtained. Because of the language problems involved, companies must make sure their telemarketing sales forces not only speak the language of the local customer but also do so fluently and with the correct local or regional accent.

However, not all countries accept the practice of soliciting business directly at home. A telemarketing directive in the EU allows consumers to place their names on a telephone preference list to eliminate telemarketing calls to their homes. Any firm that continues to call potential customers can be fined. Even so, telemarketing is already big business in Europe; total full-time employment in the field is estimated at more than 1.5 million.

Telemarketing has been intensifying elsewhere as well. In Latin America, growth has been substantial, and call centers have expanded rapidly throughout Brazil. Still, many Brazilians can be more effectively reached by loudspeaker than by telephone. Wal-Mart successfully sent out green vans to roam modest neighborhoods in São Paulo, inviting people, via loudspeaker, to apply for credit cards at the company's Todo Dia stores.[25]

On a global level, telephone sales may be particularly useful for business-to-business marketing. Because costs for overseas travel are considerable, telemarketing across countries or on a global basis may prove very cost-effective. Similarly, the Internet can further decrease customer service costs by allowing firms to respond to customers' requests via e-mail.

Similar to phone campaigns, direct-mail campaigns are largely dependent on good infrastructure. However, creativity and perseverance can sometimes overcome the obstacle of a poor mail delivery system. When the Carsa Group launched its first direct-mail campaign for financial services in Peru, it faced a postal system that was essentially nonexistent. Even using private courier firms was problematic: Such firms were known to broker clients' mailing lists to their competitors. Provincial couriers delivered mail as a sideline to their main business focus, such as fertilizer sales. Nonetheless, the Carsa Group went forward with the campaign, designing its own catalogues and establishing a call center to support the campaign. Response rates topped 26 percent—more than ten times what many U.S. campaigns would consider to be outstanding results. What was the reason for such a high response? In Peru, 69 percent of families received fewer than two pieces of mail monthly, so the impact of the campaign's personalized letters was amazing![26]

With the advent of the Internet, many marketers saw an opportunity to reach many potential customers cheaply and efficiently via e-mail. However, their would-be targets rebelled against unsolicited commercial bulk e-mail, or **spam**. Although some emerging markets, such as those in Asia, have less strict regulations on spam, laws in developing countries discourage it—as do new technologies to block incoming spam. On October 31, 2003, an EU directive went into effect requiring its member states to implement legislation banning unsolicited commercial e-mail without consumer consent or, in some cases, without a prior business relationship. The EU rule covers e-mail, faxes, automated calling systems, and mobile messaging. National governments are allowed to determine enforcement, but

Spam unsolicited commercial bulk e-mail

consumers must be allowed to claim damages.[27] Europe now has stronger privacy laws than the United States. Still, an estimated 53 percent of all e-mail in the EU is unsolicited commercial bulk e-mail. Eighty percent is in English and claims to originate in North America.[28]

Product Placement

Marketers increasingly seek to have their products appear in television shows and motion pictures. Some even pay to have discussions of their products written into scripts that air. However, global marketers are discovering that different cultures and regulatory environments may restrict the international expansion of this practice. For example, a study has shown that Chinese consumers are less accepting of product placements than are Americans.[29] And placement faces tough regulations in the United Kingdom, a society that worries about the blurring between advertising and entertainment. A brand name can be mentioned, but only if it is "editorially justified" in the opinion of the U.K.'s Independent Television Commission, the agency that licenses and regulates commercial television. For example, when Heinz sponsored a cooking series entitled "Dinner Doctors," its name appeared only in the sponsorship credits. No Heinz product could be mentioned or shown anywhere in the content of the show.[30]

Managing Word of Mouth

When importer Piaggio USA wanted to revive stagnant sales of Vespa scooters, it hired extremely attractive young women to pose as motorbike riders and frequent trendy cafés in Los Angeles. The scooter-riding models would then strike up conversations with other patrons at the cafés. When anyone complimented their bikes, they would pull out a notepad and write down the name and phone number of the local Vespa dealer. In Canada, Procter & Gamble promoted Cheer detergent by having brightly outfitted shoppers break into impromptu fashion shows in supermarkets, mentioning to onlookers that their clothes were washed in Cheer. Vodafone Netherlands used Twitter to create a dialogue with consumers and build interest in major product launches. In all three cases, marketers were attempting to catch the attention of potential customers not only to promote a sale but also to get people talking about their product to their friends. This managed word of mouth is called **buzz marketing**.

Buzz can be cheap; there are no national media to buy and no costly price promotions. Instead, product recommendations appear to come from a customer's coolest friends. Still, experts suggest that buzz marketing can backfire if consumers feel it is subversive or if too many companies are trying to do it. Then buzz can become merely annoying.[31]

In an individualistic culture such as that which prevails in the United States and Canada, one's "coolest friend" can conceivably be a person one has just met. In more collectivist cultures, where people are more wary of outsiders, marketers may need to recruit members from each target in-group very carefully to play this role. An unknown actor may not do. In Kaler, a town of three hundred families in rural India, Hyundai reached out to the village headman whose advice is sought on marriage, crops, and, more recently, which TV or car to buy. Says the head-man, "If I tell them I like a particular brand, they'll go out and get it."[32]

Word of mouth is especially crucial to marketing in many Asian cultures. In Japan, the average high school girl sends around 200 cell phone text messages a

Buzz marketing managed word of mouth in which a firm attempts both to promote a sale and to encourage people to talk about the firm's product or service

day. Word of mouth is seen as a key way to reach this market.[33] In fact, six of the top ten markets in which consumers rely most on word of mouth are in Asian countries. These include Hong Kong, Taiwan, Indonesia, India, South Korea, and the Philippines. The other four countries among the top ten are surprisingly disparate—New Zealand, Ireland, Mexico, and the United Arab Emirates.[34]

In China, Mars Inc. used buzz marketing to effectively promote its Snickers candy bar. Because older Chinese considered the candy bar to be too sweet, the company decided to target teenage boys. Mars became a sponsor of the Beijing Olympics and hosted its own outreach events. Among these were the Snickers Street Olympics and Snickers Jump Satisfaction. In the latter event, participants attempted to jump over as many Snickers bars as possible in order to win them. To promote these events to its target market, Mars created buzz on the Internet. For example, online games were linked to the Street Olympics but required four to play. This inspired one participant to reach out to three more. The company was pleased with the results. One manager remarked that teenage boys "flocked to the events like seagulls."[35]

Word of mouth can also be important in business-to-business marketing, where referrals are often crucial. However, there appear to be cultural differences in how managers seek advice concerning potential purchases. A study of U.S. and Japanese corporate buyers of financial services revealed that the Japanese used referral sources—both business and personal—almost twice as often as did U.S. corporate buyers. This supported prior research that suggested that Japanese corporate buyers use a greater variety of referral sources than their American counterparts.[36]

PUBLIC RELATIONS

When Pepsi employees noticed critical Twitter posts concerning a Pepsi ad in a German trade magazine, they notified their company. The ad for diet cola depicted a calorie killing itself. A popular commentator, whose sister had committed suicide, objected to the ad. Pepsi's global director of digital and social media quickly posted an apology.[37]

A company's public relations function consists of marketing activities that enhance brand equity by promoting (or protecting) goodwill toward the organization. In turn, this goodwill can encourage consumers to trust a company and predispose them to buy its products. Tim Horton's is a chain of doughnut and coffee stores across Canada that has successfully fought off the world's largest doughnut chain, Dunkin Donuts Inc. After 30 years in Canada, Dunkin Donuts only captured a 6 percent share of the Canadian market. Among the things that Canadian customers like about Tim Horton's is its charity work operating camps for underprivileged children.[38] In Texas, a market loyal to U.S. vehicles, Japanese automaker Toyota is trying to change consumer attitudes by becoming a major patron of the arts in the city of San Antonio.[39]

Often international marketers find that public relations activities are necessary to defend the reputation of a brand against bad publicity. With millions of Europeans afraid of contracting mad-cow disease by eating beef, McDonald's Corporation began an unusual public relations campaign. Customers were invited to visit the McDonald's meatpacking plant in France, which supplies its 860 restaurants in that country. Touring visitors learned that ground meat was made of 100 percent muscle, not of the nerve tissue that caused the risk of disease.[40]

Public relations campaigns themselves can go wrong. Instead of neutralizing bad publicity, such campaigns can sometimes increase it. In our global society, such gaffes can be heard around the world. Philip Morris's subsidiary in the Czech Republic—in an attempt to bolster goodwill with the Czech government—commissioned a study to show that cigarettes have positive financial benefits to the state. In addition to benefiting from the taxes assessed on cigarette sales, the Philip Morris subsidiary maintained that the state saves a great deal of pension money when a citizen dies prematurely from diseases attributed to smoking. When the press heard of this study, outraged editorials appeared in newspapers around the world.

One of the best-known public relations crises arose from the promotion strategy for baby formula that Nestlé employed in developing countries in the 1970s. Forty years later, the crisis still haunts the firm and its industry. In the 1970s, Nestlé and other producers of baby formula flooded maternity wards in less developed countries with free samples of their products. When new mothers ran out of the samples, they often discovered that their own breast milk had dried up. Few could afford the expensive formula. Some diluted it in an effort to make it last longer, and this sometimes resulted in the death of the baby. Activists organized a global boycott of Nestlé products, and UNICEF, the United Nations agency charged with protecting children, refused to accept cash contributions from the company.

Major formula producers agreed to comply with a voluntary marketing code devised by UNICEF and the World Health Organization that practically forbids any distribution of free formula. But the controversy hasn't stopped there. The companies have always understood this code to apply to less developed countries only, whereas UNICEF has stated that it understands the code to apply to developed countries as well. The controversy has also heated up in the shadow of the AIDS epidemic in Africa. Studies show that about 15 percent of women with HIV in Africa will transmit it to their children through breastfeeding. Nestlé claimed it had received desperate pleas from African hospitals for free formula but was afraid to violate the code. Both Nestlé and Wyeth-Ayerst Laboratories Inc. offered to donate tons of free formula to HIV-infected women in Africa. However, UNICEF

United Colors of Benetton, the Italian clothing company, is one of many global firms that associates itself with charitable causes.

refused to lend its approval because it didn't want to appear to endorse an industry it had long accused of abusive practices.[41]

International marketers often are accused of promoting products that change consumption patterns to the detriment of local cultures. Proactive public relations campaigns can often help to offset this xenophobia. After the United States began bombing raids into Afghanistan in the fall of 2001, Muslim radicals in Indonesia bombed a KFC store. No ill feeling was expressed at a McDonald's franchise in Indonesia that had established goodwill over the years in its surrounding Muslim community by donating food and dining facilities to Islamic institutions.[42] Many international firms become involved in charitable donations involving both money and employees' time. Others offer corporate-sponsored scholarships. Whatever the chosen venue, fostering goodwill for the corporation in local communities plays an increasing role in international promotion strategy.

What aspects of promotion should you consider for your product overseas? Continue with Country Market Report on our website (http://www. cengage.com/ international).

CONCLUSION

Promotion in an international context is particularly challenging because managers are constantly faced with communicating to customers with different cultural backgrounds. This tends to add to the complexity of the communications task, which demands a particular sensitivity to culture, habits, manners, and ethics.

Aside from the cultural differences that affect the content and form of communications, international firms also encounter a different set of cost constraints for the principal elements of the promotion mix, such as selling and advertising. Given such diversity from country to country, international firms have to design their communications carefully to fit each individual market. Furthermore, the availability of any one element cannot be taken for granted. The absence of any one element of the promotion mix, as a consequence of either legal considerations or level of economic development, may force the international firm to compensate with a greater reliance on other promotion tools.

When designing effective sales forces, international marketers need to compare the challenges involved in international selling with those inherent in local selling. International sales efforts can usually be maintained for companies selling highly differentiated and complex products to a clearly defined target market. In most other situations, wherein products are targeted at a broader type of business or at end users, international firms will typically have to engage a local sales force for each market. Local sales forces are usually very effective in reaching their own market or country. Establishing a local sales force and managing it are challenging tasks in most foreign markets and require managers with a special sensitivity to local laws, regulations, and trade practices.

As we saw in Chapter 13, as well as in this chapter, all forms of direct and interactive marketing apply to the international market as well. Many firms have succeeded by adopting U.S.-based or U.S.-originated direct-marketing ideas and using them skillfully abroad. With the international telecommunications infrastructure developing rapidly, the applications for telemarketing as well as Internet-based interactive marketing will expand. These will undoubtedly become important elements of the communications mix for globally active firms large and small.

QUESTIONS FOR DISCUSSION

1. What difficulties could arise if a U.S. salesperson expected to make a sale of industrial equipment during a two-week visit in China?

2. Why do you think many countries restrict the promotional use of sweepstakes and other games of chance?

3. What types of companies would you suggest sponsor the next Olympic Games? How would such firms profit from their association with the Olympic Games?

4. Do you support UNICEF's decision to oppose the donation of baby formula to African hospitals? Why or why not?

Iain Masterton/Alamy

© Imagine/18439GNG

15
Managing Global Advertising

SHORTLY AFTER THE EXXON MOBIL MERGER, the new company, based in Irving, Texas, announced plans to promote its four key brands—Exxon, Mobil, Esso, and General—with a global television advertising campaign.[1]

Global campaigns were not new to the company. Exxon's 1965 Esso tiger campaign, "Put a tiger in your tank," was launched in the United States, Europe, and the Far East.[2] However, the new campaign was aimed at 100 countries at a cost of $150 million. Five hours of film footage were developed centrally to be accessed by the company's various national subsidiaries. Up to six different casts stood by to act out essentially the same story line—with a few variations. The same scene could be shot with a Japanese man, a sub-Saharan African, a Northern European, or a Southern European. Actors varied the hand they used in a scene depicting eating. (In some cultures, food is customarily eaten only with the right hand.) A voice-over told the same story in 25 different languages. Centralized production saved considerable production costs for ExxonMobil and helped ensure that television spots would be consistent and of similar quality around the world. It also meant substantial business for the agency—in this case, Omnicon Group's DDB Worldwide—that landed the job. Not everyone agreed that centralization of advertising was a good idea. The CEO of a rival agency, Bcom3 Group's Leo Burnett Worldwide, noted that brands at different stages around the world require different messages and advertising campaigns.[3]

International marketers face an important question: Should advertising campaigns be local or global? The first part of this chapter is organized around key factors that impact this decision. The chapter continues with a discussion of the major issues relating to media choices and campaign implementation.

GLOBAL VERSUS LOCAL ADVERTISING

Global marketers are among the major advertisers today, as shown in Table 15.1. An important question facing these international firms is whether to standardize or localize advertising across national markets. Standardizing advertising across all markets has received a considerable amount of attention and is considered the most controversial topic in international advertising. One of the best—and earliest—examples of a successful standardized campaign was Philip Morris's Marlboro campaign in Europe. Marlboro's success as a leading brand began in the 1950s, when the brand was repositioned to ensure smokers that the flavor would be unchanged by the effect of the filter. The theme "Come to where the flavor is. Come to Marlboro country" became an immediate success in the United States and abroad. Similarly, Patek Philippe, maker of prestige watches, supported its brand with a standardized television campaign utilizing the theme "You never actually own a Patek Philippe. You merely look after it for the next generation." The campaign has been successful in the United States, Europe, China, Japan, Singapore, and Taiwan.

TABLE 15.1   TOP GLOBAL MARKETERS

RANK	COMPANY	HOME COUNTRY	INDUSTRY TYPE	WORLDWIDE ADVERTISING SPENDING (IN MILLIONS)
1	Procter & Gamble	United States	Cosmetics/Toiletries	$9,358
2	Unilever	United Kingdom	Cosmetics/Toiletries, Food/Beverages	5,295
3	L'Oréal	France	Cosmetics	3,426
4	General Motors	United States	Automotive	3,345
5	Toyota Motor	Japan	Automotive	3,202
6	Ford Motor	United States	Automotive	2,906
7	Johnson & Johnson	United States	Cosmetics/Toiletries	2,361
8	Nestlé	Switzerland	Food/Beverages	2,181
9	Coca-Cola	United States	Food/Beverages	2,177
10	Honda Motor	Japan	Automotive	2,047
11	Time Warner	United States	Publishers, Printers, Engravers	2,022
12	Reckitt Benckiser	United Kingdom	Cosmetics/Toiletries, Food/Beverages	1,983
13	Sony Corp.	Japan	Electronics	1,886
14	Kraft Foods	United States	Food/Beverages	1,853
15	Nissan Motor	Japan	Automotive	1,826
16	GlaxoSmithKline	United Kingdom	Pharmaceuticals/Health Care	1,802
17	McDonald's	United States	Fast Food	1,740
18	Volkswagen	Germany	Automotive	1,729
19	Mars	United States	Food/Beverages	1,708
20	Walt Disney	United States	Broadcasting, Cable, Film/Video	1,677

continued

Table 15.1 continued

RANK	COMPANY	HOME COUNTRY	INDUSTRY TYPE	WORLDWIDE ADVERTISING SPENDING (IN MILLIONS)
21	PepsiCo	United States	Food/Beverages	1,553
22	Chrysler	United States	Automotive	1,319
23	Danone Group	France	Food Processing/Manufacturing	1,306
24	PSA Peugeot Citroen	France	Automotive	1,292
25	General Electric	United States	Lighting/Utilities	1,277
26	Yum Brands	United States	Restaurants	1,238
27	News Corporation	Australia	Holding Company	1,144
28	Maxingvest	Germany	Holding Company	1,076
29	Kellogg	United States	Food/Beverages	1,054
30	Viacom	United States	Broadcasting, Cable, Film/Video	1,002
31	Panasonic	Japan	Electronics	999
32	Colgate-Palmolive	United States	Cosmetics/Toiletries	994
33	Henkel	Germany	Industrial Chemicals	993
34	Pfizer	United States	Pharmaceuticals	918
35	Vodafone Group	United Kingdom	Holding Company	913
36	France Telecom	France	Telecommunications	897
37	Sears Holding Corp.	United States	Holding Company	893
38	Renault	France	Automotive	873
39	Hyundai Motor	Korea	Automotive	848
40	SC Johnson	United States	Cleaning Agents, Cosmetics/Toiletries	843
41	Anheuser-Busch InBev	Belgium	Food/Beverages	829
42	Dell	United States	Computer/Electronics	824
43	Ferrero	Italy	Food/Beverages	820
44	Bayer	Germany	Pharmaceuticals	780
45	Canon	Japan	Computer/Electronics	760
46	Daimler	United States/Germany	Automotive	748
47	General Mills	United States	Food/Beverages	741
48	Wal-Mart Stores	United States	Retail	734
49	Vivendi	France	Media	729
50	Kao	Japan	Industrial Chemicals	719
51	Telefonica	Spain	Telecommunication	700
52	Metro Group	Germany	Retailer	667
53	Samsung Group	Korea	Computer/Electronics	656
54	American International Group	United States	Financial Services	654
55	Microsoft	United States	Computer/Electronics	628
56	Hewlett-Packard	United States	Computers/Electronics	624

continued

Table 15.1 continued

RANK	COMPANY	HOME COUNTRY	INDUSTRY TYPE	WORLDWIDE ADVERTISING SPENDING (IN MILLIONS)
57	Fiat	Italy	Automotive	613
58	Wyeth	United States	Pharmaceuticals/Health Care	610
59	Citigroup	United States	Financial Services	602
60	Suzuki Motor	Japan	Automotive	586
61	LVMH Moet Hennessy Louis Vuitton	France	Luxury goods	584
62	Campbell Soup	United States	Food/Beverages	581
63	IAC/InterActiveCorp	United States	Media	570
64	American Express	United States	Financial Services	565
65	BMW	Germany	Automotive	558
66	Schering-Plough Corp.	United States	Health Care	550
67	Mazda Motor	Japan	Automotive	548
68	Visa International	United States	Financial Services	543
69	Novartis	Switzerland	Pharmaceuticals/Health Care	518
70	Clorox	United States	Cleaning Agents	508
71	Kia Motors	Korea	Automotive	499
72	Nintendo	Japan	Games	494
73	Kimberly-Clark	United States	Paper, Packaging/Container	478
74	Mattel	United States	Games/Toys	466
75	Carrefour	France	Retailer	462

Source: Data collected from "Top 100 Global Marketers," *Advertising Age*, December 8, 2008, pp. 4–6.

Standardized campaigns have increased over the years. Most studies of international advertising standardization in the 1970s and 1980s concluded that very little standardization was being used. However, a later study of 38 multinationals revealed that about half of these companies employed extensive or total standardization when developing and executing their global advertising. Only a quarter stated that standardization was very limited or nonexistent.[4] Thus, there appears to be a trend toward more standardization. Still, many marketing executives remain skeptical of the value of global advertising campaigns, and trends can reverse themselves. For example, Coca-Cola abandoned a more standardized approach to advertising in India and now creates advertisements for the market that are made in India and tailor-made for Indian consumers.[5]

DEVELOPING GLOBAL CAMPAIGNS

Of course, firms do not need to choose solely between totally standardized worldwide campaigns and totally localized ones. Similar to developing global products, many firms adopt a modularized approach to global advertising: A company may select some features as standard for all its advertisements while localizing other features. Most common is the **global theme approach**, wherein the same advertising

Global theme approach the use of an advertising campaign in which a single advertising theme is utilized in all markets but is varied slightly with each local execution

theme is used around the world but is varied slightly with each local execution. Coke's global campaign featuring "Coke Moments" was developed and shot in a number of the brand's top markets, including Brazil, Germany, Italy, France, and South Africa, as well as the United States. In "Spanish Wedding," a demure young woman enjoys a Coke while dressing for the big day.[6] Furthermore, if a global campaign is not appropriate, a regional one might be.

When developing global (or regional) campaigns, a company should follow procedures that are similar to those utilized in developing global products. In other words, local adaptation should not be an afterthought. Input should be sought early from markets where the campaign will ultimately air and should be incorporated into the design of the campaign. This ensures that a message will indeed be appropriate for each market and that the media necessary for the campaign will be available. It also identifies what adaptations need to be made and usually shortens the time of making such adaptations.

For example, standardized campaigns launched by automaker Fiat were originally developed in Italy and adapted with minor changes (such as translation) by local agencies in different national markets. Subsequently, the company allied with Publicis Groupe to establish a Fiat-specific advertising agency for all of Europe that would create pan-European campaigns. A key mandate for the new agency was to seek input early in the development of campaigns to determine if a marketing message could use a single campaign across Europe or whether it required different campaigns for different markets.[7]

Two advertisements—one in English and the other in Spanish—promote Armstrong flooring and point potential buyers to the company's website. Different decors reflect the different cultures.

THE GLOBAL-LOCAL DECISION

A number of cost, market, regulatory, and cultural factors influence the extent to which advertising can be standardized.

Cost Savings

One advantage of a more standardized approach to advertising involves the economics of a global campaign. To develop individual campaigns in many countries is to incur duplicate costs such as those for photographs, layouts, and the production of television commercials. In a standardized approach, these production costs can be reduced, and more funds can be spent on purchasing media space.

Branding

In Chapter 11, we discussed the increased interest in global branding by multinational firms. Many companies market products under a single brand name globally or regionally. With the substantial amount of international travel occurring today, and the considerable overlap in media across national borders, companies are increasingly interested in creating a single brand image. This image can become confused if local campaigns are in conflict with each other. The following list shows some examples of companies' efforts to create a single brand image:

- H.J. Heinz developed a global campaign for Heinz ketchup to develop consistency in the brand image and advertising across its various national markets.[8]
- Jaguar found that its new S-type model appealed to similar customers around the world, so it launched the same campaign from "Chicago to Riyadh, Tokyo, and Berlin." This allowed Jaguar to enjoy a consistent image worldwide and save money by not having to develop a different theme for each market.[9]
- Disney embarked on its first global advertising campaign for its theme parks. Previously, the company advertised each park regionally. Now, Disney wants to address travelers worldwide and pull them into any Disney theme park anywhere.[10]

Target Market

Global campaigns may be more successful if the target market is relatively narrowly defined. For example, Procter & Gamble doubled the sales of Pringles potato chips in four years to $1 billion. Now one of P&G's top three global brands, Pringles is sold in over 40 countries. P&G attributes the global success of Pringles to a uniform advertising message aimed at young children and teens. The message used around the world is "Once you pop you can't stop." Although P&G allows some local differences in product market-to-market, such as flavor variations, the bulk of the advertising is standardized.[11]

Market Conditions

While cost savings, global branding, and focused target markets argue for more standardized advertising, varying market conditions may limit the utility of standardization.

Stage in Life Cycle. Because products may be at different stages of their product life cycles in different countries, different types of advertising may be necessary to take into account the various levels of customer awareness. Typically, a campaign during the earlier stages of the product life cycle concentrates on familiarizing people with the product category because many prospective customers may not have heard about it. In later stages, with more intensive competition, campaigns tend to shift toward emphasizing the product's advantages over competitors' products. Sometimes Frito-Lay's products are so unfamiliar in certain overseas markets that advertising campaigns focus on educating consumers with the goal of changing their consumption habits. For example, Chinese ads showed potatoes actually being sliced so people knew where potato chips came from. In Turkey, Frito-Lay distributed pamphlets suggesting new recipes and eating habits: "Try a tuna sandwich for lunch, and join it with a bag of chips."[12]

Similarly, when Procter & Gamble entered the Chinese market, it employed utilitarian ads such as ones that showed consumers the right way to wash their hair. However, as consumers became more sophisticated and needed less instruction, P&G changed the focus of their advertisments from instruction to evoking positive emotions towards their products.[13]

Perception of Product.   Products may also face unique challenges in certain markets requiring nationally tailored advertising campaigns. For example, Skoda automobiles are sold throughout Europe and in parts of Asia and Latin America. But in Britain, they acquired a deplorable reputation. In a consumer survey, 60 percent of respondents said they would never consider buying a Skoda—even after

WORLD BEAT 15.1

ADS THAT ALIENATE

CROSS-CULTURAL ADVERTISING carries the risk of alienating potential consumers who find a certain ad offensive. The more consumers dislike ads, the more likely they are to reject the product or brand. Even issues that seem, at first glance, to be innocuous can give global marketers sleepless nights. For example, Volvo worried that a new global advertising campaign stressing having fun with the family would alienate its traditional buyers who associated the brand with safety.

Cross-cultural differences in what is acceptable and what is not acceptable especially plague global advertising. Pepsi tried unsuccessfully to break with convention in Japan with its Pepsi Challenge advertising campaign in which it compared itself favorably to Coke. The country wasn't used to comparative advertising and continues to reject it to this day. After developing a successful U.S. campaign in which hip Mac foiled nerdy PC, Apple

Computer struggled to take the campaign overseas. The scrappy underdog image developed for PC in the U.S. market made him appear to lack class in Japan. For the Japanese audience Apple had to show PC more respect, dressing him in proper office attire and not clothes that made him look silly. Even in England, the Mac versus PC campaign fell flat. As one commentator noted, PC appeared to be rubbish but loveable, while Mac appeared to be smug and pretentious.

Of course, some ads alienate government authorities. One Pepsi advertisement portrayed boisterous young people drinking Pepsi and playing music in the courtyard of an apartment building. After tenants complained, the Pepsi drinkers responded by cranking up the music. Russia's watchdog agency that oversees advertising ordered the ad off the air, citing a law against advertisements that advocate violence and cruelty.

Sources: Geoffrey A. Fowler, Brian Steinberg, and Aaron O. Patrick, "Mac and PC's Overseas Adventures," *Wall Street Journal*, March 1, 2007, p. B1; Stephanie Kang, "Volvo Is Steering Gingerly to Seem Safe and Sexy," *Wall Street Journal*, August 30, 2007, p. B2; Jason Bush, "Wooing the Next Pepski Generation," *BusinessWeek*, October 29, 2007, pp. 74–75; and Kara Chan, Lyann Li, Sandra Diehl, and Ralf Terlutter, "Consumers' Response to Offensive Advertising: A Cross Cultural Study," *International Marketing Review*, vol. 24 no. 5 (2007), pp. 606–628.

Volkswagen AG bought the Czech car company and vastly improved the models. The solution was an ad campaign exploiting British humor and Skoda's position as the butt of many jokes. Each self-deprecating advertisement ended with "It's a Skoda. Honest." This very successful campaign improved the acceptance of the car in the British market.[14]

Regulatory Environment

In many instances, the particular regulations of a country prevent firms from using standardized approaches to advertising even when these would appear desirable. Malaysia, a country with a large Muslim population, has prohibited ads showing women in sleeveless dresses and pictures showing underarms. Malaysia also bans all profanity from television broadcasts. Television shows are subject to review by the country's Censorship Board. Events that are broadcast live, such as the World Cup, are aired with a few minutes delay in order to accommodate the censor.[15] In some European countries, candy advertisements must show a toothbrush symbol.

In China, advertising is subjected to substantial scrutiny and regulation. All outdoor advertisements have to be approved by multiple government organizations.[16] Superlative adjectives such as "best quality" and "finest ingredients" are banned. Television advertisements for "offensive products" such as hemorrhoid medications and athlete's foot ointments cannot be aired during the three daily meal times.[17] Children portrayed in commercials are required to show respect for their elders, and children's advertisement should not attempt to instill a sense of superiority for owning a certain product. And Chinese regulations can change practically overnight. In preparation for the Beijing Olympics, authorities began to remove or cover up billboards across the city, including those along the road leading to Beijing's international airport. Officials declared the ubiquitous billboards an eyesore, but advertisers and their advertising agencies were shocked by the unanticipated move.[18]

Certain industries face more regulation than others. Differing national rules govern the advertising of pharmaceuticals, alcohol, and financial services. Advertising for cigarettes and tobacco products is strictly regulated in many countries. The European Union (EU) banned all advertising of tobacco on billboards and in print advertising. One of the few areas where cigarette and tobacco advertising is still relatively restriction free is Central Asia and the Caucasus, formerly part of the Soviet Union. Most of these countries permit cigarette advertising on radio and television, although some relegate it to late-night slots. Such freedoms, however, are rare, and global marketers are well advised to check the local regulations carefully before launching any type of advertising campaign. A stunt pilot was arrested in Lithuania for illegally advertising cigarettes during his maneuvers. The national parliament had just recently banned tobacco ads.[19]

Currently, the EU is cracking down on health benefit claims in the advertisements for various food products. After examining the first 43 health claims out of an estimated 4,000, the European Food and Safety Authority determined that only 9 were valid. Not surprisingly, industry experts consider the EU's rules to be the most stringent in the world.[20]

Cultural Differences

Cultural differences can also restrict the use of standardized advertising. Taco Bell, a U.S.-based chain with 7,000 restaurants, found that Gidget, the talking Chihuahua dog used in advertisements in the United States, could not be used in Asia, where many consider dogs a food delicacy, or in Muslim countries, where many consider it taboo to even touch a dog. When Coty Inc. ran an ad aimed at the Middle East market for its Jennifer Lopez perfume, it placed the ad in the newly launched Middle East edition of *Elle*. But the ad, adapted for regional sensitvities, only showed the singer's face instead of her signature curvy silhouette, which ran in the original ad.[21] Cultural differences also stymied Western advertisers when they first entered Eastern Europe. One Western food company wanted to introduce bouillon cubes to Romania via ads featuring a happy family gathered around the dinner table. The campaign had to be changed because Romanian consumers were not familiar with the family dinner concept.[22]

Even if nudity in advertising is not prohibited by law, it can be controversial in many cultures. Sara Lee, the U.S.-based firm that owns such lingerie brands as Playtex, Cacharel, and Wonderbra, faced intense opposition to a series of billboards in Mexico. The company launched its global Wonderbra campaign, which, as part of its outdoor advertising, featured a Czech model posing in the bra. In several Mexican cities, citizens protested the ads as offensive. The company redesigned its billboards for Mexico, clothing the model in a suit.

Land of the Soft Sell: Advertising in the Japanese Market. Japan is the world's second-largest advertising market, after the United States.[23] However, many Western firms face special challenges when developing advertising themes for this important market. The dominant style of advertising in Japan is an image-oriented approach, or "soft sell." This contrasts sharply with the more factual approach, or "hard sell," typical in the United States and with the use of humor prevalent in the United Kingdom.

In Japan, as in many other Asian cultures, consumers tend to be moved more by emotion than by logic in advertisements, in contrast to North Americans or Europeans. Consequently, consumers need to be emotionally convinced about a product. This leads to advertising that rarely mentions price, shies away from comparative advertising aimed at discrediting the products of competing firms, and occasionally even omits the distinctive features or qualities of a product. According to some experts, Western advertising is designed to make the product look superior, whereas Japanese advertising is designed to make it look desirable. The Japanese language even has a separate verb to describe the process of being convinced to buy a product contrary to one's own rational judgment.

Nonetheless, the Japanese are interested in foreign countries and words, particularly those of the English language. Research conducted for the Nikkei Advertising Research Institute in Japan compared the number of foreign words appearing in advertising headlines. Japan, with 39.2 percent, used the highest number of foreign words, followed by Taiwan with 32.1 percent, Korea with 15.7 percent, and France with 9.1 percent. The United States used foreign words in only 1.8 percent of the headlines investigated.[24]

Japanese television commercials are full of U.S. themes. They frequently incorporate U.S. landscapes or backgrounds and often employ U.S. celebrities. Stars such as Meg Ryan, Brad Pitt, and Demi Moore can be seen in commercials featuring cosmetics, clothing, or drinks.[25] By using American actors in their commercials, Japanese companies give the impression that these products are very popular in the United States. Thanks to the Japanese interest in and positive attitudes toward many U.S. cultural themes, such strategies have worked out well for advertisers.

Credibility of Advertising.   English secondary schools teach students how to be "responsible consumers." Among other things, the required curriculum encourages students to criticize corporate advertising.[26]

In addition to other cultural differences among markets, there are national differences as to the credibility of advertising. A comparative survey conducted by a marketing research company investigated advertising credibility in 40 countries.[27] In the United States, 86 percent of consumers were eager to criticize advertising practices, particularly those aimed at children, whereas 75 percent of consumers praised advertising's creativity. In Asia, consumers were more positive. Forty-seven percent indicated that advertisements provided good product information, and 40 percent said that advertisers respected consumers' intelligence. Globally, the results were 38 percent and 30 percent, respectively.

Consumers in the former Soviet Union were among the most skeptical. Only 9 percent of consumers there believed that advertising provided good information, and only 10 percent said it respected consumers' intelligence. Globally, 61 percent of consumers appreciated advertising for both its creativity and its entertainment value, but only 23 percent of consumers living in the former Soviet Union agreed. Another study that examined attitudes toward online advertising in Romania revealed similar results. Romanian consumers found online advertising to be fun and interesting, but they had doubts about its credibility.[28]

Differences in the credibility of advertising in general, and in that of some media in particular, must be taken into consideration by the international firm. Companies may want to place greater reliance on advertising in countries where its credibility is very high. In other countries, the marketer should think seriously about using alternative forms of communication.

Addressing Cultural Differences.   Global firms can take a proactive approach to cultural differences when employing the global theme approach. In a major rebranding campaign for the Mars candy bar, outdoor billboards ran phrases aimed to trigger feelings of pleasure in local audiences. In Britain, the slogan ran "Saturday, 3 p.m.," referring to the much-anticipated soccer kickoff time. In France, the word "August" evoked the month when the whole country traditionally goes on vacation. In Germany, the words "the last parking space" were chosen for their particular national appeal.[29]

Another way to address the cultural challenges facing multinational advertising campaigns is to consider limiting such campaigns to countries within a single region of the world that share a single culture. A study of advertisements in Egypt, Lebanon, and the United Arab Emirates suggests that this might be possible. However, marketers should remember that countries that share some cultural attributes can differ on others. For example, literacy rates vary considerably within the Middle East, and this in turn can impact how products and services are advertised.[30]

To ensure that a message is in line with the existing cultural beliefs of the target market, companies can turn to a variety of resources. Local subsidiary personnel or local distributors can judge the cultural content and acceptability of the message. Advertising agencies with local offices can be helpful as well. Whether considering a local, regional, or a global approach, it is the responsibility of the international marketer to make sure that knowledgeable local nationals have enough input so that the mistake of using an inappropriate appeal in any given market can be avoided.

OVERCOMING LANGUAGE BARRIERS

Even when employing global campaigns, the proper translation of advertisements remains a major cultural challenge to global marketers. Even among English-speaking peoples, common words can vary, as Table 15.2 illustrates. Most translation blunders that plagued global advertising in the past were the result of literal translations performed outside the target country. Today, faulty translations can be avoided by enlisting local nationals or language experts. Global marketers typically have translations checked by a local advertising agency, by their own local subsidiary, or by an independent distributor located in the target country.

These same rules apply when translations are needed within a single country or regional market to reach consumers who speak different languages. When the California Milk Processor Board decided to translate its popular "Got milk?" campaign into Spanish, an adwoman who had moved to Los Angeles from Caracas, Venezuela, warned the board members that the slogan took on the meaning "Are you lactating?" in Spanish. The board wisely decided to adapt the campaign to ask, "And you, have you given them milk today?"[31]

In the EU, many advertisers emphasize visual communication rather than attempting to communicate their message through the region's various languages. Visual ads that incorporate pictures rather than words can be more universally understood. Visuals have the advantage of being less culture specific. For example, Cartier, the French luxury products firm, launched a campaign in 123 countries. The campaign used magazines only and featured minimal copy (words). It emphasized dramatic photography so that the same message could be conveyed in Brazil, Japan, Russia, and dozens of other countries.

Still, some managers of global brands are rethinking the power of local language. The Welsh Language Board encourages the use of the traditional language of Wales in advertisements. Although in decline through most of the 20th century, Welsh is enjoying a renaissance, and today it is spoken by half a million people in Britain. Consequently, Coke agreed to use Welsh in bilingual posters.[32]

TABLE 15.2 ENGLISH VERSUS ENGLISH

AMERICAN DIALECT	BRITISH DIALECT	AMERICAN DIALECT	BRITISH DIALECT
Apartment	Flat	Make a decision	Take a decision
Appetizer	Starter	Pantyhose	Tights
Attic	Loft	Paper towel	Kitchen towel
Baby carriage	Pram	To rent	To let
Car trunk	Boot	Realtor	Estate agent
College	University	Stove	Cooker
Commercial	Advert	Sweater	Jumper
Cookie	Biscuit	Washcloth	Flannel
Doctor's office	Surgery	Yard	Garden

GLOBAL MEDIA STRATEGY

As noted earlier, global marketers today account for major purchases of media space. A variety of media are available across the world. Still, difficulties arise because not all media are available in all countries. And if they are available, their technical capability to deliver a message to the required audience may be limited. Therefore, global marketers must consider the availability of various media for advertisers as well as the media habits of the target country.

Global Media

Marketers sometimes have the option of employing global media. Global television includes news networks, such as BBC World and CNN, and consumer channels, such as Animal Planet, Discovery, ESPN, and MTV. However, the global print media consist largely of magazines targeted at business executives, such as *Business-Week*, *The Economist*, *Fortune*, and *Time*, along with only a few consumer magazines, such as *Cosmopolitan* and *Elle*.[33] Nonetheless, these magazines can be particularly attractive for promoting global brands. A study of advertisements in national editions of *Cosmopolitan* appearing in Brazil, China, France, India, Korea, Thailand, and the United States revealed that there were more multinational product ads than domestic ones in every country except India.[34]

Satellite television channels, which are not subject to government regulations, have revolutionized television in many parts of the world. English is the common language of the majority of satellite channels. However, there is a trend toward local-language satellite broadcasts. Satellite channels are now available in several languages, such as Arabic, German, French, and Swedish.

SABAH ARAR/AFP/Getty Images

Global magazines such as *BusinessWeek*, *The Economist*, *Cosmopolitan*, and *Elle* reach literate urban consumers in different countries throughout the world.

One of the most successful global satellite ventures is MTV. This music channel, which was launched in the United States 30 years ago, now reaches about one billion people in 18 different languages and in more than 164 countries, with 80 percent of viewers living outside the United States.[35] McDonald's strategy of engaging MTV globally in some 160 countries was aimed at taking advantage of its global reach and the young audience attracted everywhere. As a result, McDonald's became the sole sponsor of MTV Advance Warning, a program focused on new musical talent and MTV's first truly global program.[36]

Local Media Availability

Advertiser's spending on media (or "adspend") varies by country, as shown in Table 15.3. Advertisers in the United States and many European countries have become accustomed to the availability of a full range of local media for advertising purposes. Aside from the traditional print media, consisting of newspapers and magazines, the U.S. advertiser has access to radio, television, billboards, cinemas,

TABLE 15.3 TOTAL ADSPEND IN SELECTED COUNTRIES

COUNTRY	ADSPEND IN MILLIONS	ADSPEND PER CAPITA	COUNTRY	ADSPEND IN MILLIONS	ADSPEND PER CAPITA
China	$18,388.3	$13.9	Columbia	$2,001.5	$42.8
India	6,215.2	5.3	Mexico	4,771.3	44.3
Indonesia	2,844.4	12.1	Venezuela	688.5	24.8
Japan	45,034.6	352.7	Egypt	1,193.3	15.8
Malaysia	1,594.6	57.7	Israel	1,062.3	145.8
Pakistan	270.1	1.6	Kenya	111.7	2.9
Philippines	4,609.6	51.1	Nigeria	88.5	0.6
Singapore	1,438.1	310.0	Saudi Arabia	1,273.0	50.3
South Korea	8,581.0	176.5	South Africa	3,981.3	81.5
Taiwan	1,607.0	70.0	United Arab Emirates	1,702.0	378.0
Thailand	3,285.0	51.1	Canada	10,999.6	330.6
Vietnam	572.3	6.6	USA	187,760.8	616.7
Australia	9,125.9	428.4	France	18,036.3	292.0
Czech Republic	3,508.2	340.1	Germany	26,157.7	318.2
Hungary	3,421.1	340.8	Italy	13,167.5	223.3
Poland	2,718.0	71.4	Norway	4,660.1	991.2
Russia	9,464.2	66.6	Spain	11,688.6	259.4
Ukraine	1,116.9	24.2	Sweden	2,938.0	320.8
Argentina	1,951.3	48.9	Turkey	2,787.0	37.5
Brazil	9,105.4	46.9	United Kingdom	23,452.4	384.4
Chile	1,138.8	67.8			

Source: Selected data from Global Market Information Database, 2008, Euromonitor International. © 2008. Euromonitor International. Reprinted with permission.

and the Internet. In addition, direct mail can be used with most prospective client groups. This wide choice among media may not be available in every country, particularly in rural regions. Therefore, a company marketing its products in several countries may find itself unable to apply the same media mix in all markets. Even when certain media are available, access may be partially restricted. In some countries, public and private television channels may devote no more than a small percentage of their airtime to advertising.

Across regions, global firms often employ different media mixes for their advertising. These differences in global advertising spending partially reflect different media availability. In light of media differences, as well as market differences, global managers must remain flexible in crafting their media plans. A company cannot expect to use its preferred medium to the fullest extent everywhere. Consequently, global advertising campaigns must be flexible enough to adapt to local situations. For example, when international insurers entered India's life insurance market, they estimated that only a quarter of the market had been tapped. As a result, advertisements explaining the benefits of life insurance proliferated. The ubiquitous ads appeared on billboards, in newspapers, on colorful websites, and on posters decorating kiosks.[37]

Media Habits

Adspend by media category varies by country, as shown in Table 15.4. The choice between using one medium or another is affected not only by availability and market penetration of various media, but also by the media habit of the national population or the target market in particular. Besides being concerned with media availability, international marketers must also consider media habits in different national markets. Substantial differences in media habits exist worldwide. Different cultures may favor one medium over another, regardless of media penetration. Accurate data concerning media usage may be unavailable in many developing countries, thus adding to the challenge of choosing national media and planning global campaigns.

The ownership or usage of television and radio can vary considerably from one country to another. The readership of print media (newspapers and magazines) varies as well and is influenced by the literacy of a country's population. Although national literacy levels are less of a concern for companies in the industrial products market, they can be a crucial factor in consumer goods advertising. In countries where large portions of the population are illiterate, the use of print media is of limited value. Both radio and television have been used by companies to circumvent the literacy problem. However, these media cannot be used in areas where the penetration of receivers is limited.

The developed industrial nations show high penetration ratios for all the major media carriers. However, media availability is becoming increasingly similar across regions. For example, the number of Internet users in North America and South America significantly converged between 2003 and 2009, resulting in about 260 million users in North America and about 200 million users in South America.[38] This has spurred the use of banner advertising and brand sponsored online games as a way to try to reach literate, online consumers in many different countries. In some countries, such as Korea, many young consumers now spend considerable time online and little time watching television.[39] This phenomenon has been observed in China as well. As a result, adspend in these countries is shifting from the older media to the newer.

TABLE 15.4   PERCENTAGE ADSPEND OF MAJOR MEDIA FOR SELECTED COUNTRIES

COUNTRY	TV	RADIO	PRINT	CINEMA	OUTDOOR	ONLINE
Argentina	48.7	2.5	37.0	1.3	8.0	2.5
Australia	29.7	9.6	43.0	0.8	4.0	13.0
Brazil	65.5	4.4	23.9	n.a.	4.5	1.8
Canada	30.0	13.1	39.4	0.0	3.5	14.0
Chile	55.7	6.4	28.7	0.3	7.3	1.6
China	39.5	6.5	31.8	0.0	13.7	8.5
Czech Republic	47.1	4.9	37.6	0.4	5.0	4.9
Egypt	35.9	6.7	57.1	0.3	0.0	n.a.
France	36.1	7.7	36.0	1.2	11.8	7.1
Germany	24.4	4.0	62.6	0.5	4.6	3.9
India	44.9	1.6	46.7	1.2	4.3	1.3
Indonesia	60.1	1.6	34.5	0.2	3.5	0.2
Italy	52.1	6.9	33.7	0.7	3.5	3.0
Japan	43.0	3.5	29.9	n.a.	8.9	14.6
Kenya	28.4	36.9	33.7	1.0	n.a.	n.a.
Malaysia	37.5	4.2	53.8	0.5	4.0	n.a.
Mexico	68.4	9.7	21.9	n.a.	n.a.	n.a.
Nigeria	14.3	0.7	80.6	0.0	4.5	n.a.
Pakistan	43.9	2.4	35.7	0.2	17.4	0.4
Poland	51.6	8.1	26.1	1.0	8.3	4.9
Russia	50.5	5.1	23.5	1.0	18.2	1.8
Saudi Arabia	6.0	2.5	66.4	n.a.	14.4	10.7
South Africa	49.3	11.8	33.0	0.8	4.3	0.7
South Korea	33.4	2.6	42.8	1.0	7.7	12.5
Sweden	22.6	2.9	57.2	0.4	5.8	11.0
Taiwan	34.3	9.2	39.9	n.a.	8.5	8.1
Turkey	53.4	3.5	24.4	1.2	6.2	1.2
United Arab Emirates	1.5	0.8	83.7	1.1	10.4	2.5
USA	32.8	11.6	43.5	0.3	3.8	8.0
United Kingdom	25.5	3.7	42.4	1.3	6.7	20.4
Venezuela	59.3	3.7	20.0	6.6	10.4	n.a.
Vietnam	72.3	0.2	22.2	0.0	5.2	0.1

n.a. = not available

Source: Selected data from Global Market Information Database, 2008, Euromonitor International. © 2008. Euromonitor International. Reprinted with permission.

WORLD BEAT 15.2

CHINA'S INTERNET ADS

EVEN CHINA'S BOOMING ECONOMY WAS HIT HARD by the global recession. This inspired marketing managers and ad agency executives to seek cheaper media outlets for advertising to the Chinese market. As a result, Nielsen Company estimates that online advertising in China grew an astounding 42 percent in a single year. Brands are also exploring unique ways to collaborate with Chinese web platforms. Although Coca-Cola still buys expensive air time on China's national television, the company also ran an Internet campaign for Coke Zero. The campaign asked users of a major social networking site to submit photos to show why they deserved to be the next James Bond. Winners received a day living like James Bond, paid for by Coca-Cola.

The new media is especially important for reaching China's young consumers who spend lots of time on the Internet and little time watching television. To this end, Estee Lauder's Clinique brand developed a 40-episode digital sitcom about a Shanghai college student to promote its cosmetics. Viewers could blog posts or send text messages stating what they thought about the challenges faced by the heroine. In three months, the series attracted more than 20 million views.

With car sales down in many major markets, automobile companies look to the growing Chinese market to support global sales. When buying a car, word of mouth is important in China, but many car buyers are the first among their family and friends to buy a car. Therefore, they look to the Internet as a key source of information. Shanghai GM increased its Internet advertising to 10 percent of total ad spending and expects to further increase its presence on social networking sites.

Sources: Geoffrey A. Fowler, "Marketers Flock to China's Biggest TV Network," *Wall Street Journal*, November 20, 2008, p. B8; Loretta Chao, "Online Advertising Gets Boost in China," *Wall Street Journal*, December 11, 2008, p. B6; Mei Fong, "Clinique, Sony Star in Web Sitcom," *Wall Street Journal*, March 27, 2009, p. B4; and Juliet Ye, "Auto Makers, Flock to the Web to Woo Chinese Buyers," *Wall Street Journal*, April 9, 2009, p. B9.

In fact, modernization in developing countries has created a number of new media opportunities. Across Asia—where cell phones have proliferated and there is little regulation of spam—advertisers increasingly reach consumers via text messages to their phones. In India, where mobile phone penetration is high compared to other media, such as television and the Internet, cell phone ads have proven effective in reaching the country's large and diverse population. Although cellular ad-spend is still low in countries such as India, it is expected to grow in the future.[40] Furthermore, the different cultures of Asia may be particularly well suited to the brevity necessary for cellular ads.[41] As we noted earlier concerning Japan, Asian cultures tend to want and expect less product information delivered in their advertisements.

Urbanization in emerging countries has created media opportunities as well. In Beijing, Communication Radio serves the needs of China's new commuters. In addition to offering traffic updates, the station plays light pop music to calm the nerves of motorists stuck in traffic. Eighty percent of Beijing drivers tune in. As private car ownership surges in China, Communication Radio has become one of the country's highest-ranked stations for advertising revenues.[42] To take advantage of Shanghai's busy subway system, which carries 2.2 million commuters a day, Starbucks created a "subopera" to run on high-tech flat screen monitors on the subways cars and station platforms. The subopera combined advertisement and soap opera.[43] In Dubai, the government opened negotiations with businesses in order to sell naming rights for two dozen stations being built as part of the emirate's new mass-transit system.[44] This could provide marketers with a unique and highly viewed medium.

An urban Chinese enters the subway. Urbanization in developing countries has created new media opportunities for global marketers, including electric billboards and even "suboperas" that air in the Shanghai subway.

The global explosion of media options has met with a backlash in some cases. For example, outdoor promotions are a good way to reach Russia's more affluent consumers. Russian businesspeople read newspapers and watch television less than their counterparts elsewhere, urbanites are often stuck in traffic, and many Russians are visually used to large posters from communist days. However, when ad posters as high as skyscrapers appeared in Moscow, it prompted an outcry from conservationists, regulators, and even some in the advertising industry. Although the ads were illegal, it would take weeks in Russia's unwieldy legal system to get them dismantled.[45]

Scheduling International Advertising

Media expenditures tend to peak before sales peak. How long before depends on the complexity of the consumers' buying decision and the length of their deliberation. This principle, though somewhat generalized here, applies to international markets as well as to domestic ones. Differences exist, however, because of varying sales peaks, national vacations, and religious holidays and because of differences in the deliberation time with regard to purchases.

Sales peaks are influenced both by climatic seasons and by customs and traditions. Winter months in North America and Europe are summer months in countries of the Southern Hemisphere, such as Australia, New Zealand, South Africa, Argentina, and Brazil. The season influences the purchase and consumption of many consumer goods such as clothing, vacation services, travel, ice cream, and soft drinks. Vacations are particularly important for some European countries. As noted in Chapter 3, religious holidays may also affect consumer purchases and, consequently, the placement or timing of advertising.

For industrial products, the timing of advertising in support of sales efforts may be affected by the budgetary cycles that prevail in a given country. Companies tend to be heavily influenced by their own budgetary cycles, which usually coincide with their fiscal years. In Japan, for example, many companies begin their fiscal year in June rather than in January. To the extent that capital budgets are completed before the new fiscal year commences, products that require budgetary approval will need advertising support in advance of budget completion.

The time needed to think about a purchase has been cited as a primary consideration in deciding how long it is appropriate for the advertising peak to precede the sales peak. In its domestic market, a company may be accustomed to a given deliberation time on the part of its customers. But because deliberation times may be determined by income level or other environmental factors, other markets may exhibit different patterns. The purchase or replacement of a small electrical household appliance may be a routine decision for a North American household, and the purchase may occur whenever the need arises. In a country with lower income levels, such a purchase may be planned several weeks or even months ahead. Consequently, a company engaged in international advertising needs to carefully evaluate the underlying assumptions of its domestic advertising policies and not automatically assume that they apply elsewhere.

ORGANIZING THE GLOBAL ADVERTISING EFFORT

A major concern for global marketing executives revolves around the organization of the company's global advertising effort. Key concerns include the role of the head office versus the roles that subsidiaries and the advertising agency should play. Marketers are aware that a more harmonious approach to the international advertising effort may enhance both the quality and the efficiency of the total effort. Organizing the effort deserves as much time as individual advertising decisions about individual products or campaigns. In this section, we look in greater detail at the selection of an advertising agency and at the managerial issues that arise in running a global advertising effort in a multinational corporation.

Selection of an Advertising Agency

Global companies have a number of options with respect to working with advertising agencies. Many companies develop an agency relationship domestically and must decide whether they expect their domestic agency to handle their global advertising business as well. In some foreign markets, companies need to select foreign agencies to work with them—a decision that may be made by the head office alone or left to the local subsidiaries. Alternatively, multinational firms can employ agencies with global reach or agencies that have banded together to form international networks.

Working with Domestic Agencies. When a company starts to grow internationally, it is not unusual for the domestic advertising agency to handle the international business as well. However, this is possible only when the domestic agency has global experience and capability. Many smaller domestic agencies do not have international experience. Companies are then forced to make other arrangements. Frequently, the global company begins by appointing individual agencies in each of the various foreign markets where it is operating. This may be done with the help

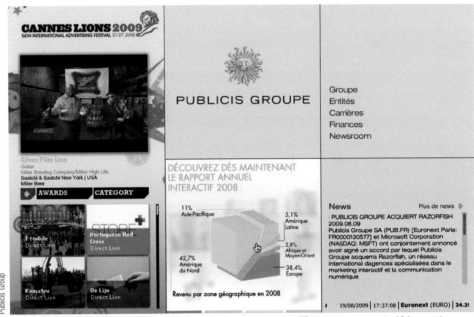

Publicis Group

Paris-based Publicis is one of the world's largest advertising groups. The group operates in 104 countries.

of the local subsidiaries or through the staff at the company's head office. Before long, however, the company will end up with a series of agency relationships that may make global coordination very difficult.

Working with Local Agencies Abroad.   The local advertising agency is expected to understand the local environment fully and is in a position to create advertisements targeted to the local market. Although it markets one of the world's best-known brands, Mercedes-Benz is one of many firms that have chosen, at times, to utilize a variety of local agencies. Prior to 1980, the company did engage heavily in global advertising, using the Ogilvy & Mather Worldwide agency. When Ogilvy & Mather pursued the business of competitor Ford Motor Company, Mercedes fired the agency. Mercedes then adopted a policy of varying its brand image from country to country and employing the most creative agency in each country.

Working with International Advertising Networks.   Many companies with extensive international operations find it too difficult and cumbersome to deal simultaneously with a large number of agencies, both domestic and international. For this reason, multinational firms have tended to concentrate their accounts with some large advertising agencies that operate their own global networks. Table 15.5 lists the world's top 50 marketing organizations/agencies.

The first generation of international networks was created by U.S.-based advertising agencies in the 1950s and 1960s, when clients encouraged their U.S. agencies to move into local markets where the advertising agencies were weak. Leaders in this process were J. Walter Thompson, Ogilvy & Mather, BBDO, and Young & Rubicam. British entrepreneurs Saatchi & Saatchi and WPP dominated the second wave of international networks. Other networks were developed by French and Japanese agencies.[46] The 1980s saw many mergers of medium-sized agencies around the world. In the 1990s, mergers and acquisitions occurred among even the largest global agencies. Some of these mergers utilized the umbrella of a holding company that allowed each agency to retain its brand identity while enjoying

			WORLDWIDE REVENUE
RANK	**AGENCY**	**HEADQUARTERS**	**IN MILLIONS**
1	WPP	U.K.	$13,600
2	Omnicom Group	USA	1,336
3	Interpublic Group of Cos.	USA	6,960
4	Publicis Groupe	France	6,900
5	Dentsu	Japan	3,300
6	Aegis Group	U.K.	2,490
7	Havas	France	2,310
8	Hakuhodo DY Holdings	Japan	1,560
9	MDC Partners	Canada/USA	584
10	Asatsu-DK	Japan	503
11	Alliance Data Systems (Epsilon)	USA	491
12	Media Consulta	Germany	427
13	Microsoft Corp. (Razorfish)	USA	409
14	Photon Group	Australia	382
15	Carlson Marketing	USA	367
16	Cheil Worldwide	South Korea	339
17	IBM Corp. (IBM Interactive)	USA	313
18	Sapient Corp. (Sapient Interactive)	USA	306
19	inVentiv Health (inVentiv Communications)	USA	280
20	Grupo ABC (ABC Group)	Brazil	279
21	STW Group	Australia	255
22	LBi International	Sweden	241
23	Clemenger Group	Australia	239
24	Cossette Communication Group	Canada	238
25	George P. Johnson Co.	USA	238
26	Aspen Marketing Services	USA	212
27	Merkle	USA	211
28	Wieden & Kennedy	USA	204
29	Chime Communications	U.K.	203
30	Mosaic Sales Solutions	USA	199
31	Commarco Holding	France	197
32	M&C Saatchi	U.K.	189
33	Serviceplan Agenturgruppe	Germany	188
34	Harte-Hanks Direct	USA	183
35	Doner	USA	181
36	Richards Group	USA	168
37	Bartle Bogle Hegarty	U.K.	169

TABLE 15.5 WORLD'S TOP 50 AGENCY COMPANIES

continued

Table 15.5 continued

RANK	AGENCY	HEADQUARTERS	WORLDWIDE REVENUE IN MILLIONS
38	Tokyu Agency	Japan	$164
39	Creston	U.K.	146
40	Cramer-Krasselt	USA	144
41	AKQA	USA	140
42	Media Square	U.K.	136
43	Marketing Store	USA	135
44	Rosetta	USA	129
45	iCrossing	USA	122
46	Derse	USA	120
47	RPA	USA	118
48	D.L. Ryan Cos. (Ryan Partnership)	USA	108
49	FullSix	France	108
50	TMP Worldwide (Veronis Suhler Stevenson)	USA	102

Source: Reprinted with permission from the August 13, 2009, issue of *Advertising Age*.

the advantages of greater size and the ability to access the full global reach of all alliance partners.[47]

Utilizing global advertising agencies or networks can be desirable in countries where advertising is not as developed as in the major markets of North America and Europe. For example, global agencies are favored in Eastern Europe, where up to 90 percent of the advertising in some markets is handled by affiliates of global agencies. They can leverage a vast knowledge within the agency network and transfer much-needed skills in order to attract business from such leading firms as Coca-Cola, Nestlé, and Unilever. When Vietnam opened to foreign advertising agencies—albeit those operating with a local, Vietnamese partner—nearly two dozen international agencies flooded into Vietnam, the world's 13th most populous country.[48]

International advertising networks are especially sought after because of their ability to execute global campaigns. Usually, one set of advertisements will be created and then circulated among the local affiliates. Working within the same agency or network guarantees consistency and a certain willingness among affiliate offices to accept direction from a central location. Therefore, as companies develop their global business and coordinate their global campaigns, they are likely to consolidate agencies.

Coordinating International Advertising

The role the international marketing executive plays in a company's international advertising effort may differ from firm to firm and depends on several factors. Outside factors, such as the nature of the market or of the competition, as well as internal factors, such as company culture or philosophy, may lead some firms to adopt a more centralized approach in international advertising. Other firms may prefer to delegate more authority to local subsidiaries and local agencies. Key factors that can cause a firm to either centralize or decentralize decision making for international advertising are reviewed in the sections that follow.

External Factors Affecting Advertising Coordination. One of the most important factors influencing how companies allocate decision making for international advertising is market diversity. For products or services where customer needs and interests are homogeneous across many countries, greater opportunities for standardization exist, and companies are more likely to centralize decision making. Companies operating in markets with very different customer needs or market systems are more likely to decentralize their international-advertising decision making. Local knowledge is more important to the success of these firms.

The nature of the competition can also affect the way an international firm plans for decision making related to advertising. Firms that essentially face local competition or different sets of competitors from country to country may find it more logical to delegate international advertising to local subsidiaries. On the other hand, if a company is competing everywhere against a small set of international firms, the company is more apt to centralize key marketing decisions in an attempt to coordinate its actions against its global competitors. In such cases, advertising decision making may be centralized as well.

Internal Factors Affecting Advertising Coordination. A company's own internal structure and organization can also greatly influence its options in terms of centralizing or decentralizing decision making about international advertising. The opportunities for centralizing are few when a company's approach is to customize advertising for each local market. However, when a company adheres to a standardized advertising format, a more centralized approach will be possible and probably even desirable.

Skill levels and efficiency concerns can also affect the level of centralization. Decentralization is possible only when the advertising skills of local subsidiaries and local agencies are sufficient for them to perform successfully. Decentralization is often believed to result in inefficiencies or decreased quality because a firm's budget may be spread over too many individual agencies. Instead of having a large budget in one agency, the firm has created mini-budgets that may not be adequate to attract the best creative talent to work on its products. Centralization often gives the firm access to better talent, though knowledge of the local markets may be sacrificed. On the other hand, international advertising cannot be centralized successfully in companies where the head-office staff does not possess a full appreciation of the international dimension of the firm's business.

The managerial style of the international company may also affect the centralization decision on advertising. Some companies pride themselves on giving considerable freedom to managers at their local subsidiaries. Under such circumstances, centralizing advertising decisions may be counterproductive. The general approach taken by the company's top management toward international markets is closely related to its desire to centralize or decentralize international advertising.

However, because the internal and external factors that characterize the company are subject to change over time, the decision to centralize or decentralize will never be a permanent one. For example, Coca-Cola shifted more advertising decision making to its subsidiaries. Then, two years later, advertising oversight shifted back to headquarters in Atlanta. Lackluster sales and some embarrassing ads—an angry grandmother streaking down a beach in Italy—proved fatal to Coke's "think local" strategy.[49]

Should advertising for your product be standardized, customized, or modularized? What adaptations might be necessary for your target market? Continue with Country Market Report on the student companion website at http://www.cengage.com/international.

CONCLUSION

The complexity of dealing simultaneously with a large number of different customers in many countries, all speaking their own languages and subject to their own cultural heritage, presents a real challenge to the international marketer. Proponents of global advertising point to the convergence of customer needs and the emergence of "world consumers," customers who are becoming ever more homogeneous whether they live in Paris, London, New York, or Tokyo. However, many aspects of the advertising environment remain considerably diverse. Although English is rapidly becoming a global language, most messages still have to be translated into local languages. Widely differing regulations in many countries on the execution, content, and format of advertisements still make it very difficult to apply standardized solutions to advertising problems. Media availability to advertisers differs substantially in different parts of the world, so global companies still need to adapt their media mix to the local situation.

Many marketers, however, realize that total customization is not desirable because it would require that each market create and implement its own advertising strategies. Top creative talent is scarce everywhere, and better creative solutions tend to be costlier ones. As a result, companies appear to be moving toward modularization, in which some elements of the advertising message are common to all advertisements, whereas other elements are tailored to local requirements. Successful modularization requires that companies plan such an integration of responsibilities from the very outset, considering the full range of possibilities and the requirements that will need to be satisfied across their major markets. This is a considerable challenge to global marketing executives and their advertising partners.

QUESTIONS FOR DISCUSSION

1. What has motivated the apparent increase in the use of standardized advertising across national markets?
2. What do you think are the reasons that attitudes about the credibility of advertising vary among countries?
3. What advice would you give to a U.S. firm interested in advertising in Japan?
4. How will the advertising industry have to react to evolving conditions in developing countries and the former Soviet bloc?
5. How will increased Internet access affect international advertising?

PART **5**

Managing the Global Marketing Effort

© Photodisc/Getty Images

Antoine Gyori/Corbis

© Inmagine/18439GNG

16
Organizing for Global Marketing

LEARNING OBJECTIVES

After studying this chapter, you should be able to:

- List and explain the internal and external factors that affect how global organizations are structured and managed.

- Note the advantages and disadvantages of the different ways of structuring a firm with international sales.

- Discuss global mandates, and note how global mandates can affect a firm's organization.

- Explain why organizational issues for born-global firms differ from those for traditional multinational companies.

- Give examples of how technology can be utilized to support internal global communications systems.

- List and explain the elements of an effective global control strategy.

- Discuss the conflicts that can arise between international headquarters and national subsidiaries.

- Consider a career in global marketing.

3M CREATED ITS INTERNATIONAL operations group in 1951, launching subsidiaries in Australia, Canada, France, Germany, Mexico, and the United Kingdom. Forty years later, it became the first foreign firm to have a wholly owned subsidiary in China. Today, half of the company's sales are outside the United States, and three-quarters of its managers have worked in a foreign country. Yet, despite its long history as an international firm, 3M still grapples with the question of how best to organize itself.

Over the years, 3M developed an organizational matrix—several structures superimposed on one another. Managers of country subsidiaries share responsibility with division managers located at headquarters in St. Paul, Minnesota. Disagreements over strategy sometimes arise. Subsidiary managers seek to maximize total sales and profits in their countries. Division managers seek to maximize the global sales and profits of their product lines. Despite the matrix, most concede that the country managers often exercise the greater power. In this respect, some are concerned that 3M has been left behind; most other global firms have centralized power over the past 20 years. However, running 3M's international business from St. Paul could prove too burdensome. The matrix allows the company to react quickly to local markets. Who better than the local manager to decide whether and how to raise prices in Germany? Thus, the debate continues. Who is better qualified to decide how to market a product abroad—the person who best knows the product or the person who best knows the country?[1]

An important aspect of global marketing is the establishment of an appropriate organization. The organization must be able to formulate and implement strategies for each local market and for the global market as well. The objective is to develop a structure and control system that will enable the firm to respond to distinct variations in each market while applying the relevant experience that the company has gained in other markets and with other products. To be successful, companies need to find a proper balance between these two needs. A number of organizational structures are suitable for different internal and external environments. No one structure is best for all situations.

ELEMENTS THAT AFFECT A GLOBAL MARKETING ORGANIZATION

The success of a global strategy will be acutely influenced by the selection of an appropriate organization to implement that strategy. The structure of an international organization should be congruent with the tasks to be performed, the need for product knowledge, and the need for market knowledge. The ideal structure of such an organization should be a function of the products or services to be sold in the marketplace, as well as of the external and internal environments. Theoretically, the way to develop a global marketing organization is to analyze the specific tasks to be accomplished within an environment and then to design a structure that will support these tasks most effectively. A number of other factors complicate the selection of an appropriate organization, however. In most cases, a company already has an existing organizational structure. As the internal and external environments change, companies will need to reevaluate that structure. The search for an appropriate organizational structure must balance local responsiveness against global integration. It is important that global managers understand the strengths and weaknesses of different organizational structures as well as the factors that usually lead to change in the structure.

Corporate Goals

Every company needs a mission. The mission is the business's framework—the values that drive the company and the vision it has for itself. The mission statement is the glue that holds the company together. Yahoo asserts that its mission is "to connect people to their passions, their communities, and the world's knowledge."[2] Starbucks' mission is "to inspire and nurture the human spirit—one person, one cup, and one neighborhood at a time."[3] Reconsidering a firm's mission can result in organizational change. When Bayer introduced a new mission statement emphasizing innovation and sustained growth, the company also announced a structural realignment to better attain these goals. Three global product divisions—health care, nutrition, and high-tech materials—were established.[4]

After declaring its mission, no company should begin establishing an international organization until it has reviewed and established its strategies and objectives. Some global firms even include strategy statements in their missions. Corporate leaders have, at times, developed strategic visions with slogans such as "Encircle Caterpillar" for Komatsu and "Beat Xerox" for Canon. If the head of a company can instill this sense of winning throughout the firm, it will inspire the organization to excel and achieve far greater goals.

Corporate Worldview

Corporate management can adopt one of several worldviews concerning global markets. These worldviews, or orientations, will significantly affect the choice of organizational structure. Some firms adopt an **ethnocentric orientation**. Management is centered on the home market. Ideas that emanate from there are considered superior to those that arise from the foreign subsidiaries. Headquarters tells its subsidiaries what to do and solicits little or no input from the subsidiaries themselves. Top managers in the foreign subsidiaries are most often managers sent from headquarters on relatively short-term assignments.

Ethnocentric orientation a corporate worldview in which management is focused on the home market and considers ideas from the home market to be superior to those from foreign subsidiaries

Procter & Gamble's Egyptian website mirrors the mission and values of the global corporation. These include "providing branded products and services of superior quality and value that improve the lives of the world's consumers."

Polycentric orientation a corporate worldview in which each market is considered unique and local subsidiaries are given power to develop and implement independent strategies

Alternatively, corporate management can take a **polycentric orientation**, wherein each market is considered unique. This is at the heart of the multidomestic strategies discussed in Chapter 1. Local subsidiaries are given great leeway to develop and implement their own strategies. Little or no interdependencies arise among subsidiaries. Management positions in local subsidiaries are usually filled by local nationals. Some polycentric firms evolve a focus that is regional rather than national. Geographic regions such as Europe and Latin America, rather than single national markets, are seen as possessing unique features that require separate marketing strategies. Decision making becomes centralized at the regional level, but regions still remain relatively independent of headquarters and of one another.

Geocentric orientation a corporate worldview in which management pursues a global marketing strategy and decision making is shared by headquarters and subsidiaries

A **geocentric orientation** returns power to global headquarters, but this orientation is very distinct from an ethnocentric orientation. A geocentric firm focuses on global markets as a whole rather than on its domestic market. Good ideas can come from any country, and the firm strives to keep communication lines open among its various units. Even top management at corporate headquarters is likely to come from many nations. Most important, all national units, including the domestic one, must consider what is best for the whole organization and act accordingly.

Other Internal Forces

Other internal factors can also affect the international marketing organization. These factors include the volume and diversity of the firm's international business, its economic commitment to international business, the available human resources, flexibility within the company, and home-country culture.

Importance of International Sales. The size and importance of a firm's international business affect its organizational structure. If only a small percentage of sales (1–10 percent) is international, a company will tend to have a simple organization such as an export department. As the proportion of international sales increases relative to total sales, a company is likely to evolve from having an export department to having an international division and then to having a worldwide organization. Companies may even consider moving global headquarters out of the home country as overseas sales become increasingly important. Oil services company Halliburton moved its global headquarters from Houston to Dubai to be closer to its growing business in the Middle East and Asia.[5]

Diversity of International Markets Served. As the number and diversity of international markets increase, it becomes necessary to have a more complex organization to manage the marketing effort, and it requires a larger number of people to understand the markets and implement the strategies.

Level of Economic Commitment. A company that is unwilling or unable to allocate adequate financial resources to its international efforts will not be able to sustain a complex or costly international structure. The less expensive organizational approaches to international marketing usually result in less control by the company at the local level. It is extremely important to build an organization that will provide the flexibility and resources to achieve the corporation's long-term goals for international markets.

Human Resources. Available and capable personnel are just as vital to a firm as financial resources. Some companies send top domestic executives to foreign operations, only to find that these expatriates do not understand the nation's culture. The hiring of local executives is also difficult, because competition for such people can be extremely intense. Motorola puts hundreds of executives through workplace simulation exercises to try to identify the best candidates with the necessary international management skills to run a global business.[6] Because people are such an important resource in international organizations, a lack of appropriate personnel can constrain a firm's organizational growth.

Flexibility. When a company devises an organizational structure, it must build in some flexibility, especially to be prepared in case reorganization becomes necessary in the future. A study of the implementation of a global strategy for 17 products found that organizational flexibility was one of the keys to success.[7] The structure must be flexible enough to respond to the needs of consumers and the challenges of global competitors. Even companies that establish a perfect design for the present find themselves in trouble later on when the firm grows or its market changes.

WORLD BEAT 16.1

CORPORATE CULTURE CHANGE

DESPITE THE FACT THAT TOYOTA'S BOARD remains Japanese, the company sometimes chooses American culture over Japanese culture. Toyota is looking to Americans to fill key jobs in Europe, Thailand, and Mexico, where they replace Japanese managers. The same is true in the Chinese market. One reason is market similarity: In the Chinese market, most sales people earn their living via commissions—similar to the United States but not to Japan.

When Chinese computer maker Lenovo bought IBM's personal computer business, it also chose to adapt its corporate culture, known for its militaristic discipline, to a more American way of doing things. In China, managers who arrived late for a meeting had to stand at the front of the room while other executives bowed their heads in silence for a full minute. Similarly, Chinese consumer appliance producer Haier had to adapt to a less authoritarian style when it expanded its business into the United States.

American employees who made mistakes refused to stand on a set of footprints outlined on the floor and publically criticize themselves out loud. Now, instead of humiliating bad workers, Haier asks its best American employees to stand in the footprints for recognition.

Increasingly, Asian firms are looking to American executives to spur corporate cultural change—even back home in Asia. Korean LG Electronics hired foreigners for top positions at global headquarters, including veterans from IBM, Hewlett-Packard, Procter & Gamble, and Unilever. Arguments among top executives, once avoided in face-saving Korean culture, are now encouraged. At Japanese Fuji Fire and Marine Insurance, the company's new Iranian-American CEO also inaugurated change, redrawing reporting lines so more managers spoke directly to him. He also outlawed the word-for-word reading of prepared reports at meetings.

Sources: Jane Spencer and Loretta Chao, "Lenovo Goes Global, with Bumps," *Wall Street Journal Europe*, November 5, 2008, p. 4; Norihiko Shirouzu, "Foreign Model," *Wall Street Journal*, May 26, 2006, p. A1; Mei Fong, "Chinese Refrigerator Maker Finds U.S. Chilly," *Wall Street Journal*, March 18, 2008, p. B1; Moon Ihlwan, "The Foreigners at the Top of LG," *BusinessWeek*, December 22, 2008; and Phred Dvorak, "Outsider CEO Translates a New Message in Japan," *Wall Street Journal*, March 10, 2008, p. B1.

Home-Country Culture. Siemens, the large German electronics and engineering conglomerate, does 80 percent of its business abroad, and 60 percent of its workforce is employed outside of Germany. Managers of most local subsidiaries are local nationals.[8] However, like many German companies, Siemens has employed a more centralized management style when dealing with its important U.S. subsidiary, with power located at headquarters in Germany and a German citizen sent to oversee the U.S. market. Keeping close control over important markets and decisions has its roots in German history. Many day-to-day issues cannot be decided by an individual but must be approved by a management board in Germany, and a separate supervisory board consisting of shareholder and employee representatives has to approve major decisions. Some managers argue that Siemens won't truly change until Americans and Asians are on the board.[9]

Appointing foreign managers to the position of chief executive is relatively rare in continental Europe. It is more common in Great Britain and the United States. For example, in 2004, McDonald's appointed an Australian as CEO, and Coca-Cola appointed an Irishman as CEO. The foreign CEO may be more common in the United States for several reasons. As we saw in Chapter 3, U.S. culture is more individualistic and, consequently, open to foreigners. Furthermore, foreign-born managers began seeking jobs in U.S. multinational corporations years ago as U.S. MNCs hired many foreigners to manage their many overseas subsidiaries. These managers often had to develop good English skills to advance, and many were willing to relocate overseas—including to the United States—in order to advance their careers.[10]

External Forces

A number of external factors can affect how global organizations are structured and managed. The most important of these are geographic distance, time zone differences, types of customers, and government regulations. In the international environment, each issue should be examined to determine its effect on the organization.

Geographic Distance.

Technological innovations have somewhat eased the problems associated with physical distance. Companies, primarily in the United States and in other developed countries, enjoy such conveniences as next-day mail and e-mail, fax machines, videoconferencing, mobile phones, mobile data transmissions, rapid transportation, and, of course, the Internet. However, these benefits cannot be taken for granted in international operations. Distance becomes a distinct barrier when operations are established in less developed countries where the telecommunications infrastructure may be more primitive. Moreover, companies invariably find it necessary to have key personnel make trips to engage in face-to-face conversations. Organizations in the same region are often grouped together to help minimize travel costs and the travel time of senior executives. Technology has shortened, but not eliminated, the distance gap.

Time Zones.

One problem even high technology cannot solve is time differences (see Figure 16.1). Managers in New York who reach an agreement over lunch will have a hard time finalizing the deal with their headquarters in London until the following day because, by that time, most executives in England will be on their way home for the evening. The five-hour time difference results in lost communication time and impedes rapid results. E-mail has contributed substantially to the interaction among far-flung units, but adaptations still need to be made. Brady Corporation of Milwaukee produces industrial sign and printing equipment. About 45 percent of its sales are outside the United States. Managers in Milwaukee commonly take conference calls at 6 a.m. and place calls late at night to catch the company's Asian managers during their workdays.[11]

Types of Customers.

Companies may need to take their "customer profiles" into account in structuring their global marketing organizations. Companies that serve very few, geographically concentrated global customers will organize their global marketing efforts differently from firms that serve a large number of small customers in country after country. For example, if a firm has key global customers, it may adjust its organization and select its office locations according to where its customers are located. Many companies that sell equipment or parts to automotive firms maintain marketing units near major concentrations of automotive activity, such as Detroit in the United States and Stuttgart in Germany. Supplier parks sit adjacent to Ford manufacturing sites in Spain, Germany, and Brazil and are increasingly planned for U.S locations.[12] On the other hand, companies that sell to large numbers of customers tend to maintain more regional, or even country-specific, organizations, with relatively less centralization. Similarly, if customer needs or competition varies greatly from country to country, there is less impetus to centralize.

FIGURE 16.1
Time Zones of the World

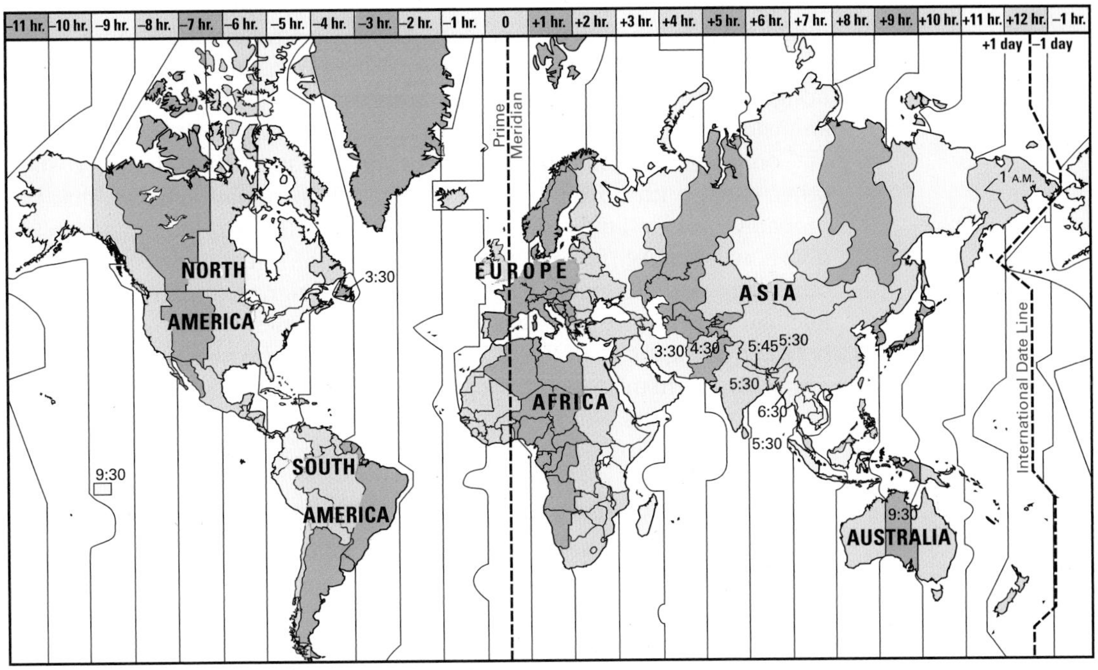

Source: From *The 1996 Information Please® Almanac.* Copyright 1995 by Information Please LLC. All rights reserved.

Government Regulations. How various countries attract or discourage foreign operations can affect the structure of the global organization. Laws involving imports, exports, taxes, and hiring differ from country to country. Local taxes, statutory holidays, and political risk can deter a company from establishing a subsidiary or management center in a country. Some countries require a firm that establishes plants on their territory to hire, train, and develop local employees and to share ownership with the government or local citizens. These requirements for local investment and ownership may dictate an organization that allows greater local decision making.

TYPES OF ORGANIZATIONAL STRUCTURES

The global marketplace offers many opportunities. To take advantage of these opportunities, a company must evaluate its options, develop a strategy, and establish an organization to implement the strategy. The organization should take into account all the factors affecting organizational design in determining which structure is best suited to its current strategic needs. In this section, we review the various options for international and global organizational structures.

Companies Without International Specialists

Many companies, when they begin selling products to foreign markets, operate without an international organization or even an international specialist. A domestically oriented company may receive inquiries from foreign buyers who saw an advertisement in a trade magazine or attended a domestic trade show. The domestic staff will respond to the inquiry in the same way they respond to any other. Product brochures will be sent to the potential buyer for review. If sufficient interest exists on the part of both buyer and seller, then more communication (e-mails, telephone calls, personal visits) may transpire. With no specific individual designated to handle international business, it may be directed to a sales manager, an inside salesperson, a product manager, or an outside salesperson.

Companies without an international organization incur limited costs, but on the other hand, with no one responsible for international business, that business will probably provide little sales and profit. When the firm attempts to respond to the occasional inquiry, no one will understand the difficulties of translation into another language, the particular needs of the foreign customer, the transfer of funds, fluctuating exchange rates, shipping, legal liabilities, or the other many differences between domestic and international business. As the number of international inquiries grows or management recognizes the potential in international markets, international specialists will have to be added to the domestic organization.

International Specialists and Export Departments

The complexities of selling a product to a variety of different countries prompt most domestically oriented firms to establish some international expertise. This can vary from retaining a part-time international specialist to having a full complement of specialists organized into an export department. Figure 16.2 is a sample organization chart for an organization operating with an international specialist.

International specialists and export departments primarily perform a sales function. They respond to inquiries, manage exhibits at international trade shows, and handle export documentation, shipping, insurance, and financial matters. International specialists may also maintain contact with embassies, export financing agencies, and various departments of commerce. The international specialist or export department may use an export agent, an export management company, or import intermediaries to assist in the process.

Hiring international specialists gives firms the ability to respond to and process foreign business. The size of this type of organization will be directly related to the amount of international business handled. The costs should be minor when compared to the potential.

However, international specialists and export departments are often reactive rather than proactive in nature. They usually respond to inquiries. Few evaluate the worldwide demand for a product or service, identify opportunities, or develop a global strategy. Also, because international sales are so small, the international specialist may have little opportunity to modify current products or services to meet international market needs. In most cases, products are sold as is, with no modification.

International Divisions

As sales to foreign markets become more important to the company, and the complexity of coordinating the international effort extends beyond the capacity of a specialist or an export department, the firm may establish an international division. The international division normally reports to the president. This gives it equal status with other functions such as marketing, finance, and production. Figure 16.3 illustrates the organizational design of a firm using an international division.

FIGURE 16.2
Organization with an International Specialist

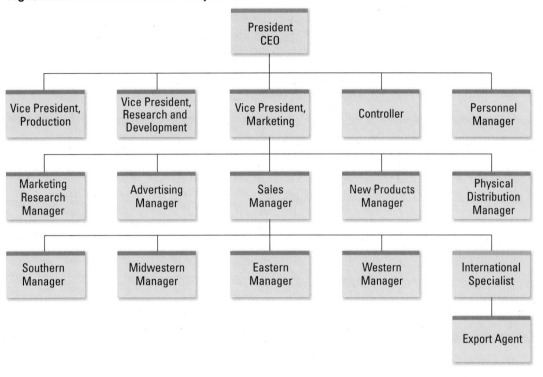

FIGURE 16.3
Organization with an International Division

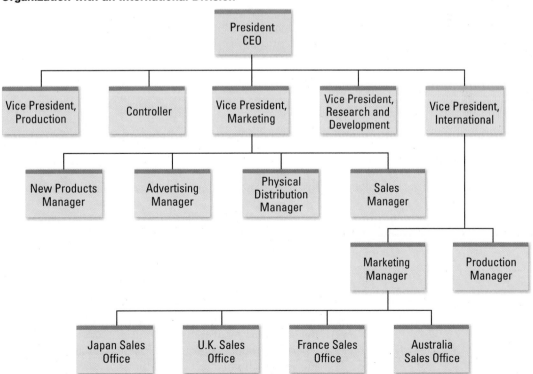

International divisions are directly involved in the development and implementation of global strategy. Heads of international divisions have marketing managers, sales managers, and perhaps even production managers reporting to them. These divisions focus all their efforts on international markets. As a result, they are often successful at increasing international sales.

The international division actively seeks out market opportunities in foreign countries. The sales and marketing efforts in each country are supported through regional or local offices. These offices understand the local environments, including legal requirements, customer needs, and competition. This close contact with the market improves the organization's ability to perform successfully. The use of an international division may be particularly appropriate for a firm with many different product lines or businesses. When none of these divisions has extensive experience outside the domestic market, all foreign business may be combined into the international division.

When Robert Iger became head of Disney's new international division (later CEO), the company's international operations represented only 20 percent of corporate sales and even less of profits. Iger soon discovered that the company's disorganized forays into foreign markets had resulted in a lack of synergy between different divisions resulting in overlap and lack of coordination. In Japan, the manager in charge of Disney's studio division didn't even know who ran the television division. In addition, local managers complained that product decisions were being made at headquarters in Burbank, California, with little regard to local tastes. Over the next decade, the international division allowed local managers to make more decisions and recruit partners to help develop more culturally attuned products.[13]

Worldwide or Global Organizations

As a firm recognizes the potential size of the global market, it begins to change from a domestic company with some business overseas to a worldwide company pursuing a global strategy. At this point, international divisions are superseded by new global structures. A company can choose to organize in terms of one of three dimensions: geography, function, or product. The matrix organization, another possible type of worldwide organization, combines two or more of these dimensions.

Geographic Organizational Structures.
The geographic organizational design is appropriate when the company needs an intimate knowledge of its customers and their environments. Such a design gives the company an opportunity to understand the local culture, economy, politics, laws, and competitive situation. Geographic organizational structures can be either regionally focused or country-based structures.

Regional Management Centers. Regional management centers enable an organization to focus on particular regions of the world such as Europe, the Middle East, Latin America, North America, the Caribbean, or the Far East. Figure 16.4 illustrates the regional structure of a worldwide geographic organization.

The reasons for using a regional geographic approach to organizational design are related to market similarity and size. A group of countries that are located close together and have similar social and cultural histories, climates, resources, and (sometimes) languages may have many similar needs for products. Sometimes these regional country groups have unified themselves for political and economic reasons. The European Union (EU) and Mercosur are such regional groupings.

FIGURE **16.4**
Geographic Organization by Regional Management Centers

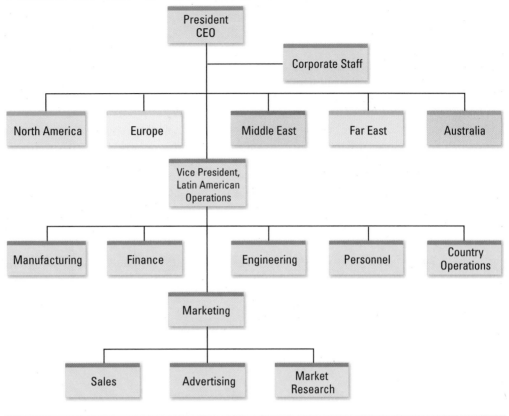

Also, once a market reaches a certain size, the firm must employ a staff dedicated to maximizing revenues from that area of the world and to protecting the firm's assets there.

Regional management can respond to local conditions and react faster than a totally centralized organization where all decisions are made at global headquarters. At the same time, a regional organization captures some of the benefits associated with greater centralization. In Europe, many large international companies were originally organized on a national basis. The national organizations, including those in France, Germany, Italy, and the United Kingdom, often were coordinated loosely through European headquarters. The development of a single European market caused companies to rethink their European organizations, often to reduce the role of the national organization in favor of a stronger pan-European management. A major benefit of a regional or pan-European structure is reduced operational costs. In addition, a study of Western European and U.S.-based firms with significant operations in Central and Eastern Europe revealed that regional management centers are an attractive organizational device to exploit market similarities and supply local offices with additional support and expertise.[14]

Regional organizations have their disadvantages, however. First, regional organization implies that many functions are duplicated at the different regional head offices. Such duplication tends to add significantly to costs. A second, more serious disadvantage is that regional organizations inherently divide global authority. In a purely regionally organized company, only the CEO has true global responsibility.

WORLD BEAT 16.2

WHERE'S HEADQUARTERS?

LENEVO USED TO BE A CHINESE COMPUTER COMPANY headquartered in China. That changed after it acquired IBM's personal computer business. The company is incorporated in Hong Kong, but headquarters is divided among Paris, Beijing, Singapore, and Raleigh in North Carolina. Similarly, fashion-apparel maker, Ports 1961, describes itself as a global brand with roots in Canada. However, that did not stop the company from moving its headquarters from New York City to Xiamen, China. Dutch pharmaceutical firm Organon moved its headquarters to New Jersey to be close to the important U.S. market. Four years later, it closed its U.S. headquarters and returned to the Netherlands to prepare for a stock-market listing. After being purchased by Schering-Plough, Organon announced that global headquarters would relocate back to the United States.

Why do global firms move their headquarters out of their home countries? The motives are varied, but the top reasons appear to be markets, mergers and acquisitions, and, of course, tax evasion. After Tyco International moved to tax-haven Bermuda, the United States passed a law that made it harder to move abroad to avoid taxes. There was a public outcry of tax evasion when oil services company Halliburton moved its CEO and headquarters from Houston to Dubai. Management rejected these claims, noting that the company was still incorporated in the United States. Management further asserted that the shift of headquarters overseas was motivated by the company's new emphasis on developing international markets.

But when it comes to value for money, it is hard to beat New York City as a site for global headquarters. NYC is rated number one among top global cities for business activity and human capital. It only ranks 22nd for cost of living.

Sources: "Lenevo Goes Global," *Dow Jones Financial Wire*, November 3, 2008; Phred Dvorak, "Why Multiple Headquarters Multiply," *Wall Street Journal*, November 19, 2007, p. B1; "Halliburton Executives Say Company Well-Positioned During Economic Downturn," *Associated Press Newswires*, November 19, 2008; Cost of Living Survey 2008, Mercer, http://www.mercer.com; and 2008 Global Cities Index, http://www.foreignplicy.com.

Developing global marketing strategies for products or services is difficult, because regional managers tend to focus on a limited regional perspective.

Country-Based Organizations. The second type of geographic organization is the country-based organization, which utilizes a separate unit for each country. Figure 16.5 illustrates a simple, country-based, geographic organization.

A country-based organization resembles a regional structure, except that the focus is on single countries rather than on a group of countries. For example, instead of having a regional management center in Brussels overseeing all European sales and operations, the company has an organizational unit in each country. The country-based organization can be extremely sensitive to local customs, laws, and needs, all of which may differ considerably even though the countries participate in a regional organization, such as the EU or NAFTA.

One difficulty that plagues a country-based organization is its higher costs. Therefore, it is important to ensure that the benefits of a local organization offset its cost. Coordination with headquarters can also prove difficult. If a company is involved in forty countries, it can be cumbersome to have all forty country-based organizational units reporting to one or a few people in the company's headquarters. Furthermore, country managers too often duplicate efforts. Before Unilever abandoned its emphasis on national market autonomy, its Chinese and Hong Kong subsidiaries each developed their own formulations for shampoo, despite the fact that hair and hair-washing habits were nearly identical in the two markets.[15]

Jose Fuste Raga

The skyline of Singapore. Whereas the nightlife of Hong Kong is popular with single expatriates, clean and orderly Singapore appeals to expatriates with families. That is one reason why Singapore remains competitive as a location for Asian headquarters of multinational firms.

FIGURE 16.5
Country-Based Geographic Organization

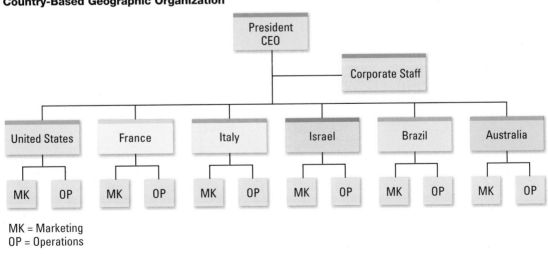

MK = Marketing
OP = Operations

Country organizations are being phased out or reduced as regional organizations emerge. For example, in response to the signing of NAFTA, many firms began to integrate their separate organizations for Canada, the United States, and Mexico. Among these was Lego, the Danish toy maker. Lego reduced the responsibility of its Canadian operation and combined some executive positions at its Enfield, Connecticut, operation. At the same time, it decided to develop its Mexican market from the U.S. location as well. Other firms have chosen the same path, integrating their Canadian subsidiaries with their U.S. companies and developing their Mexican markets from the U.S. base.

To deal with the shortcomings of a country-based structure, many firms combine the concepts of regional and country-based organizations, as shown in Figure 16.6. Combining regional and country-based approaches minimizes many of the limitations of both designs, but it also adds an additional layer of management. Some executives think that superimposing a regional headquarters makes the country-level implementation of strategy more cumbersome rather than improving it. In order for the company to benefit from a regional center in such a combined approach, there must be some value in a regional strategy. Each company must reach its own decision regarding the proper geographic organization design, its cost, and its benefits.

Functional Organizational Structures.   A second way of organizing a global firm is by function. In such an organization, the top executives in marketing, finance, production, accounting, and research and development (R&D) all have worldwide responsibilities. For international companies, this type of organization is best for narrow or homogeneous product lines, with little variation between products or geographic markets. As shown in Figure 16.7, the functional organization has a simple structure. Each functional manager has worldwide responsibility for that function. Usually, the manager supervises people responsible for the function in regions or countries around the world.

FIGURE 16.6

Organization Using Both Country-Based Units and Regionally Based Structure

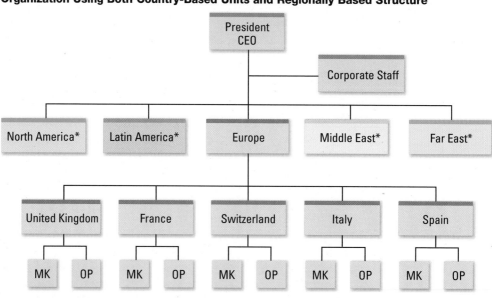

MK = Marketing
OP = Operations

* Country organizations similar to those shown for the European center would be under each regional office.

FIGURE 16.7
Functional Global Organization

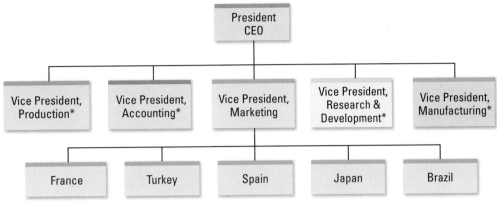

* Each functional vice president has managers of that function in the countries served reporting to
 him or her, as illustrated with the Vice President, Marketing.

Ford Motor Company abandoned its regional structure for a functional one. Previously, Ford had major operating units in North America, Europe, Latin America,
Africa, and Asia. Each regional unit was responsible for its own operations, developing and producing cars for its regional markets. Faced with strong competition
from the more efficient Japanese companies such as Toyota, Ford realized that under its regional setup it incurred a massive penalty for unnecessary duplication of
key functions and efforts. Even though Ford served almost identical customer
needs in many countries, the company was developing separate power trains and
engines and was purchasing different component parts.

The new organization of Ford Automotive called for four major functions—
marketing and sales, manufacturing, and purchasing, and product development.
The most important function was vehicle development, structured around five development centers in the United States and in Europe. The development center for
small cars was located in Europe with locations in both Germany and the United
Kingdom. The United States received the development centers for rear-wheel-drive
cars and commercial trucks, all with global development responsibility. Some
25,000 Ford managers either moved from one location to another or were reas-
signed to report to new supervisors. The company expected to cut development
costs by using fewer components, fewer engines, and fewer power trains as well
as by speeding up development cycles. As a result of this reorganization, Ford
projected savings of $2 to $3 billion per year.

Still, the reorganization termed "Ford 2000" was undergoing modifications even
before the arrival of the millennium. Ford's then chairman, Jacques Nasser, decided
to return some power to Ford's regional business units. The move was made to
enable Ford to respond more quickly to consumer trends. It would allow managers
on the ground to respond quickly without waiting for direction from headquarters.

Product Organizational Structures. A third type of worldwide marketing
organization is based on product line rather than on function or geographic area
(see Figure 16.8). Under this structure, each product group is responsible for marketing, sales, planning, and (in some cases) production and R&D. Other functions,

FIGURE 16.8
Global Product Organization

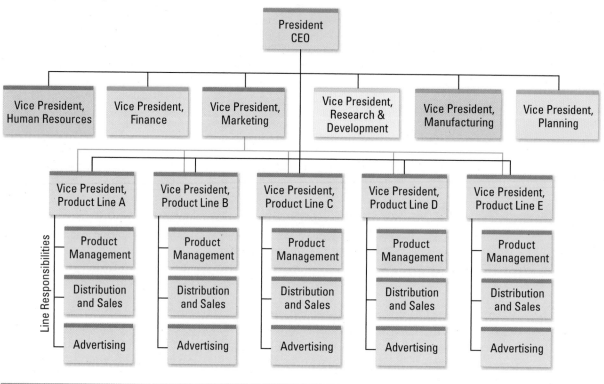

such as legal, accounting, and finance, can be included in the product group or performed by the corporate staff. Both Procter & Gamble, a leading global U.S. consumer products company, and Kraft Foods, a leading U.S. food company, have adopted the global product organization.

A firm may choose to organize by product line for several reasons. Structuring by product line is common for companies with several unrelated product lines. A product focus is also appropriate when the differences involved with marketing the various product lines are greater than the perceived differences between the geographic markets. Typically, the end users for a product organization vary by product line, so there is no advantage in having the same group handle marketing for the different product lines.

A product organization concentrates management attention on the product line, which is an advantage when the product line constantly changes with advancements in technology. Headquarters can develop global products and arrange global rollouts. A product organization is effective in monitoring competition that is globalized rather than localized. Also, the firm can add new product groups as it adds new, unrelated products through acquisition.

The product organization has limitations as well. Knowledge of specific geographic areas can be limited, because each product group may not be able to afford to maintain a large local presence in each market. Because decision making becomes more centrally located under a product structure, sensitivity to local market conditions can be diminished. This lack of knowledge and sensitivity may cause the company to miss local market opportunities. The top managers of international product divisions can themselves present a problem, particularly if they are promoted from the domestic side of the business. They can be ethnocentric and relatively uninterested in or uneasy with international markets.

Also, if each product group goes its own way, the company's international development may result in inefficiencies. For example, two product divisions may be purchasing advertising space independently in the same magazine. This will prove more expensive than combining the purchases. To offset such inefficiencies, some companies supplement their worldwide product organizations with global units that provide for coordination of activities such as advertising and customer service across countries.

Matrix Organizational Structures. As the Ford example suggests, some companies have grown frustrated with the limitations of a one-dimensional geographic, functional, or product organization structures. To overcome these drawbacks, the matrix organization was developed. As shown in Figure 16.9, the matrix organization allows for two or more dimensions of theoretically equal weight (here, geographic and product dimensions) in the organizational structure and in decision-making responsibility. A matrix organization often includes both product and geographic management components. Product management has worldwide responsibility for a specific product line, whereas geographic management is responsible for all product lines in a specific geographic area. These

FIGURE 16.9
Matrix Organization

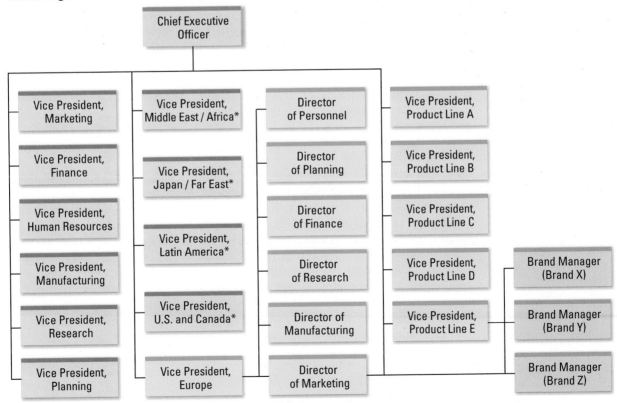

* Each regional vice president has functional managers reporting to him or her, as illustrated for the Vice President, Europe.

management structures overlap at the national product/market level. A matrix organization structure has a dual rather than a single chain of command, which means that many individuals will have two superiors. Under this organizational structure, the brand managers for brands X, Y, and Z in any European country would report directly to two different bosses—vice president product line E and the director of marketing for Europe.

Firms tend to adopt matrix organizations when they need to be highly responsive to two dimensions (such as product and geography). But matrix organizations are not without their challenges. Some critics of Unilever's matrix structure complained that its complexity—with some managers in charge of product categories, others in charge of brands, and still others in charge of geographic areas—resulted in duplication of authority and confusion of responsibility.[16] Power struggles are a common problem, especially when a matrix organization is first established. Relationships are tested as each side of the matrix attempts to "find its place" in the organization. In fact, the key to successful matrix management is the degree to which managers in an organization can resolve conflict and achieve the successful implementation of plans and programs. The matrix organization requires a change in management behavior from traditional authority to an influence system based on technical competence, interpersonal sensitivity, and leadership.

The matrix organization also requires a substantial investment in dual budgeting, accounting, transfer pricing, and personnel evaluation systems. Matrix structures may become even harder to manage as a result of corporate downsizing. Shrinking staffs add to the difficulties surrounding the multiplicity of bosses. Most companies have cut the assistants or liaison personnel who used to smooth things out and made sure everyone could get together on a certain day. As a result, some managers with more than one boss are now saddled with more work coordinating meetings and assignments, increasing their already heavy workloads.[17] Nonetheless, the additional complexity and cost of a matrix organization can sometimes be offset by the benefits of the dual focus. Overall, the matrix structure can permit an organization to function better in an uncertain and changing environment.

Global Mandates

Global mandate a responsibility assigned to a manager or team within a firm to carry out a task on a global scale

Global team a task force established to address at the global level a particular issue facing a firm

Whichever structure a firm employs, the question of who should administer **global mandates** remains an important concern. A global mandate is the expressed assignment to carry out a task on a global scale. As such, they often fit poorly into established organizations and lines of communication. Global mandates may be assigned to individual managers or to newly created **global teams**. In either case, responsibility can extend across functions and across all geographic locations, and the teams or marketing managers often make decisions that can affect all national subsidiaries. We have already discussed two types of global mandates—global brand management (Chapter 11) and global account management (Chapter 14). Global mandates can also be of a temporary nature, such as a team to determine how to respond to a major change in product technology.

Organization of the Born-Global Firm

In Chapter 8, we introduced the concept of born-global firms. From their inception or very shortly thereafter, these new firms target global markets. Almost immediately, international sales account for a large proportion of their total sales. There are several explanations for this phenomenon. Entrepreneurs are increasingly

Procter & Gamble's global business units support the company's valuable global brands. For example, a Pantene team within the Beauty Care GBU oversees global product launches and marketing campaigns that communicate the same fundamental benefits worldwide.

Corporate Info
Structure

Four Pillars

Four pillars — Global Business Units, Market Development Organizations, Global Business Services and Corporate Functions — form the heart of P&G's organizational structure.

- Global Business Units (GBU) build major global brands with robust business strategies.
- Market Development Organizations (MDO) build local understanding as a foundation for marketing campaigns.
- Global Business Services (GBS) provide business technology and services that drive business success.
- Corporate Functions (CF) work to maintain our place as a leader of our industries.

P&G approaches business knowing that we need to Think Globally (GBU) and Act Locally (MDO). This approach is supported by our commitment to operate efficiently (GBS) and our constant striving to be the best at what we do (CF). This streamlined structure allows us to get to market faster.

Click on the pillars below for more information:

▸ **Corporate Structure**

▸Four Pillars
▸How the Structure Works

© 2009 Procter & Gamble

exposed to global opportunities as a result of the communications revolution. Many global entrepreneurs have themselves worked or studied in foreign countries. Many realize that their customers and competition are global. A large number of global start-ups can be found in Silicon Valley, where rapidly changing technologies encounter worldwide demand.

Born globals can benefit from the fact that they have no organizational history. Other firms have traditionally passed through several structural reorganizations as they evolved into global firms. Born-global firms can adopt global organizations from the start. This is enviable in that structural change can entail heavy costs and business disruptions. However, there is something to be said for the more traditional, gradual evolution of a global organization. Firms that move into international markets more slowly can build up market and cultural knowledge over time. They cultivate and support ever more extensive worldwide organizations by recruiting and training knowledgeable and experienced managers and staff. Born globals attempt to do this practically overnight and can find their managerial resources stretched to the limit. As is the case with other entrepreneurial ventures, they can find themselves with fewer assets than opportunities.

CONTROLLING THE GLOBAL ORGANIZATION

As an international company becomes larger and more globally focused, maintaining control of international operations becomes increasingly important. Establishing a system to control marketing activities in numerous markets is not an easy job. However, if companies expect to implement their global strategies, they must establish a control system to regulate the many activities within their organizations.

Elements of a Control Strategy

Control is a cornerstone of organization. Control provides the means to direct, regulate, and manage business operations. The implementation of a global marketing program requires a significant amount of interaction not only among various national subsidiaries, but also among the individual areas of marketing, such as product development and advertising, and among the other functional areas, such as production and R&D. The control system is used to measure these business activities along with competitive and market reactions. Deviations from the planned activities and results are analyzed and reported so that corrective action can be taken.

A control system has three basic elements: (1) the establishment of standards, (2) the measurement of performance against those standards, and (3) the analysis and correction of any deviations from the standards. Although control is a conceptually simple aspect of the organization process, a wide variety of problems arise in international situations, resulting in inefficiencies and intra-company conflict.

Developing Standards. Corporate goals are achieved through the effective implementation of a marketing strategy in the international firm's many national markets. Standard setting is driven by these corporate goals. Standards must be clearly defined, universally accepted, and understood by managers throughout the global organization. The standards should be set through joint deliberations involving corporate headquarters personnel and each local marketing organization. Normally, the standard setting is done annually when the operational business plan is established.

Firms can employ both behavioral and performance standards. **Behavioral standards** refer to actions taken within the firm. They can include the type and amount of advertising to be developed and utilized, the market research to be performed, and the prices to be charged for a product. **Performance standards** refer to market outcomes. They extend beyond financial data and might include sales by product line, market shares, product trial rates by customers, innovation, and customer satisfaction.

Measuring and Evaluating Performance. After standards are set, performance must be monitored. In order to monitor performance against standards, management must be able to observe current performance. Much of the numerical information, such as sales and expenses, will be reported through the accounting system. Other items, such as the implementation of an advertising program, will be communicated through a report. At times, personal visits and meetings may be advisable when management is attempting to evaluate more complex issues, such as the success or failure of coordinated national actions against a global competitor.

Analyzing and Correcting Deviations from the Standards. The purpose of establishing standards and reporting performance is to ensure achievement of corporate goals. To achieve these goals, management must evaluate how well

---

Behavioral standards standards relating to actions taken within the firm

Performance standards standards relating to market outcomes

performance is living up to the standards the company has set and must initiate corrective action when performance is below those standards. As a consequence of distance, communication issues, and cultural differences, the control process can be difficult in the international setting.

Control strategy can be related to the principle of the carrot and the stick: using both positive and negative incentives. On the positive side, outstanding performance can be rewarded with increased independence, more marketing dollars, and salary increases or bonuses for the managers. On the negative side, unsatisfactory performance can mean reduction in all those items, as well as the threat that the managers responsible will lose their jobs. The key to correcting deviations is to get managers to understand and agree with the standards and then ensure that they have the means to correct the deficiencies. Therefore, the managers are often given some flexibility with resources. For example, if sales are down 10 percent, managers may need the authority to increase advertising or reduce prices to offset the sales decline.

Communication Systems

Effective communication systems facilitate control. Global strategies that require standardization and coordination across borders will need an effective communication system to support them. Headquarters staff will need to receive timely and accurate local input from national subsidiaries. Then decisions can be made quickly and transmitted back to the local management for rapid implementation.

Global information networks are now available that allow improved communication around the world. The Internet links millions of computer users and reduces many of the constraints imposed by geography. For example, Siemens operates in 190 countries and has instituted an internal system, or "sharenet," for posting knowledge throughout the global company. The sharenet came in handy when Siemens Malaysia wanted to bid on a high-speed data network linking Kuala Lumpur and its new airport. Lacking the know-how necessary for such a project, the subsidiary turned to the sharenet and discovered that Siemens was already working on a similar project in Denmark.[18]

Corporate Culture as Control

In addition to the processes we have described, many international firms attempt to establish cultural control. If an international firm can establish a strong corporate culture across its subsidiaries, then managers from its various units share a single vision and values. Some believe that this corporate socialization enables global firms to operate with less burdensome hierarchical structures and fewer time-consuming procedures.

Matsushita (Panasonic) provides managers with six months of cultural training, and Unilever's new hires go through corporate socialization as well. Such initiation programs help to build the vision and shared values of a strong corporate culture. Managers also receive ongoing training. For example, Unilever brings 400 to 500 international managers from around the world to its international management-training center. Unilever spends as much on training as it does on R&D, not only to upgrade skills but also to indoctrinate managers into the Unilever family. This helps to build personal relationships and informal contacts that can be more powerful than any formal systems or structures.

We must remember that the corporate culture of a firm mirrors to a large extent the national culture of its homeland. When a U.S. multinational socializes its local managers to "think and act American," this can make communication and control within the multinational easier. Nonetheless, local managers must still operate within many national cultures that are different from the American culture. It is equally important that they maintain their local culture and remain capable of relating to local customers, competitors, and governments. One way to encourage cultural sensitivity at the highest levels within a multinational company is to include board members who are not from the home country of the firm. One study revealed that 90 percent of Europe's largest businesses have at least one director from outside their home countries. In the United States, however, this number was only 35 percent.[19]

CONFLICT BETWEEN HEADQUARTERS AND SUBSIDIARIES

Despite attempts to build a transnational corporate culture within multinational firms, a universal problem facing international marketing managers is the internal conflict that arises between headquarters and subsidiaries. Table 16.1 summarizes several significant differences in perceptions of marketing issues between subsidiaries and home offices that emerged from a study of U.S. companies with operations in Hong Kong. The study also identified three areas in which subsidiaries perceived their autonomy as significantly less than did headquarters—pricing, logo and name, and the choice of an advertising agency.[20] This is probably not surprising, given our prior discussion of the impact of global branding, increased price coordination

TABLE 16.1 **PERCEPTIONS OF ISSUES RELATED TO MARKETING IN HOME OFFICE AND SUBSIDIARIES**

MARKETING ISSUE	HOME OFFICE	SUBSIDIARY
1. Visits from home office managers to subsidiaries are usually productive.	Agrees more	Agrees less
2. Problems come up frequently because the home office does not understand the variety of opinions that can exist at a subsidiary as a consequence of the more widely differing backgrounds there than at the home office.	Agrees less	Agrees more
3. Problems come up frequently because the home office does not understand that a subsidiary's culture can be different from that of the home office.	Agrees less	Agrees more
4. There is not enough emphasis at the subsidiaries on strategic thinking and long-term planning.	Agrees more	Agrees less
5. Subsidiaries are encouraged to suggest innovations to the home office.	Agrees more	Agrees less
6. The home office generally tries to change subsidiaries rather than trying to understand and perhaps adapt to them.	Agrees less	Agrees more
7. Subsidiaries have enough flexibility to cope effectively with changing local conditions.	Agrees more	Agrees less
8. Knowledge is transmitted freely from the home office to subsidiaries.	Agrees more	Agrees less
9. There is a lack of carryover of marketing knowledge from one subsidiary to another.	Agrees more	Agrees less
10. The home office tries to involve subsidiaries' marketing managers meaningfully in decision making.	Agrees more	Agrees less

Source: Reprinted from *Journal of World Business* 36, no. 2, Chi-Fai Chan and Neil Bruce Holbert, "Marketing Home and Away," p. 207. Copyright © 2001, with permission from Elsevier.

worldwide, and the trend among multinationals to consolidate advertising within one or a few agency networks.

Conflicts between headquarters and subsidiaries are inevitable because of the natural differences in orientation and perception between the two groups. The subsidiary manager usually wants more authority and more local differentiation, whereas headquarters wants more detailed reporting and greater unification of geographically dispersed operations. The parent is usually the more powerful in the relationship, but sometimes a subsidiary can take over a parent company. Trendy U.S. retailer Esprit watched its sales in the United States decline while sales in Asia and Europe soared to over $1 billion a year. Its Hong Kong office later bought full rights to the Esprit brand around the world for $150 million. Its first goal: Revamp strategy in the U.S. market.[21]

Conflict is not all bad. Conflict generates constant dialogue between different organizational levels during the planning and implementation of strategies. This dialogue can result in a balance between headquarters and subsidiary authority, global and local perspective, and standardization and differentiation of the global marketing mix. And it can allow new and better ideas to surface from any part of the global organization.

Under its banner, "Science for a Better Life," German-based Bayer is a major global player in health care, polymers, and crop science. It markets its products in over 120 countries. But all subsidiaries are not equal. Bayer's Brazilian subsidiary accounts for 39 percent of its Latin American sales. Its subsidiary in South Africa accounts for 50 percent of company sales in Africa.

CONSIDERING A GLOBAL MARKETING CAREER

A viable organizational structure, a unifying corporate culture, and effective control systems all enable a firm to compete in the global arena. Equally important are the individuals who manage the firm. Throughout this book, we have presented the argument that virtually all firms are affected by increased global competition. In turn, most firms will not only deal with competitors from other countries, but also will depend on sales that are increasingly multinational. Many will need to adapt to buyers who are becoming global themselves. Because of this, firms will need managers who understand the issues we have discussed here: the impact of the global environment on marketing, global strategic planning, managing a marketing mix across cultures, and effectively managing relations between headquarters and subsidiaries to ensure that global strategy is well implemented. Any marketer who eventually reaches the upper echelons of management will need an understanding of the concepts we have covered in this book.

In many companies, global marketing is not always an entry-level job, especially for recent university graduates. Firms often choose to fill globally oriented positions with marketers who have first had domestic experience. A good career strategy is to join a company that has global operations and whose culture you admire. After proving yourself in the home market, you should be eligible for a global position in only a few years. This is especially true if you are assigned to the firm's headquarters. Informal networking with international executives can be a good way to broadcast your interest in international markets and global strategy—and companies are always in need of such motivated managers.

Besides this traditional route to a career in global marketing, there are other ways to go international—even at an entry level. Consider smaller companies that need help with international markets immediately. Born-global companies are increasingly common. Export management companies are another option. For these types of firms, skills in the local language of a key target market can make you stand out. If you are an American citizen, you might join the Peace Corps. The Peace Corps offers positions that are business oriented, and you receive language and cultural training. You can also look for a job with a foreign multinational that operates in your country. Even if you do not work with foreign markets right away, you will gain the experience of working with different cultures within your organization. Or consider positions in purchasing with a company that deals extensively with foreign suppliers. Knowing about global marketing can make you a more sophisticated buyer. Many U.S. managers in entry-level positions in purchasing find themselves flying to Mexico or the Far East to help manage the buyer-supplier relationship. Finally, government positions such as those with local or national commerce departments can provide excellent experience and can put you in touch with many corporate executives working in international markets.

Whether you choose a more traditional route to a career in global marketing, or find a particular niche that is right for you, the need for a global mind-set and the numbers of challenging and exciting positions for global marketers will only increase in the future.

CONCLUSION

Organizing the marketing efforts of a company across a number of countries is a difficult process. As the scope of a company's international business changes, its organizational structure must be modified in accordance with the internal and external environments. In this chapter, we have reviewed the various types of organizations commonly used, showing the benefits of each. The dynamic nature of business requires that a company constantly re-evaluate its organizational structure and processes and make any modifications necessary to meet the objectives of the firm.

The task of molding an organization to respond to the needs of a global marketplace also involves building a shared vision and developing human resources.

A clear vision of the purpose of the company that is shared by everyone gives focus and direction to each manager. Managers can be a company's scarcest resource. A commitment to recruiting and developing managers who understand the complexities of global markets and the importance of cross-cultural sensitivity should help the international firm build a common vision and values, which in turn facilitates the implementation of a global strategy.

QUESTIONS FOR DISCUSSION

1. How does a domestic organization evolve into an international organization? What type of international organization is likely to develop first? What type is likely to develop second? Why?

2. To achieve better international sales, which accounted for about 30 percent of total revenues, the U.S.-based toy manufacturer Mattel decided to put U.S. division heads in charge of international sales. Discuss the pros and cons of such a move in general and for a firm in the toy industry in particular.

3. Apart from its formal organizational structure, in what ways can the global company ensure that it is responding to the market and achieving efficiency, local responsiveness, and global learning?

4. What are the advantages and limitations of using the Internet as a means of internal communication within a global organization?

5. What suggestions would you propose to bridge the gaps between headquarters and subsidiaries that are noted in Table 16.1?

CASES

BANANA WARS

For nearly a decade, the EU and the United States were engaged in a heated trade dispute over bananas. The EU had introduced tariffs and quotas that discriminated in favor of bananas grown in former European colonies and dependencies located in the Caribbean and Africa. The new rules were favorable to the European-based banana companies, whose production was heavily located in these preferred regions. However, the new rules were disadvantageous to the U.S.-based companies, such as Chiquita and Dole, that owned banana plantations in Latin America.

Dole responded to the crisis by shifting more banana production to West Africa. Over the next few years, Dole's market share in European bananas actually increased. Chiquita, however, asked the U.S. government to bring a complaint against the EU under GATT. The United States won two subsequent suits, but the EU used its veto power under GATT to avoid compliance. However, these veto rights were rescinded under the WTO.

The WTO then ruled on the case again in favor of the United States, calling Europe's quota system blatantly discriminatory. This time the United States was allowed to employ sanctions against the EU if it failed to comply. The EU proceeded to make what most observers believed to be cosmetic, ineffectual changes to its banana importation rules. In retaliation, the United States announced that it would levy 100 percent tariffs on 17 categories of European goods, including printed cards, cashmere clothing, coral jewelry, and chandeliers.

EU officials objected, claiming that the United States was not authorized to determine whether the EU's actions were insufficient and thus was required to take the case back to the WTO. The U.S. government believed this was a delaying tactic that the EU could employ again and again. The WTO supported the U.S. position and approved the retaliatory actions.

In Europe, the U.S. sanctions were called "silly" and a "return to the Middle Ages." Many EU manufacturers were angry that they were made to suffer over a trade issue that did not concern them. For example, thousands of jobs were at risk in the Belgian biscuit industry, where some companies exported 20 percent of their production to the United States. The sanctions also threatened Asian investors in Europe such as the British battery subsidiary of the Japanese Yuasa Corporation, which had only recently developed export sales to the United States. Now that effort would be for nothing. Only products from Denmark and the Netherlands escaped sanctions because these countries had lobbied the EU for compliance with the banana decision.

Some questioned why the United States was pursuing the banana case so vehemently. After all, no jobs were at risk in the United States. Still, Chiquita's lobbying efforts paid off. The head of Chiquita was a major donor to both the Republican and Democratic parties in the United States. A lobbyist for Greek feta cheese was less successful in his efforts to keep feta off the sanction list, despite his argument that the pain would be borne by Greek Americans, for whom feta was a dietary staple.

The United States insisted that the issue at stake in the banana wars was nothing less than the credibility of the WTO. Europe could not flaunt a WTO decision. Ironically, the U.S. trade representative had angered Europeans five years earlier by stating that WTO membership would not obligate America to obey its rules. The United States could defy WTO rules and accept retaliation from an injured party. After all, few countries would wish to initiate a trade war with the United States. Despite this rhetoric, the United States had complied with WTO rulings against it, such as one concerning U.S. restrictions affecting the import of oil from Brazil and Venezuela.

The United States was not alone in its attempts to receive redress for losses in the EU banana market. The WTO arbitration panel allowed Ecuador to impose over $200 million in sanctions, an amount equivalent to its banana exports shut out of EU markets. However, Ecuador annually imported products worth only $62 million from the EU, and these imports were mainly medicines. Consequently, the WTO authorized Ecuador to impose punitive tariffs on service providers and copyrighted material, including compact discs, from the EU. The EU trade ambassador announced that the EU would monitor Ecuador's penalties and challenge them if they were excessive.

Discussion Questions

1. Who are the winners and the losers in the banana wars?
2. Is the U.S. response silly?
3. What potential threats to the WTO are illustrated by the banana wars?

Sources: Michael M. Weinstein, "The Banana War between the United States and Europe Is More Than a Trivial Trade Spat," *New York Times*, December 24, 1998, p. 2; Helen Coopers, "Curdish War," *Wall Street Journal*, March 1, 1999, p. A1; Brian Kenety, "Trade: Banana Producers Fear Tariff Solution to EU-US Trade War," Inter Press Service, March 16, 2000; and Elizabeth Olsen, "WTO Allows Ecuador to Impose Tariffs on EU in Banana Dispute," *International Herald Tribune*, p. 13.

CASE 2.2

TROUBLE IN MERCOSUR

Since its inception, Mercosur had become Latin America's most successful integration agreement. Among its members were Latin America's largest economy, Brazil (GDP = US$1,035 billion), and its third-largest economy, Argentina (GDP = US$374 billion). From 1991 to 1998, trade between Brazil and Argentina increased 500 percent to $15 billion. However, in 1999, Mercosur trade volume fell 20 percent. Argentina and Brazil were both experiencing recessions and disagreed on which foreign exchange policy to follow. This disagreement threatened the future of Mercosur.

Argentina's Convertibility Plan pegged its peso to the U.S. dollar and banned the printing of unbacked currency. By restricting its money supply and curbing government spending, Argentina reduced inflation from 5,000 percent in 1989 to 1 percent by the year 2000. Through the early and mid-1990s, Argentina experienced an economic boom attributed to its trade liberalization, monetary and foreign exchange stability, and the privatization of previously state-owned companies.

Similarly, Brazil's Real Plan initially pegged the Brazilian real to the U.S. dollar. Inflation fell from 2,500 percent in 1993 to 2.5 percent in 1998. Trade and investment liberalization encouraged investment in Brazil, but pent-up demand for capital and consumer goods caused the country's merchandise balance to drop from a surplus of US$10.5 billion in 1994 to a deficit of US$6.3 billion in 1998. The Asian financial crisis in mid-1997 caused foreign investors to worry about the future of other developing countries. Foreign capital fled Brazil, and the country's BOP deteriorated. A subsequent recession, augmented by the failure of the Brazilian Congress to pass key spending reforms, further

eroded investor confidence in the country. Brazil's foreign exchange reserves continued to dwindle. The government responded by announcing a change to the free float of the real. The real plummeted against the dollar and consequently plummeted against the Argentine peso.

Still, the Argentine government remained committed to foreign exchange stability. Argentina even began discussing with the U.S. Treasury the possibility of formally dollarizing its economy. The idea was feasible. Panama had adopted the U.S. dollar as its currency in 1904. Already over half of the bank deposits and loans in Argentina were in dollars. Automated teller machines dispensed both pesos and dollars. The U.S. Federal Reserve shipped tons of dollar-denominated bills overseas every year. Nearly two-thirds of the almost $500 billion in U.S. currency circulated outside the United States.

Nonetheless, dollarization would be practically irreversible. Argentina would give up control over its money supply to the U.S. Federal Reserve. Critics argued that the U.S. Federal Reserve set policy to assist the U.S. economy, which had little in common with the Argentine economy. Even talking about dollarization would undermine confidence in the peso. Others noted that the alternative of allowing the peso to float freely like the real would be likely to erode confidence even more, resulting in a devaluation of the peso.

Nonetheless, costs of doing business in Brazil were soon 30 percent below those in Argentina. Argentina saw its trade surplus with Brazil disappear. The placing of quotas on certain products imported from Brazil, the first quotas in Mercosur history, had alarmed Brazil, which was investigating legal means to have them lifted. Many Argentine companies and multinational corporations, such as Philips Electronics NV and Goodyear Tire and Rubber Company, had shifted production from Argentina to Brazil. Argentina claimed to have lost 250,000 jobs since the devaluation in Brazil. Unemployed workers marched with signs saying "Made in Brazil—No!" The state governor of Buenos Aires summed up the anti-Brazilian feeling: "The Brazilians are like bad neighbors that come into our house to steal the furniture."

In December 2001, the Argentine government temporarily set limits on the amount of money that Argentines could withdraw from banks or transfer abroad. In the previous year, 20 percent of bank deposits in the country had been converted by their owners into dollars and moved to overseas accounts. Banks were concerned about how long dollar reserves would last in the country at the rate of one peso to one dollar. Rumors of a possible devaluation of the peso were rife by early 2002. But devaluation remained problematic. Many debts and contracts in Argentina were denominated in dollars.

A devaluation of the peso would increase the cost in pesos of meeting those dollar obligations. This situation in turn could cause a banking crisis.

Discussion Questions

1. What foreign exchange regime should Argentina adopt: dollarization, a freely floating peso, the status quo, or another? Why?
2. Which foreign exchange regime would you prefer to see in Argentina if you were a U.S. exporter of heavy machinery? A European exporter of cosmetics? A Brazilian exporter of automobiles? Why?
3. What problems related to regional integration agreements are illustrated in this case?

Sources: David Wessel and Craig Torres, "Passing the Buck," *Wall Street Journal*, January 18, 1999, p. A1; Craig Torres and Matt Moffet, "Neighbor-Bashing," *Wall Street Journal*, May 2, 2000, p. A1; U.S. Department of State, FY 2000 Country Commercial Guides: Argentina and Brazil; and Michelle Wallin, "Analysts Warn That a Free-Floating Peso Is Only Part of the Fix That Argentina Needs," *Wall Street Journal*, February 8, 2002, p. A16.

CASE 2.3

TEXTILE TRAUMA

When the General Agreement on Tariffs and Trade (GATT) was first signed, the textile and apparel industries were too controversial to be included within its scope. Employment in these industries was still high in Europe and the United States, and developed countries feared significant unemployment if protective measures were not continued against new producers from developing economies. As a result, textile trade was negotiated bilaterally and governed for 20 years by the rules of a separate international agreement, the Multifibre Arrangement (MFA), which allowed for the emergence of an international quota system regulating world trade in textiles and clothing.

Despite these protectionist measures, employment in these industries continued to decline in the developed world as manufacturers closed facilities or relocated production in lower-cost countries. And textile and apparel quotas were not immune from politics. After the terrorist attacks of September 11, 2001, on New York and Washington, DC, Pakistan was recruited to the U.S. war on terror.

The country was extended US$143 million in new textile quotas by the United States, and the European Union increased Pakistan's quota by 15 percent.

The MFA was later replaced by the WTO Agreement on Textiles and Clothing, which set out a transitional process for the ultimate removal of these quotas by January 1, 2005. Tariffs would remain. These were generally higher in developing countries, ranging from 5 to 30 percent in Malaysia (depending on the category), 13 to 35 percent in Mexico, and up to 44 percent in Turkey. Among developed countries, tariffs were highest in Australia, Canada, and the United States, where they ranged between 0 and 15 percent.

The end of quotas was expected to create big winners and losers. For example, sources at the WTO estimated that India's share of U.S. clothing imports would rise from 4 percent before to 15 percent after the lifting of quotas, and China's share of imports would rise from 16 percent before to 50 percent after the lifting of quotas. China was also expected to see a large increase in its position in the European Union. Estimates put that share at 29 percent of total imports the first year quotas were lifted, threatening currently strong regional producers such as Turkey. In fact, many expected China to attain a 50 percent share of world market within only a few years.

China's textile and apparel industries had several advantages over those in other developing countries. Chinese labor was often cheaper and usually more productive, which was a particular advantage in the labor-intensive apparel industry. Huge factories attained substantial economies of scale, and China provided a good transportation infrastructure with especially quick turnaround times for ships in Chinese ports. Locally produced inputs such as cotton also helped keep costs low. Productive Chinese textile mills provided cheap cloth to Chinese garment manufacturers. In addition, opponents accused China of unfairly gaining advantage by pegging its currency too low and not allowing it to revalue based on market demand. China was also notorious for massive software pirating, including software used in the textile and apparel industries, resulting in savings from the avoidance of paying royalties on the intellectual property of others. Critics argued that many Chinese manufacturers were government owned and thereby received unfair subsidization.

However, others were less sure about the ability of China to attain and sustain its projected gains in market share. Besides the possibility that its currency could be revalued, the Chinese economy showed signs of overheating and the government might decide to tighten credit to textile mills. As many foreign clothing manufacturers moved production to China, prices for materials and labor could increase. Already, clothing factories in China's more developed coastal cities were experiencing difficulty in recruiting new labor. As China's rural incomes rose, fewer Chinese migrated to its cities. Many international producers —as well as global buyers—were considering the risk (both political and economic) of relying too heavily on a single source such as China. Also, the large increases in market share predicted for China were based on actual experience in Australia, where quotas had been removed several years earlier. But some analysts believed that supplier countries near to major markets could partially defend their positions if they focused on "replenishment" products—fashion-oriented products whose buyers (such as Wal-Mart) were sensitive

to a supplier's ability to fill reorders very quickly and reliably.

Still, China presented a very real threat to the textile and apparel industries in most other countries. One report projected Mexico's share of the U.S. market to fall from 10 percent to only 3 percent, and the market share for the rest of the Americas to fall from 16 percent to 5 percent. U.S. manufacturers would suffer both directly and indirectly, as many U.S. firms supplied inputs to apparel manufactures in Latin American and the Caribbean. Also of concern was whether bilateral trade agreements between the United States and Latin American countries would allow Latin American clothing manufacturers to use Chinese textiles in clothing exports that received lower tariff rates from the United States. Even if the use of Chinese textiles were to be prohibited or penalized, many believed that Chinese textiles could be smuggled easily into Mexico or Central America due to lax customs procedures. Therefore, enforcing such a rule would be difficult.

The lifting of textile and apparel quotas threatened the economies of developing countries more than it did those of the United States or Europe. Cambodia, for example, expected its economic growth rate to be halved by expected losses in its garment sector. A system originally designed to protect jobs in Europe and the United States had become the vehicle by which many countries in the developing world could receive guaranteed, if limited, access to these developed markets. For example, if Wal-Mart sought to source a large amount of T-shirts, its preferred supplier in China might not be able to deliver the full amount due to a U.S. quota on T-shirts from China. Wal-Mart could be forced to seek additional suppliers in other developing countries, even if the output from those manufacturers was more costly and of lower quality than that of the preferred Chinese supplier.

But guaranteed market access for less-efficient developing countries was now disappearing. In response, a coalition consisting of U.S. manufacturers and those from 24 developing countries convened a Summit on Fair Trade in Brussels and issued a communiqué warning the WTO that 30 million jobs were at risk in the developing world with the passing of the Multifibre Arrangement. Not everyone was sympathetic. The executive director of the U. S. Association of Importers of Textiles and Apparel, sent a letter to the trade representatives at Brussels scoffing, "There is no 'crisis' other than the one created by those who did not prepare or who are unwilling to compete without the crutch of protection."

One of the early promoters of the summit was Mauritius, a tiny island state located off the coast of East Africa. Its population was largely ethnic Indians, many bilingual in French and English. A stable, business-friendly government had offered tax incentives to export-oriented industries, and large amounts of foreign investment in clothing manufacture had poured into the country. The garment industry grew to employ one in five working Mauritians, producing products for such global brands as Calvin Klein and Gap. As a result, the median household income of the country had doubled in ten years to US$4,560, making it one of the highest-income countries in Africa. However, the entry of China into the world market had already resulted in the closing of garment factories on the island, and unemployment had risen from 3 percent to 10 percent.

Bangladesh, a mostly Muslim country of 140 million, was another case in point. Its garment industry employed half the country's industrial workforce and supplied 80 percent of its hard-currency earnings. Bangladesh was one of the poorest countries in Asia and had been designated the most corrupt country in the world by watchdog organization Transparency International. Political tension was pervasive, and Muslim fundamentalist parties were expanding their control in parliament. Some rural areas had become essentially ungovernable harbors of militant Islamic extremists who were opposed to the neighboring governments of India and Myanmar.

Bangladesh ranked low in basic infrastructure, such as transportation and communications, and delays and strikes at its ports often forced garment exporters to employ expensive air-cargo space in order to meet order deadlines. Although its garment workers earned less than half of what Chinese garment workers earned, its garment factories had never attained the economies of a scale found in China. Unlike China, its apparel industry had no homegrown source of cotton and remained dependent on imported fabrics. Nonetheless, under the MFA, Bangladesh had become a major supplier of apparel to both the United States and Europe.

Now experts estimated that over half of the jobs in the Bangladesh apparel industry would disappear. In addition, fifteen million jobs in related industries would be lost as well. As in Mauritius, factory closings had already begun. The burden of this unemployment would fall on both men and women, as over half the workers in the industry were female. An earlier increase in female employment (attributed to the garment industry) had resulted in improvements in women's lives, such as increased enrollments in primary education. Also, studies had linked a decline in domestic violence against women in developing countries with a woman's ability to earn cash outside the home.

As the end of textile and apparel quotas approached, both the EU and the United States prepared to apply temporary restrictions on certain Chinese imports that would threaten their own manufacturers. The ability to employ such temporary restrictions had been previously negotiated as part of the agreement for China to join the WTO. However, just two weeks before quotas were due to be lifted, China announced that it would impose export duties on its garment industry. The duties would be levied by item rather than by value and would amount to somewhere between 2.4 and 6 cents per piece. Some industry observers predicted that the duties would be painful to Chinese producers without being crippling. Others believed that the impact would be negligible. Nonetheless, Chinese officials insisted that the export tariffs represented a serious attempt to limit the Chinese threat to other developing countries, such as Cambodia and Bangladesh.

Discussion Questions

1. What factors contribute to a country's success as an apparel exporter?
2. Which theory best explains a nation's success in this industry post MFA—the theory of comparative advantage or the theory of competitive advantage? Explain.
3. How will temporary restrictions help U.S. manufacturers?
4. What actions would you suggest for textile and garment producers in Mexico and Turkey?
5. Why do you think the Chinese government has imposed export tariffs on its industry?
6. Is there hope for Mauritius and Bangladesh in the global economy? What advice would you give these countries?

Sources: Farhan Bokhari, "US Rejects Pakistan Pleas on Textile Quotas," *Financial Times*, August 13, 2003, p. 8; Carlos Tejada, "Paradise Lost," *Wall Street Journal*, August 14, 2003, p. A1; Neil King Jr. and Dan Morse, "Bush Set Quotas on Some Imports of Chinese Goods," *Wall Street Journal*, November 19, 2003, p. A1; Peter Fritsch, "Looming Trouble," *Wall Street Journal*, November 20, 2003, p. A1; Rebecca Buckman, "Navigating China's Textile Trade," *Wall Street Journal*, September 10, 2004, p. A10; Greg Hitt, "American Textile Makers Mobilize Alliance of Rivals to

Counter China's Share," *Wall Street Journal*, December 14, 2004, p. A2; Andrew Browne, "China Discloses Details of Its Textile Duties," *Wall Street Journal*, December 28, 2004, p. A2; *Industrial Tariff Liberalization and the Doha Development Agenda*, World Trade Organization, 2003; and Greg Hitt, "Latin Trade Deal Has Chinese Flavor," *Wall Street Journal*, January 26, 2005, p. A4.

CASE 3.1

BANNING BARBIE

The Institute for Intellectual Development of Children and Young Adults has declared Barbie a cultural threat to Iran. The tall, blond, blue-eyed doll represents the American woman who never wants to get old or pregnant. She wears makeup and indecent clothes. She drinks champagne in the company of boyfriend doll Ken. To replace Barbie, the Institute designed Sara. Sara has darker skin and black hair, and she wears the traditional floor-length chador. Sara has no boyfriend doll. The idea of having a boyfriend is a concept not acceptable to most Middle Eastern families. Sara's brother, Dara, is dressed in the coat and turban of a Muslim cleric or *mullah*.

Since its Islamic Revolution over 30 years ago, Iran has been particularly wary of Western influences. A Coca-Cola factory was shut down for "promoting American culture." A call to ban Barbie is not popular with all Iranians, however. Some toy-store owners think Barbie is about business, not culture, and many moderate Iranians oppose attempts to protect national culture by force and prohibitions. Barbie's continued popularity results in the doll being smuggled into Iran.

For many years, Barbie remained the most popular doll among affluent consumers in the neighboring Arab world. In an attempt to give Arab girls a feeling of pride in belonging to their own culture, the Arab League sponsored feasibility studies to interest private-sector investors in producing the Leila doll. Leila was envisioned to be about ten years old with black eyes and hair. Her wardrobe options would include Western outfits as well as traditional dresses from the various Arab regions, such as Egypt, Syria, and the Gulf states. Similar to Sara, Leila would enjoy government subsidies and sell at about $10, whereas Barbie can sell for between $30 and $150 in various capitals of the Middle East. Nonetheless, Leila was never launched.

In the United States, competition to Barbie has also emerged. A manufacturer in Livonia, Michigan, introduced a Razanne doll for Muslim Americans. The doll's creator claimed that the main message of the doll was that what matters is what's inside you, not how you look. Razanne has the body of a preteen and comes in three types: fair-skinned blond, olive-skinned with black hair, and black skin with black hair. Her clothing is modest but her aspirations are those of "a modern Muslim woman." For example, there is a Girl Scout Razanne and a Teacher Razanne.

However, it would be a doll designed and sold by Newboy Studios from the Arab private sector who would finally dethrone Barbie among Muslim consumers in Arab countries. Brown-haired Fulla has a beautiful face and is shaped similarly to Barbie but with a more modest bosom. Her outside wear keeps her fully covered. The skirts of her inside clothes fall just below her knee. Similar to Sara, Fulla doesn't have a boyfriend. Though more expensive than Sara, Fulla sells for half the price of Barbie. Fulla is supported by television commercials that show her praying, reading a book, and baking a cake for a friend. In addition the remarkably successful doll has dozens of related products, such as bicycles, cereal, chewing gum, and stationary.

As Fulla prepared to make her Western debut at the Toy Fair in New York, one NewBoy manager declared Fulla to be a global doll not a Muslim doll. He noted that Fulla is sold in India wearing the traditional sari. Everyone doesn't agree, however. There have been calls to ban Fulla in France where some see Fulla as an Islamist plot to reach children in their homes and divide the nation between a majority who play with Barbie and a Muslim minority who play with Fulla.

Discussion Questions

1. Why was Barbie popular in both France and the Middle East?
2. Should Muslim countries ban Barbie? Should France ban Fulla? Why or why not?
3. Why do you think Fulla was far more successful than Sara or Razanne?

Sources: Matthew Campbell, "Barbie Hasn't a Prayer Against Devout Islam Doll," *Sunday Times*, January 22, 2006; Katie Reid, "Arab Companies Cash in on Cultural Sensitivities," *Financial Times*, February 22, 2006; Kate Gillespie, Jean-Pierre Jeannet, and David H. Hennessey, *Global Marketing* (Houghton Mifflin: New York), 2007, p. 90; Allie Shah, "The Arab Answer to Barbie," *Merced Sun-Star*, January 15, 2007, p. D1; and "Iran: Playthings of the Godless," *Maclean's*, May 12, 2008, pp. 1–9.

CASE 3.2

WORK VERSUS LEISURE

Unlike their counterparts in many countries, employers in the United States are not required by law to provide paid vacations for their employees. In fact, American culture in general appears suspicious of leisure. Some attribute this to the Protestant work ethic. Many Americans fill their free time with intellectually or physically demanding hobbies or *volunteer work*. Even on vacation, Americans stay in touch with the workplace via their cellular phones and laptop computers.

Europeans, on the other hand, hold leisure in high regard. By law, France has the shortest work week in Europe. In addition, the French spend the most time sleeping of all industrial nations. They also spend over two hours a day eating, twice the time Americans spend eating. In Germany, however, longer work weeks may soon be the norm. To Germans, prosperity once meant less work and more leisure time. However, a low birthrate has resulted in fewer workers supporting more and more retired Germans in the generous state pension system. Germans in the workforce may soon have to work longer hours to support the retirees.

The restful German Sunday is also under attack. Sunday is designated "a day for spiritual reflection" in the German constitution. This custom results in a ban on Sunday shopping. Since the reunification of Germany, former East Germans who grew up in a largely atheistic society have waged war on Sunday closings. East German cities routinely exploit loopholes in the law to allow stores to stay open; one loophole that is commonly invoked allows sales to tourists. Department stores in Berlin now welcome tens of thousands of Sunday shoppers, using the argument that their products could be of interest to tourists. Union leaders, bent on protecting leisure time for their members, have joined churches in denouncing this trend.

If Germans may soon work longer hours, Japanese are considering working less. Japanese workers take an average of only nine vacation days a year. However, many have been reconsidering the value of leisure since their prime minister suffered a stroke brought on by overwork. Japan has seen a sharp increase in suicides and *karoshi*, or death caused by overwork. Japan has also introduced "Happy Mondays," creating longer weekends by switching certain public holidays from Saturdays to Mondays. The government hopes that more holidays will deliver the added bonus of encouraging Japanese to spend more money in pursuit of leisure and thus boost the economy.

In fact, as many Asian countries have become more prosperous, employees now work less for the same salaries. As a result, the five-day work week is becoming the norm across much of Asia—with controversial results. The Korean Culture and Tourism Policy Institute provides leisure counselors to help workers learn how to adapt to time off, since many Koreans don't know what to do with their extra time. Other Koreans are finding that fewer hours at work add stress to the family as housewives complain that their husbands are around home too much. Still others have discovered that leisure can be expensive. Visits to museums, meals at restaurants, and sports lessons all add up. A survey of Koreans revealed that 63 percent of respondents worried about the economic burden resulting from their leisure-time spending.

Discussion Questions

1. What cultural factors influence a society's attitudes toward work and leisure?
2. How can different attitudes toward leisure affect the marketing of products?

Sources: Lina Yoon, "More Play, Less Toil is a Stressful Shift for Some Koreans," *Wall Street Journal*, August 10, 2006; "Sacred Work, Sacred Leisure" in Kate Gillespie, Jean-Pierre Jeannet, and David H. Hennesssey, *Global Marketing* (Houghton Mifflin: New York, 2007); and "France Wrests Title of Sleeping Giant," *Dow Jones Chinese Financial Wire*, May 5, 2009.

CASE 4.1

CUBA: REENTERING THE WORLD

In 2009, the United States government indicated its willingness to reconsider a nearly 50-year embargo on Cuba. In the 1950s, the economy of Cuba was dominated by Spanish landowning families and U.S. corporations. A communist revolution led by Fidel Castro resulted in thousands of confiscations of foreign and local properties. These confiscations included factories, plantations, mines, and real estate. The U.S. government responded to the confiscations by placing an embargo on Cuba in 1962. The embargo disallowed U.S. exports to or imports from Cuba. In addition, U.S. foreign investment in Cuba was forbidden. Castro originally offered to pay claimants with money from sugar sales to the United States, but the U.S. government refused to negotiate with the dictator. Today the United States recognizes nearly 6,000 claims against Cuba, totaling nearly $7 billion in today's prices.

For years Cuba remained a satellite of the Soviet Union. Virtually all its trade was with Russia or the Soviet bloc. With the dissolution of the Soviet Union, Cuba was left one of the few remaining communist states in the world. It lost its traditional trading partners and found itself financially destitute. Though wary of capitalism, the island nation began tentatively to encourage foreign investment in the mid-1990s. Investments, primarily from Canada and the EU, quickly grew to several hundred in number.

The United States, never having lifted its embargo on Cuba, was quick to respond. The Helms-Burton law was passed allowing U.S. citizens to sue foreign companies that used property that had been previously confiscated by the Cuban government. In addition, the U.S. government would deny visas to corporate officers of such companies. Some foreign companies quickly complied by checking for claims against their new Cuban investments. Many more ignored the U.S. threat. President Clinton eventually waived the right to sue under the Helms-Burton law in response to an EU initiative to ask for a WTO ruling against the American law.

Then, after nearly 40 years, the United States partially lifted its embargo against Cuba. The embargo had failed in its primary mission to remove Fidel Castro. Supported by a politically powerful farm lobby, the embargo was amended to allow sales of agricultural products and medicine to Cuba. Still the Cuban government remains wary of closer economic ties with the United States. Although the Cuban economy has improved somewhat, the country remains a tightly controlled society with eleven million people living at subsistence level.

Cuba has suggested that it is ready to meet its claims obligations under international law, but it is unclear where Cuba would find the money. Cuba has stated that it plans to seek redress from the United States for the economic cost inflicted by the U.S. embargo, a cost estimated at over $60 billion. Another option could be the sale of government-owned properties. Some suggest that the U.S. government should offer Cuba a bailout plan to welcome the nation back into the fold. In the meantime, a Miami financier has proposed pooling corporate and personal claims against Cuba into a fund that would issue shares to claim holders. These shares would then be speculatively bought and sold.

Discussion Questions

1. List the various issues covered in Chapter 4 that are illustrated by this case.

2. Should claim holders be compensated? If so, *who* should pay? Why?

3. If you were considering investing in the proposed claims fund, what discount rate would you apply? In other words, how many cents on the dollar do you think these claims are worth? Why?

Sources: "Cuba Reentering the World," in Kate Gillespie, Jean-Pierre Jeannet, and David H. Hennessey, *Global Marketing* (Houghton Mifflin: New York, 2007); "Patchy Blockade," *Economist,* August 16, 2008; Laura Meckler, "U.S. to Ease Curbs on Cuba Travel," *Wall Street Journal Europe,* April 6, 2009, p. 9; and Steve LeVine, "The U.S. and Cuba: A Thaw in Rhetoric, Not Trade," *BusinessWeek Online,* April 20, 2009.

CASE 4.2

COKE UNDER FIRE

For over two years, Coca-Cola struggled to acquire the soda brands of Cadbury Schweppes, which included Dr Pepper and 7-Up. The proposed purchase originally encompassed all of Cadbury Schweppes's international markets except those in the United States, France, and South Africa. A successful purchase would increase Coca-Cola's market share in soda in over 150 countries. For example, Coca-Cola's share in Canada was expected to rise from 39.4 percent to 49.1 percent. In Mexico, its share would rise from 68.4 percent to 72.6 percent.

Not everyone was pleased with the proposed purchase. Pepsi, Coke's major rival, sent letters to legislators in Canada asking the Canadian government to disallow the purchase of the Canadian operations, maintaining that it would result in weaker competition, higher prices, and the loss of three hundred jobs in Pepsi's Canadian operations. Smaller independent bottlers joined Pepsi in opposition. Canada's Federal Competition Bureau agreed to undertake a costly investigation that resulted in Coke canceling its plans in Canada. In the meantime, Australia, Belgium, and Mexico rejected the purchase. A number of European countries and the Chilean government also put it under review. As a result, Coke scaled back on its attempts to buy the brands in Europe. Instead, South Africa was added to the deal.

The Cadbury Schweppes purchase is not the only encounter Coke has had with competition regulators in Europe and elsewhere. The offices of Coca-Cola Enterprises were raided in London and Brussels. EU regulators were seeking incriminating documents related to Coke's allegedly having given German, Austrian, and Danish supermarkets illegal incentives to stock fewer rival products. A similar investigation the year before in Italy had resulted in a $16 million fine being levied on the company. If found guilty in the broader EU case, the company could be fined as much as $14.4 billion.

The new head of Coca-Cola had visited Europe and personally met with top antitrust officials at the EU and various European countries. He wanted to present Coke's case personally and to achieve a better understanding of the concerns of the officials. He stated that Coke was committed to playing by the house rules wherever they did business. However, what Coke called aggressive yet honest competition, Europe viewed as abrasive, domineering, and unacceptable American behavior.

Problems had cropped up back home in North America as well. A jury in Daingerfield, Texas, found the company guilty of breaking Texas antitrust laws and assessed a $15.6 million fine. Coke was accused of demanding exclusive advertising, displays, and vending machines from retailers. In addition, a U.S. Federal Trade Commission report concluded that acquisitions of other soft-drink brands by industry leaders resulted in higher prices to American consumers. In Mexico, Pepsi had accused Coca-Cola of forbidding its many small shopkeepers to sell rival soft drinks. After battling these allegations in the Mexican courts for several years, Coke lost the first of 70 similar cases brought against it for anticompetitive actions. Mexican antitrust authorities also rejected the plans for Coca-Cola and its Mexican bottler to purchase Mexico's second largest juice company.

Discussion Questions

1. Why do you think some countries disallowed the Cadbury Schweppes acquisition whereas others did not?
2. Given Mr. Daft's statement that Coca-Cola was committed to playing by the rules, why was the firm in trouble in so many countries?
3. What advice would you give Coca-Cola concerning its handling of government relations?

Sources: "Coke Under Fire," in Kate Gillespie, Jean-Pierre Jeannet, and David H. Hennessey, *Global Marketing* (Houghton Mifflin: New York, 2007); Mexico Antitrust Agency Rejects Coke-Femsa Buy of Juice Company," *Dow Jones International News*, May 25, 2007; and Adam Thomson, "Coke is Forced to Pay $1 Million Fine in Mexico," *Financial Times*, May 29, 2007, p. 18.

CASE 5.1

WHAT TEENS WANT

Increasingly, consumer product companies and retailers are targeting teens. In the United States alone, the teen market comprises nearly 60 million consumers, and their purchases total $170 billion a year. Some teen-specific sites, such as Delias.com, have proved successful. Delia's sells clothes that appeal to teens while providing chatrooms and links to other teen sites. Two of the most popular teen sites are Amazon.com and Gap.com. Wal-Mart.com is also popular, despite the fact that it does nothing in particular to attract teens to its site. Teens like it for its good prices.

Marketers in Europe also are trying to understand the teen market better. European teens were once seen as being closer to their parents but more irreverent than American teens. They also watched television less and were more influenced by European music trends. However, a study of German teens—thought to be indicative of most Europeans—showed the teens spending more of their leisure time watching television, talking on the phone, and listening to music. At the top of the shopping list for buyers 10 to 17 years old was a computer connected to the Internet.

Blogs, instant messaging, and social networking sites such as MySpace allow teens to instantly know what's happening to other teens around the world. But does a global teen segment really exist? Some cosmetic marketers believe in a global youth culture that is experimental by nature and open to niche brands. Clinique, a division of the cosmetics company Estée Lauder, undertook a multinational survey to determine what teens found "cool." However, early results from the United States and the United Kingdom revealed no clear product preferences that set teens apart from older consumers. Mothers and daughters appeared surprisingly similar in what they wanted in cosmetics and fragrances, although teens seemed to appreciate advertising geared to them. Teens also shopped for upscale fragrances at mass markets where prices were cheaper.

Whether it is possible to extrapolate teen consumer behavior from the developed to the developing world is even more problematic. A study comparing Asian teens to their parents discovered that the teens ranked values such as individualism, freedom, and ambition significantly higher than their parents did. However, at a United Nations convention on youth, one girl from Bangladesh described her 15-year-old sister as pregnant and working in a textile factory all day. To her, luxury products and the Internet had little meaning. However, a study of homeless street kids in Brazil revealed that the desire to own global brands was a major impetus for their leaving home for life on the streets. Those who were able to find work would usually spend their first earnings on a pair of Reebok or Nike shoes.

Discussion Questions

1. Would it be useful for global marketers to think of teens as a global segment? Why or why not?
2. Suggest ways in which teen consumer behavior is likely to differ between developed and developing countries.
3. Why do you think street kids in Brazil are attracted to global brand names?

Sources: "Europe Vision Launches New TV Channel," *Dow Jones International News*, February 15, 2007; Clayton Collins, "Status of U.S. Brands Slips Globally Among Teens," *The Christian Science Monitor*, February 16, 2006, p. 13; *Global Cosmetic Industry Report: Cosmetics and Teens* (172:3), Gale Group, 2004; Arundhati Parmar, "Global Youth United," *Marketing News*, October 28, 2002, p. 49; "Television and Telephoning Among Top Ten Adolescent Leisure Pursuits," *Deutsche Presse-Agentur*, May 11, 2000; Anne-Beatrice Clasmann, "Young People in Developing Nations Seek More Responsibility," *Deutsche Presse-Agentur*, February 26, 2000; Mario Osava, "Children—Brazil: Street Kids Are Caught Up by Consumer Fever," *Inter Press Service*, December 9, 1999 and Steve Hamm, "Children of the Web," *BusinessWeek*, July 2, 2007, pp. 50–58.

CASE 5.2

DIASPORA MARKETING

Globalization has given rise not only to an accelerated flow of goods and services around the world, but it also has fostered dramatic increases in the movements of people across borders. A *diaspora* is defined as any body of people living outside their traditional homeland. Thus a diaspora comprises migrants and their descendants who maintain a relationship to their country of origin. This broader definition reflects the changing magnitude and nature of global migration. Since 1975, world migration has more than doubled. Today, approximately 3 percent (over 150 million people) of the world's population are migrants, many of whom have emigrated from a developing country to a developed country. One in ten persons living in a developed country today is a migrant.

Diasporans, individuals living in the diaspora, are able to remain connected to their countries of origin more easily and cheaply than ever before, reinforcing and strengthening their group identity. Innovations in transportation and communication technologies now allow migrants to psychologically and physically connect with their countries of origin in ways that were virtually unimaginable in the past. Declining costs in air and other transportation modes make it easier for immigrants and their descendants to visit their countries of origin. Global media provide immigrants with a constant stream of information about their origin countries. Ethnic bulletin boards, cyber communities, and e-commerce sites on the Internet offer immigrants an opportunity to socially connect not just with each other but also with family, friends, and other individuals in their countries of origin.

Savvy global marketers are beginning to recognize and unlock the marketing potential of diasporas in several different ways. For example, many diasporans long for the products or services produced in their home countries. On Tulumba's online marketplace (http://www.tulumba.com), Turkish diasporans can satisfy their craving for Turkish food products, such as *simit* and *mantı*; purchase Turkish books, music, and movies; and even acquire "Evil Eye" jewelry. Fast-food giant, Jollibee, often actively selects its overseas locations near high concentrations of Filipino migrants. The company website (http://www.jollibee.com.ph/) describes the importance of Jollibee for overseas Filipinos as "more than home for them. It is a stronghold of heritage and a monument of Filipino victory."

Thamel.com's web portal (http://www.Thamel.com) allows Nepalese diasporans to purchase goods and services online from Nepalese suppliers and have them delivered to the homes of friends and family living in Nepal. After a huge success selling more traditional items, such as flowers, cakes, and CDs, the company has expanded its product line to enable Nepalese diasporans to purchase health insurance, arrange for limousine service, finance automobiles and household durables, or pay tuition, utility, or other bills for friends and family in Nepal.

Diasporans often visit friends or family back in their countries of origin or simply travel to learn about their cultural heritage. Wizz Air (http://wizzair.com/) is a low-cost travel airline targeting the nearly one million Eastern Europeans who have moved to Western European nations since the 2004 EU expansion. Many travel agencies are offering "cultural heritage tours" to diaspora groups. For example, the African American Travel Agency (http://www.africanamericantravelagency.com/) offers educational tours for African Americans who want to "learn about the African presence in Brazil."

Diasporans are important for non-governmental organizations (NGOs) and government marketing efforts too. To raise resources for relief efforts following the 2004 Asian tsunami, NGOs actively targeted the Indian, Thai, Indonesian, and Sri Lankan diasporas, and the Armenian government partnered with Armenian diaspora groups around the world. Coptic Orphans (http://www.copticorphans.org/) is an example of an NGO fully supported by a diaspora community. Through its fundraising efforts among Egyptians living in the United States of the Coptic Christian faith, Coptic Orphans provides tuition, tutoring, and other services to Coptic children in Egypt. Numerous governments and diaspora organizations have put on investment-promotion events for diaspora communities living abroad to encourage them to invest in existing companies or start new businesses in their countries of origin.

Discussion Questions

1. How and why might diasporans' ability to buy differ from that of individuals of a similar age who remained in their country of origin or homeland?

2. Referring to Maslow's hierarchy of needs, identify and describe the level of needs that the companies featured in this case (e.g., Tulumba, Jollibee, Thamel.com, Wizz Air, the African American Travel Agency, and Coptic Orphans) fill for the diasporans who purchase products and services from them.

3. Are the companies featured in this case (e.g., Tulumba, Jollibee, Thamel.com, Wizz Air, the African American Travel Agency, and Coptic Orphans) targeting a *global segment* when they target their diaspora communities? Why or why not?

Source: Prespared by Liesl Riddle. Used by permission.

CASE 5.3

QUESTIONABLE PAYMENTS

Scenario 1: Thomas Karel is a Swiss national who works as the export manager for a major U.S. producer of machinery and software systems for petroleum exploration. His company is bidding on a $25 million contract that could produce $5 million in profit for his firm. The potential customer is the state-owned oil company in a Latin American country. Thomas has recently heard from his company's agent in that country. The agent suggests that he can "nail down" the contract if Thomas will give him $1 million to pass on to an influential cabinet member in charge of awarding the contract. The competition, a French multinational firm, is also bidding on the contract. *What should Thomas do?*

Scenario 2: David Yang has been sent to a country in Southeast Asia to negotiate the possible sale of a large-scale traffic control system to be adopted across the country. The contract involves not only traffic lights but also their installation and servicing, as well as computer software to monitor traffic flows. Another American in the country has suggested to David that he retain the public relations firm owned by the wife of the country's prime minister. The prime minister is not directly involved with the negotiations for the traffic control system. *What should David do?*

Scenario 3: Michael Avila is the general manager of a subsidiary in the Middle East of an American shipping company. His company specializes in moving the household belongings of expatriates working for multinational companies. Michael is about to authorize the monthly slush fund for payments to customs officials to expedite the movement of his clients' goods through customs when he catches sight of an article in the local newspaper. The government has announced a crackdown on corruption. *What should Michael do?*

Scenario 4: Ana Weiss is the new general manager of DeluxDye in Taiwan. DeluxDye produces high-quality industrial paints and dyes that are used in the manufacture of such products as toys and housewares. Compared to competitors' products, DeluxDye products are relatively expensive to purchase. However, they save costs over the long run. Their higher quality ensures more consistent color and performance and less manufacturing downtime. The money customers save can more than make up for the higher initial price of the product.

Corporate guidelines, established in the United States, forbid the paying of any bribes, however small. In Taiwan, Ana's sales force is complaining that their inability to offer "tea money" is discouraging sales growth in the market. Tea money consists of small cash payments or gifts, such as tickets to rock concerts or sports events. These payments are often given to lower-level employees who act as gatekeepers to the higher-level manager—often the head of one of Taiwan's many family-owned manufacturing firms—who in turn makes the buying decision. DeluxDye believes its products are superior to those of its competitors and insists that its sales forces around the world promote the product on its merits alone. Bribery is immoral, and it casts doubts on the integrity of the briber. *What should Ana do?*

1. Explain and defend a course of action for each of the managers above.

2. When considering questionable payments, should marketers emphasize ethical concerns, legal considerations, or making the sale? Explain your answer.

CASE 6.1

JOLLIBEE GOES GLOBAL

Jollibee is the dominant fast-food restaurant chain in the Philippines, with over 60 percent share of the market. A survey revealed that 69 percent of Filipino respondents visited Jollibee most often, compared with only 16 percent for McDonald's. Jollibee's founder, Tony Tan, is ethnically Chinese. His family immigrated from China, and his father worked as a cook in a Chinese temple. Mr. Tan was just getting started with Jollibee when McDonald's entered the market in 1981. His friends suggested that he apply for a McDonald's franchise. Mr. Tan declined.

Instead, Mr. Tan went on to develop his own chain that offers unique Filipino food, such as spaghetti with meat sauce topped with smoked fish, deep-fried pork skin, bean curd, sliced boiled eggs, and spring onions. In keeping with local tastes that appreciate food with lots of sugar and salt, Jollibee hamburgers are especially sweet. Beef is served with honey and rice, and of course there are mango shakes. Jollibee is recognized by its bee icon, which symbolizes the Filipino spirit of lightheartedness and happiness as well as representing a busy worker. Besides its flagship Jollibee restaurants, Jollibee Foods Corporation (JFC) also owns a chain of Chinese restaurants, Chowking, in the Philippines. But the importance of this chain is relatively low compared to JFC. Only 2 percent of Filipino respondents in a poll replied that Chowking was their most visited restaurant.

Over 25 years after Mr. Tan declined to become a franchisee of McDonald's, Jollibee operated 1,400 restaurants in the Philippines compared to 280 run by McDonald's. During that time, the Philippines emerged as a major outsourcing destination for 24-hour call centers serving the U.S. market. Jollibee was quick to tap into this trend. It built restaurants near the call centers and kept them open day and night.

Many surveys of Asian businesses rank Jollibee high. A poll of Asian business leaders conducted by *Asian Business Magazine* rated Jollibee number one in Asia in terms of growth potential and contribution to society, number two in honesty and ethics, number three in long-term vision, and number four in financial soundness. In total, Jollibee received the highest ranking of all firms in the consumer category —ahead of major multinationals such as Coca-Cola, Nestlé, and Procter & Gamble. Another poll, this one conducted by *Far Eastern Economic Review,* ranked Jollibee the highest on its leading-companies indicator, ahead of Toyota Motor of Japan and Singapore Airlines.

Like most other fast-food chains in the Philippines, Jollibee buys most of its food inputs from overseas. Imports tend to be cheaper and of better quality than food products available locally. The company decided that it would build a $32 million food-processing plant and logistics and distribution center in the Philippines with the incentive of a four-year tax holiday from the government of the Philippines. The center would serve both local and international operations. Keeping costs low is essential to a company already working on low margins. With the country in recession, Jollibee refused to raise prices in the Philippines, opting instead to try to increase revenues through expansion. Mr. Tan announced that he would like to see JFC open at least 15 stores in every major market around the world. To finance expansion, the company has gone public, raising money by selling shares on the stock market.

Jollibee had already begun its overseas expansion in 1987 with a restaurant in Brunei, a small, oil-rich country with a relatively large Filipino migrant worker population. JFC moved on to enter other Asian and Middle East markets, such as Indonesia, Doha, Kuwait, Guam, Malaysia, and New Guinea. In 1998, the company opened its first restaurant in the United States in a location near San Francisco. Soon five more locations were opened in California, in areas with high Filipino populations where brand awareness of Jollibee was already high. For example, the clientele at the restaurant in the San Francisco Bay area is about evenly split between ethnic

Filipinos and others. All the U.S. restaurants exceeded expectations. However, an attempt to open a Jollibee restaurant in China proved less successful. The restaurant was eventually closed.

Nonetheless, overseas expansion remained a priority at Jollibee with a goal to attain half of its sales outside the Philippines. The Middle East looked particularly interesting. There were only two Jollibee restaurants in Doha despite the presence of 200,000 Filipino expatriates. Nearly 300,000 Filipinos live and work in Dubai.

Discussion Questions

1. What strategies did Jollibee follow—or consider following—during its evolution: dodger, defender, extender, and/or contender? Explain your answer.

2. Which strategy do you think is most appropriate for Jollibee? Why?

3. Why do you think Jollibee was successful in the United States but not in China?

Sources: "Buzzing Around McDonalds," Kate Gillespie, Jean-Pierre Jeannet, and H. David Hennessey, *Global Marketing* (New York: Houghton Mifflin: 2007), pp. 199–200; James Hookway, "Asia's Most Admired Companies," *Wall Street Journal Asia*, April 25, 2008; James Hookway, "Philippine's Jollibee Goes Abroad," *Wall Street Journal*, June 6, 2008, p. B2.; and Kristine J.R. Liu, "Jollibee Opening More Stores Abroad," *Business World*, April 21, 2009, p. S1.

CASE 6.2

ARMING THE GULF

At the beginning of the 21st century, U.S. defense companies held about 44 percent of the world armaments market. Nonetheless, the market was shrinking and becoming more competitive. U.S. defense purchases were down as a result of the dissolution of the Soviet Union. Low oil prices had reduced the ability of major Middle Eastern clients to purchase arms, and the Asian economic crisis had caused other major clients such as Taiwan to cut back orders. There had been few large deals in the industry for several years. U.S.-based Lockheed Martin Corporation could boast of a major contract with the United Arab Emirates (UAE), but negotiations had been tortuous.

The UAE first considered major defense purchases shortly after its neighbor Kuwait was invaded by Iraq. It proceeded to buy Mirage jets from France and invited companies from France, Sweden, Russia, and the United States to bid on an order of expensive advanced fighter planes. Six years later, the competitors were narrowed down to Lockheed and France's Dassault Aviation S.A. In an attempt to remain in the bidding, another U.S. firm, McDonnell Douglas, had offered steep price cuts but to no avail. Two years later, the UAE announced its final decision in favor of Lockheed. Still, details of the contract remained unresolved, and negotiations began that lasted two more years. At one time, Lockheed became so discouraged that its negotiators were called home. The U.S. government intervened and brought the two sides back together.

Like virtually all defense firms worldwide, Lockheed needed permission from its home government to make sales to foreign governments. Accordingly, the U.S. government closely monitored and even joined in the sales negotiations. U.S. firms could not sell to embargoed countries. Certain technologies could not even be sold to friendly countries. Yet the U.S. government under the Clinton administration played the most proactive role in assisting U.S. defense firms of any administration in 20 years. Both President Clinton and Vice President Gore became personally involved in promoting the Lockheed sale.

The UAE finally agreed to purchase Lockheed's Desert Falcon planes. To clinch the deal, Lockheed made concessions that would have seemed outlandish 20 years earlier. The company agreed to supply state-of-the-art technology and to put up a $2 billion bond to safeguard against technological failure. It also signed on to an "offset" agreement of $160 million to help the UAE expand its state-owned petroleum sector. Offset agreements had become increasingly a part of arms deals. Defense contractors found themselves agreeing to reinvest part of their earnings in the client country, participating in projects such as building hotels and factories, or, in the case of Korea, helping to upgrade the electronics industry.

As Lockheed relaxed with the Desert Falcon contract in hand, across the globe the Russian government was hosting Ural Expo Arms. Fifty foreign delegations were in attendance to view its 800 exhibits. The Expo was designed to highlight Russian defense suppliers and to help increase overseas sales. Russia's world market share was fluctuating between 2 and 4 percent, and the Russian government was eager to increase exports to generate foreign exchange. Longtime clients such as India and China appeared to show some preference for the Russians. Potential clients agreed that Russian products possessed certain advantages, such as simplicity of use, reliability, and low cost. However, Russian servicing was unreliable, and spare parts could be hard to get. The Russian bureaucracy moved very slowly in approving export licenses, and Russian firms rarely became involved in offset agreements. Furthermore, there were so many intermediaries involved in Russian defense sales that the Russian companies themselves saw only a fraction of the profits. Still, the Russian government vowed to increase armament purchases at home and to support Russia's defense industry abroad.

It would be nearly ten years between the signing of the first contract between Lockheed and the UAE and the delivery of all the ordered desert falcons. During this period the UAE emerged as an even more important defense market as the result of U.S. presence in Iraq and Iran's regional ambitions. In one day alone, the UAE presented two U.S. firms—Lockheed and Boeing—with orders totally

$2.8 billion. The emirate of Abu Dhabi in particular increasingly used its position as a major buyer to increase its own participation in the aerospace industry. Boeing based one of its subsidiaries, Integrated Defense Systems, in Abu Dhabi. Lockheed signed a Memorandum of Understanding with Mubadal Development Company to collaborate on various aerospace projects. Mubadal was wholly owned by the Abu Dhabi government.

Discussion Questions

1. How is the global arms market similar to other government markets? How does it differ?
2. How can home governments help and hurt firms competing in this market?
3. What qualities are necessary for a firm to compete in this market? Why are Russian companies relatively weak competitors?
4. Do you foresee any advantages or disadvantages to Lockheed partnering with an SOE?

Sources: "Aircraft-Maker IDS Eyes Middle East Market," *Gulf News*, February 27, 2009; Anne Marie Squeo and Daniel Pearl, "The Big Sell," *Wall Street Journal*, April 20, 2000, p. A1; Guy Chazan, "Russia's Defense Industry Launches Bid to Boost Sales," *Wall Street Journal*, July 14, 2000, p. A10; Brendan P. Rivers, "UAE Receives First Desert Falcons," *Journal of Electronic Defense*, July 1, 2005; J. Lynn Lunsford and Daniel Michaels, "Plane Makers Get Lift in Dubai," *Wall Street Journal*, November 12, 2007, p. A4; and "Boeing, Lockheed Win $2.8 Billion UAE Plane Deals," Reuters News, February 24, 2009.

CASE 6.3

THE NEW COLA WARS

For many years, the battle between Coke and Pepsi dominated the world stage. Private labels began to make inroads supported by powerful retailers, but no national or global brands arose to threaten the cola duopoly. More recently, however, newcomers with unique histories and international ambitions have emerged to challenge the status quo.

Europe and the Middle East

Mecca Cola was launched in France and the Middle East in late 2002 by a Tunisian-born businessman

who had moved to France over 20 years earlier. His goal was to make the new product the cola of choice for Muslims worldwide and to combat America's imperialism by providing a substitute for American products. The company pledged 20 percent of its profits to Palestinian and Muslim charities. Despite its desire to distance itself from competitors such as Coca-Cola, Mecca Cola's packaging was surprisingly similar to that of Coke's—white script on red cans.

In February 2003, the company dubbed itself the sponsor of the 1-million-strong peace march in London that demonstrated against U.S. involvement in Iraq. The company handed out 36,000 bottles of cola and 10,000 T-shirts bearing the messages "Stop the war" and "Not in my name." On the heels of this publicity, Mecca Cola entered the U.K. market with the stated goal of capturing 5 percent of the world's 10th-largest cola market. Distribution of Mecca Cola in Britain was primarily through small shops in communities where Britain's 1.5 million Muslims were concentrated. But succeeding in the U.K. market would not be easy. Sales of carbonated drinks had stabilized. The market was saturated with soda brands, and mineral waters and fruit juices were attacking cola's traditional position.

Qibla Cola was launched in Britain in late 2002, and by early 2004 it had plans to enter the U.S. market. Its slogan: "Qibla Cola, liberate your taste." (*Qibla* means "direction" in Arabic.) The Qibla Cola Company also called for a boycott of all American brands to protest the U.S.-led war in Iraq and proclaimed that people should switch to brands that were independent of governments and their unjust policies. Management was planning to target students and young people and claimed that through its branding and distribution it would position itself as a global rather than a Middle Eastern or ethnic brand. Qibla's early distribution was through an informal network of independent retailers, but it aspired to enter supermarkets. The company vowed to give 10 percent of profits to humanitarian causes around the world.

In the Middle East itself, Coca-Cola had already encountered a competitor that positioned itself as an Islamic alternative to Coke: Zam Zam cola from Iran. But as Zam Zam was expanding into Middle Eastern markets such as Saudi Arabia, Coke was returning to shelves in Iran. The United States still imposed trade sanctions on Iran but had exempted foodstuffs. Elsewhere in the Middle East, the Coca-Cola Company signed a franchise with the National Beverage Company to bottle and distribute Coke products throughout the West Bank and Gaza Strip. Arguably, the benefits of direct and indirect jobs created for Palestinians by this project far outweighed the charitable contributions that Palestinians would receive from Mecca Cola.

Back in Europe, Coca-Cola announced that it would take a minority stake in smoothie maker Innocent. Based in London, Innocent had become one of Britain's top brands as a result of its social commitment and ethical marketing. Innocent dedicated 10 percent of its profits to charity and used recycled bottles. Coke's investment in the company would help Innocent expand throughout Europe.

Latin America

Half a world away, Coca-Cola faced a different kind of challenge in Latin America, where Kola Real was emerging as a multinational threat. Kola Real had been established by a family who had seen its farm in southern Peru destroyed by the Shining Path terrorist group. Eduardo and Mirtha Aranos decided to turn disaster into opportunity. Rebels routinely hijacked Coca-Cola trucks, so the couple, along with their five sons, decided to make their own cola and sell it locally. By cutting costs such as advertising, the Ajegroup's new cola sold at an extremely low price compared to Pepsi and Coke. Kola Real captured 22 percent of the Peruvian market. Kola Real then moved into neighboring Ecuador and Venezuela. The new cola captured 16 percent of the market in Ecuador and 17 percent of the market in Venezuela and forced Coke to cut prices in those markets.

But it was the subsequent entry into Mexico by the Ajegroup that truly threatened the global market leader. Eleven percent of Coca-Cola's global profits came from Mexico, where Mexicans drank more Coke per capita than any other nation. A former head of Coca-Cola's Mexican operations, Vincente Fox, had even become president of Mexico. When the Ajegroup entered the market with cola prices set at 20 to 50 percent below those of competition, Pepsi experienced a rapid 5 percent drop in sales and Coca-Cola saw sales growth disappear. Still Coke was reluctant to lower prices. Regional newcomers had previously entered the soft-drink market in Brazil and eventually captured 30 percent of the market. As a result, Brazilian profit margins decreased for Coke and Pepsi. The possibility of the same thing happening in Mexico was a real threat.

Furthermore, most newcomers in Latin America had distributed through supermarkets, which were growing in strength but still held smaller market shares of the retail market than did the many small mom-and-pop stores throughout Latin America. Newcomers did price lower than the multinational brands but did not compete aggressively on price. The Ajegroup, however, introduced big bottles at very low prices (the brand was even called "Big Cola" in Mexico) and relied on hundreds of salespeople to reach the smaller stores that in Mexico accounted for 75 percent of cola sales. In a short time, they succeeded in gaining distribution in 25 percent of such outlets in Mexico City.

Some distributors declined the new cola, citing threats from the Coca-Cola Company to pull Coke products in retaliation (an allegation Coke denied). An earlier ruling by Mexico's antitrust board had ordered Coke to stop abusing its market power over distributors. As a result of this ruling, many distributors first became aware that they had a choice about what they sold. Still, Coke could buy loyalty by offering free refrigerators to chill Cokes and buying its small retailers life-insurance policies. Coca-Cola also offered free cases of Coke, and Coke employees were constantly visiting stores to help with stocking and display. The Ajegroup, on the other hand, kept an eye on costs. Even distribution was outsourced to third parties who often delivered in rundown trucks.

Just three years after entering the Mexican market, Big Cola had grabbed 7 percent market share with a stated goal of increasing market share to 10 percent. Long the largest international market for Coke and Pepsi, Mexico had come to represent 45 percent of Ajegroup's consolidated sales. Consequently, the company was opening a plant in Monterrey in order to increase its presence in the north of the country and had even decided to move its international headquarters to Mexico. In the meantime, the Ajegroup was moving quickly into Costa Rica, Panama, and Nicaragua.

Discussion Questions

1. Which do you think is the bigger threat to Coca-Cola—brands like Qibla and Mecca Cola or the Ajegroup? Why?

2. What are the strengths and weaknesses of Qibla and Mecca Cola compared to Coca-Cola?

3. Why has the new cola launched by the Ajegroup been so successful? Do you think this cola could successfully expand outside Latin America? Why or why not?

4. Evaluate Coca-Cola's response to Ajegroup. What suggestions would you give Coca-Cola?

Sources: Grant F. Smith, "Georgia Exports to Saudi Arabia: Coke, Innovation and Islam," Saudi-American Forum Essay #33, November 9, 2004; Meg Carter, "New Colas Wage Battle for Hearts and Minds," *Financial Times*, January 8, 2004, p. 13; Bill Britt, "Mecca Cola Mimics Coke," AdAge.com, February 24, 2003; Hillary Chura, "Qibla Calls for Boycott of U.S. Brands," AdAge.com, April 3, 2003; David Luhnow and Chad Terhune, "Latin Pop," *Wall Street Journal*, October 27, 2003, p. A1; Amy Guthrie, "Peru's Kola Real Sets Up Headquarters in Mexico City," Dow Jones Newswires, July 7, 2004; "Peruvian Ajegroup Holds 17 Pct Market Share in Venezuela," *Spanish News Digest*, August 30, 2004; Reuters, "Peru Bottler Ajegroup Grows in Mexico, Centam," January 20, 2005; and Aaron O. Patrick and Valerie Bauerlein, "Coke Teams Up with Socially Focused Smoothie," *Wall Street Journal*, April 8, 2009.

CASE 7.1

SURVEYING THE TURKISH CLOTHING INDUSTRY

Gretchen Renner had escaped to the serenity of a small tea garden overlooking the Bosporus Sea, which separates the European and Asian sides of Istanbul. As she sipped a glass of strong tea, she fought the urge to abandon her thesis research project and return to the United States.

Before arriving in Istanbul, Gretchen had been excited about the project. She had designed a survey to measure Turkish clothing firm owners' use and satisfaction with the services offered by the Textile Association of Istanbul (TAI). This association offers marketing, export counseling, and educational services designed to encourage producers to pursue export opportunities.

Two months before Gretchen had come to Turkey, a Turkish friend had told her that she must apply for a research visa from the Turkish government. Foreigners planning to conduct research projects in Turkey must possess a government-approved research visa to display to government officials and potential research participants. Foreigners conducting research projects without a research visa in Turkey risk arrest and deportation. Gretchen was surprised that the research visa application had to be completed prior to her arrival in Turkey. She waited four months to receive the visa, inconveniently postponing her trip.

Once in Turkey, Gretchen sought a list of Turkish clothing firm owners from which she could draw a representative sample for her survey. Although TAI was supportive of Gretchen's project, it hesitated to share its membership list. Gretchen spent months developing relationships with key officials at TAI, conducting interviews, and collecting information. TAI officials readily shared information about the organization's history, structure, and services. Yet each time she asked about the list, she was denied access. Some of Gretchen's contacts claimed that releasing such information compromised the firms' privacy. Others maintained that no precedent existed for releasing the list to a non-TAI employee. Additionally, several of her close contacts explained to her that she could not have the list because she was not Turkish. Finally, with no explanation, TAI supplied the list of names.

Problems then emerged during survey pretesting. The questionnaire was administered via the telephone by interviewers employed by *timat,* a well-known Istanbul market research firm. During this pretesting, Gretchen and her interviewers discovered that it was difficult to circumvent gatekeepers, such as secretaries and receptionists, to interview Turkish clothing firm owners.

Hoping to increase response rates, Gretchen sent potential respondents a presurvey fax introducing herself, explaining the survey's objectives, and noting the involvement of *timat.* But respondents voiced concerns about the fax. Most complained that no high-level *timat* executive had signed the fax; it had been signed only by Gretchen and an *timat* interview supervisor. Others were suspicious of Gretchen's authenticity. They remembered Turkish media reports that several Europeans recently had posed as academic researchers to expose child labor practices in Turkish clothing factories. Because of Gretchen's German name and the unfamiliar name of her university, many suspected that Gretchen was actually an industrial spy.

Even when Gretchen or the interviewers gained access to firm owners, few agreed to participate in the survey. One scoffed, "If you really valued my opinion, you would make an appointment and discuss this with me in person. I am a very busy person. I don't have time to talk on the phone about such things."

Face-to-face interviews, however, would be more time-consuming than telephone interviews. First, it would take time to get past the gatekeepers to make appointments with potential respondents. Second, because the firms were widely dispersed and Istanbul is a very large and traffic-congested city, Gretchen and her team of four *timat* interviewers could complete only ten surveys a day. Gretchen needed to complete 300 surveys. Gretchen's research funding was dwindling, and she had to return home in six weeks.

Looking toward the Asian side of Istanbul, Gretchen wondered how she could successfully complete her research project in the remaining time.

Discussion Questions

1. What cultural factors might contribute to the obstacles Gretchen encountered while attempting to execute the survey? How might Hofstede's dimensions of culture explain Gretchen's difficulties?

2. Why do you think Gretchen finally received the list of Turkish clothing exporters from TAI? If TAI had not supplied the list, where else could Gretchen have looked to find a suitable list?

3. How should Gretchen proceed with the survey? Do you think the benefits of the face-to-face option outweigh the costs? Or could changes be made to the telephone survey to increase response rates? Are there other research options that Gretchen should consider instead?

Source: Prepared by Liesl Riddle. Used by permission.

CASE 7.2   SELECTOR'S EUROPEAN DILEMMA

Ken Barbarino, CEO of Selector Inc., was ecstatic. The president of Big Burger, one of Selector's largest clients, had arranged for Ken to meet with the vice president of Big Burger's European operations. "Selector is going global," Ken smiled to himself.

Selector was a market research firm that provided market analyses to restaurant and retail chains. Selector's products helped clients select optimal geographic locations for successful chain expansion.

Although Big Burger was an international restaurant chain, currently Big Burger used Selector's services only for its U.S. operations. Specifically, Selector provided Big Burger's real estate team with trade-area profiles for prospective Big Burger locations. Because Big Burger was a quick-service hamburger restaurant, most of its customers were drawn from the homes and businesses within a two-mile radius around each location. Selector's trade-area profiles provided Big Burger with an overview of the individuals, households, and businesses within a potential location's trade area.

By purchasing and amalgamating databases from a large number of data vendors, Selector had amassed a broad warehouse of U.S. demographic, business, and consumer behavior data, and the reports were extremely detailed. For example, Selector's trade-area profile described proximal households according to their composition, annual income, type of residence, and commute time to work. It also reported the number of area households that dined at a quick-serve hamburger restaurant last year as well as the total dollars these households spent at quick-serve hamburger restaurants during that year. Selector's trade-area profiles also included a count of the total number of businesses and employees in the two-mile radius, as well as the percentage of businesses and employees within each two-digit standard industry code (SIC) and a list of all quick-serve hamburger restaurants within a five-mile radius and their gross unit sales. These trade-area profiles enabled Big Burger's real estate team to determine whether there was enough demand in the trade area to support a successful Big Burger location.

Ken waltzed into the office of Selector's research director, Katrina Walsh. "Guess what? Big Burger is sending us overseas!" he exclaimed. Ken told Katrina that the president of Big Burger had asked Selector to provide trade-area profiles for their prospective European locations. The president had arranged for Ken to meet with Big Burger's vice president of European operations in two weeks to demonstrate the trade-area profiles that could be used to assess potential European Big Burger locations. Big Burger had provided Ken with the addresses of seven potential sites (two in London, one in Madrid, and four in Berlin) so that Selector could create examples of their trade-area profiles for these sites. Katrina was excited about the international project and assured Ken she would acquire the European data that was needed to generate the trade-area profiles.

Katrina contacted Selector's data vendors—the companies that sold the various databases that Selector had compiled in its broad data warehouse—and inquired about purchasing European demographic, business, and consumer behavior data. She quickly learned that acquiring the data at a small, precise level of geography would be a greater challenge than she had anticipated.

In the United States, the U.S. Census Bureau aggregates the data it collects into a set of standard hierarchical geographic units (see Table 1). To protect individual privacy, data are released at the Zip+4 level and higher. The standardization of the Census Bureau's geographic order and the degree of detail within the Zip+4 level enable companies like Selector to extract precise data for a geographic area, such as a two-mile radius around a particular location, because the Census Bureau units are typically small enough to fit within that area.

However, as Katrina learned from her data vendors, European countries were geographically organized in a different way. All members of the European Union were organized according to the Nomenclature of Territorial Units for Statistics (NUTS) devised by the Statistical Office of the European Communities (Eurostat) in 1988. There

TABLE 1 **U.S. STATISTICAL TERRITORIAL UNITS: LOWEST FIVE GEOGRAPHIES AVAILABLE FROM THE U.S. CENSUS**

STATISTICAL UNIT	TOTAL NUMBER	APPROXIMATE NUMBER OF HOUSEHOLDS
Metropolitan standard unit	316	30,245
Zip code	41,940	3,167
Census tract	62,276	1,551
Block group	229,466	420
Zip+4	28,000,000	10

were several design challenges associated with the NUTS program because the countries possessed divergent geographic organizational systems and were reluctant to abandon their existing geographic hierarchies. Five NUTS levels were created. The geographic data of most EU countries are divided into NUTS Levels 1–3. Some countries further divide their geographic data into NUTS Levels 4 and 5.

Ideally, Eurostat would have liked to standardize units by either territorial size or population size. It proved difficult to do either. For example, the largest geographic unit, NUTS Level 1, includes British government office regions, German *länder*, and Finish *ahvenanmaa*. But the southeast government office region of England possesses over 17 million inhabitants, whereas the Finish *ahvenanmaa*, Åhland, includes only 25,000 people. These disparities also exist at lower levels of geography. Greater London, Berlin, and the Spanish provinces of Madrid and Barcelona—all NUTS Level 3 geographies—comprise populations exceeding 3 million people, whereas several NUTS Level 3 regions in Germany, Belgium, Austria, Finland, and Greece include fewer than 50,000 people. The NUTS levels also differed greatly in territorial size. For example, some Level 5 geographies could be as small as 50 square meters, and others could comprise an entire town.

Katrina also discovered that it would be challenging to acquire data for a two-mile radius around a specific address in Europe. NUTS data—even those at Levels 4 and 5—were for areas much larger than the two-mile radius that Big Burger was interested in. Even a simple analysis of the NUTS level that a prospective site resided in would not be comparable across national boundaries within the EU.

Furthermore, although she could identify data vendors that could provide demographic and "firmographic" data, such as the total population, the number of households, household composition, marital status, the sex and age distribution of the population, and the number of businesses and employees, she could not locate a data vendor that offered the more important consumer behavior data. Estimating quick-serve hamburger dollar demand would be extremely difficult—if not impossible—without a measure of the total dollars spent on quick-serve hamburger restaurants and the number of households dining at quick-serve hamburger restaurants last year. It was also unclear whether Katrina would be able to acquire a reliable database of quick-serve restaurant competitors and their unit sales, because most of the existing European restaurant databases were old and out-of-date.

With ten days left to go before Ken's meeting with Big Burger, Katrina wondered how she would generate trade-area profiles for Big Burger's seven European prospective locations.

Discussion Questions

1. What assumptions have Ken and Katrina made in their response to Big Burger's request for European trade-area data?
2. How—if at all—can Katrina use the available European data?
3. What should be included on the trade-area profiles for Big Burger's seven European locations?

Source: Prepared by Liesl Riddle. Used with permission.

CASE 8.1

INDIAN FOOD GOES GLOBAL

Mr. R. Krishnan, president of South Indian Foods Limited (SIFL), was deep in thought in his office at corporate headquarters in Coimbatore, India. Eleven years earlier he had founded SIFL with the help of his wife, Maya. Now, after returning from a weeklong business trip to the United States, Mr. Krishnan was pondering the future of his company. Should SIFL enter foreign markets? If so, which ones?

SIFL began as a company selling only three items but had quickly expanded to a dozen products. It produced and marketed batters, pastes, and flours that formed the ingredients of traditional South Indian cooking. For example, its Maami's Tamarind Mix consisted of mustard, ground nuts, asafetida, curry leaves, coriander powder, and dried chilies fried in oil and then combined with tamarind extract, salt, turmeric, and vinegar. The mix was next bottled and vacuum-sealed to preserve the traditional homemade flavor and aroma of tamarind mix.

The company began to market its products in and around Coimbatore. Soon, however, new production units were established in Bangalore and Madras to serve the whole South Indian market. Then three more manufacturing units were established in the states of Maharashtra, Andhra Pradesh, and West Bengal. SIFL estimated that its share of market varied between 19 and 27 percent across its product categories in the territories where it competed. Recently, new competitors had entered the market. Their market shares were slightly lower than those of SIFL. In response to increased competition, however, SIFL attempted to avoid adding new product lines that might have to compete head-on with aggressive competitors.

SIFL attributed part of its success to its promotional efforts. It used advertising campaigns in local radio and newspapers. Handbills, printed in the local language of the different Indian states, were distributed in newspapers in selected cities. The company also offered sample packets of its batter products. All these efforts had helped make Maami's a household name in South India.

When Mr. Krishnan raised the question of international expansion at an emergency board meeting, there was great enthusiasm but little agreement. Some of the managers' comments were as follows:

Krishnan: Why can't we think of going international? Our strategy did very well in the Indian market. With our state-of-the-art production facilities and marketing expertise, I believe we could easily create a niche overseas.

Sunder: We have to be optimistic about the U.S. market. As you know, the Indian population there is large enough to absorb our product. Our market research also reveals that our dishes are even favored by native Americans.

Shankar: I accept your views, but we are forgetting the fact that in the U.S. market we have to compete with powerful packaged-food companies.

Krishnan: What about Asia? In South Asia, the raw materials necessary for making our products are readily available.

Maya: I do not think targeting all of Asia is a viable option. Although the Chinese and Japanese are accustomed to rice, most of these Asian countries are culturally different from India. Why not the United Kingdom? It has a considerable South Indian population.

Dinakar: Why not set up production facilities in the United States or the United Kingdom? I believe production overseas would be a better choice than exporting to these markets.

Discussion Questions

1. What are SIFL's motivations for expanding abroad?
2. What are the advantages of targeting Indian populations residing in foreign countries? What problems might arise?
3. What are the pros and cons of entering the United States first? The United Kingdom? Neighboring Asian markets?
4. Is there any advantage or disadvantage to this product being "Made in India"?
5. SIFL will face competitors such as Kraft in the United States. What overall posture should SIFL adopt in relation to these strong competitors—attack, avoid, or cooperate? How might U.S. competitors respond to SIFL's entry into the market?
6. To investigate the competitive environment for these products in your country, visit a local grocery store or supermarket. What Indian foods or food products are sold there? Do they appear to be targeted at ethnic communities or at a wider segment? What firms make these products? What insights could your visit give SIFL?

Source: This case is based on *South Indian Foods Limited (A)* by K. B. Saji. Used by permission.

CASE 8.2

PROCTER & GAMBLE TARGETS EMERGING MARKETS

At the beginning of the millenium, Procter and Gamble was the world's largest consumer goods company, specializing in household products and personal care. Among its well-known brands are Tide detergent, Crest toothpaste, Olay skin care, Pantene shampoo, and Pampers disposable diapers.

However, with six billion consumers worldwide, the company was focused only on the richest one billion. Less than a quarter of company sales came from emerging markets, and those sales were mainly to the wealthier segments of those societies.

All that changed when a new CEO decided that P&G would seriously target developing countries and transitional economies. After all, it was estimated that each week 40,000 Asians used a washing machine for the first time. Long known for its product innovation in the United States, P&G now designated 30 percent of its research and development funds to the needs of these lower-income markets. Its engineers sought new ways to make products more cheaply, and P&G researchers visited homes in developing countries to better understand consumer needs. After just six years, company sales in emerging markets reached 50 percent of total sales.

China was a market of particular interest to Procter & Gamble. In just 20 years the company had established an extensive distribution system and had seen sales rise to $2.5 billion. China had become P&G's second largest market, and P&G had become China's largest consumer goods company. With a wide variety of brands and products, the company aimed at various target markets across different price ranges. Still, China often appeared to be two very distinct markets—urban China and rural China. Urban Chinese would pay $1 for toothpaste in exotic flavors. Rural Chinese might prefer to pay half as much and want salt added because they believe salt whitened teeth.

Despite its success in the Chinese market, Procter & Gamble experienced a major product crisis there involving P&G's elite SK-II line of skin care products. Chinese authorities announced that banned chemicals were found in the products sold in China. P&G denied the allegation. Almost immediately articles concerning the safety of SK-II appeared on thousands of Chinese Internet sites. Many experts believed that the banned chemicals were safe in small amounts and noted that these chemicals were not banned in the European market or Japan. Instead, they noted that SK-II products sold in China were imported from Japan and the Chinese government could be retaliating for Japan's recent adoption of stricter standards for Chinese agricultural imports.

When P&G voluntarily offered refunds to consumers for SK-II products, a number of problems arose. Some consumers tried to return counterfeit products. In some cases violence broke out. Salesclerks were attacked and sales counters robbed. Later the Chinese authorities announced that the banned substances did not pose a health hazard. However, the loss in sales and consumer trust was especially painful to P&G because beauty products accounted for 60–70 percent of the company's sales in China.

P&G's acquisition of the Gillette Company was also seen as a way to expand more quickly into emerging markets. The acquisition was P&G's largest to date. One of Gillette's major markets was Russia, another market of particular interest to P&G. However, this market had proven problematic. When a financial crisis caused the Russian ruble to plummet, Russian wholesalers could not afford to buy Gillette products. These products disappeared from retail stores, and Gillette's Russian sales plummeted 80 percent in a single month. Gillette found it could not meet its projected global profit growth of 15–20 percent that year. To save money, Gillette planned to close 14 factories and lay off 10 percent of its workforce worldwide.

Procter & Gamble believed that Gillette's brands, including its line of razors, would benefit from P&G's distribution throughout the developing world. However, in certain countries, such as India, Gillette's distribution was already very strong, and when the two companies merged there was considerable overlap. Therefore, in the years following the merger, P&G had to restructure distribution in developing countries leading to many distributors being abandoned. This resulted in a disruption of sales.

Unilever, with a much longer history of marketing in developing countries, was a formidable challenger to Procter & Gamble's aspirations in emerging markets. More Unilever sales came from developing countries than from the company's home base in Western Europe. The company also possessed a broader product line than did P&G. About half its products competed against those of P&G. The other half of its product lines were in packaged foods where Unilever competed against major multinational packaged-food companies, such as Kraft and Nestlé. Similar to Procter & Gamble, nearly half of Unilever's total sales were in emerging markets. With sales stalling in its home market, Unilever announced that it would shift even more resources to the developing world and would consider selling off some of its current brands to support this move.

One of Unilever's traditional strengths was its positioning strategy of offering different brands at different price points, successfully targeting both the poor and the rich in emerging markets. In India, Unilever had access to many small villages, where most multinational firms had no distribution. The company worked with a consortium of industry, academic, and non-governmental organizations to better understand the needs of low-income consumers. However, the company was also focused on expanding its position among the wealthier segments of developing countries, including offering more convenience foods.

Discussion Questions

1. Why do companies such as Procter & Gamble target emerging markets? Do you agree with this strategy?
2. What are the dangers of targeting emerging markets?

3. What advice would you give P&G for engaging competitor Unilever? What advice would you give Unilever?

Sources: Susanna Howard, "Consumer Giants Turn to World's Poorest Shoppers," *Dow Jones International News,* May 30, 2005; Jeremy Grant, "The Switch to the Lower-Income Consumer," *Financial Times,* November 15, 2005, p. 13; Deborah Ball, "Shelf Life," *Wall Street Journal,* March 22, 2007, p. A1; George Frey, "Feed the World," *Barron's,* March 3, 2008, p. 32; Dexter Roberts, "Scrambling to Bring Crest to the Masses," *BusinessWeek,* June 25, 2007; and Susan Tai, "Beauty and the Beast: The Brand Crisis of SK-II Cosmetics in China," *Asian Case Research Journal,* vol. 12, no. 1, 2008, pp. 57–71.

CASE 8.3

THE GLOBAL BABY BUST

Most people think that the world faces an overpopulation problem. But Phillip Longman argues otherwise in his book *The Empty Cradle.* He warns instead of a global baby bust. World population growth has fallen 40 percent since the late 1960s. The human population is expected to peak at nine billion by 2070, and many countries will see their population shrink long before that. Japan will have 49 retirees per 100 workers as early as 2025.

Falling birthrates mainly account for these declines (see Table 1). Several factors contribute to the falling birthrates. Around the world, more women are entering the workforce, and young people delay raising a family in order to attain the higher levels of education needed to compete in a global marketplace. However, a major reason for falling birthrates is the high cost of raising a middle-class child in an industrialized country—a cost estimated at more than $200,000 (exclusive of college tuition) in the United States.

As developing countries become more industrialized and urban, they too face a high cost of raising children. In Mexico, where fertility rates have declined precipitously, the population is aging five times faster than it is in the United States. By 2050, Algeria could well see its average age increase from 21.7 years to 40 years. One of the greatest declines in population growth is occurring in China, where government policy has long supported one child per family. It is predicted that 60 percent of China's

population could be over 60 years old by midcentury.

A nation may experience a "demographic dividend" when birthrates first fall. More working-age citizens support fewer children, freeing up money for consumption and investment. Many attribute the recent boom markets in Asia, such as China and South Korea, to this demographic dividend. However, as population growth continues to slow, the nation faces the problem of supporting older populations. For example, by 2040, Germany's public spending on pensions will exceed 15 percent of GNP, and Italy's working population is expected to plunge to 41 percent by 2050. Even China will have 30 retirees for every 100 persons in the workforce by 2025. The level of entrepreneurship in a nation also declines as its population ages. Japan and France, with their high ratios of retirees to workers, rate among the lowest countries for entrepreneurship. On a more positive note, a decline in terrorism is associated with an aging population. Longman points to the fact that Europe's Red Guard, a terrorist organization active in the 1970s, is now defunct.

Is immigration the answer for industrialized countries? To sustain its current ratio of workers to retirees over time, the United States would need to absorb almost 11 million immigrants a year. Such an influx would require building the equivalent of another New York City every ten

TABLE 1	BIRTHRATES FOR SELECTED COUNTRIES, 2000 AND 2025			
COUNTRY	BIRTHS PER 1000 POPULATION 2000	ANNUAL RATE OF GROWTH (%) 2000	BIRTHS PER 1000 POPULATION 2025	ANNUAL RATE OF GROWTH (%) 2025
Algeria	20	1.5	13	0.8
Argentina	18	1.1	13	0.5
Brazil	19	1.3	13	0.5
China	14	0.7	11	0.2
Czech Republic	9	−0.1	7	−0.4
Egypt	26	2.0	17	1.1
Ethiopia	42	2.5	27	1.5
France	13	0.5	10	0.1
Ghana	29	1.7	18	0.8
Greece	10	0.2	8	−0.2
Hungary	10	−0.3	8	−0.4
India	25	1.6	17	0.9
Indonesia	23	1.6	15	0.8
Iran	18	1.2	13	0.7
Italy	9	0.3	7	−0.3
Japan	10	0.2	8	−0.6
Kenya	37	2.1	19	1.2
Mexico	23	1.4	16	0.8
Poland	10	0.0	9	−0.3
Russia	9	−0.4	8	−0.6
Saudi Arabia	30	2.9	22	1.3
South Africa	22	0.6	15	−0.7
South Korea	13	0.8	9	−0.1
Spain	10	0.2	7	−0.3
Sweden	10	0.0	10	−0.1
Switzerland	11	0.5	9	0.0
Thailand	17	1.1	12	0.3
Turkey	19	1.3	12	0.6
Ukraine	9	−0.7	9	−0.5
United Kingdom	11	0.4	10	0.2
United States	14	1.0	14	0.8

Source: Adapted from U.S. Census Bureau (http://www.census.gov).

months. By 2050, 73 percent of the U.S. population would be immigrants or descendants of immigrants who arrived since 1995. However, before this occurs, a potential political backlash against immigrants could materialize. Supply is a problem also. Puerto Rico—once a major source of immigration to the United States—no longer provides a net flow of immigrants to the United States despite its lower standard of living and free access to the United States. In addition, the United States would have to compete with Europe for immigrants from the developing world. In fact, to sustain its current age structure, even South Korea would have to bring in over six million immigrants by 2050.

Discussion Questions

1. What are the implications of the global baby bust for marketers of consumer goods?
2. What are the implications of the global baby bust for marketers who sell to governments?
3. Why do you think entrepreneurship in a nation declines as its population ages? How could this impact global marketing?
4. How does the global baby bust affect the relative attractiveness of different national markets?

Sources: Phillip Longman, "The Global Baby Bust," *Foreign Affairs*, May/June 2004, pp. 64–79; Erika Kinetz, "As the World Comes of (Older) Age," *International Herald Tribune*, December 4, 2004, p. 14; and Pete Engardio and Carol Matlack, "Global Aging," *Business-Week*, January 31, 2005, pp. 44–47.

CASE 9.1

UNHAPPY MARRIAGE

Anheuser-Busch purchased 17.7 percent of Grupo Modelo for $477 million in 1993, with an option of increasing its shares to 50.2 percent. At the time of the purchase, Anheuser held 45 percent of the U.S. beer market. Modelo was the world's tenth-largest beer producer. It held 50 percent of the Mexican beer market and exported to 124 countries in every continent of the world. However, with the passing of NAFTA (North American Free Trade Agreement), Mexico's 20 percent tariffs on imported beer were to be phased out. Modelo feared that U.S. breweries would invade its market. Anheuser viewed its stake in Modelo as a profitable acquisition of brands such as Corona, as well as a way to increase Anheuser's distribution network in Mexico quickly.

Anheuser told its U.S. distributors that they would soon have access to a major imported beer. Distributors assumed this meant Corona, which was fast growing in popularity in the United States. However, in late 1996, management at Modelo renewed the firm's ten-year contract with its existing U.S. distributors, dashing Anheuser's hopes of gaining Modelo brands for its own U.S. distribution system. In December 1996, Anheuser announced that it would exercise its option to increase its stake in Modelo.

A six-month dispute over price ensued, and the parties settled for $605 million. Then in June 1997, Anheuser opted to further increase its stake, this time to the full 50.2 percent allowed under the joint venture contract. Discussions became so contentious that the two parties went into international arbitration, and the price was eventually set at $556 million. By 1998, the price of Anheuser's stake

in Modelo, as valued on the Mexican stock exchange, was twice what it had paid for the stock. However, its 50.2 percent stake in Modelo did not give Anheuser a controlling share of board votes. It held only 10 of the 21 seats on the board of directors.

Despite trade liberalization, Modelo's brands soon increased their share of the Mexican market to 55 percent. In the United States, where beer imports accounted for 14 percent of the market, Corona had pulled ahead of Heineken to become the best-selling import. Corona was enjoying 40 percent growth per year in the United States and had already become the tenth best-selling beer in that market. It was particularly successful among college students and consumers in their 20s. Anheuser's major brand, Budweiser, found itself competing against Corona. Anheuser began a campaign to disparage the freshness of Corona. It distributed display cards to thousands of bars and restaurants, noting that Corona didn't put the manufacturing date on its bottles. Anheuser also introduced three Corona clones—Azteca, Tequiza, and Rio Cristal—all produced in the United States.

The relationship between the parent companies became more confused in 2008 when Belgium-based InBev SA announced that it had arranged to acquire Anheuser-Busch. Anheuser had originally resisted the unsolicited acquisition, even attempting to convince Modelo to sell them their remaining share in the Mexican joint venture. With the Modelo share, some analysts believed that Anheuser would become too expensive for InBev to purchase. However, when the acquisition proceeded, the Modelo

Group claimed that they could choose to opt out. The Modelo Group asserted that under Mexican law a carefully crafted clause in the original joint venture agreement permitted the company to buy back the Anheuser share should the acquisition take place. Then the company could operate independently or seek a new international partner such as InBev's archrival SABMiller. The InBev acquisition of Anheuser went through in 2009, but the legal status of the Mexican joint venture remained unresolved.

Discussion Questions

1. Why did Anheuser purchase its stake in Grupo Modelo?
2. Why was Grupo Modelo willing to sell the stake?

3. What went wrong? Why?
4. What lessons about choosing international partners can be learned from this case?

Sources: "Unhappy Marriage," in Kate Gillespie, Jean-Pierre Jeannet, and H. David Hennessey, *Global Marketing* (New York: Houghton Mifflin, 2007); David Kesmodel and David Luhnow, "Anheuser Seeks Out a Mexican Ally," *Wall Street Journal*, June 13, 2008, p. B1; Cheryl Meyer, "Bud Deal Pressures the Beer World," TheDeal.com, July 28, 2008; "Grupo Modelo Announced Profit Fall," BMI Industry Insights, August 5, 2008; Aoife White, "InBev Shareholders to Vote on A-B," *Associate Press Newswires*, September 5, 2008; and "Lager Heads," *St. Louis Post-Dispatch*, May 13, 2009.

CASE 9.2

DÉJÀ VU?

Coca-Cola, the world's largest soft-drinks company, and Nestlé, the world's largest packaged-foods company, announced that they were forming a joint venture to develop and market ready-to-drink coffee and tea products. Each would contribute $50 million to the new venture. Nestlé possessed well-known trademarks in coffee and tea. It sold iced coffee in Europe and had recently test-marketed a mocha cooler in the United States. Still, it was not very active in the ready-to-drink category overall. For its part, Coke offered a global distribution system for soft drinks.

The newly formed company, Coca-Cola Nestlé Refreshment, had its headquarters in Tampa, Florida. (Coca-Cola was headquartered in Atlanta, Georgia, and Nestlé in Vevey, Switzerland.) The only market excluded from the venture was Japan, where Coke already had a position in ready-to-drink coffee. Nestlé came to the venture with prior experience with an alliance partner; it distributed General Mills cereals through its international distribution system. Coke, on the other hand, had no such alliance experience. Two years later, the venture launched its first product, Nestea Iced Tea, a single-serve tea drink. In the following two and a half years, more than a dozen tea and coffee drinks were developed.

However, after only four years, the two companies announced that they were dissolving the equity joint venture and were closing the Tampa office. Some believed the venture had moved too slowly and had been beaten to the market by an alliance between Pepsi and Lipton. Under new terms, Coke received a 100-year license to use the Nestea trademark anywhere in the world and would pay Nestlé an undisclosed royalty for Nestea sales. Nestlé would continue to try to sell Nescafé products through the Coke distribution system.

Nestlé then embarked on an aggressive acquisition strategy. But after several years, it slowed down this activity to concentrate more on the 7,000 brands it already had. In the meantime, Coca-Cola continued to dominate in worldwide soda sales but saw Pepsi dramatically expand its noncarbonated lines, including a variety of coffee and teas. To help its ailing juice business, Coca-Cola entered a joint venture with France's Groupe Danone to expand the distribution of Minute Maid refrigerated orange juice in supermarkets throughout Europe and Latin America.

Seven years after abandoning their first venture, Coke and Nestlé announced that they were resurrecting their earlier alliance and renaming the venture Beverage Partners Worldwide (BPW). The new headquarters were to be located in Zurich, Switzerland, and the revived venture would operate in 40 countries. Nestlé would develop the products, and Coke would distribute them. However, Coke would contribute the teas it developed for the

Chinese market, along with its line of Planet Java coffees. Nestlé would add its Belte tea line. This time around, the parents envisioned that the venture would operate with the "speed and culture of a start-up company."

Five years into the new venture, Nestlé reported that the venture was going well. However, the two partners decided to scale it back. Under a restructuring in which no cash changed hands, BPW was limited to producing and selling only ready-to-drink black tea products and Enviga, a new ready-to-drink green tea beverage that purported to burn calories. Coke would develop and market its own coffee products in the future that would likely compete with Nestlé's own ready-to-drink coffees. In the meantime, BPW accrued some successes. Canadians began to drink more iced tea, making Canada the third largest iced tea market in the world and boosting sales of bottled Nestea. However, Enviga was struck a blow when U.S.

courts fined BPW and its two parents $650,000 for making false claims regarding the product. Apparently, Enviga didn't really burn calories.

Discussion Questions

1. Why were Coca-Cola and Nestlé interested in forming a joint venture?
2. What do you think went wrong the first time?
3. What do you think went wrong the second time?

Sources: Betsy Mckay, "Coke, Nestlé Narrow Drink Venture," *Wall Street Journal*, November 3, 2006, p. B3; "Déjà Vu" in Kate Gillespie, Jean-Pierre Jeannet, and H. David Hennessey, *Global Marketing* (New York: Houghton Mifflin, 2007); "Canadians' Love Affair with Tea Is Turning Cold," *Canada Newswire*, May 7, 2008; "Nestlé 2008," *Dow Jones International News*, February 19, 2009; and "NJ Joins Settlement over Green Tea Diet Claims," *Associate Press Newswires*, February 26, 2009.

CASE 10.1

MAKING PRODUCTS ETHICAL

As global competition increases, consumers demand quality products at cheap prices. To lower costs, many international firms have moved production to developing countries. Much of this manufacturing is outsourced to local contractors. Increasingly, however, many consumers are factoring ethical, as well as economic, concerns into their buying decisions. To meet these new concerns of consumers, firms must now ensure that no products are produced in sweatshops, where workers are underage, overworked, or beaten.

Consumer concern over products made in sweatshops exploded in the late 1990s. Activists embarrassed famous brands with exposés of working conditions abroad. Key targets were Wal-Mart stores and Nike shoes. Student protests ensued, and consumer boycotts proved costly to the firms. Subsequently a White House task force was established, including consumer activists and industry representatives, to suggest codes of conduct for overseas production. The task force even considered allowing complying firms to label their products "not made in sweatshops."

Mattel and Disney are two companies that have adopted codes of conduct and attempt to

enforce them. Mattel hired an independent panel to monitor its factories and is considered by many to be a model for others. Social auditors visit Mattel factories three times a year. Disney has completed over 10,000 overseas inspections and has cut off subcontractors that failed to make improvements.

Even high-tech firms are concerned about ethical suppliers after a major watchdog group alleged dire working conditions at overseas factories supplying the computer industry. After auditing one supplier, Hewlett Packard asked it to decrease the noise in its factories. The supplier complied, spending tens of thousands of dollars to amend machinery and supplying workers with top-of-the-line ear protectors. Workers then complained that their ears got too hot.

In fact, a new industry of social auditing appears to have emerged overnight. Companies have hurried to become certified under the new global standard in ethical production—Social Accountability 8000. Both nongovernmental agencies operating in developing countries and major international auditing firms have become involved in overseeing firm compliance to the new standard. In a single year,

PricewaterhouseCoopers conducted 15,000 inspections related to SA 8000 in the Chinese province of Guangdong alone.

Nike formed a labor practices department and supplied Global Alliance, a Baltimore-based activist group, with a $7.9 million grant to study social problems in its contracted factories. The company released a report identifying widespread problems among its Indonesian subcontractors. Major concerns dealt with limited medical care and forced overtime. Sexual molestation was widespread in a workplace environment where female workers accounted for over 84 percent of the workforce. Nearly 14 percent of interviewed workers reported witnessing physical abuse, especially when managers were under pressure to meet production goals. Nike, with six full-time staff in Indonesia for labor practices alone, was poised to respond to the findings. However, the company noted that it had far more leverage over its shoe subcontractors, who often worked exclusively for Nike. Its clothing subcontractors were a different story. Those local firms often worked for a dozen different companies.

Gap released a report admitting problems with working conditions in many of the 3,000 factories that produce Gap clothing. Ten to 25 percent of factories in China and Taiwan were found to use psychological coercion or verbal abuse. More than 50 percent of factories in sub-Saharan Africa violated safety procedures. Ninety percent of factories

applying for contracts failed the retailer's initial evaluation. Gap also pulled 50 percent of its orders placed with one of its 200 Indian suppliers because the company determined that children were working there and in squalid conditions.

Labor-rights groups applaud this new openness on the part of the companies, but everyone does not agree. A trade minister of India insisted that reports of child labor in his country were overblown by activists determined to make India look bad.

Discussion Questions

1. What can global firms do to make their products more socially acceptable?
2. What do you think they should do? Why?
3. What are the costs to global firms of keeping their products sweatshop-free?
4. What are the possible costs of not complying with SA 8000?

Sources: Peter Burrows, "Stalking High-Tech Sweatshops," *BusinessWeek,* June 19, 2006; "'Ethical' Products," in Kate Gillespie, Jean-Pierre Jeannet, and H. David Hennessey, *Global Marketing* (New York: Houghton-Mifflin, 2007); "India Trade Minister Says Activists Hyping Child Labor Reports," *Dow Jones International News,* October 30, 2007; and "Gap Pulls Orders from Vendor Involved in Child Labor Flap," *Dow Jones International News,* November 14, 2007.

CASE 10.2 CARS FOR EMERGING MARKETS

With automobile markets maturing in the triad, both Ford and General Motors must look for growth elsewhere. Two large emerging markets, India and Russia, promise sales growth but present challenges as well.

India is the world's second most populous country and one of its poorest, with a per-capita income of only $1,000 a year. For 40 years the Indian car market was protected from foreign competition and was dominated by only two models of cars. When the government liberalized the automobile market, global competitors flocked to India. Soon there were 15 automobile firms with production in India, a phenomenon that led to considerable overcapacity in the market.

Ford was among the firms that had been attracted to India. However, the Ford Escort fared poorly in this market. The company found out firsthand that the Indian consumer wanted the best but would not spend much money for it. Ford responded by designing their first car built specifically for consumers in the developing world, the Ikon, a mid-sized automobile aimed at first-time buyers. More than 400 engineers and development personnel were assigned the task, at a cost of $500 million.

Essentially, Ford remade its Fiesta model. More headroom was added to accommodate men who wore turbans. Doors opened wider for women who wore saris. The air conditioning was adjusted to India's heat, and air-intake valves were fitted in such a way as not to be vulnerable to the flooding that accompanied India's monsoon season. Shock absorbers were toughened to withstand potholed streets. Ford even convinced certain of its suppliers to set up plants near the Ford plant in India in order to meet India's local-content requirements. Extensive product testing was done under India's harsh driving conditions.

The Ikon was priced between $9,500 and $16,000, and its sales in India quickly surpassed those of the Escort. In addition, over 50 percent of production of the Ford Ikon was exported to South America and South Africa. Despite this success, Ford had no model to compete in the small car category, which accounted for 80 percent of the Indian market. Ford announced plans to develop such a car to be priced between $7,600 and $10,200. However, local competitor, Tata Motors, had already successfully launched its mini car, Nano, priced at about $2,500.

About the time the Ikon was enjoying its first sales in India, General Motors decided to take quite a different route to the market in Russia. GM identified Russia as one of eight countries that would account for two-thirds of global growth in car sales in the coming decade. Unfortunately, Russia continued to be plagued with both political and economic risk. Furthermore, GM was concerned that a stripped-down model of a Western car—GM's traditional approach to markets in developing countries—would not be cheap enough for the Russian market. Although such a car could be assembled inexpensively in Russia, the engineering to create the adapted model would be extremely expensive. Also, market research showed that Russians thought little of cars assembled in Russia, even if they included foreign-made parts and bore a prestigious brand name. If a car were assembled in Russia, it would be attractive only if it sold at an extremely low price.

GM decided, therefore, to put its Chevrolet brand on a product developed by Avtovaz, a struggling automobile producer from the Soviet era. As the Soviet car producer, Avtovaz had dominated not only the Russian market but also the Soviet bloc market until the fall of communism, when it lost its captive export markets and the Russian market became deluged with imported cars. Avtovaz's cheapest car, priced at $3,000, was the boxy four-door "classic." Most of its models included no automatic transmission, no emission controls, and no power steering. The company developed only one new model in the 1990s. With Russia's political

uncertainty and collapsed economy, Avtovaz lacked the funds to bring the model to production.

After considerable negotiations, GM and Avtovaz agreed to enter a $333 million joint venture to produce the Niva. GM would contribute much-needed cash, as well as designing and supervising the production facilities. Avtovaz would contribute the Niva design and would also save GM the costs of developing a parts and distribution system, because the car would be sold and serviced through the Avtovaz system. Still concerned about political risk in Russia, GM convinced the European Bank for Reconstruction and Development to lend the venture $93 million and to invest another $40 million in exchange for a 17 percent equity stake.

The new Niva was noisy, delivered a rough ride, and had a low-power engine, but it passed basic safety testing, carried a GM logo, and could be sold for $7,500. The premium model would get Opel transmissions. Surveyed consumers liked the Niva better than other Russian models. In addition, GM identified, among its international operations, potential export markets for up to 25,000 of the 75,000 cars to be produced each year.

Five years after its launch, the joint venture between GM and Avtovaz shut down production temporarily over disagreements between partners. Russian state arms exporter Rosoboronexport had taken control of Avtovaz and declared itself unhappy with the financial performance of the venture. Avtovaz demanded more money for its car kits and engines. Both partners have retained global accountancy firm KPMG to assess what these inputs should cost. In addition, production targets were slashed due to cheap imports and a rise in domestic competition.

Discussion Questions

1. What are the similarities and differences between the car markets in India and Russia?
2. Which market do you think is the most difficult? Why?
3. Compare the pros and cons of Ford's model invention strategy and GM's joint venture strategy.

Sources: "Rethinking World Cars," in Kate Gillespie, Jean-Pierre Jeannet, and H. David Hennessey, *Global Marketing* (New York: Houghton Mifflin, 2007); Guy Chazan, "GM's Russian Venture Will Resume Production," *Wall Street Journal*, February 21, 2006, p. A8; "Ford India Eyes Small Car," *Dow Jones International News*, July 17, 2007; Eric Bellman, "Ford to Expand in India," *Wall Street Journal Asia*, January 9, 2008; and Erika Kinetz, "For Safety, Status, and Price, Indians Snap Up Ultra-Cheap Tata Nano," *Associated Press Newswires*, April 9, 2009.

CASE 10.3

LAUNCHING INTUITION

Estee Lauder is among the world's largest manufacturers and marketers of makeup, skincare, and fragrance products. Based in the United States, the company's overseas sales now account for nearly 60 percent of total sales. Its global reach is significant. Its Clinique brand is sold in 130 countries. When Estee Lauder launched Intuition, its biggest new fragrance in five years, the new fragrance was allotted a record-breaking $30 million advertising budget. Lauder aimed for $100 million in sales in the first year, more than double the sales of most other new fragrances.

A typical launch of a Lauder fragrance began with its introduction in the United States. The product would then be introduced to overseas markets in six months to a year. In an unprecedented move, the launch of Intuition bypassed the United States. Instead, it was introduced in France and Britain in September, with a rollout to the rest of Europe, Asia, and Latin America in October. Approximately 40 percent of sales of prestige fragrances take place in November and December. Only later would Intuition be introduced in the United States.

Estee Lauder owned five of the top ten women's fragrances sold at department stores across the United States. However, only one Lauder perfume, Pleasures, made the top ten in Europe. The U.S. fragrance market, especially for the premier lines sold in department stores, remained in a slump. For the past five years, sales had been flat or down each year. In Europe, the market had grown about 8 percent the previous year.

Lauder had established creative divisions in Paris and Tokyo to develop products for local consumer needs. Intuition was the first collaborative effort between Lauder's U.S. and European development centers. Intuition's formula was lighter than the traditionally heavy European fragrances and was targeted at the younger woman (starting in her mid twenties). It was marketed as Lauder's first fragrance with a European sensibility, although the company wanted Intuition eventually to be seen as a global fragrance. Some managers believed that future U.S. sales might even be improved if Intuition could be billed as previously "available only in Europe."

Discussion Questions

1. What are possible reasons for the unconventional development and launch of Intuition?
2. What difficulties might the company face with such a launch?

Sources: "Launching Intuition," in Kate Gillespie, Jean-Pierre Jeannet, and H. David Hennessey, *Global Marketing* (New York: Houghton-Mifflin, 2007); Loran Braverman, "The Allure of Estee Lauder," *BusinessWeek*, February 27, 2008; and Andria Cheng, "Overseas Growth Fuels Estee Launder's 36% Profit Gain," *Dow Jones Business News*, August 14, 2008.

CASE 11.1

CHASING PIRATES

Pirated software is a major challenge to Microsoft, which loses hundreds of millions of dollars a year to the practice. Piracy also costs governments in lost tax revenues. Mexico, for instance, is estimated to lose $200 million a year to pirated software. Piracy rates vary by country, the rates in developing countries being significantly higher than those in developed countries:

China	80%
Egypt	59%
European Union	35%
India	68%
Mexico	59%
Nigeria	83%
Russia	68%
Turkey	64%
United States	20%

To combat piracy, Microsoft added an edge-to-edge hologram on its CD-ROMs to ensure buyers of the product's authenticity. Still, an estimated two million websites sell pirated software. As a result, the company aggressively monitors the Internet to uncover sites for illegal downloading.

Closing down pirates overseas has taken several forms. In Bulgaria, Microsoft launched a campaign to eradicate pirated software by offering full packages discounted 60 percent off their previous price. Buyers were also entitled to the next version at no extra charge. In Pakistan, Microsoft offered to provide a training program for software instructors and to install laboratories in the top fifty universities and colleges in the country. This $150 million package would be in exchange for better government enforcement of antipiracy laws. In Malaysia, Microsoft installed a toll-free phone number and offered substantial rewards for evidence against companies using pirated software.

In Singapore, a country of only four million people, Microsoft still loses millions of dollars a year to pirates. Microsoft began a campaign in the Singapore schools to educate students concerning the illegality of piracy. Despite Singapore's excellent reputation for law enforcement in general, U.S. officials had put it on their list of countries to watch for poor enforcement of copyrights. Under similar pressure from the United States, Taiwan has been cracking down more on piracy. A firm caught exporting pirated software was fined $7.9 million, and its owner was sentenced to two years in jail. Over a period of five years, the piracy rate dropped from 42 percent to 36 percent in Singapore and from 43 percent to 29 percent in Taiwan.

The Chinese market is also of concern. Bill Gates, chairman and CEO of Microsoft, himself traveled to China to sign an agreement with the government there to promote the authentic use of software. Under the agreement, several key government entities pledged to buy Microsoft and to avoid pirated products. In exchange, Microsoft agreed to provide technical training and consulting. Later the same year, Microsoft brought its first piracy case to the Chinese courts. Engineers were found to be using pirated Microsoft products in the office building of the Yadu Group. The Yadu Group argued that they were innocent because the engineers worked not directly for them but for a sister company. The Chinese court found in favor of Yadu and ordered Microsoft to pay $60 in court costs.

Despite this setback, Microsoft appeared to be making some headway in its attempt to gain support from the Chinese government for piracy protection. The firm considerably expanded its research and development effort in China, raising it to world-class status and offering fellowships to doctoral students in China. Some industry observers believed that when the product was "made in China" the government was more motivated to support protection.

However, Microsoft's rollout of an anti-piracy program called *Windows Genuine Advantage* angered Chinese software users. The automatically installed system update turned desktops using pirated versions of Windows completely black every hour until the software was validated. This earned the product the nickname "Black Screen of Death" by critics. Within months of the product's introduction, a Chinese lawyer filed multiple complaints against Microsoft, claiming the program violated privacy and antimonopoly statutes in the country.

After pursuing various antipiracy policies, Microsoft decided to introduce a version of Windows software especially for consumers in developing countries. A multicountry launch included Malaysia, Indonesia, India, and Russia. The new software offered fewer features for a lower price. It was installed in low-cost personal computers and not sold separately. The price Microsoft charged computer manufacturers for the product was not made public, but the low-end PCs are estimated to retail for about $300. The company also decided to test market an aggressive pricing strategy in China, offering their Microsoft Office software for only $29.

Discussion Questions

1. What do you think accounts for the different piracy rates across countries?
2. Identify the different strategies Microsoft uses to combat counterfeits.
3. Why does Microsoft expect each of these efforts to be useful? What is your opinion?

Sources: "Chasing Pirates," Kate Gillespie, Jean-Pierrre Jeannet, H. David Hennessy, *Global Marketing*, (New York:: Houghton-Mifflin, 2007); Anil K. Gupta and Haiyan Wang, "How to Get China and India Right," *Wall Street Journal*, April 28, 2007, p. R4; "China Consumers' Association Discusses Possible Microsoft Infringement," *New China News Agency*, November 1, 2008; Aaron Back, "Microsoft to Add Sites in China," *Wall Street Journal Europe*, May 18, 2009, p. 8; Peter Burrows, "Microsoft's Aggressive Pricing Strategy," *BusinessWeek*, July 27, 2009, p. 51; and *Piracy Study in Brief, Business Software Alliance*, May 2009.

CASE 11.2

FIGHTING AIDS IN ASIA

Mary Foster had just resigned from her job as a global product manager at a major multinational packaged-foods company to head AIDS Prevention International (API), an NGO based in Washington, DC, dedicated to slowing the spread of HIV/AIDS in developing countries. Mary had been an active volunteer as an MBA student, raising money for AIDS awareness programs in the United States. She welcomed the opportunity to return to this early interest.

API had been recently established by a very generous U.S. philanthropist. The investment return of API's current endowment would cover annual expenses for operating a headquarters located in the United States as well as small offices in up to four developing countries. In addition, funds would remain to support modest educational programs in these countries as well as further fundraising efforts.

Mary believed that the NGO's resources could best be deployed by focusing on a few countries in Asia. She was currently in the process of prioritizing target countries and deciding which population segments within those countries to target. Other key questions involved the extent to which API should ally with local NGOs and governments and whether API should apply for funding from the U.S. government.

The Global AIDS Epidemic

HIV was first identified in the 1970s. (HIV is the virus that triggers AIDS.) The disease spread first among homosexuals, intravenous drug users, and workers in the sex industry but inevitably entered the general population. AIDS was now the world's fourth-largest infectious killer. The disease first appeared in West Africa. After remaining relatively contained in the Congo's sparsely populated jungles, it began to spread rapidly via rebel armies and truck drivers who frequented brothels. AIDS was already devastating the African continent when it first appeared in the United States in the early 1980s. Africa still remained the hardest hit area of the world. South Africa was host to one in ten new infections.

There were substantial differences in HIV prevalence rates by region. Intraregional differences at the country level could be substantial as well (see Table 1). The highest estimates for new HIV/AIDS infections were in sub-Saharan Africa, Eastern Europe, Central Asia, South Asia, and Southeast Asia. Who was most at risk could also vary by region. In Eastern Europe and Russia, 80 percent of HIV-positive people were less than 30 years of age compared with only 30 percent in Western Europe and North America. In Ukraine, drug injection was the principal mode of transmission, whereas it accounted for only 10 percent of the newly diagnosed HIV cases in Western Europe.

Besides the personal tragedy associated with the disease, the economic impact could be tremendous. For example, loss of productivity combined with increased expenditures to combat the disease contributed to a GNP decrease of 8 percent in Namibia. Kenya—where the government once hesitated in

TABLE 1	ADULT (15–49 YEARS) HIV PREVALENCE RATE BY COUNTRY
Brazil	.6 %
China	.1
Great Britain	.2
India	.3
Indonesia	.2
Russia	1.1
South Africa	18.1
Thailand	1.4
United States	.6

Source: Adapted from UNAIDS, 2008 Report on the Global AIDS Epidemic (http://www.unaids.org).

broadcasting the danger of AIDS in its sex industry for fear of scaring away tourists—saw its per-capita income drop 10 percent. In recognition of this economic impact on developing countries, the World Bank joined other transnational institutions such as the United Nations in supporting programs to halt the spread of the disease.

Prioritizing Markets

Mary had narrowed the potential countries to four: Thailand, China, India, and Indonesia.

Thailand

HIV was first detected in Thailand in the mid-1980s among male homosexuals. The government immediately began to monitor high-risk groups, including drug users and prostitutes. Accurate information alerted the authorities to rapidly soaring infection rates. The government responded quickly with a survey of sexual behavior among Thais. This survey revealed that Thai men frequently indulged in unprotected commercial sex. These results were highly publicized, and a campaign was launched to persuade prostitutes to insist on condom use. Safe sex was promoted via billboards, leaflets, and television commercials. The results were impressive. In just a few years, adult men reporting nonmarital sex dropped from 28 percent to 15 percent. Men reporting seeing a prostitute fell from 22 percent to 10 percent. The proportion claiming to have used a condom during sex with a prostitute rose to 93 percent. The number of sexually transmitted diseases in government clinics fell from over 400,000 to 50,000.

However, Virginia-based NGO International Social Justice (ISJ) claimed that many if not most of the women employed in Thailand's sex trade (estimated at 200,000) are sold or kidnapped into prostitution and asserted that these women needed liberation, not condoms. Influenced by organizations such as ISJ, the U.S. Leadership Against HIV/AIDS, Tuberculosis, and Malaria Act forbade funding for any organization that advocated the legalization of prostitution or did not have a policy explicitly opposing prostitution.

Furthermore, in the wake of the Asian financial crisis, Thailand cut its expenditures for AIDS prevention. By the mid-2000s, expenditures were still only about half of what they once were. New infection rates remained high among drug users and homosexual men. Some believed that Thailand's war on drugs, which resulted in the killing of 3,000 alleged drug dealers, had driven drug users underground and away from AIDS preventative services such as needle exchange programs. New HIV infection rates were also up

from 11 percent to 17 percent among urban youth. Because earlier campaigns had associated condoms with commercial sex, safe sex may have become stigmatized. Condom usage by young men with steady girlfriends was only 12 percent, and unprotected sex with multiple partners was on the rise among Thai teens. Local NGOs were calling for improved and expanded sex education in Thai schools.

China

HIV first entered China in the late 1980s via infected drug users. In the 1990s, a major epidemic arose in the province of Henan when villagers were recruited to donate blood. In order to donate up to four times a day, villagers were reinfused with their own blood after the plasma had been extracted. Activists estimate that one million became infected with HIV. In one village alone a third of the adult population contracted the disease. No one was ever held accountable. In fact, China's communist government was at first less than enthusiastic about raising AIDS awareness, and many AIDS prevention volunteers reported being harassed by government authorities. Statistics concerning the disease were treated as a state secret.

The government attributed most AIDS cases to intravenous drug use. However, international agencies estimated that only about 60 percent of Chinese infected with HIV/AIDS contracted the disease through use of illicit drugs. Infection from unprotected sex was rising. China's younger generation was reaching puberty earlier and marrying later. Consequently, premarital sex was on the rise. Hundreds of millions of Chinese were on the move as well, as rural Chinese poured into urban areas in search of jobs. Many of these migrants were males who left wives behind in the country. However, many migrants were women in search of jobs that often failed to materialize. The result was a booming commercial sex industry in Chinese cities.

The government announced that it would redouble efforts to educate students regarding AIDS and launched AIDS prevention websites aimed at youth. Despite the new push by the central government, many believed provincial governments were ignoring —even covering up—the problem, and a surprising number of Chinese remained unaware of the disease. Only in 2004 did the Chinese government announce that AIDS prevention would be added to the country's educational curriculum.

India

India, with an estimated five million persons infected with HIV, ranked third after South Africa and Nigeria for the highest number of infected persons. In recognition of this crisis, the government organized a Parliamentary Forum on HIV/AIDS, which brought together more than 1,200 elected political figures from across the country. As in many developing countries, controversy surrounded AIDS statistics collected by the government. To address this problem, the Indian government hired a prestigious (and independent) private company to estimate the level of HIV/AIDS in India.

Nonetheless, a government survey showed that prevention programs were only reaching about 30 percent of the population. Women who were infected by their husbands were often blamed by their in-laws. NGOs that operated homes for AIDS patients or AIDS orphans were often evicted if their landlords discovered the nature of their operations. Police were even known to harass health workers who were trying to disseminate the government's own AIDS prevention information.

Health workers in India believed that the disease was spreading fastest in rural areas where prevention programs were the weakest and record-keeping the worst. Hope Foundation was disseminating AIDS information and condoms at truck stops. India's five million truckers covered 5,000 miles of highways and reported three to five sexual partners a week. In six years, the HIV infection rate among truckers fell from 10 percent to 4 percent.

To address the threat of AIDS to young people, the government had established two national prizes to award colleges or youth groups who acted as agents of change by implementing their own AIDS awareness initiatives. Still AIDS carried a social stigma in India. When the disease first entered the country, many Indian officials declared that India's moral character and conservative sexual mores would prevent the spread of AIDS. Sex was rarely a subject of public discourse. It was largely absent from Indian films, and schools offered little or no sex education.

The Bill & Melinda Gates Foundation had pledged $100 million for a ten-year program for AIDS prevention in India. However, several years into the program, the foundation decided to turn over its network of over 100 non-profit organizations to the Indian government to run. The government was unenthusiastic, noting that the costs of the network were astronomical. They pointed to air-conditioned clinics and glossy English posters and brochures that the clinics' illiterate clientele could not read. In addition, top managers were paid salaries commensurate with MBA salaries in the West. Results were disappointing as well. Despite an expensive campaign aimed at truckers, an internal report concluded that only 12 percent of truckers were even aware of the program's services and only 7 percent ever used them.

Indonesia

Indonesia historically enjoyed a low rate of HIV infection, but that was changing fast, particularly among drug users and throughout the nation's expanding commercial sex industry, where only one man in ten used a condom. The World Health Organization had given Indonesia even a higher priority for AIDS attention than China or Thailand, and international AIDS prevention groups stated that the Indonesian government vastly underreported the cases in the country.

However, Indonesia was Islam's most populous country, and AIDS prevention endeavors were proving controversial with conservative Muslims. Islam forbade extramarital sex. One Muslim politician remarked that AIDS prevention should focus on improving people's morality and not urge them to protect themselves by using condoms. The Indonesian Ulemas' Council, the country's highest Islamic authority, proclaimed that Muslims should fight AIDS by being more religious and closer to family.

DKT Indonesia, a Washington-based NGO, produced a line of condoms that it sold at discount rates in Indonesia to truck drivers, sailors, and prostitutes. The NGO also placed a few condom advertisements with Indonesia's MTV affiliate but used dancing strawberry cartoons rather than images of real people. Attempts to get other AIDS prevention advertisements aired met with less success. Another U.S.-based NGO, Family Health International, aired a commercial briefly that depicted men visiting prostitutes. But stations immediately pulled the ad when fundamentalist Muslim clerics complained.

The Indonesian government officially proposed new education programs in schools along with better training for health-care workers and voluntary HIV testing and counseling. However, some within the government questioned spending on AIDS prevention when the country needed basic education and health care. Also, much of the country's health-care budget fell under the auspices of provincial governments sympathetic to views of Islamic fundamentalist groups. As one local AIDS activist noted: Many considered AIDS a punishment from God for wrongdoing. Others viewed it as a Western phenomenon—and nothing to do with them.

As Mary contemplated the challenges of each of these four potential Asian markets, she wondered whether any of her experience as a global product manager could be put to use in this new context of international social marketing.

Discussion Questions

1. Given that there are many multinational and local "competitors" participating in the social marketing of AIDS prevention, what role should API play? What products/services could it deliver?
2. What elements of these services might be standardized across developing countries? What elements might need to be adapted? Why?
3. What suggestions would you give Mary for prioritizing the four Asian markets?
4. Should API partner with local governments? Local NGOs? Should it pursue funding from the U.S. government?
5. How might Mary's experience as a global product manager be useful in this new setting?

Sources: "Fighting AIDS in Asia," Kate Gillespie, Jean-Pierrre Jeannet, H. David Hennessy, *Global Marketing*, (New York:: Houghton-Mifflin, 2007); Yemie Adeoye, "Country Now Second Highest in AIDS Victims," *All Africa*, July 6, 2009; "Civil Society Groups to Join Bali AIDS Meet," *Jakarta Post*, July 22, 2009, p. 4; and "Bill Gates' Indian Education," *Forbes*, August 3, 2009, p. 95.

CASE 12.1

THE PRICE OF COFFEE IN CHINA

When Starbucks, the Seattle-based coffee shop chain, first entered China, it faced a country of tea drinkers. Still, Japan too had been a country of tea drinkers but had evolved into a major coffee market. Starbucks itself had recently entered Japan and was already the top-ranked restaurant chain, according to a prestigious industry study. Top management at Starbucks was astounded at the firm's brand recognition across Asia, an awareness that had come about with virtually no investment in advertising. The company soon promoted China to a priority market.

In considering China, Starbucks noted that coffee consumption in a country is directly related to income. The firm sought to take advantage of growing disposable income in China, where per-capita income had reached $750 a year. In particular, Starbucks believed there would be substantial demand among younger urbanites in China. Confident in their decision, the firm entered the Chinese market with plans to open ten shops in Beijing in 18 months. The first Starbucks in Beijing was located in a shopping center across the street from a five-star hotel. Still, some were skeptical about the Starbucks move. Coffee sales had been growing between 5 and 8 percent a year in China. However, in the wake of the Asian financial crisis many foreign expatriates left the country. Consequently, coffee sales growth had tapered off.

When Starbucks opened in Beijing, the store offered the same coffee products and other merchandise as was available in its U.S. shops. Starbucks's stated strategy was to set prices lower than those of comparable coffee shops already opened in China. These other coffee shops targeted expatriates, tourists, and elite Chinese. China's luxury market was among the fastest growing in the world. Luxury shoppers were largely young professionals, many of whom enjoyed trying new foreign brands. Starbucks hoped to target a larger segment of Chinese society. Therefore, prices were set similar to those charged in New York City, with a grande latte priced at $4.50. A local coffee shop in the same complex that charged prices even higher than those at Starbucks announced that it would lower prices to below those of the new U.S. competitor.

Starbucks imported all its coffee beans into China, despite the fact that China was attempting to improve both the quality and the size of its own coffee harvests. Other nations, such as Vietnam, had expanded coffee production. This had resulted in a world supply of coffee beans that exceeded demand by 10 percent. Furthermore, a devaluation of Brazil's currency provided this major coffee exporter with an increased competitive edge over new entrants into the coffee market.

Discussion Questions

1. What are the possible arguments for pricing a grande latte at $4.50 in Beijing?
2. What are the possible arguments for pricing lower? For pricing higher?
3. Could purchasing Chinese coffee beans in the future affect Starbucks's pricing strategy in China? Explain.

Sources: "The Price of Coffee in China," in Kate Gillespie, Jean-Pierre Jeannet, and H. David Hennessey, *Global Marketing* (New York:: Houghton-Mifflin, 2007); John Rolfe and Tom Smithies, "Roaring China No Longer Synonymous with Cheap," *Daily Telegraph*, August 4, 2008, p.19; Jenn Abelson, "In Second Crack at China Market, Dunkin' Donuts Alters Recipe," *Boston Globe*, November 21, 2008, p. A1; and Bonnie Cao, "Luxury Brands Look to Well-Heeled Chinese," *Associated Press Newswires*, May 10, 2009.

CASE 12.2

THE PRICE OF LIFE

In a surprising announcement, the world's second largest pharmaceutical company, GlaxoSmithKline (GSK), announced that it would slash prices on the pharmaceuticals it sold in the world's poorest countries. The company challenged other pharmaceutical firms to do the same. Specifically, GSK declared that it would cut prices for all drugs in the 50 least-developed countries to a level no higher than 25 percent of the price charged in the United States. The company also pledged to redirect 20 percent of its profits from poor countries to hospitals, clinics, and medical staff in those countries. In addition to slashing prices in the very poor markets, GSK also noted that it was determined to make drug prices more affordable in what it termed to be middle-income countries, such as Brazil and Mexico.

This was not the first time a global pharmaceutical company had taken such action. Eight years earlier, Merck declared that it would cut prices 40 to 55 percent in African markets on two of its recent AIDS-fighting drugs. Merck's powerful three-drug cocktail would be available in Africa for $1,330 a year, compared to approximately $11,000 in the United States. The company noted that it would be realizing no profits at this new price. Merck also pledged to extend these discounts to poor countries elsewhere in the world. Bristol-Myers followed suit, promising to slice the price of its AIDS drug Zerit to only $54 a year in Africa. At this price, Bristol-Myers claimed to be selling below costs. The company called on donor governments in Europe, Japan, and the United States to join in a vigorous international response to the AIDS crisis in Africa, where more than 26 million people are estimated to be infected with the HIV virus that eventually causes AIDS.

Only a week before, however, 39 major pharmaceutical companies had begun litigation to stop Indian pharmaceutical firms from selling generic versions of their patented drugs, including AIDS drugs, in the South African market. India had long refused to recognize pharmaceutical patents in order to supply its vast poor population with recent pharmaceutical products at much cheaper prices. Indian firms had become adept at reverse-engineering drugs and had become efficient producers and exporters of high-quality generics. When two Indian generic drug firms, Cipla and Hetero, entered a price war in Africa, prices on some key AIDS drugs fell precipitously. India had joined the WTO, and the country consequently agreed to bring its pharmaceutical protection laws more in line with world norms. However, change was not immediate, and patent protection cases were slowly working their way through the Indian legal system.

In the meantime, the fight to keep the prices of AIDS drugs high in Africa eventually failed, resulting in embarrassing public relations missteps for many global pharmaceutical companies. Consumer boycotts had even been threatened in developed markets. Many companies that held patents on AIDS pharmaceuticals lowered their prices to below that of the Indian generics. In some cases, donor organizations, such as the United Nations, helped supplement the low prices, bolstering the margins the pharmaceutical companies made off the sales. But primarily, the global pharmaceutical companies simply agreed to lower their prices. In the years that followed, access to life-saving AIDS treatments increased significantly in Africa, and the growth of Indian generics was somewhat abated.

Nonetheless, the fact that pharmaceutical companies continued to charge different prices in different countries for the same drug fueled controversy. For example, as markets matured in developed countries, many firms were counting on substantial growth among the middle classes in the developing world, especially in middle-income countries such as Mexico. However, they faced pressure to keep prices low in these countries as well. When Abbott

Laboratories was told by the Thai government to lower its price on its latest version of the AIDS drug Kaletra, the company threatened to remove it from the Thai market. A consumer boycott of the company ensued, and Abbott agreed to lower the price to $1,000 a year. In another lower-middle-income country, Guatemala, the drug sold for $2,200. The average salary in Guatemala was $2,400.

Similarly, Bristol-Myers Squibb charged four times as much for two of its AIDS drugs in Mexico as it did in sub-Saharan Africa. An AIDS treatment in middle-income Mexico could cost $6,000 in a country where the per-capita income was only about $7,300. An AIDS organization launched an ad campaign in the United States, specifically in Los Angeles, against Bristol-Myers demanding that the company lower its prices in Mexico.

Of course, consumers in developing countries rarely pay the full price of a drug, because governments often purchase and dispense critical drugs. As major buyers, governments too were concerned with costs. However, Indian generic giant, Aurobindo, sued the South African government when it chose a local producer's bid over Aurobindo's to supply an AIDS drug. Aurobindo claimed that their bid was priced about 30 percent lower than the winner's bid. However, the South African government produced a study showing that the local producer's tax contribution, linkages with local suppliers, and job creation supported the government decision to procure locally. In fact, emerging markets enforced some of the world's highest tariffs on pharmaceuticals. Iran had tariffs of 50 percent, India of 36 percent, and Brazil and Mexico of more than 35 percent.

Controversy was not limited to emerging markets. Even in developed countries, pharmaceutical prices could differ substantially. For example, drug prices were higher in the United States than in Europe, where governments paid for most prescription drugs. Consequently, European governments negotiated prices with pharmaceutical firms. For example, the antipsychotic drug Clozaril could cost $51.94 in Spain, $89.55 in Germany, $271.08 in Canada, and $317.03 in the United States. Ironically, over-the-counter drugs and generic versions of prescription drugs whose patents had expired could be cheaper in the United States than in Europe because of greater competition in the U.S. market.

Discussion Questions

1. What factors might contribute to GlaxoSmithKline's announcement to discount prices in emerging markets? Do you think these reasons are altruistic or self-serving?
2. Should U.S. consumers pay higher prices for pharmaceuticals than Africans? Why or why not?
3. Should Mexican consumers pay higher prices for pharmaceuticals than Africans? Why or why not?
4. Should U.S. consumers pay higher prices than Europeans for pharmaceuticals? Why or why not?
5. Should national governments pay more for locally produced pharmaceuticals?
6. What challenges might pharmaceutical companies face from widely disparate prices?

Sources: Sarah Boseley, "Drug Giant Pledges Cheap Medicine for World's Poor," February 14, 2009, *The Guardian*, p. 1; "The Price of Life," in Kate Gillespie, Jean-Pierre Jeannet, and H. David Hennessey, *Global Marketing* (New York:: Houghton-Mifflin, 2007); Theresa Agovino, "AIDS Group Launches Ad Campaign," *Associated Press Newswires*, February 23, 2007; Nicholas Zamiska and James Hookway, "Abbott's Thai Pact May Augur Pricing Shift," *Wall Street Journal*, April 23, 2007, p. A3; Philip Ngunjiri, "Big Pharma Still Ignoring the Poor," *All Africa*, December 10, 2007; and Mathabo Le Roux, "Indian Firm Sues Over Aids-Drug Tender," *All Africa*, June 29, 2009.

CASE 12.3

GAMALI AIR

Jennifer Beaudreau, an account manager at Ameridere, was very excited to learn that Gamali Air was seriously considering purchasing two of her company's L700 Turboprop planes. Ameridere had been invited to bid on the contract and had subsequently offered to deliver the two planes for US$46 million. Gamali Air was to pay $12 million in cash upon delivery, $12 million one year later, and $22 million three years after delivery. Interest charges were already included in the $46 million bid.

Gamali, once a part of French West Africa, was now a multiparty democracy with a population of ten million, 85 percent of whom were Muslim. The GDP per capita in Gamali was only $1,600, and the illiteracy rate remained at about 60 percent. The main industries of Gamali were tourism, agriculture, fish processing, phosphate mining, fertilizer production, and petroleum refining. The latter required the importation of oil because Gamali had no crude oil reserves itself. The country's exports of $1.1 billion included fish, peanuts, refined petroleum products, phosphates, and cotton. Tourism was another substantial source of foreign exchange. For the past year, however, rising world oil prices caused Gamali to run a significant balance-of-trade deficit, and inflation had risen to 15 percent from a prior low of 8 percent. Inflation was also fueled by government spending to try and offset unemployment, which was currently estimated at 48 percent. High unemployment in the cities contributed to a number of social problems, including juvenile delinquency and drug addiction. Although rebel groups recently signed a peace treaty with the government, the south of Gamali was still plagued with intermittent armed conflict by separatist groups and bandits.

Gamali Air originated in 1965 when it was established as a state-owned enterprise. As a result of privatization, 30 percent of the company had been sold to a Gamali business group whose other group companies included several hotels, a trading company, and investments in construction and textiles. The Gamali government retained the remaining 70 percent of the airline. With flights to Paris, Lyons, Marseilles, London, and New York, the stated goal of Gamali Air was to become the leading carrier in Africa. The two additional planes would add to the airline's current fleet of four planes. Gamali Air had purchased Boeing and Airbus aircraft in the past, but it was now in the market for planes appropriate for medium hauls. The airline was expanding its regional service within Gamali primarily to service increased demand from tourists visiting its wildlife parks.

Jennifer had supervised the original bid for the sale. Now the vice president of Gamali Air had formally notified her that Ameridere was one of two finalists for the contract. Their remaining competitor was a Brazilian firm that Ameridere had never before bid against. However, Jennifer knew that the Brazilian firm, which was about half the size of Ameridere, was strong in Latin America and Asian markets and had recently won a substantial contract in Europe. Both firms specialized in making smaller planes for regional markets. For example

Ameridere's L700 Turboprop was designed for flights fewer than 500 miles and carried 86 passengers. Ameridere was especially well known for the comfort and quietness of its planes as well as its after-sales service. The Brazilian firm was well known for the creative financing packages it offered customers.

Although the recent communication from Gamali Air was exciting, Jennifer realized that Ameridere would have to respond quickly to three requests forwarded by its potential customer:

- Ameridere was now asked to present a bid for after-sales service and training for flight and maintenance crews.
- Management at Gamali Air also suggested that payment for the planes be made by countertrade. The airline would arrange through the Gamali government to deliver fertilizer or phosphate valued at $46 million over a period of three years. These products would be valued at their world market price less 5 percent on the day it was received by Ameridere. The 5 percent was supposed to cover the cost of shipping the products to possible markets in France or Spain.
- Finally, Ameridere was asked to agree to quote the price in Gamali dinars instead of U.S. dollars. The vice president of Gamali Air reminded Jennifer that the dinar had been pegged 1:1 to the euro three years earlier and the euro had increased 30 percent against the dollar in the past year. He noted that if the sale had been concluded a year ago, Ameridere would have realized 30 percent more dollars on its second payment had it quoted the price in dinars rather than in dollars.

Jennifer knew that her company wanted to expand out of its current markets in North America and Europe, where sales growth had slowed, and management at Gamali Air had intimated that, all things being equal, they would prefer to work with an American rather than a Brazilian supplier. However, Ameridere had never become involved in countertrade or pricing in foreign currencies. As she sat down to develop answers to the requests made by Gamali Air, Jennifer remembered what her boss had said that morning: "Let's make them a counteroffer both sides can live with."

Discussion Questions

1. Evaluate Gamali Air's countertrade proposal.

2. Evaluate the proposal to quote the price in dinars rather than in U.S. dollars.

3. How would you address each of Gamali Air's requests? Develop a counterproposal that "both sides can live with." Explain why your proposal would be reasonably attractive to both Ameridere and Gamali Air.

Source: Case prepared by Kate Gillespie and David Hennessey for class discussion.

CASE 13.1

GIANTS IN ASIA

The world's two largest retailers have targeted Asia with varying results. U.S.-based Wal-Mart and France's Carrefour both offer large stores stocked with groceries and general merchandise. Their entry into new national markets is invariably a shock to local retailers, who suddenly see the status quo of decades upset by these international competitors.

Government officials in China have credited Wal-Mart with revitalizing the retail sector. For years, government-owned retailers offered the same limited products, while employees took naps on the counters. When Wal-Mart opened its new store underneath the soccer stadium in the city of Dalian, the store was soon packed to capacity. Still, Wal-Mart chose to enter China slowly in order to learn as it went along. When it opened its first stores, customers arrived on bicycles and made only small purchases. Wal-Mart also discovered that it couldn't sell a year's supply of soy sauce to customers who lived in small apartments. Furthermore, the firm faced a variety of government restrictions. Foreign retailers needed government-backed partners, and cities often restricted the size of stores. In response to these challenges, Wal-Mart invited government officials to visit its headquarters in the United States, donated to local charities, and even built a school. Wal-Mart sourced nearly all its products locally, and nearly all employees were Chinese. To understand Chinese consumption patterns better, Wal-Mart's American manager walked the streets to see what the Chinese were buying.

Whereas Wal-Mart thrived in China, the company's decision to enter Japan proved more problematic. Wal-Mart studied the Japanese market for four years and decided it needed a local partner. It agreed to buy 6 percent of Japan's fifth-largest supermarket chain, Seiyu, with the option to increase its share to 67 percent. Still, Wal-Mart faced challenges: Japanese consumers associated low prices with poor quality. If the price of fish was low, it must be old. And employees balked at the idea of approaching customers and asking them if they needed assistance. Traditionally employees waited for the customer to ask them for assistance. Perhaps the biggest challenge was the speed at which competition responded by slashing prices, building single-story supercenters, providing acres of parking, launching "Made in Japan" campaigns, and streamlining their logistics systems.

Carrefour, which has stores in 33 countries, began its Asian operations in Taiwan and then moved into China and Korea. Carrefour entered Indonesia at the height of the Asian financial crisis, opening six stores in the capital city of Jakarta in just two years. The new stores competed on selection and low prices, and challenged both open-air markets and the city's small, Chinese-owned neighborhood grocers. The 280-member Indonesian Retail Merchant Association urged Jakarta to impose zoning restrictions on hypermarkets. Carrefour has also proved a threat to the larger, locally established grocery chains. One such chain, Hero supermarkets, admitted it couldn't compete with Carrefour on overall prices and chose instead to discount high-visibility products such as rice and to offer a variety of promotional specials. Hero also competes on freshness and has an excellent reputation among consumers for its produce.

Carrefour entered the Japanese market about the same time as Wal-mart, investing $150 million to set up its first three stores. Carrefour had avoided Japan previously because of its high land prices. Although a depressed Japanese economy had lowered land prices, it meant the stores were opening in a climate of slow retail sales. Like Wal-Mart, Carrefour found itself making adaptations to local culture. Within days of opening in Japan, the stores began selling more vegetables in packages of two or three, as other Japanese grocers do, instead of

TABLE 1	HYPERMARKET OUTLETS BY COUNTRY IN ASIA					
	2003	2004	2005	2006	2007	2008
HYPERMARKET OUTLETS						
China	714	1,075	1,318	1,660	1,909	2,138
India	14	22	36	70	122	266
Indonesia	43	56	51	74	91	116
Japan	7	8	8	8	7	7
Malaysia	29	38	50	59	78	95
Philippines	6	7	11	15	18	20
Singapore	7	9	10	12	11	12
South Korea	265	285	306	340	370	395
Taiwan	97	107	111	108	110	114
Thailand	106	109	122	130	146	163
Vietnam	3	3	4	6	7	7

Source: Selected data from Global Market Information Database, 2008, Euromonitor.

by weight. To provide competitive prices, Carrefour announced plans to buy 54 percent of its products directly from Japanese suppliers. This would circumvent the cumbersome wholesaling system of Japan, but it would require convincing Japanese producers to abandon long-standing relationships with their distributors—something that other foreign retailers previously had difficulty doing. In the meantime, Japanese grocery chains were restructuring and moving more to direct sourcing themselves.

Indonesian and Japanese competitors could take some hope in the fact that Carrefour had to retreat from the Hong Kong market. The company cited stiff competition and restrictive development laws. Analysts suggested that the hypermarkets were unable to attract enough customers, most of whom were unwilling to go out of their way to do their daily shopping. Both Carrefour and Wal-Mart had also exited South Korea, despite the fact that South Koreans were very accepting of hypermarkets (see Table 1) and had the highest penetration per capita of hypermarkets in Asia.

Local competitor E-Mart bought Wal-Mart's stores in South Korea. Wal-Mart was credited with inspiring E-Mart's cost-cutting efficiency. However, the South Korean retailer had its own unique spirit. The

atmosphere in these stores was bright, loud, and frenetic, as if E-mart was attempting to capture the feel of a traditional outdoor market. Shinsegae, the company that owns E-Mart, had also entered the Chinese market and vowed to invest nearly $500 million there by 2015.

Discussion Questions

1. Why do you think hypermarkets are more common in some countries than others?
2. What competitive advantages do foreign retailers such as Wal-Mart and Carrefour enjoy when they enter Asian markets?
3. What are some possible competitive advantages of local retailers? Are those advantages transferable to other Asian countries?
4. Why do you think governments regulate retailing practices?

Sources: Evan Ramstad, "South Korea's E-Mart Is No Wal-Mart," *Wall Street Journal*, August 10, 2006, p. B1; "Giants in Asia," in Kate Gillespie, Jean-Pierre Jeannet, and H. David Hennessey, *Global Marketing*, Houghton-Mifflin, New York, 2007; William J. Holstein, "Wal-Mart in Japan," *Fortune*, August 6, 2007, p. 73; "South Korea's Shinsegae to Open 100 Stores in China," *Agence France Presse*, September 8, 2008; and Mei Fong, "Retailers Still Expanding in China," *Wall Street Journal*, January 22, 2009, p. B1.

CASE 13.2

WHO'S TO BLAME?

Several European countries, including Germany, Italy, France, Belgium, and Finland, filed suits against U.S. tobacco giants Philip Morris and R.J. Reynolds alleging that the two firms had cooperated with smugglers of cigarettes. The countries sought compensation for unpaid custom duties as well as unpaid value-added taxes. The European Union estimated that these losses came to billions of dollars. European governments weren't the only losers. An estimated third of all cigarettes sold in the world are smuggled. Malaysia has estimated that its losses in taxes due to smuggled cigarettes amounted to $1.3 billion in one year alone. These cigarettes arrived mainly from Indonesia and Thailand and were brought in under the aegis of crime syndicates. Malaysia, like most other countries, taxed cigarettes heavily not only as a source of revenue but also as a proven method for discouraging smoking.

At the same time in India, British American Tobacco (BAT) was facing an exposé resulting from the public examination of its internal communiqués. For example, BAT products were legally restricted in India to duty-free shops and hotels but were in fact smuggled into India on an extensive scale from the United Arab Emirates. A memorandum issued by a top BAT executive discussed how the firm could advertise its brands without calling attention to the fact that most of the cigarettes were smuggled into the country. The memorandum went on to discuss contingency plans if any of the normal smuggling channels were shut down. When the *Business Standard* called BAT for comment, the company sent the following reply:

> *where governments are not prepared to address the underlying causes of the smuggling problem (excessive tax on tobacco), businesses such as ours are faced with a dilemma. If the demand for our products [is] not met, consumers will either switch to our competitor brands or there will be the kind of dramatic growth in counterfeit products that we have seen in Asian markets ... [W]here any government is unwilling to act or their efforts are unsuccessful, we act, completely within the law, on the basis that our brands will be available alongside those of our competitors in the smuggled as well as the legitimate market.*

Despite the attempts by government to stem smuggling, it continued to grow. Nearly 300 million contraband cigarettes, mostly from China, were seized at British ports in a single year. Factories in Eastern Europe and Russia were also the source of many cigarettes smuggled into Western Europe. The lost tax revenues to governments from contraband cigarettes worldwide were estimated at $50 billion annually. And cigarettes were not the only consumer product fueling the growth in smuggling. Pakistan complained to the Kenyan government that tea smuggled in from Kenya, thus avoiding a 36 percent tariff, was costing the Pakistani government millions of dollars a year. Next door in India, smuggled mobile phones not only avoided tariffs but hefty value-added taxes as well.

The Chinese government had introduced severe penalties for smuggling consumer goods into China, including life sentences and even the death penalty. China's smuggling law not only targets smugglers but also encompasses anyone who buys from smugglers. They, too, can be charged with smuggling. Vietnam is another country that has taken serious steps against smugglers. The head of a private company and the chief of the smuggling investigation bureau of Ho Chi Minh City's customs department were sentenced to death for smuggling. The case involved 74 people who were charged with smuggling $71.3 million worth of electrical goods and home appliances into Vietnam.

Discussion Questions

1. Why would BAT, or any other multinational firm, cooperate with smugglers?
2. How could smuggling hurt a multinational company?
3. Why do you think some countries are introducing stiff penalties for smuggling?
4. Whom do you think should be held responsible for smuggling—the manufacturer, the smugglers themselves, the retailers, or the final consumer?

Sources: "Who's to Blame," in Kate Gillespie, Jean-Pierre Jeannnet, and H. David Hennessey, *Global Marketing*, Houghton-Mifflin, New York, 2007; Jeff Pickett, "Chinese Burn," *Daily Star*, December 14, 2008; Denis Campbell, "Developing World Faces Black Market Cigarette Plague," *The Observer*, June 28, 2009; "VAT Hike May Boost Duplicate Mobile Market," *Times of India*, July 2, 2009; and "Pakistan Asks Kenya to Help Curb Tea Smuggling," *Pak Banker*, July 6, 2009.

CASE 14.1

THE SOUTH AMERICAN SALES DILEMMA

Shortly after his 34th birthday, Jay Bishop was promoted from director of North American sales to director of global sales at Intelicon, a worldwide provider of digital marketing services. Among the services Intelicon provided were customized e-mail campaigns, online surveys, and online customer loyalty and incentive programs. Jay moved into his new position in January. One of his first tasks was to review all global sales numbers in order to identify areas for growth and improvement. During this exercise, he noticed a number of discrepancies between the Latin American sales numbers and numbers for the rest of world. In particular, he noted that 420 sales calls in the United States had resulted in 180 actual sales, whereas in Latin America, only 40 sales had resulted from 200 such sales calls. Eager to make a good start in his new job (and under pressure from his superiors to fix the situation), Jay immediately scheduled a trip to visit offices in Brazil and Argentina in February. He was surprised, however, to receive calls from the country managers in both São Paulo and Buenos Aires, telling him to put the trip off until after the Mardi Gras season. Recognizing that he knew little about Latin American culture and not wanting to ignore the advice of his new subordinates early on, Jay followed their advice and rescheduled his trip for mid-March.

As often happens when one is busy, Jay's Latin American trip arrived quickly. Stepping off the plane in São Paulo after the ten-hour trip, he was exhausted but ready to work. Passing through customs and into the passenger arrival area, he looked furtively for Rivaldo Pessoa, the Brazilian country manager. Mr. Pessoa, however, was nowhere in sight and did not arrive for 30 minutes. Jay was quite frustrated, not to mention jet-lagged. Moreover, Mr. Pessoa did not seem very apologetic when he blamed his tardiness on traffic and rain.

Rather than stopping at the hotel so he could drop off his luggage, Jay insisted that they go straight to the office and start analyzing why sales were down in Brazil. He kept trying to bring the topic up on the long drive into the city, but Mr. Pessoa insisted on asking him questions about his family and pointing out landmarks in the city, this being Jay's first visit to Brazil. "Why does this guy

want to know my life story? Doesn't he know his job is at stake?" thought Jay. Eventually resigning himself to the fact that nothing would get done until they got to the office, Jay tried to sit back and enjoy the ride.

When they arrived at the office, Mr. Pessoa ushered Jay into the small conference room and then left for ten minutes before returning with coffee and his two salespeople, Renata Pinheiro and Joao Prestes. Both spoke English well and seemed eager to make a good impression. Jay felt that neither had any idea why he was in Brazil, other than that it might be a goodwill tour. He wanted to get to the point, so he came out and said, "The reason I'm here is that we are not meeting our sales numbers for Latin America, and we need to change that." Mr. Pessoa looked a bit surprised, as did Renata and Joao. Jay pressed on, "I need to run through a few analytical questions to determine the root causes of the challenges in the Brazilian market so that we can fix them and take some of the pressure off of you guys." All three seemed to relax at that.

"Okay, let's begin," said Jay. "First, I want to learn more about your backgrounds, what brought you to Intelicon." Mr. Pessoa began: "Well, before I joined Intelicom three years ago, I worked over 20 years in the banking sector, most recently in investment banking at BNP Paribas. I helped take a number of Brazilian companies public and worked on numerous bond issues." Impressed, Jay turned to Joao, who said, "I started in professional services at IBM and worked there for six years. As the Internet took off, I wanted to get involved in a smaller, more Web-based business, which is when I came to Intelicon." Renata finished: "I graduated from the Fundacao Getulio Vargas a year ago," she said, "and took a degree in marketing. My parents pressed me to go into the family business, but I wanted to make a name for myself and felt that consultative sales would be a great place to start. My parents, however, were shocked that I wanted to sell things rather than doing something they considered more respectable, like marketing or finance. I'm out to prove myself."

Needless to say, Jay was very impressed with his new staff and was even more confused about why they were having so much trouble selling

Intelicon's services. He decided to move on to more probing questions. Looking to Mr. Pessoa, he asked, "How do you get your sales prospects? Do you cold-call? Is that successful?" Mr. Pessoa looked a bit perplexed. "I suppose," he said, "that we could probably cold-call more. Mostly we rely on personal contacts within the different organizations." Jay was puzzled. He had heard that this was a common practice in Latin America, but felt that it could be contributing to the long sales cycles that were causing the closing rates in Latin America to be so much lower than in the rest of the world.

Jay believed he was starting to fill in the picture. However, to understand thoroughly the challenges he was facing in Latin America, he knew he would have to attend some sales calls. Mr. Pessoa mentioned that he had two meetings scheduled later in the afternoon, one with Abril, a large media conglomerate in São Paulo, and the other with CVRD, a powerful mining concern. Jay said he would like to attend, and although Pessoa looked wary for an instant, he readily agreed.

The meeting with Abril started well. Mr. Pessoa clearly had a lot of experience presenting to an audience, and he seemed to know two of the four executives in the room as they caught up on family and friends for the first few minutes of the meeting. At the end of the presentation, Mr. Pessoa and Jay asked a number of probing questions and generally felt the meeting was going well. However, the executives kept raising objections. Eventually Mr. Pessoa folded, thanking them for their time and leaving. Once again, Jay was puzzled. He made a point of mentioning to Mr. Pessoa that sometimes getting a "no" was part of sales and that to be successful he needed to find ways to turn a "no" into a

"yes." Mr. Pessoa looked a bit embarrassed but said that he did need to do more of this.

The traffic on the way to the meeting with CVRD was horrible, and much to Jay's chagrin, they arrived nearly an hour late. This did not seem to be a problem, however, because the vice president they were slated to meet was also running late. Once again, Pessoa did an excellent job in the presentation of products and services, and there was clear interest on the part of the vice president. Jay thought for sure they would close him on the spot and was getting that tingly feeling. Both sides went through the motions, discussing timelines and pricing structures, but just when Jay was ready to go in for the kill, Pessoa thanked the gentleman for his time, said he would send him a proposal, and scheduled lunch together the following week. Jay did not know what to say. He guessed that the sale would eventually happen, but he also knew he needed to get revenue as soon as possible.

Exhausted, Jay headed back to his hotel and fell fast asleep. He had learned a lot in one day but realized that he still had a long way to go if he wanted to succeed. Tomorrow, he would fly to Argentina and do it all over again.

Discussion Questions

1. What might explain the lower ratio of sales to sales calls in Latin America compared with the United States?
2. In what ways might cultural differences explain differences in personal selling between Brazil and the United States?
3. What advice would you give Jay?

Source: Case prepared by Michael Magers. Used by permission.

CASE 14.2

FLYING TO ARMENIA

British Airways (BA) is one of the world's largest international airlines, flying passengers to 143 destinations in 69 countries. One such destination was the Republic of Armenia, a small country at the crossroads of Europe and Asia. The whole territory of Armenia is only 11,506 square miles with a population of three million. However, an additional seven million ethnic Armenians live outside Armenia. This Armenian diaspora remains

intimately tied to its homeland across generations. Armenian communities around the world attend Armenian churches, teach their children the Armenian language, and celebrate Armenian national and cultural days with great passion. Many Armenians live in various countries of the Middle East and Europe, and one of the largest Armenian communities resides in the United States.

During the past 20 years, Armenia had been undergoing a rapid but difficult transition from a Soviet, centrally planned economy to a democratic society with a market economy. The 1990s were particularly difficult for the country. Armenia shared all the economic problems that resulted from the breakup of established economic relations among what had been the Soviet republics. In addition, it faced an electricity crisis combined with a military territorial conflict with neighboring Azerbaijan. These problems led to a marked lowering of the standard of living of the population in the country and to overall economic difficulties.

However, with foreign aid from the International Monetary Fund, the World Bank, the European Union, and the U.S. government, as well as substantial assistance from the diaspora, the economy began to stabilize. By the end of the decade, a legal and regulatory framework for the private sector was being created, and an increasing number of multinational corporations, including Coca-Cola, Adidas, Samsung Electronics, Mercedes-Benz, and Kodak, had established a presence in the country.

Armenia had attracted several international airlines that competed alongside its national carrier, Armenian Airlines. These carriers included BA, Swiss Air, Austrian Air, Russian Aeroflot, and Syrian Air. Although traveling was not something many Armenians could afford, it remained the only viable way to travel in and out of the country. Armenia was landlocked, and traveling through neighboring countries was not practical because of poor transportation infrastructure and intermittent political tensions. Most air travelers were employees of international aid organizations operating in Armenia, business travelers, or diaspora Armenians visiting their homeland.

British Airways first entered the Armenian market with twice-weekly service from London to Yerevan, the capital of Armenia. Along with Swiss Air and Austrian Air, BA charged higher prices than Armenian Airlines, Aeroflot, or Syrian Air. BA embarked on several successful promotions to attract customers, to establish brand recognition in the market, and to enhance its international reputation as a caring company. To mark the second anniversary of its instituting flights between London and Yerevan, BA put together a program of events designed to support cultural and humanitarian programs in Armenia. For example, it supported the Third International Chamber Music Festival, which took place in Yerevan, by bringing two leading Armenian musicians—cellist Alexander Chaoshian and pianist Seda Danyel—from London to Yerevan to participate in the event.

The company also announced a special discount rate to about a dozen destinations, substantially increasing the number of tickets sold. During this campaign, BA contributed $10 from the price of each economy-class ticket and $50 from the price of each business-class ticket to one of Armenia's largest orphanages. (For comparison, per-capita spending for a child in such institutions was around $700 per year.) A special ceremony was held to bestow the funds on the orphanage. For that ceremony, the BA hot-air balloon, a familiar ambassador around the world, was brought to Armenia for the first time. The balloon was set to spend a day in Opera Square, the foremost center for cultural activities in Yerevan. Prior to that, BA ran a competition in which questions about BA were posed in the local media. People who phoned in with the right answers could meet the crew of the balloon and go for a short ride. This event was widely covered in the Armenian press and on the television news.

British Airways also introduced the Executive Club, BA's frequent-flyer program, to the Armenian market. As with other frequent-flyer programs, members of the Executive Club could earn free flight miles by traveling via BA as well as using certain hotels and car rentals. Club membership also offered a variety of other benefits, such as priority on flight waiting lists and a special agent to handle inquiries. British Airways ran a special promotion of the Executive Club at the elite Wheel Club, a favorite dining place of expatriates working in Armenia, especially English speakers. Any member of the Executive Club who ate at the Wheel received an entry into a prize drawing. Anyone who was not a member of the Executive Club could join at the Wheel. The top prize was a pair of tickets to any destination.

British Airways also ran a "Where in the World?" competition. People were invited to write in and say where in the world they dreamed of spending Valentine's Day with the person they loved and why they wanted to go there. The three most creative, funny, or touching entries won a pair of tickets to the dream destination. The event was announced on Hay FM, one of Armenia's most popular radio channels among young people. The event enjoyed a high response rate and engendered considerable word of mouth among Hay FM listeners, as well as publicity in the local press.

Discussion Questions

1. For each of the five promotions discussed in the case, identify the target market, explain the motivation behind the promotion, and suggest ways in which to measure the success of the promotion.

2. Why do you think each of these promotions worked well in the Armenian market?

3. Would these promotions be as successful in your country? Why or why not?

Source: Case prepared by Anna V. Andriasova. Used by permission.

CASE 15.1

ADVERTISING TO KIDS

Children in the United States see an estimated 20,000 commercials a year. Marketers spend $5 billion a year directly targeting children. And much more advertising reaches children when they are not even the target audience.

An investigation by the U.S. Federal Trade Commission (FTC) discovered internal memos detailing how companies commonly target their marketing of violent games, music, and movies to children. This prompted lawmakers to reconsider tightening laws on advertising to children. In a follow-up study the next year, the FTC discovered that the movie and video-game industries had improved their practices but that the recording industry continued to show total disdain for public concerns about marketing violent and sexually explicit products to underage children. This encouraged the call for laws that would restrict advertisements—whether targeted directly to children or not—that reached large audiences under the age of 17 years.

A number of industries already set their own standards for advertising to children. The beer industry discourages placing ads on programs where half or more of the audience is under the age of 18. Several movie studios set their cutoff standard at 35 percent. Still, the Association of National Advertisers continues to lobby against any legislation that would restrict advertising for violent movies, video games, or music; it contends that such restrictions would curtail free speech, a fundamental American freedom enshrined in the American Bill of Rights. Ironically, a study conducted by the National Institute on Media and the Family discovered that 99 percent of students in grades 7 through 12 could identify Budweiser as a brand of beer—significantly more students than could identify the purpose of the Bill of Rights. Nonetheless, advertisers won a legal victory when the Supreme Court struck down the state of Massachusetts's restrictions on billboard advertising of cigars and smokeless tobacco products. The law, aimed at protecting

children, was deemed to violate the advertisers' freedom of speech.

The controversy over advertising to children is not restricted to the United States. In Britain, advertisements that provoke children to behave improperly are taboo. Regulators have no direct authority to ban advertisements, but they enjoy powerful influence with the nation's media. A television ad created by the Publicis Group for Hewlett-Packard featured children throwing snowballs at a passing train. Regulators considered this an incitement to antisocial behavior, and the spot was removed.

Greece bans toy advertising on television between 7:00 a.m. and 10:00 p.m. In Norway and Sweden, television advertising aimed at children has been illegal since the 1990s. Critics of the Swedish advertising ban are quick to point out that Swedish children have access to international channels that allow them to see ads from other countries. TV3, a Swedish channel that broadcasts from the United Kingdom, is free to advertise to children because of its British location. Even so, a number of European countries, including Greece, Belgium, Italy, and Poland, are debating tightening their restrictions. Advertisers argue that increased regulation across Europe could greatly curtail children's programming on the many private channels not subsidized by governments.

Across the world, in Indonesia, a cigarette-advertising campaign came under attack by educators and politicians. The campaign featured animated characters, including ants, roosters, and snails, dancing to music. Critics believed that the ad encouraged children, who make up the majority of cartoon lovers, to think that smoking was a good thing. The company quickly removed the offending ad. In Indonesia, the penalty for marketers who target children is a hefty fine and a jail sentence of up to five years.

Many countries are now considering restricting advertising to children by firms in the food, beverage, and fast-food industries because their products do not promote a healthy diet. A number of food companies in South Africa have voluntarily agreed not to advertise to children younger than 12 years unless the products being promoted represent healthy dietary choices. However, new online promotional options increase the chance for reaching children even when companies do not particularly target them. For example, Coca-Cola launched a campaign on Facebook that allowed users to create a "Sprite Sips" character and share it with their friends. However, the company could not control the age of the recipients when the ad went viral. Similarly, Kraft's NabiscoWorld.com, one of the world's most popular food websites, created a game around the concept of rapidly twisting, licking, and dunking an oversized Oreo cookie in a glass of milk. The site is designed for kids older than the age of 12 years, but its games appeal to children much younger.

Discussion Questions

1. Why is advertising directed at children regulated in so many cultures? Why is there so much variation in these regulations?
2. Should the EU develop a common policy toward advertising that targets children? Why or why not? What barriers to such a policy might exist?
3. What restrictions on advertising directed at children would you favor? Why?

Sources: "Advertising to Kids," in Kate Gillespie, Jean-Pierre Jeannet, and H. David Hennessey, *Global Marketing*, New York: Houghton Mifflin, 2007; *Advertising to Children*, European Advertising Alliance, http://www.easa-alliance.org, August 2008; Catherine Holahan, "Crying Foul Over Online Junk Food Marketing," *Business-Week*, August 13, 2008; Kgomotso Mathe, "Rescuing Kids from Ads," *Business Day*, June 27, 2009; and Susan Krashinsky, "Cookie Monster Has Spoken, Advertisers Have Listened," *Globe and Mail*, July 17, 2009, p. B4.

CASE 15.2

THE ALLIANCE

Dentsu, Japan's largest advertising agency, joined Leo Burnett and the MacManus Group, both headquartered in the United States, in an agreement to create one holding company, Bcom3, for the three agency networks. Although the three remained legally distinct companies, certain benefits were expected to arise from this new alliance. Leo Burnett and the MacManus Group hoped to cut costs by exploring ways to reduce redundant divisions and subsidiaries. Dentsu expected Bcom3 to expand its access to worldwide advertising networks for its clients, mainly Japanese companies. With a relatively small international presence, Dentsu could not currently serve a Japanese client in a foreign market as well as Leo Burnett or the MacManus Group could. By gaining the ability to tap into the international subsidiaries of Leo Burnett and the MacManus Group, Dentsu significantly enhanced its global presence virtually overnight.

But would this new alliance really be good for Dentsu? Dentsu Inc. was the largest independent advertising agency in the world. Founded in 1901 as a combination news and advertising agency,

Dentsu evolved into a propaganda service known as Domei News Service during World War II. Dentsu was still 48 percent owned by Kyodo and Jiji, Japan's two major wire services. In the early postwar years, Dentsu helped launch Japanese commercial television and viewership rating services. Dentsu retained equity stakes in several television stations and helped conceive and market some programming. Of Dentsu's worldwide billings, about 5 percent came from its own overseas subsidiaries.

Dentsu dominated the Japanese advertising industry. Unlike the European and the American advertising industries, the industry in Japan had a taboo against an advertising agency represed competitors. Japanese clients were generally comfortable with different divisions or teams the same ad agency handling competitor a This was one reason why the biggest ad agencies in Japan had become dispropo large compared to agencies in Western Dentsu itself handled ads for about 3,00 cluding nearly all of Japan's major According to industry estimates, De on average 31 percent of all television commercials and 20 percent of newspaper ads in Japan.

However, the past decade had been problematic for Dentsu. A recession in Japan hurt profit margins, and growth had fallen to a 25-year low. Nissan Motor Company, Dentsu's long-term client, shocked management at Dentsu when it announced it was leaving to start a new relationship with Hakuhodo Inc. Hakuhodo, the second-largest advertising agency in Japan, was half Dentsu's size. Hakuhodo had formed an alliance with the U.S.-based multinational advertising agency, TBWA, and later bought 15 percent of TBWA's equity. Management at Nissan Motor explained that Nissan wanted to consolidate its marketing activities worldwide in cooperation with Hakuhodo and TBWA. Nissan Motor recognized that Dentsu was the number one agency in Japan, but the Japanese market alone was not big enough for Nissan Motor's profit objectives. The Nissan experience was a watershed. From then on, Dentsu was concerned that other "old friends" might defect.

Bcom3 also included two major media-buying firms, Starcom Worldwide and Mediavest. Media-buying firms exercise more power in negotiating with media companies, such as newspapers, television, and radio, because of their large purchases of media space and consequent market power. Dentsu performed media buying within its own organization but had never developed the size or market power of international firms such as Starcom or Mediavest. Therefore, Dentsu could profit from discounted media prices by working through these companies. In addition, these media-buying companies possessed advanced media-planning tools to develop efficient and effective media such as the means to determine what percent of a campaign budget should go to national television, regional television, and so on.

Dentsu was involved in a 50/50 joint venture with Young and Rubicam in Asian markets.

It was the oldest surviving alliance between a Japanese and a U.S. advertising agency. Nonetheless, Dentsu's own subsidiaries in Asia competed with the joint venture. The relationship between the two partners was further strained when the WPP Group bought Young and Rubicam in 2000. Dentsu considered WPP a major competitor. WPP held a 20 percent stake in Japan's third-largest agency.

For Dentsu, an alliance with such firms as Leo Burnett and the MacManus Group offered a channel to service its clients better internationally, augmenting the business of its own overseas subsidiaries. After two years, however, management at Dentsu was reviewing the situation. The biggest advantage for Dentsu to date had been the cost savings associated with buying $100 million worth of advertising space each year in the United States for Japanese copier maker Canon. But Bcom3 was not yet capturing the many new global accounts that the partners had envisaged. Unlike Nissan Motor, most Japanese corporations had not consolidated their global advertising business within a few agencies. Most managers of Japanese subsidiaries in international markets were not Japanese. They often preferred to choose their own agencies in spite of the relationship between headquarters in Japan and Dentsu. Furthermore, most Japanese multinational corporations had already built long-term relationships with Western advertising agencies.

Discussion Questions

1. Why was Dentsu interested in the Bcom3 alliance?
2. Why would Leo Burnett and the MacManus Group be interested in an alliance with Dentsu?
3. What problems can arise when two or more advertising agencies form an alliance? How might these problems be exacerbated if the agencies are from different cultures?
4. What recommendations would you give Dentsu?

Source: Case prepared by Jaeseok Jeong. Used by permission.

SHANGHAICOSMOPOLITAN.COM

a young and successful ghai, the financial capital s job to interview young

professionals and feature their lifestyles in the newspaper where he worked. His large and well-connected social circle was full of well-educated and high-income individuals. Similar to Andy, most of these young professionals were single and lived with their parents. Their salaries were relatively high by local standards. When they were not working, they often banded together and frequented expensive restaurants, night clubs, coffee shops, and unique boutiques for clothes.

A year ago, Andy met his friend, Ma Li, to have a coffee together at Starbucks. Li was an electrical engineer who worked for a large Chinese telecommunication company. Li had extensive computer and Internet skills and always wanted to start up his own online business instead of working for a company. After a few sips of coffee, Andy asked Li:

> Do you think creating a social networking website for our friends would be a good idea? It's inconvenient to contact everyone by phone to get together somewhere. If we are able to create a website solely for young professionals in Shanghai, it would make it easier for everyone to get together. In foreign countries, user-generated social networking websites are gaining in popularity. This will surely influence the Chinese market in the future. It will be popular, at least among our circle of friends. And they have incredible buying power and like to spend money. Advertisers will be interested in such a site, too. We can make some money out of it.

Li's eyes lit up when he heard the idea. As an electrical engineer, he had been concerned about the development of Web 2.0 (user-generated online media) in China. There were already quite a few major players, such as sina.com.cn, that provided blog services, and social networking websites were beginning to become popular. Currently, only one holding company, Xiang Shu, created multiple social networking websites to target college students—similar to Facebook in the United States. However, there appeared to be no special social networking website that targeted high-income young professionals.

With about $1,000 investment in hardware, Andy and Li established their social networking website, ShanghaiCosmopolitan.com. In order to minimize the start-up investment, Andy and Li served as both the owners and employees of the site, although both kept their prior jobs. Li designed the site and Andy promoted the site to his large circle of friends. As predicted, the site became extremely popular in Shanghai among young professionals with moderate-to-high income in a short time.

In China, young professionals, in particular, were well connected offline because they relied on relationships, or *guanxi*, to develop their own careers. *Guanxi* describes a tightly integrated social network. Members within this network of trusted friends depend on each other and respect each others' opinions. Friends within a network not only develop deep feelings for each other, they also have a moral obligation to maintain the relationship, even if it requires personal sacrifice. Frequent socialization and hanging out with friends helps to nurture and strengthen *guanxi*.

Once Andy sent out news of ShanghaiCosmopolitan.com to his friends, they relayed the message to their own well-connected social circles by word of mouth. The site became popular practically overnight. Young professionals felt proud to have a social networking website designed specifically with their needs in mind.

The Advertising Challenge

With the exponential growth of its online community, ShanghaiCosmopolitan.com recently was forced to hire three full-time employees to manage the site. In contrast with the popularity of the site, however, the advertising revenues had not run as well as expected. Andy and Li needed to increase advertising revenue soon to support their growing business. They determined early on that they could not charge a membership fee for signing up for the site, because most other social networking websites in China are free of charge to their members.

Other social networking websites invited marketers to advertise in the form of banners and pop-up ads on users' personal web pages. They also set up profile pages for brands in order for a brand to come to life as a "person" and socialize with users in a more friendly and personalized way. This marketing communication strategy had been successful on Facebook as well as on the social networking sites in China that mainly targeted college students. However, many of Andy's friends told him that they regarded such promotion strategies as naïve. Only college students or childish people would fall for this type of advertising or perceive a brand to be a friend.

Andy's friends had also voiced objections to traditional banners and pop-up ads. They were quick to emphasize that ShanghaiCosmopolitan.com should be used to connect with friends and share lifestyles and hobbies. They did not want to be interrupted by a deluge of advertisements on the site unless the information being communicated was exactly the type they wanted to hear. They also complained that a site full of banners and pop-up ads made them feel as if they were being watched and used by advertisers. Despite these objections, Andy ran a trial during which he allowed certain marketers to exhibit banners on the site for free. The outcome of the trial was somewhat disappointing since the click-through rate to those banners was relatively low, about one-fifth of the click-through rate on websites such as Yahoo.com.cn.

Group Bargaining Zone

ShanghaiCosmopolitan.com currently received most of its advertising revenues from a single site feature: group bargaining zone (GBZ). There were two ways that marketers could participate in the site's group bargaining option. First, site users could post their wants and needs for a group discount on the GBZ. A list of marketers was then allowed to browse those needs every day. These marketers signed contracts with ShanghaiCosmopolitan.com and were regarded as credible by Andy. If a firm saw that there was demand from site members for their goods, the firm paid ShanghaiCosmopolitan.com a fee to be connected to those consumers. However, marketers were not allowed to directly contact site members. Members' personal information, including contact information, was not made available to marketers. However, ShanghaiCosmopolitan.com allowed participating marketers to use its instant chatting software to make counter offers to consumer groups. A second way in which firms could participate on the site was to regularly post quantity discount offers on the GBZ. These firms paid ShanghaiCosmopolitan.com for advertising space on a monthly basis. Consumers could then browse those offers. If interested, they would seek out their friends to see if they could reach the required number of buyers to qualify for the discounted price.

Andy believed that young Shanghai professionals liked the GBZ for several reasons. They could save money and have fun with friends at the same time. It also allowed them to feel like superachievers by overpowering marketers. The major advertisers on the GBZ were taxi companies and upscale restaurants. Most of ShanghaiCosmopolitan's young clientele worked close to each other in fashionable business districts where jammed subways favored commuting by taxi. However, most young professionals could not afford to take taxis by themselves to work and back on a daily basis because the fees were too high. Restaurants supported the GBZ because it helped them to maximize profits. Some restaurants in Shanghai were mainly set up with four-person table settings. If an individual customer, or even a couple, visited the restaurant they most likely would be seated at a four-person table. If

four people would agree to come in and sit together, the restaurants could offer a group discount. Furthermore, in Shanghai, the number of consumers eating in a restaurant was considered a good indicator of the restaurant's quality. Restaurants especially welcomed the patronage of large groups of diners. Following the success that restaurants and taxi companies experienced on the site, gyms and travel agencies also showed interest in advertising on the GBZ.

Although ShanghaiCosmopolitan.com enjoyed steady advertising revenues from local restaurants as well as transportation, gym, and tourism companies, Andy wanted to expand the advertising revenue and attract more multinational firms as advertisers. One idea was to approach brands that targeted women. Andy observed that women were more active than men on his social networking website. Young female professionals liked to purchase luxury goods such as Louis Vuitton handbags and Christian Dior makeup. However, on average, a classic Louis Vuitton handbag was priced more than $1,000 in the Chinese market, while high-income young professionals in Shanghai only earned $1,500 to $2,000 per month. Andy realized that many marketers of luxury goods disparaged group bargaining. However, he did note that some of those same marketers would hold an end-of-the-year clearance sale. At these sales, items could sell for 20 to 40 percent off list price.

Andy also needed to reply to a request from a friend, Wang Hong. Hong now worked for a Chinese contract manufacturer that produced for a multinational firm operating in China. The local company routinely manufactured 20 percent more products than were ordered by its multinational client. This practice was not uncommon in China because contract manufacturers were uncertain whether or not all the products they produced would meet their clients' standards. However, contract manufacturers rarely destroyed the surplus inventory that they produced. Hong was inquiring whether he could sell his company's surplus on the GBZ.

Discussion Questions

1. Why do you think young Chinese professionals frequent expensive restaurants and purchase luxury goods? What are the implications for multinational firms that wish to communicate to this market segment?
2. Evaluate Andy's option of promoting banner and pop-up ads for increasing advertising revenue.
3. Why do you think the group bargaining zone appears to work in a social networking site in China? Would the

group bargaining zone work in social networking websites in your country? Why or why not?

4. Why would a multinational firm be interested in participating in the group bargaining zone? Why might not they be interested?

5. Should Andy allow Wang Hong to sell surplus products on the group bargaining zone? Why or why not?

Source: Case prepared by Jie Zhang for the purpose of class discussion. Used by permission.

CASE 16.1

HOW LOCAL SHOULD COKE BE?

For 20 years, Coke had expanded its soft-drinks business rapidly overseas. It had consolidated its bottling networks to cover increasingly large territories in response to an increasingly centralized retail trade. Many decisions about advertising and packaging were dictated from Atlanta. With the purchase of Minute Maid orange juice in the late 1990s, Coke was hoping to gain economies of scale for global dominance in the juice business in addition to its presence in soft drinks.

By the new millennium, however, Coke was rethinking its U.S.-based centralized approach to running its global business. For the first time in its 114-year history, Coke's top executives met together outside Atlanta headquarters. It was a harbinger of things to come. From then on, the Coke board would meet outside the United States once a year. This change was one of many instigated by Coke's new CEO, Douglas Daft, who was attempting to turn the company around after two years of poor profits. Daft himself was an Australian who had attracted attention with his successful management of Coke's Japanese subsidiary, where his localization approach had built a successful tea and coffee business. Under Daft, Atlanta was envisioned as a support to Coke's national subsidiaries, rather than as the traditional central headquarters that would mandate and direct the company's worldwide operations. Coke would cease to be big, slow, and out of touch and would instead be light on its feet and sensitive to local markets. One immediate effect of Daft's more localized strategy was the cut of 2,500 jobs at Atlanta headquarters. Asian and Middle East operations, previously managed out of Atlanta, would be transferred to Hong Kong and London, respectively.

The backlash against Coke's centralized approach first emerged in Europe, where the company sells 17 percent of its case volume of soft drinks. Europe's contribution to corporate profits is even higher. Two incidents caused Coke's new management to reconsider its European policy. As a result of various court rulings across Europe, Coke had to significantly scale back its attempt to buy Cadbury Schweppes's beverage brands. A contamination scare also forced Coke to destroy 17 million cases of Coke at a cost of $200 million. Amid the bad publicity that arose from this incident, Coke was accused of being evasive and arrogant and of delaying too long in its response while waiting for direction from Atlanta.

Daft decided to break up responsibility for Europe, which had long been handled by a single division that oversaw 49 markets. Ten new geographic groups were formed on the basis of culturally and economically clustered markets. After all, what did Finland and Italy have in common? Furthermore, per capita consumption of Coca-Cola beverage products varies greatly across European countries. France's per capita consumption stands at 130 glasses a year. In Germany, this number rises to 179 and in Spain, to 303. Growth rates vary as well. In Italy, consumption doubled in ten years. Growth during the same period in Turkey was even greater. Consumption was up from 12 glasses per capita to 140.

In another break with the past, nine of the new European groups were to be run by non-Americans. Previously, half of the top executives in Europe had been sent over from the United States. Europe would be the test case to see whether Coke could get closer to its consumers by altering its organization. The new European groups were still under orders to push Coke's four core brands—Coca-Cola, Fanta, Sprite, and Diet Coke—but they were encouraged to explore new products and develop flavors with local appeal. Germany responded with a berry-flavored Fanta, and Turkey developed a pear-flavored beverage.

Soon other changes were evident. The formal suits seen at headquarters in Atlanta were replaced by more informal attire. Local lawyers were employed instead of lawyers sent from the United States. Reporters seeking a Coke spokesperson could contact expanded communications offices in European countries instead of having to contact Atlanta. Previously, only a single global website had been allowed; now local subsidiaries could run their own websites. Coke's Belgian site—in Dutch, French, and English—received three million hits in its first month. One manager noted that developing the website took only a few weeks, whereas it would have taken eight months under the old centralized system. Belgium was also the site for a new localized promotion idea. Coke hostesses were sent to discos at night to hand out bottles of Coke and promote the idea of a "Coke pause" in a night of otherwise hard drinking. A local spokesman supported the new promotional idea, noting that Belgians were party animals—something Atlanta headquarters might have been slow to appreciate.

Although a euphoric freedom appeared to spread across Europe, the success of the new organizational structure was less clear when it came to the bottom line. Sales slipped slightly in Europe just as localization was being put in place. Some believed that Coke's restructuring of Europe was an overreaction to some bad publicity. They argued that Coke would always be a foreign target. McDonald's had tried to assuage French farmers with a local purchasing campaign, only to meet with indifference. Was Coke doomed to face similar indifference as it attempted to localize? As for the contaminated-bottles crisis, a year later in Belgium, sales had returned to normal levels, and schools where students had reported getting sick had renewed their contracts with Coke. And Atlanta was sending further messages that there would be limits to localization. One top executive at the German operations was fired for running television advertisements aimed at the radical youth movement.

Another early challenge to localization would likely be Coke's launch of its sports drink Powerade in Europe. The sports-drink market in Europe was only $1 billion, compared to $61 billion in the United States, but it was growing fast. Competition in Europe was fragmented but included Powerade's archrival Gatorade, owned by Coke's archrival PepsiCo. Gatorade held 78 percent of the U.S. market and was strong in Europe as well. Powerade would essentially retain its American formula but would taste slightly different because of ingredient regulations of the European Union. The new launch might possibly cannibalize Aquarius, Coke's other recent launch into the sports-drink market in Europe. However, a company spokesperson noted that Aquarius was meant to be drunk after exercising, whereas Powerade was to be drunk while exercising as well. At headquarters, managers envisioned the target market for their new introduction as European males ages 13 to 29 years. Powerade was scheduled to debut in Europe in nine national markets—France, Germany, Greece, Hungary, Italy, Poland, Spain, Sweden, and Turkey.

Discussion Questions

1. What are the pros and cons of changing Coke's single European structure into ten different regional groups?
2. Do you agree with Coke's firing of the executive in Germany? Why or why not? How should Coke avoid incidents like this in the future?
3. If you were the manager of Coke in Germany or Turkey, where would you invest your greatest effort, behind the launch of Powerade or behind the launch of your locally developed fruit-flavored drinks? What factors would guide your decision?
4. What suggestions would you offer to Coke about its global organizational structure and control?

Sources: "How Local Should Coke Be?" in Kate Gillespie, Jean-Pierre Jeannet, and H. David Hennessey, *Global Marketing*, Houghton Mifflin, 2007; "Operating Group Overview," *2008 Year in Review, The Coca-Cola Company*, http://www.thecoca-cola company.com; and "Europe," *2008 Year in Review, The Coca-Cola Company*, http://www.thecoca-colacompany.com.

CASE 16.2

THE GLOBALIZATION OF INDIAN IT

Wipro Ltd. originated as an Indian firm operating in the vegetable oils trade about half a century ago. By the beginning of the 21st century, it had evolved into one of India's largest software services companies, employing 6,700 software engineers. Located in India's high-tech city of

Bangalore, Wipro began in the software business by writing code on contract, handling multimillion-dollar contracts with international companies such as General Electric, Nokia, and Home Depot. However, its president, Vivek Paul, aspired to bring the company up the value-added chain to become one of the top ten information technology (IT) companies in the world. Instead of simply writing code, Wipro would expand into the more lucrative area of business process consulting, offering supply chain management and deciphering customer trends from sales data—and competing with the likes of IBM Global Services and Electronic Data Services. But was this vision viable? Could Wipro go from an Indian firm with overseas clients to a truly global corporation virtually overnight? One estimate suggested that Wipro would need to hire an additional 30,000 employees worldwide in order to accomplish this goal.

Key Indian software development companies such as Wipro Ltd. and Infosys Technologies Ltd. had already captured a lucrative market by handling code-writing jobs from larger international companies. Working from sites such as a high-technology industrial park in India's high-tech showcase Bangalore, Indian software companies could take advantage of both lower-paid Indian talent and the telecommunications revolution in order to service overseas markets quickly and effectively. In addition, these companies had invested heavily in training their workforces, which resulted in dramatic improvements in productivity and quality.

Indian IT firms faced several challenges, however. Infrastructure problems, such as electricity shortages and poor roads, still plagued Bangalore. Although programmers in Bangalore were cheap by Western standards, their salaries had been rising at a rate of 15 percent a year, at least until the global recession hit. Indian IT now faced competition from such other low-cost countries as China, the Philippines, Vietnam, and Western consulting companies were challenging the competitive advantage of Indian firms by opening Asian software centers. In addition, some U.S. clients had decided to move their IT outsourcing to Latin American locations such as Cost Rica, because they found the time zone differences between India and the United States were too difficult to handle. Despite their successes, Indian IT increasingly competed with IBM and Accenture for multinational contracts, and, unlike these global rivals, Indian firms remained far more dependent on short-term contracts.

Therefore, moving into more sophisticated and higher-margin IT products was attractive to Indian firms, but it meant both converting current clients and attracting new ones. Wipro convinced Thomas Cook Financial Services not only to use them for designing a system for automating Thomas Cook's foreign currency transactions, but also to hire them to install the system within the British multinational. But new, smaller accounts would also be necessary if Indian firms were to carve out a significant global market share. VideosDotCom sent some work to Wipro when its Texas-based staff was too busy. Subsequently, it switched most of its development work to Bangalore, citing Wipro's extensive e-commerce experience, development skills, pricing, and overall quality. Infosys won a contract from EveryD.com, a Japanese online shopping and banking service for housewives. Its job encompassed developing the business plan, designing the portal, and writing the operational software. The Japanese customer noted that Infosys wasn't the cheapest of alternatives but that it had the necessary expertise and delivered the product on time.

In addition to these more established companies, Indian start-up software companies were developing their own products and taking them directly to the largest national market—the United States. Some executives of these Indian start-up companies found themselves moving overseas almost immediately. The chairman of Bombay-based I-Flex Solutions, a financial services software developer, moved to New Jersey in order to be able to call on potential clients personally. Over a period of just a few years, the company had posted 25 percent of its 1,425 employees to four continents. Despite being an Indian start-up, Talisma Corporation, a customer relations management software developer, was established and based in Seattle, where it could employ U.S. salespeople to promote its made-in-India product. One year later, Talisma had 19 offices in seven countries.

Such IT start-ups contributed to the fact that India had become one of Asia's major destinations for venture capital. Still, Indian capital markets were generally noted for their conservatism. Firms were expected to post profits consistently. A loss of money, even in the short term, was considered unacceptable. Laying out large sums of money, such as those needed for the acquisition of other firms, was often judged to be very risky.

Some of the venture capital flowing into India came from expatriate Indians. Many Indian IT engineers worked or had worked in the United

States. Silicon Valley's Indian high-tech population numbered around 200,000 and was considered to be the area's most successful immigrant community. Many Indians working in the IT industry in the United States believed that despite their technical expertise—or possibly because of it—they were being overlooked for management positions. Ironically, American companies considered their technical skills to be too valuable to lose by transferring them to management. Partially as a reaction to this, many Indians working in the United States considered starting their own businesses either in India or in the United States. Indians living in the United States often invested in each other's start-up companies, sat on each other's boards, and hired each other for key jobs. In fact, companies with Indian founders could often hire teams of developers more rapidly than the average U.S. company without the benefit of ethnic ties to the Indian community. IndUS Entrepreneurs (TIE) of Santa Clara emerged as one of the preeminent networking groups for Indian entrepreneurs. It hosted monthly Angel Forums at which entrepreneurs could pitch plans to potential investors. The IndUS Entrepreneurs website stated as the group's goal the duplication of the Silicon Valley success story in India.

Discussion Questions

1. Why will Indian IT firms have to transform themselves into more global corporations in the future?
2. How will their internationalization experience differ from the experience of U.S.-based firms in the latter half of 20th century?
3. What unique advantages and disadvantages do these firms possess?
4. Which organizational structure do you think would be appropriate for a more global Wipro? Why?

Sources: "The Globalization of Indian IT," in Kate Gillespie, Jean-Pierre Jeannet, and H. David Hennessey, *Global Marketing*, Houghton Mifflin, 2007; Amy Barrett, "Heading South," Business Week.com, February 20, 2008; Vivek Wadhwa, "India: Toward High-End Outsourcing," BusinessWeek.com, December 17, 2008; Pankaj Mishra, "Indian IT Companies Bid against MNC Rivals for $1 Billion BP Deals," *Economic Times*, July 25, 2009; and Mehul Srivastava and Steve Hamm, "Using the Slump to Get Bigger in Bangalore," *BusinessWeek*, August 3, 2009, p. 50.

APPENDIX:

Cases

CASE 1

GUEST-TEK INTERACTIVE ENTERTAINMENT: INTERNATIONAL SALES

Guest-Tek and the Global Opportunity

The chief executive officer (CEO) of Calgary-based Guest-Tek Interactive Entertainment Ltd. (Guest-Tek) considered whether and how his company should grow its business overseas. Ninety-seven percent of Guest-Tek's 2003 revenue was derived from North American hotels — a market he knew would eventually become saturated. Guest-Tek had listed publicly several weeks earlier, in January 2004. Both internal and external investors now demanded results. Other geographic markets held the promise of new growth and competitors were already pursuing those opportunities. The CEO had to decide on a course of action.

Company Background

Guest-Tek was founded in Calgary, Canada, in March 1997, and since then had established itself as a leading provider of high-speed Internet access in hotels in North America and, to a lesser extent, abroad. Guest-Tek sold its Internet solution, which was branded as GlobalSuite, to three-, four- and five-star hotels and installed access points in guest rooms, meeting rooms and common areas. Guest-Tek then maintained a post-installation network and provided technical support for GlobalSuite users through a toll-free, 24-hour telephone line. Users were typically business travelers who connected with their own laptop computers. GlobalSuite was a premium high-speed Internet access solution that was easy to use for travelers and convenient for hotel managers.

Laurie Milton prepared this case under the supervision of Nigel Goodwin solely to provide material for class discussion. The authors do not intend to illustrate either effective or ineffective handling of a managerial situation. The authors may have disguised certain names and other identifying information to protect confidentiality.

EXHIBIT 1 GUEST-TEK CLIENT LIST, 2003

OWNERSHIP GROUP/CHAIN	PROPERTIES
Marriott International	132
Hyatt Corporation/Hyatt International Corporation	42
InterContinental Hotels Group	37
Hilton Hotels Corporation	34
Starwood Hotels & Resorts Worldwide	20
Accor Hotels	20
Carlson Companies	18
Best Western International	8
Ritz-Carlton Hotel Company	6
Independent, boutique and other	87
Total	404

GEOGRAPHIC REGION	PROPERTIES
North America	358
International	46
Total	404
Guestrooms	80,700

Note: Figures as of November 30, 2003.

Source: Guest-Tek Prospectus, January 30, 2004.

GlobalSuite's industry-leading 99 percent user success rate,[1] together with Guest-Tek's comprehensive service package for both guests and hotel managers, had secured some of the world's finest hotel chains and management groups as clients (see Exhibit 1 for Guest-Tek's client list). The company had also raised sales to $17.2 million[2] for the nine months ending December 31, 2003 (see Exhibit 2 for Guest-Tek's income statement) and successfully completed an initial public offering (IPO) of $44.6 million. Virtually all of the company's activities were run from the head office in Calgary with a staff of fewer than 150 (see Exhibit 3 for an allocation of Guest-Tek's staff by department).

[1] Guest-Tek measured user success as the percentage of users achieving a high-speed Internet connection when using GlobalSuite; user success rates among Guest-Tek's competitors were typically much lower, and in some cases were as low as 50 percent.
[2] Financial figures in this case are presented in Canadian dollars, unless otherwise noted.

EXHIBIT 2 GUEST-TEK INCOME STATEMENT, FY2001 - FY2003 (in Cdn$)

	YEAR ENDED MARCH 31			SIX MONTHS ENDED SEPTEMBER 30	
	2003	2002	2001	2003	2002
Revenue:					
New installations	$7,294,666	$2,733,589	$1,134,780	$9,705,524	$2,615,911
Recurring revenue	1,406,428	810,783	400,917	1,333,641	591,972
	8,701,094	3,544,372	1,535,697	11,039,165	3,207,883
Expenses:					
Cost of goods and services sold	4,597,565	2,032,882	1,194,804	6,147,837	1,633,172
Selling, general and administrative	2,694,619	1,922,727	1,728,720	1,897,504	1,130,086
Research and development	551,216	556,804	456,467	273,488	270,079
Foreign currency loss	37,558	1,320	—	175,144	1,942
Interest expense (income), net	37,726	(6,468)	171,277	53,256	15,464
Write-down of property and equipment	—	—	810,544	—	—
Amortization of property and equipment	151,687	122,100	264,360	85,964	67,644
	8,070,371	4,629,365	4,626,172	8,633,193	3,118,387
Income (loss) from operations	630,723	(1,084,993)	(3,090,475)	2,405,972	89,496
Government assistance for research & development	175,709	—	—	—	54,803
Income (loss) before income taxes	806,432	(1,084,993)	(3,090,475)	2,405,972	144,299
Income taxes (recovery)	(440,000)	—	—	(185,122)	—
Net income (loss)	$1,246,432	$(1,084,993)	$(3,090,475)	$2,591,094	$ 144,299

Note: Six month figures are unaudited.

Source: Guest-Tek Prospectus, January 30, 2004.

The Hospitality Industry

The hospitality industry encompassed many segments, including hotels, rental properties, military housing, student housing and timeshare units, plus bars, coffee shops, restaurants, airports and train stations. Guest-Tek focused its efforts on serving hotels and, more specifically, on those in the three-, four- and five-star range. To this point in time, the company had concentrated almost exclusively on its home continent, North America (see Exhibit 4 for Guest-Tek's revenue by geographic region). The company had left the other geographic markets in Europe, Asia-Pacific and South America largely unexplored, with limited direct sales to date.

Business travelers who frequented North American three-, four- and five-star hotels had come to expect or even require Internet access. One industry survey found that as many as 87 percent of business travelers checked e-mail or accessed the Internet from their laptops on a daily basis while on the road. There was general agreement in the industry that these travelers preferred high-speed Internet access to dial-up access for speed, convenience and cost effectiveness. Many travelers cited broadband services as an important factor in selecting accommodations. As a result, hotel

EXHIBIT 3 GUEST-TEK STAFF BY DEPARTMENT

EXHIBIT 4 GUEST-TEK REVENUE BY GEOGRAPHIC REGION, FY2001 - FY2003

	YEAR ENDED MARCH 31			SIX MONTHS ENDED SEPTEMBER 30	
	2003	2002	2001	2003	2002
Canada	$1,192,855	$ 977,309	$ 907,240	$ 781,478	$ 812,562
United States	7,203,772	2,567,063	628,457	10,021,236	2,343,616
Other	304,407	—	—	236,451	51,705
Total	$8,701,034	$3,544,372	$1,535,697	$11,039,165	$3,207,883

Source: Guest-Tek Prospectus, January 30, 2004.

managers were adopting high-speed Internet access as a way of attracting guests, competing with other properties and deriving additional revenue. This competitive edge had been particularly important for hotel managers during the recent downturn in the industry when Severe Acute Respiratory Syndrome (SARS), global security concerns and other political, social and economic events had raised anxiety about travel. Hotel managers hoped that high-speed Internet access would position them to capitalize on the expected recovery.

The North American Market

With 64,500 hotels and more than five million hotel rooms, North America was second only to Europe on both dimensions. More importantly from Guest-Tek's perspective, though, was the fact that 40 percent of the world's business travel was conducted in North America — more than in any other geographic region.

North America led the world in terms of both the proportion of total hotels equipped with high-speed Internet access (referred to as the penetration rate) and the frequency with which the service was used by guests (referred to as the usage rate). Both penetration and usage rates were rising sharply. Also, hotel managers increasingly viewed such access as a competitive necessity or a guest amenity and were cutting user fees or offering access for free.

High-speed Internet access-enabled properties were typically in the four- and five-star hotel categories. These hotels normally installed the service in all of their guestrooms as well as in meeting rooms and common areas. When installation in four- and five-star hotels approached saturation (which was expected to happen within two to three years), several access providers planned to reach out to the two- and three-star categories for more growth opportunities. Fewer hotels in those categories could afford 100 percent installation. Consequently, many opted to install services in a portion of rooms, to be used either on a trial basis or in rooms reserved for business travelers.

North America was home to 85 different hotel brands (see Exhibit 5 for more information on the North American hotel industry) as well as independent boutique hotels. Guest-Tek was a certified supplier to eight of those brands: Accor, Carlson Hospitality, Choice, Hilton, Hyatt, InterContinental Hotel Groups, Marriott and Starwood. In total, GlobalSuite had been installed with 35 different brands and 40 independent hotels. In fiscal year (FY) 2003, no single brand represented more than 11 percent of Guest-Tek's revenue.

GlobalSuite Solution

To answer the demand for high-speed Internet access, Guest-Tek's research and development team had developed GlobalSuite as an easy-to-use or "plug-and-play" solution. In other words, hotel guests could connect their own laptops and gain access to the Internet, corporate e-mail and other applications quickly and without changing their settings. Guests typically connected by plugging their laptops into ports or "nodes" located in the guestrooms and public areas, including conference rooms and business centers; those ports were in turn connected to a network throughout the hotel.

Wireless solutions were becoming increasingly common in the industry, allowing guests with wireless network interface cards to connect from hotspots located in lobbies, bars and other public areas and sometimes in the guestrooms themselves. Not only were wireless solutions convenient for guests, they were less demanding in terms of infrastructure and were therefore less expensive for hotels. By February 2004, 70 percent of Guest-Tek's installations involved some degree of wireless functionality.

The wide variety of laptop configurations and network settings often made access difficult, but

EXHIBIT 5 NORTH AMERICAN HOTEL INDUSTRY BY SEGMENT (AS OF NOVEMBER 2003)

SEGMENT	UPPER UPSCALE	UPSCALE	MIDSCALE w/ F&B	MIDSCALE w/out F&B	ECONOMY	INDEPENDENT
Rating	5 – 4 star	4 star	3 star	3 star	2 star	Various
Representative brands	Four Seasons	Crown Plaza	Best Western	Amerihost	Budget Inn	Various
	Hilton	Doubletree	Four Points	Comfort Inn	Days Inn	
	Hyatt	Novotel	Holiday Inn	Country Inn	Econo Lodge	
	InterContinental	Radisson	Park Plaza	Hampton Inn	Motel 6	
	Ritz-Carlton	Residence Inn	Ramada	Signature Inn	Super 8	
Target client	Luxury/corporate	Corporate	Ec. bus. traveler	Ec. bus. traveler	Traveling sales	Various
Hotels	1,794	2,370	5,097	6,980	10,330	29,271
Rooms	658,316	380,236	643,490	628,155	810,445	1,728,300
Rooms per hotel	367	160	126	90	78	59

Notes: Figures for US and Canada only. F&B refers to food and beverage service. Ec. bus. traveler refers to economy business traveler.

Source: Smith Travel Research Database, November 26, 2003. Cited in Guest-Tek Prospectus, January 30, 2004.

GlobalSuite's technology was reliable and easy to use regardless of laptop settings and technical challenges. Guests who still experienced difficulty could call the technical support desk and receive help in a variety of languages, including English, French, Spanish, Dutch, Cantonese, Mandarin, Japanese, Arabic and Hindi. GlobalSuite was also a secure solution suitable for business use. The proprietary software was regarded as best-in-class technology and was guarded closely as intellectual property.

GlobalSuite had been developed with the hotel manager in mind as a complete or "turnkey" system requiring little knowledge or effort on the manager's part. Installation services were provided by Guest-Tek's highly skilled operations and deployment teams. Network equipment was sourced from high-quality manufacturers, including Cisco Systems, Hewlett Packard, Dell and Paradyne Networks. Following an installation, Guest-Tek trained hotel staff to use the system, monitored and managed the system, acted as an Internet service provider (ISP) and offered free software upgrades. Guest-Tek thus offered a complete solution designed for high-quality service and peace of mind.

Additional features and benefits were designed to appeal to hotel managers who had the option to set access prices or provide the service free of charge, to track and report on usage and to customize the user interface with the hotel's own brand. GlobalSuite was a best-in-class solution designed for clients who were willing to pay a premium. Depending on the size of an installation and the user fees that a hotel manager was willing to pay, payback for the system could be achieved within 12 to 18 months.

Business Model

Once a hotel had signed a contract to purchase GlobalSuite, Guest-Tek deployed its own project managers and installation professionals to the hotel to set the system up. By managing the installation with its own people, Guest-Tek maintained control over the timelines, costs and quality. Installation work required only a few days and typically took place within four to six weeks of a contract being signed. The company could install the solution in 40 to 50 hotels per month. Installation capacity had doubled over the previous year, due to better processes and the addition of new staff.

An installation typically generated one-time revenues for Guest-Tek from the software license, installation services and networking equipment. These revenues could total between US$100 and US$350 per room, depending on the hardware involved, with a gross margin of 35 to 45 percent. Guest-Tek also derived recurring revenues from ongoing software and hardware maintenance and from call center support. Recurring revenues totaled between US$3 and US$4 per room, per month. A 99 percent customer retention rate ensured the sustainability of the recurring revenue.

EXHIBIT 6 HSIA INSTALLATIONS IN NORTH AMERICA, BY COMPANY (AS OF NOVEMBER/DECEMBER 2003)

	UPPER UPSCALE	UPSCALE	MIDSCALE w/ F&B	MIDSCALE w/out F&B	ECONOMY	UNCLASSIFIED	TOTAL
Wayport	296	101	78	53	12	56	596
STSN	254	277	7	28	—	24	590
Guest-Tek	100	145	21	26	9	57	358
GoldenTree	17	95	25	78	8	21	244
Stay Online	8	79	17	7	1	11	123
Broadband Hospitality	4	37	8	63	—	4	116
V-Link	78	—	—	—	—	1	79
Suite Speed	3	4	4	9	—	10	30
Indirect competitors	368	350	469	581	209	418	2,395
Total	1,128	1,088	629	845	239	602	4,531

Notes: Figures for US and Canada only. GoldenTree had 142 pending installations under construction. F&B refers to food and beverage service.

Source: Roger Sharma, "North American Market Analysis," *Guest-Tek*, December 2003.

North American Competition

Guest-Tek faced direct competition in North America from a number of other Internet solution providers. Chief among these were Wayport and STSN. These companies were running systems in approximately 600 North American hotels each, as of December 2003, as compared to Guest-Tek's roughly 360 installations at that time. Other providers trailed behind (see Exhibit 6 for a breakdown of the competition in North America).

Wayport, based in Austin, Texas, provided wired access but was also a leader in wireless solutions. Wayport had preferred vendor status with Four Seasons and was also building the Wayport brand by providing access in airports and 75 McDonald's restaurants in California. STSN, of Salt Lake City, Utah, was partially owned by Marriott and most of STSN's installations were at Marriott hotels. Golden-Tree Communications, a spin-off of a Korean hardware manufacturer, was also a notable competitor in North America. With low prices and what Guest-Tek's executives believed to be a more basic solution, GoldenTree appealed to three-star hotels as well as budget-conscious four-star hotels. StayOnline, another notable North American provider, was similar to Wayport in its focus on wireless applications.

In-room entertainment companies, cable companies, ISPs, data networking companies and local telephone network operators also offered Internet access. These companies used different technology and offered a variety of benefits to various segments of the market. In-room entertainment companies, for example, provided Internet access through television sets outfitted with keyboards. This rudimentary solution did not allow users to connect with their own laptops. Some of these companies, particularly the telecommunications companies (telcos), were attempting to include hotels in their broader strategy to set up wireless public access points, known as hotspots. Hotspots could be set up at virtually any location, including coffee shops, airports, office buildings and shopping malls. Guest-Tek, as a niche solution provider, recognized that these companies were penetrating the market but did not consider them to be direct competitors.

In the CEO's estimation, Guest-Tek was very strong compared to its competitors on key competitive elements, which included comprehensive solutions, ease of deployment, wireless capability, security, connectivity rates and end-user support. The subsequent supplier certification from various hotel brands, including Hilton, Hyatt and Marriott, gave Guest-Tek a strong competitive message. Finally, Guest-Tek was reasonably priced, relative to other premium service providers.

Guest-Tek's Sales and Marketing Department

Guest-Tek's revenue generation was overseen by the vice president of Sales and Marketing. He held an undergraduate finance degree and an MBA in Enterprise

Development from the University of Calgary. Known as an ambitious and energetic entrepreneur, he was keenly interested in growing Guest-Tek.

The VP of Sales and Marketing had a staff of 24 and was responsible for all geographic regions. Within North America, the VP had the help of a sales director; the sales director managed the sales staff directly while the VP managed the region at a strategic level and actively participated in major deals. The VP also had the help of a consultant who provided advice on the European market. There were no sales and marketing staff allocated to the other geographic regions.

Sales were pursued through direct and indirect channels, with direct being the principal channel in North America and indirect being the principal channel in the other geographic regions. Direct sales were conducted by Guest-Tek sales representatives working at Guest-Tek's head office and traveling to visit potential customers. Indirect sales were pursued through partnerships and alliances with complementary service providers and through independent agents who sold GlobalSuite on a freelance basis.

A marketing director reported to the VP of Sales and Marketing and supported the sales activities by managing the Guest-Tek brand and creating demand for GlobalSuite. Marketing activities included telemarketing, direct mail, communication with media and industry analysts, advertising and trade shows. The marketing director had a total staff of eight.

The VP of Sales and Marketing additionally oversaw a value-added solutions director. This manager was charged with finding ways to sell new products and services to existing clients. This function was seen as a way to derive additional revenue in a market that was becoming saturated. Value-added solutions were also viewed as tools for enhancing customer loyalty and ensuring recurring service and maintenance revenue for GlobalSuite installations. The value-added solutions director was assisted by two other staff members.

Direct Sales

The direct sales process began with Guest-Tek inside sales representatives contacting groups of hotels that shared common ownership or common management and contacting individual hotels. The inside sales representatives' objective was to generate leads for Guest-Tek's direct sales representatives. There were five inside sales representatives working under the direction of a coordinator. The direct sales representatives followed up on those leads, promoted GlobalSuite to the hotel owners and managers and attempted to close deals. Guest-Tek employed 10 direct

sales representatives. All inside and direct sales representatives reported to the sales director for North America. The direct sales method was the exclusive method employed in North America, and the sales team was now extending this method to Latin America as well. All direct sales activities were managed out of Guest-Tek's head office.

Inside and direct sales representatives preferred to work with hotel ownership and management groups rather than individual hotels. Convincing one such group to purchase GlobalSuite usually resulted in sales to multiple properties. The sales representatives also targeted hotels that fell under brands such as Hilton, Hyatt and Marriott, which had granted Guest-Tek preferred vendor status and wished to see consistency across their properties. While the hotels under these brands did not necessarily have to follow advice from the brand level, preferred vendor status was a strong selling point for Guest-Tek.

Inside and direct sales employees had revenue quotas and were compensated partly through commission. All North American sales were priced and recorded in U.S. dollars but overseas sales could also be priced and recorded in local currency.

The direct sales approach had driven Guest-Tek's rapid growth despite an inherently long sales cycle. A contract required a significant capital commitment from the hotel's decision maker, who typically had to obtain approval from many layers of ownership and management. The direct sales approach allowed Guest-Tek representatives to build relationships with clients and influence them throughout the decision-making process. The full process, from generating interest to building a relationship and finally signing a contract, could take between four and 12 months and occasionally even longer.

Indirect Sales through Resellers

The indirect sales method most commonly involved partnerships with technology resellers who licensed GlobalSuite software as part of their own solution. In this case, Guest-Tek collected one-time revenue for the software license but took no other part in the deal and undertook no other efforts for marketing, operations or otherwise. Guest-Tek's only activity in this process was to manage the relationship with the reseller. This method had been employed in Europe, the Middle East and Africa through French technology reseller Locatel.

The relationship with Locatel had been relatively easy to manage. Initial meetings to broker the deal had been conducted at Guest-Tek's office in Calgary and at Locatel's office in Paris, France, and a Guest-Tek technical representative had later been sent to Paris to train Locatel personnel. The relationship was managed by Guest-Tek's business development team, and since Locatel installed the solution, Guest-Tek project managers and operations teams were not involved.

The reseller channel was a low-cost and low-risk method of entering new markets, particularly when Guest-Tek did not have expertise or presence in those markets. As the CEO explained, "Inbound demand mitigates risk, because a knowledgeable partner is coming to us with opportunities." However, the reseller retained a significant portion of the revenue and Guest-Tek had no control over the installation or support aspects of the solution and consequently could not control the quality, the customer experience or the user experience. Furthermore, the CEO felt that this channel was too passive.

Indirect Sales through Agents

Guest-Tek also sold GlobalSuite indirectly through agents, although this method was less common. Agents were independent technology salespeople selling the full GlobalSuite solution as well as other products and solutions from other vendors. They were self-employed freelancers who took a percentage of the revenue from each sale. Agents were familiar with GlobalSuite but under no obligation to sell it over other solutions.

Guest-Tek did not drive this strategy and any sales generated this way were essentially viewed as bonus sales. The company's efforts were limited to providing the agents with information to help them sell Global-Suite and offering the agents better commissions to encourage them to favor it. There were currently two agents operating for Guest-Tek in the Latin American region: one in Argentina and the other in Trinidad.

The Expansion Challenge

Guest-Tek's share offering, completed on February 6, 2004, brought the company net proceeds of $28.3 million (see Exhibit 7 for the intended allocation of the funds). These funds would allow Guest-Tek to grow by eliminating some of the financial constraints that had inhibited the company in the past. However, public status brought new shareholders and higher expectations and the CEO knew that these people were watching Guest-Tek's market position very closely. The company's sales had grown quickly over the past two years, and the CEO felt pressure to continue that pace.

EXHIBIT 7 INTENDED ALLOCATION OF PROCEEDS FROM GUEST-TEK'S IPO (FIGURES IN CDN$)

MILLIONS	ALLOCATION
$ 2.0	Increasing operational capacity for deployments
3.0	Expanding international sales and marketing initiatives
5.0	Advancing new product offerings
15.0	Funding disciplined, strategic acquisitions
3.3	Supplying working capital for general corporate purposes
$28.3	Proceeds to the corporation

One promising avenue for growth was the international market. "Guest-Tek has established a strong position with the industry in North America," the CEO stated in a recent earnings release. "We are working aggressively to repeat this success on a global scale." To that end, $3.0 million of the IPO proceeds had specifically been allocated for international sales and marketing initiatives. Guest-Tek had young, energetic and entrepreneurial leaders and employees, and there was a general feeling within the ranks that the company could "take on the world." Also, the company's executives believed that they could make up for their lack of international experience with their superior technology, turnkey solution, technical expertise, sales skills and hotel market expertise.

However, international sales could be framed as both an opportunity and a competitive requirement because the North American branches of hotel brands wanted the solutions they chose to also be available to their international branches. In other words, hotel brands wanted to deal with global players. Finally, international sales could also be considered as a risk because Guest-Tek was unfamiliar with those markets.

Key Decision Makers

As a rapidly growing company with expectations to match, Guest-Tek's business decisions were driven principally by the sales, marketing and business development personnel. The CEO would ultimately make the decision with substantial input from the VP of Sales and Marketing, who viewed international expansion as an excellent opportunity and the most natural avenue for growing the company.

Guest-Tek's founder, who was also the former CEO and the former executive vice president of Business Development, would also have some input in the decision-making process. While no longer an executive of the company, the founder held a seat on the board of directors. He held a bachelor of commerce degree specializing in the hospitality industry. Prior to founding Guest-Tek, he had spent several years as an analyst for economic diversification and business development. The founder strongly favored international expansion. The founder and the VP of Sales and Marketing had known each other for years, even before the VP of Sales and Marketing joined the company, and the two had held many positive conversations about international expansion.

Feasibility and practical aspects had to be considered as well as market potential; therefore, the CEO would also consider the opinions of several other executives. These executives were supportive of international expansion but cautioned that there would be challenges. There was a general feeling that risks could be mitigated by working with partners such as Locatel and by selling to international hotel management groups, ownership groups and brands that were already customers in North America.

Guest-Tek's vice president of Operations was an industrial engineer with an MBA from the same graduating class as the VP of Sales and Marketing. She had joined Guest-Tek in 2000. With her dual training, she provided a balanced opinion of both operations and business. She believed that the required changes to the software would be minimal but cautioned that hardware standards and prices would vary considerably between countries. The company would face a learning curve upon entering each new region and each new country. The VP of Operations accepted these challenges and was supportive of international expansion.

The vice president of Research and Development was also supportive of international expansion. With a doctorate in computer science from the University of Calgary, postdoctoral fellowships at both MIT and Stanford University and experience with several high-tech startups, he had a deep understanding of the technological ramifications facing Guest-Tek. He suggested that his department's only challenge would lie in translating GlobalSuite's user and manager interfaces into multiple languages. GlobalSuite's user interface was already available in English, French and Spanish, and additional translation would be a straightforward task. Translation of the management interface — that part of the solution used by hotel managers for pricing and billing, reporting and other administrative work — would be a much more complicated, expensive and time-consuming project.

There was also the question of multilingual service through Guest-Tek's user support hotline. Support was currently offered in the same three languages — English, French and Spanish — on a full-time basis and only partial coverage was available in other languages.

Guest-Tek's chief financial officer was also an important figure in the decision-making process and a supporter of international expansion. She was a chartered accountant with a strong business background. She was keenly aware of the expectations that Guest-Tek now faced from investors and analysts and recognized the need for revenue growth. Additional funds from the IPO had been allocated to expanding Guest-Tek's operational capacity, so growth could be achieved profitably.

Geographic Choices

The outstanding questions to those involved revolved around which markets were the most attractive, how those markets should be pursued and how the overseas business should be managed. These were difficult questions to answer because Guest-Tek had only basic information on the overseas markets and had no staff with overseas experience or expertise aside from a recently retained consultant for the European region. The CEO preferred to gather as much information as possible before making a decision in an unfamiliar area, but in this case adequate information was not to be found internally. Without reasonable information, he was more reactive and preferred to entertain proposals from knowledgeable partners, but as explained previously, that was considered a passive strategy. The CEO had set an ambitious goal of deriving 15 to 20 percent of new installation revenue outside North America in FY2005 — a goal that might require more proactive efforts. With this in mind, the CEO considered what he did know about the opportunities before him.

European Market

Guest-Tek had historically looked beyond North America to the European market as a possible avenue for expansion. Europe featured 67,500 hotel properties and nearly six million hotel rooms, which were often combined with the 14,000 properties and roughly 670,000 rooms in the Middle East and Africa, and referred to as the broader Europe, Middle East and Africa (EMEA) region. However, a higher concentration of hotels and steeper demand for high-speed Internet access made the United Kingdom and continental Europe the focus.

Penetration and usage rates were growing in Europe, but trailed behind North American rates and were not expected to fully catch up. In general, there was less business travel in Europe than in North America, and guests demanded less Internet service. However, European hotel managers were beginning to perceive high-speed Internet access as a necessary service offering, and the market was becoming more demand-driven, with strong growth expected for 2004 and beyond. European hotel managers were also more inclined to pay higher prices for better solutions. Industry sources suggested that growth in high-speed Internet access in homes and offices was particularly noticeable in France and Italy. The CEO also knew that within Europe, the busiest destinations for both European and American business travelers were the United Kingdom and Germany. The proliferation of wireless technology was expected to bolster the European industry since many of Europe's hotels were historic and managers preferred less intrusive and less damaging infrastructure.

Guest-Tek's CEO resisted the temptation to discuss Europe as a single market since he perceived little homogeneity across the continent. Countries varied considerably in culture, language, business practices, the balance between business and pleasure travel, Internet use, and broadband penetration among the general population (see Exhibit 8 for a comparison of broadband access in OECD [Organisation for Economic Cooperation and Development] countries). Adoption of high-speed Internet access in hotels also varied accordingly. Hotel communities in different countries varied in the extent to which they welcomed a solution provider from North America. Some did not mind, while others preferred to deal with local providers or at least local offices of global providers.

European countries also differed from Canada and the United States in terms of hotel structure. Firstly, the majority of European hotels were independent or affiliated with voluntary chains that demanded less in terms of conformity and standards. Guest-Tek's preferred provider approach might not be as effective in these situations.

Secondly, European hotels tended to be smaller than North American hotels, resulting in smaller sales. It was often more difficult to convince a manager of a small hotel to accept the high price of a premium high-speed Internet access solution. Furthermore, the CEO believed that the European property and room totals had been inflated by small lodging establishments catering only to leisure travelers. Thus, while the totals for Europe were higher than those for North America, the CEO believed that the effective market for Guest-Tek was actually smaller in Europe.

A variety of providers were now targeting Europe, most notably European telcos, such as British Telecom

EXHIBIT 8 BROADBAND ACCESS IN OECD COUNTRIES (AS OF JUNE 2003)

COUNTRY	PENETRATION
Korea	23.2%
Canada	13.3%
Iceland	11.2%
Denmark	11.1%
Belgium	10.3%
Netherlands	9.2%
Sweden	9.2%
Switzerland	9.1%
Japan	8.6%
United States	8.3%
Austria	7.0%
Finland	6.6%
OECD	6.1%
Norway	5.4%
Germany	4.8%
EU	4.6%
Spain	4.2%
France	4.1%
Portugal	3.7%
United Kingdom	3.6%
Italy	2.8%
Luxembourg	2.3%

Note: Penetration figures per 100 inhabitants. Only countries with at least 1.0% penetration are shown.

Source: OECD.

and France Telecom, offering hotspots and other technologies. However, Guest-Tek perceived its most direct competition in the European market as coming from North American solution providers who viewed Europe as a natural growth area as the North American market approached saturation. As the most notable example, STSN was believed to have at least 100 European installations. Wayport was smaller than STSN in Europe but also had a presence. Several Asian niche providers were also entering Europe. One such company, inter-touch, had completed 36 installations by mid-2003.

Guest-Tek had so far approached EMEA sales indirectly through a partnership with Locatel, which had a relationship with the Accor hotels and had installed

GlobalSuite in 33 hotels as of January 2004. As explained previously, indirect sales had been a low-cost and low-risk method of introducing GlobalSuite to the market. The CEO wondered whether the time had come to sell more proactively. Guest-Tek was not prohibited from selling directly in markets where Locatel had a presence.

Latin American Market

High-speed Internet access penetration and usage rates among Latin America's 21,000 hotels and nearly one million hotel rooms were widely believed to trail behind North America's rates, although exact figures for Latin America were unavailable. A higher ratio of pleasure travel to business travel in Latin America resulted in lower demand for high-speed Internet access among travelers. Lower penetration in Latin homes and offices also limited demand in hotels. The low demand was exacerbated by a poor communications infrastructure that raised the cost for a solution. Hotel managers charged higher users fees to fund cost recovery, and this practice further discouraged use.

In a more positive light, the CEO viewed Latin America as a relatively easier market to approach than Europe or Asia-Pacific because he believed Latin America had more internal homogeneity. However, in his experience, this internal homogeneity sometimes led Latin American clients to favor Latin American vendors.

Guest-Tek has thus far approached South America as an extension of the company's North American activities. Activity had been modest to date. Since beginning direct sales efforts to Latin America from its Calgary headquarters in June 2003, Guest-Tek had sold at least one major hotel in Aruba, Chile, Costa Rica, Dominican Republic, Mexico, Panama and Puerto Rico. Some additional demand came from Hilton and other existing customers and from the two agents who sold GlobalSuite among other solutions. Each opportunity was carefully and individually evaluated and only accepted if it presented a comfortable return on investment. In this way, Guest-Tek had mitigated its risk by reacting to inbound opportunities. In total, Guest-Tek had nearly a dozen installations in Latin America. Based on these results, the CEO considered the establishment of a regional office with a larger direct sales force.

Asia-Pacific Market

The Asia-Pacific region, with 54,700 hotel properties and nearly four million hotel rooms, also caught the CEO's attention. Its usage rate actually rivaled that of North America and both usage and penetration rates were expected to rise quickly in a revived economy. Guests were demanding high-speed Internet access in spite of user fees that doubled or even tripled North American fees. Many foreign and local providers were stepping in to answer the demand.

The Asia-Pacific region, like Europe, was diverse. Cultures, languages, business communication styles and high-speed Internet access penetration and usage varied widely. Some countries or districts within the region, including Hong Kong, were approaching hotel high-speed Internet access saturation while the market in other countries was still nascent. Countries with high residential and business broadband adoption reportedly had high hotel adoption as well, and Japanese hotel managers in particular demanded the service.

Unfortunately, Guest-Tek had little knowledge of the region and detailed assessments of the various countries were not available; in fact, the CEO ventured to say that this was the region that Guest-Tek understood least. Guest-Tek had few relationships in the area and no staff members with Asian expertise. This lack of familiarity and knowledge had clearly influenced Guest-Tek's approach to the region in the past. Guest-Tek had not proactively pursued deals and had only installed services when approached by hotels. As with opportunities in Latin America, inbound opportunities were carefully evaluated on an individual basis and only accepted on the grounds of a comfortable return on investment. Although the CEO didn't know for certain, Guest-Tek's experience in Asia-Pacific so far supported the widely held belief that it was a difficult market for foreigners to enter.

The Asian preference for a different business model was one aspect of the market that was known to Guest-Tek. In this region, solution providers were often expected to provide the solution, including software, hardware and installation services, at no charge in exchange for a share of the user fees. This model, usually referred to as "revenue share," required a great deal of capital and involved a high degree of risk for the solution provider. This model had been commonplace in North America five years earlier, but had proved to be unsustainable, and many providers following that model had filed for bankruptcy. In fact, Guest-Tek had employed that model to some degree in the company's early stages, but had abandoned it before shifting to its current model. The demand for revenue share contracts on the part of Asian hotel managers ran counter to Guest-Tek's proven strategy, and the CEO was reluctant to revisit the matter.

Most of the high-speed Internet access solutions in Asia were provided by larger telcos, including China Mobile, China Telecom, NTT Communications, Japan Telecom and Yahoo! Broadband Japan, and most of the solutions were based on different technologies including hotspots. There were only a few providers in the region that were similar to Guest-Tek in terms of their solution and business model. They were generally locally based, like Australia's inter-touch, which had more than 100 installations in the region.

Management of International Business

International expansion not only posed questions of how and where to sell GlobalSuite but also how to manage the business and actually install the solution. Up to that time, Guest-Tek's direct sales activities had been conducted from Guest-Tek's head office in Calgary with personal visits by sales and account managers to the hotel properties as necessary. When a contract was signed, a project manager and an operations team were dispatched from the Calgary office to the hotel property to install the solution. Travel to overseas properties for both sales and installations could be costly due to the time and distance involved. Since, to date, international sales were relatively rare, coordination from the head office had been wise and feasible.

This situation could change, however, if Guest-Tek were to make a more concerted effort overseas. The option that immediately came to mind was to set up local offices with local presence, knowledge, connections and acceptance. Such offices, though difficult to staff, might provide a competitive advantage. An overseas office could be built with transplanted North American personnel, local personnel or some mix of the two. Present Guest-Tek employees had little overseas experience. None of the executives had worked overseas, and beyond the one direct salesperson pursuing Latin America and the consultant providing advice on Europe, there were no employees with significant international knowledge. The CEO preferred to promote people from within the company but knew also that international expansion would require an international experience base.

The establishment of overseas offices would also force questions about management and control. International offices could operate as closely managed extensions of the North American office under the CEO or the VP of Sales and Marketing, or they could be run as relatively autonomous units. The CEO wanted to replicate the Guest-Tek culture and ensure quality of operations, but with limited information about the markets, he was unsure of how well the North American management style would translate into the regions in question. He was also unsure of what level of overseas activity could effectively be managed by executives in the head office and at what point a region required or deserved its own autonomous leadership.

Of course, the option of pursuing indirect sales was still available and was somewhat attractive. Reseller and agent relationships were relatively easy to manage and would not require a buildup of staff levels. Resellers and agents would already have presence and expertise in the markets in question. However, the CEO was not certain that the more passive nature of indirect sales would fulfill his mandate for expansion.

The Ceo's Challenge

Understanding the new investors' demands for revenue growth, the CEO had to decide whether or not Guest-Tek should pursue overseas opportunities. He felt he had to decide quickly, given that the North American market would eventually become saturated and competitors were already pursuing international opportunities. Should Guest-Tek expand overseas? If so, which markets should it enter? And how should the overseas operations be managed?

CASE 2

AGT, INC.

AGT, Inc. is a marketing research company, located in the city of Karachi, Pakistan. Jeff Sons Trading Company (JST) has approached it to look at the potential market for an amusement park in Karachi. As the city is very crowded and real estate costs are very high, it will be difficult to find a large enough piece of land to locate such a facility. Even if there is some land available, it will be very expensive and that will have a detrimental effect on the overall costs of the project. JST wants to know the potential of this type of investment. They want the market research to identify if a need for the amusement park exists and, if so, what is the public's attitude toward that type of recreational facility. If a need is found and support is sufficient, then they want to know what type of an amusement park is required by the potential customers. JST will make its investment decision based on the results of this study.

Background

Pakistan is a country that qualifies as a less-developed country (LDC). It is a typical developing country of the Third World faced with the usual problems of rapidly increasing population, sizable government deficit and heavy dependence on foreign aid. The economy of Pakistan has grown rapidly in the last decade, with GDP expanding at 6.7 percent annually, more than twice the population growth. Like any other LDC, it has dualism in its economic system. For example, the cities have all the facilities of modern times, whereas the smaller towns have some or none. Such is also true for income distribution patterns. Real per capita GDP is Rupees 10,000 or $400 annually. There is a small wealthy class (1%–3%), a middle class consisting of another 20%, while the remainder of the population is poor. Half of the population lives below the poverty line. Most of the middle class is an urban working class.

Karachi, the largest city with a very dense population of over 6 million, has been chosen for the first large-scale amusement park in Pakistan. The recreational facilities in Karachi are very small, including a poorly maintained zoo, and people with families avoid visiting most facilities due to the crowds. There are other small parks but not enough to cater to such a large population. The main place people go for recreation is the beach. The beaches are not well developed and are regularly polluted by oil slicks from the nearby port. There seems to be a growing need for recreational activity for people to spend their leisure time. It is also true that many of the people in the higher social classes take vacations with their families and spend money on recreational activities abroad. To see that there is a true need for this type of recreational facility, we propose to conduct a marketing research study of its feasibility. Other potential problems facing the project include:

- Communication system is very poor.
- Only a small percentage of the people own their own transportation.
- Public and private systems of transportation are not efficient.
- Law and order is a problem, described as similar to Los Angeles.

Research Objectives

In order to make an investment decision, JST outlined its research objectives necessary to design a marketing strategy that would accomplish the desired return on investment goals. These objectives are as follows:

1. Identify the potential demand for this project.
2. Identify the primary target market and what they expect in an amusement area.

Information Needs

To fulfill our objectives we will need the following information:

Market

a. Is there a need for this project in this market?
b. How large is the potential market?
c. Is this market sufficient to be profitable?

Consumer

a. Are the potential customers satisfied with the existing facilities in the city?
b. Will these potential consumers utilize an amusement park?
c. Which segment of the population is most interested in this type of facility?
d. Is the population ready to support this type of project?
e. What media could be used to get the message across successfully to the potential customers?

Location

a. Where should this project be built to attract the most visitors?
b. How will the consumer's existing attitudes on location influence the viability and cost of this project?
c. Will the company have to arrange for the transportation to and from the facility if location is outside the city area?
d. Is security a factor in location of the facility?

Recreation Facilities

a. What type of attractions should the company provide at the park to attract customers?
b. Should there be some overnight facility within the park?
c. Should the facility be available only to certain segments of the population or be open to all?

Proposal

With the objectives outlined above in mind, AGT, Inc. presented the following proposal:

The city of Karachi's population has its different economic clusters scattered haphazardly throughout the city. To conduct the marketing research in this type of city and get accurate results will be very difficult. We recommend an extensive study to make sure we have an adequate sampling of the opinion of the target market. Given the parameters above we recommend that the target market be defined as follows:

Desired Respondent Characteristics

- Upper Class—1% (around 60,000)
- Middle Class—15% to 20% (around 900,000 to 1,200,000)
- Male and female
- Age: 15 to 50 years (for survey; market includes all age groups)
- Income level: Rs 25,000 and above per year (Rs: 2,000 per month)
- Household size—with family will be better for sample
- Involved in entertainment activities
- Involved in recreational activities
- Actively participates in social activities
- Members of different clubs
- Involved in outdoor activities

To obtain accurate information regarding respondent's characteristics, we have to approach the market very carefully because of the prevailing circumstances and existing cultural practices. People have little or no knowledge of market surveys. Getting their cooperation, even without the cultural barriers, through a phone or mail survey will be very difficult. In the following paragraphs we will be discussing negative and positive points of all types of surveys and select the appropriate form for our study.

The first, and possibly best, method to conduct the survey under these circumstances will be through the mail, which will not only be cheaper but can also cover all the clusters of population easily. We can not rely totally on a mail survey, as the mail system in Pakistan is unreliable and inefficient. We can go through courier services or registered mail but it will skyrocket the cost. It will not be wise to conduct a mail survey alone.

The other option is to conduct a survey by telephone. In the city of 6 million there are around 200,000 working telephones (1 per 152 persons). Most of the telephones are in businesses or in government offices. It is not that the people cannot afford a telephone, but that they cannot get one because of short supply. Another problem with a telephone survey is

cultural; it is not considered polite to call someone and start asking questions. It is even more of a problem if a male survey member were to reach a female household member. People are not familiar with marketing surveys and would not be willing to volunteer the information we require on telephone. The positive point in telephone survey is that most of the upper class women do not work and can be reached easily. However, we must use a female survey staff. Overall, the chances of cooperation through a telephone survey are very low.

A mall/bazaar intercept could also be used. Again, however, we will face some cultural problems. It's not considered ethical for a male to approach a female in the mall. The only people willing to talk in public are likely to be the males and we will miss female opinion.

To gather respondent data by survey in a country such as Pakistan, we will have to tailor our existing data collecting methods and make them fit accordingly to the circumstances and cultural practices of the marketplace. As a company based in Pakistan with the experience of living under these cultural practices, we propose the following design for the study and questionnaire.

Design of the Study

Our study's design will be such that it will have a mixture of three different types of the surveys. Each survey will focus on a different method. The following are the types of surveys we recommend, tailored to fit in the prevailing circumstances.

Mail Survey

We plan to modify this type of survey to fit into existing circumstances and to be more efficient. The changes made are to counter the inefficient postal system and to generate a better percentage of responses. We plan to deliver the surveys to the respondents through the newspapermen. We know that average circulations of the various newspapers is 50,000 to 200,000 per day. The two dailies chosen have the largest circulation in the city.

A questionnaire will be placed in each newspaper and delivered to the respondent. This will assure that the questionnaire has reached its destination. This questionnaire will introduce us to the respondent and ask for his cooperation. The questionnaire will have return postage and the firm's address. This will give the respondent some confidence that they are not volunteering information to someone unknown. A small promotional gift will be promised on returning the completed survey. Since respondents who will claim the gift will give us their address, this will help us maintain a list of respondents for future surveys. Delivery through newspapermen will also allow us to easily focus on specific clusters.

We except some loss in return mail because there is no acceptable way to get the questionnaires back except through the government postal system. We plan to deliver 5,000 questionnaires to the respondents to counter the loss in return mail. The cost of this survey will be less than it would be if we mailed the questionnaires. As this will be the first exposure for many respondents which allows them to give their views about a nonexistent product, we do not have any return percentage on which to base our survey response expectations. In fact, this may well be the base for future studies.

Door-to-Door Interviews

We will have to tailor the mall/bazaar intercept, as we did in the mail survey, to get the highest possible response percentage. Instead of intercepting at malls, it will be better to send surveyors from door-to-door. This can generate a better percentage of responses and we can be sure who the respondent is. To conduct this survey we will solicit the cooperation of the local business schools. By using these young students we stand a better chance of generating a higher response. Also, we plan to hire some additional personnel, mostly females, and train them to conduct this survey.

Additional Mail Survey

We are planning to conduct this part of the survey to identify different groups of people already involved in similar types of activity. There are eight to ten exclusive clubs in the city of Karachi. A few of them focus solely on some outdoor activity such as yachting and boating, golf, etc. Their membership numbers vary from 3,000 to 5,000. High membership cost and monthly fees have made these clubs restricted to the upper middle class and wealthy. We can safely say that the people using these clubs belong to the 90th percentile of income level. We propose to visit these clubs and personally ask for the members' cooperation. We also plan to get the member list and have the questionnaire delivered to them. They will be asked to return the completed questionnaire to the club office or to mail it in the postage paid reply envelope. We believe that this group will cooperate and give us quality feedback.

The second delivered survey will be to local schools. With the schools' cooperation, we will ask that this questionnaire be delivered by their pupils to the parents. The cover letter will request that the parents fill out the questionnaire and return it to school. This will provide a good sample of people who want outdoor activities for their children. We hope to generate a substantial response through this method.

Questionnaire Design

The type of questions asked should help our client make the decision of whether to invest in the project. (See proposed questionnaire.) Through the survey questionnaires, we should answer the question "Is the population ready for this project and are they willing to support it?" The questionnaire will be a mixture of both open-ended and close-ended questions. It will help to answer the following questions:

- Is there a market for this type of project?
- Is the market substantial?
- Is the market profitable?
- Will this project fill a real need?
- Will this project be only a momentary fad?
- Is the market evenly distributed in all segments/clusters or is there a higher demand in some segments?
- Is the population geared toward and willing to spend money on this type of entertainment facility? If so, how much?
- What is the best location for this project?
- Are people willing to travel some distance to reach this type of facility? Or do they want it within city limits?
- What types of entertainment/rides do people want to see in this amusement park?
- Through what type of media or promotion can prospective customers best be reached?

Discussion Questions

1. What are the objectives of the research project? Does the survey satisfy these objectives?
2. How do elements of culture affect the research design, collection of data, and analysis? Contrast this with the design, collection of data, and analysis of a similar survey project in a more developed country such as the United States.
3. What alternative data collection methods might be useful to pursue? What are the strengths and weaknesses of these alternative methods?

Case prepared by William J. Carner. Used by permission.

QUESTIONNAIRE: Please check appropriate box. Thank you.

1. Are there adequate recreational facilities in the city?
    Yes ☐   No ☐

2. How satisfied are you with the present recreational facilities?
    (Please rate at 0 – 10 degrees)
    0—1—2—3—4—5—6—7—8—9—10
    Poor   Excellent

3. How often do visit the present recreational facilities? (Please check)
    Weekly   ☐
    Fortnightly   ☐
    Monthly   ☐
    Once in two months   ☐
    Yearly   ☐
    More (indicate number)_____ ☐
    Not at all   ☐

4. Do you visit recreational areas with your family?
    Yes ☐   No ☐

    If no, why not?
    Security   ☐
    Distance   ☐
    Expense   ☐
    Crowd (not family type)   ☐
    Poor Service   ☐
    Other (Please specify)   ☐

    _____

4a. Do you stay overnight?
    Yes ☐   No ☐

    If yes, how long? _____
    (Please indicate number of days)

4b. If no, would you have stayed if provided the right circumstances or facilities?
    Yes ☐   No ☐

5. Have you ever visited an amusement park?
    (Here in Pakistan ☐ Abroad ☐)
    Yes   ☐ (Please go to question 5b)
    No   ☐ (Please go to question 5a)

5a. If no, why not?
    Security   ☐
    Distance   ☐
    Expense   ☐
    Crowd (not family type)   ☐
    Poor Service   ☐
    Other (Please specify) _____ ☐

    _____

5b. If yes, when did you last visit an amusement park?
    Last month   ☐
    Last six months   ☐
    Within a year   ☐
    More (specify number)   ☐

    WHERE? _____

6. What did you enjoy the most in that park?
    Roller Coasters   ☐
    Water Slides   ☐
    Children Play Areas   ☐
    Shows   ☐
    Games   ☐
    Simulators   ☐
    Other_____   ☐

6a. How much did you spend in that park? (approximately)
    Rs 50 or less   ☐
    51 to 100   ☐
    101 to 150   ☐
    151 to 200   ☐
    More than 200   ☐

    WHERE?_____

6b. How would you rate the value received?
    (Please rate at 0 – 10 degrees)
    0—1—2—3—4—5—6—7—8—9—10
    Poor   Excellent

7. Would you utilize an amusement park if one was built locally?
    Yes   ☐   No ☐

8. What would you like to see in an amusement park? (Please give us your six best choices.)

a._____   d._____

b._____   e._____

c._____   f._____

9. Where would you like its location to be?

Within city area	☐
Beach area	☐
Suburbs	☐
Outskirts of city	☐
Indifferent	☐

10. How many kilometers will you be willing to travel to the park?

Under 10 K	☐
11 to 20	☐
21 to 35	☐
36 to 55	☐
56 to 65	☐
More than 65	☐

11. How often do you take vacations for recreation purposes?

Never	☐
Once a year	☐
Twice a year	☐
More (please specify) _____	☐

Please Tell Us About Yourself:

12. Please indicate your age.

Under 15	☐
16 to 21	☐
22 to 29	☐
30 to 49	☐
50 to 60	☐
Over 60	☐

13. Please indicate your gender:

Male ☐   Female ☐

14. Are you married?

Yes ☐   No ☐

15. How many children do you have?

Please indicate number_____

16. Please indicate your total family income. (Yearly)

Under 12,000	☐
Over 12,000 to 15,000	☐
Over 15,000 to 20,000	☐
Over 20,000 to 25,000	☐
Over 25,000 to 40,000	☐
Over 40,000 to 60,000	☐
Over 60,000 to 80,000	☐
Over 80,000	☐

17. Do you own a transport?

Yes ☐   No ☐

18. Any other comments?

(If you need more space, please attach additional sheet.)

_____

_____

_____

_____

_____

_____

Thank you, we appreciate your time!

Important:

If you want us to contact you again in later stages of this project, or will be interested in its results give us your name and address and we will be glad to keep you informed. Thank you.

_____

_____

_____

_____

_____

CASE 3

SHANGHAI TANG: THE FIRST GLOBAL CHINESE LUXURY BRAND?

When he created Shanghai Tang in 1994, Hong Kong businessman David Tang intended to launch China's first bona-fide luxury brand. The idea was "to create the first global Chinese lifestyle brand by revitalising Chinese designs—interweaving traditional Chinese culture with the dynamism of the 21st century".[1] In the first few years, Tang's flamboyant, cross-cultural style and ties to international celebrities fuelled the buzz surrounding the label. But the company was unable to establish its core customer outside its home market, Hong Kong,[2] and it struggled to find a niche among successful, established global brands [see the **Appendix** for descriptions of a selection of successful global luxury brands].

In 2005, under new leadership and revised creative direction, Shanghai Tang expanded into several regional markets, with a particular focus on Asia. But was the company on track to become the first global Chinese luxury brand? Would David Tang's vision be realised?

The Story

I just thought to myself, that if you agree that China will eventually be the largest economy in the world, it was time to start a brand that was quintessentially Chinese.[3]

— David Tang, founder of Shanghai Tang

David Tang's vision was to create a lifestyle brand that reintroduced traditional Chinese aesthetics to a new consumer audience. A self-described "broker between East and West," Tang said that he constantly reconciled the various cultural influences he absorbed throughout his life.[4] Born into privileged Hong Kong society, Tang's grandfather made his fortune from the Kowloon Motor Bus Company. Tang's father owned racehorses, and his mother was a Hong Kong socialite. At the age of 14, Tang was sent to England to attend boarding school. Initially unable to speak English, Tang quickly adapted to the habits of well-bred British society and spent weekends visiting friends' families at their country houses while attending the Pure School in Cambridge.[5] He studied law and philosophy at King's College in London and then returned to China as a lecturer in philosophy at Peking University.[6]

Tired of academia, Tang ventured into business, beginning with a job at Cluff Oil. He also became the exclusive importer of Cuban cigars to Asia and Canada and managed "a family investment fund, an oil-drilling business and a gold mine in Africa."[7] While he enjoyed success in these ventures, Tang felt a wave of opportunity flowing from China and set his sights on the creation of a lifestyle brand that was quintessentially Chinese. He was determined to create a brand that embodied everything he loved about the beauty and mystery of China from days past. The idea was to reintroduce this aesthetic and the impeccable Chinese sartorial tradition to an entirely new audience in a way that was relevant to modern tastes. Tang's aesthetic was inspired by the Art Deco Shanghai of the 1930s, when the city was considered "the pearl of the Orient."[8]

In August 1994, his vision was realised. The Shanghai Tang flagship, a 12,000-square-foot store on Hong Kong's Pedder Street, opened its doors to the public. Tang created Shanghai Tang as a lifestyle emporium where shoppers could purchase photo albums, watches, bedding, a sweater or a tailor-made *qipao* (a traditional Chinese dress) in one shop [see **Exhibit 1** for product categories and price ranges]. He also sold communist era kitsch at upscale prices, like Mao Tse Tung watches and goods emblazoned with a red communist star, like the items sold in small side street shops in Hong Kong long popular with Western tourists. To elevate their country-of-origin status and mitigate China's reputation for making cheap, low-quality products, the items carried the label "Made by Chinese." Wealthy tourists visiting Hong Kong, Shanghai Tang's core customer, often stopped at

[1]Shanghai Tang company website http://www.shanghaitang.com (accessed 5 February 2006).

[2]Shanghai Tang's core customer in its home market was wealthy western tourists.

[3]Wong, T. (19 April 2003) "Chic Chinoiserie," *Toronto Star*.

[4]Leris, S. (16 September 2005) "Chairman Tang," *Evening Standard*.

Monica Park prepared this case under the supervision of Dr. Chi Kin (Bennett) Yim for class discussion. This case is not intended to show effective or ineffective handling of decision or business processes.

[5]Ibid.

[6]Ibid.

[7]Ibid.

[8]Management Today (5 May 2006) "MT in China: Silk Route to Success (Luxury Goods)," http://www.turnitin.com/viewGale.asp?r=4.26767452 89107&svr=8&lang=en_us&oid=40377352&key=ed4c906c537619b43f19 3e6292b323fd (accessed 23 May 2006).

EXHIBIT 1 SHANGHAI TANG
PRODUCT CATEGORIES AND PRICE RANGE (US$)

WOMEN'S	MEN'S	CHILDREN'S	ACCESSORIES	HOME
Coats: 435–625	Jackets: 290–770	Jackets: 130–265	Pouches & Cases: 25–50	Candles & Fragrances: 20–155
Jackets: 170–880	Shirts & T-shirts: 60–155	Shirts & Tops: 40	Handbags: 155–430	Bed & Bath: 65–1,350
Blouses: 125–270	Sleepwear: 170–295	Sleepwear: 75–150	Cufflinks: 60	Tableware: 40–205
Tops: 65–240	Sweaters: 120–675	Toys: 20–35	Handkerchiefs: 125	Frames & Albums: 45–205
Dresses: 295–515			Wallets: 40–125	Travel: 55–155
Sleepwear: 170–295			Footwear: 70	CDs: 25
Sweaters: 140–550			Hats & Caps: 30	Boxes: 45–610
			Scarves: 110–290	Stationery: 40–50
			Watches: 90–315	

Source: Shanghai Tang company website: www.shanghaitang.com.

Shanghai Tang's flagship store to buy the signature Tang Jacket, a tunic with a mandarin collar in shockingly bright colours, or a silk handbag embroidered with cherry blossoms.

In 1995, Swiss luxury conglomerate Compagnie Financiere Richemont SA (Richemont), the parent company of prominent luxury brands such as Cartier, Alfred Dunhill, Montblanc, Van Cleef & Arpels and Chloe [see **Exhibit 2** for brands by product category], became a major shareholder in Tang's company. The company paid Tang US$13.1 million for a 40% stake and then bought out another partner to raise its stake to a controlling position.[9] The company owned brands under four major segments: jewellery, watches, writing instruments and leather goods and apparel. With a big luxury goods player like Richemont behind it, Tang's brand obtained something significant that no other Chinese fashion house had achieved: the financial and symbolic backing of a European luxury conglomerate. Tang dismissed speculation that, under Richemont's leadership, Shanghai Tang would showcase more mainstream fashions detached from Chinese influence.

Our business is to always be quintessentially Chinese and to find our place within the mainstream. If we stop being Chinese, we will completely lose ourselves.[10]

— David Tang

Riding the wave of self-created momentum (and with Richemont's deep pockets backing him), Tang once again dreamed big. Shanghai Tang began a rapid expansion, with plans to open stores in New York, London and several Asian cities. Tang's particular focus was the US. "I want to take New York. I want to pick it up and embrace it with a big squeeze and a sloppy wet kiss," Tang said.[11] In December of 1997, at a star-studded event that rivalled Hollywood premiers, Shanghai Tang's 12,500 square foot store opened. Sarah Ferguson appeared on the Oprah Winfrey show and gave Oprah a pair of Shanghai Tang's signature silk pyjamas.[12] To coincide with the store opening, high-profile Chinese actress Gong Li was

[9]McBride, S. (23 July 2003) "Shanghai Tang Wants Its Buzz Back," *The Wall Street Journal.*

[10]Wong, T. (19 April 2003) "Chic Chinoiserie," *Toronto Star.*
[11]Hays, C. (19 August 1999) "A Fashion Mistake on Madison Avenue," *The New York Times.*
[12]Seno, A. (5 December 1997) "Doing the Right Tang in New York," *Asiaweek.*

EXHIBIT 2 RICHEMONT BRANDS BY PRODUCT CATEGORY

JEWELRY	WATCHES	WRITING INSTRUMENTS	LEATHER, APPAREL & ACCESSORIES
Cartier	Cartier	Montblanc	Alfred Dunhill
Piaget	Van Cleef & Arpels	Montegrappa	Lancel
Van Cleef & Arpels	Piaget		Chloe
	A. Lange & Shone		Old England
	Vacheron Constantin		Shanghai Tang
	Jaeger-LeCoultre		Purdey
	Panerai		Hacket
	Baume & Mercier		
	IWC		
	Mont Blanc		
	Dunhill		

featured in a print campaign, which included ads in *The New York Times, Vanity Fair, Harper's Bazaar* and *W*.[13]

Situated on Madison Avenue—prime fashion real estate—the New York store was poised to be the western beacon to its sister stores in the east. As was typical, Tang's excitement and vision were bold, but the dream proved too big for reality. In July 1999, the high-profile New York flagship closed only 19 months after it had opened and relocated to a smaller space down the road from the original.[14]

There were several reasons why sales did not meet expectations. First, the company overestimated American consumers' interest in upscale Chinoiserie. Kristina Stewart, editor-in-chief of *Quest* magazine in New York, was quoted in an article saying, "they certainly courted the Upper East Side scene and threw lavish parties there, but at the end of the day those lime-green Nehru jackets made better wallpaper. You can't wear that stuff."[15] Second, the Shanghai Tang style was confusing for customers. There was incongruity in presenting both pre-revolutionary and cultural revolution styles in the same store, and the tongue-in-cheek, post-modern take on China's

heritage was ultimately lost on the wealthy American buyer. Third, it was difficult to justify the prices for high-end Chinese trinkets because cheaper alternatives were readily available in Chinatown at the Pearl River department store on Canal Street. Finally, the choice of retail space on Madison Avenue meant high rent (US$2.7 million annually), which ultimately sales revenue could not cover.

> It's tough to start a brand. In one sense fashion is easy, but the competition is intense. Retail is a tough business, and we've pumped a lot of money into the brand, and I guess we shouldn't be surprised if it's a struggle. You look at something like Ralph Lauren. It took them 30 years to become established as a global brand.[16]
>
> — David Tang

New Direction

Leadership

Despite missteps in the American retail market, the Shanghai Tang Hong Kong flagship continued to do steady business and the company maintained its relationship with Richemont. In 2001, Tang decided to devote his time and energy towards other business ventures but he maintained a position on the board and was the brand's largest shareholder after Richemont. Richemont executives assumed a more active role in the company's direction. In 2001, CEO Raphael

[13]Sutton, J. (2 March 1998) "East to East Coast: Tang Sells Fine China," *Marketing News*.
[14]*WWD* (25 February 2005) "Shanghai Tang Reinvented," http://www.turnitin.com/viewGale.asp?r=4.2676745289107&svr=8&lang=en_us&oid=21911753&key=128b94a0e28af65c90a629fd3645776d (accessed 23 May 2006).
[15]Hays, C. (19 August 1999) "A Fashion Mistake on Madison Avenue," *The New York Times*.
[16]Wong, T. (19 April 2003) "Chic Chinoiserie," *Toronto Star*.

le Masne de Chermont was recruited from another Richemont brand, Piaget, to refocus and redirect the ailing Shanghai Tang brand. Le Masne had stark but complementary contrast to Tang's flamboyant leadership style and quietly transformed the company into "a lifestyle brand" of more aesthetic subtlety during the first few years that would be relevant to the discerning taste of the global luxury customer.[17] But le Masne took from Tang's mistake the lesson that would guide the brand going forward: "we need to be more modern".[18]

In step with the company's evolution, top management embodied the cross-cultural blending that would become the brand's signature: David Tang from Hong Kong, le Masne from France, creative director Joanne Ooi from America and marketing director Camilla Hammar from Sweden. As le Masne noted, "We're a melting pot of multicultural people who work on the same vision: a Chinese lifestyle brand that's relevant."[19]

Planned Growth

Le Masne reported that worldwide sales for Shanghai Tang in 2005 grew 43% from the previous year, and American sales (at boutiques in Honolulu and New York) were up 50%.[20] According to one source, yearly sales were somewhere between US$20–$30 million, with the majority of sales at the Hong Kong flagship. In 2005, new stores opened in Zurich, Shanghai, Tokyo and Bangkok, with stores in Beijing and Milan planned to open in 2006[21] [see **Exhibit 3** for retail store locations]. The overall expansion included 11 new stores in the next two years bringing the total to 30.[22] The Asian market was "responsible for 80% of the brand's sales. Richemont's latest annual report stated that overall sales in Asia (outside Japan) grew 20%, compared to 10% in Europe, 7% in the Americas and 3% in Japan, for the fiscal year that ended in March 2004"[23] [see **Exhibit 4**].

Unlike Tang, le Masne was less concerned with dominance in America and set his sights on the rapidly

EXHIBIT 3 SHANGHAI TANG RETAIL SPACE

CITY	RETAIL LOCATION	TYPE OF RETAIL SPACE
Shanghai	Promenade on Mao Ming	shop
	Shangri-La Hotel	shop
	Xintiandi Plaza	free-standing store
New York	Madison Avenue	free-standing store
Paris	Rue Bonaparte	free-standing store
London	Sloane Street	free-standing store
	Selfridges	shop
Hong Kong	Pedder Building	free-standing store
	The Peninsula Hotel	shop
	Hong Kong International Airport	shop
	Intercontinental Hotel	shop
Tokyo	Chuo-Ku	free-standing store
Singapore	Ngee Ann City	free-standing store
Bangkok	The Emporium	shop
	Four Seasons Hotel	shop
Beijing	Beijing Capital International Airport	shop
Honolulu	Ala Moana Shopping Center	shop
Jakarta	Plaza Senayan	shop
Zurich	Globus Schweizergasse	free-standing store

Notes: A free-standing store sells one brand under one roof. A shop is retail space leased to a company usually located in a department store, hotel or shopping mall.

Source: Shanghai Tang.

growing wealthy class in China. This shift in regional focus, particularly for the luxury goods segment, appeared to be on track. "A 2005 Ernst & Young analysis of luxury goods consumption [estimated] that sales in China [would] grow 20% annually from 2005 to 2008."[24] According to the report, by 2015 China would overtake the United States as the world's second-largest consumer market of luxury goods after Japan.[25]

However, the brand had to be relevant to both wealthy Chinese customers and wealthy non-Chinese customers, who had different points of reference for what was considered elegant Chinese style. Chinese consumers in the apparel market still seemed to belong to two extremes. Angelica Cheung, editor of *Vogue China*, said these two groups were "a very

---

[17]*WWD* (25 February 2005) "Shanghai Tang Reinvented," http://www. turnitin.com/viewGale.asp?r=4.2676745289107&svr=8&lang=en_us& oid=21911753&key=128b94a0e28af65c90a629fd3645776d (accessed May 23, 2006).

[18]Tischler, L. (January–February 2006) "The Gucci Killers," *Fast Company*, 102, pp. 42–48.

[19]Ibid.

[20]Jana, R. (1 December 2005) "Shanghai Tang: A Taste of China," [www document] http://www.businessweek.com (accessed 23 February 2006).

[21]Ibid.

[22]Edelson, S. (25 February 2005) "Shanghai Tang Reinvented," *WWD*.

[23]Jana, R. (1 December 2005) "Shanghai Tang: A Taste of China," [www document] http://www.businessweek.com (accessed 23 February 2006).

[24]Ibid.

[25]Ibid.

EXHIBIT 4 RICHEMONT SALES

	2001 US$ M	2002 US$ M	2003 US$ M	2004 US$ M	2005 US$ M
SALES	3341	3415	3632	3967	4679
Cost of Sales	(1103)	(1223)	(1360)	(1508)	(1668)
Gross Profit	2238	2193	2272	2459	3011
SALES BY PRODUCT LINE					
Jewelry	809	776	833	927	1064
Watches	1499	1587	1696	1834	2233
Writing Instruments	239	252	276	321	375
Leather Goods	283	268	269	282	326
Clothing and other	512	532	559	603	681
Total	3341	3415	3632	3967	4679
SALES BY GEOGRAPHIC REGION					
Europe	1368	1513	1550	1714	2023
Japan	655	658	701	735	808
Asia-Pacific	648	628	691	749	964
Americas	671	616	689	770	884
Total	3341	3415	3632	3967	4679
Average Exchange Rate	2001	2002	2003	2004	2005
EUR/US$	0.907	0.8848	0.9947	1.1754	1.2589

Note: Figures from year ending March 2005.

Source: Richemont (2005) "Annual Report."

moneyed minority seduced by foreign luxury labels, and the overwhelming majority who are interested only in cheap, affordable clothing. There's not much for anyone in between."[26] The company's three Shanghai stores sold 50% of their merchandise to local young, urban professionals. The other half was sold to westerners looking for Asian-inspired garments in rich fabrics and colours. Courting wealthy Chinese consumers appeared to be a good idea, but when attempting to build a luxury apparel brand translatable in several markets, it was easier said than done. "Young Chinese women wish to be modern and chic," Cheung said. "Westerners might think that Chinese women look great in a *cheongsam* or similar Chinese clichés but that sort of clothing reminds

modern women of their grandmothers. Instead everyone today wants to look like Kate Moss."[27] Consumer segments in Asian cities outside China also needed convincing, though of a different sort. For example, in Japan, the world's largest luxury goods market, le Masne said customers wouldn't embrace a Chinese brand unless it had a certain cachet in France and Italy.[28]

To stay relevant in the high-end fashion market, Shanghai Tang expanded its fashion horizons and collaborated with several top designers. The Shanghai Tang jewellery range, made by Sandra d'Auriol, a French designer based in Hong Kong, sold well. Philip Treacy, famed accessories designer, made hats for winter 2005 and worked on another collection for

[26]Asome, C. (10 May 2006) "Chinese Whispers Turn Out to be Exaggerated," *The Times.*

[27]Ibid.
[28]McBride, S. (23 July 2003) "Shanghai Tang Wants its Buzz Back," *The Wall Street Journal.*

spring 2006. A line of trendy, embellished T-shirts for spring 2005 came from Studd by Gabby Harris. And introduced exclusively to Shanghai Tang stores in May 2005 was a collection of special edition Puma shoes, the Shanghai Tang Peony. Le Masne expressed the intention to start lines of licensed products, such as eyewear and fragrances, that tended to significantly increase sales figures while at the same time introducing the brand to a wider audience who could afford the relatively cheaper products. The high-profile collaborations and possible line extensions, along with new stores, were intended to raise awareness of the brand.

Rather than grand store openings and costly celebrity endorsements, Shanghai Tang focused on localised public relations and sponsored events relevant to each regional market. Also, prime retail locations remained central to its channel strategy of maintaining access to luxury consumers. In addition to its freestanding stores, Shanghai Tang opened shops in world-renowned hotels such as the Peninsula and the Four Seasons and, to court the wealthy traveller, it also opened shops in Hong Kong International Airport and Beijing Capital International Airport.

Design

Much of the credit for Shanghai Tang's sales turnaround went to creative director, Joanne Ooi, who was recruited by le Masne in 2001. As the brand outgrew its kitschy image, Ooi introduced design statements that "combined Chinese culture references and sleek, contemporary clothes"[29] [see **Exhibit 5** for a selection of products]. It was reported that Ooi was offered her directorship after submitting the following comments on the Shanghai Tang flagship to le Masne:

> It's an overpriced Chinese emporium that has no credibility with local Chinese people, let alone with fashion people. Its very narrow market is high-end tourists. It's a once-in-a-lifetime destination shopping experience, a kind of fashion Disneyland. Plus, it's unwearable and eccentric.[30]
>
> — Joanne Ooi, creative director, Shanghai Tang

At the creative helm of the brand she once found risible, Ooi was clear on Shanghai Tang's international image, saying, "the goal is to be the ambassador of modern Chinese style."[31] To achieve this, Ooi conducted her research for collections in art museums and read books on regional history. To serve as inspiration for the autumn 2005 collection, Ooi commissioned artwork "by established Chinese contemporary artists and young art students."[32]

For one collection, Ooi focused on Chinese calligraphy by turning traditional Chinese characters into decorative patterns.[33] "Ethnic tribes in China's Hunan province" inspired another collection of clothes, as did the "fur-lined clothing worn by Mongolian and Tibetan nomads."[34] Ooi preferred these design sources to fashion magazines and of-the-moment trends. More important, however, was that this established the credibility of the brand's intention to become an ambassador of China's national aesthetic. On this point, Ooi said, "I try to stay away from a pastiche of what Westerners think of as Chinese culture."[35]

Branding Chinese culture could be an effective point upon which to differentiate from European and American luxury brands. However, as the company expanded, the cultural branding angle became complicated and ran the risk of alienating potential customers in Asia. In short, exoticised images of Asia were less appealing to Asian consumers. While popular with a portion of Hong Kong's wealthy class, Shanghai Tang had not yet proved popular among Chinese consumers unconvinced as to why they should pay top-dollar for Shanghai Tang's reinvented Chinese style.

China's First Global Luxury Brand?

Since China had both economic and cultural cachet, Shanghai Tang and other Chinese brands were poised to enter a new era of heightened global interest in all things Chinese.[36] Would Shanghai Tang follow in the tradition of established global luxury brands associated with a national aesthetic? As le Masne said, "If Hermes is a representation of French lifestyle-chic, or [Ralph] Lauren is [a representation] for the Americans, and Armani is for the Italians, why not Shanghai Tang for the Chinese?"[37] Was the company on track to become the first global Chinese luxury brand?

[29]Jana, R. (1 December 2005) "Shanghai Tang: A Taste of China," [www document] http://www.businessweek.com (accessed 23 February 2006).

[30]Tischler, L. (January–February 2006) "The Gucci Killers," *Fast Company*, 102, pp. 42–48.

[31]Jana, R. (1 December 2005) "Shanghai Tang: A Taste of China," [www document] http://www.businessweek.com (accessed 23 February 2006).

[32]Ibid.
[33]Ibid.
[34]Ibid.
[35]Ibid.
[36]Ibid.
[37]McBride, S. (24 July 2003) "Shanghai Shocker," *Far Eastern Economic Review*.

EXHIBIT 5 SHANGHAI TANG SPRING SUMMER 2006 (SELECT IETMS)

"PEONY" MAGIC COAT

Silk dupioni three-quarter length coat with "Peony" flower print, frog button closure and beading along the trim, US$625.

SILK LINEN COAT

Simple and elegant three-quarter length coat in exquisite silk linen, US$435.

DENIM "MAO" JACKET

Light, modernised denim "Mao" jacket with four front patch pockets and no lining, US$290.

COTTON PAJAMAS

Cotton poplin pajamas with mandarin collar, frog buttons and contrast piping, US$170.

SILK FAN CLUTCH

Fan shaped clutch with "Cherry Blossom" silk jacquard and jade and Chinese knot tassel. Zip closure, US$175.

TOPSTITCHED "DOUBLE FISH" CUSHION

Vivid cotton cushions with intricate "Double Fish" motif topstitching, US$95.

Source: Shanghai Tang company website: www.shanghaitang.com.

Appendix: Selection of Successful Global Luxury Brands

LVMH Moet Hennessy Louis Vuitton

LVMH was the world's largest luxury goods company with more than 1,500 retail outlets (including 280-plus Louis Vuitton stores), around 150 DFS Group duty-free shops, Le Bon Marche department stores and hundreds of designer boutiques worldwide.

In 1854, woodworker Louis Vuitton started with a store in Paris to sell his handcrafted luggage. Vuitton introduced the LV monogram in 1896 and opened stores in the United States and England by 1900. In 1977 Henry Recamier, who was a former executive and married into the Vuitton family, entered the business and transformed the business from little-known status symbols to designer must-haves. Within ten years, sales soared from US$20 million to nearly US$2.5 billion. In 1987 Recamier merged Louis Vuitton with Moet Hennessy (maker of wines, spirits and fragrances) and all were under the name LVMH Moet Hennessy Louis Vuitton. When Bernard Arnault became chairman in 1989, LVMH increased its fashion holdings by buying Givenchy, Christian Lacroix and Kenzo. Arnault is credited for transforming the LVMH Group from a small producer of clothing and champagne to a global luxury conglomerate made up of the world's most powerful luxury brands. LVMH owns such fashion brands as Berluti, Celine, Christian Dior, Donna Karan, Emilio Pucci, Fendi, Marc Jacobs and Thomas Pink. Central to the group's strategy is management of its "star brands" paired with product quality and a culture of innovation. According to Arnault, a star brand is a brand that is "timeless, modern, fast-growing, and highly profitable."[38] The majority of LVMH brands have a long history of craftsmanship and were originated in Europe. The LVMH management strategy was to build a work environment that supported creativity while at the same time enforcing strict business discipline. Worldwide revenue in 2005 totalled US$ 16.8 billion, up 11% from 2004.

Ralph Lauren

Polo Ralph Lauren Corporation originated the concept of the lifestyle brand. Ralph Lauren, born Ralph Lifshitz, grounded his brand in a quintessentially American image of wealth and status and consistently carried this aesthetic throughout his retail stores and product lines. He began his career as a sales representative for Rivetz, a Boston tie maker, and in 1967 he began designing ties for Beau Brummel of New York. He named his own style division "Polo" because of the upper class image it evoked. In the early 1970s, Lauren partnered with Peter Strom to form Polo Fashions and focused on tailored menswear. In 1971 Lauren introduced his signature polo logo and his women's line. In the same year, the first licensed Polo store on Rodeo Drive in Beverly Hills and his first in-store boutique at Bloomingdale's in New York City were opened. In 1980, Polo Ralph Lauren expanded further into licensed products, including home furnishings, jeans, fragrance and eyewear. In 1997 Polo went public and, following a large restructuring, bought back its European licensee to reclaim greater control of the Polo brand. The company's brands were: Polo by Ralph Lauren, Ralph Lauren, Ralph Lauren Purple Label, Black Label, Blue Label, Lauren by Ralph Lauren, Polo Jeans Co., Rugby, Chaps, RRL, RLX, RL Childrenswear, and Club Monaco. Net revenue for fiscal year 2005 was US$3.3 billion.

Giorgio Armani

Giorgio Armani was the sole shareholder of his US$ 1.7 billion lifestyle business. The company licensed its name for perfume, watches and accessories, but continued to earn more than half of its revenues from apparel.[39] In 2003, 53% of his total sales were generated by garments, from sporty AX/Armani Exchange to the luxurious Giorgio Armani brand. Armani had stores in more than 35 countries. The company's brands included: Giorgio Armani, Armani Exchange, Emporio Armani, Armani Jeans, Armani Collezioni, Armani Junior, Armani Casa and a Giorgio Armani Accessories store. To control the integrity of the brand, Armani owned Simint, the Italian holder of the Armani jeans license, and had several joint ventures with Italian manufacturing companies to bring its apparel production in-house while allowing for a controlled expansion of product lines.

Armani studied medicine and was in the Italian army before starting working as a window dresser for La Rinascente department stores, where he later became a menswear buyer. His first design position was at Nino Cerruti. In 1975 Armani partnered with Sergio Galeotti and established Giorgio Armani S.p.A. The Armani label became known for its unstructured

[38]Som, A. (Winter 2005) "Personal Touch That Built an Empire of Style and Luxury," *European Business Forum.*

[39]The paradox of the fashion business at the luxury level is that it is difficult to build a successful business on clothes alone. Successful brands usually make most of their revenue from accessories and fragrance.

tailored suits. The business went global in the 1980s and gained greater recognition when the designer dressed actor Richard Gere in the film *American Gigolo*. Armani was successful in creating a true lifestyle brand, extending his design aesthetic into multiple product categories, even expanding beyond fashion and home furnishing. In 2004, Armani announced his intent to develop a series of Armani-branded and styled hotels.

Hermes

Hermes International sold a wide range of luxury goods, including scarves, ties, leather goods, watches, stationery and men's and women's apparel. There were approximately 215 Hermes stores worldwide and around 40 retail outlets that sold Hermes products. The company did not grant licenses and made most of the products it sold. Famous for its leather goods, Hermes was founded in 1837 in France by harness-maker Thierry Hermes. Hermes won acclaim for its unique carriage design and its saddle stitch became a trademark. Thierry's son, Emile-Maurice, expanded the product range to include travel-related leather goods, including saddlebags, luggage, wallets, handbags and even jewelry. Emile also chose the well-known logo, the horse-drawn carriage. Clothing was introduced in the 1920s when Emile's son-in-law, Robert Dumas, took over the company. Dumas introduced the first Hermes scarf in 1937, which became one of the design house's signature pieces. Dumas' son, Jean-Louis, took control of the company in 1978 when his father passed away. He brought in young designers to reinvigorate the brand's image. When the company went public in 1993, the family retained more than 80% of the share holdings. Hermes also owned crystal-maker Les Cristalleries de Saint-Louis, silversmith L'Orfevrerie Puiforcat, shoemaker John Lobb, 35% of Jean-Paul Gaultier's fashion business and 32% of German camera maker Leica. In 2002, the company expanded its leather-working business and, through public campaigns, promoted the craftsmen and women behind its products. In 2005, net profit totaled US$298.3 million, up 15% from 2004. As of 2005, descendants of founder Thierry Hermes owned 75% of the company.

Source: Hoover's Company Information [www document] http://www. hoovers.com (accessed 15 January 2006) and 2005 Company Annual Reports [www documents] http://www.hermes.com (accessed 15 January 2006); http://www.armani.com (accessed 15 January 2006); http://www.lvmh.com (accessed 15 January 2006); http://www.polo.com (accessed 15 January 2006).

CASE 4

IKEA: FURNITURE RETAILER TO THE WORLD

Introduction

IKEA is one of the world's most successful global retailers. In 2007, IKEA had 300 home furnishing superstores in 35 countries and was visited by some 583 million shoppers. IKEA's low-priced, elegantly designed merchandise, displayed in large warehouse stores, generated sales of €21.2 billion in 2008, up from €4.4 billion in 1994. Although the privately held company refuses to publish figures on profitability, its net profit margins were rumored to be approximately 10%, high for a retailer. The founder, Ingvar Kamprad, now in his 80s but still an active "advisor" to the company, is rumored to be one of the world's richest men.

Company Background

IKEA was established by Ingvar Kamprad in Sweden in 1943 when he was just 17 years old. The fledgling company sold fish, Christmas magazines, and seeds from his family farm. His first business had been selling matches; the enterprising Kamprad purchased them wholesale in 100-box lots (with help from his grandmother who financed the enterprise) and then resold individually at a higher markup. The name IKEA was an acronym: I and K his initials; E stood for Elmtaryd, the name of the family farm; and A stood for Agunnaryd, the name of the village in southern Sweden where the farm was located. Before long, Kamprad had added ballpoint pens to his list and was selling his products via mail order. His warehouse was a shed on the family farm. The customer fulfillment system used the local milk truck, which picked up goods daily and took them to the train station.

In 1948, Kamprad added furniture to his product line; in 1949, he published his first catalog, distributed then as now, for free. In 1953, Kamprad was struggling with a problem: the milk truck had changed its route, and he could no longer use it to take goods to the train station. His solution was to buy an idle factory in nearby Almhult and convert it into a warehouse. With business now growing rapidly, Kamprad hired a 22-year-old designer, Gillis Lundgren. Lundgren originally helped Kamprad do photo shoots for the early IKEA catalogs, but he started to design more and more furniture for IKEA, eventually designing as many as 400 pieces, including many best sellers.

This case was prepared by Charles W. L. Hill, School of Business, University of Washington. Reprinted by permission.

IKEA's goal over time was to provide stylish functional designs with minimalist lines that could be cost-efficiently manufactured under contract by suppliers and priced low enough to allow most people to afford them. Kamprad's theory was that "good furniture could be priced so that the man with a flat wallet would make a place for it in his spending and could afford it."[1] Kamprad was struck by the fact that furniture in Sweden was expensive at the time, something that he attributed to a fragmented industry dominated by small retailers. Furniture was also often considered family heirlooms, passed down across the generations. He wanted to change this: to make it possible for people of modest means to buy their own furniture. Ultimately, this led to the concept of what IKEA calls "democratic design"—a design that, according to Kamprad, "was not just good, but also from the start adapted to machine production and thus cheap to assemble."[2] Gillis Lundgren was instrumental in the implementation of this concept. Time and time again, he would find ways to alter the design of furniture to save on manufacturing costs.

Gillis Lundgren also stumbled on what was to become a key feature of IKEA furniture: self-assembly. Trying to efficiently pack and ship a long–legged table, he hit upon the idea of taking the legs off and mailing them packed flat under the tabletop. Kamprad quickly realized that flat-packed furniture reduced transport and warehouse costs, and damage (IKEA had been having a lot of problems with furniture damaged during the shipping process). Moreover, customers seemed willing to take on the task of assembly in return for lower prices. By 1956, self-assembly was integral to the IKEA concept.

In 1957, IKEA started to exhibit and sell its products at home furnishing fairs in Sweden. By cutting retailers out of the equation and using the self-assembly concept, Kamprad could undercut the prices of established retail outlets, much to their chagrin. Established retailers responded by prohibiting IKEA from taking orders at the annual furniture trade in Stockholm. Established outlets claimed that IKEA was imitating their designs. This was to no avail, however, so the retailers went further, pressuring furniture manufacturers not to sell to IKEA. This had two unintended consequences. First, without access to the designs of many manufacturers, IKEA was forced to design more of its products in-house. Second, Kamprad looked for a manufacturer who would produce

IKEA-designed furniture. Ultimately, he found one in Poland.

To his delight, Kamprad discovered that furniture manufactured in Poland was as much as 50% cheaper than furniture made in Sweden, allowing him to cut prices even more. Kamprad also found that doing business with the Poles required the consumption of considerable amounts of vodka to celebrate business transactions, and for the next 40 years his drinking was legendary. Alcohol consumption apart, the relationship that IKEA established with the Poles was to become the archetype for future relationships with suppliers. According to one of the Polish managers, there were three advantages of doing business with IKEA: "One concerned the decision making; it was always one man's decision, and you could rely upon what had been decided. We were given long-term contracts, and were able to plan in peace and quiet.... A third advantage was that IKEA introduced new technology. One revolutionary idea, for instance, was a way of treating the surface of wood. They also mastered the ability to recognize cost savings that could trim the price."[3] By the early 1960s, Polish-made goods were to be found on more than half of the pages of the IKEA catalog.

By 1958, an expanded facility at the Almhult location became the first IKEA store. The original idea behind the store was to have a location where customers could come and see IKEA furniture set up. It was a supplement to IKEA's main mail-order business; but it very quickly became an important sales point in its own right. The store soon started to sell car roof racks so customers could leave with flat-packed furniture loaded on top. Noticing that a trip to an IKEA store was something of an outing for many shoppers (Almhult was not a major population center, and people often drove in from long distances), Kamprad experimented with adding a restaurant to the store so that customers could relax and refresh themselves while shopping. The restaurant was a hit, and it became an integral feature of all IKEA stores.

The response of IKEA's competitors to its success was to argue that IKEA products were of low quality. In 1964, just after 800,000 IKEA catalogs had been mailed to Swedish homes, the widely read Swedish magazine *Allt i Hemmet* (Everything for the Home) published a comparison of IKEA furniture to that sold in traditional Swedish retailers. The furniture was tested for quality in a Swedish design laboratory. The magazine's analysis, detailed in a 16-page spread, was that not only was IKEA's quality as good if not

[1] Quoted in R. Heller, "Folk Fortune," *Forbes*, September 4, 2000, 67.
[2] B. Torekull, *Leading by Design: The IKEA Story* (New York: HarperCollins, 1998), 53.
[3] Ibid.

better than that from other Swedish furniture manufacturers, the prices were much lower. For example, the magazine concluded that a chair bought at IKEA for 33 kronor ($4) was better than a virtually identical one bought in a more expensive store for 168 kronor ($21). The magazine also showed how a living room furnished with IKEA products was as much as 65% less expensive than one furnished with equivalent products from four other stores. This publicity made IKEA acceptable in middle-class households, and sales began to take off.

In 1965, IKEA opened its first store in Stockholm, Sweden's capital. By now, IKEA was generating the equivalent of €25 million and had already opened a store in neighboring Norway. The Stockholm store, its third, was the largest furniture store in Europe and had an innovative circular design that was modeled on the famous Guggenheim Art Museum in New York. The location of the store was to set the pattern at IKEA for decades. The store was situated on the outskirts of the city, rather than downtown, with ample space for parking and good access roads. The new store generated a large amount of traffic, so much so that employees could not keep up with customer orders, and long lines formed at the checkouts and merchandise pick-up areas. To try and reduce the lines, IKEA experimented with a self-service pick-up solution, allowing shoppers to enter the warehouse, load flat-packed furniture onto trolleys, and then take them through the checkout. It was so successful that this soon became the company norm in all stores.

International Expansion

By 1973, IKEA was the largest furniture retailer in Scandinavia with nine stores. The company enjoyed a market share of 15% in Sweden. Kamprad, however, felt that growth opportunities were limited. Starting with a single store in Switzerland over the next 15 years, the company expanded rapidly in Western Europe. IKEA met with considerable success, particularly in West Germany, where it had 15 stores by the late 1980s. As in Scandinavia, Western European furniture markets were largely fragmented and served by high-cost retailers located in expensive downtown stores, selling relatively expensive furniture that was not always immediately available for delivery. IKEA's elegant functional designs with their clean lines, low prices, and immediate availability, were a breath of fresh air, as was the self-service store format. The company was met with almost universal success even though, as one former manager put it: "We made every mistake in the book, but money nevertheless poured in. We lived frugally, drinking now and

again, yes perhaps too much, but we were on our feet bright and cheery when the doors were open for the first customers, competing in good Ikean spirit for the cheapest solutions."[4]

The man in charge of the European expansion was Jan Aulino, Kamprad's former assistant, who was just 34 years old when the expansion started. Aulino surrounded himself with a young team. Aulino recalled that the expansion was so fast paced that the stores were rarely ready when IKEA moved in. Moreover, it was hard to get capital out of Sweden due to capital controls; the trick was to make a quick profit and get a positive cash flow going as soon as possible. In the haste to expand, Aulino and his team did not always pay attention to detail. He reportedly clashed with Kamprad on several occasions and considered himself fired at least four times, although he never was. Eventually the European business was reorganized, and tighter controls were introduced.

IKEA was slow to expand in the United Kingdom, however, where the locally grown company Habitat had built a business that was similar in many respects to IKEA, offering stylish furniture at a relatively low price. IKEA also entered North America, opening seven stores in Canada between 1976 and 1982. Emboldened by this success, in 1985, the company entered the United States. It proved to be a challenge of an entirely different nature.

On the face of it, America looked to be fertile territory for IKEA. As in Western Europe, furniture retailing was a very fragmented business in the United States. At the low end of the market were the general discount retailers, such as Walmart, Costco, and Office Depot, who sold a limited product line of basic furniture, often at very low prices. This furniture was very functional, lacked the design elegance associated with IKEA, and was generally of a fairly low quality. Then there were higher-end retailers, such as Ethan Allen, that offered high-quality, well-designed, high-priced furniture. They sold this furniture in full-service stores staffed by knowledgeable salespeople. High-end retailers would often sell ancillary services as well, such as interior design. Typically these retailers would offer home delivery service, including set-up in the home, either for free or a small additional charge. Because it was expensive to keep large inventories of high-end furniture, much of what was on display in stores was not readily available, and the client would often have to wait a few weeks before it was delivered.

IKEA opened its first U.S. store in 1985 in Philadelphia. The company had decided to locate on the

[4]Ibid.

coasts. Surveys of American consumers suggested that IKEA buyers were more likely to be people who had travelled abroad, considered themselves risk-takers, and liked fine food and wine. These people were concentrated on the coasts. As one manager put it, "There are more Buicks driven in the middle than on the coasts."[5]

Although IKEA initially garnered favorable reviews, and enough sales to persuade it to start opening additional stores, by the early 1990s, it was clear that things were not going well in America. The company found that its European-style offerings did not always resonate with American consumers. Beds were measured in centimeters, not the king, queen, and twin sizes with which Americans are familiar. American sheets did not fit on IKEA beds. Sofas were not big enough, wardrobe drawers not deep enough, glasses too small, curtains too short, and kitchens did not fit American-size appliances. In a story often repeated at IKEA, managers noted that customers were buying glass vases and using them to drink out of, rather than the small glasses for sale at IKEA. The glasses were apparently too small for Americans who like to add liberal quantities of ice to their drinks. To make matters worse, IKEA was sourcing many of the goods from overseas, priced in the Swedish kronor, which was strengthening against the American dollar. This drove up the price of goods in IKEA's American stores. Moreover, some of the stores were poorly located, and not large enough to offer the full IKEA experience familiar to Europeans.

Turning around its American operations required IKEA to take some decisive actions. Many products had to be redesigned to fit with American needs. Newer and larger store locations were chosen. To bring prices down, goods were sourced from lower-cost locations and priced in dollars. IKEA also started to source some products from factories in the United States to reduce both transport costs and dependency on the value of the dollar. At the same time, IKEA noticed a change in American culture. Americans were becoming more concerned with design, and more open to the idea of disposable furniture. It used to be said that Americans changed their spouses about as often as they changed their dining room tables, about 1.5 times in a lifetime, but something was shifting in American culture. Younger people were more open to risks and more willing to experiment. There was a thirst for design elegance and quality. Starbucks was tapping into this, as was Apple Computer, and so did IKEA. According to one manager at IKEA, "Ten or

15 years ago, traveling in the United States, you couldn't eat well. You couldn't get good coffee. Now you can get good bread in the supermarket, and people think that is normal. I like that very much. That is more important to good life than the availability of expensive wines. That is what IKEA is about."[6]

To tap into America's shifting culture, IKEA reemphasized design and started promoting the brand with a series of quirky hip advertisements aimed at a younger demographic: young married couples, college students, and 20- to 30-something singles. One IKEA commercial, called "Unboring," made fun of the reluctance of Americans to part with their furniture. One famous ad featured a discarded lamp, forlorn and forsaken in some rainy American city. A man turned to the camera sympathetically. "Many of you feel bad for this lamp," he said in thick Swedish accent. "That is because you are crazy." Hip people, the commercial implied, bought furniture at IKEA. Hip people did not hang onto their furniture either; after a while they discarded it and replaced it with something else from IKEA.

The shift in tactics worked. IKEA's revenues doubled in a four-year period to $1.27 billion in 2001, up from $600 million in 1997. By 2008, the United States was IKEA's second-largest market after Germany, with 35 stores accounting for 10% of its total revenues, or around $2.4 billion, and expansion plans called for 50-plus stores in the United States by 2012.

Having learned vital lessons about competing in foreign countries outside continental Western Europe, IKEA continued to expand internationally in the 1990s and 2000s. It first entered the United Kingdom in 1987, and by 2008, it had 17 stores in the country. IKEA also acquired Britain's Habitat in the early 1990s and continued to run it under the Habitat brand name. In 1998, IKEA entered China, where it had four stores by 2008, followed by Russia in 2000 (11 stores by 2008), and Japan in 2006, a country where it had failed miserably 30 years earlier (by 2008 IKEA had four stores in Japan). In total, by 2008, there were 285 IKEA stores in 36 countries and territories. The company had plans to continue opening between 20 and 25 stores a year for the foreseeable future. According to one manager, an important limiting factor on the pace of expansion was building the supply network.

As with the United States, some local customization has been the order of the day. In China, for example, the store layout reflected the layout of many Chinese apartments, and because many Chinese apartments have balconies, IKEA's Chinese stores

[5]J. Leland, "How the Disposable Sofa Conquered America," *New York Times Magazine*, October 5, 2005, 45.

[6]Ibid.

included a balcony section. IKEA also has had to adapt its locations in China, where car ownership is still not widespread. In the West, IKEA stores are generally located in suburban areas and have lots of parking space. In China, stores are located near public transportation, and IKEA offers delivery services so that Chinese customers can get their purchases home. IKEA has also adopted a deep price discounting model in China, pricing some items as much as 70% below their price in IKEA stores outside China. To make this work, IKEA has sourced a large percentage of its products sold in China from local suppliers.

The IKEA Concept and Business Model

IKEA's target market is the young, upwardly mobile global middle class who are looking for low-priced but attractively designed furniture and household items. This group is targeted with somewhat wacky, offbeat advertisements that help to drive traffic into the stores. The stores themselves are large warehouses festooned in the blue and yellow colors of the Swedish flag that offer 8,000 to 10,000 items, from kitchen cabinets to candlesticks. There is plenty of parking outside, and the stores are located with good access to major roads.

The interior of the stores is configured almost like a maze that requires customers to pass through each department to get to the checkout. The goal is simple; to get customers to make more impulse purchases as they wander through the IKEA wonderland. Customers who enter the store planning to buy a $40 coffee table can end up spending $500 on everything from storage units to kitchenware. The flow of departments is constructed with an eye to boosting sales. For example, when IKEA managers noticed that men would get bored while their wives stopped in the home textile department, they added a tool section just outside the textile department, and sales of tools skyrocketed. At the end of the maze, just before the checkout, is the warehouse where customers can pick up their flat-packed furniture. IKEA stores also have restaurants (located in the middle of the store) and child-care facilities (located at the entrance for easy drop off) so that shoppers stay as long as possible.

Products are designed to reflect the clean Swedish lines that have become IKEA's trademark. IKEA has a product strategy council, which is a group of senior managers who establish priorities for IKEA's product lineup. Once a priority is established, product developers survey the competition and then set a price point that is 30% to 50% below that of rivals. As IKEA's Web site states, "We design the price tag first, then the product." Once the price tag is set, designers

work with a network of suppliers to drive down the cost of producing the unit. The goal is to identify the appropriate suppliers and the least-costly materials, a trial and error process that can take as long as three years. By 2008, IKEA had 1,380 suppliers in 54 countries. The top sourcing countries were China (21% of supplies), Poland (17%), Italy (8%), Sweden (6%), and Germany (6%).

IKEA devotes considerable attention to finding the right supplier for each item. Consider the company's best-selling Klippan love seat. Designed in 1980, the Klippan, with its clean lines, bright colors, simple legs, and compact size, has sold some 1.5 million units since its introduction. IKEA originally manufactured the product in Sweden but soon transferred production to lower-cost suppliers in Poland. As demand for the Klippan grew, IKEA then decided that it made more sense to work with suppliers in each of the company's big markets to avoid the costs associated with shipping the product all over the world. Today, there are five suppliers of the frames in Europe, plus three in the United States and two in China. To reduce the cost of the cotton slipcovers, IKEA has concentrated production in four core suppliers in China and Europe. The resulting efficiencies from these global sourcing decisions enabled IKEA to reduce the price of the Klippan by some 40% between 1999 and 2005.

Although IKEA contracts out manufacturing for most of its products, since the early 1990s, a certain proportion of goods have been made internally (in 2008, about 90% of all products were sourced from independent suppliers, with 10% being produced internally). The integration into manufacturing was born out of the collapse of communist governments in Eastern Europe after the fall of the Berlin Wall in 1989. By 1991, IKEA was sourcing some 25% of its goods from Eastern European manufacturers. It had invested considerable energy in building long-term relationships with these suppliers, and had often helped them to develop and purchase new technology so that they could make IKEA products at a lower cost. As communism collapsed and new bosses came in to the factories, many did not feel bound by the relationships with IKEA. They effectively tore up contracts, tried to raise prices, and underinvested in new technology.

With its supply base at risk, IKEA purchased a Swedish manufacturer, Swedwood. IKEA then used Swedwood as the vehicle to buy and run furniture manufacturers across Eastern Europe, with the largest investments being made in Poland. IKEA invested heavily in its Swedwood plants, equipping them with the most modern technology. Beyond the obvious benefits of giving IKEA a low-cost source of supply, Swedwood has also enabled IKEA to acquire knowledge about manufacturing processes that are useful both in product design and in relationships with other suppliers, giving IKEA the ability to help suppliers adopt new technology and drive down their costs.

For illustration, consider IKEA's relationship with suppliers in Vietnam. IKEA has expanded its supply base in Vietnam to help support its growing Asian presence. IKEA was attracted to Vietnam by the combination of low-cost labor and inexpensive raw materials. IKEA drives a tough bargain with its suppliers, many of whom say that they make thinner margins on their sales to IKEA than they do to other foreign buyers. IKEA demands high quality at a low price. But there is an upside; IKEA offers the prospect of forging a long-term, high-volume business relationship. Moreover, IKEA regularly advises its Vietnamese suppliers on how to seek out the best and cheapest raw materials, how to set up and expand factories, what equipment to purchase, and how to boost productivity through technology investments and management process.

Organization and Management

In many ways, IKEA's organization and management practices reflect the personal philosophy of its founder. A 2004 article in *Fortune* describes Kamprad, then one of the world's richest men, as an informal and frugal man who "insists on flying coach, takes the subway to work, drives a 10-year-old Volvo, and avoids suits of any kind. It has long been rumored in Sweden that when his self-discipline fails and he drinks an overpriced Coke out of a hotel minibar, he will go down to a grocery store to buy a replacement."[7] Kamprad's thriftiness is attributed to his upbringing in Smaland, a traditionally poor region of Sweden. Kamprad's frugality is now part of IKEA's DNA. Managers are forbidden to fly first class and are expected to share hotel rooms.

Under Kamprad, IKEA became mission driven. He had a cause, and those who worked with him adopted it too. It was to make life better for the masses, to democratize furniture. Kamprad's management style was informal, nonhierarchical, and team based. Titles and privileges are taboo at IKEA. There are no special perks for senior managers. Pay is not particularly high, and people generally work there because they like the atmosphere. Suits and ties have always been absent, from the head office to the loading docks. The culture is egalitarian. Offices have an open plan and are furnished with IKEA furniture; private offices are rare. Everyone is called a "co-worker," and first names are used throughout. IKEA regularly stages antibureaucracy weeks during which executives work on the store floor or tend to registers. In a 2005 *BusinessWeek* article Andres Dahlvig, the CEO, described how he spent time earlier in the year unloading trucks and selling beds and mattresses.[8] Creativity is highly valued, and the company is replete with stories of individuals taking the initiative; from Gillis Lundgren's pioneering of the self-assembly concept to the store manager in the Stockholm store who let customers go into the warehouse to pick up their own furniture. To solidify this culture, IKEA had a preference for hiring younger people who had not worked for other enterprises and then promoting from within. IKEA has historically tended to shy away from hiring the highly educated, status-oriented elite, because they often adapted poorly to the company.

Kamprad seems to have viewed his team as extended family. Back in 1957, he bankrolled a weeklong trip to Spain for all 80 employees and their families as reward for hard work. The early team of employees all lived near each other. They worked together, played together, drank together, and talked about IKEA around the clock. When asked by an academic researcher what the fundamental key was to good leadership, Kamprad replied "Love." Recollecting the early days, he noted that "When we were working as a small family in Almhult, we were as if in love. Nothing whatsoever to do with eroticism. We just liked each other so damn much."[9] Another manager noted that "We who wanted to join IKEA did so because the company suits our way of life. To escape thinking about status, grandeur and smart clothes."[10]

As IKEA grew, the question of taking the company public arose. While there were obvious advantages associated with doing so, including access to capital, Kamprad decided against it. His belief was that the stock market would impose short-term pressures on IKEA that would not be good for the company. The constant demands to produce profits, regardless of the business cycle, would, in Kamprad's view, make it more difficult for IKEA to take bold decisions. At the same time, as early as 1970, Kamprad started to worry about what would happen if he died. He decided that he did not want his sons to inherit the business. His worry was that they would either sell the company, or they might squabble over control of the company, and

[7]C. Daniels and A. Edstrom, "Create IKEA, Make Billions, Take a Bus," *Fortune*, May 3, 2006, 44.

[8]K. Capell et al., "Ikea," *BusinessWeek*, November 14, 2005, 96–106.
[9]B. Torekull, *Leading by Design: The IKEA Story*, 82.
[10]Ibid., p 83.

thus destroy it. All three of his sons, it should be noted, went to work at IKEA as managers.

The solution to this dilemma created one of the most unusual corporate structures in the world. In 1982, Kamprad transferred his interest in IKEA to a Dutch-based charitable foundation, Stichting INGKA Foundation. This is a tax-exempt, nonprofit legal entity that in turn owns INGKA Holding, a private Dutch firm that is the legal owner of IKEA. A five-person committee, chaired by Kamprad and including his wife, runs the foundation. In addition, the IKEA trademark and concept was transferred to IKEA Systems, another private Dutch company, whose parent company, Inter-IKEA, is based in Luxembourg. The Luxembourg company is, in turn, owned by an identically named company in the Netherlands Antilles, whose beneficial owners remain hidden from public view, but they are almost certainly the Kamprad family. Inter-IKEA earns its money from a franchise agreement it has with each IKEA store. The largest franchisee is none other than INGKA Holdings. IKEA states that franchisees pay 3% of sales to Inter-IKEA. Thus, Kamprad has effectively moved ownership of IKEA out of Sweden, although the company's identity and headquarters remain there, and established a mechanism for transferring funds to himself and his family from the franchising of the IKEA concept. Kamprad himself moved to Switzerland in the 1980s to escape Sweden's high taxes, and he has lived there ever since.

In 1986, Kamprad gave up day-to-day control of IKEA to Andres Moberg, a 36-year-old Swede who had dropped out of college to join IKEA's mail-order department. Despite relinquishing management control, Kamprad continued to exert influence over the company as an advisor to senior management and as an ambassador for IKEA, a role he was still pursuing with vigor in 2008, despite being in his 80s.

Looking Forward

In its half century, IKEA had established an enviable position for itself. It had become one of the most successful retail establishments in the world. It had expanded into numerous foreign markets (Exhibit 2), learning from its failures and building on its successes. It had brought affordable, well-designed, functional furniture to the masses, helping them to, in Kamprad's words, achieve a better everyday life. IKEA's goal was to continue to grow by opening 20 to 25 stores a year for the foreseeable future. Achieving that growth would mean expansion into non-Western markets, including most notably China where it had recently established a beachhead. Could the company continue to do so? Was its competitive advantage secure?

EXHIBIT 1 IKEA BY THE NUMBERS IN 2008

IKEA Stores	285 in 35 countries
IKEA Sales	€21.2 billion
IKEA Suppliers	1,380 in 54 countries
The IKEA Range	9,500 products
IKEA Coworkers	127,800 in 39 countries

Source: http://franchisor.ikea.com/showContent.asp?swfId=facts9.

EXHIBIT 2 SALES AND SUPPLIERS

TOP FIVE SALES COUNTRIES		TOP FIVE SUPPLYING COUNTRIES	
Germany	15%	China	21%
United States	10%	Poland	17%
France	10%	Italy	8%
United Kingdom	7%	Sweden	6%
Sweden	6%	Germany	6%

Source: http://www.ikea.com/ms/en_GB/about_ikea/facts_and_figures/index.html.

References and Reading

1. Anonymous, "Furnishing the World," *The Economist*, November 19, 1995, 79–80.
2. Anonymous. "Flat pack accounting," *The Economist*, May 13, 2006, 69–70.
3. K. Capell, A. Sains, C. Lindblad, and A. T. Palmer, "IKEA," *BusinessWeek*, November 14, 2005, 96–101.
4. K. Capell et al., "What a Sweetheart of a Love Seat," *BusinessWeek*, November 14, 2005, 101.
5. C. Daniels, "Create IKEA, Make Billions, Take Bus," *Fortune*, May 3, 2004, 44.
6. J. Flynn and L. Bongiorno, "IKEA's New Game Plan," *BusinessWeek*, October 6, 1997, 99–102.
7. R. Heller, "Folk Fortune," *Forbes*, September 4, 2000, 67.
8. IKEA Documents at www.ikea.com.
9. J. Leland, "How the Disposable Sofa Conquered America," *New York Times Magazine*, October 5, 2005, 40–50.
10. P. M. Miller, "IKEA with Chinese Characteristics," *Chinese Business Review*, July–August 2004, 36–69.
11. B. Torekull, *Leading by Design: The IKEA Story* (New York: HarperCollins, 1998).

CASE 5

YUHAN-KIMBERLY: "KEEP KOREA GREEN"[1]

By Dae Ryun Chang and Bernd Schmitt

Introduction

On a hot summer day in 1984, Eun-Wook Lee and hundreds of other employees at Yuhan-Kimberly labored under the sun planting trees on a barren mountainside as part of a new corporate initiative called "Keep Korea Green." Lee had just joined the company, which made personal care items such as tissues, diapers, and feminine hygiene products. "I didn't study business to plant trees," he thought angrily.

Coming back to the same mountainside 25 years later as Vice President of Corporate Communications, Lee could only laugh and be slightly embarrassed at how shortsighted he had been. Thanks to Yuhan-Kimberly, this mountain and scores of others had been reforested so well that now the trees had to be pruned. Looking at the lush forest, Mr. Lee felt immense pride in his company and in the corporate social responsibility campaign (CSR) he had, if unwillingly, helped seed.

But he also felt deeply worried. The world had changed a lot since that backbreaking day in 1984: many companies were now proclaiming themselves "green," and some voices in the general public were coming to see Yuhan-Kimberly not as the environmental pioneer it fancied itself, but rather as a model of corporate hypocrisy—a company that made inherently wasteful products while making small, PR-inspired gestures toward sustainability. Was "Keep Korea Green" becoming an empty slogan, and if so, what could the company do?

Back in his office, Lee had various proposals for alternative CSR campaigns sitting on his desk, but one general decision to make. Would his company best be served by a new CSR campaign—or should it keep and develop the current CSR campaign? Also, what role could the campaign play in the green reinvention of its very products? Top management expected a decision from corporate communications regarding the future CSR campaign and suggestions from Lee about how the CSR campaign could help with the launch of new products.

The Origins of Yuhan-Kimberly

Yuhan Corporation was founded in 1926, making it one of the oldest companies in Korea. Its founder, Il-han New, had gone to the United States to pursue his studies. After graduating from the University of Michigan, he joined GE as the company's first Asian accountant.[2]

While New was in Korea on a business trip, his life took a fateful turn. At that time, Korea was under Japanese colonial rule, and New witnessed the misery of the occupation firsthand. In 1926, he decided to come back to Korea for good and start a pharmaceutical business. His management philosophy was, "Profit-seeking is worthwhile only when it results not just in individual wealth but also in national prosperity."

Yuhan took heed of this directive. Starting in 1936, the company offered an employee stock ownership plan. In 1954, New began promoting educational projects: he established a technical high school and a boarding school. Upon his death in March 1971, his fortune was, at his direction, given to charity. More than 80 years since Il-han New started his business, he was still held in high esteem for his business acumen, his contributions to Korean self-sufficiency, and his generosity.

The Start of Yuhan-Kimberly

In 1970, one year before the death of Il-han New, Yuhan Corporation entered into a joint venture with Kimberly-Clark, one of the world's leading manufacturers of personal care products. The venture was motivated more by politics than economics: in the 1970s, with South Korea under the dictatorial rule of President Jung-Hee Park, it was almost impossible for companies to survive without currying governmental favor. New faced a moral dilemma: to protect his company, he would have to pay bribes to the government, and to protect his integrity, he would have to put his company in danger. Faced with this terrible choice, he came up with a creative solution: a joint venture with a U.S. corporation. After all, Korea was a staunch American ally. New figured that it would be impossible for President Park to pressure a local company that had a joint venture with a major U.S. corporation. What's more, New coveted the manufacturing technologies that a marriage with Kimberly-Clark would afford him.

The Growth of Yuhan-Kimberly

Yuhan-Kimberly opened its first factory in Kunpo in 1970 and started producing toilet paper, facial tissues,

[1]This case appears as case #090503 in the Columbia CaseWorks collection. Reprinted with permission.

[2]"Great Men in Korean Culture" (in Korean), June 1996, http://person. mct.go.kr/person/data/person_view.jsp?cp_seq=61.

and feminine napkins. Sales in its first year were a modest 0.3 billion won, but fueled by the rapid growth of South Korea's middle class, the company tapped into the emerging demand for paper-based family products hitherto considered too extravagant or exotic by Korean consumers. As Koreans adopted a more Western lifestyle, their need for more specialized paper products expanded.

In 1980, Yuhan-Kimberly built its second factory in Kimchon and began manufacturing Huggies diapers. At the time, South Korea had a birthrate per married couple of about 4.0. (The government, concerned about overpopulation, would soon create propaganda espousing the desirability of having fewer children.) With further expansion of its product lines, Yuhan-Kimberly set up a third plant in Daejon in 1994. By this time, the company had annual sales of 268.2 billion won.

Competition with P&G

Other multinational companies now wanted in on South Korea's burgeoning consumer market. Procter & Gamble entered Korea in 1989 through a joint venture with Seotong Battery. Soon after, P&G parted ways with Seotong and established a wholly-owned subsidiary to begin a drive into Korea's personal product markets. The formidable P&G had many established brands, such as Whisper (feminine napkins) and Pampers (baby diapers), big advertising budgets, and a time-tested marketing management system.

By 2000, Yuhan-Kimberly dominated the major paper categories (see Exhibit 1), but during its 20 years of competition with P&G, it did lose a few fights, as with one over feminine hygiene products. P&G boldly decided to use an overt advertising approach that emphasized the functional user benefits of its Whisper brand. The ads shocked conservative Koreans, but they worked: in 1997, P&G held close to a 60%

market share. In response, Yuhan-Kimberly spent more than US$ 10 million developing a product that was not only functionally superior according to universal specifications, but also more comfortable in use as perceived by local consumers. Yuhan-Kimberly's advertising of its "White" brand was subtle when compared to P&G's strategy; instead of talking about and showing the product, it emphasized the sensory benefits of its usage. Moreover, whereas P&G used celebrity spokeswomen for its ads, Yuhan-Kimberly opted for a testimonial campaign where non-celebrities, usually college women, talked about their positive experiences using the product (see Exhibit 2 for a storyboard comparison).

Performance in 2007

In 2007, Yuhan-Kimberly had net sales of nearly 905 billion won and a net income of about 105 billion won, representing annual increases of 8.5% and 16.3% respectively. In fact, the key financial performance indicators for Yuhan-Kimberly (see Exhibit 3) had been positive for the last few years. Yuhan-Kimberly's business portfolio consisted of eight sectors (see Exhibit 4). The most successful products continued to be the *Big Three* paper markets of infant care (baby diapers), family care (facial and bathroom tissue), and feminine care (feminine napkins). For the last three years, these products had captured nearly 80% of the total revenues for the company.

Even though Kimberly Clark owned 70% of Yuhan-Kimberly, most South Koreans perceived it to be primarily a Korean company. Since Yuhan-Kimberly maintained relative management autonomy, Kimberly Clark had not imposed restrictions on Yuhan-Kimberly's administrative policy and activities. For example, Yuhan-Kimberly launched its own local brands, such as White—which attained over 50% market share in its segment in Korea. Also, Yuhan-Kimberly

EXHIBIT 1 YUHAN-KIMBERLY VS. P&G MARKET SHARES IN THE KEY KOREAN PAPER CATEGORIES

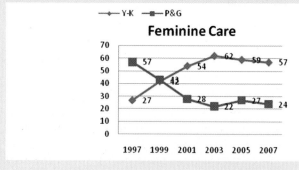

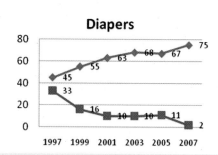

EXHIBIT 2 TV STORYBOARDS FOR YUHAN-KIMBERLY'S "WHITE" AND P&G'S "WHISPER"

Source: White (Yuhan-Kimberly, 2001), Whisper (P&G, 2001).

export products had outperformed Kimberly Clark in 52 countries.[3]

[3]Nakhoon Kim, "Opportunities to Jump to Asia No.1," *HanKyung Business* (in Korean), November 27, 2008. http://www.kbizweek.com/cp/view. asp?vol_no=678&art_no=11&sec_cd=1659.

Since 2003, Yuhan-Kimberly had, at the request of Kimberly Clark, assumed management control of the North Asia region. The company at first declined this request, preferring to concentrate on its domestic market. It acquiesced only after Kimberly Clark guaranteed Yuhan-Kimberly management control in each

EXHIBIT 3 YUHAN-KIMBERLY'S KEY FINANCIAL PERFORMANCE INDICATORS FOR 2004–2007

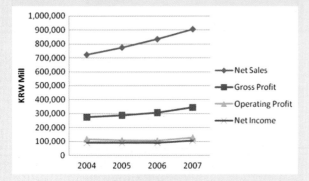

EXHIBIT 4 YUHAN-KIMBERLY'S BUSINESS PORTFOLIO FOR 2005–2007

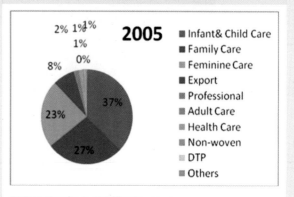

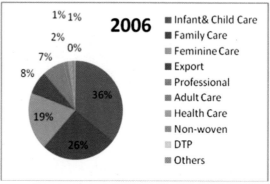

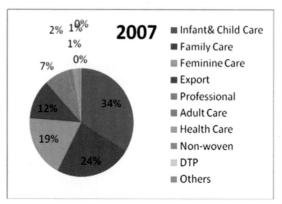

country. One year after Yuhan-Kimberly had taken the helm of the North Asia management, Kimberly Clark Taiwan turned a profit and Kimberly Clark China saw a 30% increase in productivity.[4]

Sustainability Management

Yuhan-Kimberly thought about sustainability in economic, social, and environmental terms. It believed its economic responsibilities were to innovate, compete, increase revenue, and create jobs. It understood its social responsibility to center on the quality of life of its employees—which could best be improved through ethical management, transparency, and the promotion of lifelong learning—and of its customers, who were best served with products that promoted health and hygiene. Finally, the company viewed its environmental responsibilities as hinging on its ability to use natural resources as carefully as possible, reduce energy consumption to alleviate global warming, and lead the industry in using new technology to "green" its manufacturing processes.

Yuhan-Kimberly's Family Friendly Management programs and policies included flexible work schedules, lifelong learning, non-gender bias, maternity protection, an employee assistance program, and volunteer opportunities. The flexible work schedule program allowed employees time to rest or to enroll in work-related or lifelong educational programs and to spend more time with their families. The costs of the lifelong programs were subsidized by Yuhan-Kimberly not only for the employees, but also their dependents. This program lowered the fatigue level of

employees and thus improved both productivity and product quality.[5]

Yuhan-Kimberly made sure that there was no gender bias in the company for any of the worker benefits. Moreover, the company adopted a miscarriage/stillbirth leave program that pre-dated by two years the mandatory regulation started by the Korean government in 2006. Furthermore, Yuhan-Kimberly

[4]Jinnam Choi, Sunyoung Sun, *How Did Moon Kook Hyun Recreate Yuhan-Kimberly¿* p. 212 (in Korean), 2008.

[5]*The Ministry of Family and Women*, "A Shortcut to Develop a Company," 2006.

provided female employees with the opportunity of a two-month pre-maternity leave which was unique in Korea. Other maternity-related programs included the subsidy of Caesarian birth surgery costs, the company-wide sharing of news of employees giving birth, and the provision of special rooms for breastfeeding. These efforts had a measurable impact: the birthrate at Yuhan-Kimberly in 2007 was 1.89 per married couple, whereas the national average was 1.16.

"Keep Korea Green" Campaign

In 1984, when Yuhan-Kimberly began its green campaign, critics were skeptical: it did not make sense to them that Yuhan-Kimberly, as a large health and hygiene company, would embark on an environmental initiative. Yuhan-Kimberly stakeholders, including its major shareholders, its business partners, some of its top executives, and even the Ministry of Forestry, were dumbfounded. There were also grumblings by tree-planting "volunteer" employees at Yuhan-Kimberly who, like Lee, thought they had better things to do.

Ironically, even at that time Koreans were well aware of the need for reforestation. Thirty-six years of Japanese rule in the early 1900s and the Korean War in the 1950s had devastated much of the land. Moreover, the industrialization of Korea during the 1960s and 1970s had taken place without much consideration for the environment. As a result, in the early 1980s only one-third of Korea's mountainside, which amounted to 65% of all land, had been reforested. Despite the misgivings both within and outside Yuhan-Kimberly, the CEO and his chief lieutenants considered it a moral obligation to push the "Keep Korea Green" campaign. According to Lee, there was a collective sense that if *they* did not do something, no one would. "People can care and talk about societal problems all they like," he explained, "but will have little power to effect change. That is why companies must play a more proactive role to promote societal progress and make a difference."

The program started with a reforestation program under the slogan "Sharing a vision: love for trees." This phrase was designed not only to restore the original look and conditions for some key locales, but also to inspire in the general population a love for trees. From 1984–2008, Yuhan-Kimberly planted and nurtured over 21 million trees on 7,533 hectares of public and state-owned areas (see Exhibit 5 for a "before and after" example of a reforested area).

The second phase began in 1998, when Yuhan-Kimberly turned "Keep Korea Green" into a national effort focused on "nurturing" trees instead of just planting them. The company also provided environmental awareness education for Korean youth. Students from 2,012 schools participated in this program.

In the third phase, the company extended the campaign to North Korea, China, and Mongolia. After the

EXHIBIT 5 "BEFORE AND AFTER" PICTURE OF TREE PLANTING IN A "KEEP KOREA GREEN" AREA

1985

2005

EXHIBIT 6 PREVENTION OF DESERTIFICATION IN NORTHEAST ASIA—TREE PLANTING IN MONGOLIA

YEAR	2001	2002	2003	2004	2005	2006	2007
No. of trees planted	500	1,000	200,000	150,000	150,000	150,000	800,000
Area	Inside the children's park in Mongolia	Avenues in Ulaan Bataar	Tujiin Nars in Selenge State				
Tree Type	Fir trees/ Larch trees	Pine trees/ Fir trees	65 ha Pine trees	50 ha Pine/ larch trees	50 ha Pine trees	50 ha Pine trees	250 ha Pine trees

Korean War, North Korea cleared its mountains for farming; this left its mountains almost totally ravaged. The impoverished soil caused by the lack of trees was chiefly responsible for the chronic food shortage in North Korea. Since 1999, Yuhan-Kimberly had helped, and in a very public fashion: part of its reforestation plan centered on famous Mt. Keumkang, a symbol of North Korean pride.

The company also tackled an important regional problem. Every year around March, Koreans suffer from the health effects of yellow dust that blows into Korea from northern Asia. Yellow dust is also a serious environmental concern in China and sometimes even finds its way to the Western United States. Desertification in North Asia is a contributing factor to this phenomenon. In recognition of this problem, Yuhan-Kimberly helped to plant over 2.6 million trees in China and Mongolia to prevent further desertification in these countries (see Exhibit 6 for results in Mongolia).

"Keep Korea Green" had been good for Yuhan-Kimberly. According to a consumer survey on corporate image in 2002, the company ranked first among Korean companies for goodwill, trust, and contribution to society. Also, a study in 2007 conducted by Gallup Korea showed that Yuhan-Kimberly was perceived as being the most eco-friendly corporation in Korea, beating out much bigger companies such as Samsung, LG, and Hyundai[6] (see Exhibit 7).

Yuhan-Kimberly was also perceived as outperforming many of its rivals in terms of workplace environment (see Exhibits 8 and 9). A 1999 internal study on the link between the "Keep Korea Green" campaign and brand equity showed correlations between the campaign and its corporate as well as individual category brand equity measures (see Exhibit 10). Moreover, a study by the LG Economic Institute showed that almost 90% of consumers were willing to pay a premium for the products of environmentally-friendly companies.

[6]*Yuhan-Kimberly Corporate Reputation & CSR Report*, 2009.

Now What?

As Lee looked out across a mountain thick with trees he had helped plant 25 years ago, he realized that Yuhan-Kimberly's "Keep Korea Green" campaign had found itself part of the national zeitgeist. What's more, Yuhan-Kimberly's attention to its social responsibilities had not been incompatible with the attainment of its economic objectives; its sales, profits, and brand image had all benefited from its CSR campaign.

Lee, however, still worried. "Sure," he thought, "people know about 'Keep Korea Green' and they know it is what made Yuhan-Kimberly special. But back in the 80s and 90s, we were the only ones talking about green. Now, with even the President of Korea making it a national prerogative, every company is coming out with something green. We are no longer so special."

Lee was thinking in particular of the globally popular green management and green marketing craze that had reached South Korea. Ever since the "wellness/well-being" trend—which emphasized the harmony of physical and mental life—had hit South Korea around 2002, South Korean customers had become more interested in environmental issues, and almost all corporations had been trying to take advantage of this by coming out with purportedly environmental products. The problem with all this was that it

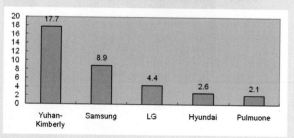

EXHIBIT 7 ECO-FRIENDLY IMAGE FOR SELECTED KOREAN COMPANIES

Source: Gallup Korea, 2007.

EXHIBIT 8 SOCIAL INVESTMENT OUTLAYS BY YUHAN-KIMBERLY

(UNIT: 1,000 KOREAN *WON*)

	2007	2006
(1) Donations to society		
Keep Korea Green Campaign	6,787,055	5,398,693
Environmental Protection Campaign	3,171,634	1,969,099
Family Friendship and Social Evolution	2,195,418	3,156,075
Literature Mecenat	662,714	721,950
Subtotal	12,816,821	11,245,817
(2) Employees welfare		
Scholarship	1,912,600	1,621,778
Expenses for Congratulations and Condolences	579,410	479,962
Group Term Insurance	83,844	119,619
Physical Examination Fee	502,581	14,644
Transference Bonus/Relocation Expenses	132,082	163,176
Building Costs of Rest Home	88,022	7,922
Subtotal	3,298,539	2,407,101
Total	16,115,360	13,652,918

Source: Korea Financial Supervisory Service.

became increasingly difficult to separate the authentic CSR campaigns from the fake ones.

Moreover, "Keep Korea Green" itself had been criticized by environmentalist and civic groups that saw the campaign as a cynical attempt to compensate for the serious environmental damage caused by both the

EXHIBIT 9 PERCEPTION OF WORKPLACE ENVIRONMENT FOR KOREAN COMPANIES

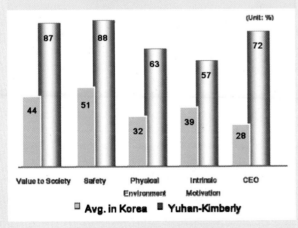

Source: Hewitt Associates, Best Employers in Asia Research, 2003.

production and disposal of paper products. In this newly hostile environment, Yuhan-Kimberly had to weigh the pros and cons of continuing the "Keep Korea Green" campaign.

One new idea that Yuhan-Kimberly played with was "Project Birthrate 2.0." Korea's birth rate of 1.2 per married couple was the lowest in the world among the Organisation for Economic Co-operation and Development (OECD) countries, according to the United Nations Population Fund. Some executives at Yuhan-Kimberly hoped that the prospective campaign could arouse a nationwide awareness about this societal problem and restore the company's image. Nonetheless, executives faced daunting implementation challenges. "Keep Korea Green" had been sustained for about 25 years. Would the company have to wait that long to achieve a similar success with this campaign?

As executives thought through the viability of this and other proposed campaigns, they returned frequently to a central question: What is the ideal relationship between a corporate social responsibility campaign—be it "Keep Korea Green," or "Project Birthrate 2.0," or something else entirely—and the launch of new products? Was it time for the company to stop thinking of CSR campaigns and product innovation as wholly separate efforts? Perhaps, they

EXHIBIT 10 COMPANY STUDY ON THE CORRELATION OF "KEEP KOREA GREEN" (KKG) AND ITS CORPORATE AND PRODUCT BRAND EQUITY

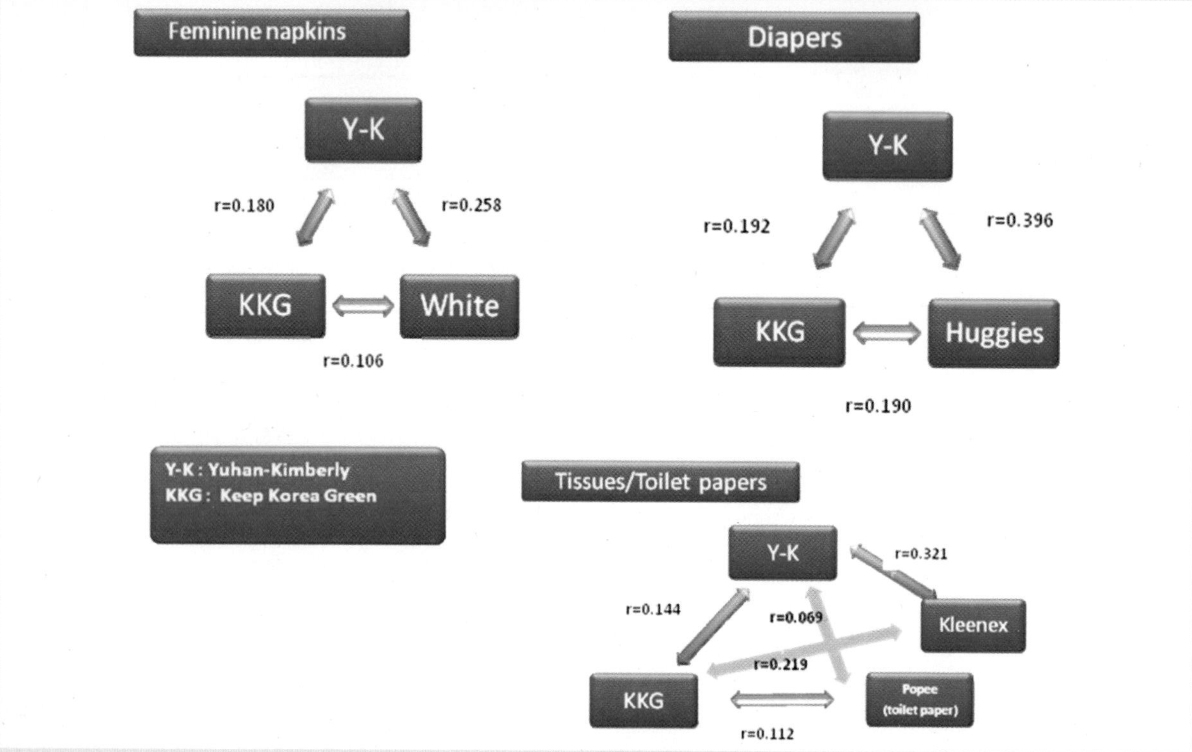

Source: Company document.

thought, a joining of these two areas might provide the company with exactly the public image it needed: that of a company whose environmental commitment was revealed in the very products it produced.

This line of thinking had the virtue of being in tune with efforts already under way. In July 2007, the company had entered the cosmetics business with the launch of a new skin care brand called "Green Finger." The product, which contained mostly herbal ingredients, was based on four years of intensive research and development, much of which centered on the benefits of ingredients found in forests, data that Yuhan-Kimberly had gleaned from its "Keep Korea Green" campaign. Yuhan-Kimberly found itself in the wonderful position of being able to trumpet the genuine roots of its new push toward environmentally-friendly products.[7]

And in October 2008, Yuhan-Kimberly had launched a line extension called "Green Finger My Kids." In South Korea, cosmetics companies seldom launched a kid's line, because they did not think that they needed to separate the infant and kid segments. However, Yuhan-Kimberly seized the opportunity to market a skin care line dedicated to 4–10 year olds. Their attempt was based on product differentiation that would place emphasis on its organic ingredients and take advantage of its eco-friendly corporate image. When Yuhan-Kimberly promoted the new product, they highlighted its *Forest Relaxing Recipe*, trying to remind customers of the "Keep Korea Green" campaign.

As Lee thought all of this through, he found himself walking more briskly into the peaceful forest. Inhaling the fresh air, he contemplated what the next steps for Yuhan-Kimberly should be. He had to decide soon whether to continue with the green CSR campaign or whether to embark on a new flagship campaign such as "Birthrate 2.0." Moreover, senior management expected that he address the value and future contribution of a CSR campaign to new product development.

[7]Jinyup Baek, "Yuhan-Kimberly's Penetration of the Cosmetic Market," *Money Today News* (in Korean), July 9, 2007, http://www.moneytoday.co.kr/view/mtview.php?type=1&no=2007070913501969078&outlinek=1.

Notes

Chapter 1

1. Charles Goldsmith, "MTV Seeks Global Appeal," *Wall Street Journal*, July 21, 2003, p. B1.

2. Carol Matlock, "Free Paper, Costly Competition," *BusinessWeek*, November 19, 2007, p. 94.

3. Yuri Kageyama, "Japan Imports American Culture via Calories," *Marketing News*, May 1, 2007, p. 11.

4. Janet Adamy, "Dunkin' Begins New Push into Asia," *Wall Street Journal*, January 17, 2007, p. A4.

5. Steve Hamm, "IBM vs. Tata: Which is More American," *BusinessWeek*, May 5, 2008, p. 28.

6. David Gregorcyk, "Internationalization of Conglomerates from Emerging Markets" (honors thesis, Teresa Lozano Long Institute of Latin American Studies, The University of Texas at Austin, 2005).

7. Geoffrey A. Fowler and Evan Ramstad, "Online Auctioneer to Buy Korean Site as It Refocuses on E-Commerce, PayPal," *Wall Street Journal*, April 16, 2009, p. B2.

Chapter 2

1. Gordon Fairclough, "The Global Downturn Lands with a Zud on Mongolia's Nomads," *Wall Street Journal Europe*, April 21, 2009, p. 30.

2. Bob Donath, "Don't Miss Opportunities in Global Market," *Marketing News*, July 21, 2003, p. 7.

3. Frances Williams, "WTO Predicts 9% Fall in World Trade," *Financial Times*, March 24, 2009, p. 8.

4. "Garlic Wars," CBSNEWS.com (accessed July 23, 2003).

5. Michael E. Porter, *The Competitive Advantage of Nations* (New York: Macmillan, 1990), pp. 69–175.

6. Moon Ihlwan, "A Nation of Digital Guinea Pigs," *BusinessWeek*, February 4, 2002, p. 50.

7. Yuka Hayashi, "Japan's Energy Advantage," *Wall Street Journal*, October 7, 2005, p. A13.

8. Dexter Roberts, "China's Factory Blues," *BusinessWeek*, April 7, 2008, pp. 78–81.

9. Aaron Bernstein, "Shaking Up Trade Theory," *BusinessWeek*, December 6, 2004, pp. 116–120.

10. Niraj Sheth, "Outsourcers Hone European Savvy," *Wall Street Journal*, July 29, 2008, p. B2.

11. Christopher B. Clott, "Perspectives on Global Outsourcing and the Changing Nature of Work," *Business and Society Review* 109, no. 2 (2004), pp. 153–170.

12. Diana Farrell, "How Germany Can Win from Outsourcing," *McKinsey Quarterly*, no. 4 (2004).

13. Bernstein, "Shaking Up Trade Theory," pp. 118, 120.

14. Marc Lifsher, "Venezuela's Ills Confound Foreigners," *Wall Street Journal*, June 23, 2003, p. A13.

15. Phillip Day, "Yuan's Drop Propels China's Export Powerhouse," *Wall Street Journal*, May 28, 2003, p. A11.

16. Marcus Walker, "Exchange-Rate Policy Gains Currency as an Urgent Global Issue," *Wall Street Journal*, February 1, 2005, p. A11.

17. Betsy McKay, "Coke Bets on Russia," *Wall Street Journal*, January 28, 2009, p. A1.

18. Kelly Evans and Sara Murray, "Weak Dollar Crimps Study Abroad," *Wall Street Journal*, May 14, 2008, p. D1.

19. Manjeet Kripalani and Nandini Lakshman, "Rise of the Rupee," *BusinessWeek*, August 6, 2007, p. 66.

20. Timothy Aeppel, "Survival Tactics," *Wall Street Journal*, January 22, 2002, p. A1.

21. Neal Sandler, "Israel: Attack of the Super-Shekel," *BusinessWeek*, February 25, 2008, p. 38.

22. Christopher J. Chipello and Mark Heinzl, "As Canada's Dollar Surges, the Country's Exporters Pay a Steep Price," *Wall Street Journal*, June 14, 2003, p. A14.

23. Katy McLaughlin, "The Rising Cost of Being Fabulous," *Wall Street Journal*, May 13, 2003, p. D1.

24. Darren Everson, "Foreign Travel Deals on a Weak Dollar," *Wall Street Journal*, January 4, 2007, p. B7.

25. Consumer Expenditures on Leisure and Recreation, *Euromonitor International*, 2007.

26. Samantha Gross, "Global Sales Pitch Promotes N.Y. Diversity," *Marketing News*, April 2, 2007, p. 34.

27. Matt Moffett and Bob Davis, "Insufficient Fund," *Wall Street Journal*, April 21, 2006, p. A1.

28. Marc Champion, "Euro-Zone Debate Keeps Britain Abuzz," *Wall Street Journal*, May 21, 2003, p. A1.

29. Bob Davis, "Surge in Protectionism Threatens to Deepen World-Wide Crisis," *Wall Street Journal*, January 12, 2009, p. A2.

30. Michael Casey and Matt Moffett, "Argentine Farmers Call a Truce," *Wall Street Journal*, April 3, 2008, p. A8.

31. Taos Turner and Michael Casey, "Argentine Judge Rules against Ban," *Wall Street Journal*, April 6, 2006, p. A7.

32. Helene Cooper, "Russia Agrees to Limit Steel Shipments," *Wall Street Journal*, February 23, 1999, p. A8.

33. David Murphy, "Car Makers Worry China Is Planning a U-Turn," *Wall Street Journal*, July 31, 2003, p. A14.

34. Ken Smith, "Eye on Beijing: Can China Liberalize Its Culture Industry?" *Wall Street Journal*, March 28, 2002, p. A18.

35. Jagdish Bhagwati and Arvind Panagariya, "Bilateral Trade Treaties Are a Sham," *Financial Times*, July 14, 2003, p. 17.

36. Paul Magnusson, "The Highest Court You've Never Heard Of," *BusinessWeek*, April 1, 2002, pp. 76–77.

37. Andrew Marshall, "Southeast Asia Talks Free Trade, but Progress Slow," *Reuters English News Service*, April 5, 2002.

38. Adam Schwarz and Roland Villinger, "Integrating Southeast Asia's Economies," *McKinsey Quarterly*, no. 1 (2004).

39. Geri Smith and Paul Magnusson, "Fox's Dream," *BusinessWeek*, August 14, 2000, p. 56.

40. Paul Blustein, "A Quiet Round in Qatar?" *Washington Post*, January 30, 2001.

41. William Drozdiak, "Poor Nations May Not Buy Trade Talks," *Washington Post*, May 15, 2001.

42. Paul Magnusson, "States' Rights vs. Free Trade," *BusinessWeek*, March 7, 2005, pp. 102, 104.

43. Geoffrey Garrett, "Globalization's Missing Middle," *Foreign Affairs* 83, no. 6 (November/December 2004), pp. 84–97.

44. Bob Davis and John Lyons, "Wealth of Nations," *Wall Street Journal*, May 24, 2007, p. A1.

45. Gordon Fairclough, "Korea Torn over Open Markets," *Wall Street Journal*, November 18, 2005, p. A14.

Chapter 3

1. Paula Prada and Bruce Orwall, "A Certain 'Je Ne Sais Quoi' at Disney's New Park," *Wall Street Journal*, March 12, 2002, p. B1.

2. Geoffrey A. Fowler and Merissa Marr, "Disney and the Great Wall," *Wall Street Journal*, February 9, 2006, p. B1.

3. Jonathan Cheng, "Hong Kong Disneyland Gets New Manager," *Wall Street Journal*, August 15, 2008, p. B4.

4. "Give Me a Big Mac but Hold the Beef," *Guardian*, December 28, 2000, p. 4.

5. "Cultural Explanations: The Man in the Baghdad Café," *The Economist*, November 9, 1996, pp. 23–26.

6. Francis Fukuyama, *Trust: The Social Virtues and the Creation of Prosperity* (New York: Free Press, 1996), p. 6.

7. David Murphy, "Selling Christmas in China," *Wall Street Journal*, December 24, 2002, p. B1.

8. Geoffrey A. Fowler, "China's Yuletide Revolution," *Wall Street Journal*, December 22, 2005, p. B1.

9. Hugh Pope, "A New Holiday Hit in Muslim Turkey," *Wall Street Journal*, December 24, 2003, p. A1.

10. Farnaz Fassihi, "As Authorities Frown, Valentine's Day Finds Place in Iran's Heart," *Wall Street Journal*, February 12, 2004, p. A1.

11. Ibid.

12. Joel Greenberg, "Who in Israel Loves the Orthodox? Their Grocers," *New York Times*, October 17, 1997, p. 4.

13. Sarmad Ali, "New Cellphone Services Put God on the Line," *Wall Street Journal*, March 27, 2006, p. B1.

14. Carla Power and Ioannis Gatsiounis, "Meeting the Halal Test," *Forbes Asia*, April 16, 2007, pp. 38–40.

15. Shahidan Shafie and Osman Mohamed, "'Halal'— The Case of the Malaysian Muslim Consumers' Quest for Peace of Mind," *Proceedings of the American Marketing Association* (Winter 2002), p. 118.

16. Ibid.

17. Ibid.

18. Lauren Etter and John Lyons, "Brazilian Beef Clan Goes Global as Trouble Hit Market," *Wall Street Journal*, August 1, 2008, p. A1.

19. "Halal Growth Means Big Things for the UAE," *Al-Bawaba News*, October 9, 2007.

20. Yasmine El-Rashidi, "Ramadan Turns into Big Business," *Wall Street Journal*, October 6, 2006, p. B3.

21. Kang Siew Li, "Coca-Cola's Global Ramadhan Commercial," *Business Times, The New York Straits Times Press*, January 14, 1998, p. 17.

22. Anna Slater, "Indian Monsoon Drenches the Land; Marketers Drench the Consumer," *Wall Street Journal*, July 24, 2003, p. A12.

23. Henry Sender, "Foreign Car Makers Make Mark in India," *Asian Wall Street Journal*, August 22, 2000, p. 1.

24. "U.S. Company Criticized for Misusing Images of Indian Hindu Deities," *BBC Monitoring*, November 18, 2000.

25. John Pomfret, "80-Year-Old Cashes In on Famous Name," *Seattle Times*, August 25, 1998, p. A13.

26. "Trouble Brewing," *Newsweek*, July 19, 1999, p. 40.

27. Karin Esterhammer, "Fall Festivals Fill Japan's Streets with Pageantry," *Los Angeles Times*, June 10, 2001, p. L6.

28. Sheryl Wu Dunn, "Korean Women Still Feel Demands to Bear a Son," *New York Times International*, January 14, 1997, p. A3.

29. Fuq-in Bian, John R. Logan, and Yanjie Bian, "Intergenerational Relations in Urban China," *Demography* 35, no. 1 (February 1998), pp. 119–122.

30. Simon Saulkin, "Chinese Walls," *Management Today* (September 1996), pp. 62–68.

31. Fukuyama, *Trust*, pp. 62, 98.

32. Scheherazade Daneshkhu, "Poor Communication and Bureaucracy Make Eastern Europe Frustrating," *Financial Times*, September 9, 1996, p. 12.

33. Glen H. Brodowsky, Beverlee B. Anderson, Camille P. Schuster, Ofer Meilich, and M. Ven Venkatesan, "If Time Is Money, Is It a Common Currency? Time in Anglo, Asian and Latin Cultures," *Journal of Global Marketing* 21 no. 4, 2008, pp. 245–257.

34. Ibid.

35. Jo Johnson and Ralph Atkins, "Workers at French Plant Vote for a Longer Week," *Financial Times,* July 20, 2004, p. 1.

36. K. Sivakumar and Cheryl Nakata, "The Stampede towards Hofstede's Framework: Avoiding the Sample Design Pit in Cross-Cultural Research," *Journal of International Business Studies* 32, no. 3 (2001), p. 555.

37. Geert Hofstede, *Culture and Organizations: Software of the Mind* (New York: McGraw-Hill, 1991), p. 23.

38. "Move Over, Myspace; Korean Social Site Targets U.S. Teenagers," *Marketing News,* September 15, 2006, pp. 52–53.

39. Hofstede, *Culture and Organizations*, p. 50.

40. Ibid., p. 123.

41. Sivakumar and Nakata, pp. 555–574.

42. Tomasz Lenartowicz, James P. Johnson, and Carolyn T. White, "The Neglect of Intracountry Cultural Variation in International Management Research," *Journal of Business Research* 56, no. 12 (2003), pp. 999–1008.

43. Joyce S. Osland and Allan Bird, "Beyond Sophisticated Stereotyping: Cultural Sensemaking in Context," *Academy of Management Executive* 14, no. 1, 2000, pp. 65–79.

44. Samuel P. Huntington, *Who Are We?: The Challenges to America's National Identity* (New York: Simon and Schuster, 2004), pp. 365–366.

45. Ronald Inglehart and Wayne E. Baker, "Modernization, Culture Change, and the Persistence of Traditional Values," *American Sociological Review* 65 (February 2000), p. 31.

46. Merissa Marr, "Small World," *Wall Street Journal*, 11 June 2007, p. A1.

47. Jean-Claude Usunier, *Marketing Across Cultures* (New York: Prentice-Hall, 2000), pp. 416–420.

48. Harry C. Triandis, "The Many Dimensions of Culture," *Academy of Management Executive* 18, no. 1 (2004), p. 90.

49. Judith Bowman, "Before Going Overseas, Be Ready: Know the Protocol," *Mass High Tech*, April 26, 1999, p. 31.

50. Valerie Reitman, "Japanese Workers Take Classes on the Grim Art of Grinning," *Los Angeles Times,* April 8, 1999, p. E4.

51. "Se Habla Ingles," *Wall Street Journal*, December 30, 2004, p. A8.

52. "English and Electronic Commerce: The Default Language," *The Economist*, May 15, 1999, p. 67.

53. "It's Barbara Calling," *The Economist*, April 29, 2000.

54. Phred Dvorak, "Plain English Gets Harder in Global Era," *Wall Street Journal*, November 5, 2007, p. B1.

55. Kevin Voigt, "Japanese Firms Want English Competency," *Wall Street Journal*, June 11, 2001, p. B7.

56. Kathryn Kranhold, Dan Bilefsky, Matthew Karnitschnig, and Ginny Parker, "Lost in Translation?" *Wall Street Journal*, May 18, 2004, p. B1.

57. Robert Frank, "Big Boy's Adventures in Thailand," *Wall Street Journal*, April 12, 2000, p. B1.

58. Ibid.

59. Michael Schuman, "Foreign Flavor," *Wall Street Journal*, July 24, 2000, p. A1.

60. Philip R. Harris and Robert T. Moran, *Managing Cultural Differences*, 4th ed. (Houston, TX: Gulf, 1996), pp. 218–223.

Chapter 4

1. Kerry A. Dolan, "Dancing with Chavez," *Forbes*, November 13, 2000, p. 72.

2. Jose de Cordoba and Joe Millman, "Cemex to Fight Venezuela's Nationalization Effort," *Wall Street Journal*, August 20, 2008, p. A10.

3. Joel Millman, "Chavez Tasks Food Producers amid Shortage," *Wall Street Journal*, February 19, 2008, p. A11.

4. Vern Terpstra and Kenneth David, *The Cultural Environment of International Business*, 3rd ed. (Cincinnati: Southwestern, 1992), p. 203.

5. "YouTube Confronts Censors Overseas," *Dow Jones Chinese Financial Wire*, March 21, 2008.

6. Greg Ip and Neil King Jr., "Ports Deal Shows Roadblocks for Globalization," *Wall Street Journal*, March 11, 2006, p. A1.

7. Norihiko Shirouzu, "Toyota's New U.S. Plan," *Wall Street Journal Asia*, June 21, 2007, p. 1.

8. "Bill, Borrow, and Embezzle," *The Economist*, February 17, 2001.

9. "About Face," *The Economist*, December 9, 2000.

10. Kevin J. Delaney and Andres Cala, "France Mobilizes, Seeks European Allies to Fend Off Google," *Wall Street Journal*, May 12, 2005, p. B1.

11. Stephen Castle, "Europe Puts Its Culture Online from Books to Art," *International Herald Tribune*, November 20, 2008, p. 4.

12. Jane Spencer, "Chinese Activists Launch Drive to Shame Polluters," *Wall Street Journal*, March 28, 2007, p. B3A.

13. Helene Cooper, "Looming Battle," *Wall Street Journal*, October 29, 2001, p. A1.

14. Geofrey A. Fowler, "It's Called the Forbidden City for a Reason," *Wall Street Journal*, January 19, 2007, p. B1.

15. Neil King Jr., "Iraq's Business Elite Gropes in Dark," *Wall Street Journal*, June 25, 2003, p. A4.

16. Matt Moffett, "In Argentine Province, Fashion Police Say Small Isn't Beautiful," *Wall Street Journal*, November 26, 2005, p. A1.

17. Mei Fong, "Avon's Calling," *Wall Street Journal*, February 26, 2007, p. B1.

18. "Chinese Defense Firm Banned for Selling Tech to Iran," *Dow Jones Business News*, May 22, 2003.

19. "Coke Opens Saudi Plant in Cola War," *Agence France-Presse*, May 5, 1999, p. 1.

20. Bhushan Bahree, "Exxon, Shell Poised to Win Saudi Deals," *Wall Street Journal*, June 1, 2001, p. A11.

21. "U.S. Bans Sales of iPods to North Korea," *ABC News Online*, November 29, 2006.

22. "Wal-Mart, NY Yankees, Others Settle Charges of Illegal Trading," CNN.com, April 14, 2003.

23. "U.S. Court Hears Appeal of Massachusetts' Burma Law," *Dow Jones News Service*, May 4, 1999.

24. Leslie Chang, "Chinese Lawyers Plan to Take On Big Tobacco," *Wall Street Journal*, May 16, 2001, p. A17.

25. Peter Wonacott, "As WTO Entry Looms, China Rushes to Adjust Legal System," *Wall Street Journal*, November 9, 2001, p. A13.

26. David Ahlstrom, Michael N. Young, and Anil Nair, "Deceptive Managerial Practices in China: Strategies for Foreign Firms," *Business Horizons*, November–December, 2002, pp. 49–59.

27. Michael Schroeder, "Regulatory Rules Stifle Business in Poor Countries," *Wall Street Journal*, September 8, 2004, p. A17.

28. Sebastian Moffett, "Taking on Japan's Red Tape," *Wall Street Journal*, September 8, 2004, p. A17.

29. Ichiko Fuyuno, "Japan Grooms New Lawyers," *Wall Street Journal*, April 3, 2004, p. A18.

30. "Of Laws and Men," *The Economist*, April 7, 2001.

31. Charlene Barshefsky, "Trade Policy for a Networked World," *Foreign Affairs*, March/April 2001, p. 141.

32. Stephen J. Kobrin, "Territoriality and the Governance of Cyberspace," *Journal of International Business Studies* 32, no. 4 (2001), pp. 687–704.

33. "Telecom, Web Firms Want Cautious Moves on Global Legal Pact," *Wall Street Journal*, June 6, 2001, p. A28.

34. Susan Postlewaite, "A Crackdown on Madcap Drivers," *BusinessWeek International Editions*, April 30, 2001, p. 5.

35. Jean-Claude Usunier, *Marketing Across Cultures* (New York: Prentice-Hall, 2000), pp. 83–85.

36. Harry C. Triandis, "The Many Dimensions of Culture," *Academy of Management Executive* 18, no. 1 (2004), p. 92.

37. James E. Austin, *Managing in Developing Countries* (New York: The Free Press, 1990), p. 166.

38. Glenn R. Simpson, "Multinational Firms Take Steps to Avert Boycotts over War," *Wall Street Journal,* April 4, 2003, p. A1.

39. Austin, *Managing in Developing Countries*, pp. 148–153.

40. Peter Wonacott, "Chinese Firms Find Their Iraq Projects in Limbo," *Wall Street Journal,* July 10, 2003, p. A8.

41. Usha C. V. Haley, "Assessing and Controlling Business Risks in China," *Journal of International Management* 9 (2003), p. 243.

42. Ravi Ramamurti, "The Obsolescing 'Bargaining Model'? MNC-Host Developing Country Relations Revisited," *Journal of International Business Studies* 21, no. 1 (2001), pp. 23–39.

43. David B. Yoffie and John J. Coleman, "Motorola and Japan," Harvard Business School Case No. 9-388-056.

44. Orit Gadiesh and Jean-Marie Pean, "Manager's Journal: Think Globally, Market Locally," *Wall Street Journal,* September 9, 2003, p. B2.

45. "A Long Arm for Securities Law," *The Economist,* May 19, 2001.

46. Chip Cummins, "Business Mobilizes for Iraq," *Wall Street Journal,* March 24, 2003, p. B1.

47. Joel Millman, "Gangs Plague Central America," *Wall Street Journal*, December 11, 2003, p. A14.

48. "Slow Progress on Iran Claims," *New York Times,* November 14, 1984, pp. D1, D5.

49. Stephen J. Kobrin et al., "The Assessment and Evaluation of Noneconomic Environments by American Firms: A Preliminary Report," *Journal of International Business Studies* 11 (Spring–Summer 1980), pp. 32–47.

50. "Business in Difficult Places," *The Economist,* May 20, 2000.

51. "Political Risk Insurers Fear Crisis Escalation," *Business Insurance* 24, no. 33a (1990), p. 1.

52. Vanessa Houlder, "Climate Change Could Be Next Legal Battlefield," *Financial Times,* July 14, 2003, p. 10.

53. Gary Fields, "Protecting 'Soft Targets,'" *Wall Street Journal,* November 26, 2003, p. A4.

54. Kathryn Kranhold and Carla Anne Robbins, "GE to Stop Seeking Business in Iran," *Wall Street Journal*, February 3, 2005, p. A3.

55. Jay Soloman and Mariam Fam, "Air Battle," *Wall Street Journal*, July 28, 2006, p. A1.

56. Michael R, Czinkota, Gary A. Knight, Peter W. Liesch, and John Steen, "Positioning Terrorism in Management and Marketing: Research Propositions," *Journal of International Management* 11 (2005), pp. 581–604.

57. "Starbucks Plots Global Conquests," *Kitchener-Waterloo Record,* April 16, 2003, p. E4.

58. Laurie P. Cohen, "Chiquita Under the Gun," *Wall Street Journal*, August 2, 2007, p. A1.

59. John Lyons, "Mexico's Safety Wins Tourists," *Wall Street Journal,* April 28, 2004, p. A15.

60. John Krich, "Malaysia Draws New Tourists," *Wall Street Journal,* April 23, 2004, p. A13.

61. "Fight for Global Education Pie Gets Fiercer," *Straits Times*, February 14, 2005.

62. Thomas Mucha, "10 Ways to Protect Your Business from Terror," *Business* 3, no. 1 (January 2002), pp. 50–51.

63. Michael Czinkota and Gary Knight, "Managing the Terrorism Threat," *European Business Forum*, no. 20 (Winter 2005), p. 45.

64. Gabriel Kahn, "A Case Study of How One Company Prepared for War," *Wall Street Journal*, March 25, 2003, p. A14.

65. Sherry L. Harowitz, "The New Centurions," *Security Management,* January 1, 2003, p. 50.

66. Howard Winn, "Risk Management: The Quest for Quality," *Far Eastern Economic Review*, October 21, 2004, p. 46.

67. Nanette Byrnes, "The High Cost of Fear," *BusinessWeek,* November 6, 2006, p. 16.

68. Harowitz, "The New Centurions," p. 50.

69. Paul Magnusson, "What Companies Need to Do," *BusinessWeek*, August 16, 2004, p. 26.

70. "Terrorism Insurance Deemed Reasonable but Many Firms Don't Have It," *Security Director's Report*, December 2008, p. 9.

Chapter 5

1. Brendan M. Case, "Latin Flavor Brewing," *Dallas Morning News*, March 26, 2002, p. 1D.

2. Brian Dumaine, "P&G Rewrites the Rules of Marketing," *Fortune*, November 6, 1989, p. 48.

3. Euromonitor International Global Marketing Information Database, viewed January 4, 2008.

4. "Distribution of Income or Consumption," *2001 World Development Indicators* (Washington, DC: World Bank, 2001), p. 70.

5. Jeremy Schwartz, "Mexico City Seeks to Corral an Army of Street Vendors," *Austin American Statesman,* May 6, 2007.

6. Jessi Hemple, "The Indian Paradox," *BusinessWeek*, February 12, 2007, p. 102.

7. C.K. Prahalad, *The Fortune at the Bottom of the Pyramid: Eradicating Poverty through Profits*, Wharton School Publishing, Upper Saddle River, NJ, 2004.

8. Van R. Wood, Dennis A. Pitta, Frank F. Franzak, "Successful Marketing by Multinational Firms to the Bottom of the Pyramid: Connecting Share of Heart, Global 'Umbrella Brands,' and Responsible Marketing," *Journal of Consumer Marketing* 25, no. 7, p. 421.

9. John Ireland, "Lessons for Successful BOP Marketing from Caracas' Slums," *Journal of Consumer Marketing* 25, no. 7, pp. 430–438.

10. Jean-Claude Usunier, *Marketing Across Cultures* (New York: Prentice-Hall, 2000), p. 104.

11. Julie J. Li and Chenting Su, "How Face Influences Consumption," *International Journal of Market Research* 49, no. 2, pp. 237–256.

12. David McHardy Reid, "Consumer Change in Japan: A Longitudinal Study," *Thunderbird International Business Review*, 49, 1, (2007), pp. 77–101.

13. Thomas J. Madden, Kelly Hewlett, and Martin S. Roth, "Managing Images in Different Cultures: A Cross-National Study of Color Meaning and Preferences," *Journal of International Marketing* 8, no. 4 (2000), pp. 90–107.

14. Michael Fielding, "Special Delivery: UPS Conducts Surveys to Help Customers Export to China," *Marketing News*, February 1, 2007, pp. 14–15.

15. Joseph T. Hallinan, "Imported Beers Win Converts in the Heartland," *Wall Street Journal,* July 25, 2006, p. B1.

16. Eric Bellman, "Suzuki's Stylish Compacts Captivate India's Women," *Wall Street Journal,* May 11, 2007, p. B1.

17. Christina Passariello, "Dior to Unveil Line of Mobile Phones," *Wall Street Journal*, May 21, 2008, p. B9.

18. Jack Ewing, "Mad Dash for the Low End," *BusinessWeek*, February 18, 2008, p. 30.

19. C.K. Prahalad and Allen Hammond, "Serving the World's Poor, Profitably," *Harvard Business Review*, September 2002, pp. 48.

20. Annel Karnani, "The Mirage of the Bottom of the Pyramid: How the Private Sector Can Help Alleviate Poverty," *California Business Review* (49, 4), Summer 2007, and C.K. Prahalad and Allen Hammond, "Selling to the Poor," *Foreign Policy*, May/June 2004.

21. Christina Passariello, "Beauty Fix," *Wall Street Journal*, July 13, 2007, p. A1.

22. Wal-Mart de Mexico Social Responsibility and Sustainable Development, 2007 Annual Report, p. 9.

23. Jan-Benedict E. M. Steenkamp, Rajeev Batra, and Dana L. Alden, "How Perceived Brand Globalness Creates Brand Value," *Journal of International Business Studies* 34, 1 (2003), pp. 53–65.

24. Margot Cohen, "Urban Vietnamese Get Rich Quick," *Wall Street Journal*, October 26, 2004, p. A22.

25. Yuliya Strizhakova, Robin A. Coulter, and Linda L. Price, "Branded Products as a Passport to Global Citizenship: Perspectives from Developed and Developing Countries," *Journal of International Marketing* (2008), 19, 4, pp. 57–85.

26. Niraj Dawar and Philip Parker, "Marketing Universals: Consumers' Use of Brand Name, Price, Physical Appearance, and Retailer Reputation as Signals of Product Quality," *Journal of Marketing* 58, no. 2 (April 1994), pp. 81–95.

27. Steve Hamm, "Children of the Web," *BusinessWeek*, July 2, 2007, p. 52.

28. Michael Fielding, "Explore New Territory," *Marketing News*, March 1, 2007, p. 26.

29. Vijay Mahajan and Kamini Banga, *The 86% Solution* (Upper Saddle River, NJ: Wharton School of Publishing, 2006), p. 68.

30. Gail Edmondson, Paulo Prada, and Karen Nickel Anhalt, "Lexus: Still Looking for Traction in Europe," *BusinessWeek*, November 17, 2003, p. 122.

31. Leslie Chang, "In China, Adults Find Comfort as Toys Become More Available," *Wall Street Journal,* September 12, 2002, p. A13.

32. Allen K. K. Chan, Luther Denton, and Alex S. L. Tsang, "The Art of Gift Giving in China," *Business Horizons*, July–August, 2003, pp. 47–52.

33. Douglas Bowman, John U. Farley, and David C. Schmittlein, "Cross-National Empirical Generalization in Business Services Buyer Behavior," *Journal of International Business Studies* 31, 4 (2000), pp. 667–685.

34. Lawrence H. Wortzel, "Marketing to Firms in Developing Asian Countries," *Industrial Marketing Management* 12 (1983), pp. 113–123.

35. Desirée Blankenburg Holm, Kent Eriksson, and Jan Johanson, "Business Networks and Cooperation in International Business Relationships," *Journal of International Business Studies* 27 (1996), pp. 1033–1053.

36. James K. Sebenius, Rebecca Green, and Randall Fine, "Doing Business in Russia: Negotiating in the Wild East," Harvard Business School, Note #9-899-048 1999, pp. 6–7.

37. John L. Graham and N. Mark Lam, "The Chinese Negotiation," *Harvard Business Review*, October 2003, pp. 82–91.

38. George S. Yip, *Total Global Strategy II* (Englewood Cliffs, NJ: Prentice-Hall, 2003), pp. 36–39.

39. "GM Network Unifies Auto Parts Buys," Dow Jones Newswire, June 11, 2002.

40. *Selling to the Government Markets: Local, State, Federal* (Cleveland: Government Product News, 1975), p. 2.

41. Mushtaq Luqmani, Ghazi M. Habib, and Sami Kassem, "Marketing to LDC Governments," *International Marketing Review* 5, no.1 (Spring 1988), pp. 56–67.

42. U.S. Commercial Service, Malaysia Country Commercial Guide, 2009.

43. David Lague and Susan V. Lawrence, "China's Russian-Arms Spree," *Wall Street Journal,* December 10, 2002, p. A15.

44. U.S. Commercial Service, Mexico Country Commercial Guide, 2009.

45. U.S. Commercial Service, Brazil Country Commercial Guide, 2008.

46. Stefania Bianchi, "Mideast Widens Aircraft Ventures," *Wall Street Journal*, July 30, 2008, p. B2.

47. U.S. Commercial Service, Egypt Country Commercial Guide, 2007.

48. Daniel Pearl, "In India, Roads Become All the Rage," *Wall Street Journal*, January 3, 2001, p. A10.

49. Bryan W. Husted, "Wealth, Culture, and Corruption," *Journal of International Business Studies* 30, no. 2 (1999), pp. 339–359.

50. Mohsin Habib and Leon Zurawicki, "Corruption and Foreign Direct Investment," *Journal of International Business Studies* 33, no. 2 (2002), pp. 291–307.

51. Jonathan P. Doh, Peter Rodriguez, Klaus Uhlenbruck, Jamie Collins, and Lorraine Eden, "Coping with Corruption in Foreign Markets," *Academy of Management Executive* 17, no. 3 (2003), pp. 114–127.

52. Benjamin Norris, "Don't Ignore the FCPA," *Journal of Commerce*, February 27, 2006.

53. Russell Gold and David Crawford, "U.S., Other Nations Step Up Bribery Battle," *Wall Street Journal*, September 12, 2008, p. B1.

54. Kara Scannell, "Swiss Lawyer Faces Charges in Bribery Case," *Wall Street Journal*, September 15, 2003, p. A16.

55. "Two Companies Admit Payments to Officials," *New York Times,* January 11, 2001, p. CP 10.

56. Kate Gillespie, "Middle East Response to the U.S. Foreign Corrupt Practices Act," *California Management Review* 29, 4 (1987), pp. 9–30.

57. "Thirty-four Nations Sign Anti-Bribery Agreement at OECD," Dow Jones Newswire, December 17, 1997.

58. Associated Press, "U.N. Anticorruption Treaty Aims to Ease Retrieval of Dirty Money," *Wall Street Journal*, December 9, 2003, p. A10.

59. Michael Peel, "Hurdles in Countering Cross-Border Corruption," *Financial Times* (London), August 14, 2006, p. 10.

60. Ibid.

Chapter 6

1. Michael Flagg, "Enjoy Shinier Hair! Chinese Brands Arrive," *Wall Street Journal*, May 24, 2001, p. A17.

2. Merissa Marr and Geoffrey A. Fowler, "Chinese Lessons for Disney," *Wall Street Journal*, June 12, 2006, p. B1.

3. Shaun Rein, "Lessons for Chinese Companies as They Go Global," *BusinessWeek Online*, December 2, 2008.

4. George S. Yip, *Total Global Strategy* (New York: Prentice-Hall, 2002), pp. 171–175.

5. Betsy McCay, "Pepsi Uncaps Russian Juice Deal," *Wall Street Journal*, March 21, 2008, p. B4.

6. Geoffrey A. Fowler and Betsy McKay, "Coke Pins China Hopes on Blitz in Beijing," *Wall Street Journal*, August 19, 2008, p. A1.

7. Manjeet Kripalani and Mark L. Clifford, "Finally Coke Gets It Right," *BusinessWeek,* February 10, 2003, p. 18.

8. Cecille Rohwedder, "Stores of Knowledge," *Wall Street Journal*, June 6, 2006, p. A1.

9. Arindam K. Bhattacharya and David C. Michael, "How Local Companies Keep Multinationals at Bay," *Harvard Business Review*, March 2008, p. 86.

10. Eric Bellman, "Why Indian Retailers May Thrive Alongside Many Big New Rivals, *Wall Street Journal*, December 13, 2006.

11. Niraj Dawar and Tony Frost, "Competing with Giants," *Harvard Business Review* 77 (March-April 1999), pp. 119–129.

12. Guliz Ger, "Localizing in the Global Village: Local Firms Competing in Global Markets," *California Management Review* 41, no. 4 (Summer 1999), pp. 64–83.

13. Jason Dean, "China's Web Retailers Beat U.S. Rivals at Their Own Game," *Wall Street Journal*, August 22, 2006, p. B1.

14. Tomas Elewaut, Patricia Lindenboim, and Damian L. Scokin, "Chile's Lesson in Lean Banking," *McKinsey Quarterly*, no. 3 (2003).

15. Jack Ewing and Joseph Weber, "The Beer Wars Come to a Head," *BusinessWeek,* May 24, 2004, p. 68.

16. Dawar and Frost, "Competing with Giants," p. 124.

17. Jaime Mejia and Gabriel Sama, "Media Players Say 'Si' to Latino Magazines," *Wall Street Journal*, May 15, 2002, p. B4.

18. David C. Gregorcyk, "Internationalization of Conglomerates from Emerging Markets: Success Stories from Mexico" (honors thesis, Teresa Lozano Long Institute of Latin American Studies, The University of Texas at Austin, 2005).

19. Hugh Pope, "Turkish Surprise," *Wall Street Journal*, September 7, 2004, p. A1.

20. Steven Gray, "In Indonesia, a Fight for the Soy-Sauce Crown," *Wall Street Journal*, April 20, 2007, p. B3.

21. Marcus Walker and Martin Gelnar, "Europe's Dysfunctional Family Businesses," *Wall Street Journal*, December 22, 2003, p. A13.

22. Hannah Karp and Andrew Wallmeyer, "Europe Firms Enjoy Homegrown Edge," *Wall Street Journal*, November 17, 2004.

23. Charles Forelle, "Microsoft Loss in Europe Raises American Fears," *Wall Street Journal*, September 18, 2007, p. A1.

24. Nikki Tait, "European Takeover Rulings Have Not Been 'Biased,'" *Financial Times*, July 14, 2003, p. 10.

25. Carol Matlack, Joseph Weber, and Wendy Zellner, "In Fighting Trim," *BusinessWeek*, April 28, 2003, p. 26.

26. Hiroyuki Tezuka, "Success as the Source of Failure? Competition and Cooperation in the Japanese Economy," *Sloan Management Review* 38 (Winter 1997), pp. 83–93.

27. Ibid.

28. J. McGuire and S. Dow, "The Persistence and Implications of Japanese Keiretsus," *Journal of International Business Studies* 34 (2003), pp. 374–388.

29. Ibid.

30. Betsy McKay and David Luhnow, "Mexico Finds Coke and Its Bottlers Guilty of Abusing Dominant Position in Market," *Wall Street Journal*, March 8, 2002, p. B3.

31. Gary S. Becker, "Is Europe Starting to Play by U.S. Rules?" *BusinessWeek*, April 22, 2002, p. 24.

32. Peter Fritsch, "Hard Profits," *Wall Street Journal*, April 22, 2002, p. A1.

33. Ilan Berman, "A Dangerous Partnership," *Wall Street Journal*, February 22, 2007, p. A14.

34. Josh Gerstein, "Chinese Law Delivers Shipping Controversy," *USA Today*, April 5, 2002, p. B8.

35. Joe McDonald, "Chinese Auto Makers Announce Mergers," Associated Press, December 27, 2007.

36. Jane Spencer, "Why Lenevo Can't Tame U.S.," *Wall Street Journal*, February 2, 2007. p. A14.

37. James E. Austin, *Managing in Developing Countries* (New York: The Free Press, 1990), pp. 127–129.

38. James M. Dorsey, "Turkish Conglomerate Prepares to Slim Down," *Wall Street Journal*, August 14, 2000, p. A14.

39. James Hookway, "Vietnam Pushes State-Owned Firms to Diversity," *Wall Street Journal*, December 19, 2007, p. A11.

40. Bruce Einhorn, Stuart Young, and David Rocks, "Another About-Face for Acer," *BusinessWeek*, April 24, 2000, p. 146.

41. Eugene D. Jaffe and Israel D. Nebenzahl, *National Image and Competitive Advantage* (Copenhagen: Copenhagen Business School Press, 2001), p. 53.

42. Elizabeth Woyke, "Flunking Brand Geography," *BusinessWeek*, June 18, 2007, p. 14.

43. Rajshekhar G. Javalgi, Bob D. Cultler, and William A. Winans, "At Your Service! Does Country of Origin Research Apply to Services?" *Journal of Services Marketing* 15, no. 6/7 (2001), pp. 565–582.

44. Dae Ryun Chang and Ik-Tae Rim, "A Study on the Rating of Import Sources for Industrial Products in a Newly Industrialized Country: The Case of South Korea," *Journal of Business Research* 32 (1995), pp. 31–39.

45. Hans B. Thorelli and Aleksandra Glowaka, "Willingness of American Industrial Buyers to Source Internationally," *Journal of Business Research* 32 (1995), pp. 21–30.

46. Chike Okechuku and Vincent Oneyemah, "Nigerian Consumer Attitudes toward Foreign and Domestic Products," *Journal of International Business Studies* 30, 3 (1999), pp. 611–622.

47. Gary S. Inch and J. Brad McBride, "The Impact of Country-of-Origin Cues on Consumer Perceptions of Product Quality: A Binational Test of the Decomposed Country-of-Origin Construct," *Journal of Business Research* 57 (2004), pp. 256–265.

48. Michael A. Kamins and Akira Nagashima, "Perceptions of Products Made in Japan versus Those Made in the United States among Japanese and American Executives: A Longitudinal Perspective," *Asia Pacific Journal of Management* 12, no. 1 (1995), pp. 49–68; and Inder Khera, "A Broadening Base of U.S. Consumer Acceptance of Korean Products" in Kenneth D. Bahn and M. Joseph Sirsy (eds.), *World Marketing Congress* (Blacksburg, VA: Academy of Marketing Science, 1986), pp. 136–141.

49. Owen Brown, "China Consumers Rate Japan Cars, Electronics Tops," *Wall Street Journal*, June 7, 2004, p. A17.

50. Jim Rendon, "When Nations Need a Little Marketing," *New York Times*, November 23, 2003, p. 5.

51. Sarah McBride, "Kia's Audacious Sorento Plan," *Wall Street Journal*, April 8, 2002, p. A12.

52. Janeen E. Olsen, Linda Nowak, and T. K. Clarke, "Country of Origin Effects and Complimentary Marketing Channels: Is Mexican Wine More Enjoyable When Served with Mexican Food?" *International Journal of Wine Marketing* 14, no. 1 (2002), pp. 23–34.

53. Hugh Pope, "Turkish Delight," *Wall Street Journal*, September 7, 2004, p. A1.

54. Massoud M. Saghafi, Fanis Varvoglis, and Tomas Vega, "Why U.S. Firms Don't Buy from Latin American Companies," *Industrial Marketing Management* 20 (1991), pp. 207–213.

55. Shawn Thelen, John B. Ford, and Earl D. Honeycutt Jr., "Assessing Russian Imported versus Domestic Product Bias," *Thunderbird International Business Review* 48, no. 5, 2006, pp. 687–704.

56. Lyn S. Amine, Mike C. H. Chao, and Mark J. Arnold, "Exploring the Practical Effects of Country of Origin, Animosity, and Price-Quality Issues," *Journal of International Marketing* 113, no. 2, 2005, pp. 114–150.

57. Jill G. Klein, Richard Ettenson, and Marlene D. Morris, "The Animosity Model of Foreign Product Purchase: An Empirical Test in the People's Republic of China," *Journal of Marketing* 62 (1998), pp. 89–100.

58. Ibid.

59. John Quelch, "The Return of the Global Brand," *Harvard Business Review* 81 (August 2003), pp. 22–23.

60. John Carreyrou and Jenny E. Heller, "U.S. Rift Hits Bottom Line," *Wall Street Journal*, June 16, 2003, p. A13.

61. Salah AlShebil, Abdul A. Rasheed, and Hussam Al-Shammari, "Battling Boycotts," *Wall Street Journal*, April 28, 2007, p. R6.

62. Carreyrou and Heller.

63. Tamsin Carlisle and Joel Baglole, "Canadian Businesses Fear Fallout of Iraq Stance," *Wall Street Journal*, March 28, 2003, p. A11.

64. Peter Wonacott and Chad Terhune, "Path to India's Market Dotted with Potholes," *Wall Street Journal*, September 12, 2006, p. A6.

65. T. Kenn Gaither and Patricia A. Curtin, "Examining the Heuristic Value of Models of International Public Relations Practice: A Case Study of the Arla Foods Crisis," *Journal of Public Relations Research* 20 (2008), pp. 115–137.

Chapter 7

1. Carlta Vitzthum, "Just-in-Time Fashion," *Wall Street Journal*, May 23, 2001, p. B1.

2. Rohwedder, Cecile, "Zara Grows as Retail Rivals Struggle," *Wall Street Journal*, March 26, 2009, p. B1.

3. Balaji R. Koka, John E. Prescott, and Ravindranath Madhavan, "Contagion Influence on Trade and Investment Policy: A Network Perspective," *Journal of International Business Studies* 30, no. 1 (1999), pp. 127–148.

4. David A. Ricks, *Blunders in International Business*, 3rd ed. (New York: Blackwell, 1999), pp. 130–136.

5. Merissa Marr and Geoffrey A. Fowler, "Chinese Lessons for Disney," *Wall Street Journal*, June 12, 2006, p. B1.

6. Pierre Berthon, Leyland Pitt, Constantine S. Katsikeas, and Jean Paul Berthon, "Virtual Services Go International," *Journal of International Marketing* 7, no. 3 (1999), p. 98.

7. C. Samuel Craig and Susan P. Douglas, *International Marketing Research: Concepts and Methods* (New York: Wiley, 1999), pp. 16–19.

8. "Russia's Unemployment Rate Rises Year-on-Year," *Interfax News Agency*, June 21, 1999, p. 1.

9. Leonard Gurevich, "Focus on Central Asia: Conducting Research in the Post-Soviet Era," *Quirk's Marketing Research Review*, no. 1048 (November 2002).

10. Brian Palmer, "What the Chinese Want," *Fortune*, October 11, 1999.

11. Geoffrey A. Fowler, "China Radio Is Wave of Future for Advertising," *Wall Street Journal*, April 28, 2004, p. A6.

12. "Sharp as a Razor in Central Asia," *The Economist*, June 5, 1993, p. 36.

13. Geraldo Samor, Cecille Rohwedder, and Ann Zimmerman, "Innocents Abroad?" *Wall Street Journal*, May 16, 2006, p. B1.

14. Gordon Fairclough, "McDonald's Marketing Chief in China Preaches On-the-Ground Experience," *Wall Street Journal*, May 7, 2007, p. B4.

15. Elizabeth Robles, "In Cuba, the Usual MR Methods Don't Work," *Marketing News*, June 10, 2002, p. 12.

16. Tim Plowman, Adrien Lanusse, and Astrid Cruz, "Observing the World," *Quirk's Marketing Research Review*, no. 1171 (November 2003).

17. Michael Fielding, "In One's Element," *Marketing News*, February 1, 2006. pp. 15–20.

18. Emily Nelson, "P&G Checks Out Real Life," *Wall Street Journal*, May 17, 2001, p. B1.

19. Michael Fielding, "Shift the Focus," *Marketing News*, September 1, 2006, p. 18.

20. Dana James, "Back to Vietnam," *Marketing News*, May 13, 2002, p. 1.

21. Gurevich, "Focus on Central Asia."

22. Rod Davies, "Focus Groups in Asia," Posted on *Orient Pacific Century*, 2005, http://www.orientpacific.com (accessed June 1, 2005).

23. Sharon Seidler, "Qualitatively Speaking: Conducting Qualitative Research on a Global Scale," *Quirk's Marketing Research Review*, no. 1182 (December 2003).

24. Lyn Montgomery, "Simplifying Research in Japan," *Quirk's Marketing Research Review*, no. 729 (November 2001).

25. Eileen Moran, "Managing the Minefields of Global Product Development," *Quirk's Marketing Research Review*, no. 625 (November 2000).

26. Kevin Reagan, "In Asia, Think Globally, Communicate Locally," *Marketing News*, July 19, 1999, pp. 12–14.

27. Robert B. Young and Rajshekhar G. Javalgi, "International Marketing Research: A Global Project Management Perspective," *Business Horizons*, 50, 2007, p. 118.

28. J. Brad McBride and Kate Gillespie, "Consumer Innovativeness among Street Vendors in Mexico City," *Latin American Business Review* 1, no. 3 (2000), pp. 71–94.

29. Moran, "Managing the Minefields."

30. Dana James, "Back to Vietnam," *Marketing News*, May 13, 2002, pp. 1, 13–14.

31. Moran, "Managing the Minefields."

32. See, for example, N. L. Reynolds, A. C. Simintiras, and A. Diamantopoulos, "Sampling Choices in International Marketing: Key Issues and Guidelines for Research," *Journal of International Business Studies* 34 (2003), p. 81.

33. Craig and Douglas, *International Marketing Research*, p. 282.

34. Geraldo Samor, "In Brazil, Ford Has Discovered the Way Forward," *Wall Street Journal*, July 10, 2006, p. B1.

35. Tim R. Davis and Robert B. Young, "International Marketing Research: A Management Briefing," *Business Horizons*, March–April 2002, p. 33.

36. Craig and Douglas, *International Marketing Research*, p. 286.

37. Arundhati Parmar, "South African Research," *Marketing News*, September 15, 2003, p. 19.

38. Gurevich, "Focus on Central Asia."

39. Robin Cobb, "Marketing Shares," *Marketing*, February 22, 1990, p. 44.

40. "Russian Researchers Do Not Enter Internet," *Kommersant International*, September 22, 2007.

41. Gary S. Insch and Stewart R. Miller, "Perception of Foreignness: Benefit or Liability?" *Journal of Managerial Issues*, (17/4), pp. 423–438.

42. McBride and Gillespie, "Consumer Innovativeness," p. 80.

43. "Research in Denmark, Germany and the Netherlands," *Quirk's Marketing Research Review*, no. 731 (November 2001).

44. Gabriel Kahn, "Chinese Puzzle: Spotty Consumer Data," *Wall Street Journal*, October 15, 2003, p. B1.

45. James Heckman, "Marketers Waiting, Will See on EU Privacy," *Marketing News*, June 7, 1999, p. 4.

46. "Japan-Market Research-Competitive Landscape," *Data-monitor Market Research Profiles*, November 1, 2004.

47. J. M. Batista-Foguet, J. Fortiana, C. Currie, and J. R. Villalba, "Socio-Economic Indexes in Surveys for Comparisons between Countries," *Social Indicators Research* 67 (2004), p. 328.

48. Jennifer Mitchell, "Reaching across Borders," *Marketing News*, May 10, 1999, p. 19.

49. Irvine Clarke III, "Global Marketing Research: Is Extreme Response Style Influencing Your Results?" *Journal of International Consumer Marketing* 12, no. 4 (2000), pp. 91–111.

50. Peter Landers, "Merck, Pfizer in Japan," *Wall Street Journal*, October 2, 2003, p. B4.

51. "High Price of Industrial Espionage," *Times of London*, June 5, 1999, p. 31.

52. C. K. Prahalad and Gary Hamel, "The Core Competence of the Corporation," *Harvard Business Review* 68 (May–June 1990), pp. 79–91.

53. Ibid.

54. Geoffrey A. Fowler, "Copies 'R' Us," *Wall Street Journal*, January 31, 2003, p. B1.

55. Barton Lee, Soumya Saklini, and David Tatterson, "Research: Growing in Guangzhou," *Marketing News*, June 10, 2002, pp. 12–13.

56. Thomas Rideg, "Traditional Survey Instruments Encounter Difficulties When Applied to LatAm," *Info-americas*, December 7, 2004.

57. Jack Honomichl, "Acquisitions Help Firms' Global Share Increase," *Marketing News*, August 18, 2003, p. H3.

58. Bob Violino, "Extended Enterprise: Coca-Cola Is Linking Its IT System with Those of Worldwide Bottling Partners As It Strives to Stay One Step Ahead of the Competition," *Information Week*, March 22, 1999, pp. 46–54.

59. Gabriel Kahn, "Made to Measure," *Wall Street Journal*, September 11, 2003, p. A1.

Chapter 8

1. "Kraft to Focus on Ten Brands Overseas," *Reuters News*, September 3, 2008.

2. Julie Forster and Becky Gaylord, "Can Kraft Be a Big Cheese Abroad as Well?" *BusinessWeek,* June 4, 2001, pp. 63–67.

3. Geoffrey A. Fowler, "Friendster Didn't Die," *Wall Street Journal*, June 6, 2007, p. B1.

4. "Chinese Firms Seek to Expand Overseas," *Dow Jones Commodities Service*, April 4, 2006.

5. Peter Landers, "U.S. Is Tonic for Japan's Top Pharmaceuticals," *Wall Street Journal*, May 21, 2002, p. B6.

6. Michael Zielenziger, "DHL Worldwide Express Starts Service in Kabul, Afghanistan," *San Jose Mercury News*, April 6, 2002.

7. Geri Smith and Michael Arndt, "Wrapping the Globe in Tortillas," *BusinessWeek*, February 26, 2007, p. 54.

8. Anil K. Gupta and Haiyan Wang, "How to Get China and India Right," *Wall Street Journal,* April 28, 2007, p. R4.

9. "Boss Talk: It's a Grande-Latte World," *Wall Street Journal*, December 15, 2003, p. B1.

10. Amy Chozick, "Japan's Auto Giants Steer toward China," *Wall Street Journal*, May 16, 2007, p. A12.

11. George S. Yip, *Total Global Strategy II* (Upper Saddle River, NJ: Prentice-Hall, 2003), p. 76.

12. Cris Prystay, "In Bid to Globalize, U.S. Colleges Offer Degrees in Asia," *Wall Street Journal*, July 12, 2005, p. B1.

13. "Manager's Hands-Off Tactics Right Touch for Italian Unit," *Nikkei Weekly*, February 3, 1997, p. 17.

14. Amy Chozick, "Cold Stone Aims to Be Hip in Japan," *Wall Street Journal*, December 14, 2006, p. B10.

15. Kenichi Ohmae, *Triad Power: The Coming Shape of Global Competition* (New York: Free Press, 1985).

16. "Alcatel Open to More Acquisitions," *Business World*, March 25, 1999.

17. Gail Edmondson and Adeline Bonnet, "Toyota's New Traction in Europe," *BusinessWeek*, June 7, 2004, p. 64.

18. "Whirlpool Says Net Fell by 65 Percent on Impact of Brazil Devaluation," *Wall Street Journal*, April 16, 1999, p. B2.

19. Russell Gold, "Exxon to Boost Spending, Broaden Exploration," *Wall Street Journal*, March 6, 2008, p. B1.

20. Christos Pantzalis, "Does Location Matter? An Empirical Analysis of Geographic Scope and MNC Market Valuation," *Journal of International Business Studies* 32, no. 1 (2001), pp. 133–155.

21. Joel Millman, "Latin Americans Boost Home Coffers," *Wall Street Journal*, March 17, 2003, p. A2.

22. "Fast Drive Out of the Shadows," *Financial Times*, June 17, 1996, p. 17.

23. "Carlsberg A/S," *Food and Drink Weekly*, October 26, 1998.

24. Pamela Druckerman, "As Brazil Booms, Citibank Is Racing to Catch Up," *Wall Street Journal*, September 11, 2000, p. A30.

25. "Acer's Semiconductor Unit Weighs Market Listing as Picture Brightens," *Dow Jones Business News*, January 20, 1999.

26. Katrijn Gielens and Marnik G. DeKimpe, "The Entry Strategy of Retail Firms into Transition Economies," *Journal of Marketing* 71 (2007), pp. 196–212.

27. Sarah Ellison, "Cadbury Schweppes Works to Tempt More Sweet Tooths," *Wall Street Journal*, April 24, 2001, p. B4.

28. Agnes Akkerman, "Union Competition and Strikes," *Industrial & Labor Relations Review*, July 2008, vol. 61, no. 4, (July 2008) p. 452–453.

29. William H. Davidson, "Market Similarity and Market Selection: Implications for International Market Strategy," *Journal of Business Research* 11, no. 4 (1983), p. 446.

30. Sylvie Chetty and Colin Campbell-Hunt, "A Strategic Approach to Internationalization: A Traditional Versus a 'Born-Global' Approach," *Journal of International Marketing* 12, no. 1 (2004), pp. 57–81.

31. Daniel Michaels, "Landing Rights," *Wall Street Journal*, April 30, 2002, p. A1.

32. "Boss Talk: It's a Grande-Latte World," *Wall Street Journal*, December 15, 2003, p. B1.

33. Shawna O'Grady and Henry L. Lane, "The Psychic Distance Paradox," *Journal of International Business Studies* 27, no. 2 (1996), pp. 319, 324–325.

34. Torben Pedersen and Bent Petersen, "Learning about Foreign Markets: Are Entrant Firms Exposed to a 'Shock Effect'?" *Journal of International Marketing*, 12, no. 1 (2004), pp. 103–123.

35. "The Caucasus, a Region Where Worlds Collide," *The Economist*, August 19, 2000.

36. Neal M. Ashkanasy, Edwin Trevor-Roberts, and Louise Earnshaw, "The Anglo Cluster: Legacy of the British Empire," *Journal of World Business,* 37, no. 28-39 (2002).

Chapter 9

1. Anne L. Souchon, Adamantios Diamantopoulos, Hartman H. Holzmuller, Catherine N. Axinn, James M. Sinkula, Heike Simmet, and Geoffrey R. Durden, "Export Information Use: A Five-Country Investigation of Key Determinants," *Journal of International Marketing* 11, no. 3 (2003), pp. 106–127.

2. "Eye Surgery the Material Difference," *Metalworking Production*, March 15, 2004, p. 13.

3. Niles Hansen, Kate Gillespie, and Esra Gencturk, "SMEs and Export Involvement: Market Responsiveness, Technology and Alliances," *Journal of Global Marketing* 7, no. 4 (1994), pp. 7–27.

4. Steve Hamm, "Children of the Web," *BusinessWeek*, July 2, 2007, p. 54.

5. Edward G. Thomas, "Internet Marketing in the International Arena: A Cross-Cultural Comparison," *International Journal of Business Strategy* 8, no. 3 (2008), pp. 84–98.

6. "World Internet Penetration Rates by Geographic Region," Internet World Stats, Miniwatts Marketing Group, 2009.

7. Chandrani Ghosh, "E-Trade Routes Planning to Do Global Business on the Web? Next Linx Will Ease the Way," *Forbes,* August 7, 2000, p. 108.

8. "Harvard Business School Publishing and New York Times Syndicate Announce Harvard Business Review to Be Published in Mandarin Chinese," *Businesswire*, July 17, 2001.

9. "Everlast Worldwide Inc. Announces New Head of Global Licensing," PR Newswire, October 25, 2000.

10. "Roche Grows Position in Japan," *Chemical Market Reporter*, December 22–29, 2003, p. 10.

11. Nick Wingfield, "Priceline.com Plans Asia Partnership with Hutchinson," *Wall Street Journal*, January 26, 2000, p. A19.

12. "NZ Fonterra Signs Deal with Egypt's Arab Dairy," *Dow Jones International News*, April 7, 2009.

13. "Franchise Services Sector in Mexico," *U.S. Commercial Service*, April 2008.

14. "Franchising Now Accounts for 5% of Philippine GDP," *Manila Bulletin*, July 10, 2008.

15. "Morocco Franchise Market," *U.S Commercial Service*, 2009.

16. "Happy Hookahs," *The Economist*, May 5, 2001.

17. Lawrence Bivens, "U.S. Franchisors Are Making Major Global Inroads," *Wall Street Journal*, April 10, 2008, p. D4.

18. Oxana Parshina, "Franchising in Kazakhstan," *U.S. Commercial Service*, April 2009.

19. Ibid.

20. Judith Rehak, "Franchising the World: Services and Internet Fuel of Global Boom," *International Herald Tribune*, October 14, 2000, p. 20.

21. "Nokian Tyres Expands Contract Manufacturing in Slovakia," *Nordic Business Report*, November 8, 2004, p. 1.

22. "BMW Testing the Water for Local Facilities," *Businessline* (Islamabad), May 17, 2002.

23. Joel Millman, "Go North," *Wall Street Journal*, May 10, 2004, p. A1.

24. "Europe First Stop? Novartis Win Kindles Deutsch Global Plan," *Advertising Age*, November 1, 2004, p. 3.

25. Doreen Hemlock, "Florida, Brazil Compete in Citrus Industry," *Knight Ridder/Tribune Business News*, July 11, 2001.

26. Andrew Meadows, "Florida Citrus Processors Concentrate on Brazilian Juice Invasion," *Knight Ridder/Tribune Business News*, June 9, 2001.

27. Neal Sandler, "An Israeli Coffee Outfit Goes Global," *BusinessWeek*, August 14, 2008.

28. Claude Obadia and Irena Vida, "Endogenous Opportunism in Small and Medium-Sized Enterprises' Foreign Subsidiaries: Classification and Research Propositions," *Journal of International Marketing* 14, no. 4, (2006), pp. 57–86.

29. Anthony Goerzen, "Managing Alliance Networks: Emerging Practices of Multinational Corporations," *Academy of Management Executive* 19, no. 2 (2005), pp. 94–107.

30. Margaret Popper, "Flying Solo Overseas," *BusinessWeek*, May 20, 2002, p. 28.

31. Prashant Kale and Jaideep Anand, "The Decline of Emerging Economy Joint Ventures," *California Management Review* 49, no. 3 (2006), pp. 62–68.

32. Gordon Fairclough, "Passing Lane," *Wall Street Journal*, April 20, 2007, p. A1.

33. David Ahlstrom, Michael N. Young, and Anil Nair, "Deceptive Managerial Practices in China: Strategies for Foreign Firms," *Business Horizons*, November–December 2002, pp. 49–59.

34. Dana James, "Back to Vietnam," *Marketing News*, May 13, 2002, p. 13.

35. Geoffrey A. Fowler and Jason Dean, "In China, MySpace May Have to Be 'OurSpace,'" *Wall Street Journal*, February 2, 2007, p. B1.

36. Aimin Yan and Yadong Luo, *International Joint Ventures* (Armonk, NY: M.E. Sharpe, 2001), p. 223.

37. Usha C.V. Haley, "Assessing and Controlling Business Risks in China," *Journal of International Management* 9 (2003), pp. 237–252.

38. "Starbucks Calls China Its Top Growth Focus," *Wall Street Journal*, February 14, 2006, p. B4.

39. Starbucks Coffee Co. corporate website, http://www.starbucks.com (accessed June 9, 2005).

40. Elizabeth M. Gillespie, "Back as CEO, Can Howard Schultz Save Starbucks?" *Associated Press Newswires*, January 8, 2008.

41. "The Advantages of Marrying Local," *Financial Times*, December 21, 2000, p. 16.

42. Janine Brewis, "Brasil Telecom Fears Takeover Bid," *Financial Times*, November 16, 2003, p. 1.

43. Yan and Luo, *International Joint Ventures*, p. 281.

44. "Alliance Tips for a Beautiful Relationship," Financial Times-FT.com (accessed July 11, 2001).

45. Rajneesh Narula, "Globalisation and Trends in International R&D Alliances," MERIT-Infonomics Research Memorandum Series, 2003, pp. 2–7.

46. Dean Takahashi, "New Chip called a Threat to Intel," *Knight Ridder/Tribune Business News* (Washington), February 8, 2005, p. 1.

47. Neal E. Boudette, "Road Less Travelled," *Wall Street Journal,* August 4, 2003, p. A1.

48. "Starbucks Starts Sales of Bottled Coffee in China," *China Knowledge Press*, November 2, 2007.

49. Justin Wastnage, "Star Alliance in Defining Moment," *Flight International* 166, no. 4965 (January 3, 2005), p. 15.

50. General Mills corporate website, http://www.generalmills.com (viewed June 24, 2009).

51. Wastnage, "Star Alliance in Defining Moment."

52. "SABMiller to Buy Stake in Italian Brewer," *International Herald Tribune*, May 15, 2003, p. 3.

53. Chris Nuttall, "EBay Backs Its $100 million Outlay in China," *Financial Times*, February 11, 2005, p. 19.

54. Mahmoud Kassem, "Banks Seek Takeover Targets in Egypt," *Wall Street Journal Europe*, July 11, 2001.

55. Peter Wonacott and Henny Sender, "Indian Firms See Acquisition as Path to World-Wide Growth," *Wall Street Journal*, May 1, 2006, p. A6.

56. Gary McWilliams and Evan Ramstad, "China's Aggressive Buyers Suffer Setbacks on Some Overseas Deals," *Wall Street Journal*, August 22, 2006, p. A1.

57. Pete Engardio, "Emerging Giants," *BusinessWeek,* July 31, 2006, p. 49.

58. Internet World Stats, Miniwatts Marketing Group, http://www.internetworldstats.com/stats3.htm#asia (accessed February 22, 2005).

59. Alex Roth and Mike Esterl, "DHL Beats a Retreat from U.S." *Wall Street Journal*, November 11, 2008, p. B1.

60. Evette Treewater, "Global Retailers Refocus on Latin America," *Infoamericas*, November 16, 2007.

61. Nick Wingfield and Mylene Mangalindan, "Yahoo Agrees to Cede Most Auction in Europe to eBay," *Wall Street Journal Europe*, May 24, 2002, p. A5.

62. Andrea Welsh and Ann Zimmerman, "Wal-Mart Snaps Up Brazilian Chain," *Wall Street Journal*, March 2, 2004, p. B3.

63. William A. Orme, "A Grocer amid Mideast Outrage," *New York Times*, January 25, 2001, p. C1.

64. "Sainsbury's to Pull Out of Egypt," *Jerusalem Post Daily*, April 10, 2001, p. 10.

65. "DHL Resumes Afghanistan Service," *Jakarta Post*, March 20, 2002, p. 12.

66. Yuri Kageyama, "Japan Imports American Culture via Calories," *Marketing News,* May 1, 2007, p. 11.

67. Jenn Abelson, "In 2nd Crack at China Market, Dunkin' Donuts Alters Recipe," *Boston Globe*, November 21, 2008, p. A1.

68. Kwon, Yung-Chul and Michael Y. Hu, "Comparative Analysis of Export-Oriented and Foreign Production-Oriented Firms' Foreign Market Entry Decisions," *Management International Review* 35, no. 4 (1995), pp. 325–336.

Chapter 10

1. Bruce Orwall, "Can Grinch Steal Christmas Abroad?" *Wall Street Journal*, November 16, 2000, p. B1.

2. Yasmine El-Rashidi, "D'oh! Arabized Simpsons Aren't Getting Many Laughs," *Wall Street Journal*, October 17, 2005, p. A42.

3. Amy Chozick, "Cold Stone Aims to Be Hip in Japan," *Wall Street Journal*, December 14, 2006, p. B10.

4. Carol Matlack, "Bordeaux Goes to the Lab," *BusinessWeek*, April 9, 2007, p. 10.

5. Pierre Berthon, Leyland Pitt, Constantine S. Katsikeas, and Jean Paul Berthon, "Virtual Services Go International: International Services in the Marketspace," *Journal of International Marketing*, 7, no. 3 (1999), p. 96.

6. Mylene Mangalindan and Kevin Delaney, "Yahoo! Ordered to Bar the French from Nazi Items," *Wall Street Journal*, November 21, 2000, p. B1.

7. Peter Ford, "Need Software in, Say, Icelandic? Call the Irish," *Christian Science Monitor*, February 6, 2001, p. 1.

8. Geoffrey A. Fowler and Ramin Setoodeh, "Outsiders Get Smarter about China's Tastes," *Wall Street Journal*, August 5, 2004, p. B1.

9. Ford, "Need Software in, Say, Icelandic?"

10. Julie Jargon, "Kraft Reinvents Iconic Oreo to Win in China," *Wall Street Journal Asia*, May 1, 2008, p. 28.

11. Arundhati Parmar, "Dependent Variable," *Marketing News*, September 16, 2002, p. 4.

12. Fowler and Setoodeh, "Outsiders Get Smarter About China's Tastes."

13. Deborah Ball, Sarah Ellison, Janet Adamy, and Geoffrey A. Fowler, "Recipes without Borders?" *Wall Street Journal*, August 19, 2004, p. A6.

14. Ford, "Need Software in, Say, Icelandic?"

15. Catherine Arnold, "Foreign Exchange," *Marketing News*, May 15, 2004, p. 13.

16. Antonio Regalado, "Marketers Pursue the Shallow-Pocketed," *Wall Street Journal*, January 26, 2007, p. B3.

17. Parmar, "Dependent Variable."

18. Deborah Ball, "Shelf Life," *Wall Street Journal*, March 22, 2007, p. A1.

19. Ball, "Shelf Life."

20. Ellen Byron, "Emerging Ambitions," *Wall Street Journal*, July 16, 2007, p. A1.

21. Norihiko Shirouzu, "What Prosperity Has to Do with Price of Cars in China, *Wall Street Journal*, April 17, 2008, p. B1.

22. Cris Prystay, "Companies Market to India's Have-Littles," *Wall Street Journal*, June 5, 2003, p. B1.

23. Elisabeth Malkin, "Mexico Goes Top-Flight," *BusinessWeek*, June 26, 2000.

24. Claudia Puig, "'Hannibal' Ignites Worldwide Controversy," *USA Today*, March 7, 2001, p. D6.

25. International Standards Organization website, http://www.iso.ch.

26. Barbara Carton, "No Yolk," *Wall Street Journal*, June 24, 2002, p. A1.

27. Jim Carlton, "EU Directive Will Hit Electronics Industry Hard," *Wall Street Journal*, June 29, 2006, p. B5.

28. Brandon Mitchener, "Increasingly, Rules of Global Economy Are Set in Brussels," *Wall Street Journal Europe*, April 23, 2002, p. A1.

29. Ford, "Need Software in, Say, Icelandic?"

30. John O'Neil, "Reducing Drug Overdoses, by Packaging," *New York Times*, May 29, 2001, p. 8.

31. Kathy Chen, "Cashmere Clothes to Undergo More FTC Monitoring," *Wall Street Journal*, May 4, 2001, p. B1.

32. "Coca-Cola Poland Details Scope of Product Recalls," *Wall Street Journal*, July 14, 1999, p. A17.

33. "Boss Talk: It's a Grande-Latte World," *Wall Street Journal*, December 15, 2003, p. B1.

34. Jason Singer and Martin Fackler, "In Japan, Adding Beer, Wine to Latte List," *Wall Street Journal*, July 14, 2003, p. B1.

35. David Twiddy, "Payless ShoeSource Opens in Middle East," Associated Press Newswire, March 31, 2009.

36. James T. Areddy and Peter Sanders, "Chinese Learn English the Disney Way," *Wall Street Journal*, April 20, 2009, p. B1.

37. Lee Hawkins Jr., "New Driver," *Wall Street Journal*, October 6, 2004, p. A1.

38. "Winners for 2003" *BusinessWeek*, July 7, 2003, p. 70.

39. "GM Innovations Recognized," PR Newswire, April 25, 2001.

40. Jason Bush, "Mouse Ears over Moscow," *BusinessWeek*, June 11, 2007, p. 42.

41. Bruce Einhorn, "A Dragon in R&D," *BusinessWeek*, November 6, 2006, p. 45.

42. Kathy Chen and Jason Dean, "Low Costs, Plentiful Talent Make China a Global Magnet for R&D," *Wall Street Journal*, March 13, 2006, p. A1.

43. Kasra Ferdows, "Making the Most of Foreign Factories," *Harvard Business Review*, 75 (March–April 1997), pp. 73–88.

44. Keith Johnson, "The Business-Spanish Lessons: An Entrepreneur Wants to Bring U.S. Universities to Spaniards," *Wall Street Journal*, March 12, 2001, p. R18.

45. "Heineken Signs Deal with Femsa to Import Beers," *Wall Street Journal*, June 22, 2004, p. B3.

46. Nandini Lakshman, "Here Come the Bride Sites," *BusinessWeek*, November 6, 2006, p. 42.

47. Julie Jargon, "General Mills Tries to Convince Americans to Cook Chinese," *Wall Street Journal*, May 29, 2007, p. B1.

48. Rajneesh Narula and Geert Duysters, "Globalisation and Trends in International R&D Alliances," *Journal of International Management* 10 (2004), p. 213.

49. "Airlines Move toward Buying Planes in Alliances," *Dow Jones Business News*, May 19, 2003.

50. Tim R. V. Davis and Robert B. Young, "International Marketing Research: A Management Briefing," *Business Horizons*, March–April 2002, pp. 31–38.

51. "Test It in Paris, France, Launch It in Paris, Texas," *Advertising Age*, May 31, 1999, p. 28.

52. Marian Beise and Thomas Cleff, "Assessing the Lead Market Potential of Countries for Innovation Projects," *Journal of International Management* 10 (2004), pp. 453–477.

53. Jathon Sapsford, "Toyota Introduces a New Luxury Brand in Japan: Lexus," *Wall Street Journal*, August 3, 2005, p. B1.

54. Chad Terhune, "Coca-Cola Posts 11% Increase in Profit," *Wall Street Journal*, July 18, 2003, p. B2.

55. Charles Goldsmith, "Latest Madonna Release," *Wall Street Journal*, September 4, 2003, p. B1.

56. "DHL and EXE Begin Global Roll-Out," Business Wire, February 13, 2002.

57. Nanette Byrnes, "Panning for Gold in Local Markets," *BusinessWeek*, September 18, 2000, p. 54.

Chapter 11

1. Pui-Wing Tam, "H-P Lands $3 Billion Contract to Manage P&G Tech Services," *Wall Street Journal*, April 14, 2003, p. B4.

2. Cassell Bryan-Low, "Microsoft Battles Piracy in Developing Markets," *Wall Street Journal*, December 25, 2004, p. B4.

3. Philip Makutsa, Kilungu Nzaku, Paul Ogutu, Peter Barasa, Sam Ombeki, Alex Mwaki, and Robert E. Quick, "Challenges in Implementing a Point-of-Use Water Quality Intervention in Rural Kenya," *American Journal of Public Health* 91, no. 10 (October 2001), pp. 1571–1573.

4. Mary Anne Raymond and John D. Mittelstaedt, "Perceptions of Factors Driving Success for Multinational Professional Services Firms in Korea," *Journal of Consumer Marketing* 14, no. 1 (2001), p. 24.

5. Peggy Cloninger, "The Effect of Service Intangibility on Revenue from Foreign Markets," *Journal of International Management* 10 (2004), p. 126.

6. Martin Fackler and Ichiko Fuyuno, "Japan Lawyers See Seismic Shift," *Wall Street Journal*, September 16, 2004, p. A15.

7. David Murphy, "Chinese Builders Go Global," *Far Eastern Economic Review*, May 13, 2004, p. 30.

8. John Lyons, "Siting a Call Center? Check Out the Mall First," *Wall Street Journal*, July 3, 2006, p. B1.

9. Pierre Berthon, Leyland Pitt, Constantine S. Katsikeas, and Jean-Paul Berthon, "Virtual Services Go International: Services in the Marketspace," *Journal of International Marketing* 7, no. 3 (1999), pp. 85–86.

10. Raymond and Mittelstaedt, "Perceptions of Factors," p. 26.

11. Michael Laroche, Linda C. Ueltschy, Shuzo Abe, Mark Cleveland, and Peter P. Yannopoulos, "Service Quality Perceptions and Customer Satisfaction: Evaluating the Role of Culture," *Journal of International Marketing* 12, no. 3 (2004), pp. 58–85.

12. Ibid; and Raymond and Mittelstaedt, "Perceptions of Factors," p. 39.

13. Laroche et al., "Service Quality Perceptions," p. 77.

14. Mary Yoko Brannen, "When Mickey Loses Face: Recontextualization, Semantic Fit, and Semiotics of Foreignness," *Academy of Management Review* 29, no. 4 (2004), pp. 593–616.

15. Betsy Morris, "The Brand's the Thing," *Fortune*, March 4, 1996, p. 75.

16. Bernd Schmitt, "Language and Visual Imagery: Issues of Corporate Identity in East Asia," *Columbia Journal of World Business* 30 (Winter 1995), pp. 2–36.

17. "Google Becomes Gu Ge in China," *Financial Times*, April 13, 2006, p. 19.

18. Jean-Claude Usunier and Janer Shaner, "Using Linguistics for Creating Better International Brand Names," *Journal of Marketing Communications* 8, no. 4 (2002), pp. 211–229.

19. George W. Cooper, "On Your 'Mark,'" *Columbia Journal of World Business* 5 (March–April 1970), pp. 67–76.

20. "Darkie No, Darlie Yes," *South China Morning Post*, May 16, 1999, p. 2.

21. Gary McWilliams and Evan Ramstad, "China's Aggressive Buyers Suffer Setbacks on Some Overseas Deals," *Wall Street Journal*, August 22, 2006, p. A1.

22. Ernest Beck, "Unilever Renames Cleanser," *Wall Street Journal*, December 27, 2000, p. B8.

23. Alice Z. Cuneo, "Landor: Experts on Identity Crisis," *Ad Age International*, March 1997, pp. 1–44.

24. Michael Fielding, "Walk the Line," *Marketing News*, September 1, 2006, pp. 8 and 10.

25. David A. Aaker and Erich Joachimsthaler, "The Lure of Global Branding," *Harvard Business Review* 77 (November–December 1999), pp. 137–144.

26. Ibid.

27. Susan P. Douglas, C. Samuel Craig, and Edwin J. Nijssen, "Integrating Branding Strategy across Markets: Building International Brand Architecture," *Journal of International Marketing* 9, 2 (2001), p. 110.

28. Johnny Johansson and Ilkka A. Ronkainen, "Consider Implications of Local Brands," *Marketing News*, May 15, 2004, p. 46.

29. Douglas B. Holt, John A. Quelch, and Earl L. Taylor, "How Global Brands Compete," *Harvard Business Review* 82 (September 2004), pp. 68–75.

30. Isabelle Schuiling and Jean-Noel Kapferer, "Real Differences between Local and International Brands: Strategic Implications for International Marketers," *Journal of International Marketing* 12, no. 4 (2004), pp. 97–112.

31. Holt, Quelch, and Taylor, "How Global Brands Compete," p. 69.

32. Ibid, p. 71.

33. Yuliya Strizhakova, Robin A. Coulter, and Linda L. Price, "Branded Products as a Passport to Global Citizenship: Perspectives from Developed and Developing

Countries," *Journal of International Marketing* 16, no. 4 (2008), pp. 57–85.

34. Claudiu V. Dimofte, Johny K. Johansson, and Ilkka A. Ronkainen, "Cognitive and Affective Reactions of U.S. Consumers to Global Brands," *Journal of International Marketing* 16, no. 1 (2008), pp. 113–135.

35. Claudia Penteado, "Regional Brands: Varig Eyes the Skies outside of Brazil," *Advertising Age International,* March 1997, pp. 1–19.

36. Jane Blennerhassett, "Shangri-La on Earth," *Advertising Age International,* March 1997, pp. 1–24.

37. Julien Cayla and Giana M. Eckhardt, "Asian Brands without Borders: Regional Opportunities and Challenges," *International Marketing Review* 24, no. 4 (2007), pp. 444–456.

38. Ibid.

39. "Who Favors Branding with Euro Approach?" *Advertising Age International,* May 25, 1992, pp. 1–16.

40. Schuiling and Kapferer, "Local and International Brands."

41. Ibid.

42. Marta Karenova, "Nostalgia Revives Soviet-Era Brands," *Wall Street Journal,* November 19, 2004, p. A12.

43. Leslie Chang and Peter Wonacott, "Cracking China's Market," *Wall Street Journal,* January 9, 2003, p. B1.

44. Rajeev Batra, Venkatram Ramaswamy, Dana Alden, Jan-Benedict Steenkamp, and S. Ramachander, "Effects of Brand Local and Nonlocal Origin on Consumer Attitudes in Developing Countries," *Journal of Consumer Psychology* 9, no. 2 (2000), pp. 83–95.

45. Paul Gao, Jonathan R. Woetzel, and Yibing Wu, "Can Chinese Brands Make It Abroad?" in "Global Directions," *McKinsey Quarterly,* Special Edition, no. 4 (2003), pp. 52–65.

46. "M&M to Drive Specialty Retailing Biz via Global Brands," *Businessline,* Chennai, January 22, 2009.

47. Geoffrey A. Fowler, "A Starck Vision of Asia's Future as Elite Producer of Brands," *Wall Street Journal,* April 7, 2004, p. B1.

48. Kate Gillespie, Kishore Krishma, and Susan Jarvis, "Protecting Global Brands: Toward a Global Norm," *Journal of International Marketing* 10, 2 (2002), pp. 99–112.

49. Guy Chazan, "Philip Morris Suffers a Setback in Russian Suit on Trademarks," *Wall Street Journal,* October 13, 1999, p. A26.

50. Gordon Fairclough, "From Hongda to Wumart, Brands in China Have Familiar, if Off-Key, Ring," *Wall Street Journal,* October 19, 2006, p. B1.

51. Bart A. Lazar, "Protect Trademarks When Marketing in China," *Marketing News,* June 15, 2006, p. 7.

52. "Starbucks Victory Opens Door to Russian Cafes," *Wall Street Journal,* November 18, 2005, p. A14.

53. Frederik Balfour, "Fakes," *BusinessWeek,* February 7, 2005, pp. 54–64.

54. Cliff Edwards, "HP Declares War on Counterfeiters," *BusinessWeek,* June 8, 2009, p. 44.

55. Barry Berman, "Strategies to Detect and Reduce Counterfeiting Activity," *Business Horizons* 51, no. 3 (2008), pp. 191–199.

56. Bruce Einhorn and Xiang Ji, "Deaf to Music Piracy," *BusinessWeek,* September 10, 2007, pp. 42–44.

57. Geoffrey A. Fowler and Jason Dean, "In China, MySpace May Need to Be 'OurSpace,'" *Wall Street Journal,* February 2, 2007, p. B1.

58. Bruce Einhorn, "Google Hits a Chinese Wall," *BusinessWeek,* September 10, 2007, p. 24.

59. Balfour, "Fakes," p. 56.

60. "Vietnam's Prolific Counterfeiters Take a Walk on 'LaVile' Side," *Asian Wall Street Journal,* June 4, 1998, p. 1.

61. "Sleaze E-Commerce," *Wall Street Journal,* May 14, 1999, p. W1.

62. Glenn R. Simpson, "EBay to Police Site for Sales of Pirated Items," *Wall Street Journal,* February 28, 2000, p. A3.

63. Christina Passariello, "EBay Fined over Selling Counterfeits," *Wall Street Journal,* July 1, 2008, p. 1.

64. The first eight suggestions listed here are forwarded by Robert T. Green and Tasman Smith, "Countering Brand Counterfeiters," *Journal of International Marketing* 10, no. 4 (2002), pp. 89–106.

65. Gabriel Kahn, "Factory Fight," *Wall Street Journal,* December 19, 2002, p. A1.

66. Peggy Chaudhry, Victor Cordell, and Alan Zimmerman, "Modeling Anti-Counterfeiting Strategies in Response to Protecting Intellectual Property Rights in the Global Environment," *Marketing Review* 5, no. 1 (2005), pp. 59–72.

67. Balfour, "Fakes," p. 62.

68. Diana Farrell, "The Hidden Dangers of the Informal Economy," *McKinsey Quarterly,* no. 3 (2004), pp. 26–38.

69. Ibid.

70. Dexter Roberts, Frederik Balfour, Bruce Einhorn, and Michael Arndt, "China's Power Brands," *BusinessWeek,* November 8, 2004, p. 50.

71. Matt Forney, "Harry Potter, Meet 'Ha-li Bo-te,'" *Wall Street Journal,* September 21, 2000, p. B1.

72. Geoffrey A. Fowler, "Disney Tries New Antipiracy Tack," *Wall Street Journal,* May 31, 2006, p. B3.

73. Geoffrey A. Fowler, "Hollywood's Burning Issue," *Wall Street Journal*, September 18, 2003, p. B1.

74. Green and Smith, "Countering Brand Counterfeiters," pp. 91, 101.

75. "Businesses Battle Bogus Products," AP Online, January 26, 1999.

76. Balfour, "Fakes," p. 62.

77. Ken Bensinger, "Film Companies Take to Mexico's Streets to Fight Piracy," *Wall Street Journal*, December 17, 2003, p. B1.

78. Cassell Bryan-Low, "Microsoft Battles Piracy in Developing Markets," *Wall Street Journal*, December 23, 2004, p. B4.

79. Alan R. Andreasen, "Social Marketing: Its Definition and Domain," *Journal of Public Policy and Marketing* 13, no. 1 (Spring 1994), pp. 110–111.

80. George G. Brenkert, "Ethical Challenges of Social Marketing," *Journal of Public Policy and Marketing* 21, no. 1 (Spring 2002), pp. 14–25.

81. "AIDS Prevention Programs Can Be Transferred to Developing Countries," *Ascribe News*, September 23, 2004.

82. Steven G. Friedenberg, Charles Jordan, and Vivek Mohindra, "Easing Coffee Farmers' Woes," *McKinsey Quarterly*, no. 2 (2004), pp. 8–11.

83. Makutsa et al., "Water Quality Intervention in Rural Kenya."

84. "Facebook, Google, YouTube, MTV, Howcast, Columbia Law School and U.S. Department of State Convene the Alliance of Youth Movements Summit," http://www.marketwatch.com, November 18, 2008.

85. Parveen Ahmed, "Affluence Leads to Alcohol Abuse in SE Asia, Report Says," *Marketing News,* September 15, 2006, p. 18.

86. Gerald Hastings, "Relational Paradigms in Social Marketing," *Journal of Macromarketing* 23, no. 1 (2003), pp. 6–15.

Chapter 12

1. Stephen Labaton, "The World Gets Tough on Fixing Prices," *New York Times*, June 3, 2001, p. 1.

2. Ian McDonald, Liam Pleven, and Eric Bellman, "Agents of Change," *Wall Street Journal*, February 12, 2007, p. A1.

3. Kerry Capell, "Fashion Conquistador," *BusinessWeek*, September 4, 2006, p. 38.

4. Mary Anne Raymond, John F. Tanner Jr., and Jonghoo Kim, "Cost Complexity in Pricing Decisions for Exporters in Developed and Emerging Markets," *Journal of International Marketing* 9, no. 3 (2001), pp. 19–40.

5. "Arbitrage," *Wall Street Journal*, June 10, 2008, p. D10.

6. Joel Millman, "Visions of Sugar Plums South of the Border," *Wall Street Journal*, February 13, 2002, p. A15.

7. "Poland Consents to High Prices," *Polish News Bulletin*, September 8, 2008.

8. Jay Solomon, "From Its Base in India, Private-Hospital Chain Enjoys Global Reach," *Wall Street Journal Europe*, April 26, 2004, p. A1.

9. Philip R. Cateora and John L. Graham, *International Marketing*, 11th ed. (Boston: Irwin McGraw-Hill, 2004), p. 553.

10. Ruth Bolton and Matthew B. Myers, "Price-Based Global Segmentation for Services, *Journal of Marketing*, 67 (July 2003), pp. 108–128.

11. Karby Leggett, "In Rural China, GM Sees a Frugal but Huge Market," *Wall Street Journal*, January 16, 2001, p. A19.

12. Lee C. Simmons and Robert M. Schindler, "Cultural Superstitions and the Price Endings Used in Chinese Advertising," *Journal of International Marketing* 11, no. 2 (2003), pp. 101–111.

13. Jathon Sapsford, "Toyota Introduces a New Luxury Brand in Japan: Lexus," *Wall Street Journal*, August 3, 2005, p. B1.

14. Rujirutana Mandhachitara, Randall M. Shannon, and Costas Hadjicharalambous, "Why Private Label Grocery Brands Have Not Succeeded in Asia," *Journal of Global Marketing* 20, no. 2/3 (2007), pp. 71–87.

15. James T. Areddy, "Chinese Consumers Overwhelm Retailers with Team Tactics," *Wall Street Journal*, February 28, 2006, p. A1.

16. Cecilie Rohwedder, Aaron O. Patrick, and Timothy W. Martin, "Grocer Battles Unilever on Pricing," *Wall Street Journal*, February 11, 2009, p. B1.

17. Gordon Fairclough, "China's Car-Price Wars Dent Profits," *Wall Street Journal*, September 18, 2007, p. A11.

18. Ian Young, "… Charges 18 Firms with Operating Hydrogen Peroxide Price-Fixing Cartel," *Chemical Week,* February 9, 2005, p. 12.

19. Eva Perez and Corey Boles, "US Fines British, Korean Airlines for Price Fixing," Dow Jones Financial Wire, August 1, 2007.

20. OandaFXTrade (http://oanda.com), Currency Exchange Rates, Historical Rates, viewed November 12, 2009.

21. Betsy McKay, "Ruble's Decline Energizes Firms Who Manage to Win Back Consumers," *Wall Street Journal*, April 23, 1999, p. B7.

22. James T. Areddy, "China's Inflation Weapon," *Wall Street Journal*, August 20, 2004, p. A10.

23. Phusadee Arunmas, "Cement Producers Agree to Ceiling on Prices," *Bangkok Post,* April 26, 2002, p. P1.

24. Gireesh Chandra Prasad, "Patented Drugs to Cost Same Here as Overseas," *Knight Ridder/Tribune Business News*, February 2, 2005, p. 1.

25. Geri Smith and Michael Arndt, "Wrapping the Globe in Tortillas," *BusinessWeek*, February 26, 2007, p. 54.

26. "S. Korean Trade Panel Finds Japanese Robot-Makers Dumping," *Knight Ridder/Tribune Business News*, February 25, 2005, p. 1.

27. Eric Bellman, "Rural India Snaps Up Mobile Phones," *Wall Street Journal*, February 9, 2009, p. B1.

28. Anna Smolchenko, "They've Driven a Ford Lately," *BusinessWeek*, February 26, 2007, p. 52.

29. Eric Bellman, "A Dollar Store's Rich Allure in India," *Wall Street Journal*, January 23, 2007, p. B1.

30. For a conceptual treatment, see *Transfer Pricing* (Washington, DC: Tax Management, Inc., 1995).

31. Michael Happell, "Asia: An Overview," *International Tax Review* 10 (February 1999), pp. 7–9.

32. Foo Eu Jin, "Transfer Pricing Poses Threat to Firms," *Business Times* (Malaysia), March 10, 1999, p. 3.

33. Jeanne Whalen, "GlaxoSmithKline Gets New Tax Bill from U.S. Agency," *Wall Street Journal Europe*, January 27, 2005, p. A4.

34. Saeed Samiee, Patrick Anckar, and Abo Akademi, "Currency Choice in Industrial Pricing: A Cross-National Evaluation," *Journal of Marketing* 62, no. 3 (July 1998), pp. 25–27.

35. "Market Data: Currency Futures," *Financial Times*, March 3, 2005, p. 27.

36. Philip Shishkin, "Europe Decides to Fine Nintendo," *Wall Street Journal*, October 25, 2002, p. B5.

37. Keith E. Maskus and Yongmin Chen, "Parallel Imports in a Model of Vertical Distribution: Theory, Evidence, and Policy," *Pacific Economic Review* 7, no. 2 (2002), pp. 319–334.

38. Mary L. Kevlin, "United States: Parallel Imports," *Mondaq Business Briefing,* June 22, 2001.

39. Mathew B. Myers, "Incidents of Gray Market Activity among U.S. Exporters: Occurrences, Characteristics, and Consequences," *Journal of International Business Studies* 30, no. 1 (1999), pp. 105–126.

40. Samuel Ee, "Porsche Offers Benchmark Warranty to Beat Grey Imports," *Business Times*, October 29, 2008.

41. Mark Maremont, "Blind Ambition," *BusinessWeek*, October 23, 1995, pp. 78–92.

42. Lyse Comins, "Consumer Groups Welcome New 'Grey Goods' Legislation," *The Mercury*, February 15, 2007, p. 6.

43. Sarah Houlton, "Parallel Trade Setback," *Pharmaceutical Executive* 24 (March 2004), p. 46.

44. Marios Theodosiou and Constantine S. Katsikeas, "Factors Influencing the Degree of International Pricing Strategy Standardization of Multinational Corporations," *Journal of International Marketing* 9, no. 3 (2001), pp. 1–18.

45. Das Narayandas, John Quelch, and Gordon Swartz, "Prepare Your Company for Global Pricing," *Sloan Management Review* 42 (Fall 2000), pp. 61–70.

46. "Countertrade Program for Farm Sector Urged," *BusinessWorld* (Manila), November 29, 2004, p. 1.

47. Aspy P. Palia and Peter W. Liesch, "*Survey of Countertrade Practices in Australia*," http://www.netspeed.com.au/jholmes/default.htm (accessed March 4, 2005).

Chapter 13

1. Marc Lifsher, "Will Venezuelans Shun Mom and Pop for the Hypermarket?" *Wall Street Journal,* June 28, 2001, p. A13.

2. Euromonitor International Global Information Database, 2005, http://www.euromonitor.com/GMID (accessed March 9, 2005).

3. "Overview of the Current State and Potential of China's Cosmetics and Toiletries Market," *Household and Personal Products Industry* 39, no. 2 (February 2002), p. 1.

4. "Tecnica Acquires Nordica," *Powder Magazine*, January 14, 2002, http://www.powdermag.com (accessed March 9, 2005).

5. Warren Keegan, *Global Marketing Management*, 7th edition (Englewood Cliffs, NJ: Prentice-Hall, 2001), p. 183.

6. "Seiko Epson Clones Strategy of U.S. Rival," *Nikkei Weekly*, January 17, 1994, p. 8.

7. Linda Doke, "Millions Make Their Living through Sales," *The Times*, August 31, 2008.

8. Richard C. Cheung, T. C. Chu, and Jacques Penhirin, "Wholesale Moves in China," *McKinsey Quarterly*, no. 3 (2002), pp. 16–18.

9. "Arbitrator Fines Vulcan $23 Million," *Chemical Week*, March 14, 2001, p. 13.

10. Keysuk Kim and Changho Oh, "On Distributor Commitment in Marketing Channels for Industrial Products: Contrast between the United States and Japan," *Journal of International Marketing* 10, no. 1 (2002), pp. 72–97.

11. Bridget Finn, "A More Profitable Harvest," *Business 2.0 Magazine*, May 1, 2005.

12. Preet S. Aulakh and Esra F. Gencturk, "International Principal-Agent Relationships," *Industrial Marketing Management* 29 (2000), pp. 521–538.

13. Karl Edmunds, "How to Tell When Channel Conflict Is Destructive," *Frank Lynn & Associates*, March 2008.

14. Kim and Oh, "On Distributor Commitment" p. 89.

15. David Arnold, "Seven Rules of International Distribution," *Harvard Business Review* 78 (November–December 2000), pp. 132–133.

16. "Kodak Japan to Make Chinon Fully Owned Subsidiary," *Knight Ridder/Tribune Business News*, January 22, 2004, p. 1.

17. "American Standard Succeeds in Korea by Outflanking Local Firms' Lockout," *Financial Times,* August 26, 1993, p. A6.

18. Leslie Chang and Peter Wonacott, "Cracking China's Market," *Wall Street Journal*, January 9, 2003, p. B1.

19. Donald G. McNeil Jr., "Coca-Cola Joins AIDS Fight in Africa," *New York Times*, June 21, 2001, p. 8.

20. "Japan Drug Maker to Buy Rival for $7.7 Billion," *New York Times*, February 26, 2005, p. 3.

21. "The Cost of Moving Goods: Road Transportation, Regulations and Charges in Indonesia," *The Asia Foundation*, April 2008, pp. 47–50.

22. Ben Dolven, "The Perils of Delivering the Goods," *Far Eastern Economic Review,* July 25, 2002, p. 29.

23. "Importing with a Little Help from Friends," *Modern Plastics*, February 1, 2005, p. 50.

24. "Swisscom Slashes Order Processing Time through Process Monitoring with ARIS PPM from IDS Scheer," *IDS Scheer Press Release*, April 29, 2008 (accessed March 26, 2009), http://www.ids-scheer.com/en/News/Swiss com_slashes_order_processing_time_through_process_ monitoring_with_ARIS_PPM_from_IDS_Scheer/113211. html?referer=3673.

25. "RFID Advances Worldwide," *Information Week*, March 7, 2005, p. 1.

26. Dale Rogers, "Supply Chain Management: Retrospective and Prospective," *Journal of Marketing Theory and Practice* 2, no. 4 (2004), pp. 60–65.

27. Linda C. Ueltschy, Monique L. Ueltschy, and Ana Christina Fachinelli, "The Impact of Culture on the Generation of Trust in Global Supply Chain Relationships," *Marketing Management Journal* 17, no. 1, (2007), pp. 15–26.

28. Edward Morash and Daniel Lynch, "Public Policy and Global Supply Chain Capabilities and Performance: A Resource-Based View," *Journal of International Marketing* 10, no. 1 (2002), pp. 25–51.

29. Evette Treewater and John Price, "Navigating Latin American Distribution Channels," *Logistics Today* 48, no. 9 (2007), pp. 1–43.

30. Ellen Byron, "Emerging Ambitions—P&G's Global Target: Shelves of Tiny Stores," *Wall Street Journal*, July 16, 2007, p. A1.

31. Dexter Roberts, "Scrambling to Bring Crest to the Masses," *BusinessWeek*, June 25, 2007.

32. Timothy Aeppel, "Too Good for Lowe's and Home Depot?" *Wall Street Journal,* July 24, 2006, p. B1.

33. Cecilie Rohwedder, "Style and Substance, The Chic of Arabia," *Wall Street Journal*, January 23, 2004, p. A11.

34. Ernest Beck, "Stores Told to Lift Prices in Germany," *Wall Street Journal*, September 11, 2000, p. A27.

35. Mei Fong, "Chinese Rules May Tie Up Foreign Retailers," *Wall Street Journal*, July 17, 2006, p. A6.

36. Kerry A. Dolan, "Latin America: Bumps in Brazil," *Forbes*, April 12, 2004.

37. The section on replicators, performance managers, and reinventors is taken from Luciano Catoni, Nora F. Larssen, James Naylor, and Andrea Zocchi, "Travel Tips for Retailers," *McKinsey Quarterly*, no. 3 (2002).

38. Irena Vida, James Reardon, and Ann Fairhurst, "Determinants of International Retail Involvement: The Case of Large U.S. Retail Chains," *Journal of International Marketing* 8, no. 4 (2000), pp. 37–60.

39. "International Direct Marketing in a Rapidly Changing World," *Direct Marketing*, March 1, 1999, p. 44.

40. Miriam Jordan, "Knock Knock," *Wall Street Journal*, February 19, 2003, p. A1.

41. Chandra Devi and Siti Syameen Md Khalili, "Is e-shopping Safe?," *The New Straits Times*, October 3, 2008.

42. Treewater and Price, "Navigating Latin American Distribution Channels."

43. Evan Ramstad and Gary McWilliams, "Computer Savvy: For Dell, Success in China Tells Tale of Maturing Market," *Wall Street Journal*, July 5, 2005, p. A1.

44. Louise Lee, "Dell May Have to Reboot in China," *BusinessWeek*, November 7, 2005, p. 46.

45. Christopher Lawton and Mei Fong, "Dell to Sell PCs through China Retail Titan," *Wall Street Journal*, September 24, 2007, p. A4.

46. Miriam Jordan, "Web Sites Revive Fading Handicrafts," *Wall Street Journal*, June 12, 2000, p. B1.

47. Jenny Deam, "Beads for Life: Two Coloradans Discover a Way to Help the Women of Uganda, One Colorful Bead at a Time," *Denver Post*, January 25, 2005, p. F1.

48. This section is largely taken from Kate Gillespie and J. Brad McBride, "Smuggling in Emerging Markets: Global Implications," *Columbia Journal of World Business* 31 (Winter 1996), pp. 40–54.

49. "Beef Importers: Banned Offal Smuggled into Malaysia," *Dow Jones Newswire*, January 22, 2006.

50. Meredith Derby and Liza Casabona, "Counterfeiting Wars Heat Up for Shoe Players," *Footwear News*, October 3, 2006, p. 1.

51. Maud S. Beelman, Duncan Campbell, Maria Teresa Ronderos, and Erik J. Schelzig, "Major Tobacco Multinational Implicated in Cigarette Smuggling, Tax Evasion, Documents Show," Investigative Report, The Center for Public Integrity, http://www.public-i.org/story_01_013100.htm.

52. For more on smuggling, see Kate Gillespie, "Smuggling and the Global Firm," *Journal of International Management* 9, no. 3 (2003), pp. 317–333.

53. Marek Strzelecki, "'Ants' Carry Contraband into Poland," *Wall Street Journal*, October 9, 2002, p. B31.

54. Guy Chazan, "Suddenly Boxed In, Russian Smugglers Plot Their Next Move," *Wall Street Journal*, May 4, 2004, p. A1.

55. Lowell Bergman, "U.S. Companies Tangled in Web of Drug Dollars," *New York Times*, October 10, 2000, p. 1.

Chapter 14

1. J. Lynn Lunsford, Daniel Michaels, and Andy Pasztor, "At the Paris Air Show, Boeing–Airbus Duel Has New Twist," *Wall Street Journal*, June 15, 2001, p. B4.

2. "Sealed Air Taiwan (A)," Harvard Business School, Case No. 9-399-058.

3. Michael Ewing, Albert Caruana, and Henry Wong, "Some Consequences of Guanxi: A Sino-Singaporian Perspective," *Journal of International Consumer Marketing* 12, no. 4 (2000), pp. 75–89.

4. Hussain G. Rammal, "International Business Negotiations: The Case of Pakistan," *International Journal of Consumer Marketing* 15, no. 2 (2005), pp. 129–140.

5. Lynn E. Metcalf, Allan Bird, Mark F. Peterson, Mahesh Shankarmahesh, and Terri. R. Lituchy, "Cultural Influences in Negotiations: A Four Country Comparative Analysis," *International Journal of Cross-Cultural Management* 7, no. 2 (2007), pp. 147–168.

6. Kelly Hewett, R. Bruce Money, and Subhash Sharma, "National Culture and Industrial Buyer-Seller Relationships in the United States and Latin America," *Journal of the Academy of Marketing Science* 34, no. 3, pp. 386–402.

7. Jonathan Friedland, "Sweet Solution," *Wall Street Journal*, March 2, 1999, p. A1.

8. Jean-Pierre Jeannet, "Siemens Automotive Systems: Brazil Strategy" (Lausanne: IMD Institute, European Case Clearinghouse).

9. Jean-Pierre Jeannet and Robert Collins, "Deloitte Touche Tohmatsu International Europe" (Lausanne: IMD Institute, European Case Clearinghouse).

10. H. David Hennessey, "Discovering the Hidden Value in Global Account Management," unpublished working paper, Babson College, 2004.

11. Except where otherwise noted, ideas from this section are taken from H. David Hennessey, "Discovering the Hidden Value in Global Account Management," and H. David Hennessey and Jean-Pierre Jeannet, *Global Account Management* (Chichester, UK: John Wiley & Sons, 2003).

12. David Arnold, Julian Birkinshaw, and Omar Toulan, "Can Selling Be Globalized?: The Pitfalls of Global Account Management," *California Management Review* 44, 1 (Fall 2001), pp. 8–20.

13. Roger Daniels, "MT Survey of Surveys: Trade Fairs," *Management Today*, February 7, 2005, p. 62.

14. Iris Kapustein, "Selling and Exhibiting across the Globe," *Doors and Hardware*, September 1, 1998, p. 34.

15. Peter Fritsch, "Hard Profits," *Wall Street Journal*, April 22, 2002, p. A1.

16. R. Bruce Money and Deborah Colton, "The Response of the 'New Consumer' to Promotion in the Transition Economies of the Former Soviet Bloc," *Journal of World Business* 35, no. 2 (2000), pp. 189–205.

17. David Wessel, "Capital: German Shoppers Get Coupons," *Wall Street Journal*, April 5, 2001, p. A1.

18. Lenard C. Huff and Dana L. Alden, "An Investigation of Consumer Response to Sales Promotion in Developing Markets," *Journal of Advertising Research* 38 (May/June 1998), pp. 47–57.

19. Lisa Bertagnoli, "Continental Spendthrifts," *Marketing News*, October 22, 2001, p. 15.

20. David A. Griffith and John K. Ryans Jr., "Organizing Global Communications to Minimize Private Spill-Over Damage to Brand Equity," *Journal of World Business* 32, no. 3 (1997), pp. 189–202.

21. William Fenton, "The Global Sponsorship Market," *Journal of Sponsorship* 2, no. 2 (2009), pp. 120–130.

22. Arundhati Parmar, "Jiminy, Cricket!" *Marketing News*, March 17, 2003, pp. 4–5.

23. Frederik Balfour, "It's Time for a New Playbook," *BusinessWeek*, September 15, 2003, p. 56.

24. Stephanie Kang and Mike Esterl, "Pitched Battle," *Wall Street Journal*, May 23, 2006, p. A1.

25. Miriam Jordan, "Wal-Mart Gets Aggressive about Brazil," *Wall Street Journal*, May 25, 2001, p. A8.

26. William A. Kotas, "Starting from Scratch," *Marketing News,* September 30, 2002, p. 16.

27. Catherine Arnold, "The Spam Update," *Marketing News,* December 8, 2003, p. 9.

28. Brandon Mitchener, "Europe Blames Weaker U.S. Law for Spam Surge," *Wall Street Journal,* February 3, 2004, p. B1.

29. Sally A. McKechnie and Jia Zhou, "Product Placement in Movies: A Comparison of Chinese and American Consumer Attitudes," *International Journal of Advertising* 22 (2003), pp. 349–374.

30. Erin White, "U.K. TV Can Pose Tricky Hurdles," *Wall Street Journal,* June 27, 2003, p. B7.

31. Gerry Khermouch and Jeff Green, "Buzz Marketing," *BusinessWeek,* July 30, 2001, pp. 50–56.

32. Cris Prystay, "Companies Market to India's Have-Littles," *Wall Street Journal,* June 5, 2003, p. B1.

33. Amy Chozick, "Cold Stone Aims to Be Hip in Japan," *Wall Street Journal,* December 14, 2006, p. B10.

34. *Word-of-Mouth the Most Powerful Selling Tool: Nielsen Global Survey,* October 1, 2007.

35. Hiroko Tabuchi, "Mars's Snickers Gets Olympic Lift," *Wall Street Journal,* August 22, 2008, p. B6.

36. R. Bruce Money, "Word-of-Mouth Referral Sources for Buyers of International Corporate Financial Services," *Journal of World Business* 35, no. 3 (Fall 2000), pp. 314–329.

37. Sarah E. Needleman, "For Companies, a Tweet in Time Can Avert PR Mess," *Wall Street Journal,* August 3, 2009, p. B6.

38. Joel Baglole, "War of the Doughnuts," *Wall Street Journal,* August 23, 2001, p. B1.

39. Sholnn Freeman, "Toyota Tackles Texas with Ad Blitz, Charitable Donations," *Wall Street Journal,* July 28, 2005, p. B1.

40. John Carreyrou and Geoff Winestock, "In France, McDonald's Takes Mad-Cow Fears by the Horns," *Wall Street Journal,* April 5, 2001, p. A17.

41. Alix M. Freedman and Steve Stocklow, "Bottled Up," *Wall Street Journal,* December 5, 2000, p. A1.

42. Jay Solomon, "How Mr. Bambang Markets Big Macs in Muslim Indonesia," *Wall Street Journal,* October 26, 2001, p. A1.

Chapter 15

1. "ExxonMobil Launches Advertising Campaign to Announce New Company," PR Newswire, December 3, 1999.

2. Bill Chase, "Letters to the Editor," *Wall Street Journal Europe,* July 24, 2001, p. 9.

3. Vanessa O'Connell, "Exxon 'Centralizes' New Global Campaign," July 7, 2001, *Wall Street Journal,* p. B6.

4. Greg Harris, "International Advertising Standardization: What Do Multinationals Actually Standardize?" *Journal of International Marketing* 12, no. 4 (1994), pp. 13–30.

5. Stephanie Kang, "Indian Ads Come into Their Own," *Wall Street Journal,* December 19, 2007, p. B4.

6. Hillary Chura and Richard Linnett, "Coca-Cola Readies Global Assault," *Advertising Age,* April 2, 2001, p. 1.

7. Erin White, "Publicis Groupe Creates Agency Dedicated Just to Serve Fiat," *Wall Street Journal,* July 11, 2003, p. B4.

8. Patricia Sabatini, "Heinz Re-enlists Leo Burnett for Global Campaign," *Pittsburgh Post-Gazette,* March 27, 1999, p. C1.

9. Bradford Wernie, "Jaguar Goes Global," *Automotive News Europe,* April 12, 1999, p. v.

10. Suzanne Vranica and Bruce Orwall, "Disney Will Launch Global Campaign to Boost Ailing Parks," *Asian Wall Street Journal,* December 30, 2004, p. A6.

11. Judann Pollack, "Pringles Wins Worldwide with One Message," *Ad Age International,* January 11, 1999, p. 14.

12. "Using Potato Chips to Spread the Spirit of Free Enterprise," ABCNEWS.com (accessed September 9, 2002).

13. Geoffrey A Fowler, "For P&G in China, It's Wash, Rinse, and Don't Repeat," *Wall Street Journal,* April 7, 2006, p. B3.

14. Dana James, "Skoda Taken from Trash to Treasure," *Marketing News,* February 18, 2002, pp. 4–5.

15. Deborah L. Vence, "Match Game," *Marketing News,* November 11, 2002, pp. 1, 12.

16. Philip J. Kitchen and Tao Li, "Perceptions of Integrated Marketing Communications: A Chinese Ad and PR Perspective," *International Journal of Advertising* 21, no. 1 (2005), p. 68.

17. Geoffrey A. Fowler, "Advertising: China Cracks Down on Commercials," *Wall Street Journal,* February 19, 2004, p. B7.

18. Jason Leow, "Beijing Mystery: What's Happening to the Billboards?" *Wall Street Journal,* June 25, 2007, p. A1.

19. "Cigarette Stunt Pilot Fined for Airborne Cigarette Advertising," Associated Press, September 20, 2000.

20. Matthew Dalton, "In EU, Food Claims Aren't Taken Lightly," *Wall Street Journal,* February 4, 2009, p. B5A.

21. Christina Passariello, "Chic under Wraps," *Wall Street Journal,* June 20, 2006, p. B1.

22. Normandy Madden and Andrew Hornery, "As Taco Bell Enters Singapore, Gidget Avoids the Ad Limelight," *Ad Age International*, January 11, 1999, p. 13.

23. "Dentsu Ventures Abroad," *Asian Wall Street Journal*, March 29, 2001, p. N1.

24. Jae W. Hong, Aydin Muderrisoglu, and George M. Zinkhan, "Cultural Differences and Advertising Expression: A Comparative Content Analysis of Japanese and U.S. Magazine Advertising," *Journal of Advertising* 16, no. 1 (1987), pp. 55–62.

25. "Movie Stars Moonlight in Japan," *Forbes*, March 14, 2001.

26. Erin White, "U.K. Gives Lessons on Ad Messages," *Wall Street Journal*, December 2, 2002, p. B6.

27. Leah Rickard, "Ex-Soviet States Lead World in Ad Cynicism," *Advertising Age*, June 5, 1995, p. 3.

28. Ying Wang, Timothy J. Wilkinson, Nicolae Al. Pop, and Sebastian A. Vaduva, "Romanian Consumers' Perceptions and Attitudes toward Online Advertising," *Marketing Management Journal* 19, no. 1 (2009), pp. 73–83.

29. Dagmar Mussey, "Mars Goes Local," *Ad Age Global*, May 10, 2002.

30. Kiran Karande, Khalid A. Almurshidee, and Fahad Al-Olayan, "Advertising Standardization in Culturally Similar Markets," *International Journal of Advertising* 25, no. 4 (2006), pp. 489–512.

31. Christopher Woodward, "Got Spanish? Anita Santiago Helps Advertisers Bridge the Gap between Anglo and Latino Cultures," *BusinessWeek*, August 14, 2000, p. F12.

32. Jim Pickard, "Coca-Cola to Use Welsh in Adverts," *Financial Times*, July 6, 2000.

33. Juliana Koranteng, "Global Media," *Ad Age International*, February 8, 1999, p. 23.

34. Michelle R. Nelson and Hye-Jin Paek, "A Content Analysis of Advertising in a Global Magazine across Seven Countries," *International Marketing Review* 24, no. 1 (2007), pp. 64–86.

35. Kerry Capell, "MTV's World," *BusinessWeek*, February 18, 2002, p. 81.

36. "McDonald's Strikes Sweeping International Music Deal," *Ad Age Online*, February 15, 2005.

37. Beverly Matthews, "Foreign Life Insurers Eye India," Reuters English News Service, April 3, 2001.

38. "How to Buy ... Selling: Consumers as 'Sellsumers' in the Americas," Euromonitor International, August 12, 2009.

39. Dae Ryun Chang, "The 'We-Me' Culture: Marketing to Korean Consumers," *Advances in International Marketing* 18 (2007), pp. 145–161.

40. Eric Bellman and Tariq Engineer, "India Appears Ripe for Cellphone Ads," *Wall Street Journal*, March 10, 2008, p. B3.

41. Yung Kyun Choi, Jang-Sun Hwang, and Sally J. McMillan, "Gearing Up for Mobile Advertising: A Cross-Cultural Examination of Key Factors that Drive Mobile Messages Home to Consumers," *Psychology & Marketing* 25, no. 8 (2008), pp. 756–768.

42. Kathy Chen, "Beyond the Traffic Report," *Wall Street Journal*, January 2, 2003, p. A9.

43. James T. Areddy, "Starbucks, Pepsico Bring 'Sub-opera' to Shanghai," *Wall Street Journal*, November 1, 2007, p. B1.

44. Margaret Cocker, "Dubai Pulls Out the Stops," *Wall Street Journal*, August 8, 2008, p. B8.

45. Guy Chazan, "Moscow, City of Billboards,"*Wall Street Journal*, July 18, 2005, p. B1.

46. Andreas Grein and Robert Ducoffe, "Strategic Responses to Market Globalisation among Advertising Agencies," *International Journal of Advertising* 17, no. 3 (1998), pp. 301–319.

47. Marye Tharp and Jaeseok Jeong, "The Global Network Communications Agency," *Journal of International Marketing* 9, no. 4 (2001), p. 113.

48. Michael Flagg, "Vietnam Opens Industry to Foreigners," *Wall Street Journal*, August 28, 2000, p. B8.

49. Betsy McKay, "Coke Hunts for Talent to Re-Establish Its Marketing Might," *Wall Street Journal*, March 6, 2002, p. B4.

Chapter 16

1. Kevin Maler, "3M Looks to Expand Global Sales," *Knight Ridder/Tribune Business News*, June 17, 2001.

2. Adam Lashinksy, "Yahoo's Mission Quest," *Fortune*, February 2, 2007.

3. "Mission Statement, Starbucks Coffee Company," http://www.starbucks,com (accessed August 5, 2009).

4. "Science for a Better Life: Mission Statement for the Bayer Group," http://www.bayer.com (accessed August 5, 2009).

5. Jim Krane, "Halliburton CEO Moves from Houston to Dubai to Focus on Mideast, Asian Ventures," Associated Press Newswires, March 11, 2007.

6. David Woodruff, "Your Career Matters," *Wall Street Journal*, November 11, 2000, p. B1.

7. Kamran Kashani, "Why Does Global Marketing Work—or Not Work?" *European Journal of Management* 8, no. 2 (1990), pp. 150–155.

8. Carol Hymowitz, "European Executives Give Some Advice on Crossing Borders," *Wall Street Journal*, December 2, 2003, p. B1.

9. Matthew Karnitschnig, "Identity Question," *Wall Street Journal*, September 8, 2003, p. A1.

10. Carol Hymowitz, "Foreign-Born CEOs Are Increasing in U.S., Rarer Overseas," *Wall Street Journal*, May 25, 2004, p. B1.

11. Jason Gertzen, "Milwaukee-Based Manufacturer Seeks Overseas Expansion," *Knight Ridder/Tribune Business News*, June 11, 2001.

12. Will Pinkston, "Ford Mulls Suppliers Park Near Atlanta," *Wall Street Journal*, July 12, 2000, p. S1.

13. Merissa Marr, "Small World," *Wall Street Journal*, June 11, 2007, p. A1.

14. Arnold Schuh, "Global Standardization as a Success Formula for Marketing in Central Eastern Europe?" *Journal of World Business* 35, no. 2 (Summer 2000), pp. 133–148.

15. "The Legacy that Got Left on the Shelf: Unilever and Emerging Markets," *Economist Intelligence Unit Executive Briefing*, February 12, 2008.

16. Ernest Beck, "Familiar Cry to Unilever: Split It Up!" *Wall Street Journal*, August 4, 2000, p. A7.

17. Carol Hymowitz, "In the Lead: Managers Suddenly Have to Answer to a Crowd of Bosses," *Wall Street Journal*, August 12, 2003, p. B1.

18. "Electric Glue," *The Economist*, June 2, 2001.

19. Joann S. Lublin, "Globalizing the Boardroom," *Wall Street Journal*, October 31, 2005, p. B1.

20. Chi-fai Chan and Neil Bruce Holbert, "Marketing Home and Away: Perceptions of Managers in Headquarters and Subsidiaries," *Journal of World Business* 36, 2 (Summer 2001), pp. 205–221.

21. Sarah McBride, "Can Esprit Be Hip Again?" *Wall Street Journal*, June 17, 2002, p. B1.

Company and Name Index

Subject Index

Key terms and the page references where their definitions appear are given in bold.